GEORGES PEREC
A Life in Words

ᵹ

Georges Perec

A LIFE
IN WORDS

A BIOGRAPHY BY
David Bellos

DAVID R. GODINE, PUBLISHER
Boston

First U.S. edition published in 1993 by
DAVID R. GODINE, PUBLISHER, INC.
Horticultural Hall
300 Massachusetts Avenue
Boston, Massachusetts 02115

Originally published in the United Kingdom
by Harvill, a division of HarperCollins Publishers
Copyright © 1993 by David Bellos

LIBRARY OF CONGRESS CATALOGING-IN-PUBLICATION DATA
Bellos, David.
Georges Perec : a life in words / David Bellos.
p.   cm.
Includes bibliographical references and index.
ISBN 0-87923-980-8
1. Perec, Georges, 1936-1982—Biography. 2. Authors, French—20th
century—Biography. I. Title.
PQ2676.E67Z53   1993
848'.91409—dc20   [B]   93-11604   CIP

First U.S. edition
Printed and bound in the United States of America

For my father

This book is a life of Georges Perec, the author of *Life A User's Manual*, one of the most exhilarating works of fiction ever to have been written. Perec often likened literature to a jigsaw puzzle, and once, with a chuckle, cast himself in the same light: *All I know is that the puzzle is called* The Life and Works of Georges Perec, he said. *But I don't know what the solution is.*

Contents

Part III: 1975–1982

Prof, Dept. French Studies
Univ, of Manchester.

Acknowledgments

The University of Manchester and the British Academy supported some of the costs of the research that led to the writing of this book, and their assistance is gratefully acknowledged.

Eric Beaumatin guided me through the collections of the Association Georges Perec, and I received much-needed help at the Bibliothèque de l'Arsenal.

I received assistance from a great number of people in my search for the traces of Georges Perec in libraries and archives of different kinds in many parts of the world: in Australia, from Margaret O'Hagan at Queensland University Library, and from members of the French Departments at the Universities of Queensland and Melbourne; in Britain, from the Department of French Studies at the University of Warwick; in France, from Marcel Benabou on behalf of OuLiPo, from Olivier Bétourné at Editions du Seuil, from Madame Bonazzi at the Archives Nationales, from R. P. Bonvallet at Villard-de-Lans, from the Centre de Documentation Juive Contemporaine, from Lieutenant-Colonel Destours at the Caserne de Reuilly, from Madame Anne-Marie Duhard at the Ministry of Defence, from Robert Gallimard at Editions Gallimard, from Professor André Hugelin and the secretarial staff of CNRS LA 38 at CHU Saint-Antoine, from Thérèse Mairesse at Editions Denoël, from Mémoire Juive de Belleville, from M. Niborsky at MEDEM, from Madame Pezet at Radio-France, from Madame Rivaud at Lycée Henri-IV, and from the Croix-rouge française in Paris and Grenoble; in Germany, from Dr Robert Karge, Steffie Hoster, and Petra Stein at Saarländischer Rundfunk, Saarbrücken, from Verlag der Autoren in Frankfurt-am-Main, and from Herr Treichel at the Landesrentenbehörde Nordrhein-Westfalen in Düsseldorf; in Italy, from ACIF in Bologna; in Tunisia, from the British embassy; and in Yugoslavia, from Kasimir Klarić at Radio Zagreb and from Katarina Ciric-Petrović at Novi Sad.

I was fortunate to have a research assistant during the first two years (1988–90) of the work which led to this book: Patrizia Molteni gave invaluable support during that time, and has been a treasured collaborator ever since. I was also able to call on the expertise of other colleagues at the University of Manchester and elsewhere, among them Professor Philip Alexander (Jewish Studies), Helmut Weber (German), Terry Lewis (French), Steve Wharton (documentary film), David Shepherd (Russian), and Claudia Nocentini (Italian). Christiane Dancie shared with me the results of her research in and around Etampes. I also gained many insights from work done by students in my department, notably Jane Byrne, Susan Glover, and Heather Mawhinney.

Many letters, manuscripts, and other items relating to the life and work of Georges Perec are in the possession of individuals, and I am grateful to the many who allowed me to consult, transcribe, photocopy, and on occasion even to borrow documents: in America, Laurent de Brunhoff and Kate Manheim; in Australia, Jacques Birnberg and Jean-Michel Raynaud; in Belgrade, Milka Čanak-Medić and Mladen Srbinovic; at La Rochelle, Jean Duvignaud; in Paris, Pascal Aubier, Stella Baruk, Claude Berge, Catherine Binet, Robert Bober, Christian Bourgois, Marie-Claude de Brunhoff, Henri Chavranski, Philippe Drogoz, Dr Henry Gautier, Pierre Getzler, Alain Guérin, Philippe Guérinat, Serge Klarsfeld, Bernard Quilliet, Bernard Queysanne, Bianca Lamblin, Sylvia Lamblin-Richardson, Jacques Lederer, Christine Lipinska, Bruno Marcenac, Michel Martens, Harry Mathews, Jean Mailland, Bernard Mirabel, Paul Otchakovsky-Laurens, Paulette Perec, Jean-Paul Rappeneau, Dr Suzanne Tyc-Dumont, Paul Virilio, and Gérard Zingg; in Saarbrücken, Eugen Helmle; at Saint-Jean-de-Sauves, Huguette Moralès; and at Saint-Pierre-du-Vauvray, Suzanne Lipinska. Marc Zaffran at Souillé, Wolfgang Schenck at Davos, Claus Henneberg at Hof, and Johann-Maria Kamps at Cologne sent me copies of precious documents and tape recordings. From Australia, C. B. Thornton-Smith sent me a tape recording of Perec's talk at the University of Adelaide. In New York, Saul Steinberg himself found and sent me a copy of *The Art of Living*.

My understanding of Perec's work has been formed by my own efforts as a reader and as a translator, and by the research of numerous colleagues. Points borrowed from published papers are acknowledged in notes within the body of the text, but I would also like to acknowledge here the many direct and indirect contributions made by speakers and participants at the Séminaire Georges-Perec, held at the University of Paris-VII, and all that I learnt from the informal discussions that often follow the meetings.

Like all who take an interest in Perec's work, I owe much to Bernard Magné. Without the stream of conference papers and articles he has published, the formal aspects of the later work would be far less well understood. Philippe Lejeune's sensitive research on the drafts and manuscripts of *W or The Memory of Childhood*, *Lieux*, and *Je me souviens* has been no less important in guiding my steps. I found much to nourish my own reflections in Claude Burgelin's *Georges Perec* (Paris, Le Seuil, Les Contemporains, 1988), the best introductory study available in French. I am grateful as well to Warren Motte, Marcel Benabou, Jürgen Ritte, and Andrew Leak for helping me to grasp many different aspects of Perec's work.

I have relied as much as possible on written and recorded sources, but a great deal of the biographical information given in this book is necessarily drawn from conversations and from private correspondence with about 150 of Perec's friends, relations, colleagues, and collaborators in America, Australia, England, France, Germany, Israel, Italy, Tunisia, and Yugoslavia. I should like to thank them collectively for the time and consideration each of them gave me even when he or she had misgivings about the appropriateness of a biography of Georges Perec, or about my ability to write one.

Most chapters of this book end with a brief list of sources not acknowledged in the text or footnotes. These lists, printed in smaller face, are not exhaustive. One informant requested not to be named; another is referred to by initials. In any case, as most of the information I give has more than one source, the attribution of specific points to named individuals would be inappropriate. The sources lists do no more than indicate a selection of documents and individuals whose contributions were of particular importance to the chapter.

It was not within my power to talk to all the people who knew Georges Perec, and there are many who could make corrections or add further details, if not whole chapters, to the story that I tell. I hope they will do so when they feel the time is right. This is the first biography of Georges Perec, not the last.

Drafts of parts of this book have been read and commented upon by a number of the people who figure in it, and I have done my best to take account of their reactions. The errors and infelicities remaining are my responsibility entirely.

I am especially grateful to Madame Ela Bienenfeld for her role in the work that has led to this book. Despite her initial reservations about the project of a biography of her cousin, she gave me access to many of the papers in the "Fonds Perec", she shared with me detailed memories of her own past, and alerted me to many misapprehensions on my part in early drafts, which would otherwise have gone uncorrected.

It is impossible to acknowledge adequately all the help that I was given by Catherine Binet. Not only did she give me access to numerous documents as well as practical assistance in finding many of Perec's friends, but she also engaged me in copious correspondence, conversations and arguments on the interpretation of Perec's life and work. Several points made in this book derive from her unpublished work, *La Commande ou projet d'un voyage à W (Montage)*, and many others first arose in debate with Catherine Binet and thus belong as much to her as to me. However, that does not mean that every part of this book has her unqualified approval. It is not an "authorised" biography, nor was it written for the people who helped me to write it. It was written for all those who have been bowled over or will yet be moved by *Life A User's Manual*, by *Things*, by *A Man Asleep*, or by *W or The Memory of Childhood*, and who, like myself, never met their living author.

Christopher MacLehose, Dorothy Straight, Guido Waldman, Vera Brice, Susan Lendrum, Joseph West, and Olivia Bellos all played roles far beyond the call of their professional or family commitment to this biography and to its author. I am more grateful to them than words can say for their support, advice, and practical help, without which this book might never have been begun, let alone edited, corrected, indexed, illustrated, and, at long last, actually brought to completion.

User's Guide

References and Quotations

Quotations from books by Georges Perec that are currently available in English translation are set in italic and attributed by an abbreviated English title and page number in square brackets following. A key to the abbreviations used may be found on page xxi.

Quotations from books by Georges Perec that are not yet available in English are given in translation, set in italic, and attributed by an abbreviated French title and page number in square brackets following (except for *Je me souviens*, where paragraph numbers are used). A key to the abbreviations used may be found on pages xxiff. All translations are my own unless otherwise stated.

Other written and recorded sources are given in notes, either at the foot of the relevant page or at the end of the chapter. Perec's written and spoken words are set in italic, without quotation marks; quotations from other sources are set in roman, either with quotation marks or in a distinctive layout.

On the few occasions where I have reconstructed dialogues in which Georges Perec speaks, I give his words in italic only when I believe them to represent exactly what he said. Other reconstructed dialogues (involving Perec and other speakers) are presented in quotation marks and in roman type.

Titles of works

I refer to the titles of Perec's works by their English translations if English translations are available in 1992. I refer to other published and unpublished works by Perec by their original titles and give a translation in parentheses following the first mention only. However, the index of titles includes both original and translated titles, which will allow the reader to find all mentions of the relevant work in the book as a whole by looking up either name.

English-language editions of foreign works by other authors are used whenever possible, and these, too, are indexed under both their original and their translated titles.

The conventions outlined above have certain consequences. *Life A User's Manual* is available in English translation, and so, when I describe Perec opening a fresh ledger on 29 October 1976 and writing the first words of his masterpiece, I write, on p. 620 below, that he "copied out first of all the words he had scribbled down on the train:

In Memory of Raymond Queneau
Life A User's Manual."

But that is not quite true. What he wrote was:

A la mémoire de Raymond Queneau.
La Vie mode d'emploi.

I have found no solution to the language puzzles I have set myself by writing between two (or rather, three) languages. If the clashes my conventions have created annoy some readers sufficiently to make them wish to learn French (or German) and be done with it, I shall not be the one to complain.

The Parts

Part I of this book deals with Perec's family history and with his life up to the age of thirty or thereabouts. It is a historical narrative, based on archival as well as literary research, and covers many matters that cannot be reconstructed with certainty. My intention, in this part, is to present what I have found as fully as I can. (Other documentation is thought to exist but is not accessible.) I use the memories that Perec confined to texts not intended for publication as documentary evidence; I treat his autobiographical words in literary texts with greater circumspection.

Part II presents a more selective account of Perec's life and work between 1965 and 1975. In this period, when Perec was a published writer, the course of events can be plotted more comprehensively from written and recorded sources. The narrative is ordered by the flow of time but does not reproduce everything that was written or said by or about or in connection with Perec in those years.

Part III deals with Perec's life after 1975, the period of his greatest achievements, and it is structured in a different way. In this part, I have chosen to forsake strict chronological sequence in order to present Perec's life and work in a more thematic way. I have reproduced only a selection of the anecdotes that Perec's many friends have recorded in writing elsewhere. My intention in this part, and my broadest aim in the book as a whole, is to tell the prodigious tale of a life in words.

Perec's posthumous life – the growth of Perec studies, the rediscovery of his manuscripts, the publication of his works, the translation of his texts into other languages and into other forms (plays, radio serials, recitals, films) is not the explicit subject of any part of this book. But it is not the least remarkable feature in the life of Georges Perec, which, in that sense, is still only at its beginning.

Although he had little formal contact with higher education and never got a degree, Georges Perec possessed a culture of staggering breadth. In presenting his life and work, I have drawn a map of Perec's mind that is necessarily limited by my own cultural boundaries, with dark continents corresponding to blind spots in me. For instance, there should probably be more mention of Raymond Roussel and Michel Leiris than there is in this book, and film culture no doubt pervades Perec's writing more extensively than I can see. Conversely, the connections that I make between Perec and, for example, Nabokov and Balzac, may, in some cases, reflect patterns that belong mainly to me.

Key to Abbreviations Used in the Text

Works by Georges Perec Available in English

53D   "53 Days", trans. David Bellos (Boston: David R. Godine, forth-coming). Originally published as "53 jours" (Paris: P.O.L., 1989).

L   Life A User's Manual, trans. David Bellos (Boston: David R. Godine, 1987). Originally published as La Vie mode d'emploi (Paris: Hachette, 1978).

MA A Man Asleep, trans. Andrew Leak (published in one volume with Things. A Story of the Sixties, trans. David Bellos; Boston: David R. Godine, 1990). Originally published as Un Homme qui dort (Paris: Denoël, 1967).

T   Things. A Story of the Sixties, trans. David Bellos (Boston: David R. Godine, 1990). Originally published as Les Choses. Une histoire des années soixante (Paris: René Julliard, 1965).

W   W or The Memory of Childhood, trans. David Bellos (Boston: David R. Godine, 1988). Originally published as W ou le souvenir d'enfance (Paris: Denoël, 1975).

These translations are all also published in London by Harvill, an imprint of HarperCollins. The British editions have the same page numbering and the same text as the American editions.

Works by Georges Perec Available in French (or German)

BO   La Boutique obscure (Paris: Denoël, 1973)

Clô   La Clôture et autres poèmes (Paris: Hachette, 1980)

CSL   Cantatrix Sopranica L et autres écrits scientifiques (Paris: Le Seuil, 1991)

D   La Disparition (Paris: Denoël, 1969)

EsEs   Espèces d'espaces (Paris: Galilée, 1974)

inf   l'infra-ordinaire (Paris: Le Seuil, 1989)

Jms   Je me souviens (Paris: Hachette, 1978)

Jsn   Je suis né (Paris: Le Seuil, 1990)

M   Die Maschine (Stuttgart: Reklam's Universal-Bibliothek, 1972)

MC I   Les Mots croisés I. Précédés par des considérations de l'auteur sur l'art et la manière de croiser les mots (Paris: Mazarine, 1979)

MC II   *Les Mots croisés II* (Paris: P.O.L./Mazarine, 1986)

PC   *Penser/Classer* (Paris: Hachette, 1985)

PTG   *Petit Traité invitant à la découverte de l'art subtil du go* (Paris: Christian Bourgois, 1969)

QPV   *Quel Petit Vélo à guidon chromé au fond de la cour?* (Paris: Denoël, 1966)

REI   *Récits d'Ellis Island. Histoires d'errance et d'espoir* (Paris: Le Sorbier, 1981)

Th   *Théâtre I* (Paris: Hachette, 1980)

UCDA   *Un Cabinet d'amateur* (Paris: Balland, 1979)

V   *Voeux* (Paris: Le Seuil, 1990)

Other Sources

AGP   Refers to the Association Georges Perec

Atlas   Refers to *Atlas de littérature potentielle* (Paris: Gallimard, Collection Idées, 1981)

CGP   Refers to the *Cahiers Georges Perec*, a series further issues of which are in course of preparation:

    CGP I   (Paris: P.O.L, 1985)

    CGP II   *Textuel 34/44* (Université de Paris-VII), no. 21 (1988)

    CGP III   *Presbytères et prolétaires. Le Dossier P.A.L.F.* (Paris: Editions du Limon, 1989)

    CGP IV   *Mélanges* (Paris: Editions du Limon, 1990)

    CGP 5   Bernard Magné, Mireille Ribière, *Les Poèmes hétérogrammatiques* (Paris: Editions du Limon, 1992)

FP   Refers to the "Fonds Perec", the archive of Perec's papers currently located at the Arsenal Library in Paris. The numbers following an appearance of the abbreviation FP indicate the location of the document in the inventory established by the Association Georges Perec

MO   Refers to Philippe Lejeune, *La Mémoire et l'oblique. Georges Perec autobiographe* (Paris: P.O.L., 1991)

OCR   Refers to *Oulipo. Créations, Re-créations, Récréations* (Paris: Gallimard, Collection Idées, 1973)

PAP   Refers to Mireille Ribière, ed., *Parcours Perec: Actes du*

Colloque de Londres (Lyon: Presses universitaires, 1990)

RCF   Refers to David Bellos, ed., "Georges Perec Number", *Review of Contemporary Fiction* XIII.1 (Naperville, IL: Dalkey Archive Press, forthcoming 1993)

Other Abbreviations and Acronyms Used in the Text

ACR	Atelier de création radiophonique
AdP	Archives de Paris
AL	Arsenal Library, Paris
AN	Archives Nationales, Paris
BBC	British Broadcasting Corporation
BCA	Brigade des Chasseurs Alpins
BEA	British European Airways
BETAP	Ecole des Troupes Aéroportées (Pau)
BFI	British Film Institute
BibOl	La Bibliothèque Oulipienne
BN	Bibliothèque Nationale, Paris
CAR	Commission d'Avances sur Recettes
CDJC	Centre de Documentation Juive Contemporaine
CGQJ	Commissariat Général aux Questions Juives
CGT	Confédération Générale du Travail
CHU	Centre Hospitalo-Universitaire
CNC	Centre National de la Cinématographie
CNRS	Centre National de la Recherche Scientifique
CO	commanding officer
CPSU	Communist Party of the Soviet Union
CRF	Croix-rouge française
CRS	Compagnie Républicaine de Sécurité
CSN	see SNC
DES	Diplôme d'Etudes Supérieures
DOM et TOM	Domaines et Territoires d'Outremer
EPHE	Ecole Pratique de Hautes Etudes
ETMAR	Etudes de marché
EV	engagé volontaire
FFI	Forces Françaises de l'Intérieur
FK	Franz Kafka
FLL	François Le Lionnais
FLN	Front de Libération Nationale

FTP	Francs-Tireurs-Partisans
GCSE	General Certificate of Secondary Education
GERM	Groupe d'Etudes et de Réalisations musicales
GPRA	Gouvernement Provisoire de la République Algérienne
IFOP	Institut Français de l'Opinion Publique
IRES	Institut de Recherches et d'Etudes Sociales
IS	Internationale Situationniste
JBSA	Jacques Bienenfeld Société Anonyme
JCML	Jeunesses Communistes Marxistes-Léninistes
LA	Laboratoire Associé
LN	Les Lettres Nouvelles
NCO	non-commissioned officer
nrf	*Nouvelle Revue française*
NYPL	New York Public Library
OAS	Organisation de l'Armée Secrète
ORTF	Organisation de la Radio-Télédiffusion Française
OuLiPo	Ouvroir de Littérature Potentielle
PCF	Parti Communiste Français
QGAC	Quartier Général – Administration Centrale
RAF	Royal Air Force
RCP	Régiment de Chasseurs Parachutistes
REI	Régiment Etranger d'Infanterie
RER	Réseau Express Régional
RN	Route Nationale
RTB	Radio-Télévision Belge
SHAFE	Supreme Headquarters of Allied Forces in Europe
SMN	Société Minière de Normandie
SNC	système nerveux central
SNCF	Société Nationale des Chemins de Fer Français
SR	Saarländischer Rundfunk
STO	Service du Travail Obligatoire
TamS	Theater am Sozialamt
TEE	Trans-Europ-Express
UEC	Union des Etudiants Communistes
USAF	United States Air Force
WDR	Westdeutscher Rundfunk
ZNO	zone non-occupée
ZO	zone occupée

In addition, the following self-invented abbreviations appear in the text:

GA   *La Grande Aventure*
Lg   La Ligne générale

List of Illustrations

2: Photographs
Between pages 322–323

By courtesy of the Association Georges-Perec: figure 9 and photographs 7, 8,
    9, 14, 20, and 22.
By courtesy of Marcel Benabou: photograph 40
By courtesy of R. P. Bonvallet: figure 8.
By courtesy of Christian Bourgois (Photo: Michel J. Philippot): photograph
    47
By courtesy of Henri Chavranski: photographs 2 and 6.
By courtesy of Christiane Dancie: photographs 15, 16, and 17.
By courtesy of Philippe Drogoz: photograph 33.
By courtesy of Jean Duvignaud: photograph 32.
By courtesy of Patrick Fréchet (Photo Pascal Lemaître): photograph 31
By courtesy of Eugen Helmle: figure 23 and photograph 34.
By courtesy of Claus Henneberg: figure 26.
By courtesy of Bianca Lamblin: photographs 1, 3, 4, 5, 10, 11, and 13.
By courtesy of the Landesrentenbehörde Nordrhein-Westfalen: figure 7 and
    photograph 12.
By courtesy of Suzanne Lipinska: photograph 30.
By courtesy of the Mairie du XXe Arrondissement: figure 5.
By courtesy of Leila Menchari (Photo: Michelangelo Durazzo): photographs
    26 and 27.
By courtesy of Huguette Moralès: photograph 18.
By courtesy of Bernard Quilliet: figure 10.
By courtesy of Saarländischer Rundfunk: figure 27.
By courtesy of Suzanne Tyc-Dumont: figure 12.

PART I
1936–1965

Poland in 1915.
(The dotted line shows the border
of Poland in 1945.)

CHAPTER 1

The Name

Georges Perec was born in Paris on 7 March 1936, four years and three months before German troops entered the city. He had a French forename and a surname that spells "perrek" in French. As written, as pronounced, Perec seems to match names like Bellec and Perros-Guirec, which come from Brittany, as every French-speaker knows. So when you see the name Perec written or when you hear it said, you assume that the person who bears it has ethnic roots in France's Celtic fringe. In fact, there were no Bretons at all amongst Georges Perec's forebears. He was the French son of Jewish immigrants from Poland, and it was his bizarre fortune to be called by a Hebrew word spelt in Polish, which, when pronounced in French, sounds Breton.

> *I knew nothing of the outside world except that there was a war, and that, because of the war, there were refugees: one of these refugees was called Normand and lived in a room in a house that belonged to a man called Breton. That's the first joke I can remember.* [W 88]

In his teens, Perec played with his Celtic potential, signing some of his letters "Pereq" and others, it seems, "Perrec'h". A little later, he tried out a cross-Channel identity, writing letters to friends and mentors in a variety of English. Of course, the adult Georges Perec was a French writer, a writer of French, but Frenchness was not quite something simply given to him.

Georges Perec's paternal grandfather was called David Peretz, and he lived in Lubartów, a small town near the city of Lublin, in Poland, which was at that time part of Russia. The name Peretz is of biblical origin. By tradition, all the branches of the Peretz clan (whose members spelt their surname Perez, Peres, Perutz, Peiresc, and so on, in the various countries where they settled) are descended from one of Judah's twin sons by his daughter-in-law Tamar. According to the Bible story, when Tamar went into labour with twins, the midwife placed a red thread on the first infant hand to emerge, and said, "this one will be the firstborn". But the infant withdrew its hand, and the other twin was born before him. Surprised at such agility, the midwife declared, "How hast thou broken forth? This name be upon thee!" [Genesis 38:28]. The Hebrew word for "break forth" is made of the same letters as the word for gap, hole, or breach, so what the midwife called the infant, in a rare instance of Old Testament humour, was Gap, Gapman, or Breacher.

The Hebrew root **פרץ** (P - R - Ts, "perets") is represented

| in Greek as Φαρεσ ("phares") whence in the King James Bible Pharez [Numbers 26:20] Phares [Matthew 1:33] Perez [Luke 3:33] | in Russian as in Polish as in German as in Spanish as and in English as | Перец ("perets") Perec ("perets") Peretz Perez Peretz or Perets |

In Russian, the official language of Lubartów and Lublin from 1831 to 1915, Georges Perec's grandfather's name was written Перец, representing exactly the same sound as Perec in Polish, in which, as in Hungarian, the unaccented letter *c* makes an English "ts" or "tz".

David Peretz, his wife, Rojza, and his three children, Esther, Lejzor and Icek, Georges Perec's father, all left Poland between 1918 and 1929. Esther was married, and already Esther Bienenfeld, by the time she emigrated. Lejzor went to Palestine, then under British mandate, where his name was spelt Peretz. Icek, the youngest, went to school in the newly independent state of Poland and then left for France with identity papers written in Polish.

It is a rule of the French language (called the rule of assimilation) that any word, insofar as it is written in a Latin alphabet, is assumed to be written according to the French system of spelling. Icek Perec, whose name was pronounced "Itzek Peretz" in Polish, became "Issek Perrek" the moment he handed his papers to the *police des frontières*. Nobody distorted Georges Perec's family name. Nobody mangled it on purpose. It just changed, automatically, through the introduction of a Polish spelling into French.

Georges Perec's father seems to have adopted the new sound of his name without demur. When he enlisted in the French foreign legion in 1939, he must have said "Perrek" when he got to the head of the queue, where a sympathetic recruiting clerk adjusted the spelling to what it would have been had the name been pronounced "Perrek" in Polish. Perec's father's passbook thus bears the name Isek Perek.

In his strange and moving "autobiographical fiction", *W or The Memory of Childhood*, Perec gives a brief and tangled account of the linguistic history of his name. He points out, correctly but quite irrelevantly, that in Russian the word *peretz* (more usually transcribed from Cyrillic as *p'erets*) means "pepper". He also volunteers the information that in Hungarian, *perec*, pronounced "peretz", as in Polish, refers to a bread-ring. In fact, *perec* is more commonly heard in Hungarian in the compound word *sósperec*, pronounced "shoshper-ets", literally a "salt-bread ring" – that is to say, a pretzel. It makes just the sort of approximate pun that Perec loved playing with in French, for *sósperec* is about as near as you can get to Georges Perec's own name pronounced with a Hungarian, or Serbian, or Polish accent: "shoshperets" versus "zhorzhperets".

A pretzel is a length of dough baked in a double loop, more or less like a figure-of-eight: just holes tied together with bread. Polish-spelt *Perec* is Hebrew for "hole" – and Hungarian *sósperec* is a roll with two holes. The "peretz connection" is pure coincidence, since the languages involved are unrelated, but when Perec was in Belgrade – and in love, at the age of twenty-one – his Yugoslav friends teased him without mercy for being just a *petit pain*. He took an obscure revenge years later by putting a few pretzels as well as linguistic half-truths into *W or The Memory of Childhood*. Perec turned a multi-lingual pun into a kind of destiny, as if he had been called "man of gaps" twice over by his name.

Nor is the double name game abandoned in Perec's masterpiece, *Life A User's Manual*. The novel's main story concerns Percival Bartle-booth, a man who devotes his life to jigsaw puzzles. Perec explained that the novel itself was constructed like a jigsaw puzzle, and he also made it clear that it was but a piece in the larger puzzle of his own life and works. For instance, in one scene, Kleber, Bartlebooth's superannuated chauffeur, places an American novel face down on a green leather bench seat in the antechamber where he waits. Its title – *The Wanderers* – can thus be seen on the cover, and it is given in English in the French text. The first novel Perec wrote, which he never dared submit to a publisher, was called *Les Errants* ("The Wan-derers"). But the "self-inscription" of Perec the novice writer into his later novel is signalled by the name of the fictitious author of *The*

Wanderers, George Bretzlee. Although he cannot be found in the catalogue of the Library of Congress, "George Bretzlee" can easily be read, for the letters of his surname can be rearranged to spell the French (and Viennese) word for *sósperec*, which Perec had already given in *W or The Memory of Childhood* as one of the (false) cognates of his own patronym: Bretzlee ⇒ Beretzele = *bretzel* ("pretzel") ⇒ Perec.

In fact, there were Polish Jews whose name really *was* Pretzel, a name presumably derived from Hebrew *Peretz* by the same circuitous pun as Perec's self-inflicted pet name. One survived the Nazi camps, emigrated to Australia, and published an autobiography entitled *Portrait of a Young Forger*.[1]

Georges Perec's mother came from Warsaw, and her maiden name was Cyrla Szulewicz. With that spelling, it should be pronounced in Polish as "Shoolevich", with an ending of the same Slavic kind as *Yurevich* or *Malevich*; but it is obviously a Yiddish name,[2] amended on purpose during the long Russian annexation of Poland, and its proper sound was "Shoolevits", which would be written in German or English transcription as *Schulewitz*. That is the sound that Perec tried to represent in quasi-French when he misspelled his mother's name as *Schulevitz* in an early autobiographical essay [*W* 30–33], and it is also the source of the more Frenchified *Choulevisse* ("shooleyveess"), a name found in one of his unfinished sketches [see *MO* 31].

Schulewitz is no less full of meaning than *Peretz*. In Yiddish, a *schul* is a synagogue, school, or classroom (from the German *Schule*, "school"); *witz* refers to wit, cleverness, humour, or a joke or pun. So Perec's mother's family were "learned jokers", or "synagogue wits", or "classroom punsters". Even if he had lost all memory of his childhood languages, the adult Perec had several Jewish friends who understood Yiddish, as well as many German colleagues who could have told him what *Schulewitz* might mean; and by the time he wrote his childhood autobiography, Perec himself could understand German reasonably well. It is inconceivable that he never grasped

[1] Marian Pretzel, *Portrait of a Young Forger* (Brisbane: University of Queensland Press, 1989).

[2] Yiddish is a dialect of German spoken until recent times by Jewish communities in the Pale of Settlement (Poland, the Baltic States, the Ukraine) and farther afield. Although structurally unrelated to Hebrew, Yiddish is traditionally written in Hebrew characters, from right to left. Transcriptions from Yiddish into the English alphabet normally follow German spelling rules.

the extraordinary predestination that his maternal line seems to have mapped out for him through its name, but nowhere does he mention it. Perec's silence is eloquent. What Perec tells the reader about his father's name announces a game of gaps. He also tells us that his mother disappeared.

The name Pérec, with an acute accent on the first e, seems to be a genuine, if rather rare French-Breton name, and is born by a celebrated woman athlete from the French West Indies, who is of course unrelated to the writer Georges Perec. His relationship to a character called Perec who turns up in in a recent English travelogue is less clear. This is how Andrew Harvey's Georges Perec takes his leave, somewhere in the Himalayas:

> Perec stood flexing his biceps (very small) in the light. He said, "I am going. We will never meet again. Be careful. You are very enthusiastic, and a great fool, you will be eaten alive if you don't watch out. I wish you all the melancholy wisdoms and a relatively early death! Ha! Yes!" and ran out into the morning laughing and slapping his thighs. "All the melancholy wisdoms and a relatively early death! What rhythm! What stytle!"[1]

From this imaginative passage comes the surmise, made by a Danish anthropologist, that towards the end of his life Perec became a "wild proto-lama" tramping the roads of Ladakh.[2] But in the wide range of endearingly childish ambitions which the adult Perec admitted to having – crossing the intersection of the international date-line and the equator, travelling by hot-air balloon, scripting a movie in which five thousand Kirghiz horsemen sweep across the steppe – there is not a word about becoming a Buddhist.

The signature "Pereq" is on a letter to Jean Duvignaud dated 9 April 1956; "Geroges [sic] Perrec'h" is the name on a letter dated 8 October 1956, now FP 31,1,35d; Perec wrote whole letters in English to Jean Paris, and parts of letters to Jacques Lederer and Philippe Guérinat, in 1957–59.

The *fiche matricule* of "Isek Perek" is in the archives of the French Ministry of Defence.

---

[1] Andrew Harvey, *A Journey in Ladakh* (London: Cape, 1983), p. 90.

[2] Poul Pedersen, "A Propos *Ting*", *Tiddskrift Antropologi* 21–22 (1990), p. 183.

CHAPTER 2

Lubartów, Lublin, Vienna

I would so much like to retire to my country estate like Athos, Perec once noted wistfully [FP 57, 37], but for most of his life he avoided going back to Lubartów to look for his Polish roots. His first published novel, *Things,* was swiftly translated into Hungarian, Bulgarian, Romanian, Estonian, Russian, Czech, and Polish, and it was also published in French in the Soviet Union, in an annotated edition for use in schools; it would not have been hard for Perec to find an excuse for travelling behind the Iron Curtain in the later 1960s and the 1970s. He did not bother. It was not until 1981 that he accepted an invitation from the French government to undertake a speaking tour of Poland, and thereby gave himself the opportunity or the provocation that he needed to cease deferring his pilgrimage to the place that had been his family's home for many generations.

When Perec got back to Warsaw after an exhausting day-trip to Lubartów and Puławy, he found his colleague Claude Roy waiting for him at their hotel, the Europejski. "Did you find anything?" Claude asked. *Nothing,* Perec replied. *All wiped out.*[1]

> *Like near and distant cousins of mine, I might have been born in*
> *Haifa, Baltimore or Vancouver*
> *I might have been Australian, Argentinian, English or Swedish,*
> *but in the almost unlimited range of potentials,*
> *one thing was specifically denied me:*
> *I could not be born in the country of my ancestors*
> *in Lubartów or Warsaw*
> *or grow up there, in the continuum provided*
> *by tradition, community and language.*   [REI 44][2]

Before the great turmoils of this century, Lubartów was a town of about ten thousand people, roughly half of them Jewish. Thirty-five hundred Jews were still living there in 1942. All of them were

---

[1] Claude Roy, *Permis de séjour, 1977–1982* (Paris: Gallimard, 1983), p. 208.
[2] Translated by Harry Mathews.

deported, in a single operation, to Belzec and Sobibor, then gassed and incinerated. None of the Jewish population survived, apart from the few who took to the woods and joined the partisans. Some of these brave *levertover* (as Lubartów Jews are called in Yiddish) survived the chaos of the war's end and got themselves to Paris, where they found those earlier émigrés from Lubartów who had avoided deportation during the German occupation of France. They set up an association, Les Amis de Lubartów, through which they published a memorial volume to their vanished kinsfolk. *Our Martyrs* contains photographs of old Lubartów and of many of its Jewish inhabitants and gives long lists of those who perished, amongst them the households of Shmuel Peretz, Gedaliah Peretz, Rashi Peretz, and Moshe Peretz. Were any of these Peretzes second, third, or nth cousins of Georges Perec? Was the writer related to the one Peretz – Joynah – who, according to the Yiddish text of *Our Martyrs*, joined a *Royte Verband* ("Red Brigade", or partisan group) and turned up in Paris before 1947? Perec might have found out had he responded to a letter he received in the 1960s on the headed notepaper of Les Amis de Lubartów from a man who claimed to have known his father, Icek Perec, at school. But Perec did not respond. He thought the claim was obviously untrue, *since my father left L when he was four or five. The lie filled me with outrage. Everything that concerns my father fills me with outrage* [*CGP II* 167]. History, at least, provides no grounds for Perec's emotions. His father was born in 1909 and attended school in Poland in the period from 1915 to 1925, and it is far from impossible that one of his school friends was alive (not many survived, but some certainly did) and well and in Paris in the 1960s. But perhaps Georges Perec did not want to know at that stage in his own life that not every trace of his father had vanished.

In the spring of 1967, Georges Perec began to make lengthy enquiries into his Polish background. He planned to write a family history, a kind of saga or chronicle, to which he gave the working title *L'Arbre* ("The Tree"). He conducted regular interviews with his aunt Esther, made copious notes, and interviewed several other relatives, but there is no evidence that he ever tried to get in touch with Les Amis de Lubartów. Despite that, Perec's notes for *L'Arbre* show that he knew much more about his family than he chose to include in *W or The Memory of Childhood*.

★

David Peretz, Georges Perec's grandfather, was born in Lubartów in 1870. The branch of the Peretz family into which he was born was not poor and lived in a large house of its own. It was almost a ranch house, built in the shape of a U; one wing was let out as a billet for Russian soldiers. The Lubartów Peretzes were not ghetto Jews, for there had never been a ghetto there. Like many Jews in the parts of Poland annexed by Russia, the Peretzes seem to have done rather well by the occupying army. The Russians mistrusted the Jews rather less than they mistrusted the Poles: after all, the Jews were not Catholics and did not speak the "local dialect" that the Russian Empire was determined to suppress.

It cannot be said for certain whence came David Peretz's forebears, for in the official register of the population of the city of Lubartów, drawn up after Polish independence, there is a tear across the part of the page where the parentage of David Peretz should appear.[1] However, the family tree that Georges Perec put at the head of his family saga shows David's father, Menachem, as the nephew of the most famous of all Polish Peretzes of modern times: Isaak Leib Peretz, the founding father of Yiddish literature. There was not much contact between the Lubartów Peretzes and the Zamość branch, from which Isaak Leib Peretz came, but it was a connection of which every Peretz was proud. Georges Perec himself went on using it throughout his life as a test of relatedness whenever he came across someone called Perec, Perc, Peretz, or such like on his travels. In Saarbrücken, for example, the owner of the town's main antiques store proved to be a distant cousin because he, too, could demonstrate that he was a descendant of I. L. Peretz. On the other hand, the Kurt Peretz whom Perec found in the telephone directory in Sydney turned out to be unrelated, since Isaak Leib was nowhere on his family tree.

One of the first presents that Georges Perec gave to his German translator, Eugen Helmle, in 1966 or 1967, was a fine hand-printed German edition of Peretz's *The Golem*, the first, and the briefest, literary version of the Yiddish folk-myth that inspired Gustav Meyrink's great panorama of Jewish life. Amongst the collection of books in Perec's rue Linné flat is a well-thumbed paperback of

---

[1] The French translation of this document, made in 1927 in connection with naturalisation procedures, states that "la rubrique relative à la filiation des 3 premières personnes . . . manque par suite d'une déchirure" ("the column relating to the ascendance of the first three persons . . . is missing owing to a tear"). David Peretz is the first of the three people referred to.

Meyrink's novel in French. And yet as late as 1980, Perec mentioned that amongst the projects he had yet to begin was *a study of The Golem*, which, he added, he had *never really read*. [1] There are so many versions of the Golem in European literature and music that it is impossible to know what it was that Perec hadn't yet studied, but he must have known the basic story as told by his great-grand-uncle, which goes like this: in the attic of the synagogue in Prague, there is a clay statue – the Golem – which had come alive and defended the Jews against the Gentiles when the right word was whispered in its ear by the great Rabbi Loeb, its creator:

> But the Name by which it could be called to life in a day of need, the Name has disappeared. And the cobwebs grow, and no-one may touch them. What are we to do? [2]

David Peretz was a traditional Jew and a pious man, an unworldly observer of the Talmud and Torah, of the kind gently mocked in many of I. L. Peretz's stories of life in the shtetl. It is quite possible that he was a Hasid, or close to the Hasidic movement (as were the Zamość Peretzes), since his daughter, Esther, when explaining the family background to her nephew in 1967, spoke at some length about what Hasidism was: a cult of joy through prayer and song, a fervently religious branch of orthodox Judaism, intent on achieving spiritual elevation through strict observance of the law. Long after the family had left Poland, when David Peretz was a kindly old man behind the counter of a Paris grocery store, his wife was not keen to leave him in sole charge. He might give away the whole stock of sweets to children who came in and asked for them.

David Peretz, who held a position as a minor official in Lubartów, was married in 1895. His bride, Sura Rojza Walersztejn, was short, dark-haired, energetic, and just sixteen. She became a mother within a year. She held different views from her husband and soon became the family provider, setting up a business to supply timber to local builders. David spent much of his time in prayer rooms but was not allowed to bring his piety into the home: Jewish rites were not

---

[1] G. Perec, "Questions-réponses", in *Action poétique* 81 (1980), p. 39.

[2] Isaak Leib Peretz, "The Golem", trans. Irving Howe, in E. Litvinoff, ed., *The Penguin Book of Jewish Short Stories* (London: Penguin Books, 1979), p. 16.

observed by Rojza, according to Esther's later account of her home life in Poland. In fact, if we are to believe a scribbled line opposite Rojza's name in Perec's notes, his grandmother refused even to give alms to the poor. Giving alms is the very basis of traditional Jewish social life; you cannot refuse to give alms without making quite a stir in the world in which David and Rojza lived. In the eyes of a Hasid, or an orthodox Jew, refusing to give alms is tantamount to refusing to be Jewish.

The Polish revolt of 1905 was the first upheaval that modern history imposed on the Peretzes. Russian troops withdrew from Lubartów during the revolt and left the town to the Poles. David was dismissed from his official position and came close to being executed for having collaborated with the Russians; Rojza's timber business had to be abandoned. So the family – David and Rojza had two children already, Chaja Esther, aged nine, and Lejzor, born in 1904 – trekked on foot, with their pots and pans, to Puławy, about thirty miles away, on the banks of the River Vistula. It was a pretty little town with a fortress, a university, and an agricultural school. It was also a Russian garrison town, which gave Jews some protection from Polish resentment. The Peretzes lived in a house on the edge of the town. They had a backyard, and chickens, and a garden with flowers. Esther remembered her years in Puławy, from the age of nine to the age of eighteen, as the happiest of her life. Rojza adapted to her new situation, and opened a boardinghouse. David returned to prayer.

Another child, a son, was born in 1909, whilst the family was still in Puławy. However, the few surviving official documents concerning the third-born of the children, Icek Judko, Georges Perec's father, give Lubartów, not Puławy, as his place of birth. It is possible that Rojza returned to her own family, the Walersztejns, for confinement and delivery. Alternatively, the exile in Puławy may not have lasted as long as Esther remembered in her conversations with Georges Perec more than half a century later. And it is also possible that Icek was born in Puławy but Lubartów was entered on the birth certificate because the family regarded Lubartów as its true home and place of origin. For how many more years did David's father, Menachem, go on living in the great house shaped like a U? For how long did that ranch house still stand? When Perec went back in 1981, there was no trace of it. But he was amused to discover (since he had decided long before to call his family history "The Tree") that the arms of his family's home town depicted two lions on either side of a tree.

Chaja Esther Peretz was thirteen when Icek was born. It is said that she played a larger role in bringing him up than her mother did, for Rojza was busy with the boardinghouse, the family's sole source of income. Esther was to play a vital role, too, in the life of the young Georges Perec, but it seems fair to say that her influence on the writer actually began long before, in Puławy, in the years when she helped to rear and to educate Georges's father.

Like her mother, Esther was dark-haired and dark-eyed, and had striking good looks. Like Rojza, too, Esther was full of energy and the will to get on in the world. She did not inherit her father's submissiveness and never sought to emulate his pious spirituality. Her childhood ambition was to get a proper education, become a teacher, and be recognised as a full member of lay society. She would also have loved to learn to play a musical instrument. She must have told her nephew Georges (though it is not recorded in the 1967 interview notes) that she went on a hunger strike to obtain her father's permission to attend the lyceum, or grammar school, in Puławy [CGP II 168]. She did well there and in the summer of 1914 was about to begin her final year of study, leading to the Russian matriculation certificate, when Gavrilo Princip shot Archduke Ferdinand as he crossed the bridge at Sarajevo, plunging Europe into war. Austrian armies gathered in Galicia and threatened Russia's western elbow in central Poland. Puławy was a garrison town, with a fortress and a river crossing: an obvious battle site. The civilian population was evacuated, and the Peretzes once again piled their mattresses, their pots, their pans, and their linen onto a horse-drawn cart and trudged alongside it to the nearest big city, Lublin. They had relatives there who took them in. They lived on Kowalska, near the synagogue; Rojza opened a grocery store in the same street. For the first time in many generations, the Lubartów Peretzes were living in a ghetto.

Early in 1915, Lublin was taken by the Austrian army, and there followed three years of relatively benign Hapsburg rule. The Austrians had more money than the Russians, and they handled Poland more liberally: Esther remembers those years, her first city years, as a period of euphoria. However, Austrian occupation had one serious consequence for her. The Hapsburgs were in alliance with the Polish army raised in Galicia by Pilsudski and were vaguely committed to the establishment of an independent Poland after the war. The Austrians had never tried to impose German as a common language on their ramshackle empire, and Polish thus became the language of administration, education, and examination in Austrian-occupied Lublin. Esther found herself obliged to repeat a year of lyceum and to pass her matriculation in Polish, which she had learned as a girl by taking private lessons but which was neither the language of her family (Yiddish), nor the main language of her education (Russian). She succeeded nonetheless and was able to begin a career as a primary schoolteacher.

Esther taught young children to read and write in a clandestine school, in an attic, but it is not clear whether she taught them in Yiddish or in Polish. She also taught in a school organised by the Bund; perhaps it was the same one. The Bund was a Jewish workers' movement that was active in Russia, Poland, and the Baltic states, fighting for a socialist society in which Jews would be fully emancipated but not assimilated. Esther dreamed of being a qualified schoolteacher in an established post, in public employ. No doubt the Bund came closest to offering her the possibility of fulfilling that dream. In Russia, the movement was liquidated by Lenin in October 1917; in Poland, it remained active throughout the 1920s.

The second Peretz child, Lejzor, was a clever boy with a special gift for mathematics. One of the first acts of the provisional government of the independent Republic of Poland, proclaimed on 7 November 1918 in Lublin itself, was to exclude all Jews from the lyceum. It also became illegal for Jews to walk in public parks. Lejzor got into fights, and, like many Jewish boys, he got beaten up. After a bad beating, perhaps, he decided that he had had enough of being a second-class citizen. He did not dare tell his family, for his father was a traditional Jew and therefore anti-Zionist, and his elder sister was a Bund socialist and therefore likewise anti-Zionist. He did not say farewell before he set off, in the dark of night, with half-a-dozen companions no older than he, to walk to Warsaw and then, with the help of the Zionist networks, by way of Prague, to Vienna. It took months. In Vienna he stayed a whole year and apprenticed himself to a locksmith, in order to have a trade before the last stage of his journey to Palestine. He was just eighteen when he got there, in 1922, and joined Kibbutz Ein Shemer, near Hadera, on the coastal plain. He began his new life as a farm guard, but his mathematical talents did not go unnoticed: after catching malaria, he was sent back to Europe to learn to be a civil engineer. He arrived in Paris in 1925, where he found his sister once again, who had reached France by a very different route.

In the last year of the Great War, Esther had got to know an Austrian soldier who was stationed in Lublin, by the name of Marc Bienenfeld. Marc was from Galicia and was, in effect, like the Peretzes, a Polish Jew. Marc's brother David came to visit him, on a month's leave from his unit, which was posted in the southernmost part of the Austro-Hungarian Empire. The Bienenfelds were poor Jews, but in Austrian Galicia it was not impossible even for Jews to make their way through education. David had been through primary and secondary school in Polish and German, and had begun medical studies at Vienna University before the outbreak of war. He served in the army as a medical auxiliary, and, in Esther's eyes, he cut a dashing figure on horseback. After their first meetings in Lublin, David wrote postcards in Polish to his schoolteacher sweetheart (he spoke no Russian and did not use Yiddish, though he must have understood it) and also sent her books about the Montessori method of educating young children. At the war's end, David returned to his medical studies at Vienna University. At first he did not dare return to Lublin to see Esther, for fear of being conscripted once again into the army – this time, the Polish one, which was fighting a "small" war with Russia for control of the western Ukraine. Esther sent him money to help him continue his studies.

David Bienenfeld and Chaja Esther Peretz (now written Perec, in independent Poland) were married in Lublin in 1919. David went back to Vienna, while Esther stayed on in Poland. During school holidays she joined her husband and worked as a waitress to support him through his final years of study. They had their first child in 1921 and called her Bianca.

It is an unusual name for the child of Polish Jews. One story that has been handed down has it that David and Esther intended to name their daughter after a Polish friend of theirs called Branca, but the registrar's clerk got it wrong and wrote *Bianca* instead. But that would not explain why the "wrong" name survived in the family. Another story, included in Perec's draft notes for *L'Arbre*, is that David Bienenfeld had distant cousins in Italy and wished to choose an Italian name for his first child. A third story holds that *Bianca* was simply a name that appealed to Esther's romantic imagination. Whatever the truth of it, the name that David and Esther adopted for their daughter, whether by mistake or by design, can be seen as a symptom of their desire to be Western, to be educated, to envisage a future that would be free of the Polish, German, Jewish, and

Hebrew past. Perhaps they would have made their lives in Poland or Austria as assimilated Jews had that proved to be possible. But when David Bienenfeld reached his medical finals in 1922, he found his way barred. The Polish government had passed a decree making it illegal for medicine to be practised by Jews. Since David was regarded as a Pole in Austria, he was obliged to sign a deed renouncing his right to practise medicine in order to obtain a medical degree.

The rest of David Bienenfeld's life, of which a decade and more was spent as Georges Perec's guardian and effective father, must be seen in the light of this harsh twist of fate. He was twenty-nine, and because of the war he had waited nearly ten years to qualify. He could have practised in Palestine, but that would have called for a commitment to Zionism, and to the pioneering life, that he was not prepared to make. He might have been able to practise in Argentina or America, but there were no Bienenfelds, or for that matter Peretzes, settled there then. He had had visits and insistent letters from a distant cousin in Paris, offering him training and a career with good prospects. It was not a medical career, but he had a wife and a daughter to provide for. With regret – with bitterness, even – David accepted his family responsibilities and abandoned the profession he had worked so hard to enter. He would make a new and quite different life for himself, and for the whole family, in France.

David's brother Marc had been gone for two years already and now wanted his wife and baby son to join him in Paris. So there were five in the Bienenfeld group that sat for three days and three nights in third-class carriages trundling on from Lublin to Warsaw, to Vienna, to Munich and Strasbourg and finally to Paris, the City of Light: David, Esther, and Bianca, Ada, Marc's wife, and their baby boy, Nehemias, or Nicha. Jews were leaving places like Lublin by the thousand in those years. Many of them were uneducated and poor. The Bienenfelds were not among the most desperate; at least they knew what their destination was, and had jobs and relatives waiting for them there. All the same, it was a fearsome uprooting. None of them would ever see Poland again.

Esther said later that she left her Jewish life behind her at the station in Lublin "like a locked suitcase", and that she forgot every word of Polish the moment she stepped off the train at Gare de l'Est. It was a huge transition; perhaps the threads had to be cut sharply to make it manageable. But Esther also said to Georges Perec in those later years of her life that it had all been too hard, that one lifetime was not enough to travel "from the ghetto to the light".

Within a few years, the whole Peretz family had left Poland, and all of David Bienenfeld's brothers and sisters were in Paris. No close relatives were left in the East by the time Georges Perec was born, in 1936. All the same, the family into which he was born and the family in which he was brought up had their roots in Lubartów and Lublin, roots that could never be severed completely, even if what most of the branches chiefly desired was to grow into fully-fledged American, British, Argentinian, Israeli, or French citizens.

David **Peretz** Lubartów 1870 – disappeared 1943	m.1895	Sura Rojza (*Rose*) **Walersztejn** Lubartów 1879 – Tel Aviv 1964
Chaja Esther Lubartów 1896 – Paris 1974 m.1920 David **Bienenfeld** 1893–1973	Lejzor (*Léon*) **Peretz** Lubartów 1904 – Haifa 1964 m.Esther	Icek Judko (*Isie*) **Perec** Lubartów 1909 – Nogent-sur-Seine 1940 m.1934
Bianca Lublin 1921– m. 1941 Bernard **Lamblin**	Ela (*Lili*) Paris 1927–	Uriel Haifa 1936– Daniel Haifa 1942– Gabriel Haifa 1945–	Cyrla (*Cécile*) **Szulewicz** Warsaw 1913 – Auschwitz 1943
Marianne 1945– m.Abir **Saluden**	Sylvia 1952– m.James **Richardson**		Georges Paris 1936– Paris 1982 Jeannine (*Irène*) 1938

Letters from David Bienenfeld to Esther Perec are in FP 48.

"Like a locked suitcase": *vie juive comme valise fermée*, from Perec's notes, FP 58, 11+; "from the ghetto to the light": *du ghetto vers la lumière – une génération trop courte*, from Perec's notes, FP 69,6,26 rº.

Arms of Lubartów: undated letter from Perec to Ela Bienenfeld, from Warsaw [1981].

Our Martyrs was kindly provided by M. Niborski and translated from the Yiddish by Sally Barnett and N. Bellos.

CHAPTER 3

Perec and the Persian Gulf

On his way to Australia in August 1981, Georges Perec broke his journey for a day and a night at Bahrain. He was hoping to plug one of the gaps in his research for *L'Arbre*. Some of Perec's friends suspected that the family saga was a trick that he played on his own writing plans, the great work that would always be the one to be tackled next, when the decks had been cleared of the projects in hand – a psychological subterfuge for getting on with something else. In fact, Perec never ceased to use his trips abroad to gather material for the history of his numerous and enterprising collateral relations. His cousin Ela had given him names and addresses of former contacts of the family in the Persian Gulf. When he got to Bahrain, he found it hot and sticky, as might be expected. Also, it was Friday. He saw the airport and the Hilton Hotel; everything else was shut.

Why Bahrain? Before it grew rich as an exporter of oil, the island had long been a trading post for the pearls found in the warm, clear waters of the Persian Gulf, and it was to work in the pearl trade that first Marc and then David Bienenfeld abandoned Lublin and Vienna for Paris. Marc became a buyer of South American pearls and spent time in Venezuela; David did his tour of overseas duty in the Gulf, mostly in Bahrain. Both brothers worked for a cousin of theirs, the founder of the Bienenfeld fortune, a buccaneering businessman known to all as Big Jacques.

Jacques Bienenfeld's story is an extraordinary one. He was born a poor Jew in Kalusz, in eastern Galicia (now Kalush, in the Ukraine), and trekked west at the age of fourteen. He arrived in Paris in around 1890, without a sou, without an education, and without a word of French, but he was strong, and clever, and determined.[1] He began

---

[1] It is possible that Jacques had relatives in Paris already. In 1891, a Bienenfeld wrote to Arthur Rimbaud and offered to send a caravan to meet the poet-trader at Harrar in Abyssinia, but no connection has been established between this Bienenfeld and Big Jacques. As a curiosity, see Arthur Rimbaud, *Œuvres complètes* (Paris: Gallimard, Bibliothèque de la Pléiade, 1954), pp. 533 and 787. The references were noted by Perec, FP 58, 41 v.

buying and selling secondhand jewellery – maybe, at the start, on the pavement. He must have done very well at it. He soon had a shop on the ground floor of 62 Rue Lafayette, a good commercial site in a central business area, in the ninth arrondissement. It is said that his first big deal was to buy an African king's crown jewels on credit and sell them for cash. He began to specialise in pearls, eventually abandoning retail for the richer pickings, and greater risks, of the wholesale trade. He consulted experts on the biology and ecology of the oyster and became an expert in his own right. His business grew, and he took over the fifth, sixth, and seventh floors of 62 Rue Lafayette. He came to own the whole block, a prime commercial property. He was the very model of the self-made man.

Jacques Bienenfeld was probably a millionaire before the First World War, when he was interned (for a time) as an enemy alien. Naturalisation was difficult in France in those days, and Jacques's application was not granted until 1922. In addition to the annoyance it caused him, however, the war also brought him great rewards, for in times of turmoil, small objects of value such as pearls – easily carried, easily hidden, easily recognised – command a high premium over other, more cumbersome forms of wealth and over all forms of paper money. Simultaneously, the course of history forced formerly wealthy families to part with their jewels. Jacques Bienenfeld acquired some of the fabulous trinkets of the fallen Hapsburgs. One of his former employees recalls a jewel-encrusted umbrella handle; to Esther, Jacques gave a bracelet that had once belonged to Queen Zita of Hungary. It is possible that these wartime bargains turned Big Jacques from a merely rich man into the master of a colossal fortune. In the immediate postwar period, he set off for eastern Europe to look for his roots and transplant them to the West. He wanted all his (male) relatives to work for him. He wanted the firm to remain the Maison Bienenfeld, however large it grew.

Pearl trading calls for special skills and a good deal of courage. Natural pearls form in oysters in warm waters, and they are found in commercial quantities in various corners of the tropical and subtropical world, from the Persian Gulf to the coast of Venezuela, from the south island of Japan to Palawan in the Philippines. The value of a raw pearl is not easily guessed. Pearls are laminated, like onions – that is to say they consist of layer upon layer of minutely thin skin. (*Hamlet*, act 5, scene 2, contains a famously obscure pun on *onion* in the sense of "pearl" [*unio* in Latin]; Perec incorporates the whole passage, though the pun is entirely lost in French, in his stage play *La Poche Parmentier* ["The Warp"].) Each pearl-skin takes its colour from the conditions prevailing during its slow growth – the temperature of the water and the food ingested by the oyster. The grown pearl acquires its shimmering hue from the layering of skins of many different shades. The outermost skin is often not the finest; a raw pearl may have a potential beauty that cannot be seen without careful study, a beauty that sometimes cannot be seen at all but can only be guessed at on the basis of long experience and intuition. The pearl buyer out in the field, in an Arabian or Venezuelan trading post, takes a guess and decides what to settle for with the pearl fisher or, more usually, the middleman. The pearl trader, in Paris, takes a second guess and decides whether or not to peel the pearl. Though it is performed only rarely, peeling represents the summit of the pearlman's art. Since a pearl can no more be put back together again than can a peeled onion, the decision requires courage. By peeling the right number of layers of tightly compacted pearl skin, an expert pearler can transform something dull and barely saleable into an object worth a hundred times more. By peeling when he should not, however, or by peeling too much, he may, of course, achieve the opposite result.

Whether peeled or not, raw pearls have to be polished and then, for the most part, pierced for stringing into necklaces. Weighing, sorting by colour and by size, polishing, piercing, pricing, and stringing are specialised jobs done by different workers whose training is itself a long-term investment. Hand-polishing and hand-piercing used to result in occasional damage. Big Jacques Bienenfeld consulted experts and then designed electrical polishing and piercing machines of his own. He had them built in Switzerland. They were beautiful precision tools of wood and brass, and they remained standard trade equipment for many decades.

On his family recruiting campaign in 1918–19, Jacques first tracked down Marc Bienenfeld, who was only too glad to make a career and a new life in the West. In his hometown, Jacques found a cousin in his teens who bore a different name, Lieberman, and he invited him to come over for training in the pearl trade all the same. Simon Lieberman did well. He had a good eye, a good head, and a gift for languages. Ten years later, Jacques gave him the task of setting up a branch of the firm in New York, where Simon stayed, and many years later, after becoming an American citizen, went into business on his own account, specialising in Japanese cultured pearls. Simon Lieberman wrote his memoirs after retiring from business. One evening in 1979, he showed the typescript to a visiting French writer who was also a distant relative and an old friend. Georges Perec was delighted; he sat up all night in the Abbey Victoria Hotel reading Simon's explanations of his early history, which was also the early history of one part of Perec's own family. He would have to include much of it in *L'Arbre*, he wrote to his lover, Catherine Binet, *the book about my family that I'm hoping I'll finally begin to complete one day*. He had at least discovered how to establish his degree of relationship to Simon Lieberman:

> *Whereas David Bienenfeld [. . .] is the pearlman Jacques Bienen-feld's father's brother's grandson, Simon Lieberman is the grandson of the pearlman Jacques Bienenfeld's mother's sister. Simon's grand-mother's sister married my father's sister's husband's grandfather's brother. It's as simple as pie.*

For many Poles, France was not just another foreign land. It played a special role in Polish history: the ill-fated Warsaw uprising of 1831 had been directly inspired by France's liberal revolution of 1830, and Paris had become a haven for Polish exiles of all kinds – political dissidents, dispossessed aristocrats, revolutionaries, Jews. The Polish community in France was already large and growing by the day in the 1920s, as the new republic in the east tried to solve its unemployment problem by exporting labour to the old republic, which had lost its young men in the trenches of the First World War. In eastern Euro-pean imaginations, France was a beacon of hope, a land of prosperity, and, unlike America, the home of revolutions. There were therefore several strands in David and Esther's decision to leave for Paris. They were refugees from Polish anti-Semitism as well as economic migrants, but there was also a measure of Polish idealism in their departure for France, a streak of Francophilia, a conviction that they were moving to a *better* land. They looked forward to making their way in a lay society in which their Jewishness would not be an obstacle to their becoming French.

Big Jacques Bienenfeld was, sporadically, a generous man, but he did not offer an easy living to his relatives the moment they set foot in France. He paid for David and Esther to learn French at the Berlitz

School (which both of them did quickly, and effectively); then he took David on as a trainee and paid him a trainee's wage. David and Esther found an attic flat on the sixth floor of a block without a lift in Rue Michel-Ange, in the sixteenth arrondissement, and moved in with Marc, Ada, and Nicha. It was cramped; each family lived in a room, and they shared the kitchen, with Esther and Ada taking weekly turns at shopping and at cooking. At least they had a bathroom. They told themselves that it was better than what they would have had in Poland. Later, the Bienenfelds moved to a flat of their own near Gare de l'Est, then moved again to Rue Lamartine, almost next to the business premises in Rue Lafayette, which were always called *le bureau*. It was not until the very end of the 1920s that David and Esther settled on the west side of Paris, renting a small villa in the suburban town of Suresnes, immediately opposite the vast palace where their cousin Jacques lived in splendour.

How rich was the founder and chairman of Jacques Bienenfeld Société Anonyme? His employees whispered that he was worth five hundred million francs, but their guess probably left the firm's debts out of account. The company, called JBSA for short, funded its huge operations with bank loans secured against the pearls purchased. As long as the market continued to rise, as it did for a decade after the war, it was a profitable procedure for both parties, and Jacques lived in appropriate style. He brought Italian craftsman and painters to Suresnes to redecorate his château, which had a staff comprising a cook, a maid, a butler, three gardeners, and a chauffeur, who drove him to *le bureau* every day in a grand old Unic.

Jacques had been married and divorced before the First World War, and in 1922 he married again. His wife, Germaine Franck, came from an established French-Jewish family with its roots in Alsace, and she bore Jacques a son. Through her he acquired relatives who had been French for generations, and a nephew, Robert Franck, who was to become an enterprising journalist for *L'Express* and, from 1972, *Le Point*. In fact, it was Robert Franck who smoothed the path of Georges Perec towards the achievement of one of his most intensely held ambitions: to become a regular, weekly, published crossword-puzzle setter, and to rival the great Robert Scipion.

Jacques Bienenfeld was a barrel-shaped man, who according to the legends handed down about him, looked like Orson Welles and lived like Citizen Kane. He was a brilliant talker, an expansive personality, and an intuitive rather than a calculating financier. He had made a fortune from nothing, and he had the faults of an empire builder, too: a degree of megalomania, a short temper, a rough and imperious manner, and an unpredictable streak. In the 1920s, he ruled over more than sixty people at 62 Rue Lafayette, and he terrified them all.

Jacques was broad; David was slim. Jacques was self-taught; David was an educated man. Jacques was bold, and David was cautious by nature. If Jacques was a figure out of Dickens or Balzac, almost the caricature of a captain of industry, David was a man more suited to the twentieth century, to an age of accountants and bankers, who came very soon to control much of his life.

David Bienenfeld spent his first years in the pearl trade in Rue Lafayette learning how to recognise different kinds and grades of pearls, how to weigh them in a complicated exponential scale of "times", how to see through outer skins into hidden beauty, and how to price the merchandise. Just as Simon Lieberman was sent after training to buy in Massawa, and Marc to buy in Venezuela, so David was dispatched to Bahrain as the buying agent for the JBSA. The journey alone took three weeks, and he was away for many months more in that dry and desolate outpost of the British Empire. Pearl buying was an infinitely slow process of muted haggling with Arab middlemen, who took tea with the suave European but never stated their prices in words, communicating instead in that ancient Oriental code (Rousseau mentioned it two centuries earlier, in his essay on the origins of language) that consists of pressing different fingers during the parting handshake.

It must have been a strange and empty life, waiting, in a tropical climate, in a place with virtually no distractions, for the next telegram from Paris and the next oblique and muffled negotiation with a white-robed pearl-fisher's emissary. More than thirty years later, David's nephew Georges Perec was stranded in a somewhat similar place on the coast of Tunisia. In an oversized, almost empty, concrete-walled flat – not unlike the one lived in by Jérôme and Sylvie in the second part of his novel, *Things* – Perec planned and perhaps even drafted a novel about a pearl trader posted to an exotic location who tries, three times over, to write the story of his life. That novel, which was to be set in Palawan if it was ever completed, is now lost, but a long letter describing it in detail has survived. It was entitled *J'avance masqué*, a French version of the motto of the philosopher Descartes, *Larvatus prodeo* ("I go forward in disguise"). It could have served as Perec's own motto; perhaps it also serves to explain something of

David Bienenfeld, whose respectable business career masked a lost vocation in medicine. Perec never acknowledged openly the great role that David had played in his life (he barely mentions his name in *W or The Memory of Childhood*), but the plan of *J'avance masqué* suggests that he did make at least one attempt to imagine something like his uncle's life.

In 1927, a new and more liberal nationality law was introduced in France. It was now possible to become French by naturalisation after four years' residence, which the Bienenfelds had already completed. Before leaving for Bahrain, David applied for French nationality for himself, for Esther, and for Bianca. He had numerous documents sent over from Poland and translated officially by the law firm of Victor Borten. The application was granted. When David returned from Bahrain in 1928, he and his family were no longer foreign, but French.

During David's absence, in October 1927, Esther gave birth to their second child, a daughter. Ela was the first of the Peretz and Bienenfeld clans to be born in the West, and she had French nationality by her birth; that is perhaps why she was given, as a kind of farewell, a characteristically Jewish and eastern European name.

Esther fell ill with pleurisy before Ela was born. Pregnancy and childbirth did not cure her, and so Jacques, stepping into David's shoes, had her seen by the leading chest specialist of the day. The distinguished professor treated the pleurisy by pneumothorax, which did not improve matters one bit, and then recommended convalescence in pure mountain air. Jacques paid for Esther to go to a sanatorium at Leysin, in the Swiss Alps; the girls were looked after by a mademoiselle, first in Paris and then in a family hotel at Leysin, so that they could be near their mother. Esther's convalescence lasted nearly two years. The family was not permanently reunited in Paris – or rather, in the rented villa at Suresnes – until 1929.

On his long buying trip in Bahrain, David Bienenfeld was not impressed by the quality of the pearl harvest on offer that season. He would have preferred to buy rather little of it and was reluctant to execute the orders that he had from Big Jacques, to buy everything he could. He knew that a huge, speculative plot had been hatched. Jacques had borrowed heavily in order to command a sufficient proportion of world supplies of raw pearls to enable him to penetrate and then dominate the biggest market of them all, America. He had sent Simon Lieberman to open the New York branch of the JBSA.

David's role in the plot was to bring back enough merchandise to keep Simon supplied. Negotiations with the Arabs were conducted in less than whispers, but orders from Jacques always came by telegram, with cordite: HAVE COURAGE BUY BUY BUY; or MONKEY DONKEY IDIOT FOOL; or ON RECONSIDERATION BELIEVE YOU ACTED WISELY STOP PAY YOURSELF SPECIAL COMMISSION $2,000 TO COMPENSATE FOR INSULTS.

There was not much David could do other than follow his master's orders. He bought out the entire stock of his Bahraini trading partner, Ali Reza, and returned to Paris in 1928 with more than four million dollars' worth of pearls, most of which turned out to be not particularly suitable for the American market, as he had feared. By the time they had all been made ready for shipment (sorted, graded, polished, pierced, and priced), the Wall Street crash was bringing down with it the fortunes of those people who might otherwise have bought the luxuries the Bienenfelds had to sell. CONFIDENTIAL PEARL PRICE CRASHING SELL WHATEVER YOU CAN REGARDLESS OF COST ONLY FOR CASH OR TOP UNQUESTIONABLE CREDITS, Jacques cabled to Simon, who knew as much already.

The end came in 1933. Jacques's fabled wealth bled away in unsaleable stock of declining value and in ever-rising interest payments to the banks that had financed his bid for world domination of the pearl trade. Jacques Bienenfeld himself died in December of that year, at the nadir of the Great Depression, allegedly a few minutes after a delegation of bankers had come to the great house at Suresnes to demand his resignation as chairman of the JBSA. "It was the right time to die," wrote Simon Lieberman, "Jacques could not have lived disgraced."

David Bienenfeld ran the company from 1933 until his death, in 1973. He ran it very differently from Jacques, because he was a different kind of man, and also because the stock now belonged to the banks on whose loans the company had defaulted. He gave up part of the building in Rue Lafayette and continued trading, on a much-reduced scale, effectively on behalf of the company's creditors. It was David's respectability, his obvious trustworthiness – his rigidity, even – that persuaded the bankers to let him get on with recouping the losses by trading, instead of keeping the pearls locked up in vaults. David was no doubt fairly well matched to the circumstances he found himself in, but those circumstances must also have reinforced character traits that saved his financial skin, and thus indirectly saved his life and the lives of his family. They were traits that Georges Perec would later find hard to bear.

Jacques Bienenfeld, the business genius, the king of the pearl trade, was brought down by the same quality that had made him rich: a willingness to gamble, to take a risk, to stretch himself to the limit. He had been right many times, and he had been handsomely rewarded for the risks he had taken. He got it badly wrong only once. Despite the mess he made of his business in his last years, it has to be said – and it is Georges Perec who says it, at the head of the Bienenfeld section of *L'Arbre* – that it was to Big Jacques Bienenfeld, the pearl king, and to him alone, that all the Bienenfelds (and, as a consequence, Georges Perec too) owed their French or American nationalities, and their lives.

Ali Reza remained a trading partner of David's, almost a family friend, and after the Second World War he sent the Bienenfelds crates of candied mangoes every year. Once he came to Paris and took a flat on the Champs-Elysées. He invited all the Bienenfelds to watch the Armistice Day parade from his balcony, and gave David's ten-year-old nephew his first glimpse of outrageous luxury. Women hovered around the Oriental gentleman, popping candies and chocolates into his mouth. And into Georges Perec's, too.

Bahrain in 1981: Jean-Michel Raynaud, *Pour un Perec lettré, chiffré* (Lille: Presses universitaires de Lille, 1984); letter from Georges Perec to Catherine Binet, from Sydney, 30 August 1981.

The pearl trade: Simon Lieberman, "People, Pearls and Places", unpublished typescript in the possession of Bianca Lamblin.

L'Arbre: letter from Georges Perec to Catherine Binet, from New York, 18 May 1979; FP 58.

Poles and the French: Janine Ponty, *Polonais méconnus. Histoire des travailleurs immigrés en France dans l'entre-deux-guerres* (Paris: Publications de la Sorbonne, 1988). About 250,000 Poles were brought to France by intergovernmental treaty between 1919 and 1926, excluding dependents and individual and clandestine immigrants.

J'avance masqué: letter from Georges Perec to Pierre Getzler, from Sfax, 8 February 1961.

Candied mangoes: FP 57, 75 (16 April 1972).

CHAPTER 4

Belleville and Passy

Esther was the eldest of the three Peretz children, David Bienenfeld was the eldest of five. Though they left their Jewish lives behind them in Lublin, they did not abandon the responsibility they felt for their siblings and parents. In establishing themselves professionally and financially in Paris, they were also establishing a French bridgehead for the whole family group. Apart from David Bienenfeld's father, Pinkas, who died in 1923, and Esther's brother Lejzor, who had already emigrated to Palestine, every member of the Bienenfeld couple's two close families moved to Paris before 1930.

In fact, the first to arrive was Lejzor. He came in 1925, on release from his kibbutz in Palestine, with his wife, also called Esther, and spent his days at the Ecole des Travaux publics, the civil-engineering college. To earn his keep, he spent his nights as a watchman (in a garage, with a loaded gun in his belt, according to one memory; at the premises of the JBSA, according to another). Esther (Georges Perec's *other* aunt Esther) worked in the basement of a gramophone shop in Boulevard Saint-Michel, putting 78-rpm records onto turntables for customers upstairs to listen to for a sou a time. Acute poverty did not stop Lejzor – who now called himself Léon, as we, too, will call him henceforth – from carrying off the highest honours in his final diploma. He knew what he wanted to do with his brains, and for what purpose. He returned to Palestine in 1928 or 1929, joined the Palestine Road Company as an engineer, and played a major role in the draining of the 'Emeq Hula, the malarial swamp north of Lake Tiberias in Galilee. He rose to become general manager of the company, and, after the State of Israel won independence in 1948, its outright owner. He grew rich, had three sons, and built a huge villa on the slopes of Mount Carmel, overlooking the Bay of Haifa. It was there that his only nephew, a French teenager called Georges Perec, came to stay for the summer holidays in 1952. It was an unfortunate experience. Georges was sent off to a scout camp with his cousin Uriel to help gather the sunflower harvest. He did not like the outdoor labouring life at all. He ate too much watermelon and drank litres of water on top of it – an old trick that gave him the violent colic he must have been warned of. Georges was sent back to Haifa to recover and then packed off home again. On his return to "civilisation", he declared that he would never again go to live "in boy-scout-land". And that seems to have closed the whole issue of Israel for him, for good.

In the course of the 1920s, David Bienenfeld's twin sisters, Berthe and Gisèle, and his youngest brother, Jacques (called Jacquot, to distinguish him from Big Jacques) settled in Paris. Jacquot began a career in the pearl trade, as David had done, working for the JBSA. The husbands of Berthe and Gisèle went into the jewellery business as well, though not with the Bienenfeld firm; David helped get them established. David's mother, Rebecca (*Rifka* in Yiddish), came last. She lived on her own; her granddaughters remember the candles she lit on Friday nights. She died in Paris before the outbreak of the Second World War. Only the grave of Pinkas remained in the East.

Pinkas **Bienenfeld** 1868–1923			m.		Rebecca (*Rifka*) **Schleifer** 1870 – Paris 1934
David 1893– Paris 1973	Marc 1897– Paris 1978 m. Ada	Berthe 1904– Paris 1969 m. Robert **Chavranski**	Gisèle 1904– New York 1958 m. Lery **Arnold**		Jacques (*Jacquot*) 1907– m. Estelle
Nehemias (*Nicha*) 1921– Paris 1956	Paul Paris 1926–	Henri Paris 1930–	Simone Paris 1934–		Donald New York 1945–

Esther's family followed the same track, for the same reasons, at much the same time. Her younger brother, Icek, called Izie, or Isi, or Izzy, came when he was about eighteen, probably towards the end of 1927, and her parents, David and Rojza (now called Rose, or Grandma Rose) arrived in 1929 or perhaps 1930.[1] With their arrival, the transplantation of the two clans was complete. As such things go,

[1] Rose also came for a visit in 1925 or 1926, when Léon was still in Paris. See illustration 1.

it seems to have been a remarkably well-organised and successful transfer. In less than a decade, David and Esther had got themselves and nearly all their close relatives into new lives in the West. But not quite everything went according to plan.

Esther could not look after her young brother Izie during his first years in Paris, for she was in Switzerland, convalescing from pleurisy. Later on, she would often blame herself for not having guided Izie's first steps in the West; unlike most of the others, the youngest of the Peretz children made no giant strides.

Very little is known for sure about the attitudes, the character, or the experiences of Georges Perec's father. According to Perec, who no doubt got the information from his aunt Esther, Izie left school when he was quite young (though in any case, being Jewish, he could not have gone to a lyceum) and completed all or part of an apprenticeship to a hatter in Warsaw. In Paris, David Bienenfeld got him taken on in the jewellery business, though there is no record of what branch or even what firm he worked for. By the time Esther got back from Leysin, in 1929, Izie had already dropped out of that career. When his parents immigrated shortly after and settled in Belleville, Izie joined them. He seems to have chosen to live in Paris as he had lived as a child in Lublin: with his meek and pious father and his dynamic mother, Rose. Ever the family provider, she promptly opened another grocery store.

Izie was a handsome young man, in Bianca's recollection, and a happy-go-lucky sort of fellow. Esther told Georges that his father preferred playing cards and gambling on horses to the struggle for financial security; perhaps he had transferred his father's trust in the Lord to trust in his luck. There is no reason to suppose that he was lacking in intelligence: he learnt French quickly and came to speak it with no trace of accent, an achievement that escaped even the accomplished Esther. Nor was he lazy. He helped his mother with the grocery store; it was he who got up at four in the morning to fetch the fresh produce from the central wholesale market at Les Halles, before going off to his own job.

My aunt [. . .] told me once that he was a poet; that he played truant; that he didn't like to wear a tie; that he was more at ease with his pals than with diamond traders (which still doesn't tell me why he didn't pick his pals from the diamond trade). [W 28]

David Bienenfeld must have provided the money, and Esther certainly helped to find accommodation and business premises for David and Rose. They moved into a tiny flat – barely more than a ground-floor room, perhaps a former concierge's *loge* – giving onto the court-yard at 24 Rue Vilin, in the twentieth arrondissement, in the heart of Belleville. There is no documentary trace of Izie's address before 1932, but from that date for sure, if not from earlier, he lived in the same house, probably even in the same room, as his parents. Esther, meanwhile, moved with her husband and daughters from Suresnes to a flat in Boulevard Delessert, in the middle-class, west-side quarter of Passy.

Belleville is a working-class area on the eastern edge of central Paris. In the 1920s and 1930s, it was inhabited very largely by recently arrived immigrants, almost all of them from eastern Europe and almost all of them Jewish. Its function was similar to that of London's East End or New York's Lower East Side, but with its narrow, cobbled streets winding up the steep slope of Ménilmontant, Belleville was probably even more like Warsaw or Łodz than any of the Jewish ghettos of the English-speaking world. The shops carried signs in Hebrew characters, the newsagents sold Yiddish newspapers, bearded men in top hats and black coats chatted on street corners in Yiddish: it was a whole Yiddish town within sight of the Eiffel Tower, shtetl-sur-Seine.

Grandma Rose opened a grocery store just round the corner from Rue Vilin, at the junction of Rue des Couronnes, Rue Julien-Lacroix, and Passage Julien-Lacroix. There were barrels of cucumber and herring in brine on the pavement outside. Ela and Bianca remember going there from time to time as little girls, in the 1930s. They remember the unfamiliar smells of Belleville – the smells of pickles and eastern European food, without doubt, but like Whitechapel and the Lower East Side, the place must also have smelled of over-crowding, and of poverty.

Rue Vilin was a shortish cul-de-sac for vehicles, ending in steep steps that led up to a platform at the junction of Rue Olivier Metra and Rue du Transvaal. Until quite recently, you could see over the whole of Paris from that promontory and could pick out in the middle distance the Panthéon, the Institut, and the golden dome of the Invalides. It was much the same as the perspective that Eugène de Rastignac contemplates at the end of Balzac's *Old Goriot*, from the Père Lachaise cemetery, less than a mile to the south.

The decay of old Belleville was a deliberate part of postwar town planning. Much of it has been rebuilt, and all that now remains of the street in which Georges Perec spent the first years of his life is a few cobbles forming part of a path across a postmodern hillside park. Georges Perec observed the progressive dereliction of Rue Vilin at first hand, for it was one of the twelve places in Paris which he chose to visit once a year, in connection with a writing project that he began in 1969. After each visit he would write meticulous descriptions that he would then put away, under seal.[1] He also had the street photographed several times between 1970 and 1980, when number 24 was one of the few houses still standing. He knew what the final act would be:

> The demolition men will come and their heavy hammers will smash the stucco and the tiles, will punch through the partitions, twist the ironwork, displace the beams and rafters, rip out the breeze blocks and the stone: grotesque images of a building torn down, reduced to piles of raw materials which scrap merchants in thick gloves will come to quarrel over: lead from the plumbing, marble from the mantelpieces, wood from the structure and the floors, the doors and the skirting boards, brass and cast iron from handles and taps, large mirrors and the gilt of their frames, basin stones, bathtubs, the wrought iron of the stair rail . . .
>
> The tireless bulldozers of the site-levellers will come to shovel off the rest: tons and tons of scree and dust.   [L 131]

In old Belleville, Izie Perec – perhaps already called André by his café acquaintances – became a worker. He obtained a work permit, a *carte d'identité de travailleur industriel*, which gave his trade as that of caster (in a foundry, presumably). Nothing is known about where he worked, nor about any other jobs he may have held, nor about his political views, nor, in fact, about what sort of man he really was. When Esther told Georges Perec that his father had been a "poet", did she mean that he recited verse, or that he lied to her? Bianca remembers her mother being anxious about Izie; but it is impossible to tell whether she was worried about his low status and income or about some trouble he may have been in. Izie never applied for naturalisation. He remained a working-class lad, and a foreigner.

In Rue Vilin, Izie met a Polish girl who had come to Paris before

---

[1] The project, entitled *Lieux* ("Places") is described in *Eses* 76–77 and in chapter 42 below.

he had, sometime in the 1920s. Like him, she spoke French without an accent. She lived at number 1, with her father and mother and her several brothers and sisters, the youngest of whom, called Fanny, was still a little girl. Cyrla (in Yiddish, Tzirele) Szulewicz called herself Cécile and was a hairdresser (or at least was training to become one). She was not a striking young woman either in looks or in character; Bianca, the only person now alive who knew Georges Perec's mother, remembers her as being almost the opposite of Izie's own mother, the purposeful Grandma Rose.

Nothing is known about the courtship of Izie and Cécile – how long it went on, whether it met with parental approval, whether it was in fact arranged. All that survives is the formal record of their marriage in the register of the twentieth arrondissement. It took place at 10:35 A.M. on Thursday, 30 August 1934, ten days after Cécile's twenty-first birthday (which may mean that the young couple waited until parental consent was no longer required by law). The civil ceremony lasted exactly five minutes; French registry-office marriages are pretty formal events. The witnesses at the civil ceremony were near neighbours: Chaim Kohn, a hairdresser – perhaps it was he who had taught Cécile her trade – and a tailor, Aaron Hang. After the relevant paragraphs of the civil code had been read out by one of the deputy mayors, Izie and Cécile signed the book:

Izie's signature is firm, even elegant; Cécile's is wobbly, whether from emotion, from an unfamiliar quill, or, as seems most probable, from unfamiliarity with writing. Though she spoke French with native ease, Cécile never wrote it well; Bianca gave her spelling and grammar lessons later on, to little effect. In her signature, Cécile shows the same hesitation over the spelling of her surname that her son was to display in *W or The Memory of Childhood*. It seems she began to write the Yiddish sound of -*witz*, then had to correct it to make the Polish-Russianised ending -*wicz*. It is plausible, or more than likely, perhaps even a foregone conclusion, that Perec's parents were also married in a religious ceremony at the synagogue: living in Jewish Belleville, the unrebellious children of Jewish immigrants could hardly have avoided a "proper" wedding. There is no record of such an event, however. Esther did not mention it in her conversations with her nephew about his family background, yet, if it happened, Esther would doubtless have been there. It would have been a grand gathering of both parts of the family, now split between the western suburb of Passy, and the east-side slum called Belleville.

> *I remember having laughed out loud, much later on, at a cartoon (probably when I was twelve or thirteen) showing a Paris urchin saying to another: For the long vacation I shall visit my aunt at La République (or at Opéra, or at Passy, etc.) [. . .] The idea of taking a holiday in a posh part of the city, of going from a wretched quarter to a middle-class one, was familiar to me; I could have been that street urchin just as, to resuscitate another similarly familiar and quite outmoded anecdote, I could have been the little boy who shows off to his pals by telling them how, one day, he went for a ride in his uncle's motor car.* [FP 57, 15]

Obviously Izie had been expected to do better; Esther and David Bienenfeld were disappointed by his lack of ambition and of application. He had not walked over the bridge they had built for him. Something of the outsider's awkwardness can be seen in the poorly focused photograph of a family gathering, somewhere in Paris, taken very probably in the winter of 1930 (illustration 5). Standing in the back row, from right to left, are David Bienenfeld, then Esther, then David's sister Berthe, then Izie. This was perhaps the photograph that made Georges Perec think that his father looked like Franz Kafka. What is more certain is that with his dark curly hair, his prominent ears, and his asymmetric posture, Izie looked just like his son.

Izie and Cécile lived at number 24 Rue Vilin, perhaps in a different room from Rose and David. They rented the ground-floor, street-side room of the house and opened a ladies' hairdressing business. The business was officially registered in the name of Icek Perec in February 1935, but that was probably only a formality: it was Cécile who ran the salon, single-handed.

The social and cultural disparity between the Perecs of Belleville and the Bienenfelds of Passy was already great, but there were nonetheless plenty of links between the two branches of the family in the 1930s. Esther went to see her mother in Rue Vilin and took her daughters along. Grandma Rose called on Esther and David when they were living in Boulevard Delessert and, later on, in Rue des Eaux. They all liked to play cards, and there were Sunday afternoons when the whole Paris clan – David's brothers, sisters and in-laws, Esther's parents and her brother – gathered in the smoke-filled Bienenfeld lounge for long sessions of belote. The fortunes of the different members of the family may have been varied, but it was not a family divided.

A year after she was married, Cécile became pregnant, and she gave birth to a boy at 9:00 P.M. on 7 March 1936, in a maternity clinic in Rue de l'Atlas, in the neighbouring nineteenth arrondissement. The birth was declared three days later by the sixteen-year-old assistant midwife who had delivered the child, who was named Georges. The midwife gave his parents' address as number 1 Rue Vilin, which was in fact the address of Cécile's parents. It may have been a simple mistake on her part; it may have been Cécile's error, in a postnatal haze; or it may be that Cécile had moved back to be with her own family during confinement (a similar speculation has been made about the place of birth listed on Izie's identity documents). But it is certain that the house in which Georges Perec spent his first years was not number 1, but number 24 Rue Vilin.

Izie and Cécile had their son circumcised. The ritual operation would have been carried out by the *mohil* in the family home, within a few days of the infant's birth.

Izie forgot one thing at first: to take advantage of French nationality laws and to have the boy registered as French at birth. Perhaps it was Esther who reminded him of the formalities that needed completing; at all events, five months later, on 18 August 1936, Izie went to see the justice of the peace of the twentieth arrondissement to declare before witnesses that his son, having been born in France, was of French nationality. The official term used for Georges Perec's nationality status for the rest of his life was *Français par déclaration, fils d'étrangers*. There is virtually no difference between that status and just plain French nationality – except in quite special circumstances. The wafer-thin gap between being French by parentage and French by declaration was to affect the course of Perec's life only once, but then in a rather substantial way: it obliged him, indirectly, to do two years' military service in the French army, which briefly turned him into a parachute trooper.

A second child was born in 1938 but lived for only a few weeks. According to Esther, Georges's sister was called Irène, but according to the only document unearthed so far that mentions this brief life (her birth was not registered in either the nineteenth or the twentieth arrondissement), she was called Jeannine.

In one sense at least, Georges Perec had a privileged start to his life. He was surrounded as an infant by a large extended family: his two parents, three of his four grandparents[1] and several uncles and aunts on his mother's side were all in close proximity, and an aunt, uncle and two cousins on his father's side lived not too far away for frequent contact. *I've been told that I stayed for longer or shorter periods, but really quite often, with my aunt Esther [. . .] over towards Passy* [FP 57, 15].

> *I must note down this true or false memory which has come back to me: in the morning I used to get into my parents' bed; my mother would get up, but my father, who had already been to Les Halles, slept in. My favourite game consisted of plunging completely under the sheets and going to my father's feet, which I tickled, with great bursts of laughter.* [Quoted in MO 221]

Georges Perec spent his first years in a multilingual environment. Izie and Cécile spoke French to each other (as did Georges's aunt Esther and uncle David). Grandma Rose and David Peretz, who probably spoke Yiddish to each other, used Polish to talk with Esther and David (whose other language was German, not Yiddish) and presumably either one or the other with Izie and Cécile; they never learnt more than very basic French and spoke it with thick accents. In the street, the infant Perec would have heard some French but much more Yiddish, along with sprinklings of Polish, and snatches of Russian, German, Czech, Hungarian, and Romanian. It is not known what language his Szulewicz relatives used with each other, or with him, but the predominance of Yiddish and Polish as the languages of the older generation, and of Yiddish as the language of the broader environment, is beyond doubt.

Perec forgot a great deal but not quite everything about his early years in Rue Vilin. He must have learnt to understand Yiddish, if not to speak it, and there is later evidence that he knew at least some words of Polish as well. It is also quite possible that he began to learn to read at the age of three or four, and that the first letters he

---

[1] It is not known when Georges Perec's maternal grandmother died, save that it was before the German occupation of Paris.

recognised and deciphered were Hebrew characters, not Latin ones. The fact that he later forgot whatever Hebrew and Yiddish he had picked up as an infant is not, in itself, at all surprising. But something stuck in his mind and, despite its internal contradictions and probably secondary elaborations, seemed to him to constitute the first trace of his own existence:

> *I am three. I am sitting in the middle of* [the back room of my grandmother's shop] *with Yiddish newspapers scattered around me. The family circle surrounds me wholly, but the sensation of encirclement does not cause me any fear or feeling of being smothered; on the contrary, it is warm, protective, loving: all the family – the entirety, the totality of the family – is there, gathered like an impregnable battlement around the child who has just been born (but didn't I say a moment ago that I was three?).*
>
> *Everyone is in raptures over the fact that I have pointed to a Hebrew character and called it by its name: the sign was suppos-edly shaped like a square with a gap in its lower left-hand corner, something like* פ *and its name was apparently gammeth, or gammel. The subject, the softness, the lighting of the whole scene are, for me, reminiscent of a painting, maybe a Rembrandt or maybe an invented one, which might have been called "Jesus amid the Doctors".* [W 13]

Perec's character does not exist in the Hebrew alphabet; as he points out in a footnote, the shape represented could at best be a very poorly made mem,[1] מ . Four or five times already, before finalising *W or The Memory of Childhood*, Perec had grappled with the evanescent memory of the first, false letter of his life, in texts placed in sealed envelopes. Some of his sketches looked more like a tav than a mem, some looked like nothing much at all, and he wondered whether it was a gimmel or a yod that he had learned to name. Yod? A sign of *youd* (*Jude*, "Jew"), Perec surmises. Gimmel? The letter for G, which (French pronunciation left aside) could be the initial letter of Perec's forename, Georges. Perhaps it is not really surprising, therefore, that the letter-shape represented in the published version of Perec's first memory of childhood is less like a badly drawn tav, mem, gimmel

---

[1] The French text says *men*, not mem. The English translator should not have corrected Perec's "mistake"! See chapter 52 below.

or yod than like a left-for-right inversion (as Catherine Binet saw long ago) of the shape that the adult Perec made when signing his initial G.

AdP: *Registre de commerce*, entry number 631320

Authenticated copy of Icek Judko Perec's work permit number 37AC19031 dated 10 September 1939, from the records of the French Ministry of Defence.

The development of Perec's memory of "The Hebrew Letter" is studied by Philippe Lejeune in *MO* 210–230, and also in chapter 52 below.

CHAPTER 5

The Collapse of France

Cécile and Izie, and therefore everyone else, called Georges Jojo. How was he brought up? His mother worked full-time at her hairdressing business; his father had a job and a half labouring as a foundryman and giving a hand to Grandma Rose, who must have put in long hours at her grocery shop. Old David Peretz was probably more interested in playing with his grandson than in minding the store; no doubt he dandled *dos Kind* on his knee, and told him Bible stories. Perhaps he also sang him the Polish lullaby, "Ay, ah, kotki dva", which is the last fading trace of the family's origins in the present-day memory of David Peretz's eldest French great-granddaughter. There are no memories of Georges's maternal grandmother, Laja, nor of his grandfather, Aaron Szulewicz; the only written record states his occupation as *marchand ambulant*, perhaps of fruit and vegetables, since Perec corrects himself, in *W or The Memory of Childhood*, to say that Aaron was not a craftsman but a greengrocer. Cécile's young sister Fanny, only ten years older than her nephew, acted as nanny to Jojo and often took him to Passy to see his aunt Esther and to play.

It was but a thirty-minute trip on the metro from one world to another, from a warm, working-class, immigrant slum to an area of comfortable balconied apartment blocks. At Passy, Jojo played in the sandpiles by the Seine near the Pont de Grenelle, and on one occasion was taught to ride a bicycle by his cousin Ela, whom he called Lili. Though the bicycle had stabilising side-wheels, Ela thought it necessary to instruct her cousin in every movement at the top of her voice; people came to their windows to see what the fuss was about. As an adult, Georges Perec remembered the screaming but thought it had been his [*W* 51].

In the first years of Georges Perec's life, refugees poured into Belleville, telling ever grimmer tales of the situations in Poland, in Germany, in Czechoslovakia, in Austria. Even if its roads were not paved with gold, even if anti-Semitism was not absent from the banks of the Seine, France was a haven still. As Austria and Czechoslovakia fell into German hands, the Belleville community believed as much as their French hosts in the invincibility of the Maginot line.

Hitler invaded Poland in September 1939, and France and Britain, joint guarantors of Polish sovereignty, declared war on Germany. There was an immediate general mobilisation in France. Even the half-blind philosopher Jean-Paul Sartre was called up to watch weatherballoons over eastern France. David Bienenfeld did not have to volunteer, for, as a naturalised Frenchman with military experience in the old Austrian army, he was in the reserve and was mobilised straightaway. His unit was stationed near Meaux, where he served for nearly six months as a medical officer. At long last his early training in Vienna found some practical use. Izie, on the other hand, could not join the regular French army, as he held Polish nationality. But the rules of enlistment into the foreign legion were altered to permit large numbers of eager immigrants to bolster the defence of France: on declaration of war, the legion allowed men to join up "for the duration of the hostilities". And that is precisely what Icek Judko Perec did.

Izie was an able-bodied man of thirty, and one of many thousands of Jews who joined up in the first few days of the war. Why did he do so? In *W or The Memory of Childhood*, Georges Perec writes that Izie was *un brave à trois poils,* "a doughty fighter" in the English translation, which misses the sense of perhaps foolish bravado in the French, but he gives none of the reasons that might have prompted his father to throw in his lot with the French army. However, it is not hard to see what they might have been. France had declared war on Germany; Germany was an enemy of the Jews; Izie was a Jew; ergo, he should join up. Second, France was going to war for the defence of Poland; Izie was a Pole; ergo, he should join up. (Given the attitudes of the other members of the family toward Poland, this seems a less likely motive). Third, Izie was still a foreigner in a country that his family had made its own. Esther probably encouraged her brother to enlist, as it would make it easier for him to become French. She certainly approved of his decision to do so, out of loyalty to the country that had become hers, or as her daughters put it, out of idealism and gratitude.

It is also possible that Izie was swept along by the propaganda of the French press, or by the excitement of the crowd; he may have been dragged to the recruiting office by his workmates; or maybe, like Ernie Levy, the Jewish immigrant in André Schwarz-Bart's novel

The Last of the Just, Izie joined up because there was not much else to do. But to judge by the guilt to which Esther subsequently admitted, Izie's enlistment was not a sudden or a private decision but one discussed, approved, and supported by the elders of the family.

The documentary evidence suggests that Izie planned to enlist in the foreign legion even before war was declared, before the German-Soviet pact of August 1939 which made the invasion of Poland a near certainty. On 18 July 1939, he went to the local police station with two shopkeepers from Rue Julien-Lacroix – Jean Jaillot from number 3, and Jean Andrieu, from number 46, both of them *marchands de vins* – to obtain a certificate of residence in Paris *"pour s'engager volontaire"* ("to enlist"). Izie did not use the certificate for two months. Perhaps the recruiting offices were closed for the summer holiday; perhaps Izie (or Esther, or Cécile) had second thoughts; or perhaps the certificate was in fact obtained for some other purpose. Whatever the reason for the delay, the certificate was presented on 19 September, when Izie attended the foreign legion's recruiting office at the Fort of Vincennes and signed a cyclostyled piece of paper on which he requested enlistment in the legion for the duration of the war.

On 5 October he went through his medical examination: he was found to be one metre sixty-seven in height (his son, Georges, would be slightly shorter, one metre sixty-six), to have brown hair (Georges's was black), brown eyes (Georges's were green), good teeth (Georges's were terrible), and an oval face, to weigh sixty-two kilos, to have no distinguishing features, and to be fit for service. He signed the contract of engagement later that day. He must have left almost immediately, as he arrived at the legion's mainland base and training camp at Valbonne, near Cannes, on 8 October 1939.

Whilst Izie went through basic training in the south of France, Cécile carried on her business, Rose carried on running her shop, and Georges no doubt carried on playing in the street under the eye of his teenage aunt Fanny. But during that first winter of the war – the period known as the phony war, since there was no action on the Western front – Georges no longer went to Rue des Eaux to see his aunt Esther and her daughters. They had been on holiday at Annecy in the French Alps on the day war was declared, and although David had returned forthwith to Paris and then joined his unit as a mobilised officer of the reserve, Esther had decided that it would be safer for the rest of the family to get as far away from the German border as possible. Travelling cross-country, without passing through Paris (which was something of a feat in itself, given the way the French have built their roads and railways), Esther, Bianca and Ela took up residence at Quimper, in Brittany, on the Atlantic coast. Bianca remembers that they saw women crying at the news of war at every stop on their journey: in rural France, the memory of the terrible losses of the 1914–18 war was still acute.

Bianca had obtained her baccalaureate at the Lycée de Neuilly, where she was taught by Simone de Beauvoir, and had done the first year of a degree in philosophy. The Sorbonne was evacuated to Rennes, and so Bianca moved there to take her second-year courses in the winter of 1939–40. Ela went to school at Quimper, whilst Esther, free for the first time, in a curious sense, to pursue her own education, trained as a nurse in the minor-injuries ward of a military hospital and obtained an official certificate of competence from the Red Cross.

Esther's brother Léon was in Haifa, far away from the war; and David's brother Jacquot was settled in New York, working alongside Simon Lieberman. As for the other Bienenfelds, Gisèle, with her husband and her daughter, Simone, was in Paris, as was Marc, with his wife, Ada, and their two sons, Nicha and Paul; Berthe, Gisèle's twin, was also in Paris with her husband, Robert Chavranski – but their son, Henri, who suffered from chronic asthma, was at school that year, as he had been for some time already, at Villard-de-Lans, in the clean mountain air of the French Alps.

Much reorganisation took place in the French army in the course of that winter. Some reservists were demobilised on account of their age – David Bienenfeld was one of them – and whole new regiments were formed to accommodate all the volunteers. Izie was put into one of these, the XIIe Régiment Etranger d'Infanterie, created on 25 February 1940 and composed (on paper, at least) of 84 officers, 321 NCOs, 173 horses, and 2,685 other ranks from the Valbonne base, supplemented (and no doubt led) by 9 officers, 198 NCOs and 407 other ranks from the foreign legion's main base at Sidi-bel-Abbès in Algeria. In March, Izie (*Isek Perek,* according to his passbook) went with his company for further training and "amalgamation" at the military camp at Sathonay, near Lyon. He spent two months there. None of the letters he must have written to his wife or to his sister has come to light.

The German offensive began on 10 May 1940. Instead of attacking France through the plains of Flanders, as military planners had expected them to do, the Germans pushed their tank columns through the allegedly uncrossable hills of the Ardennes and made straight for the Channel coast at the level of Abbeville. The French and British forces to the north of them were cut off within a few days.

French and British strategy was in tatters. A new defensive line was improvised by General Gamelin, but he was sacked and replaced by Weygand a week later. The XIIᵉ REI got its marching orders on 11 May and set off northwards from Valbonne and from Lyon, but such were the ditherings and the difficulties of the French forces that the legionnaires did not get dug into their final positions on the Somme-Aisne line until 24 May. The task of Izie's regiment was to defend the sector around the town of Soissons, about a hundred kilometres north-northeast of Paris. On 27 May, the British began evacuating their forces from Dunkirk. Izie was in a fighting unit facing what was now the main – indeed the only – active front left in the war.

The Germans came into contact with the French forces around Soissons in the first days of June. Much of northern France was already occupied, and refugees were flooding south along all the main and secondary roads leading towards Paris, making the defence of river crossings all the more awkward. Soissons itself came under aerial bombardment and the the decision was taken, after a few days of resistance, to pull the defensive line back, further south, to the next major river. The XIIᵉ REI began moving to the Ourcq on 7 June. The Luftwaffe had mastery of the skies; the infantry protected itself from the planes by spreading out and moving south across fields and through woods, but the horse-drawn vehicles were easy targets. Thirteen of the regiment's fifteen mess wagons were destroyed from the air on 8 June. The retreat was becoming a rout. The foreign legion held the Ourcq for only a few hours and then moved back still further, to the natural barrier formed by the Marne. It was not a barrier on the route to Paris any longer: the position taken up for the last real resistance to the German advance was less than fifty miles from Belleville but not north of it at all, just a shade south of the same latitude.

The XIIᵉ REI had a day of quiet before the attack began, at first light on 13 June. The French came under continuous shelling from artillery; then motorcycles with sidecar machinegunners swooped in from the north and east. By four o'clock the order to retreat had been given once again. Izie survived all of this and must have marched with his company through the night, across the plain of the Brie, halting briefly at Marolles before pushing on to the river Seine, a mile or two downstream from Bray. The regiment crossed the river and dug in on the south bank, aiming to halt any German advance over the bridges between Bazoches and Balloy. The officers believed that the XIIᵉ REI was part of a French line holding the Seine to the west, towards Paris. On the morning of 15 June, a message brought the news that the line had been abandoned. The Italian, Spanish, Polish, and Jewish volunteers led by the desert desperadoes of the XIIᵉ REI were the only defenders left on the Seine. There would be no further support, and no further contact. Izie was apparently a signaller; it may have been he who transmitted the disastrous message to his superiors. But before the soldiers of the XIIᵉ REI could organise their withdrawal, German motorcycle machinegunners were upon them.

Meanwhile, the population of Paris was struck with panic. Bianca had returned there at the end of the academic year at Rennes, to be with her father. She saw the refugees from northern France coming into the city with their handcarts laden. Like many Parisians, she and her father realised only after a day or two that the peasants were not stopping but carrying straight on, down the Boulevard Saint-Michel and out the other side. What would happen if the Germans got to the gates of Paris? It did not occur to them that defeat was a foregone conclusion. Surely the French army would put up a massive resistance to protect their capital; there would be a huge battle for Paris. It was time to get out. Along with almost every other Parisian who had a car, David Bienenfeld got away before the expected battle. He took Bianca with him, and his treasured assistant from the JBSA, Jacqueline Benoît-Lévy, and Bianca's friend and former schoolteacher, Simone de Beauvoir. The latter mentions this flight in her memoirs in a surprisingly offhand way, saying that she accepted the lift "as a matter of course" because her lycée was being evacuated to Nantes.[1] It is not likely that anything, in those few days of mass panic when more than a third of the population of Paris took to the roads, could have been called a matter of course. Simone de Beauvoir was dropped off at Angers, not Nantes; Jacqueline was left with friends at Le Mans; David and Bianca made for Quimper, to join Esther and Ela.

---

[1] Simone de Beauvoir, *Tout compte fait* (Paris: Gallimard, 1962), p. 33. A fuller account is given in Beauvoir's *Journal de guerre* (Paris: Gallimard, 1990), in which the Bienenfelds appear under altered names.

From Belleville, too, people fled to the countryside, where the risks of shelling and aerial bombardment were thought to be less. Cécile entrusted Jojo to a lady who lived in Rue Vilin, a friend of Grandma Rose's whose daughter worked as a pearl stringer for the JBSA.

> *Personally, I have no memory of that great flight from Paris, but I do have a photo which bears its trace [. . .]*
>
> *I am at the wheel of a toy car, which I remember as red but which here is obviously light in colour, perhaps with some red trim (air intake slats on the side of the bonnet). I have a kind of one-button jersey on, either with short sleeves or with the sleeves rolled up [. . .]*
>
> *I don't know where this village was. For years I believed it was in Normandy, but I rather think it was east or north of Paris. Several times, in fact, there were air raids nearby. A friend of my grandmother's had fled there with her children and had taken me with her. She told my aunt that she hid me under the eiderdown each time there was a raid, and that the Germans who occupied the village liked me a lot and played with me, and that one of them spent his time giving me rides on his shoulders. She was very afraid, she said to my aunt, who subsequently told me, that I might say something I shouldn't say, and she didn't know how to get me to understand the secret I had to keep.* [W 51–52]

At 11:20 A.M. on 15 June, Izie's regiment, under heavy machine-gun fire and without any cover, made a dash from its position behind the Seine to the bridge over the Yonne at Champigny, about eight kilometres behind them. It is not likely that Izie got as far as the Yonne. He was hit at some point on that day by a piece of shrapnel and was taken to Nogent-sur-Seine, about thirty kilometres to the east of the position defended on the morning of 15 June, along the main road, the RN 59. When his comrades reached the Yonne later that day, they found French tanks positioned at the bridge, but no one ordered the tank crews to give the XIIᵉ REI covering fire from the Germans who were pursuing them; on the contrary, when the officer commanding the Champigny crossing saw that the Germans were approaching, he had the bridge blown up straightaway. A very large part of the retreating French regiment was consequently cut off. Some men swam across; one brave soldier even found a punt and made four or five crossings under enemy fire to bring men over. Only a quarter of what was left of the regiment made it to the south side of Yonne – about 150 men and a few motorised vehicles. When they got to the main road, which runs parallel to the Yonne at that point, they found themselves trapped: German tanks and armoured vehicles were coming towards them from both directions, from Paris and from Sens. They were summoned to surrender by loud-hailer, they were told they had been betrayed, but the last rump of the foreign legion shot its way out and continued to press on to the south and west, to Montargis on the Loing and then down to Gien. They were stuck for twenty-four hours in a ten-kilometre-long jam of soldiers, civilians, cars, tanks, motorcycles, bicycles, handcarts, and pack mules, all desperate to cross the bridge, which had been set alight by German incendiary bombs. A tiny remnant of the XIIe REI got to Vierzon on 22 June, the day the armistice was signed. The regimental log states that some of the stragglers who had been cut off – "including muleteers, pack bearers, horses and Jews" – caught up with the regiment there. On 24 June, the XIIe REI was at Saint-Amand, where it was demobilised and disestablished under the terms of the armistice. The volunteers returned to civilian life; the few professional soldiers went back to Sidi-bel-Abbès. The débâcle was over. The worse catastrophe had not yet begun.

To judge from the map, it seems unlikely that Izie would have been taken to Nogent-sur-Seine had he fallen after midday on 15 June, because from then on his regiment was moving south at the best speed it could, further and further away from any roads leading to Nogent. (The next main road they came to would have given access to Montereau in the west and Sens to the southeast.) When Izie fell, as his death certificate makes clear, he was taken prisoner and then to a field hospital at the church at Nogent-sur-Seine, behind German lines. According to Georges Perec, who was told this by his aunt, who heard it from one of Izie's fellow legionnaires, the field hospital was full of dying men attended to by a single medical orderly [W 37]. Izie was bleeding badly, and someone had pinned a label onto his tunic that said (in German, necessarily) OPERATE IMMEDI-ATELY. But there was no time. Izie died on 16 June 1940, and was buried in the military section of the municipal graveyard, beneath a simple wooden cross on which his name and his regimental number were stencilled: PEREC ICEK JUDKO E.V. 3716.

Of the three-thousand-odd men of the XIIe REI, the majority were taken prisoner by the Germans, some as early as the battle of the Aisne, others at the defeat on the Marne, and about three quarters of

the survivors of those battles at the bungled crossing of the Yonne.
The official list of "losses of the Twelfth Foreign Infantry Regiment",
drawn up a few days after the armistice, shows that there were also
many deaths amongst the officers and men, men with names like
Davidovitch, Pravassoudovitch, Reciniti, Rieffel, Garaguani and
Perez. Izie's name is not on the list; the officer who drew it up noted,
"From 15 June, record incomplete".

The fifteenth and sixteenth of June were the last days of French
military resistance to the German advance, but it is not true to say
that 16 June was the last day of hostilities, and it is even less accurate
to call it the day of the armistice, as Georges Perec does in *W or The
Memory of Childhood*. The shooting and bombing went on for several
more days, and many hundreds of soldiers and civilians were still to
lose their lives before the armistice was signed, on 22 June. The effect
of Perec's error in writing about his father's death is to make it seem
an absurd irony, an unnecessary death, as if had Izie just waited
another few hours, he could have escaped unscathed. The actual
record of the regiment tells a different story. Izie died in a volunteer
regiment consisting exclusively of foreigners, fighting to hold back
the Germans, ill supported, to put it mildly, by their French colleagues in arms. On the Marne and on the Seine, the XIIe REI was
the last unit to give up. On the Yonne, the foreign legion was simply
abandoned to the Germans by French tank and bridge officers.

There is absolutely no written trace of Perec's ever having asked
himself, or historians, "Who was responsible for the death of my
father?" But that does not necessarily mean that he did not know, or
guess, or fear the answer.

The ignominious armistice signed at Rethondes on 22 June divided
France into two zones: the ZO (*zone occupée*), comprising all of France
north of the Loire and the Atlantic coastal strip down to the Spanish
border, and the ZNO, or *zone nono*, the so-called free zone, stretching
from the Loire to the south coast. France was to be ruled by a puppet
government under the now decrepit victor of Verdun, Maréchal
Pétain, from Vichy, a spa town in the Massif Central, far from the
main centres of population and industry. Officially, French law
would hold sway over the whole country; in practice, the ZO came
under German military administration, and Vichy France soon introduced legislation to bring it into line with National Socialist policies,
especially with respect to Jews.

Many of the French who had moved south of the Loire to escape

VILLE DE NOGENT-SUR-SEINE

DÉPARTEMENT
DE
L'AUBE

SERVICE
administratif.

EXTRAIT

DES REGISTRES DES ACTES DE DÉCÈS

de la Ville de Nogent-sur-Seine (Aube)

L'an mil *neuf cent quarante*

le *seize Juin :*

est décédé Rue *à l'Hôpital des Prisonniers de guerre (Eglise).*

M. *Pérec   Icek, Judko .*

Soldat au 12ème Régiment étranger, recrutement E.V. n° matricule 3716

profession de *fondeur.*

domicilié à *Paris rue Velin n° 24.*

né le *dix neuf juin mil neuf cent neuf.*

à *Lubar   (Pologne.)*

fils de *David Pérec*

et de *Sura Rojza Wabesztein*

(Etat civil)

Mention   " Mort pour la France ".

Certifié conforme aux Registres de l'Etat civil, et délivré gratuitement sur papier libre,

pour service *administratif*

Nogent-sur-Seine, le *vingt neuf Septembre*

mil neuf cent *quarante sept*

Le Maire,
POUR LE MAIRE,
L'ADJOINT.

N° *13.460/58*

"NE VARIETUR"

EXPERT TRADUCTEUR JURÉ
près le
Tribu...
de ...
34, Avenue ...
PARIS - 8-
Victor BORTEN

MAIRIE de NOGENT-sur-SEINE
(AUBE)

The Death Certificate of Icec Judko Perec

the German advance and the expected battle for Paris breathed a sigh of relief at the terms of the armistice and stayed where they were. David Bienenfeld's sister Berthe stayed put in Villard-de-Lans, where she had gone to be with her son, Henri. Her twin sister, Gisèle, had been in the south of France at the time of the invasion; with her husband and daughter, she decided to leave Europe straightaway and crossed into Spain to embark for the United States. They got as far as Cuba, where they were held up for three years whilst waiting for U.S. entry permits. But they arrived in the end, settled in New York, and eventually became American citizens.

David and Esther had fled west, not south, and therefore found themselves in the occupied zone, even if they were as far from Paris as Berthe was. They were offered passage on a boat to Britain but they did not take it. As Esther explained to Georges Perec in 1967, David Bienenfeld considered that he had no right to do so, for he had brought with him to Quimper either all or part of the stock of pearls of the JBSA, and those pearls really belonged to the company's creditors, the banks. To leave them buried at Quimper was unthinkable; to take them to Britain would be like stealing.

David's reasoning was specious – or rather, it was no less specious than the opposite argument, that taking the pearls to London would be the best way to serve the banks' legitimate interests, by putting the treasure in the only safe vaults left in Europe. But huge decisions are not necessarily rational. David and Esther were deeply committed to France and preferred to stay. Had they been offered passage to America, where they now had relatives and a business to join, they might have made a different decision, but at that time they did not have U.S. visas.

Since Quimper was in the occupied zone, it was no safer than Paris, and a lot less interesting. So, like a significant proportion of Parisians who had left the city during the exodus, the Bienenfelds returned to their flat and their jobs towards the end of July 1940. They were amazed, and overjoyed, to see that the city had survived without a scratch. There had been no battle for Paris; not a single monument or building had been bombed. For a brief moment, the euphoria of relief blotted out the grimmer truth of defeat. Bianca went to a party on their first night home, with all her old friends from the Sorbonne. They felt they had something to celebrate.

Georges Perec was probably brought back to Belleville at much the same time by the *very kind and very fat woman* from Rue Vilin who had taken him off to the country during the hostilities [*W* 52]. News of his father's death could not have been long in coming; Cécile probably received the official notification by the end of June. What sense could a little boy have made of his father's death "on the field of honour"? Small children can seem quite unaffected by such tragedies, and can appear take it in their stride. It is unlikely that the news was kept from the child: it was wartime, and his father was a soldier. Jojo would have had the sympathy of everyone on the street, and a kind of understanding. It is quite probable that he was told his father had died a hero, in the defence of France and of the Jews. He may have been made to feel just a little bit proud.

On the other hand, a boy bereft of his father at the age of four can also feel omnipotent: he is now the man of the house, the sole possessor of his mother. Or he can feel very suddenly a bottomless pit of guilt. Had Jojo never wished that his father were dead? Had he? And who then was really responsible for Izie's death? Perec would not have been the only bereaved child to take upon himself the guilt for a parent's death and to bury it very deeply, where it would do the most harm.

For Cécile, for Rose, and for Esther, Izie's death was a grievous blow. It brought them closer to each other; the difference between middle-class Passy and working-class Belleville must have seemed of little consequence beside the loss of a husband, son, and brother, a man whose life had hardly begun. Izie died just before his thirty-first birthday.

Esther took Cécile to Franck's, a dress shop in the sixteenth arrondissement, to buy her widow's weeds. Lili went along, too, and thinks that the dress bought at Franck's was the one worn by Cécile in the last known photograph of her, taken in Montsouris Park sometime in 1940:

> *My mother is wearing a big black beret. Her coat may be the same one she has on in the photograph taken at Bois de Vincennes,[1] to judge by the button, but this time she has it done up. Handbag, gloves, stockings and lace-up shoes are all black. My mother is a widow. Her face is the only light spot in the photograph. She is smiling.* [*W* 52–53]

One Sunday in the summer of 1940, before the start of the school year at the end of September, Lili had a school friend to play at her

---

[1] Illustration 7

home in Rue des Eaux. She said to her friend, "I have to introduce you to my relatives." In the lounge there was a very tiny old lady dressed all in black, with her white hair drawn into a tight chignon; a slim, modest, perhaps rather shy young woman, also dressed in black, with large, brown, sad eyes; and a little boy with curly black hair and eyes that had a bright intensity (they are remembered as having been blue at the time, though they must have turned green already, by the age of four). The little boy, Lili said, was her favourite cousin. His name was Jojo.

The debacle was over, and it had left Jojo fatherless, and his mild and hapless mother a widow. Rose had lost the son who had stayed closest to her and had helped her manage; David Peretz, her husband, had never given her much support and now spent ever more of his time in prayer. Esther felt that she should bear part of the blame for the disaster, and that she carried a double responsibility for the boy – because she was his father's elder sister and because she had encouraged his father to enlist. The situation was grave. What would become of the child?

Izie's enlistment and training: archives of the French foreign legion (Aubagne), kindly located and copied by Madame Duhard, Ministry of Defence, Paris.

The formation, complement, campaigns, losses and dissolution of the XIIᵉ Régiment Etranger d'Infanterie: Service Historique des Armées de Terre (Vincennes).

Other information was provided by Ela Bienenfeld, Marie-Thérèse Jost, Bianca Lamblin, Marianne Saluden, and by Georges Perec himself, in his notes on his conversations with Esther Bienenfeld in 1967.

CHAPTER 6

Vichy-Auschwitz

Defeated and divided, France remained only nominally a sovereign state in the summer of 1940. The prospects, for those with eyes to see, from Passy or from Belleville, were grim indeed. On the day the Bienenfelds returned to Paris from Quimper, the German military administration of the city confiscated their car, a front-wheel-drive Citroën B14. In August, Germany, disregarding the terms of the armistice it had signed six weeks earlier, annexed the departments of Alsace and Lorraine, and made the Pas-de-Calais and the Nord part of occupied Belgium, under direct German rule. The Law of 3 October 1940, enacted at Vichy, banned Jews from public appointments and the professions. The Law of 4 October 1940 gave departmental prefects powers of arbitrary internment of Jews in special camps. These laws held force in all that was left of France, in both the occupied and the non-occupied zone.

Who were the Jews in France? The Jewish community itself had no list. French civil records – as befits a country that had long before made a firm distinction between church and state – carried no mention of an individual's religious beliefs or ethnic background. Jewishness was not a fact that existed about French residents, and so the facts had to be created, administratively. Posters were put up in both zones to inform Jews that they were required to declare themselves at police stations or else be liable for unspecified penalties. After much anguished discussion, the Bienenfeld family decided to obey the instructions. David Bienenfeld declared himself, his wife, and their two daughters. The majority of Jews in Paris did likewise, out of respect for the law, out of respect for bureaucracy, out of common sense: what could be the point, in dangerous times, of getting on the wrong side of regulations? It is very probable that Cécile also went to the local commissariat and declared herself and her son; her parents-in-law, Rose and David, almost certainly did. By the end of March 1941, 139,979 people in the Paris region alone had declared themselves to be Jewish. A punched-card system was used by the French police to store and sort all the information collected by this childishly simple means; it was the first time such a device had been used in the administration of France, and it worked well, allowing retrieval under four different headings: name, address, nationality, and profession. The Germans were impressed by this "Tulard Index" of the Jews in France. SS Sturmbannführer Lischka minuted on 30 January 1941, "The French can be safely left to proceed with the rest".[1]

In the autumn of 1940 and the following months, Jojo was a frequent visitor to the Bienenfeld flat. It does not appear that he came to live there – except perhaps for a day or two at a time – but Esther did what she could to take the burden of the child off her sister-in-law and her mother, whose lives in Belleville were becoming harder by the day. It is not easy to run a grocery store under military rationing, nor to run a hairdressing salon when people have hardly enough for bare essentials.

Esther was the first to express her anxiety; she had always been more expressive, and more anxious, than her husband, David. An opportunity arose to get one of the children, at least, to safety: a marriage of convenience was arranged between Bianca and an American journalist in Paris. It would have given Bianca a U.S. passport, and, since the United States was still neutral, the legal right to leave France for America. The journalist was paid his fee, but he never turned up at the *mairie*. Bianca was relieved, for she was in love with a fellow student, Bernard Lamblin, who was French, and not Jewish, and not leaving. They married in February 1941. The Lamblin parents knew their son had married a declared Jewess.

In *W or The Memory of Childhood*, Georges Perec writes of four memories he has of his days at school in Paris. These memories can only have come from the school year 1940–41, when Georges was four and five. French school education normally starts at the age of six, but many French primary schools have a "preschool class" for five-year-olds, and nursery classes for even younger children are not rare. It is also possible that Georges was jumped up a year – he was a child with every sign of high intelligence – and put into the first class in the summer term of 1941, after his fifth birthday in March. Three of the four memories seem ordinary enough: gas-mask practice in the basement; pride and excitement in an early work of art, a

[1] Quoted in Serge Klarsfeld, *Vichy-Auschwitz. Le Rôle de Vichy dans la solution finale de la question juive en France*, vol. 1 (Paris: Fayard, 1983), p. 19.

painting of a brown bear on a dark-brown background (and presumably interpretable, as many infant visions are, only by the infant himself!); and pleasure in understanding how to make paper place mats by weaving strips of coloured cardboard together.

In the course of that winter, Vichy France embraced outright anti-Semitism. After being banned from the professions, made subject to internment, and listed, Jews were legally expropriated. The fictional justification was a fine of one billion francs on the Jewish community for acts of terrorism (committed in fact by *agents provocateurs*); the property of all Jews in the occupied zone was forfeit in payment of this astronomical sum. David Bienenfeld transferred the administration of the JBSA to his "Aryan" accountant, Tournier, and carried on business as usual. It is not known what happened to Rose's grocery store, or to Cécile's *salon de coiffure*: there is no trace of them in the records of the French "Commission for Jewish Questions". But there cannot be much doubt that they had to close down.

The first arrests of Jews in Paris took place on 14 May 1941. Using the "Tulard Index", the French police delivered 6,494 summonses requiring the recipients to present themselves, with a relative or close friend, at one of six offices for an *"examen de situation"* – a vague phrase of officialese that might have meant anything. Three thousand seven hundred obeyed the summons, only to find that it meant immediate internment in French camps at Pithiviers and Beaune-la-Rolande. The Germans asked the French to report on civilian reaction to this first step. Most people approved; the only criticism voiced was that too many heads of household had been taken and that their dependents would be a burden on the public purse.

> People say that it would have been better either to leave the Jews alone, or to intern them all without regard for age or sex, pending the European decisions on the Jewish problem to which certain newspapers have alluded.[1]

With his car confiscated, his name listed, and his business under "Aryan" administration, and with people now disappearing into prison camps, David Bienenfeld admitted to being alarmed, as Esther had been for some time already. In the early summer of 1941, he took

[1] Quoted in Serge Klarsfeld, *Vichy-Auschwitz. Le Rôle de Vichy dans la solution finale de la question juive en France*, vol. 1 (Paris: Fayard, 1983), p. 14.

action: he obtained visas that would allow him, Esther, and Ela to enter the United States.

The second major roundup of Jews in Paris took place in August 1941. Areas of the city were cordoned off, and people caught in the dragnet were asked to show their papers. Those who had identity cards with the word *Juif* marked on them were taken away to Drancy, a housing estate not far from Le Bourget Airport. David Bienenfeld was on his way to work. Normally, he got off the metro at Cadet, the nearest stop to his *bureau* in Rue Lafayette, but that day he got off at Le Pelletier because he had a call to make first. Had he stayed on the train, he would have been caught in the net. It was the last warning he needed. It is true that many people believed that only foreign Jews were at risk, and the Bienenfelds had French nationality. But there were also strong rumours that recent naturalisations – the exact details had not yet been fixed, maybe it would be all naturalisations since 1927 – were to be annulled by decree of the Vichy government.

It was time for them to go. The Bienenfelds were fortunate to have a stepping-stone in the free zone: David's sister Berthe, at Villard-de-Lans, near Grenoble, in the French Alps. David went first, crossing the Loire clandestinely near Angers, with the help of a *passeur* who was paid for his services. Esther and Lili followed by a different route before the start of the school year (that is to say before the end of September 1941). From their crossing point, Lili rang her school friend, Marie-Thérèse, to say that she was sorry she would not be able to see her, as she had had to go away.

The company's main stock-in-trade, which had been taken to Quimper, buried in a garden, dug up, brought back to Paris, hidden for a time with the parents of Bernard Lamblin, and finally kept in David's own hands, was now sent by registered post to a trusted company client in Grenoble. The package arrived safe and sound. But it would not have been wise to put all the eggs in one basket, so David Bienenfeld entrusted those jewels that belonged to him, not to the company, to the firm's commercial traveller, who agreed to smuggle them to the south. The man, a notorious homosexual, got the treasure as far as Marseille, where, it is said, he went to a transvestite party. It seems he bedecked his party companions with the necklaces he had brought along, and they ran off with them before changing back into male attire. The story, whether accurate or not, was retold many times, until Georges Perec transformed it entirely

in an uproarious novelette, *Les Revenentes* ("The Revenents"), written
without any of the vowels except e.

David, Esther, and Ela lodged first with Berthe and Robert Chavranski, at the house they had rented at Villard-de-Lans. Marc and Ada
Bienenfeld also got across the line, and took up residence with their
children, Nicha and Paul, at a farmhouse nearby. Jacquot, Gisèle and
their families were already in America, or on their way there. Aside
from Bianca, who had stayed behind with her husband Bernard, that
left only Esther's family – Rose, David, Cécile and Jojo – in Paris.
Jojo was French and, unlike Bianca, not under threat of denaturalisa-
tion, but he was far too young to cross alone.

In late 1940, the French Red Cross, or CRF, had at last been
authorised to begin its traditional work of reuniting families separated by war, and CRF "interzone convoys" shuttled back and forth
across the demarcation line, carrying children, invalids, and the
aged. At first these convoys were not closely inspected by the
Germans who controlled the border of the occupied zone. Since
the CRF did not convey family groups or adults other than the sick
and the old, their convoys presented no serious risk of becoming an
escape route for "enemies" or Jews. But they did offer a lifeline
to Georges Perec.

How did Cécile come to know of these convoys? Esther may have
heard about them through her contacts in the Red Cross, or the Red
Cross itself may have sought out eligible infants in Belleville. Or it
may just have been common knowledge that such things existed, a
story repeated from ear to ear: since the CRF transported more than
87,000 children and 18,400 invalids over the line in the first ten
months of 1941, the trains cannot possibly have been at all secret.

Georges was a war orphan and thus entitled to the assistance of the
Red Cross. There is no need to speculate that he used a false name,
or that he was given false identity papers; children under sixteen did
not have identity cards. Cécile must have had some luck, or some
help, or a good deal of determination to get her son onto the convoy,
since the demand for seats far outstripped their availability. But in
other respects, Georges's escape from German-occupied Paris was
straightforward. The account he gives of it in *W or The Memory of
Childhood* is not.

The convoy service was halted by the Germans on 28 October

1941. There were suspicions that the racial laws were not being properly observed. Stricter rules were drawn up and more cumbersome bureaucratic measures introduced before the convoys were allowed to resume. As the Red Cross's own understated history of its wartime activity in France puts the matter, from 28 October 1941 "the implementation of the racial laws made . . . surveillance [of the interzone convoys] even stricter".[1] It is very probable, therefore, that the curly-haired, obviously Jewish Jojo crossed the line before 28 October 1941.

In his childhood autobiography, Perec places his departure for Grenoble in 1942. Perhaps it is of no consequence that his chronology is hazy. However, his fourth memory of school in Paris is of being unfairly punished for causing a little girl to fall down the stairs. It was not his fault; he had been shoved in the back by the crowd and had lost his balance. He had worked hard to earn a little merit badge that was fastened on his jacket; his punishment was to have it torn off. Even in 1969, he could still feel the injustice of it all and protested his innocence to himself in a text that remains unpublished. He elaborated further in 1974:

> *I can still physically* feel *that shove in the back, that flagrant proof of injustice; and the sensation in my whole body of a loss of balance imposed by others, coming from above and falling on to me, remains so deeply imprinted on my body that I wonder if this memory does not in fact conceal its precise opposite: not the memory of a medal torn off, but the memory of a star pinned on.*   [W 54]

Put in that way, as a speculation about a memory so painful as to have been repressed, Perec's paragraph engages the reader's trust and sentiment. But Perec's memory of a medal torn off cannot conceal a memory of the yellow star that the Nazis forced Jews in occupied Europe to wear. For one thing, Perec uses the wrong word: the star of David was not *pinned* on, but *stitched*. And second, the regulation obliging Jews to wear the yellow star did not come into effect in France until 29 May 1942, by which time Georges Perec had been in

---

[1] Mme Gillet, *Au Service de la Croix-Rouge Française sous l'Occupation, 1940–1944* (Paris: Benefit of the Croix-Rouge, 1948), p. 11. The CRF kept no records of the names of the children transported on the interzone convoys, for its own security.

the French Alps for several months.[1] The misdating of the departure for Grenoble in *W or The Memory of Childhood* is not a mistake at all; by shifting his departure from Paris from 1941 to 1942, Perec makes the yellow star explanation plausible – for those readers who miss the little flag of deception pinned onto it by the word *pinned*. Perec warns his readers at the start of *W or The Memory of Childhood* that he is *like a child playing hide-and-seek, who doesn't know what he fears or wants more: to stay hidden, or to be found* [*W* 7]. It is part of the book's design to keep the child most hidden at precisely those points where he seems nearest to being found.

Bianca Lamblin accompanied Cécile and Jojo to the Gare de Lyon. It was in autumn 1941.

Cécile could not go by the same route as Jojo; she would have to find another way out. It seems strange that she did not try sooner than she did, but then she was not an adventurous kind of person, and she preferred to stay near her family even as things were getting worse – and they *were* getting worse.

The Belleville that Jojo left that day and to which Cécile returned was a place of stark poverty. There was not a lot of food in Paris, and in Jewish quarters there was even less. Jewish businesses had been seized and closed down; few people had jobs any more; money was not worth much, and there was not much of it around in any case. Undernourishment was common in Belleville; there were epidemics of disease. Cécile must have been relieved to see her son go to a place of relative safety, to a part of France where there was at least enough to eat and no German soldiers. She no doubt hoped to see him again soon.

Georges Perec describes his departure from the Gare de Lyon three times in *W or The Memory of Childhood* (on pages 26, 32 and 54), and many more times in his notes and drafts for the book. The paragraphs do not repeat each other word for word: there are variations in the memory, which is in one sense *the* memory of childhood referred to by the book's singular title. What makes this particular memory a delicate crux for the writer and for his reader is that it becomes crucial only in retrospect. At the Gare de Lyon, in 1941, Cécile may have feared for her own future, but her fears can have been only vaguely focussed. Jojo, for his part, cannot have imagined that it would be

---

[1] This explains Lejeune's statement that Perec "never wore the yellow star" [*MO* 79n].

the last time he would see his mother. From his point of view, it was his first trip on an express train, a great adventure to go and see his aunt, whom he knew and loved, and his cousin Lili, and the mountains, which he had never seen before. Perhaps Jojo was so taken with the excitement of travel and of steam trains that he did not say farewell to his mother sincerely. We can only guess what the five-year-old boy's true feelings were, but whatever they were, they must have been inappropriate to the real meaning of his departure, which he would begin to understand only years later. It was the wrong farewell. He must have come to feel that it was he who had abandoned his mother, that he should have looked after her better, brought her along, stayed behind, or done something. No wonder he could not really remember his departure from the Gare de Lyon.

Bianca remembers seeing Jojo at the station with a card strung round his neck stating his destination (GRENOBLE), much like a Londoner being evacuated from the Blitz. He did not have his arm in a sling, as he claims in one version of the memory. Perhaps Cécile did get her son a comic to read on the train; Bianca does not recall. But if she did, she cannot possibly have got him an issue of *Charlie*, *with a cover showing Charlie Chaplin, with his walking stick, his hat, his shoes and his little moustache, doing a parachute jump* [*W* 54], as Perec purports to remember

The Great Dictator, Charlie Chaplin's lampoon of Hitler, was released in 1940 and made the bowler-hatted clown an unperson in Nazi-occupied Europe. All his films were banned; no comic showing him on its cover could have been on open sale at the Gare de Lyon in 1941. The mention of *The Great Dictator* on page 77 of *W or The Memory of Childhood* is probably another one of Perec's flags or clues to the kind of work he expects his readers to do. That is not to say that Perec simply invented the cover design. According to Philippe Lejeune [*MO* 82], there was a *Charlot détective* which showed the clown as Perec describes him, doing a parachute jump, but the relevant number of the magazine, first published in 1935, was not reissued until after 1945. By the time Jojo read that comic, parachutes had become objects of some significance for him, as had his absent memory of the Gare de Lyon. The departure from Paris as recounted in Perec's childhood autobiography probably superimposes details from a later memory onto an earlier and fainter one. At any rate, at a dinner party towards the end of the 1970s, Perec said that he was sad not to have any memories from before the time he was five years old, and he maintained that the first thing he could really recall was reading a comic on a long train journey to the south. The host of the dinner party, Pascal Aubier, has no doubt about the accuracy of his memory of what Perec said next: he said that the comic he remembered reading featured Mickey Mouse.[1]

Jojo's departure left Cécile bereft of both men in her life, and she clung to what was left of her family: her father, her sister Fanny, and other brothers and sisters about whom almost nothing is known. She found a factory job, and started work on 11 November 1941. She was on the assembly line of the Compagnie industrielle de mécanique horlogère at Suresnes, in the western suburbs, not far from Jacques Bienenfeld's old palace, which was now abandoned and rotting away. It was a long journey to work, on metros that were jam-packed and on which Jews were allowed to travel only in the end carriage. Bianca saw Cécile quite often in the winter of 1941–42. She helped her with her French writing and spelling. Why, she asked her, do you not use your war widow's card to get yourself a furnished room on the west side? You would be safer than in Belleville, and save the time and expense of travel, too. Bianca and Cécile both thought that the French would respect the widow of a man who had died fighting for France. But Cécile did not want to leave her own folk in what was, for them all, an hour of need. After 29 May 1942, Cécile wore the yellow star [W 32]. Bianca collected her three cloth stars from the commissariat, but refused to wear them, ever. Shortly thereafter, Bianca and Bernard crossed the line. Cécile stayed on in Paris with Grandma Rose and David Peretz, the only members of the Perec-Bienenfeld family to be left in the occupied zone.

In the summer and autumn of 1942, arrests of foreign Jews in France proceeded in ever larger numbers. Trains were now leaving the main holding camp at Drancy for the east, their true destination known only to a very few. Most French people did not like what they saw happening, but they believed that the Jews were being shipped off to work in German factories, in support of the war effort against bolshevism, imperialism, and so on. By the end of the year it became illegal for French firms to employ foreign Jews, and so Cécile lost her factory job. It was only then that she tried to escape. She was not left to her own devices entirely: Bianca's father-in-law,

[1] Lejeune also speculates about a "Mickey" [MO 83] but does not give any source.

M. Lamblin, gave her money with which to pay a *passeur*, either a ferry-man over the Loire or a peasant who would guide her through the fields. Perec says that his mother failed to find her *passeur* when she called, and returned to Paris [*W* 33]. By the time that Cécile got to the Loire, however, the whole business of clandestine crossings had ceased. The demarcation line was suppressed in November 1942. From then on, German troops moved freely across the whole of France, to "protect" it from Allied landings from North Africa. That is probably why the *passeur* was not in. Cécile returned to Belleville, to her family and her fearful and starving community.

Perhaps she knew the end was coming. She probably knew that *Drancy* was not just the insignificant name of an ordinary station in suburban Paris. Ernie Levy, André Schwarz-Bart's "last of the just", goes to turn himself in at Drancy, so convinced is he that he is no more than a dog and deserves only to be in the same kennel as the other dogs. Cécile waited until her turn came, on 23 January 1943. She was arrested in the same raid that netted her sister Fanny and her father, Aaron. She was taken away by French policemen in the blue uniforms she had first seen as a little girl, on her arrival in the land of liberty. They took her now to a double block of buildings surrounded by barbed wire, standing amongst ordinary back gardens and vacant lots like a bronze fortress: Drancy.

Grandma Rose was not taken. There are two accounts of her escape, neither of them verifiable. When the police came to Rue Vilin, one story goes, Grandma Rose was out seeing a friend. On hearing news of the raid, instead of returning home, she took refuge in a Catholic basilica, the Sacré-Coeur. That is the story told by Georges Perec in *W or The Memory of Childhood*. The other version has it that Grandma Rose was at home at 24 Rue Vilin on the night of 23 January 1943. The policeman had only David Peretz's name on his list. Grandma Rose pleaded to be taken with him, but the policeman was firm: he could take only those whose names were listed. Grandma Rose would have to stay behind.

★

Cécile, now Cyrla once again on the meticulous list of "entries" kept by the French police, survived for nineteen days at Drancy. Perhaps she heard the stories that were current amongst the children of the camp about the kingdom of Pitchipoi, where all the Jews who were being deported would be allowed to start new lives under the guardianship of their tall blond shepherds. Perhaps she learned or guessed the truth of the indescribably squalid and simultaneously smooth-running transit camp. But if she did, she did not throw herself from an upper storey onto the concrete yard, as many did. On 11 February 1943, the next transport to the east was ready. It was a cattle-truck train, for a consignment of 1000 Jews. Convoy 47 left at 10:15 A.M., with 998 on board: 10 Bulgarian, 15 Belgian, 16 Austrian, 20 Czech, 32 Hungarian, 40 Greek, 65 Dutch, 109 Russian, 41 Turkish, 56 German, 64 Romanian, 154 denaturalised French, and 372 Polish Jews. Many were children; many were sick; some were mentally deranged. Their names were all neatly entered on the "exit" list kept by the French police to prove to the Germans that their orders were being carried out to the letter. Cyrla Perec née Szulewicz was number 464, Aaron Szulewicz number 636, and Fanny Szulewicz number 637 on the list for convoy 47. The conditions preceding their departure were so abominable that one of the deportees, Linda Gebler, aged sixty-four, perished on the station platform at Le Bourget/Drancy. After departure, there were three escape attempts before the train crossed the French border. All failed. When the convoy got to its final destination, in Poland, not so far from Lublin, at a place that Cyrla would have known as Oswiecim, 143 men and 53 women were taken out of the mass to have camp numbers branded on their right forearms, which numbers would henceforth replace their names. The term used by the SS for this operation was *selection*. The unselected were made to undress, sent into the shower room, and gassed immediately with Zyklon-B.

When Red Army soldiers liberated Auschwitz-Birkenau in 1945, they found a handful of half-dead survivors, skeletons in striped pyjamas. One of them was Primo Levi. There were fourteen still alive from the selection of 196 workers taken from convoy 47; thirteen of them were men and one was a woman. She was not Cyrla Perec. Jojo's young mother, Cécile, had disappeared.

Photocopies of the Drancy entry list for 23 January 1943 were kindly provided by S. Klarsfeld. A reproduction of the Drancy 2 exit list for 11 February 1943 is given in S. Klarsfeld, *Mémorial de la Déportation*, French edition. The constitution of convoy 47 and its fate is taken from S. Klarsfeld, *Memorial of the Deportation* (New York: Klarsfeld Foundation, n.d.), pp. 361–363.

For a description of Drancy, see André Schwarz-Bart, *The Last of the Just*, trans. Stephen Becker. (London: Secker and Warburg, 1960).

The records of the CGQJ are not open to public inspection; they were searched for us by Madame Bonazzi of the Archives Nationales.

Perec's accounts of his departure from Paris in 1941 are discussed in detail by Lejeune, *MO* pp. 79–85.

Other material is from FP 57, 15 (22 August 1969); from Georges Perec's notes on conversations with Esther Bienenfeld; from Jacqueline Benoît-Lévy, Marie-Thérèse Jost, Ela Bienenfeld, and Bianca Lamblin, and from documents in her possession.

CHAPTER 7

Villard-de-Lans

1941–1945

Grenoble, Stendhal's hated birthplace, stands at the crux of a flat-bottomed Alpine valley shaped like a Y. Three great mountain massifs look down upon it: from between the arms of the Y, to the north of the city, looms the Chartreuse; to the east, the Belledonne range; and to the west, behind an almost sheer wall rising to 2,400 metres, the Vercors. There are only eight roads into the Vercors, each one a feat of engineering. The most direct road from Grenoble, a staircase of hairpin bends, brings you first to the village of Lans-en-Vercors, at an altitude of about 1,000 metres. There you discover not a further steep rise up to the crags that can be seen from the city, but a verdant sanctuary, about five kilometres wide, called *le plateau* by those who live between the high ridges that protect it from wind, foul weather and easy encroachment. The air here is crystalline and uncannily still. One part of Perec's description of the island of W, in the fictional part of *W or The Memory of Childhood*, suits the Vercors to a tee:

> *The profoundly hostile nature of the lands all around it – a craggy, tortured, arid, glacial landscape, perpetually shrouded in fog – makes the sight of this cool and happy countryside seem all the more miraculous.* [W 65]

From Lans, a straight, flat road brings you to Villard-de-Lans, the main town of the Vercors. In 1941, it was no more than a large village with a church, a post office, a *mairie,* and a *café-tabac* set around a main square and serving a scatter of convalescent homes, boarding schools, hotels, and guesthouses for winter sportsmen and summer ramblers. During the Occupation, illegal refugees filled all the hotels and boardinghouses that had not been taken over at the start of the war by official evacuees from northern France. (The Hôtel du Parc et du Château, for example, housed a school of Polish children whose fathers worked in the coalmines of the Pas-de-Calais.) There were also a number of handsome chalets and villas in and around Villard, the skiing lodges and retirement homes of well-heeled *Grenoblois*. If you take the left turn up the hill away from the square, past a few shops and restaurants, you will find yourself on a narrow road lined by just such chalets, all with balconies, gables, and gardens. "L'Igloo" is not far, on the left. This is where Georges Perec came, towards the end of 1941, to live with his aunt Esther and his uncle David, in one half of the house rented by David's sister and brother-in-law, Berthe and Robert Chavranski.

Anything less like Belleville could not be imagined. From the steps at the top end of Rue Vilin, it is true, Jojo had had a hazy view over Paris, and on very clear days he could have seen as far as the Citroën factory on Quai de Javel. But from the windows of "L'Igloo", he could now see cows grazing, crops growing and forests of spruce and fir stretching up towards snow-capped ridges. He had been used to the smells of the ghetto; here, the air was so crisp it almost scorched the inside of your lungs. An adult would have known it was paradise, but who knows what a five-year-old city boy may have thought? Perhaps Jojo hated it at first sight, at first sniff; the sudden transition from grimy Belleville to the white and green Vercors may have been the source of some of his later sarcasms about rural scenery.

The boy whom Esther Bienenfeld collected from the Red Cross nurse at Grenoble railway station was all skin and bone; and the bones were in bad shape.[1] Jojo was thin, and he had rickets, a disease caused by vitamin D deficiency (not enough milk, not enough sunlight) and characterised by a softening of the bones. There would be enough Alpine sun and enough milk to halt the disease and to repair most of the damage it had done: Jojo did not wear the splints and straps prescribed for rickety children in prewar manuals of pediatric medicine. Rickets left Georges Perec with nothing worse than knock-knees for most of his life; his childhood malnutrition did not take its full revenge until he finally stopped ignoring his dreadful dental problems, in the 1970s. Because Perec's jawbone had been weakened in childhood, the dentist was unable to save what was then left of his teeth.

---

[1] Esther's recollection, as it appears in Georges Perec's telegraphic note on a conversation he had with her on 10 March 1967 [FP 69, 6], is: *Croix rouge transfert Infirmière m'amène à Grenoble Sous-alimenté rachitique* ("Red Cross transfer Nurse takes me to Grenoble Underfed rickety").

Jojo's rickets, discernible in a later photograph of him (illustration 9) on the balcony of his aunt's villa at Villard-de-Lans (a photograph that Perec allowed to be published to illustrate an interview concerned principally with the theme of memory in his work), is not mentioned in the autobiographical chapters of *W or The Memory of Childhood*. Instead, Perec tries to untangle a muddled memory of a hernia he may or may not have had on his arrival at Villard-de-Lans. Nothing in Perec's notes adds to his published words on the matter:

> *Perhaps I had a rupture and was wearing a truss [. . .] I think that on arrival in Grenoble I had an operation – for years I believed that Professor Mondor[1] had performed the operation, a detail I lifted from I don't know which other member of my adoptive family – for hernia and appendicitis at the same time [. . .] It was definitely not straight after my arrival in Grenoble. According to Esther, it was later, and for appendicitis. According to Ela, it was for a rupture, but much earlier, in Paris, when I still had my parents.*
>
> [Footnote:] *Actually I was wearing a truss. I had the operation in Grenoble, a few months later, and my appendix was taken out at the same time . . .* [W 55–56]

David Bienenfeld was a frustrated medical man. It is certain that he looked carefully at the condition of the five-year-old refugee from Belleville, and that all due steps were taken to set Jojo on the road to recovery. At some point in his childhood, according to a much later medical report, Perec had a primary infection of tuberculosis, which left scar tissue on his lung. There is no written trace or living memory of Jojo having been tubercular on his arrival at Villard. It seems more likely that he had a bout of tuberculosis later on, when he was a boarder in an ill-heated school, but it remains possible that he picked up the disease in Belleville. It is not certain that Perec ever knew that he had had a form of tuberculosis.

Apart from rickets, a hypothetical hernia, and a conjectural chest infection, Jojo also suffered then, as ever after, from colds in the head. The sharpest visual memory reported of the curly-haired scamp playing in the house of David Bienenfeld at Villard-de-Lans is of *l'éternel enrhumé*, a boy with an ever-dripping nose. Hardly serious, but chronic nonetheless.

[1] Henri Mondor (1885–1962) was a celebrated surgeon and also the biographer of the French poet, Stéphane Mallarmé.

Not long after Jojo arrived at "L'Igloo", David and Esther moved with him and Ela to a rented chalet of their own, to have more room. "Les Frimas" is a few hundred metres uphill from "L'Igloo", further away from the town, overlooking open fields. It has been enlarged since then and is now a family hotel, but even in 1942 it was a spacious and splendid place, with a large balcony facing southwest giving fine views of *le plateau*. How did the Bienenfelds manage to live so well in times that were so hard?

Jacqueline Benoît-Lévy, David's assistant at the JBSA, crossed the demarcation line in 1942 and went to Grenoble, where she rented a flat and recovered the parcel containing the company's stock-in-trade. She made contact with customers and other jewellers, and David himself came down from Villard by bus and did business in the city, authenticating and valuing privately owned pearls and precious stones, selling individual pieces from stock to people who had money and wanted to protect it against inflation, buying pearls and stones from people who needed to liquidate inheritances or investments. It was done quietly, without offices or paperwork, in people's flats, in back rooms, sometimes in cafés, such as Le Globe, on Place Grenette, where David's brother Marc often dropped in for a game of cards. Jacqueline developed the contacts; David provided the expertise. His skill, and no doubt his cautiousness, too, earned him enough to keep his own family comfortable and perhaps also to prop up the other Bienenfeld families on *le plateau*.

David's personal property had vanished in Marseille. It was to have formed the basis of a new business in America, for it would not have been impossible for the family to get from the free zone into Spain, and from there, using the visas obtained earlier in 1941, to the United States. But David would neither emigrate with the company stock nor face being penniless in America, and so they stayed in France, in spite of the danger. In any case, the reason always given for the Bienenfelds' not having followed a large part of the family to New York was that after the loss of what had been sent to Marseille, they could not afford to go. That seems to be the main reason why Georges Perec became a French and not an American writer.

In the Vercors, in 1941–44, nobody had much money, and there was not much to buy. The Bienenfelds had more than most; David used to cycle to farms all over *le plateau* to buy eggs, and milk, and freshly made butter, and he paid cash. But someone must have pulled Jojo's leg about his uncle's prowess as a pedaller and made him believe that the fifty-year-old jeweller could cycle down to Grenoble and back again in a day – returning via a route that, in the ranking of professional cyclists, is *hors catégorie*: thirty-two kilometres of uninterrupted climbing, a total elevation of 809 metres, and a gradient that in places is as steep as 12 per cent. Perec says that as a little boy he thought it an "amazing feat" [*W* 79]: it would have been!

The Bienenfelds put Jojo in a nursery school to begin with, a school that is still flourishing today, only a short distance away from "Les Frimas". It was called Le Clos-Margot, and in Perec's memory – and Ela's too – it was run by a Swiss teacher called Pfister. (Perec used the name several times in his writing, for one of the champion runners of W and for the name of a hotel in the Swiss Alps, at Ascona, where Léon Marcia discovers a taste for encyclopaedic learning whilst recovering from tubercular pleurisy [*L* 172].) Then, probably at the start of the school-year 1942–43, he was enrolled in a Catholic boarding school for boys called Collège Turenne. Presumably it was for the purposes of his registration at that school that Cécile sent Esther an authenticated copy of Jojo's declaration of nationality. The copy, dated 23 September 1942, was the last written trace that Perec had of his mother's life [*W* 20]. Collège Turenne has since been converted into an apartment house named Immeuble Diamant, but the building still has the tower that earned the school its nickname, "Le Clocher" ("The Belltower"). David Bienenfeld paid the school two years' fees in advance. The school authorities must have known that the child they were taking on on such terms was a Jewish refugee, but what about the other boys? If any one of them knew, he might say something unguarded to a parent, who might repeat it and put not just Jojo but the whole school at risk. Villard-de-Lans, in the Department of Isère, was in the non-occupied zone of Vichy France, where, as elsewhere, strict anti-Semitic legislation was in force.

In practice, outside of Switzerland and Portugal, the Vercors was about the safest place to be in mainland Europe. There were not many policemen stationed on the *plateau*; raiding parties from Grenoble could be seen long before they reached the summit, putt-putting up the approach roads. Some Jews were snatched away from time to time "because their papers were not in order", but the majority of the irregular residents of Villard-de-Lans needed to take only elementary precautions in order to stay relatively undisturbed during the first years of the Occupation. David and Esther did not think it necessary to obtain false papers for themselves, or to use false names.

For a child, however, and for the sake of the school, precautions had to be taken. During the exodus from Belleville in 1940, the lady who had hidden Jojo under the eiderdown had not known how to tell the boy what it was that he had to keep secret [*W* 52]; it has to be supposed that before Jojo went to board at Collège Turenne, someone – perhaps his uncle – found a way to make him understand what he must not ever reveal. Georges Perec had no memory of this, because the means he had to use to follow the injunction was – to forget. The injunction, however it was put, must have had the force of a command: You must forget . . .

How else do you tell a child that it is dangerous for him to reveal, (even incidentally, by things he does not say but merely lets slip, by the movement of an eye, or an eyebrow), that he understands Yiddish, that he knows what the Hebrew letters are, that his father's name was Izie, that he lives in Belleville, that his family comes from Poland, that his grandmother sells pickled cucumbers, salt herring, and halva, that his grandfather is never around on Saturdays, that most of his friends are Jewish – in a word, that he too is a Jew? Presumably you tell him that he must set aside all his memories of the past, that he is starting a new life, that his name is Breton, that he is French, and that he must never even think of what he has left behind.

It was a vitally necessary act of forgetting, and it was also an act of inner betrayal. Jojo did not sniffle only because of nasal congestion; he was a desperately unhappy child. On school outings on Thursday afternoons, he was often the one dragging his feet at the tail of the line. "Who's that poor wee chap at the back?", one of Lili's friends asked her when they came across the crocodile. "That's my cousin, my little brother," she replied.

Guilt attached itself to the self-inflicted eradication of Jojo's warmest memories. He grew into a man always puzzled by memory and sometimes obsessed with the fear of forgetting. In 1974, for example, Perec kept a full list of the dishes he ate at every meal throughout the year. He turned it into an insane and brilliant inventory-poem, "*Tentative d'inventaire des aliments liquides et solides que j'ai ingurgités au cours de l'année 1974*" ("Draft inventory of liquid and solid nourishment ingested in the year 1974"). But even this madly meticulous listing is incomplete, for it omits an otherwise unforgettable bottle of 1961 Clos Saint-Denis, drunk with Harry Mathews, out of huge Baccarat glasses.[1]

[1] Harry Mathews, *The Orchard* (Flint, MI: Bamberger Books, 1988), p. 27.

Collège Turenne seemed large, and it was cold, and it was run by a nun who was a member of the Resistance.[1] Jojo was taken under the wing of a friar called Father David and he received the same Catholic education as the other boys in the school. In his first year there, he saw his aunt and uncle quite frequently, perhaps every weekend. It was a year during which, by a strange fortune of war, the Vercors became rather safer than it had been before. In November 1942, when the demarcation line between the ZO and the ZNO was suppressed, the eight southeasternmost departments of France[2] were occupied not by the Germans but by their Italian allies. Villard-de-Lans, in the department of Isère, thus came under Italian occupation. As a child, Perec knew nothing of these events, or so he maintained:

I knew nothing of the outside world, except that there was a war [. . .] There were also Italian soldiers, the Alpine light infantry, in uniforms, I think, of garish green. They weren't much in evidence. They were said to be stupid and harmless. [W 88]

In fact (and it would be extraordinary if the adult Perec did not know this) the Italians were determined not to implement the anti-Jewish measures of the Vichy government. They refused to allow Jews to be deported and ensured that arrest warrants for named individuals were not executed. The Italian consul in Nice, Angelo Donati, had a whole community of Jews moved from the more vulnerable coastal towns to the remote ski resort of Mégève for safety. The same event that made it almost impossible for Cécile to escape – the suppression of the ZNO – also rendered the rest of the family's Alpine refuge much safer, at least for a while.

It must have been towards the end of Jojo's first school year at Collège Turenne, in the spring or summer of 1943, that the last of the family to escape made her way to Villard-de-Lans. Quite how Grandma Rose did it is still a mystery. She spoke almost no French and had only to open her mouth to reveal that she was foreign, and Jewish. The story given in *W or The Memory of Childhood* is that she got a train driver to hide her in his cab. Maybe; it is not a story that either Bianca or Ela heard at first hand. The only known fact is that

[1] Perec remembers *two sisters (perhaps in the ordinary as well as the religious sense of the word)* [W 94], but the recollections of others are of only one headmistress.

[2] Savoie, Haute-Savoie, Isère, Drôme, Hautes-Alpes, Basses-Alpes, Alpes-Maritimes, Var.

a tiny old lady with white hair and less than basic French had the wit, the courage, and the luck to travel 640 kilometres through Nazi-occupied France to the Italian zone. First she stayed at "Les Frimas" and then she moved into a room of her own in the town. She brought news of Belleville, and of the disaster: her husband, David, taken, and her daughter-in-law Cécile, and so many of her friends. She did not know what had happened to them; no one knew. It could not have been imagined. Rose and Esther and David must have feared the worst, but fears are not facts, and Jojo's aunt and uncle would not have wanted to upset the boy unnecessarily. In *W or The Memory of Childhood*, Perec says that he *had to deduce hypocritically* the news of his father's death from *the commiserating whispers and sighing kisses of the ladies* [*W* 38]. An atmosphere of muffled sympathy must have surrounded him in Villard as well, after Grandma Rose's arrival. The "ladies" – Esther, Berthe, Rose, and Ada – must have suspected that little Jojo was now doubly orphaned, but they did not know enough to be able to tell him outright. What else could they do but whisper their sorrow to each other, and sigh for the child?

Jojo presumably spent the summer holidays of 1943 with his aunt and uncle, and his cousin Lili, at "Les Frimas". There were trips to the farms to get milk and eggs, and expeditions to pick blackberries, and currants, and fruit. The Vercors can be a magical place for children's holidays.

American forces landed in Sicily in July 1943. The Italian army retreated, and soon the Italian Fascist leader, Mussolini, was overthrown and imprisoned. The king of Italy appointed Marshal Badoglio to negotiate a separate peace with the Allies. The treaty was made public on 3 September 1943; it weakened substantially the hold of the Axis over the continent. Hitler responded by invading northern Italy. The Germans had Mussolini released and reinstated, brought the Italian army back into the war, and established a defensive line – called the Gustav line – on the Garigliano, south of Naples, to hold back the Allied advance. (In *Life A User's Manual*, Perec has Gaspard Winckler's nephew, a man with the Shakespearean name of Voltimand, lose his life on the Gustav line.) A corollary to the separate peace of the brief Badoglio regime was the withdrawal of Italian troops from the eight departments of south-eastern France, where they were replaced by Germans. The Gestapo arrived in Grenoble in September 1943, the Wehrmacht in early October. Georges Perec's second year at Collège Turenne was set in a quite different context from the first.

With the Germans near at hand, both Bienenfeld families (David's and Marc's) as well as the Chavranskis decided that it was safer to take cover. David bought new identity cards from the doorman at one of the grander hotels in the town. He became "Dr Blanchard", Esther "Madame Beauchamps", and Lili became "Elisabeth Beauchamps". They abandoned "Les Frimas" for a house in a smaller and more remote Alpine village, Saint-Martin-en-Vercors. Lili was sent to school at Saint-Marcellin, under her false name. The Chavranskis – now "Servais" and "Sergent" – dispersed to La Chappelle-en-Vercors. Marc, Ada and their children went to Saint-Julien-en-Vercors. They kept away from the towns and lived on what resources they had saved. Georges had nowhere to go at weekends or during school holidays. That is why he came to find himself all alone in the school on Christmas Eve in 1943 [*W* 66].

During his first school year at Collège Turenne, Georges learned his catechism, which he tackled *with exaggerated keenness and piety* [*W* 94–95]. He was eventually baptised. Was he baptised simply in the normal course of a belated Catholic education? Is it right that a whole year's instruction was necessary before he could be baptised? Or was the decision to baptise a boy whom the headmistress and Father David knew to be Jewish taken by them, or perhaps by his aunt Esther, for more practical reasons?

In the later 1960s, Perec made it seem to at least some of his acquaintances that he resented his childhood conversion, saying, with some bitterness, that his protectors had "taken advantage" of the wartime situation to "slap a baptism on him". That resentment is barely perceptible in *W or The Memory of Childhood*, where Perec states that he still has *an extremely detailed memory of my baptism, which was performed sometime in the summer of 1943* [*W* 93]. Sometime in the summer of 1943, Villard ceased to be a relatively safe town under Italian occupation and became a far more perilous place, under German control. Perec was baptised at the end of October (can that really be counted as "summer"?). In all probability, the sacrament was performed at that time so as to provide the boy with additional protection, and some documentary camouflage.

Once, the Germans came to the school. It was one morning. From
very far away we saw two of them – officers – crossing the yard
with one of the headmistresses. We went to lessons as usual and
didn't see them again. At lunchtime the rumour spread that they had
only looked at the school register.   [W 103]

What the register would have shown, after 30 October 1943, was a
boy with an obviously Breton name, baptised Georges, the son of
parents named André and Cécile: nothing to alert the visitor, nothing
to give him reason for taking down the boy's trousers,[1] as he might
have done had the register shown parents with names such as Icek
Judko and Cyrla. The boy's parents' names could now be substan-
tiated, for those were the names entered on his certificate of baptism.

Georges Perec's baptism certificate.
From the register of the parish church of Villard-de-Lans

---

[1] Circumcision was considered proof of Jewishness by the Gestapo.

Perec the autobiographer spends a whole page puzzling over why he was the only member of his family who believed for many years that his father was called André. The baptism certificate answers the question: Izie was called André on an official document recording an event at which Georges was the principal actor. Perec speculates also that his father may have called himself André with his workmates and café acquaintances. That is perfectly plausible, and it would explain why *André*, rather than *Jean* or *Claude*, was given to the school for the baptism, and no doubt at Georges's first registration, too. The mystery is not why Perec attached the name André to his memory of his father; the mystery, if there is one at all, is why Perec forgot, or claimed to have forgotten, that his father was also called Izie.

Once again, Perec obliges his reader to pay meticulous and wary attention to a name. *André* is not just given, in *W or The Memory of Childhood*, as a false name (falsely given, in a sense, since it really was attributed to Perec's father in one important document), but it is also connected up (or "sewn", or "stitched"[1]) to a letter of the alphabet that plays a fundamental role in all of Perec's writings. The main stitch comes in the following passage:

> *Near the house* ["Les Frimas"], *on the other side of the road, there was a farm* [. . .] *where there lived an old man with grey whiskers. He wore collarless shirts.* [. . .] *and I remember him clearly: he sawed his wood on a sawhorse made of a pair of upended parallel crosses, each in the shape of an X (called a "Saint Andrew's Cross" in French), connected by a perpendicular crossbar, the whole device being called, quite simply, an x.*   [W 76]

The information that the cross of a sawhorse makes the shape called after Saint Andrew (*Saint André* in French) is gratuitous at the level of the story, but it is not so in the construction of Perec's text, or in the only half-hidden reconstruction of his own identity. By this addition to the story of the grey-whiskered old man (Grandfather time? The mythical figure of the father? of God?), the name and the shape of the letter x are attached not so much to Perec's real father as to his supposedly imaginary and private *name* for his father. Perec goes on to talk of all the other meanings that x has: it is the sign of the word deleted (*the string of x's crossing out the word you didn't mean*

---

[1] The term comes from Bernard Magné, "Les Sutures dans *W ou le souvenir d'enfance*", *CGP II* 39-55.

to write), the sign of multiplication, of sorting (the x-axis), and of the mathematical unknown (as in "Let x be the sum of . . ."). It is also the sign of ablation, of excision, of things cut away. It is all rather neat: the unknown father, the father cut away and crossed out, is called André, whose symbol is an x, the symbol of the unknown, the crossed-out, the cut-away. This does not mean that the stories of the sawhorse and of Perec's memory of his father's name are only literary fabrications. For it is clearly the case that the form of the letter x was, as Perec says, *the starting point for a geometrical fantasy, whose basic figure is the double V [. . .] two Vs joined tip to tip make the shape of an X.* [*W* 77]. The last paragraph of *Life A User's Manual* seems to have been plotted long before, not just in that vast book but in Perec's earlier book of memory, and even earlier, between Rue Vilin and Villard, and the sawhorse of Saint Andrew with its one-letter name, or earlier still, in the naming of the mythical ancestor as Gapman or Hole:

> *It is the twenty-third of June nineteen seventy-five, and it is eight o'clock in the evening. Seated at his jigsaw puzzle, Bartlebooth has just died. On the tablecloth, somewhere in the crepuscular sky of the four hundred and thirty-ninth puzzle, the black hole of the sole piece not yet filled in has the almost perfect shape of an X. But the ironical thing, which could have been foreseen long ago, is that the piece the dead man holds between his fingers is shaped like a W.* [L 497]

After the suppression of the demarcation line in November 1942, young Frenchmen were required to do forced labour in German factories in place of military service. Some preferred to join the maquis rather than fulfil the *Service du travail obligatoire*, and many such "deserters" made their way to the sanctuary of the Vercors in the course of that winter. By April 1943 there were 350 armed men in nine separate camps in the woods along the edge of the plateau, mostly under the command of former officers of the Chasseurs Alpins, the Alpine light infantry which had been demobilised after the armistice. From autumn 1943, the number of *maquisards* on the plateau began to grow, and the Resistance began to organise itself there as the spearhead of an internal uprising against the Germans. London and Algiers made contact and were supposed to be ready to supply arms and ammunition by parachute when the time was ripe. The first drops came from Algiers on 13 November 1943, at a place known as

Arbounouze. The Vercors adventure, one of France's national myths of heroism and stupidity, was about to begin.

In the spring of 1944, Bianca and her husband, Bernard Lamblin, who had been moving around the former free zone under false identities since 1942, joined the Bienenfelds in Saint-Martin. They used the aliases Elizabeth Davet and Gaston Cavanna. By that time the Resistance was almost ready to take control of the whole mountain fastness. The Secret Army, the FFI, the FTP, and the BCA were all working together to prepare a breakout from "fortress Vercors" (set to coincide with the Allied landings that were expected somewhere on the northern coast of Europe), and to lead the uprising of the French against the German oppressors. An advance party of British, American and Free French officers and technicians was dropped by parachute. The group dined one night with the Bienenfelds, for the Secret Army had established its HQ in the house next door to them in Saint-Martin. On 5 June 1944, Radio-Londres broadcast, but only once, the code for preparing the uprising; the message was not repeated, as it should have been, to signal the start of the uprising itself. On 6 June, the D-day landings began. London went silent. No planes appeared in the sky over the Vercors, bringing arms or men. Hundreds more volunteers clambered up the road and the tracks from the valleys below to join the Resistance on the plateau. By the end of June, the tricolour was openly flown at Villard-de-Lans. At last the airlift began: fourteen sorties were made by Free French aircraft squadrons based in Algeria, delivering weapons and ammunition by parachute, and from bases in England, American Flying Fortresses dropped no fewer than 2,160 containers on the "southern sector", most of them directly onto the Vercors plateau, between 25 and 28 June. Some of the parachutes used in the daylight spectacular on Sunday, 25 June, were red, white, and blue. It was a sight to soften the hearts of old soldiers. Did the eight-year-old Georges Perec see the silk canopies float onto the fields and woods? How could he not have heard forty-four Flying Fortresses overhead, and not rushed to the window to see? Quite easily, Henri Chavranski says. He himself was fourteen at the time, in the same place, and has no recollection of the planes or parachutes. No doubt this is partly because the American pilots flew very high (to avoid anti-aircraft fire; RAF pilots were reputed to hedgehop, but the RAF was not involved in the Vercors); partly because the landing-zones were several kilometres south of Villard-de-Lans; partly because all the drops, except the morale-boosting display on 25 June, were at night; and partly because, for security reasons, people kept quiet about what they knew. Jojo could easily have missed the sight of those thousands of silk parachutes, which came to clothe the whole population of the area after the Liberation and to be traded in small pieces in the playgrounds of the Vercors for months if not years afterward. Nonetheless, Perec's fascination with parachutes, both real and fictional, perhaps had its origin in those days of June 1944 when it could be believed that freedom and safety were going to come down from the sky.

Not all the containers that landed were of much use for achieving liberty. Some were full of berets; others, of light weapons missing some of their parts. The entire army on the plateau – now about three thousand strong – had but one bazooka. A message came to make ready a landing strip so that heavy arms not suitable for parachute drops could be brought in by transport aircraft. A site was chosen near the village of Vassieux, and the whole adult population of the area was conscripted to prepare the ground. By mid-July there was enough of a runway for a transport plane to land. On 14 July, Bastille Day was celebrated in great pomp on the main square of Villard, with a mounted military parade. On 21 July, the landing strip was used. At the last minute, the waiting partisans saw not the red, white, and blue bull's-eye but the swastika of the SS on the sides of the gliders coming in. Storm troopers spilled out shooting and massacred the entire population of Vassieux in a few minutes.

It took two armoured divisions of the Wehrmacht three days to subjugate the three thousand ill-equipped and completely trapped fighters of the Vercors. Seven hundred of the Free French perished. Were they heroes, or were they just foolish? Were they betrayed? By whom? Why were they told to prepare a runway if it was to be left unused? Why were they encouraged to concentrate their forces in a place from which there was no possibility of retreat? The advantages of the Vercors massif as a sanctuary for guerrillas turned into a disastrous handicap for a small army. What did their action achieve? Did they really delay German preparations for defending the south coast against Allied landings, or were they simply sacrificed once the bridgeheads in Normandy were established? These are some of the questions asked with passion in France over the past fifty years. The story of the Vercors continues to arouse strong feelings even now, and is the nub of contested confessions and revelations about betrayal in the Resistance movement. It is a subject on which Georges

Perec made notes in the autumn of 1981 in the library of the University of Queensland where he was writer in residence, and working on a "literary thriller" entitled "53 Days". It was Perec's last book, and it leads back to the historical circumstances of his departure as an eight-year-old boy from Villard-de-Lans, of which he says elsewhere that has no personal memory:

> One summer's day I was back on the road, with my grandmother. She was carrying a large suitcase, and I had a small one. It was hot. We stopped often; my grandmother sat on her case, and I sat on the ground or on a milestone. That went on for a markedly long time. I must have been eight and my grandmother at least sixty-five, and it took us an entire afternoon to cover the seven kilometres between Villard-de-Lans and Lans-en-Vercors . . . [W 128]

The walk took place, without a doubt, at the end of the school year 1943–44 (that is to say, the end of June: French schoolchildren then had three months' summer holidays). The decision had been taken by the Secret Army not to attempt to defend Lans-en-Vercors or Villard-de-Lans against a German attack, since that would have put the lives of the hundreds of children in the schools and convalescent homes there at risk. How did Grandma Rose know that it was safer to go towards Lans than towards the south or west? Who organised the journey, and who set up the job (as a cook in a children's home) that gave Rose and Jojo their cover? Maybe it was all just miraculous good fortune; maybe the headmistress of Collège Turenne knew what to do; maybe Rose had a message from David and Esther. But even if it was all set up for her, Grandma Rose must have had uncommon pluck to make the move with a boy in tow. In Lans, Rose and Georges were safe: the German tanks rolled through on 21 July without a shot being fired.

The four weeks that followed the German assault turned the beautiful plateau of the Vercors into a cruel rat-trap. Peasants suspected of harbouring partisans were executed on the spot. Ukrainian troops were used to mop up the remnants of the Secret Army, which meant shooting more or less anything that moved in the woods or on the road. At one point, they caught Berthe and Robert Chavranski between their line of fire and a group of partisans; Berthe fell, with a bullet in her ankle. A young German soldier came up to finish her off, as per standing orders. Berthe then did what everyone had said she must not on any account do: she shouted at the soldier, in German. He was taken aback, perhaps moved to hear his mother tongue spoken by a woman in a foreign land. Instead of shooting, he helped her up and took her to shelter. One night during those abysmal weeks, Marc heard soldiers chatting in Ukrainian outside the hut where he was hiding. They were talking about home, a part of the Ukraine that had once been Galicia. Marc could understand their dialect: they were talking about the village in which he was born.

Whilst Georges lived in a children's home at Lans and his grandmother worked silently in the kitchen, pretending to be deaf and dumb, his aunt and uncle took refuge higher up, behind Saint-Martin. A peasant family allowed Bianca and Esther to shelter in their house and showed David and Bernard a well-camouflaged hole in the ground where they could hide. Bianca brought them food at night, when it was safe. But the two men actually spent much of their time in the open, reading and playing cards.

The American army landed at Toulon on 15 August 1944. The troops moved quickly up the Rhône Valley and over the Route Napoléon through the Alps. Grenoble was liberated on 22 August. On 25 August 1944, the great bell of Notre-Dame celebrated the arrival of Général Leclerc's First Armoured Division in Paris.

David and Esther left the Vercors not long after the Liberation. Jojo was to stay with his grandmother in her flat in Villard-de-Lans for the time being, but as the Jewish refugees began heading back to Paris and Brussels and all the other places they had come from, Rose had no one left to talk to in Polish or Yiddish. She was anxious to find out what had happened to Belleville, and to be there when her husband and her daughter-in-law and her friends returned from deportation. So Rose entrusted Jojo to David's sister Berthe, and went back to Rue Vilin.

These were months of hope in France. The eastern front had not reached Poland. No one in the West knew what Eichmann was still doing in Budapest. No one had returned to tell the truth about what had been happening, and would go on happening for several months more, in Auschwitz and Belzec, Sobibor and Chelmno.

Jojo went to live with Berthe and Henri for the whole school year of 1944–45. To judge by the two separate accounts that exist of this year (Georges's, and Henri's), it was not far short of a childhood idyll. *For almost a year, Berthe was my mother*, Perec wrote in a draft of *L'Arbre*, and *mother* is not a word that he could use lightly. Henri remembers Jojo at that time as "an open, affectionate, uncomplicated" second son for Berthe. There were obvious reasons for Jojo to be as happy as a lark in spring. France had been liberated, and there was euphoria in the air; the dreadful difficulties that prevailed in almost every domain of daily life are not likely to have affected an eight-year-old very much. Jojo had been released from lonely months in a Spartan boarding school and could now wallow in homely comforts: he could be ill and get looked after (*it couldn't have been anything very serious*, Perec noted); he could sit in the kitchen and watch biscuits and *croissants fourrés* being made; and in Henri he had a big brother to look up to. Robert Chavranski, when he was there, exercised little authority: it seems to have been a household without a father figure. Jojo attended the village primary school, had pals and maybe fights, traded parachute silk and U.S. insignia in the playground. There was skiing and a ride in a bobsleigh that Jojo caused to capsize through his incapacity to tell left from right; there were berries and mushrooms to be picked, and milk to be got from the farm in a dented aluminium churn. There was news, and Henri to explain it all: he had pinned a map of Europe to the wall, and together with his little cousin he plotted the advance of the Allied armies from east and west towards Berlin. There were books, and from this period date Perec's first recorded reading experiences: Jack London, Dumas, and a serial novel called something like *Le Tour du monde d'un petit parisien* ("A Paris Lad Goes round the World"). From these books he learned that there were other books, with stories that came before, or went on after, some of which his cousin Henri had read already:

> I was transported most, and in the literal sense as well, by the death of d'Artagnan, since Henri told it and, with my assistance, acted out its main episodes whilst pushing me around in a little handcart on our long tramps around and about Villard from one farmyard to another to obtain supplies of eggs, milk and butter.   [W 144]

For France, the war was as good as over, and amazingly, about two thirds of the Jewish population was still alive. The Peretz-Bienenfeld clan had done better than average: all but three of its French-based members had survived. There had been some narrow escapes. Without a stroke of luck, David Bienenfeld would have got off at his usual metro station and then been taken to Drancy, for onward transport to the east. Without a stroke of luck, Berthe and Robert would have been shot in the head. Without the heroism of a train driver (perhaps), Rose would never have got to the Italian zone. Without the courage of a Red Cross nurse and a headmistress who was prepared to compromise herself for a Jew, Jojo might well not have been kept alive in the Vercors. All of them had come within a whisker of death during the German attack. They had all been very lucky.

The ones who had died were Jojo's grandfather David, his father, and his mother, and, on the Szulewicz side, his grandfather Aaron and his aunt Fanny – though it was not until later on, in 1945, that anyone really knew what had become of any of them except Izie. Can the child, the adolescent, the young man have accepted that it was only *by accident* that the ones who died were the poorest members of the whole extended family? What sense could be made of the distribution of luck and misfortune in his family under the Nazi occupation of France? It is important to understand the kinds of explanations that helped Georges Perec to manage his grief and his anger. They account for some of the tangles he sought to unravel in his writing. Economic factors alone do not explain the different fates that befell the Bienenfelds, the Perecs and the Szulewiczes, but to diminish the pain of loss, any explanation can seem better than none at all.

Georges Perec, "Le Travail de la mémoire", *Monsieur Bloom* № 3 (March 1979), pp. 72–75, reprinted (without the photographs) in *Jsn* 81–93; "Tentative d'inventaire des aliments liquides et solides que j'ai ingurgités au cours de l'année 1974", *Action poétique*, no. 65 (1976), reprinted in *inf* 97–106.

Serge Klarsfeld, *Vichy-Auschwitz. Le Rôle de Vichy dans la solution finale de la question juive en France*, vol. 2 (Paris: Fayard, 1985), pp. 11–64, is the standard account of the Italian treatment of Jews in the eight departments. See also Michel Mazor, "Les Juifs dans la clandestinité sous l'occupation italienne en France", *Le Monde Juif*, no. 59 (July-September 1970), p. 23.

Claude Chambard, "Le Vercors", in *Histoire mondiale des maquis* (Paris: Editions France-Empire, 1970), pp. 379–410; Paul Dreyfus, *Vercors, Citadelle de la Liberté*; Commandant Pierre Tanant, *Vercors. Haut-Lieu de France. Souvenirs.* (1947; reprint, Paris: Arthaud, 1971).

Other information from Jacqueline Benoît-Lévy, Ela Bienenfeld, R.P Bonvallet, Henri Chavranski, Nicole Doukhan, Michelle Georges, "Mme L", Bianca Lamblin, Harry Mathews.

CHAPTER 8

Hôtel Lutetia

1945

"Pearls around the neck, stones in the heart"

Yiddish proverb

In the early autumn of 1944, David and Esther Bienenfeld returned to Paris with their daughter Lili, now a girl of seventeen and already a very competent pianist. Paris was half starving still, but joy was in the air. No one doubted that the war would soon be won; emigration was off the family's agenda. The Bienenfelds rented a house in a western suburb, Neuilly-sur-Seine, from Bianca's parents-in-law and got down to rebuilding their lives in France.

David went back to work at 62 Rue Lafayette and took up the reins of the JBSA once again. Tournier had kept the firm going under the Occupation, but all sorts of things had changed. David found it hard to get back into his old routines. Where was his right-hand woman? He had never needed Jacqueline's assistance so much. She had come back from Grenoble, but distraught at what she then saw in Belleville, she was planning to start a new life in Chicago. David pleaded with her to stay and help him put the firm back on its feet. He touched her sense of loyalty, and she suspended her emigration plans – forever, in fact. The JBSA was reorganised, giving Jacqueline 10 per cent, and Tournier 30 per cent of the equity. The trade in pearls and precious stones was buoyant in the postwar period, as it had been in 1918: within months, business was booming.

The city itself had been left largely unscathed by the German occupation, but life in liberated Paris was chaotic. Food was scarce and tightly rationed. People suspected of having collaborated with the Nazis were being rounded up by vigilantes, tried in kangaroo courts, and shot. A surprising number of citizens turned out to have been in the Resistance. Murky scores were being settled, often violently, and the future was most unclear. Would the Communists take power in France? Would America invade the Soviet Union once Nazi Germany had been destroyed? Would the tens of thousands of deportees be liberated by the Americans, the British, or the Russians? There were rumours about what had happened to them, but no facts. Would they be seen alive again?

The governments of the Allied powers had had detailed intelligence for some time on how the Germans had implemented their final solution to the Jewish problem, but they had chosen either to disbelieve it or to keep it secret. Some French officials also knew exactly what fate had befallen the Jews deported from Drancy – but in 1944– 45, those particular Frenchmen were on the run, or living under false identities. The French authorities would only state, during most of that last year of the war in Europe, that the deportees had been deported; that they were believed to be in forced labour; and that they would be returned to France once Germany had been conquered. In Paris, it must have been easy to disregard the quite unbelievable scare-stories about extermination camps, especially if you did not want to believe them.

All that could be known about Jojo's mother was that she had disappeared without a trace. Esther must have battled long and hard to get the first document issued, on 23 February 1945. It stated baldly that "at the request of Mme Bienenfeld née Perec Chaja Esther born 24 October 1895 at Lubartów and of French nationality, residing at 16 Rue Saint-Pierre at Neuilly-sur-Seine, the Prefecture of Police declares that her sister-in-law Mme Perec née Szulewicz Cyrla born 28 August 1913 at Warsaw and of Polish nationality was interned as a Jewess at Drancy camp on 23 January 1943 by order of the German Occupying Authorities then deported on 11 February following" [FP 48,5,1,60]. The accuracy of the dates means that the Prefecture of Police had continuing access to the Drancy entry and exit lists, now archived in New York. The lists had been made by French policemen, maybe by the same officials who issued Esther with this document "for obtaining military rations" from the "military bureau" of the twentieth arrondissement.

David Bienenfeld, for his part, got a different authority, the Ministry of Veterans and War Victims, to issue a similar certificate a few days later. It stated only that Cyrla Szulewicz, "departed 11 II 43 as a political deportee, has not been repatriated at the present time" [FP 48,5,1,65].

These two documents had a bureaucratic meaning that is not immediately obvious. They declared, in effect, that Cécile was known to have been *alive* in France on 11 February 1943. Of course, that did not imply that she was still alive in 1945, but it did mean, and would go on meaning for many years, that Cécile was not exactly dead, administratively speaking. There had to be more than a presumption of death for a death certificate to be issued. Perhaps we do not have to imagine a sallow-faced clerk in the back room of the missing-persons' annex of the Ministry of War Victims snarling at Esther, "How do you know your sister-in-law isn't alive and well and living in South America?" But that sort of question (which in a handful of cases turned out to have a happy answer) was partly responsible for the extreme difficulty that survivors of the Final Solution had in obtaining official recognition of the loss of their relatives, as well as for the unprecedented nature of the grief they had to manage. Their grieving could have no formal beginning; what has no beginning has no end.

In talking to Georges Perec in 1967, Esther said that she first learnt of Auschwitz "at the end of the war". That may mean in August 1944 (the liberation of Paris and much of France), or in May 1945 (the fall of Berlin), or in September 1945 (the global end of the war). Esther also said that she remembered meeting survivors of the camps: one who had been sterilised, and another who told her that all of the passengers in the cattle truck in which Cécile was deported had been taken straight to the gas chamber [FP 69, 6]. She could not have learnt of Auschwitz from such survivors before April 1945, when the first few reached Paris. They were put up in the Hôtel Lutetia, to which crowds flocked throughout that summer, searching for familiar faces. Esther must have been one amongst them, putting a photograph, a name, and a request for information up on the wall where a plaque now commemorates those mostly vain searches for more than seventy-six thousand murdered French Jews.

The most heartbreaking plight in the whole family was that of Jojo. What was to be done, and who should do it? Esther acted from the start, and with absolute consistency, on the premise that she and her husband were responsible for the boy. What options were there? The arrangement with Berthe was only temporary. Grandma Rose – Jojo's closest surviving relative – could not be expected to start bringing up a bright and boisterous nine-year-old when she was sixty-five, with no husband, no means of support, and not much French. Léon, genealogically as close a relative as Esther, had never met the boy, and in any case, sending a child to Palestine in the dramatic circumstances of the period was hardly sensible. Jojo also had uncles and

aunts on his mother's side; it turned out later that at least two of them
had also survived the war, but they were not to be found in Paris in
1945. (One of them was in Lyon and resurfaced in Paris in 1946,
according to *W or The Memory of Childhood*; all contact was subsequently lost between the surviving Szulewiczes and their nephew
Georges. By an irony of the French laws of inheritance, the flat in
which *Life A User's Manual* was written now belongs to a descendant
of one of Cécile's brothers, who never met Georges Perec.) If the
Bienenfelds did not become Jojo's effective parents, then the boy's
only prospect would be the grim walls of a state orphanage. Esther's
commitment to Jojo had begun decades before, when she had raised
his father in Puławy; she had brought Izie over and was to blame –
or so she said to her daughters, and doubtless at greater length to
herself – for his bad start in French life. It was her fault – or at least
her fault in part – that he had joined the foreign legion: she should
have known he would get himself killed! She had cared for Jojo since
his birth, she had looked after him at Rue des Eaux, she had given
him a home at Villard, she had made sure he would be safe at Collège
Turenne. Of course he was her burden. There could be no question
of that. Her involvement with the boy's future was natural, historical,
fundamental, beyond rationalisation. David's commitment to Jojo
may have been less deeply rooted in emotion, but there is no doubt
that it was real.

On 2 May 1945 – a week before the fall of Berlin – there appeared
before the justice of the peace of the twentieth arrondissement of
Paris one Madame Sura Rojza Walersztejn, wife of Perec (sic), who
declared, in her capacity of "paternal ascendant of the minor Georges
Perec":

> "That Monsieur Perec father of the aforementioned minor,
> by trade a caster, having died in the service of France
>
> And Madame Perec widowed mother of the aforemen-
> tioned minor being presently deported to Germany and thus
> unable to exercise legal guardianship over the person of her
> son as prescribed by the law
>
> There is consequently and in accordance with article 405
> of the Civil Code grounds for providing Madame Perec with
> a provisional guardian to be chosen and appointed by a
> Family Council"[1]

---

[1] This document is constituted by FP 48,5,1,50 then 62 then 49 then 63.

The family council was comprised, "in the absence in Paris or within two myriameters of that city of any other or closer relatives of the aforementioned minor", of Rose, Esther, and Bianca, representing the paternal side, and three others, Jeanne Hoffman, Maxime Kahn, and Jacqueline Benoît-Lévy, representing the maternal side as friends of the boy's mother. They may indeed have been Cécile's friends, but they were all also connected to the JBSA. The family council appointed David Bienenfeld as the legal guardian of Georges Perec and made Maxime Kahn (Jacqueline's brother-in-law) the *subrogé tuteur*, to stand in David's shoes should he be prevented from exercising his duties as guardian. In fact, Maxime was never called upon and apparently never even met Georges Perec. The family council was never reconvened. At its one and only meeting, in May 1945, it empowered David Bienenfeld to receive and administer the boy's "inheritance", which consisted, at that stage, only of his right to a state pension in respect of his father's death in active service. David pursued that entitlement, had Georges "adopted by the Nation" on 13 June 1945,[1] and banked the monthly payments that began in 1947 and did not cease entirely until 1957, on Georges's twenty-first birthday. Esther kept the payment stubs and handed them all over to Georges when he had grown up, as if to say, I looked after your money, too.

Georges Perec referred to the arrangements made for him by his aunt and uncle as adoption. To a child, what Esther and David did may have seemed indistinguishable from adoption, but in law it was quite distinct. At that time, in any case, it was not legally possible to adopt a blood relative. If it had been possible, adoption by the Bienenfelds would have ruled out Georges's adoption "by the Nation" and deprived the boy of his state pension. He would have become one of David Bienenfeld's heirs and he would have had nothing that did not come directly from his uncle. Guardianship was a clearer arrangement, one that kept what was Georges's formally separate from what was David's. David and Esther never pretended they were father and mother to the boy; he always called them Tante (or Tata in child language) and Oncle (or Tonton). The only confusion arose with Lili, whom Jojo called his sister: that cannot have been only for simplicity's sake. All the formal moves were made whilst Jojo enjoyed his yearlong idyll in the Alps, bracketed out from the

---

[1] The certificate is archived as FP 48,5,1,53.

grimmer realities of his life, which may account for the rather hazy way he referred to them later on, and for his almost certainly mistaken belief that there had been an alternative plan for him to be adopted by his uncle Léon in Haifa. Had the idea of giving Jojo a home been put to Léon, he would have agreed enthusiastically. Léon was a committed Zionist and would have been delighted to help his nephew make aliyah. He helped many other immigrants in those years; his spacious villa on the slopes of Mount Carmel was never empty of new arrivals. It would have been especially suitable for Jojo, for it was a whole household of little boys: Uriel, the eldest, was exactly the same age as Georges, and there were two younger boys, Dany and Gabriel. Grandma Rose intended to emigrate and in fact went to live with Léon in 1946. The documents that have been quoted from above, however, show that in May 1945, at least, Rose was not planning to take her grandson with her. If there was ever any idea of taking Georges to Palestine, it could have been entertained only briefly, and was never communicated to the family in Haifa. It may have been one of Jojo's childhood fantasies; it may also be that the story told in *W or The Memory of Childhood* of Léon's rejection of his nephew belongs more to the fictional construction of that text than to the story of Perec's own childhood.

When David and Esther organised the legal framework for caring for Jojo, they did not yet know what terrible secrets waited in Poland, in places not far from Lublin and Lubartów: Oswiecim, Belzec, Sobibor, Chelmno . . . The first exhibition in Paris about German camps, held in November 1944, had concerned only the POW camps where French and Allied soldiers had been held more or less in accordance with the Geneva convention. In June 1945, the formerly clandestine Resistance newspaper *Libération* published a brochure containing first-person narratives by survivors of the extermination camps, together with some horrific photographs of a crematorium and of a man carbonised by a flamethrower. These narratives were all penned by French political deportees; no specific mention was made of the treatment of Jews. Later that month, the government sponsored a huge exhibition, filling twenty-nine rooms of the Grand-Palais, entitled "Hitler's Crimes". One of the rooms (but only one) was devoted, according to the catalogue, to "The Jews". It presented a chronology of the internment of Jews in the French camps of Pithiviers, Beaune-la-Rolande, and Drancy, in the occupied zone, and at Gurs, near Navarrenx, in southwestern France, under the rule of

Vichy. It also gave a tally of deportations from Drancy to Germany: 62,608. Although the catalogue reproduced photographs only of the French holding camps, the exhibition itself was dominated by two wall-size enlargements of photographs of Belsen-Bergen, on loan from the British embassy; there were other images as well of Buchenwald, Nordhausen, Mittelgladbach, and Maidanek. Though there were no pictures yet available of Auschwitz, it must have been obvious what fate had befallen the French Jews deported there from Drancy.

Bianca remembers that exhibition, and remembers it as the experience that first really opened her eyes to what had happened. It is probable that all the adult Bienenfelds went to see it, as did a large part of the population of Paris. But Jojo could not have gone, at least not this time. He was in the French Alps, and in any event, the exhibition was closed to those under sixteen.

By the time David, Esther, and Lili settled into their new apartment in Rue de l'Assomption, in the summer of 1945, they knew that they had a heavy task to carry out. They had no reluctance about bringing Jojo into the family, but there were things they had to tell him that were beyond comprehension. There must have been stones in Esther's heart when she went with David to meet the little boy at the Gare de Lyon.

L'Ame des camps. Exposition de la vie intellectuelle, spirituelle et sociale dans les camps de prisonniers, exhibition catalogue, Paris, November 1944 [BN 4º L⁴h 3145].

Témoignages de déportés politiques en Allemagne. Les Camps d'Extermination, exhibition catalogue, Paris, June 1945 [BN 8º M 26723].

Crimes hitlériens, exhibition catalogue, Grand-Palais, 1945 [CDJC B 4237].

Maurice Chérié, "L'Exposition des crimes hitlériens", *Le Monde*, 10–11 June 1945, p. 2.

Other information from, amongst others, Jacqueline Benoît-Lévy, Catherine Binet, Uriel and Daniel Peretz.

CHAPTER 9

Rue de l'Assomption

1945–1948

> "Are you as lonely as that?" I asked.
> Kafka nodded.
> "Like Caspar Hauser?"
> Kafka laughed. "Much worse than Caspar Hauser. I'm as lonely as . . .
> as Franz Kafka."
>
> – Gustav Janouch, *Conversations with Franz Kafka*

Towards the end of the summer of 1945, after the capitulation of Japan and the end of the Second World War, Robert Chavranski went down to the Vercors by train to bring Berthe, Henri, and Jojo back to Paris. France was a country wrecked by war, and its railways, sabotaged by the Resistance and then plundered of rolling stock by the retreating Germans, were barely working.

> *The journey up to Paris took a very long time. Henri taught me to count the kilometres by observing to the outside edge of the right-hand track (when travelling towards Paris; they are virtually impossible to observe when travelling from Paris since the signs are then too close to the carriage you're looking out from) the signboards with white figures on blue which mark the number of kilometres to go to Paris, one-hundred-metre divisons being marked by white stakes, except the fifth, which is red. It's a habit I've kept.* [W 156–157]

In fact, the game as Perec tried to play it as an adult, on a train from Dinard to Paris, was to count only the hundred-metre posts and to work out from that how far distant he still was from the capital. He jotted down his guesses as he sat in his compartment next to his dear Tunisian friend Noureddine Mechri (*Nour is my brother*, he often said by way of introduction) in the midst of notes about a place he had lived in as a young man, and he also noted how wrong his guesses were [FP 57, 83]. But he was trying, he insisted, to play the game exactly as Henri had taught him long before.

When Jojo's train finally steamed into the Gare de Lyon in 1945,

Esther and David were waiting on the station platform. The nine-year-old had not seen Paris since he was five and he had forgotten it almost entirely, along with everything else he had made himself forget at Collège Turenne. He must have been wide-eyed with curiosity: *As we came out of the station I asked what that monument was called: I was told that it wasn't a monument, just the Gare de Lyon* [W 157].

Jojo made a child's mistake in his use of the word *monument*. As an adult, Perec seems to have given his verbal slip a deeper meaning, as if he had already begun to build a monument in his nine-year-old mind on the site of his last memory, his lost memory, of his mother.

The Bienenfelds had a black Citroen 11 HP, the long-snouted, front-wheel-drive model used by the police, by gangsters, and by Inspector Maigret; Jojo memorised the number-plate: 7070 RL2 [*Jms* 2]. In it they drove from the station to Avenue Junot, to drop Robert, Berthe, and Henri Chavranski at their flat. Who was Junot? asked the inquisitive child. Another piece of information to memorise on that memorable day: *I remember Junot was the duke of Abrantès* [*Jms* 203].[1] From Avenue Junot, David and Esther drove Georges back to their new home, which was to be his, too, in the sixteenth arrondissement of Paris. Rue de l'Assomption is a quiet residential street in the western part of the city, running gently downhill in a southeasterly direction from the modest heights of Passy towards the Seine. It was developed towards the end of the nineteenth century; its six-storey blocks of good-sized flats, with maid's rooms attached, are graced with balconies, wrought-iron balustrades, and (in those days, soot-blackened) caryatids. Unlike Belleville or the Latin Quarter, the sixteenth does not have much street life. Cafés are few around Rue de l'Assomption, and on winter evenings, or summer weekends, the whole *quartier* can be as silent as a provincial backwater.

Nowadays, to judge by estate agents' window displays, you would need a win on the national lottery to be able to buy a flat from scratch in any of the better parts of the sixteenth arrondissement. In 1945, property prices were lower by several orders of magnitude, in real terms. The area was certainly comfortable and quiet, but it was predominantly if not exclusively middle-class, not at all the millionaires' ghetto that it seems to have become since then.

The Bienenfeld flat was at number 18, third floor right. The block

---

[1] Junot was an artillery sergeant who impressed Napoleon at the siege of Toulon. He ended up a *maréchal de France* as well as a duke.

has an entrance hall with a large mirror and an old lift in a wrought-iron lift cage, around which the broad and carpeted staircase winds. Esther's daughters, Bianca and Lili, were there to welcome their cousin Jojo. He was to have the middle bedroom, a modest, rather narrow room with a door at one end and a window at the other. It had been kitted out as a ship's cabin. The bed was a bunk that when folded away turned into a little writing desk. Lili had knotted a nautical rope around the central-heating pipe that passed vertically through one corner of the room. Another corner was draped with a fishing net and some of those old glass globes that used to serve as fishermen's floats. Was the wall painted in trompe-l'oeil (white railings, blue sky)? Perhaps it was just panelled. Bianca had been to the Institut géographique national and bought a reproduction of an old mariner's chart – a *portulan* – which she had framed and hung on the wall of her cousin's new bedroom. Georges kept that old chart forever after. He rehung it in every one of his flats, installed it over the black sofa in the ideal home imagined by Jérôme and Sylvie in the opening chapter of *Things*, and he also pasted it into *Life A User's Manual*, on page 329.

These details are omitted from *W or The Memory of Childhood*. The only story about Rue de l'Assomption in Perec's autobiographical chapters is of an ordinary, predictable childhood experience of getting lost in a new neighbourhood:

> *My aunt sent me to the end of the street to get the bread. As I came out of the baker's shop I turned the wrong way, and instead of going back up Rue de l'Assomption I went down Rue de Boulainvilliers: it took me more than an hour to find my way back home.*   [W 157]

This minimal story is told without a hint of retrospective irony. There is no reason to doubt that it is an authentic memory, but its flatness and isolation are calculated to make us hear the writer saying that in his new home he was a little boy lost.

At the start of the new school year, in October, Jojo joined the final-year class at the state primary school in Rue des Bauches, a short walk from Rue de l'Assomption. He became friendly with a near neighbour, Michel. One morning the boys got up at 4:00 A.M. to go fishing in the Seine. Michel's mother cooked the boys' catch of fresh crayfish, but Esther forbade Jojo to eat it [FP 57, 3].[1] Then there was

---

[1] Esther did not keep a kosher kitchen, but she may have remained suspicious of shellfish.

Smith, the English boy who lived at number 8, with his English Monopoly set [FP 57, 26]. From it, Perec learned that Whitechapel[1] stood for Belleville, in the set of properties which have the lowest rents and values. Passy is the French counterpart of Vine Street.[2]

At the end of the year, Jojo passed his *brevet*, the now discontinued French equivalent of the equally obsolete English eleven-plus; he does not seem to have had any educational difficulties that year, or social ones, either. He played Prince Charming in the school pageant, grinning slyly when the photographer caught him (illustration 13). He joined the Wolf Cubs and went every Sunday afternoon to play with his pack at the disused railway station at the top of Rue de Boulainvilliers. He did not become the leader of his pack, nor did he acquire many skill badges for Esther or Lili to sew on his shoulder; practical applications of manual dexterity would never be Perec's forte. Jojo's chum from number 16 remembers the fun they had trekking through the Bois de Boulogne, making campfires and playing semiorganised games in the woods – including, no doubt, cub versions of hide-and-seek.

The boy knew that his mother was dead, though Esther had not taken him aside, or out for a walk, or a treat, and said: Listen, this is what happened. There was no scene or ceremony in which the great gap in his life was spoken aloud.

Izie and Cécile were not blanked out from the child's new life at Rue de l'Assomption, however. One of the first presents Esther gave her nephew in his new home was a photograph of his father in a little leather frame, which always stood on his bedside table; the photograph of his mother stood beside it.

Esther took Jojo to see an exhibition of photographs of the concentration camps. They cannot have gone to the major event at the Grand-Palais, which closed in November 1945; Jojo would have been refused entry since he was manifestly underage. The exhibition he was taken to, Perec recalls in *W or The Memory of Childhood*, was *somewhere near La Motte-Picquet-Grenelle* . . . What the writer picks out from his memory of that exhibition is the photographs *of the walls of the gas chambers showing scratchmarks made by the victims' fingernails* [*W* 158]. Of course the little boy would have liked to believe that his mother had tried to resist her fate, to escape, to come back to him.

---

[1] Baltic Avenue, in the American version.
[2] Tennessee Avenue, in the American version.

But despite the implication of this brief passage in *W or The Memory of Childhood*, with its echo of the death of Cæcilia Winckler (a character in the fictional section of the same book, who tries to claw her way out of the cabin of a shipwrecked yacht), the real photographs are not directly relevant to Perec's mother's death at Auschwitz, as the adult writer and perhaps even the nine- or ten-year-old boy knew. One of the peculiar horrors of Auschwitz for the relatives of its victims is that there are no photographs of the *Fließband des Todes*[1] that was at the centre of the Nazis' largest industrial-mortuary complex. The SS dismantled and destroyed the gas chambers and crematoria before the Red Army arrived. All that the Russian soldiers found in the main part of the camp was *piles of gold teeth, rings, and spectacles, thousands and thousands of clothes in heaps, dusty card indexes, and stocks of poor-quality soap* [*W* 162]. The photograph mentioned by Perec is of the gas chamber at Maidanek, first shown in France at the Grand-Palais exhibition, but reproduced and reexhibited many times after that. Black streaks can be seen on the raw concrete ceiling, streaks that for many years were claimed to be evidence of victims' attempts to scrape their way out. Historians of the Final Solution do not now take the claim seriously.

The visit to the exhibition may have opened Jojo's eyes, or just underscored what he knew or had guessed already. His tragedy was something that was taken as understood in the family, something not needing to be restated, or talked over, or confronted, or bewailed. Indeed, by the time anything could be said about it, Cécile's disappearance was a story of the distant past, one that had already gone on for half the boy's life. It seems as if Jojo's bereavement and grieving were muffled, displaced, almost absent affairs. There was little the Bienenfelds could have done to make it any different.[2]

New life came to the family in October 1946, when Bianca gave birth to a daughter, who was named Marianne – the name, as it happens,

---

[1] "Production line of death": the phrase is used without irony by the SS commander interviewed in Berlin by Claude Lanzman in the film *Shoah*.

[2] See Bruno Bettelheim, "Children of the Holocaust" in *Recollections and Reflections* (London: Thames & Hudson, 1990), pp. 214–229. This essay was written as the preface to Claudine Vegh, *Je ne leur ai pas dit au revoir* (Paris: Gallimard, 1979), a collection of memoirs by French men and women bereaved in childhood by the *shoah*.

of the incarnation of France, represented on many standard-issue French postage stamps. Bianca and Bernard had only a tiny flat to live in, and they were both still cramming for the *agrégation* in philosophy. The baby was looked after first by Bernard's parents and then, from the spring of 1947, during Jojo's first year of secondary schooling, by Esther, who resurrected her memory of Polish to sing lullabies to her first granddaughter. When Marianne came to live at 18 Rue de l'Assomption, Jojo ceased to be the baby of the house.

Esther's concern for Jojo, and for his future, never wavered. When the Federal Republic of Germany was established in 1947, with a Basic Law committing the new country to pay compensation to the victims of Nazi atrocities, Esther set about collecting documentary evidence of Jojo's loss. From the synagogue in Rue Pavée she obtained a certificate of Cécile's Jewishness. From the *mairie* at Nogent-sur-Seine she acquired a copy of Izie's death certificate (*see* p. 47). From the twentieth arrondissement she got a duplicate copy of Jojo's birth certificate.[1] It turned out in practice that compensation for cases such as Georges's would not be available for another decade, but Lili nonetheless has a chronologically hazy though emotionally quite precise memory of Jojo as a little boy refusing to sign some document relating to reparations for Cécile's death. Lili understood Jojo's resistance instinctively: it was, she says, the first sign of the free man asserting himself inside the orphaned boy.

There can be no doubt that in his early years at Rue de l'Assomption, Georges Perec missed the affection of his real parents profoundly. At other levels, though, and not only at the most superficial, his life was not devoid of affection and love. The strongest of Jojo's ties was with Lili; there was between them, Bianca says, fondness, complicity, and solid feelings of brotherly and sisterly affection – and of solidarity, too, in a family that had its normal share of domestic conflicts.

Jojo's most difficult relationship was with his uncle David. Jojo had missed out on a father figure for the previous six years: in Rue Vilin, from September 1939, he had lived with his mother; at Collège Turenne, authority had been represented by a headmistress; and in 1944–45, by Berthe. (Her husband Robert was absent for most of the year.) The boy who arrived at Rue de l'Assomption in September

---

[1] These documents, all dated 1947, were consulted at the Landesrentenbehörde Nordrhein-Westfalen in Düsseldorf.

1945 was a lively nine-year-old who had not known a father since the age of three – a tricky case.

David Bienenfeld did not express his feelings with any ease. He had come to be of a piece with his business persona: sensible, cautious, absolutely proper, and somewhat rigid, well defended beneath smart but never extravagant suits. A little boy could easily jump to the conclusion that there was no warmth in him at all.

David had been too close to poverty in the course of his life to look with indulgence on waste, or on superfluities, and he was too much of a medical man not to disapprove of habits that he considered self-destructive. He had principles, some of which, inevitably, seemed old-fashioned and strict to the younger generation: eating in restaurants was to be abhorred, and makeup was not something *his* daughters would wear, any more than high heels or stockings. He never put on weight, never smoked to excess, never let himself go. He was a man to admire, a man to fear, but not a man that a boy could feel close to.

What David kept bottled up, Esther came out with. David took his extensive family responsibilities seriously but was mostly silent about them; Esther worried aloud, she fussed, she laughed, she cried. Some of the people who remember Esther well make her sound like a *yiddishe mama*, transforming ordinary life into a succession of dramas. Others emphasise that she was good at crisis management (she had managed many crises already, as we have seen), that she had a funda-mental strength of character, like her own mother Rose, and that she was actually tougher and more determined than her husband, David. She smoked too much, she was busy, she was interested in every-thing, she was never still: an infuriating person, and one you could not help being fond of. Jojo may perhaps have harboured some murky resentment towards his aunt for being Esther and not Cécile, but he could resent his uncle more easily.

Hostilities would mostly break out over meals. Jojo would not come when he was called, not sit at table properly, not use his napkin, or would say something impertinent or just look at his uncle with the bright eyes of an insubordinate scamp. Sometimes it was just too much, and David's temper would flare. He never spanked the lad, but his anger, when it boiled over ("like milk soup", in the French idiom), was quite terrifying. He would have liked to have had a son; he was doing what he could to help Jojo grow into a man.

Perec says almost nothing in *W or The Memory of Childhood* of the place David Bienenfeld played in his emotional life; indeed, he barely mentions his uncle's name in all he ever wrote. He was far more forth-coming about the imaginary relationship he had with his real father:

> At a particular time in my life.[. . .] the love I felt for my father
> became bound up with a passionate craze for tin soldiers. One day
> my aunt confronted me with a choice for Christmas between roller
> skates and a set of infantrymen. I chose the infantry; she didn't even
> bother to talk me out of it, went into the shop, and bought the skates,
> for which I took a long time to forgive her. Later, when I began
> going to grammar school, she used to give me two francs every
> morning. [. . .] for the bus. But I pocketed the money and walked
> to school, which made me late but enabled me three times a week to
> buy a toy soldier (made of clay, alas!) in a little shop on my way.
> Indeed, one day I saw in the window a crouching soldier carrying a
> field telephone. I remembered my father had been in the communi-
> cations corps, and this toy soldier, which I bought the very next
> day, became the regular centrepiece of all the tactical and strategic
> manoeuvres which I performed with my little army.   [W 28–29]

It must have been at much the same time, in the years between 1945 and 1950, that Jojo *regularly maintained a quite extraordinary imaginary relationship* [with his] *maternal branch* [W 30] about which he says nothing further except that he *would not put things that way now, obviously* [W 39]. Perec's silence about his mother in his autobio-graphical work is so striking as to constitute a palpable, self-designating gap, and it is hardly surprising that his readers are moved to seek clues to Perec's feelings in his fictions, where a few hints may in fact be found. In *Life A User's Manual*, for example, there is a character called Celia Crespi, whose name contains all the letters in *Cécile, Perec, Caecilia,* and *Isie*. Celia Crespi gives birth to a son of father unknown in 1936; the boy is brought up out of Paris, perhaps by foster parents, and dies at the Liberation whilst helping a German officer load looted champagne onto a motorcycle sidecar. The names and dates involved in this brief but poignant episode seem to invite biographical and psychological interpretation: the fate of Celia's unnamed son, the exact contemporary of Georges Perec, suggests that Jojo, too, bore a burden of guilt – for having survived.[1]

*

---

[1] This seems to be the sense in which the episode is used by Catherine Binet in her *Film sur Georges Perec* (INA/FR3/La Sept, 1991).

In October 1946 Jojo began his secondary education at Lycée Claude-Bernard, a reputable state school on the western edge of Paris, next to the great stadium of Parc des Princes, one of the city's principal venues for national and international sporting events, including track cycling. None of Perec's school reports from Lycée Claude-Bernard has come to light; all that is known for sure is that Jojo did not live up to the expectations aroused by his intelligence, which neither he nor anyone else in the family ever doubted. He became listless, careless, and inattentive. One day Lili went to see the director of the Centre Claude-Bernard, a child-guidance clinic that was located inside the school building but which was not administratively dependent on it. She took along an exercise book that Jojo had filled with strange, disjointed drawings of athletes, vehicles, and machines of war. She spoke to Dr Berge, the director, about her cousin-brother. She was told that as far as the school was concerned, Jojo was a normal child, obtaining normal results, giving no particular cause for concern. However, the exercise book Lili had brought along attracted Berge's attention since one of his staff had a research interest in art therapy. It was because of those drawings – the original story of the island society of W, forgotten thereafter and only recalled again one evening in Venice, in 1967 – that Georges Perec was referred to Françoise Dolto, a psychotherapist already well known as an expert on the problems of adolescence. For a year, perhaps two, or perhaps even longer, Jojo went once a week to see Dr Dolto in her consulting rooms in Rue Saint-Jacques, in the Latin Quarter. By bus? By metro? With his aunt? On his own? The adult Perec had to admit to himself that he really could not remember.

Jojo's physical health was attended to also. He had constant colds and headaches; he was given every known treatment for sinusitis and even sent to take the waters at the spa town of Enghien, to no avail [PC 28–29]. He had unending problems with his teeth, which were compounded by his difficult behaviour in the dentist's chair: on one occasion he bit – hard – the hand that was trying to help him. That episode probably explains why Jojo's childhood fillings were botched jobs, and the memory of such shameful behaviour may also account for the fact that as a grown man Perec put off going back to the dentist for as long as he possibly could.

One day Jojo ran away from home. In the story he wrote about

"Gorgetty", an athlete of W. About 1948.
*For years I did drawings of sportsmen with stiff bodies and
inhuman facial features . . .* [*W* 163]
Four of these drawings have been found; for a different example, see Claude
Burgelin, *Georges Perec* (Paris: Le Seuil, Les Contemporains, 1988), p. 155.

it nearly twenty years later, Perec situates the event very precisely
on Wednesday, 11 May 1947 – a few weeks after the arrival of
baby Marianne in the flat. In other texts written to be slipped into
envelopes that were to be sealed twelve years, however, he noted:

> *I say '47, but it could have been '48 or '49. I would have to make
> complicated calculations to work it out, and I can't be bothered.*
>
> [FP 57, 53]

The eleventh of May 1947 was a Sunday, not a Wednesday. But Jojo
must have run away on an ordinary school day (that is to say, not
on a Sunday or a Thursday), because the stamp market at which he
was proposing to sell his choicest pieces was closed. Perhaps the

escapade happened in 1947 but not on 11 May;[1] perhaps it happened in 1948; it could not have happened in 1949 since Bianca, who remembers the day very well, had by then left for Algiers. What is certain is that it took place when Jojo was already in therapy with Françoise Dolto.

According to Perec's account [*Jsn* 15–31], he left for school at the usual time, dressed in a grey cloth jacket, navy-blue short trousers, brown shoes, and blue woollen socks. He was due to have one hour of French and Latin with M. Bourguignon (the two subjects of *lettres* are normally taken by the same teacher), one hour of English with M. Normand, one hour of drawing with M. Joly, and one hour of science with M. Léonard. And also a history lesson with M. Poirier, who will reappear a little later under the pen-name Julien Gracq. Jojo went up Rue de l'Assomption to Avenue Mozart and boarded the metro at Ranelagh station, going in the direction of Porte de Saint-Cloud, his normal itinerary to Lycée Claude-Bernard. But on his runaway day he changed platforms at the next stop and headed back towards the city. He knew that the stamp collectors' open-air market at the Carré Marigny, just by the Franklin.-D.-Roosevelt metro station on the Champs-Elysées, was closed, but he thought he might meet someone there who would buy the items he had taken from his stamp album, which his aunt Esther kept in the big wardrobe, allegedly under lock and key. He met no one. He threw his satchel of school books into the bushes behind the puppet theatre nearby. He spent the few francs he had in his pocket on some bread, which he chewed slowly. He sat on a bench and watched a merry-go-round being assembled. He kicked his heels and examined the contents of gutters. He found a mysterious object, *a metal part, a kind of articulated copper tube with a spring-flap at one end and a threaded stem at the other* [*Jsn* 26]. Perec hid the same lost property in *Life A User's Manual*, amongst the possessions left behind in the attic room abandoned by the *Young Man from Thonon who just stopped doing anything* [*L* 240–241]; it bears a suspicious likeness to the piece that the heating engineer is cleaning, or perhaps mending or replacing, down in the boiler room: *a little cylindrical part having a ribbed tube to one side and a spring-loaded flap to the other* [*L* 73]. From what machine was it miss-

---

[1] Bernard Magné has pointed out that the number 11 seems to have a special significance for Perec, presumably in commemoration of the date of his mother's deportation.

ing? It is the "missing piece" from the day when Jojo himself went missing.

It was a lonely and pointless day. Esther was alerted by the school that Jojo had played truant. Lili went straight to the Carré Marigny to look for her "brother", as his passion for stamp collecting made that the most likely place for him to be. But Jojo was gone by the time she got there. He had moved on to the Parc de Saint-Cloud, to make a den in a thicket. Then he took long rides around the metro system, thanks to charitable ticket collectors (there were still ticket collectors then, with little hole-punching devices to perforate your ticket). He ended up on a bench more or less where he had started, on the Champs-Elysées, opposite the offices of *Le Figaro*. Late in the evening he was picked up, cold and hungry, by a passerby who took him to the police station. Jojo blurted out his story straightaway; a constable went to Rue de l'Assomption to tell the concierge, who came up to the flat, where Esther was faint with anxiety. David drove with Lili to the commissariat, and waited outside in the car while she went in. As Lili walked down the long corridors towards the back room where Jojo had been given a bowl of coffee and a buttered slice of bread, a policeman asked her who had ironed the boy's shirt for him. Lili took her brother-cousin by the hand and led him out in silence. Bianca, alerted by telephone, was waiting on the balcony with her mother when David drove Jojo back home.

Perec's retelling of this adventure, which he says he forgot for nearly twenty years, speaks explicitly only of the actions performed, the places visited, and the objects seen that day; it gives no direct description of the feelings he had as a truant, or as an adult recalling his childhood escapade. That does not make the tale inexpressive. Perec's flight from his life at Rue de l'Assomption was not carefree truancy, not a game played to any boyish purpose, but a sad and lonely provocation. The plan to sell the stamps was abandoned at the first hurdle; he had only gone to the Carré Marigny, he surmised in later years, because he knew that Lili or Esther would come to look for him there. The runaway child sank into a defensive, almost autistic silence: he spoke to nobody, did not answer those who spoke to him. He lost himself in the city, so as to say, without having to say it, I am lost.

Once upon a time, Perec wrote, *and like everyone else, I guess*
[. . .]
I wrote my address like this:
> *Georges Perec*
> *18 Rue de l'Assomption*
> *Staircase A*
> *3rd floor*
> *Right flat*
> *Paris 16*
> *Seine*
> *France*
> *Europe*
> *The World*
> *The Universe*   [*EsEs* 113]

During one of the many telephone conversations Esther had with Françoise Dolto in the course of Jojo's psychotherapy, Lili heard her mother exclaim, "But he's forever losing all his pencils!"

Dolto's reply was, "But he's lost himself, absolutely!"

Based in part on the recollections of Ela Bienenfeld, Bernard Jaulin, Marie-Thérèse Jost, Simone Kaplan, and Bianca Lamblin. Other information from Henri Chavranski, Philippe Guérinat, Olive Lieberman, and Serge Klarsfeld.

CHAPTER 10

Etampes

1949–1952

There was a contingent reason, as well as a deeper one, for Jojo's runaway day. French schoolchildren's marks, together with their teachers' comments on their classwork, are entered in a little booklet that has to be taken home, shown to parents, signed by them, and brought back to school. One day Jojo brought his school booklet home, but did not dare show it to his uncle David. The next day he played truant and threw away his *cahier de classe* in the satchel he abandoned near the Rond-Point des Champs-Elysées – so we shall never know how unflattering Jojo's teachers had been about him. The "child" (Perec seems to have been hurt by being referred to as *l'enfant* behind his back, but it was just a French translation of the customary and affectionate Yiddish phrase, *dos Kind*) was scared of his uncle: perhaps of being punished by him, certainly of his stern disapproval. Jojo was not without pride, but he cannot have been ready to stand up for himself.

Perec told the tale of his running away many times over to his classmates in later years. There were several different versions; the story acquired new twists at each retelling. Some of Perec's teenage friends thought that he had run away more than once.

Perec passed his year-end exams in June 1948, and in October he entered *quatrième*, or third form, at Lycée Claude-Bernard. That year he began Greek; he failed the course, and failed the whole year of study, too [*W* 134]. He would have to repeat the year – not an unusual occurrence in the French school system, and since Jojo was quite young for the class he was in, not really such a disaster. As the boy was also in therapy, Françoise Dolto's advice was sought on what should be done. She recommended sending Jojo to boarding school. (She may have been advising it even before he failed his examination.) She said to Esther, who discussed it with Lili, that distance would help the child to get his feelings about Rue de l'Assomption into better perspective, and that he might appreciate home life more if he was sent away.

Not many children with a home in Paris are sent to board elsewhere; France has nothing resembling British public schools. But at that time the state required every *préfecture* in the land to have a *lycée de garçons* and a *lycée de jeunes filles* with boarding facilities, and every *sous-préfecture* to have a mixed *collège* with boarding provision for boys. There were therefore a good number of boarding schools in France, but by and large they did not educate the children of the urban middle class; the boarding provision was mainly intended for that still considerable population which lived on the land, in far-flung villages and on farms from which daily travel to school was not feasible. It was just a coincidence that Jojo was sent to boarding school at the age of thirteen, the age when he might have had his bar mitzvah had his family emigrated to Israel or America, and when he would have started at Harrow or Malvern had the Bienenfelds been British and of the same social class. Perec's Israeli cousin Uriel began at Bedales at exactly the same time.

Two alternatives emerged for Jojo's schooling. He was not entitled to a boarding place in Paris since he had his home address in the city; he could go either to the large and prestigious Lycée Hoche at Versailles, which was then the *préfecture* of the now vanished department of Seine-et-Oise, or to a much smaller *collège* at Etampes, in a former *sous-préfecture* of the same department. Lili consulted Françoise Dolto about the alternatives. The therapist was in favour of the smaller and less daunting of the two.

For the following three years, Jojo's home for two thirds of his days was a dilapidated dorm under the eaves of Collège Geoffroy-Saint-Hilaire at Etampes, a much smaller town then than now, about fifty kilometres south of Paris, on the main railway line to Orléans, Tours, and Bordeaux. Most weekends he would go home to Rue de l'Assomption, returning on Sunday nights with his week's clean bedsheets and cottons in a cardboard suitcase, on the dismal stopping train, hearing stationmasters call out in the dark: "Marolles-en-Hurepoix!" "Bouray!" "Chamarande!" "Lardy!" "Etréchy!" "Etampes!"

In those days, the boardinghouse and canteen facilities of a state-funded *collège* (though not of a *lycée*) were run by the headmaster, on his own account, as a private business. Tuition was free, of course, but the boarding fees at the *collège* were paid directly to M. Bireau, the headmaster until 1953. His wife did the shopping for the canteen at the market and collected the boys' ration coupons before each meal.

For three years Jojo's six-day week would be divided up for him by a timetable that left hardly a minute spare. On Mondays, Tuesdays, Wednesdays, and Fridays, boarders were woken by the hand bell at 6:30 A.M., and from 7:00 they had to be at their desks in the study room, doing revision, exercises, or homework in complete silence, under the supervision of a *maître d'internat* – usually an ex-student earning his bed and board. The dorm was locked at 7:00, and the boys had only a tiny cupboard in the study-room for the things they would need during the long day. Breakfast was at 7:45; classes began at 8:15 and went on until 12:00. After lunch in the canteen, there was a break until 2:00, when afternoon classes began. There was no question of going off-premises during the break. The boys (joined by the *demi-pensionnaires*, day-boys and day-girls who lived too far away to go home for lunch) played in the yard, or stood under the "shed" (*le préau*) when it rained. Lessons ended at 5:00 P.M., when the day-pupils and *demi-pensionnaires* would leave for home. The boarders had an hour to kick a ball around the yard and then had to settle down for another silent study period. Dinner at 7:00, but it cannot have been much more than a snack, since study began again at 7:15; the working day ended at 9:00, when the dormitory doors were unlocked. Lights out at 11:00. The *maître d'internat* slept with the boys, in a cubbyhole with a door that could not be opened from the boys' side. They slept in separate beds, not tiered bunks, but there was not even a curtain to give a scrap of privacy. It was not a punishment regime; it was normal. Every French boardinghouse for schoolboys ran to the same Spartan schedule.

On the other two schooldays, the routine was different but hardly less strict. On Thursdays lessons began later, and finished at noon. After the break, the less senior boys (from first- to fourth-formers, *sixièmes* to *troisièmes*) were taken on their weekly "outing". They would form a crocodile, two by two, with the teacher at the head and the *maître d'internat* at the tail, and process through the little town to one or another of its open spaces: the stadium, for games; or the Tour de Guinette, a ruined medieval keep with open ground all around; or down by the banks of the river Juine, for games of hide-and-seek under strict supervision. More senior boys, from *seconde* upwards, were allowed out on their own on Thursday afternoons. They could drop into the shops or chat in cafés. Going to the local cinema, however, was a risk: by arrangement with the school, Thursday afternoon programmes were timed to end at 5:15, which meant that the boys either had to walk out twenty minutes before the end of a gripping adventure or be twenty minutes late for the 5:00 P.M. study period and get punished by detention on the following Thursday afternoon.

Saturday morning kept to the schedule of a normal school day, but the afternoon was given over to gym, followed by two hours of handicraft. Boarders were not free to go home for the weekend until 6:00 P.M.

When Jojo reentered *quatrième* at Collège Geoffroy-Saint-Hilaire, in October 1949, he chose German to replace Greek as his optional language. (He had been doing Latin and English since first form and would continue with them until the baccalaureate.) *All I now remember of it, says the narrator of "53 Days", is Der-die-das, Nouns-take-a-capital-Letter, and*

> Ich weiß nicht was soll es bedeuten,
> Daß ich so traurig bin
> Ein Märchen aus alten Zeiten
> Das kommt mir nicht aus dem Sinn.[1]

[53D 33]

Fifteen years before Perec wrote that apparent reminiscence, he told his first German acquaintances in Saarbrücken that he knew no German apart from three words he remembered from school: *Bier, Gemütlichkeit,* and *Konzentrationslager.*[2] Both of Perec's assertions about German must be taken with a pinch of salt. It was David Bienenfeld's language of education and culture; in the mesh-fronted bookcase in the dining room at Rue de l'Assomption, there was a set of books bound in grey leather that Perec remembered well [FP 53, 103]: Flaubert's *Letters,* Sinclair Lewis in English, *The Brothers Karamazov,* and also Thomas Mann's *The Magic Mountain,* which Perec later replaced, with some care, on Bartlebooth's bookshelf, in chapter 99 of *Life A User's Manual.* Perec had far more familiarity with German language and culture than he admitted to openly, either in Germany or in his books. Some of it must have sunk in from

---

[1] The opening lines of Heinrich Heine's poem, "Die Lorelei": "I do not know what it betokens/ that I am so sad/ a tale from times of old/ keeps going round in my head" (my translation).

[2] "Beer, cosiness and concentration camp".

school, but most came from his German-speaking uncle David, who in later years read his nephew's works in German translation, and wrote to congratulate the translator. But when Perec was at dinner with his translator, and had had more vodka than was wise, he snarled, in response to some forgotten conversational provocation, *I don't like German Jews.*

All the girls at the school in Etampes were from the town, as there was boarding for boys only. Of the latter, about half were also from local homes. There were 90 boarders out of a total school roll of 350, split up into three dormitories by age group (the "littles", the "middles", and the "bigs"). Most of the boarders came from outlying villages in the rich farmland of Beauce, the wheat-basket of France, on the plateau that begins around Etampes and stretches south and west towards Vendôme and Blois. There was in addition a small contingent from the French colonies, mostly Indochina, and from the three countries of the Maghreb (Tunisia, Algeria, and Morocco).[1] Jojo was an oddity: a Parisian, and a Jew. He was the only such in his class.

Perec can be seen on the class photograph of IIIB (illustration 15), aged fourteen, in the fourth row, second from the right, with his head leaning, as it always did, to the left (our right). Behind him is an Indochinese boy called Pho. Squatting in the front row, second from the right, is Bellec, the terror of the class, whose name really was Breton. Perec and Bellec were often confused. It is hard not to spoonerise the two names if you spit them out like an exasperated schoolmaster: Bellec! Pellec! Perec! Berec! The art teacher must have muddled them up, since he marked Bellec's work as Perec's and then handed it back to the latter, who kept it [FP 71, 4]. Does this mean that somewhere there is a M. Bellec, who has the adolescent artwork of one of France's most painterly writers in his trunk of childhood souvenirs? Or did Jojo, the terror, sign his own artwork with Bellec's name, to exasperate his teacher yet further, as he exasperated the gym teacher to the limits of pedagogical endurance?[2]

In *troisième*, in 1950–51, Jojo found himself sitting next to a new boy called Philippe, the brother of the school's recently appointed

---

[1] The group of Corsicans and black Africans who appear at Etampes in "53 Days" are fictional additions.

[2] Perec's school friend Philippe Guérinat suspects that the second hypothesis is the better one.

English teacher, Huguette Guérinat. Philippe had not done well at his previous school, in the west of France, and had been sent by his parents to be watched over by his sister, an attractive divorcee in her mid-twenties. Jojo and Philippe became bosom pals and formed a trio of unconventional imps with Michel Georges, a local boy from a working-class background. They were distinguished by extreme scruffiness – a calculated unkemptness, their teachers reckoned, as contrived as any other adolescent fashion, except that in those days it wasn't yet fashionable to be scruffy. Jojo kept abreast of his school-work but showed no signs of brilliance. "He didn't try to shine", Huguette recalls. "He was really very shy."

Jojo's blushing did not prevent him from having the same excitements and escapades as other pubescent boys. He smoked in the lavatories, traded Latin translations for supplies of cigarettes, had fights in the playground, and misbehaved in class. There were masturbation contests in the little locker-room next to the dorm; stains on bedsheets were called *cartes de géographie*.

The staff of the *collège* were not *agrégés,* but they taught exactly the same syllabus as their better-qualified (and better-paid) colleagues in the *lycées* of larger towns. The art teacher, Pierre Le Mars, exhibited his own work in Etampes, mostly landscapes in the manner of Cézanne. One of the English teachers, Jean-Jacques July, was a friend of the poet René Char and himself published several volumes of verse, concerned mostly with his sufferings in a German POW camp during the Second World War. One of the teachers of French and Latin could be found in the town on Sunday afternoons, hawking the anarchist newssheet *Libertaire* to *Etampois* out for a stroll. The gym teacher, a former NCO, was a first-rate coach who got the school team to win numerous cups and medals; unfortunately, he treated the unco-ordinated with stinging contempt. Worse still, for Perec, was the woodwork master, Guitton, an outstanding craftsman who took a stern view of ham-fistedness, whether intentional or not. The memory of *a pair of book ends (a ghastly application of what was supposed to be dovetailing) which I took a whole year to sabotage,* that comes back to the narrator of *"53 Days",* is perhaps a real memory of Perec's first years at Etampes.

Perec's clumsiness as a child (and as an adult) when faced with woodwork or with changing a plug may have been related to his inability to tell left from right. He had a theory about that: he was a natural left-hander who had been taught to write with his right hand

[*W* 135]. The story is plausible (until recent times, French children – like Arab children nowadays – were not *allowed* to write left-handed), and it is also possible that Perec began to learn to write from right to left, in Hebrew letters, from his grandfather David, before he went to school. But although Perec enjoyed acting up to his disability (once, when told to admire the scenery to the left in a light aircraft piloted by a friend, he looked *ostentatiously* to the right), he was not without manual dexterity for things he enjoyed doing. He played at painting, he assembled bookshelves from a kit, using the instruction manual, he typed well and fast, he could shuffle and deal cards with professional flourish. But Perec seems to have decided early on that manual skills of a practical kind were not going to be his. His frequent later comparisons of the craft of writing to carpentry and of literature to a skilfully cut jigsaw are perhaps tinged with regret.

The puzzles that Perec tackled in and out of class at Etampes were of a different kind.

> *[One year] I spent three weeks drawing a huge ground-plan of ancient Rome; another time, we all tried to solve an impossible problem: you trace six squares onto a piece of paper, to represent three houses and three utilities – the waterworks, the gasworks, and the power station. The problem was to supply each of the houses with all of the utilities without the supply lines crossing over each other at any point: nine lines in all. We tried it every which way: it wasn't at all difficult to cope with eight, but the ninth, with inexorable and depressing consistency, came up every time against one of the others. Or again, for several weeks, there was a craze for sending each other coded letters that had to be decrypted by the use of "windows" applied four times in succession, in different ways (as explained at the beginning of* Mathias Sandorf)   [*53D* 37]

Perec's results after his first two years at Etampes don't show much sign of his having yet become a champion puzzle solver, as the school memories selected for inclusion in "*53 Days*" seem to suggest. In May 1951, he obtained the *brevet*,[1] the now defunct "first baccalaureate" (equivalent to a a set of English GCSEs), but only by a narrow margin. The pass mark was 10 out of 20. Perec's best scores were in English (15.25) and in "observational sciences" (13). In French composition he got a mediocre 11.25, and in Latin 11. He failed

---

[1] The certificate is FP 48,5,1,55.

mathematics with a mark of 7.5, and for French dictation he sank to 7.25. Without the good mark in English, he would have passed over-all, but by only the barest whisker. Jojo's knowledge of English did not come from paying attention in class: as we shall see, he had spent no less than three months in England already, with relatives who spoke no French.

The French literature on which Perec was tested at the age of fifteen consisted not of whole books, but of selected extracts: lines 401–430, 588, 609, 830, 860, 1169, 1203, 1789, and 1806 of Corneille's *Nicomède*; lines 63, 96, 531–578, 897–948, 1174–1220, 1433, 1452, 1537, and 1638 of Racine's *Iphigénie*; lines 203–277, 428–510, 558–614, and 726–842 of Molière's comedy *Les Femmes savantes*; three extracts from *La Princesse de Clèves*; two passages from Chateaubriand; one poem each from Lamartine, Vigny, Hugo, and Baudelaire, and two from the reputedly easier poet Verlaine, with whom French literature – for the *troisième*, at least – came to a stop, around 1890. Little from that syllabus kept a place in Perec's adult literary culture; Racine and Corneille, for example, come into *Life A User's Manual* only in the form of three garbled gobbets recalled by a dunce. But Verlaine must have appealed to him. Some years later, Perec asked his friend Philippe, who had sat through the same course with him in *troisième*, to remember to bring him the volume containing this particular poem by Verlaine:

Gaspard Hauser chante

Je suis venu, calme orphelin
Riche de mes seuls yeux tranquilles
Vers les hommes des grandes villes:
Ils ne m'ont pas trouvé malin.

A vingt ans un trouble nouveau
Sous le nom d'amoureuses flammes
M'a fait trouver belles les femmes
Elles ne m'ont pas trouvé beau.

Bien que sans patrie et sans roi
Et très brave ne l'étant guère
J'ai voulu mourir à la guerre
La mort n'a pas voulu de moi.

Suis-je né trop tôt ou trop tard?
Qu'est-ce que je fais en ce monde?
O vous tous, ma peine est profonde
Priez pour le pauvre Gaspard.[1]

Gaspard Hauser Sings

I came as a peaceful orphan/With quiet eyes for my only fortune/ Towards the men of the cities:/ They did not find me clever.

At twenty, a new disturbance/ Called the flames of love/ Made me see beauty in women/ They saw none in me.

Though without a king or a country/ And hardly courageous/ I wanted to die in war/ Death had no use of me.

Was I born too soon or too late?/ What am I doing in this world?/ Everyone, hear my deep pain/ And pray for poor Gaspard.

Based in part on the recollections of Huguette and Antonio Moralès, formerly teachers at Collège Geoffroy-Saint-Hilaire, on other information from Ela Bienenfeld, Henry Gautier, Philippe Guérinat, Eugen Helmle, and Bianca Lamblin, and on a letter from Georges Perec to Philippe Guérinat, from Pau, 1958.

[1] Paul Verlaine, *Oeuvres poétiques* (Paris: Gallimard, Bibliothèque de la Pléïade, 1962), p. 279. In the prose story Verlaine elaborated from this subject ("Scénario pour ballet", in *Oeuvres en prose* [Paris: Gallimard, Bibliothèque de la Pléïade, 1972] pp. 97–102), Gaspard Hauser murders his natural father, an English millionaire, and is hanged for it.

CHAPTER 11

Open Doors

1948–1952

The pearl trade prospered in the postwar period, and the Bienenfelds' businesses, in France and America, produced comfortable middle-class incomes for the family. In the new state of Israel, the Palestine Road Company made Uncle Léon a wealthy man until he ran into trouble in the mid-1950s, over the construction of an airport and hospital at Larnaca (Cyprus); in Paris, Uncle David took fewer risks and never amassed a large fortune. Japanese cultured pearls first became available in the 1950s and rapidly displaced the natural variety. From New York, Simon Lieberman went to Japan to learn about them and became one of the leading importers of these smaller and more affordable jewels. To the untutored eye, a cultured pearl looks much like the real thing, but David Bienenfeld could tell a natural one at ten yards, across a crowded *salon*, and he refused to let a cultured pearl into his *bureau*. Other pearlers imported large quantities of cultured pearls into France, but David stuck to what he knew and continued to specialise in what was an increasingly recondite market. By the 1960s the JBSA was the only firm in the world trading exclusively in natural pearls, and David Bienenfeld was proud to call himself "the last of the Mohicans". He was never poor, but he was not as rich as he knew he could have been had he not applied principles about *nature* and *culture* to his business activities.

There were family holidays away from home every year: in 1946 and 1947 at the seaside, on the Atlantic coast, and in 1948 in the Vercors. The Bienenfelds stayed at the Splendid-Hotel at Villard-de-Lans and walked back up the mountainside behind Saint-Martin to renew their ties of gratitude and friendship with the peasants who had sheltered four of them during the murderous days of August 1944. A lot had changed since then, and Jojo had, too. *When I went back to Villard-de-Lans (two or three years after) I didn't recognise anything. Where is Collège Turenne?* he wondered [FP 57, 37].

Jojo spent the following summer holidays in England. It was the first of his *séjours linguistiques,* and the first of his travels abroad to make the acquaintance of more or less distant relatives scattered by History. David's maternal uncle Wolo had died in a concentration camp; his son had been brought to Britain at the end of the war and had become a market gardener. He lived in a caravan next to his plot, at South Godstone, in Surrey. Jojo boarded with a neighbour, Mrs Brown, but spent much of his time with David's British cousin, going with him in the van to sell produce at street markets all over the southern home counties. Once, Mrs Brown and her sister took their young French guest up to town:

> *The first time I saw London, I found it downright ugly.* [. . .] *I can't really remember what made me so disappointed; perhaps it was because the whole day was spent mainly going round the shops, an activity that at the time was of little interest to me. I remember that we went to see the changing of the Guard, that we walked through Hyde Park, that I learnt that the pond was called the Serpentine, and that the name of Rotten Row, the main walk in the park, simply came from its old French name, Route du Roi. I am fairly sure we also went to see the waxworks of Madame Tussaud. At any rate, by the end of the day, I was worn out.* [*inf* 77–78]

The foundations of Perec's knowledge of English were laid during those three months in Surrey; David's cousin probably spoke no French, and he had an English wife. No wonder Perec did better in English than in his other subjects at school, though he never talked about his stay in Surrey in class, and his English teacher had no idea that Perec had had a headstart over the other children at Etampes.

Jojo was raised in a musical home. Esther was always sad not to have learnt to play an instrument as a child; her gramophone was the first treasure that her new life in France had brought her. Over the years she built up a collection of records and acquired an extensive musical culture. Bianca was taught piano; Lili was more talented and took to the instrument with ease. Her lessons were hardly interrupted by war, occupation, or flight. At Villard-de-Lans, she went down to Grenoble every week for piano practice, travelling on an antiquated bus full of diesel fumes. At Rue de l'Assomption, the flat resounded for several hours every day with Lili's scales and exercises on the baby grand in the lounge. Whereas Lili might have become a concert pianist – she spent hours and hours perfecting her rendition of Schumann's *Kreisleriana* – Jojo, by contrast, was no musician. He did not lack ear, or interest, but since he could not tell his left hand from his right, the only thing he ever learnt to play was his aunt Esther's gramophone.

The flat itself was comfortably furnished and decorated with taste. In the lounge there were two canvases by Jean Le Moal, *L'Invitation au Voyage* ("Invitation to a Journey") and *La Jeune Pianiste* ("Girl Playing the Piano"); the piano itself, when not in use, was draped with a magnificent tasselled cloth, which Perec believed to have been embroidered by Grandma Rose. The corridor walls were hung with two sets of humorous cartoons, which Jojo often contemplated and was able to recall nearly thirty years later:

> *One was based on the theme of the last: the last (in the class), the last day (of the holidays), the last role (you marry her), the last trip (to the cemetery), the last bus (missed), the last word (of an argument). The other set was more varied and I had the devil of a business understanding it:* Taedium vitae *(a morose individual, seated),* Nemesis *(anger[. . .]),* Idyll *(a couple of concierges on the front step of their building), etc.*   [FP 57, 125]

David's sister Gisèle returned from New York for long summer breaks in Paris in 1946, 1948, and 1951. She came with her daughter, Simone, who was much the same age as Jojo, and often brought her round to Rue de l'Assomption to play with her French "cousin". Simone wanted to be a ballet dancer when she grew up, but her mother would not even come to watch her at rehearsals. Jojo was in a painterly phase on one of those Paris holidays, probably in 1948. He took Simone into his room to show her his latest abstract, a thing of lines and colours, mauve, pink, and brown, which he had pinned, somehow, onto the ceiling. The two of them lay side by side on the floor to admire it. Esther opened the door: On the floor, with a girl! At your age! What next! Simone thought Esther scolded the twelve-year-old Jojo too harshly for what was in her American eyes hardly a crime. A bond was forged between the two partners in adolescent gloom.

Jojo also acquired an "American uncle", through friendship rather than genealogy. David Landes had been in France with American forces in the last year of the war, and he returned there, first in 1946, then for a longer period beginning in 1948, on a junior fellowship from Harvard. He was a historian and had a letter of introduction, through family contacts, to the Bienenfelds of 18 Rue de l'Assomption. He and his wife, Sonya, became close friends of David and Esther's. Though of different generations, both women had a baby to care for, and they would wheel their prams together in the park. On Sunday afternoons the Landeses would often join the Bienenfelds at home for tea and bridge.

Card games were part of the family tradition and also a part of David's business, with some of the best deals being struck over a hand of bridge or belote at the pearl traders' club in Rue Cadet. At home, there were games after dinner and on Sunday afternoons, when the *salon* at Rue de l'Assomption would resound with the strange language of French cards: "Belote!" – "Et reu!" – "Et dix de der!" What would a Swede with school French make of his uncle calling the score at *la lyonnaise*, Perec wondered:

> *one* toutou, *one* pigeon, *three* sans, *then pass twice, put four on the ace, makes ten and two, and four and five and ten and fifty and ten, ninety-one makes nine, and thirty-five plus three* pigeons *adds up to one hundred and forty-four, which means you owe me four thousand francs, or something like that.* [FP 119, 21, 28]

David Bienenfeld was the kindest, most generous and straightforward of men for David and Sonya Landes; and Jojo, to begin with, was an amusing if occasionally infuriating imp.[1] But Landes was taken aback when, on his first Yom Kippur in France, he asked his French and Jewish friend if he could borrow a skullcap. David Bienenfeld could not oblige. He did not have a spare one; in fact, he did not have one at all. He and Esther had left all that behind them, in Lublin.

In Britain and America, most first-generation Jewish immigrants kept the symbols of their origins, whether or not they kept their faith. Even in secularised Jewish households of the second and third generation, there is often a menorah on a sideboard, a skullcap in a bottom drawer, or perhaps a mezzuzah on the door-jamb with its inscription (beginning *Shadai*) telling evil spirits to stay away. But France is a lay republic that makes greater demands on those who wish to integrate, and the Bienenfelds aspired wholeheartedly to a French cultural identity. Though their parents had continued to light candles on Friday nights and to go to shul on the Sabbath and the high holy days, David and Esther eradicated religious practices from

---

[1] Landes uses the French *espiègle*, "cheerfully mischievous".

their own French lives. In this they were not unusual amongst French Jews. They did not become indistinguishable from the French bourgeoisie, and they retained Jewish attitudes towards their families and themselves, but they kept none of the *signs* (except their accents) that would have announced their Jewishness to strangers. In America the distinction between integrated and assimilated Jews would not be very clear; in Paris it had, and still has, a real meaning.

Bianca married into the genuinely French bourgeoisie, became a teacher in public employ (as her mother had wished to do), and was influenced by Sartre (she knew him well for a time), who held Jewishness to be a contingent quality bestowed by others, by "the Other". Lili had no religious interests, either. But what of Jojo?

Perec's feelings about Jewishness were awkward and contradictory, but not uniquely or mysteriously so, since many others have lived not entirely dissimilar lives and have written about them at length. Jewishness was the subject that Perec tackled with the least spontaneity in his own writing until he was past the age of forty: for much of his life he was stuck with impulses of assertion and denial, which nearly cancelled each other out and left him largely silent on the issue.[1] Whatever Jewish culture he had acquired in Belleville was almost entirely forgotten, and at Rue de l'Assomption, though he heard Polish and English and perhaps other tongues, he never heard Yiddish or Hebrew spoken. In between his two homes, Perec had been (briefly) converted to Catholicism, and he kept a long grudge against those who had baptised him. He took a minor and artful revenge on them in later years by writing a perfidiously autobiographical "exercise" about the skiing trip he went on in December 1949, to Sankt-Anton, in the Austrian Alps.

It was a school party. Unlike most of the group from Etampes, Jojo was an experienced skier from his time at Villard, and he was keen to show off as soon as they all tumbled off the train, in the late afternoon. With a couple of other boys, he took three ski lifts to the topmost of the runs, and tried to ski back down before dark. The other two made it, but Jojo found he could no longer whizz down with his previous ease. He lost sight of his companions and then heard the ski-lift mechanism stop for the night. In the dark, the unfamiliar *piste* was impossibly hard. He fell and lost one of his skis. Frightened, wet, and cold, he sat on his remaining ski and used it as

[1] See Marcel Benabou, "Perec's Jewishness", *RCF* 76–87.

a sled. He made for a winking light he could see below. It was not the inn where the Etampes party was staying, but a far more luxurious hotel. The manager took in the lost child, gave him a bowl of hot soup and a warm bed, for it was Christmas Eve . . . and Perec allows the reader to think, if the reader likes to believe such things, that the first-person narrator of the tale was a very special kind of Christmas child. His aunt didn't even have to pay for his extra night in a comfortable manger.

Perec is just teasing in this seasonal tale cooked up for the Christmas issue of a magazine, but he was probably teasing himself at the same time, for his mythical ascendant, Peretz son of Judah, is also the direct ascendant of Jesus.[1] As a child Jojo may well have fantasised, after his bible study at Collège Turenne, that since he was not the son of the man whom other people treated as his father, he was, like Jesus, a rather special kind of "nobody's boy" [W 12]. As an adult he tried out a pseudo-messianic identity for himself when he ran into a block on the draft of his autobiography:

> I was born on 25 December oooo. My father, so they say, was a carpenter. Shortly after my birth, the Gentiles became less gentle, and we had to flee to Egypt. That is how I learnt I was Jewish, and in those dramatic circumstances lies the origin of my firm decision not to remain so. The rest is history . . .   [Jsn 10]

In troisième, in 1950–51, Philippe Guérinat and his friend Jojo often talked about their father problems. Jojo imagined his real father to be so elevated and admirable that he could only be inadequate as a son. When caught out for this or that failing or misdemeanour, the only Jewish boy in IIIB would often say, or moan: je suis un mauvais fils, "I am a bad son": at that age, and maybe earlier and later on, too, Perec needed to believe there was some reason for his feeling as though he had been crucified.

One summer (1950?) the Bienenfelds rented Bianca's mother-in-law's house at Nivillers, in the Oise, for the family holiday. There Jojo began to read some of the paperback volumes of detective fiction that Bianca's father-in-law had stored in the big cupboard just next to the room where he slept, which he later described in some detail [PC 27–28]. One afternoon Bianca and Bernard, on holiday leave from their teaching posts in Algeria, took Jojo out for a drive. The

[1] Luke 3:33, Matthew 1:3.

boy was in the backseat. He stretched forward and clapped his hands over Bernard's eyes. Bianca screamed; she turned, pushed the child back, and saw him grinning like a little devil. Didn't he realise he could have killed all three of them? she shouted. Why had he done such a stupid thing? He would not explain, except to say that he had done it *just to see*.

Perec records that the family's stay at Nivillers coincided with the height of his passion for cycling; he rode all the way back to Paris in a day, dreaming of being the next Louison Bobet [*PC* 28]. It was a fortunate coincidence: who would have had him in a car?

He spent the summer of 1951 partly at Château d'Oex, in Switzerland, at a language school where he went to learn English (again) and his cousin Uriel came from Haifa (and Bedales) to learn French [cf. *Jms* 8 and *L* 140]. The boys played table tennis with a one-armed Englishman called David Howard and lost every time, and the fifteen-year old Jojo had his first sweetheart, a girl from Geneva called Rose. But the following summer's holiday would have a bigger impact on Georges Perec.

> *My invariant basis in time is the summer of '52: I had finished* seconde *(at Etampes), and I went to Israel for two months. But I have no idea why this trip serves as my point of departure.*
>
> [FP 57, 14]

Perec spent part of his Israeli summer at his uncle Léon's home overlooking the Bay of Haifa, and part of it with his cousin Uriel's scout group at Kibbutz Ne'ot Mordechai, in Upper Galilee, bringing in the sunflower harvest. Perec behaved childishly when faced with camp life and hard labour, and he had to be brought back to Haifa with self-induced colic (*see* pp. 27–28). But the story Perec told to his friends in later life to account for his bad feelings about Israel was quite different. His uncle, he said, drove him and his cousins to the Negev, to see what a desert was like. It was hot, and stuffy, and stressful; Jojo was not at ease, and in a foul mood. When the car finally stopped, he burst out and slammed the door hard behind him. *Aie!!!* One of his cousins had had his hand on the doorpost, and a finger had come clean off. They got down on all fours to look for it in the sand, but to no avail. Perec had amputated his cousin's finger, and he would never cease to have muddled feelings of guilt and hostility as far as Israel was concerned.

But Léon would not have taken the time off work to drive boys

to the Negev; moreover, his company had not yet built the roads
that go there. Uriel, Dany, and Gabriel Peretz have, at the present
time, thirty fingers and thumbs between them. Perec's tall story is
but a desert transposition of Gogol's *The Nose*. According to one of
Perec's schoolteachers, the difficult boy once confided that he would
never go back to Israel because he had "met people there of the kind
who killed my mother". Really? *I'll never go to live in boy-scout-
land . . .*

What Jojo did get out of his Israeli escapade was the only camera
he ever owned until he crossed the Atlantic by boat, in 1979. Uncle
Léon had asked him in English what present he would like to go
home with, and Jojo had answered in *Franglais: a* caméra, *please.* He
thought the word meant a movie camera, as it does in French. He
was disappointed by his uncle's gift and hardly used it.

In 1951 David and Esther had bought a weekend house at Blévy,
a quiet village not far from Dreux, and from then on many of Perec's
shorter and longer holiday breaks were spent there, in the rolling
countryside at the edge of the plateau of the Beauce. The house stands
near the centre of the village, on the road leading out to Maillebois,
and it has gardens and orchards behind it, going down to a stream.
Jojo's room, on the first floor, with a view over the road, was stacked
with detective fiction, some of it relocated from Nivillers. Perec's
later recall of the titles that he devoured on the narrow bed would have
been quite staggering if he had not stayed at Blévy periodically over the
following twenty-five years and seen the same books on the shelves
(where, indeed, many of them still are), and perhaps even dipped into
them again from time to time. Like the Dumas that Perec had encountered at Villard-de-Lans and the Verne he read as a boy, the popular
fiction he gulped down in the bedroom at Blévy had as much to do
with his mature writing as the classics he studied at school.

Perec's first acquaintance with modern French literature took place
in Avenue Junot, at the Chavranski flat. Jojo's cousin Henri *read a lot
of novels and especially new novels.*

> *He first introduced me above all to Leiris but also to Butor, Yves
> Velan (*Je*), Saporta (*Le Furet*), Ollier (*Le Maintien de l'Ordre*),
> Howlett (*Le Théâtre des Opérations*), Michel Henry (*Le Jeune
> Officier*) and others. He used to buy the books soon after they had
> appeared (review copies sold off through second-hand dealers).*
>
> [FP 57, 107]

Perec did not plough through all these "new" novels before the age of sixteen (some were not published until later), but he also bolted down a good deal of more traditional fare in his early teens. Before leaving for Israel in July 1952, for example, he had a few weeks' holiday at home, during which he went every day with Esther and her granddaughter Marianne to the park at Pré Catelan, where he sat and read *the whole of Balzac.* [. . .] *skip-reading, actually. Every day I took one volume (the set must have been Bernard* [Lamblin]*'s) and finished it by the end of the afternoon.* [FP 57, 14]

It was Bernard Lamblin, too, who brought two other interests into the young life of Georges Perec, for Bernard was a passionate collector of everything connected to the surrealist movement, as well as a great lover of American jazz. It must have been from Bernard that Jojo learnt that the doctor who had treated him for dermatitis (induced by a strawberry binge) was a friend of André Breton, and that the pictures on his walls were examples of surrealist art. And it was most certainly from Bernard that Perec borrowed the first 78 rpm recordings of Lester Young that he heard, and from him that he acquired the first elements of his substantial jazz culture.

Bernard and Bianca had a second daughter in 1952, and Bernard's parents wished for her to be christened. Would any member of a Jewish and atheist family be acceptable as a godfather? the priest was asked. He took the view that baptism was all that was required, provided the godfather did not make a point of having "lost the faith". Everyone thought that it would be good for Jojo to have a formal role linking him to this new life in the family: and so, at the age of sixteen, he became godfather to his aunt's granddaughter, Sylvia Lamblin, whom he usually referred to, for simplicity's sake, as his niece.

Georges Perec's background between the ages of nine and sixteen was not an ordinary one. It had very little of the Jewish about it, yet it was all the same a Jewish-Polish home, with parent figures whose foreign accents were quite perceptible. It was not like a French middle-class background, if only because the relatives who came to visit were American and Israeli. It opened doors for the boy, onto high culture – classical music, modern painting, Thomas Mann, surrealism, and the new novel – and onto an uncommonly wide world: by the age of sixteen, Perec had seen England, Israel, Austria, and

Switzerland, and he had also travelled across France, from the Atlantic coast to the Alps. Like any normal child, Jojo found cycle racing, detective fiction, jazz, and films (especially forbidden ones, like *Les Enfants du Paradis*)[1] more enthralling than what was put on his plate at school and at home. What he explored for himself in the street stuck in his mind: an exhibition of monochrome paintings by Yves Klein, for example, at the Allendy Gallery, a few doors down from number 18 Rue de l'Assomption. But he was also aware that the life he was given by David and Esther was not exactly his own. He was not heir to these cultural riches, but was rather "the child", the "adopted one". If he read Camus – and who did not! – he could have cast himself as the "outsider"; if he read Balzac – which he did – he could have borrowed the title of "poor relation". It would not have been easy for him to establish an identity without the help of the images offered by art and literature, and the teenage orphan must have tried on many of these, from Rumpelstiltskin to Cinderella, from the crucified saint to the wandering Jew.

David and Esther both worried about what Jojo would become in reality. David was not especially keen to see his nephew proceed through a *grande école* into a safe job in the civil service; he would have liked him to carry on with the business. One day Simon Lieberman, in Paris with his American wife, Olive, came to dinner at Rue de l'Assomption. Jojo was all agog as Simon told fascinating stories of his stay in Japan. He turned to the boy and said, "So, would you like to come with me on my next trip and see the fabulous Orient?" Jojo nodded, his eyes bright with excitement. "That's great", Simon replied. "Then I'll be able to teach you all about the pearl business, just as your uncle would want." The boy's face fell. He looked his would-be American mentor in the eye and declared:

Excuse me, sir. I heard the word business. *I won't have anything to do with it.*

---

[1] It is a mystery why this film was held to be unsuitable for children, but when Perec saw it, years later, he still had the sensation of breaking a taboo.

Georges Perec, "Mon plus beau souvenir de Noël", *Le Nouvel Observateur* Nº 737 (December 1978), pp. 60–61.

S. Lieberman, "People, Pearls, and Places", unpublished typescript in the possession of Bianca Lamblin.

Other information from Simone Kaplan, Huguette Moralès, Uriel Peretz, Dany Peretz, Olive Lieberman and Henri Chavranski.

Books at Blévy

Based on research by Heather Mawhinney

Perec recalls in a fragment of an unfinished work, *Lieux où j'ai dormi* (*see* pp. 436–437), that it was at Blévy that he consumed *practically all the detective novels I have ever read* and he goes on to list what he can remember of them [*PC* 25–27]. Perec's memory was less approximate than he makes it seem:

Bill Ballinger, *Une Dent contre lui* (Paris: Presses de la Cité, Collection Un Mystère, 1956) is still at Blévy and is the French translation of Bill S. [William Sanborn] Ballinger, *The Tooth and the Nail* (New York: Harper and Row/London: Reinhardt and Evans, 1955).

Midi gare centrale is the French translation (Paris: Collection Le Masque number 1872) of Thomas Walsh, *Nightmare in Manhattan* (Boston: Little Brown, 1950/London: Hamish Hamilton, 1951), on which the film *Union Station* (Paramount, 1950) is based. Perec's transformation of *Walsh* into *Irish* must be a joke, for English readers only. *William Irish* is the pen-name of another crime writer, Cornell Woolrich.

Bonnes à tuer (Paris: Flammarion, "Detective Club", 1951) is also still at Blévy and is the French version of Patricia McGerr, *Follow, As the Night* (New York: Doubleday, 1951), published in Britain as *Your Loving Victim* (London: Collins, 1951). Perec highlights his own misspelling of the author's surname.

Le 9 de pique (Paris: Gallimard, "Rayon fantastique", 1956) is the only science-fiction story written by Jean Amila (the pseudonym of Jean Meckert), a French author of detective fiction. Amila anglicises his name to John Amila for this novel.

Cristal qui songe is the French title of a work that fascinated several members of OuLiPo, *The Dreaming Jewels* (New York: Greenberg, 1950), by Theodore Sturgeon, whose real name was Edward Hamilton Waldo. The novel was republished in New York in 1957 as *The Synthetic Man*.

The Dreaming Jewels is alluded to in *Life A User's Manual*, and *The Tooth and the Nail* is recapitulated in *"53 Days"*.

The magazines that Perec recalls reading in his room at Blévy also really exist. *Mystère-magazine* (nos. 62, 66, 74, 78 are at Blévy) is the French offshoot of *Ellery Queen's Mystery Magazine*, edited by Frederic Dannay and Manfred B. Lee; *Suspense* (subsequently *Choc-Suspense*, nos. 2 and 4 at Blévy) is the French edition of *Manhunt*; *Alfred Hitchcock Magazine*, edited by Alain Dorémieux, and then by Luc Geslin (nos. 44, 50, and 62 at Blévy) is the French edition of *Alfred Hitchcock's Mystery Magazine*; *Fiction* (nos. 7,10,14, and 19 at Blévy) began as a French edition of *The Magazine of Fantasy and Science Fiction*; and *Galaxie* (nos. 4 and 20 at Blévy) is the French edition of a magazine that has had many titles in its long and continuing life: *Galaxy Science Fiction*, *Galaxy Magazine*, *Galaxy Science Fiction Magazine*, *Galaxy*, and *Galaxy, Incorporating Worlds of If*.

CHAPTER 12

Dreams and Decisions

1952–1954

Jojo and his best friend, Philippe, left Etampes at the end of *seconde*, in June 1952. Philippe entered Lycée Louis-le-grand in Paris for the two years of study leading to the "group C" baccalaureate (in mathematics and natural sciences); Jojo went back home, to attend Lycée Claude-Bernard as a day-boy in the "group B" arts stream. French schools all teach the same national curriculum, but there is a recognised hierarchy among them. The Paris lycées are more demanding of their pupils and more intellectually stimulating than the provincial *collèges*. Ambitious or simply solicitous parents naturally seek to place intelligent children at the best possible schools, especially for the crucial year or two leading to the baccalaureate. Philippe and Jojo "went up" to Paris for *première* out of academic ambition – though perhaps not so much their own as their parents' and guardians'. Many *Etampois* had done the same before them; it was quite normal.

Within two years of his departure from Etampes, Georges Perec had made his decision to be a writer. It seems reasonable to set Perec's turning point in the context of his last two years of secondary education and in relation to the friendships he formed during that period. But Perec himself never claimed to understand *why* he had decided to be a writer. *I know roughly how I became a writer*, he said. *I do not know exactly why. Did I really need to line up words and sentences in order to be?* [Jsn 72].

Not long after the start of the school year in October 1952, Lycée Claude-Bernard was buzzing with excitement. One of the history masters, M. Poirier, had just been awarded France's foremost literary prize, the Prix Goncourt, for *Le Rivage des Syrtes*, published under the pen name of Julien Gracq. Did this unusual event at school give Georges his literary vocation? There's not a shred of evidence to suggest it. Perec did not read *Le Rivage des Syrtes* for another eight years, and when he did he thought it *admirable, majestic, and a bit thin.*

Nor is it certain that Perec was taught in *première* by the uncharismatic M. Poirier, who probably played no role at all in Georges's later decision to take history for his first degree.

In French lessons, Georges learnt the technique of *explication de texte*, a formalised commentary on the relationship between the gist of a passage cunningly severed from its context and the devices of language used to communicate its content to the reader. Woe betide the boy who failed to demonstrate the necessary harmony between content and style, between *fond* and *forme*! The technique, and the texts to which it was applied, had barely changed in half a century and Perec and his classmates in *première* B probably did the same work, at the same desks, as the corresponding class at any lycée in 1932, 1922, and maybe even 1902. French education in general was not innovative in the 1950s, and Lycée Claude-Bernard was no exception.

Perec made only a few new friends at his old school. They never talked very much about the parents they had lost at Auschwitz. At lunchbreaks they would saunter to a sports ground, Stade Géo André, and discuss what seemed to them a far more important matter: the international calendar of "classic" road races leading up through the year to *la grande boucle,* the Tour de France, which starts at the same time as the school holidays and closes the season. There was the Liège-Bastogne-Liège (a bone-crushing race over the infamous Belgian pavés), then the Bordeaux-Paris, the Paris-Brest-Paris, the Milan-San Remo, and the Tour du Dauphiné, often a good predicter of the outcome of the great race itself since it takes riders over excruciating Alpine roads, such as the zigzag climb from Grenoble to Villard-de-Lans, which Perec knew well. Several of the races had their start or finish at the Parc des Princes, next door to Lycée Claude-Bernard. Once Georges dared to approach Louison Bobet, and got his autograph [*Jms* 27].

The pals with whom Perec sat on the grass swapping gossip about Zatopek (the marathon champion of the 1952 Helsinki Olympics) and discussing the merits of triple chain wheels as compared to high gear ratios, were named Jean-Jacques Weiss and Serge Klarsfeld. Klarsfeld was not interested in being Jewish or in learning about what had happened to his father. The workload of *première* at Claude-Bernard (requiring long evening and weekend hours of homework and revision), as well as the nature of the work itself, insulated him completely from the real world, Klarsfeld says, as if his mind had been smothered under a blanket of *explication de texte*. Georges, a shy and scruffy dreamer with a wispy beard that came and went, gave no sign of having a greater purchase on the present or a greater interest in the recent past. Football, athletics, and cycle-racing form were his main extracurricular concerns.

When Klarsfeld woke up to the world, and to history, he put his formidable energies into establishing the facts about the deportation of Jews from France in the period of the German occupation, and into bringing French war criminals to trial. Perec took longer to find a way of relating to his own lost past, and he never had Klarsfeld's bulldozing obsession with justice and retribution. All the same, the work Perec did as a writer is built on the same historical ground as Klarsfeld's monument of scholarship and detection. In the mid-1970s, when Perec visited Robert Bober to discuss the film they were planning to make together, he saw the weighty tomes of Klarsfeld's *Mémorial de la Déportation* on the bookshelf in his study. He reached over, took it down, flicked through the pages as far as convoy 47, ran his finger down the column to find PEREC CYRLA née SZULEWICZ, gave a grunt, slammed the book shut, and put it back.

In the summer of 1953 Esther Bienenfeld telephoned Huguette Guérinat at Etampes and asked if Georges could return to Collège Geoffroy-Saint-Hilaire for his final year of secondary school. Huguette saw no difficulty from the academic side, but she told Esther that decisions about boarding were the headmaster's, not hers. The new headmaster, Beaurenaud, must have consulted his *surveillant général*, responsible for discipline and the good order of the dorms. There must not have been any problems there, either. Perec returned to Etampes as a final-year boarder in October 1953.

Nobody remembers why Georges went back to his boarding school. He had not failed at Claude-Bernard, nor had he been thrown out. He did not go back to be with Philippe, since that scatterbrain had failed his *première* and had to repeat it at Louis-le-grand. There are only speculations, vague rumours that Georges had smelled a "whiff of anti-semitism" at Claude-Bernard; that he felt lost in a big school; that he preferred the mixed *collège* to the boys-only lycée. Perhaps he could not stand being under the same roof as his uncle David, or being asked, Will you try for a *grande école*? What will your subject be? Have you thought about the law? Medicine? Or engineering, like your cousins? Or perhaps it was David Bienenfeld who did not want the dreamy, disconsolate and chain-smoking adolescent at home any more.

The *classe de philosophie* that Perec entered at Etampes was not the same as the class he had left in June 1952. Many pupils, including Michel Georges and Bellec, had left; other, older pupils, who had had to resit either *seconde* or *première*, had taken some of their places, but, even so, it was a much smaller class. There were also some new boys, from Tunisia.

M'hammed Chaker, Amor Fezzani, Ridha Jemmali, and Noureddine Mechri had all been pupils at Sadiki College, the North African Eton, when it was closed down during the pro-independence riots of 1951. They were identified as ringleaders, and warrants were put out for their arrest; they fled to France and went underground, helped by a network of French supporters of the Destour, the pro-independence party led by Habib Bourguiba. One of the four was the son of Hedi Chaker, Bourguiba's right-hand man and the leading member of the Destour still active inside Tunisia. The network hid the young Chaker in a quiet provincial *collège* for his baccalaureate year. The other Tunisians, who had applied for Lycée Hoche or Lycée Lakanal, found that their papers had been forwarded for them to Collège Geoffroy-Saint-Hilaire. Chaker would be safer with camouflage around him.

Perec and Mechri – Nour to his friends – became bosom pals and drinking companions and remained so for the rest of their lives. Nour was a handsome young man with a gift for getting girls. He could not stand the rigours of the boarding-school life and soon moved into a room of his own in the town; Chaker likewise hated the draughts, the flaking paint on the walls and the repulsive food in the canteen, but he had no choice. In the end, all four of these young men from politically prominent backgrounds found delightful peace at Etampes. They stuck together, with another Tunisian, Abd-el-Kader Zghal, and the shy Parisian Georges Perec, rounding out their fine band of friends. They felt quite safe as they sauntered through the town on Thursday afternoons. They noticed lace curtains twitching as they walked past, but it did not occur to them that the townsfolk might be racists. They were quietly convinced that the *Etampois* had never had such a handsome, exotic, and brilliant bunch in their midst before.

For a while Georges was taken under the wing of a tall, strong lad called Grappinet, and he also got to know Jacques Lederer, the only other Jewish boy in the class, who was a talented pianist and a keen follower of jazz. The friendship with Grappinet did not last beyond Perec's school days, but Jacques Lederer, like Nour, became a lifelong companion and confidant, a founding member of Perec's family of friends.

Jacques had lost his father in the camps and had been adopted by his mother's second husband, a tailor by trade. He had had a more traditional Jewish upbringing than Georges, who first sought to convert his new friend to the atheism which was, in effect, his own family tradition. The two *philosophes* would talk of the great issues as they walked around the yard during the break.

"But what happens after death?" Jacques would ask.

Georges would give a shrug of his shoulders and turn his hands palm-outward, to show how plain and obvious the answer was:

Life goes on.

Life goes on was Georges's pet phrase, Jacques remembers, just as Philippe recalls the refrain *I am a bad son.* But "Life goes on" is not only Georges Perec's phrase; it is also the sentence which begins the memorial volume published by *Les Amis de Lubartów* (*see* p. 9). "*Dos Lebn geht waiter*" is a traditional Yiddish saying; perhaps it is a typical saying in Lubartów Yiddish. Georges must have got it, together with his atheism, from his aunt Esther.

Then there were girls. Georges fell in love with a tall, blue-eyed mathematician – the local baker's daughter – who was more interested in Jemmali. He had a crush on the café owner's daughter but never got further than holding hands. Jojo was not an Adonis, that was clear; he began to think of himself as an ugly duckling. He had sinusitis and warts, ears that stuck out (he refers to them in nearly every memory chapter of *W or The Memory of Childhood*, as if they were a particular disgrace), and a thickish nose. At seventeen, he must have worried that no one would ever find him attractive.

Georges and Philippe Guérinat, who met at weekends in Paris that year, felt more than just friendly affection for each other, and it made them wonder if they were heading for a homosexual affair. They talked it through, many times over, and agreed that their feelings for each other could be called love. The outcome seemed inexorable but at the same time absolutely unappealing, and they decided therefore that neither of them was homosexual by nature. "If we could have, we would have," Philippe says. But they never did.

Philippe informed his sister, Huguette, once again Georges's English teacher, that his best friend was in great anguish. She understood him to mean that Perec was terrified that he would turn out to be gay. What happened next can't be said, but Georges soon had a serious crush on Madame Guérinat, his senior by twelve years. On his eighteenth birthday, in March 1954, he called at her flat, and offered his hand in marriage. Needless to say, it was declined, with a smile.

The philosophy master was a new man, Jean Duvignaud, who gave the whole senior class an outstanding year. Duvignaud talked to his pupils as if they were as interested as he was in literature, politics, current affairs, and the theatre. It is a pedagogic trick invented afresh by every gifted teacher; it worked that year at Etampes, as it usually does, and awoke the cultural appetites of every member of the class. Duvignaud's lessons were out of the ordinary routine. The class must have learnt at least some philosophy, but what stuck most in the pupils' minds was the master's digressions – on forthcoming plays on the Paris stage, on the exhibitions he had just seen, on recent issues of literary periodicals – and his gossip about writers, artists, and intellectuals, all of whom he treated as personal friends. Georges Perec lapped up the information, and the stimulation, that Duvignaud handed out with such liberality. He acquired enough confidence to let his teacher know what his dream was: might he, too, become a writer one day?

Perec told stories about his past to his teacher and to his friends, claiming, for example, that he had been mistaken for a non-Jewish child, who had been sent to the gas chamber in his place. Duvignaud had no reason to disbelieve this guilt-laden fantasy, for there were many who really had escaped deportation by just such a miracle, or just such a mistake. Another one of Perec's teenage fantasies came from the notorious Finaly case [see *Jms* 248]. The Finaly children had been entrusted by their Jewish parents, who had subsequently been deported and gassed, to a Catholic spinster, Mademoiselle Brun, who brought them up as her own, and as Catholics. An uncle had meanwhile emigrated to New Zealand, and long after the war's end he tracked down Mademoiselle Brun and requested that she return the children to what was left of their real family. The spinster refused, the uncle took her to court, and the Finaly case became an international tangle of accusations and appeals. It was not at all like what had happened to Georges Perec, but at the age of eighteen he was not averse to having people believe that he, too, had been kidnapped.

When did Perec decide that he would be a writer? David Landes remembers a tense and nervous Jojo calling on him in Paris, perhaps in 1953, for avuncular advice. He had to decide what to do with his life. What should he become? Landes said, "Tell me, Jojo, what do *you* want to do with your life?"

I want to write, the young man replied, with a blush but without hesitation.

"Then that is what you should do."

Landes thought nothing of that brief interview until Perec reminded him of it twenty-five years later and thanked the historian for having helped him to find his path.

Georges also told Esther what his dream was. She was alarmed and telephoned the boy's teacher Jean Duvignaud to request a summit meeting at the Closerie des Lilas, a well-known brasserie on Boulevard Montparnasse. Esther, in her fur coat, looked thin and anxious.

"Georges says he wants to be a writer. Can we take him seriously?" she asked.

"Madame," Duvignaud replied, "You must give him your trust. Georges has the makings of a writer. Let him try."

Duvignaud based his advice on the liberal view that youngsters should be allowed to do what they wanted, but he must also have been influenced to some extent by what he had seen of Perec's written work in that final year at Etampes, which, he says, was very good. Jacques Lederer remembers in particular a class paper that Perec did for Duvignaud on the topic "Elevation in Stendhal". Georges began timidly, plodding through Stendhal's conception of the sublime, Stendhal's moral philosophy, the meaning of spiritual elevation –

"No, no, no," the teacher interrupted. "That's not what I meant at all. Have you forgotten Julien Sorel in his eyrie? Fabrice in the tower in *The Charterhouse of Parma*? I meant you to talk about *elevation* in Stendhal!"

Georges blushed to the nape of his neck (Jacques was sitting behind him) and laughed out loud at his mistake. Duvignaud let him continue with the paper he had prepared. The second part of Perec's first essay on Stendhal took Jacques's breath away. It made him certain that his shy Parisian friend was a hidden giant.

Jacques had been dazzled by Georges at the start of the year, in his first playground conversation with this boy who had not previously been in his class. He had thought to impress the younger lad with knowing references to Charlie Parker and Lester Young. Georges knew exactly what Jacques was talking about; in fact, he knew as much about jazz as Jacques did, and it was Jacques who was impressed and delighted. They got together to persuade the school to let them run a *discothèque* – that is, a record lending library, not a "disco". Their collection consisted exclusively of jazz and pop. Georges (like his sister-cousin Lili) was forever humming "You go to my head"; in fact, that is all that some of his former classmates remember about him. Jacques is remembered musically as well: the jazz concert he was allowed to give in the school hall at the end of the year, with his band the Hot Peppers, is recalled not only by former classmates at Etampes, but by Perec himself, in *Life A User's Manual*, where Rémi Rorschach's music-hall act is renamed with each passing fashion, metamorphosing from Albert Greenfield and His Jolly Rogers to Paco Domingo and the Three Caballeros, Fedor Kowalski and his Magyar Minstrels and Barry Jefferson and His Hot Pepper Seven [L 43].

A month before the baccalaureate examinations began, Chaker's father was assassinated in his home town of Sfax. Duvignaud had to break the news to the boy. All the cloak-and-daggery surrounding the "Tunisian tribe" at the school had not been mere paranoia. But his friend's bereavement was not what caused Perec to call one of the streets of Sfax Avenue Hedi-Chaker in *Things*: one of the streets of Sfax *is* called Avenue Hedi-Chaker.

Georges sat his baccalaureate examinations and did very well; he also won the school prize for philosophy. When their last exam was over, he wandered into the town with Jacques and Nour. They sat in the formal gardens in the centre of the main square. It was one of those moments in life when you can almost hear a leaf turning; the boys played at guessing what the next chapters would bring.

Jacques, you'll be a famous jazz pianist. And Nour, you'll go into the movies.

And Georges, what would he do? He did not pause for a second. *Moi, je serai écrivain.*

Based on information from Ela Bienenfeld, H.E. M'hammed Chaker, Jean Duvignaud, Philippe Guérinat, Ridha Jemmali, Serge Klarsfeld, David and Sonya Landes, Jacques Lederer, and Huguette Moralès, and on additional research in Etampes by Christiane Dancie.

CHAPTER 13

Tilt

1954–1955

Perec did not move into a writer's garret in the Latin Quarter or the Marais to acquire genius as soon as his decision to be a writer was made. He went first on a summer holiday, to Rock (a tiny harbour-town on the Camel estuary, in Cornwall) to learn English (again!); he spent his time drinking pinks, flirting rather unsuccessfully with a cotton spinner's daughter, and using a portable harmonium to prac-tise a Bach prelude, the first fifty-four notes of which constituted the only keyboard piece he ever learnt to play [*EsEs* 32]. On his return to Paris for the start of the new school year, he was allowed to move downstairs, to one of the two maid's rooms on the second floor at Rue de l'Assomption. The rooms had always been used for guests and for domestic overflow, as Esther had not had live-in servants since the war. It was a step towards the independence to which the eighteen-year-old naturally aspired: Georges would be able to come and go by way of the "servants' stair". Nonetheless, he let his pals believe that he had been cast out of his home and into the lower depths. He quite liked to be seen as Cinderella; it earned him sympa-thetic affection and helped to deflect the guilt he felt for having such a comfortable, liberal, and international adoptive home.

Had Georges not done so well in his baccalaureate examination, he might have begun his university studies that year. However, he had gained good enough results to enter the race for a place at one of France's *grandes écoles*. Since he had not carried on with Greek, he was not in the running for the Ecole Normale Supérieure in Rue d'Ulm (called ENS, or Normal' Sup', or just by its address, Rue d'Ulm), but he could try for the only slightly less prestigious Ecole Normale Supérieure de Saint-Cloud. He entered the preparatory class – called *hypokhâgne* – at Lycée Henri-IV, an antiquated and over-crowded forcing house in the Latin Quarter, in October 1954. He had an open mind about it and was even keen for a new educational experience. The syllabus looked daunting, he wrote to Philippe, and the teachers seemed not bad at all, but the other boys were undisciplined and kept talking in class, and he was fed up already with the jargon of the educational elite. (After *hypokhâgne* comes *khâgne*; a *bisuth* – or first-year student – becomes a *ka* or even a *bikka*, unless he is a mathematician, in which case he is a *cube* or, with the passage of time, *hypercube*, and so on.) Very soon, however, Georges's interest waned; he became as disappointed with Henri-IV as Henri-IV grew disenchanted with him.

Perec was able to drop mathematics, with relief, and no longer needed to do any science, art, or woodwork. He took English, French, and philosophy and was obliged in principle to carry on also with gym, alongside his major subject, history. The syllabus covered England in the eighteenth century and the Balkans from 1815 to 1933. He scored reasonable marks for his history essays but not for anything else. In French literature he studied Racine and Prévost under a teacher named Simon, who saw little talent in the work of the boy from Etampes. In the first term report he commented that Perec could write coherently, but should pay more attention to style and spelling. By the end of the year he had given up hope: Perec's mark was 6 out of 20, and the teacher's comment: "Still very clumsy".

Philosophy was taught by Georges Spire, a distinguished aesthetician who lacked elementary pedagogic skills. He lectured in a drone, with his eyes on his notes, and made no attempt to keep order in a crowded class of boisterous eighteen-to-twenty-year-olds. He did not even notice their impertinence when they answered, from his own books, in plainchant, as if in church. In class Georges sat next to a *bikka* (short for *bi-carré*, "bi-square", that is a fourth-year student for the entrance examination to Saint-Cloud) by the name of Bernard Quilliet, called K (pronounced "ka") for short. Like Georges, K planned to be a writer, and intended to knock off his first masterpiece that year. K was keen on the theatre but not on the classical dramas studied in school – skimpy, feeble things, he said, admired only by sheep-brained academics. Real theatre, in Quilliet's view, was baroque, rococo, preromantic: *Wenceslas*, by Rotrou, for example, or Lemercier's *Agamemnon*. In break-time discussions he enthused over the forgotten seventeenth- and eighteenth-century playwrights whose fulsome, energetic dramas had played to packed houses right up to end of the nineteenth century, when the Third Republic had smothered them beneath Racine and the "other" Corneille – writers such as Collin d'Harleville, Lefranc de Pompignan, Guimond de la Touche,

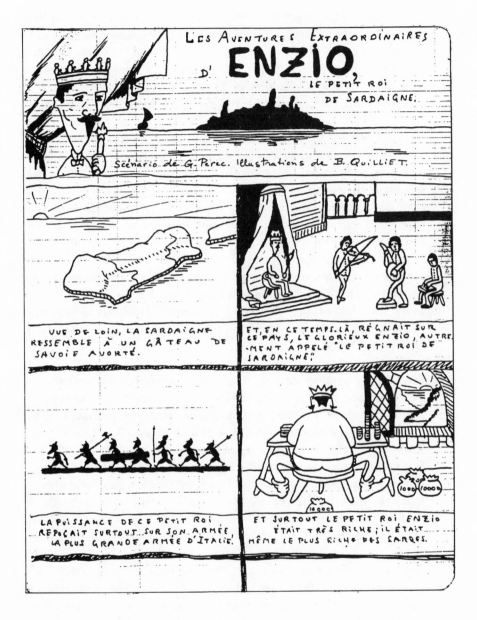

Lamotte-Houdar, Malte d'Istillerie . . . [see L 364]. Georges and Bernard may have chatted about writing tragedies, and comedies, and about the history of burlesque, but what they actually wrote together that year was a strip cartoon, "Les Aventures d'Enzio, le petit roi de Sardaigne" ("The Adventures of Enzio, the Wee King of Sardinia"). It is just about the earliest piece of Perec's written work to have come to light so far.

Enzio (circa 1220–71), the son of Frederick II and Bianca Lanzia, was king of Sardinia from 1242 to 1249. Neither Bernard nor Georges had ever been to Sardinia, but they both liked the sound of it, and especially the sound of Enzio's name. Perec wrote out the story, and then Bernard drew the cartoon pictures, which he brought into class. Using the broad shoulders of the boy in front of him as a screen, Georges would ink in the captions whilst Monsieur Spire mumbled on about the philosophy of art. Maybe Georges and Bernard would have produced a rival to Tintin had they taken Enzio beyond page 14. But it is hardly surprising that Perec came forty-second in Philosophy, in a class of forty-two boys, and finished the year with a mark of 5 out of 20 and a one-word and probably euphemistic report from M. Spire: "Weak".

Decent marks in history and English were not enough to raise his average to a passing mark of 10, and he was politely informed in the year-end report that his time at Henri-IV was over. In June 1955, he also sat *propédeutique*, the "common core" first-year examination for university arts students, which was of lower status – and lower standard – than the entrance competition for Saint-Cloud or Normal' Sup'. The results were to be posted on 14 July, Bastille Day. Georges, dressed all in black, took along his cousin Simone, freshly graduated from New York University and on her first Paris vacation alone, to read the results sheet on the notice board at the Sorbonne. A miracle! He had passed! They then went to meet the Bienenfeld family, who were assembled by the banks of the Seine to watch the firework display. Georges asked his uncle for some money to celebrate, and it turned into a row; David held his ground. That did not stop Georges and "Simonette" from undertaking a corkscrew tour of the festive city by night. At Mabillon, a café-owner had put his jukebox on the pavement, and there was dancing in the street. Georges and Simonette did not finish celebrating until dawn.

Perec's academic career never recovered from Henri-IV. In October 1955 he began a history degree at the Sorbonne; he remained a registered student for two years, but his heart was never in it. He should have attended lectures by Mousnier, de Perroy, and Rodolphe Guilland on modern, medieval and Byzantine history, respectively; instead he got hold of their cyclostyled lecture notes, passed one of the courses that he took in 1955–56, failed the others, resat the following September, did no better, and then abdicated from academic study, long before the end of his official registration. The only thing that Perec remembered with affection from his history courses, apart from a fair amount about the Balkans, was learning how to read medieval manuscripts from a model rental contract beginning with the grandiloquent announcement *"Connue chose soit a tous ceuz qui ces lettres varront et oiront . . ."*[1]. The reference work he used was a huge diplomatic dictionary compiled by a Benedictine monk, Dom Mabillon; eventually it dawned on Perec that the street, the metro station, and the whole corner in the Latin Quarter were not called Mabillon by coincidence. Paris place names now began to come alive for him as the traces of past lives. Avenue Junot, he knew, was named after a Napoleonic general; Rue Pestalozzi, near Place de la Contrescarpe, his favourite spot in the Latin Quarter in those years, was named after an educationalist. But Rue Vilin? Even in 1970 he still had not found out why the place where he was born bore that name.

It was not the wild social life of Paris that caused Perec to make a mess of *hypokhâgne* and of his history degree. On the contrary, Jacques Lederer recalls: Georges and he were more like little boys lost, ill adjusted to the size and impersonality of the big city. In the summer of 1954 Jacques's mother and stepfather had moved their home and business to Paris, to Avenue du Maine in Montparnasse. Jacques moved with them and did his *propédeutique* at the Sorbonne whilst Georges was at Henri-IV. Georges often dropped in on the Lederers, usually around dinnertime. Jacques's *yiddishe mama* would pile food on Georges's plate; it made a change from lunches in the school canteen, and also from Esther's more frugal cuisine.

Noureddine Mechri and Amor Fezzani had also moved to Paris and were living in the Tunisian students' residence in Rue Blainville, just off Place de la Contrescarpe. Georges hung around there a lot in his early student years, making friends amongst the other Tunisians and loitering in front of an incredibly dilapidated building (long since

---

[1] "Let this be known unto all who see and hear the present letters . . .". Used again in *L* 437.

demolished) with a brass nameplate announcing that it was the home of the Centre Mondial de Synthèse. For a boy who had done philosophy and not chemistry for his baccalaureate, it must have seemed to be the World Centre for Conclusions.

Some of the Tunisians still commuted to Etampes, taking their *classe de philosophie* again, and some *Etampois* – such as Philippe Guérinat, who had returned for his final year there in 1954–55 – were often up in Paris. The crowd had a rendezvous point at the crossroads of Boulevard Saint-Germain and Boulevard Saint-Michel, in the two corner cafés. Georges established his own social headquarters not far away, in the café on the corner of Rue de la Bûcherie and Rue Saint-Jacques, next door to Shakespeare & Co, the English bookshop frequented by many famous expatriate writers. The *patron* of La Bûcherie allowed impecunious students to sit by the open fire for hours on end over a single cup of tea, reading, writing, or just gazing into the flames or at the Lurçat tapestry on the wall, with its mysterious inscription, *"La nuit cache le jour à l'envers de son noir"* ("Night hides day behind its dark") [recalled in *Jms* 200]. It was a place where Nour and Amor also brought their friends, among them a red-haired student of Czechoslovak parentage called Paulette Petras, who would get to know Georges Perec better in later years.

Perec's emotions were focussed for a time on the blue-eyed mathematician from Etampes, who had now also moved to Paris but who continued to keep him at arm's length. One day she called on Georges at Rue de l'Assomption and let him kiss her. Then she went away.

Perec was lonely in Paris, and he spent a great deal of his time with his two really close pals, Jacques Lederer and Philippe Guérinat. They hung around together in bars and cafés, trying drinks of all kinds (sometimes with dramatic consequences) and, above all, going to one or another of the huge number of picture houses that Paris then enjoyed. They were not art-movie buffs in the way that students of the 1960s or 1970s would be; they went to the cinema for entertainment, for excitement, and because they were a bit lost for other things to do: concerts were too costly, and television barely existed. What they adored most especially were the comedies, the romances, the adventures, and the musicals made in Hollywood. During these foot-loose years of youth in the pavement queues of what was still a far more American city than can now be imagined (until the 1960s, when de Gaulle withdrew France from NATO, SHAFE was at Versailles, and Paris was full of GIs and PXs), Perec acquired a huge mental repertoire of the last great period of Hollywood. Reminiscences of film scenes and titles run through all of his mature writing, not just his "story of the sixties", *Things*, in which the passion for American cinema is an explicit theme.

Perec seems to have made no new friends in his first student years. He went to the movies, talked, and played cards for hours on end with Jacques, Philippe, and Nour, or by himself. He quarrelled with Jacques from time to time, sometimes quite sharply, with much screaming and waving of the arms. But they always made it up. Perec's behaviour could also be a bit odd: he always carried a handkerchief and would bite into it in moments of flamboyantly childish frustration. And when he had had a drink or two, or more, he would describe his own plight in mime. Arms out straight, hands loose, as if the wrists were broken; head flopping down on his chest, slightly sideways; eyes squinting upwards: it is the pose depicted by Grünewald on the altar at Issenheim, the famously realistic image of Christ on the cross.

Georges's year at Henri-IV uncoupled him from the train he had joined only lately, in his *classe de philosophie* – the train which would take others on to a *grande école*, the *agrégation* and a secure academic job to underpin the writing life. It was the straight track that almost all established French intellectuals had followed, the only track that was already laid down for an aspiring writer. How else did one become a French intellectual, if not by passing examinations? Georges Perec would follow a less obvious and less certain route to the destination he had chosen for himself at the age of eighteen. The kind of writer that he became bears the mark of that renunciation: *Life A User's Manual* is neither typically French nor the work of an intellectual in the sense that the French give to that term. Though his prospects looked dim in the mid-1950s, Perec was already marching to his own drummer. You can't blame his aunt and uncle for not hearing its muffled beat, but Perec himself probably did.

He wasted vast amounts of time in cafés, playing pinball machines. *Billard électrique*, "electrical billiards", is the official French term for these noisy imported toys, but they were called *flippers* by addicts, even though the earliest models lacked actual flippers and had to be banged and shunted to alter the path of the shiny steel ball – whence their other name in Franglais, *tilts*. Georges would often hold forth mock-philosophically that his life could be compared to the brief and violent path of a ball in a *tilt*, rejected unpredictably by one blinking, spring-loaded pin after another before plunging – too soon! – into the black hole where all balls must eventually come to rest. He would play for hours at a time on the clattering machines. He got blisters on his button-fingers and sores on his thumbs; the only cure was a period of abstinence, which never held for very long. Soon he would be back, with Philippe and Jacques, trying for ever higher scores and ever longer runs on a single coin. It was an obsession, an empty passion, an almost worrying addiction. But perhaps the headaches it gave him alongside his bruised hands helped him put off contemplating the other sources of his pain.

Based mainly on unpublished reminiscences by Georges Perec in FP 57, 14, FP 57, 24, FP 57, 47, and FP 57, 69; a letter from Georges Perec to Philippe Guérinat, Paris, 5 October [1954]; and a lecture given by Perec at the University of Adelaide (Australia) on 1 October 1981, together with his school report from the archives of Lycée Henri-IV and the recollections of Philippe Guérinat, Jacques Lederer, Bernard Quilliet and Simone Kaplan.

CHAPTER 14

In Tow

1955–1956

It is one thing to decide to be a writer, and quite another to become one. When Perec declared his decision to Jacques and Nour in the square at Etampes, did he know what he was saying? Would-be writers have always been ten-a-penny in France, where the profession of letters commands high esteem. Perhaps he did not realise that he was but one of many hundreds of youngsters leaving their last *explication de texte* behind them and dreaming of the cream covers of Gallimard's *nrf* collection, of the Goncourt Prize, of fame and fortune. But only one in every two hundred manuscripts submitted to French publishers is accepted, and of the couple of hundred literary works by new writers put into Paris bookshops each year, the vast majority go unnoticed and unread. Their authors carry on with careers as classicists, or historians, or advertising executives; writing is not a career you can bank on.

However it arose inside Perec's mind, the decision to be a writer, once made, engaged his whole being and opened the tap of his dormant energy. When he looked back on the summer of 1954 and tried to explain to a friend what it had meant to him to resolve to make his life in words, Perec said that with the very first sentence of fiction he penned, he had felt he was entering an awesome and magical new world. For reasons he would never cease to explore, writing gave him from the start a sense of doing *something irremediably serious . . .* Perec's decision turned out to be quite unlike the heady dreams of other youngsters of eighteen. He stuck to it through years of disappointment and obscurity; he went on reading and writing, writing and reading. Long before he had anything of significance published, when he was asked, "What do you do in life?", he never blushed to reply, *I write.* More like Honoré de Balzac than he ever cared to admit, Georges Perec became a writer for himself by decision, and for the world by tenacity. Albert Einstein defined genius as the capacity to take infinite pains; the idle student, the self-pitying Cinderella, the pinball boy, turned out to have Einstein's kind of genius, for writing.

During his student years Perec devoted his real energies to acquiring a literary education outside of the institutions to which he was nominally attached, and to obtaining a toehold in the literary establishment of Paris. Jean Duvignaud, his former teacher, was his mentor, his facilitator, and his pilot. Perec became his *poulain* – literally, a yearling, a race-horse-in-waiting – a young man in tow.

Duvignaud spent only one year at Etampes, the year of Perec's *classe de philosophie*. Thereafter he was a lecturer in sociology at the Sorbonne, in Georges Gurvitch's department, but he also spent a good part of his time in and around the theatre, and it was towards the stage, not towards sociology, that he first led Georges Perec.

Duvignaud was on the editorial board of a politically committed and innovative theatrical journal, *Théâtre populaire*. In front of his philosophy class at Etampes, he must have digressed from Descartes's *Metaphysical Speculations* to the intellectual and political import of the plays of Berthold Brecht, which his journal was about to bring out in French. Roland Barthes ("*mon ami Barthes*", Duvignaud would call him, to the annoyance of the other teachers at Etampes, who ragged him behind his back by referring to "*mon ami Bevan*", "*mon ami Bourguiba*") wrote the first essays on Brecht for a French audience; they were published in *Théâtre populaire*[1] in advance of the the Berliner Ensemble's first brief visit to Paris in the summer of 1954, when it played *Mother Courage* at the Festival of Nations. *Théâtre populaire* then published the whole of *The Caucasian Chalk Circle* in French translation in a special Brecht issue in January 1955, prior to its French première at the Théâtre Sarah-Bernhardt, attended by Brecht himself. It was the theatrical sensation of the year. There was a reception to honour the great man of the militant stage at the publishers' offices in Rue Saint-André-des-Arts. Georges Perec was in the crowd of onlookers spilling from the narrow street onto Place Saint-Michel, trying to catch a glimpse of Bert Brecht posing for the press photographers, shaking hands with Roland Barthes and his teacher Jean Duvignaud.[2]

---

[1] Some are reprinted in R. Barthes, *Critique et vérité* (Paris: Le Seuil, 1964), pp. 48–52.

[2] Perec was spotted there by a classmate from Etampes. (Information from Christiane Dancie.)

The Brecht of Duvignaud and Barthes gave Georges Perec his first grasp of "alienation". Brecht's theatre abandons the conventions designed to maintain the suspension of disbelief and makes the audience aware that what is on stage is not life but its theatrical representation. It is highly stylised, non-naturalistic theatre, using techniques reminiscent of grand opera and the Japanese tradition of masks. The desired effect of "alienation", or awareness of theatricality, goes hand in hand with Brecht's intention to raise the audience's political consciousness. His plays deal with the great subjects of epic – war, uprising, revolution – from a partisan, Marxist point of view. The coincidence of Brecht's arrival on the Paris stage and Perec's decision to be a writer, the coincidence of Perec's education at Etampes and the role of his teacher in promoting Brecht in France, can easily be considered sufficient reason for Perec's adoption of a left-wing position at the very start of his career. It may also explain in large measure why Perec's first literary ambitions – as he related them to his classmate at Lycée Henri-IV – were of a theatrical nature.

None of Perec's early efforts at writing for the stage has come to light, and the only known traces of these works are indirect. Perec told one friend that his very first writing during his *classe de philosophie* had been the first lines of a play, *straight out of Pirandello*. To another friend Perec said that he had written a whole tragedy, thought it dreadful, and put it away in a bottom drawer. Perec's surviving letters from 1955–56 have quotations from Rostand's *Cyrano de Bergerac* and from Molière, and they mention more than once his interest in the history of burlesque. The manager of Paris's principal theatrical bookshop, Les Deux Masques, knew Perec by name as one of the most assiduous standing readers at the shelves long before he knew he was a writer. Perec read theatre, thought about theatre, and must have had a few stabs at writing for the theatre before he decided on a different course. He would not return to dramatic literature until he had his next encounter with German culture.

Perec also tried out and abandoned two other avocations. The first is of a hypothetical nature. In a talk he gave in 1981,[1] in a "self-portrait" penned in 1972 [*Jsn* 67–74], and in other places, too, Perec said that he had wanted to be a painter before he wanted to be a writer. The people who remember the Perec of 1954 remember only

---

[1] Georges Perec, "A propos de la description", in A. Reniès, ed., *Espace et Représentation: Actes du Colloque d'Albi* (Paris: Editions de la Villette, 1982).

that he was determined to be a writer; he must have kept his painterly ambitions to himself. The designs he did for record sleeves, both for and with his jazz-loving pals Jacques and Philippe, do not add up to much, but the intense eye of Perec's mature writing (*Things* begins, *Your eye, first of all* . . .) makes it quite likely that at some point the writer entertained more or less seriously the idea of learning to paint.

Perec also wrote teenage poetry. There is hardly a letter or postcard from him before 1957 that does not contain a bad quatrain or a limping alexandrine. He tried to write serious verse, too. A poem in blank verse (and semi-English) entitled "Sommeil" ("Sleep") is the only one that has been found, but it was probably not the only one written. Perec soon turned his back on poetry, perhaps because of its association with adolescent emotions that he wished likewise to put away; he returned to it in later years only by an almost impossibly arduous path. From 1955 or thereabouts, Perec envisaged his future career as a writer in terms of fiction. His ambition, his intention, his will, was to be a novelist.

Jean Duvignaud gave his *poulain* Perec his first opportunity to appear in print, not in *Théâtre populaire* (though he got Nour to write for it[1] and Jemmali to do reports for him on productions in the Paris suburbs), but in *Nouvelle Nrf*, the new version of the monthly that had been founded long before by André Gide as *La Nouvelle Revue française*. Duvignaud was its regular theatre columnist in 1954, and he put his ex-pupil up to join the team of regular book reviewers contributing to what was once again a prestigious literary journal.

The reviews Perec published from January to December 1955, of books by Vidalie, Audiberti, Curtius, Jean-Pierre Richard, Donald Wyndham, Marcel Lallemand, Félicien Marceau, René de Obaldia, Driss Chraibi and Henri Thomas are competent five-hundred-word reader's reports. Perec must have been proud to see his name in print whilst he was still a senior schoolboy at Lycée Henri-IV. In some of the pieces he made his opinions quite plain. He disliked Driss Chraibi's *Les Boucs,* for example, a novel celebrated more for its social import than for its writing. He was impressed by *La Cible*, a collection of short stories by Henri Thomas, whose style, he said, was designed to suggest states of mind rather than to narrate events, and recalled Kafka's, Hemingway's and Marcel Arland's (simul-

[1] N. Michri [*sic*], review of *Scheherezade* by Tewfik el Hakim. *Théâtre populaire* no. 16 (November 1955), pp. 89–90.

taneously?). Perec was to retain his interest in Henri Thomas who, though he has won the Médicis Prize and produced a substantial oeuvre, has not attracted much critical attention even now.

No youngster in search of culture in the 1950s could have avoided an encounter with André Gide (1869–1951), whose anticolonialist and pro-Communist position, as well as his libertarian attitude towards sexual behaviour, made his stylishly ironical fictions all the more attractive. Jacques Lederer was for a time a fervent Gidean; moreover, Gide was the founder and tutelary god of the periodical that gave Perec his first access to print, and so it is hardly surprising that when it was Perec's turn to give a paper on a book of his own choosing in M. Simon's French class at Henri-IV, he talked about Gide's *Counterfeiters*.

The Counterfeiters (1925) is the first large-scale example in French literature of the explicitly self-reflective work of art, containing through the diary of Edouard the story of the composition of a novel called . . . *The Counterfeiters*. Gide's later *Journal des Faux-Monnayeurs* ("Journal of The Counterfeiters"), a critical reflection on how he wrote the novel, adds another mirror to his maze of "counterfeit" reflections.

According to his classmate Bernard Quilliet, Perec presented Gide's novel to the *hypokhâgne* class as transposed literary gossip. Drawing lines and arrows, circles and boxes on the blackboard, he demonstrated that the fictional Strouvilhou was "really" André Breton, the father of surrealism, that Passavent was none other than Jean Cocteau, and that the secrets of Alfred Jarry, the mysterious originator of pataphysics, were also hidden in the novel.

The disappointing thing about *The Counterfeiters* is that it is largely silent on the craft or crime that its title announces. At the time when Perec read Gide's metaphorically counterfeit novel, however, the Paris police were aptly providing the interested public with a large amount of information about real fakes and forgeries. The first exhibition, *Le Musée des faux artistiques* ("Gallery of Art Fakes"), was held on police premises from 13 to 27 February 1954, and it showed forged Andrea del Sartos, Cranachs, Goyas, Corots, Daumiers, Degases, Van Goghs, and much else. A larger "definitive" exhibition was held at the Grand Palais the following year at the Salon International de la Police; a specialist art-historian who was also a police inspector, Guy Isnard, brought out a book, *Les Pirates de la Peinture* ("The Pirates of Painting") to coincide. The art of faking might seem a rather obscure interest, fraught with psychological meaning, for a young man seeking to find his way as a writer. But the coincidence of Perec's first steps in writing with a broad wave of Parisian interest in the curious cases of van Meegeren, Icilio and the Lübeck frescoes was at least as important for the path he eventually took as his early passion for a novel entitled *The Counterfeiters*.

Some of the firmest foundations of Perec's literary culture were laid during his student years in Paris. No doubt he read more than those books that can be listed from the memory of his friends and from references in a few dozen letters: but the list that can be compiled in that way looks already strikingly Perecquian. During his year at Henri-IV Georges read Dante, in Lamennais's translation, and James Joyce's *Ulysses*. There was a copy of the latter at Rue de l'Assomption; a year or two later, he recommended that Bernard Quilliet (at that time an admirer of Anatole France) read an illustrated introduction to Joyce (Jean Paris's *Joyce par lui-même*) before attempting the great book itself. In return, Bernard urged Georges to try Thomas Mann. He began, it seems, with *Doktor Faustus*, in the French translation by Louise Servicen, and a few years later tackled *The Magic Mountain* – another book from his uncle David's collection. Perec reread Joyce and Mann many times in the course of his life, never ceasing to explore and, in a sense, to rewrite them, even when later literary friends found his enduring passion for them in poor taste. Perec's literary culture was acquired mostly through the medium of French, but it was international in scope; to find out what writing could be, he began by looking elsewhere.

Since Zola's intervention in the Dreyfus affair, if not since Voltaire, there has been a strong link in French culture between literature and politics. Sartre taught that abstinence from politics was itself a political act: you cannot choose not to choose, since the refusal to choose was itself a choice. Could you be an intellectual on the right? The question was purely rhetorical; no one was expected to answer yes, or even maybe, and in the 1950s, with the exception of Mauriac, no one did.

That does not make Perec's espousal of the left simply a matter of following the trend: his beliefs were no less sincerely held for being the beliefs of all his friends and mentors. It was perhaps also psychologically convenient for him to be on the far left, since a political rift lent a dimension that was easily understood in French society to Perec's antagonism towards his "bourgeois" uncle David. Still, it was not a shallow conversion. Although party politics came to interest him less and less as he grew older, Perec remained as faithful to his self-definition as a socialist as he did to his decision to be a writer. On the night of 13 May 1981, when France acquired its first elected socialist president, Perec joined the crowds in Place de la Bastille to celebrate.

In the 1950s the French left was dominated by the Communist party, or PCF, which presented itself as the only true bastion of defence against a resurgence of fascism. Had it not been the Red Army that brought Hitler down in the end? Had the PCF not been the backbone of the French Resistance? The counter-arguments were not widely known at the time. In the mid-1950s to be on the left was, for most people, to be a supporter of the Communist party. Perec never actually joined the PCF or any political party. But between 1954 and 1957 – between the loss of Indochina and the intensification of the war in Algeria – he was not far from being a fellow traveller.

French politics were then dominated by colonial questions. Whether and how to shore up France's crumbling empire were the issues on which coalition after coalition foundered under the Fourth Republic. Perec naturally took the side of the decolonisers: several of his best friends were Tunisian, and his cousin Bianca had shared with him her disquiet over the policies she had seen implemented by the French in Algeria. Bianca returned from her North African posting in 1954, and her disquiet turned to outrage when the government put in ever larger divisions of the army to quell the "terrorist" insurgents of the FLN, the Algerian National Liberation Front. She set up something called the "Committee for Peace in Algeria and for Self-Determination", collected a thousand signatures from amongst the corps of secondary schoolteachers in Paris, and sent her petition to France's erstwhile and future leader Charles de Gaulle, in his "retirement" at Colombey-les-deux-Eglises.

Georges could not join Bianca's committee, as it was a committee of teachers, but he shared its opposition both to the idea of *Algérie française* and to the military means being used to maintain it. It was already an unpopular war amongst young Frenchmen facing twenty-four months' national service in the army, navy or air force; it would soon become a national trauma. The Algerian War was the experience that defined Georges Perec's generation.

Perec already owed much to Jean Duvignaud: a philosophy prize, Stendhal, Brecht, and his first toehold in the literary world, on the *Nouvelle Nrf.* Now it was time for the *poulain* to be brought out onto the track, for Perec to be towed into the channel. Duvignaud took him along to the Royaumont Centre, probably in the summer of 1955. Royaumont is one of many rural piles in the French countryside which serve as residential retreats for artists, writers, and intellectuals. At Royaumont Perec would meet the people he would need to know in order to get on in literary society. Many of them were good friends of Jean Duvignaud's; he was able to introduce Perec to Roland Barthes, to get him talking to René de Obaldia, to the psychoanalyst Michel de M'Uzan, and to Marthe Robert, the translator of Freud and of the diaries of Kafka. None of these remarkable people became close friends of Georges Perec, who was never particularly interested in literary society, even when literary society became interested in him. However, he did more than shake hands shyly with the people to whom he was introduced; he also read their books. The influence of these works – from Barthes's *Mythologies* to Obaldia's *Fugue à Waterloo,* from Freud to Franz Kafka – can be tracked through different parts of Perec's own subsequent life and work. Duvignaud did Georges much more than a social service by taking him to Royaumont. He also showed him, indirectly, some of the paths he would follow to find his own world of culture, and his own images of himself.

Sources include letters from Georges Perec to Philippe Guérinat (1954–55), to Pierre Getzler (from Pau, 7 August 1959) and to Bernard Quilliet (19 December [1956]) and the recollections of Georges Dupré, Bianca Lamblin, Jacques Lederer, René de Obaldia, and Huguette Moralès.

Information on fakes and forgeries kindly provided in part by Patrizia Molteni and Pierre Getzler. On van Meegeren, see also André Chastel, "L'Etonnante affaire Van Meegeren et ses suites", *Le Monde,* 5 March 1955 and Mark Jones, ed., *Fake? The Art of Deception* (London: British Museum, 1990), pp. 237–240.

CHAPTER 15

Depression

1956

The earliest piece of Perec's fiction to have survived is a three-page short story entitled "Les Barques" ("The Boats") [FP 48, 9, 3, 2], written in the autumn of 1954. It tells of twenty-three boats that lie moored in the Seine, presumably beneath the Pont de Grenelle, at the bottom of Rue de l'Assomption. One day they are no longer there. There is no explanation at all; the story is made of description and creates an atmosphere of uncanny sadness. It could have been written by a talented schoolboy who was familiar with Gide or Stendhal and able to cast sentences in well-turned, literary French. It would most likely have been singled out for praise by a schoolmaster marking a set of free compositions; maybe he would also have taken the author aside to find out just what lay behind the defensive restraint of his literary exercise.

Perec's first novel was called *Les Errants* ("The Wanderers"). It was begun in the summer of 1955, when the war against Communist insurgents in the Central American state of Guatemala (the so-called United Fruit War) was at its height, and finished before mid-February 1956. The day he completed it, Georges walked home to Rue de l'Assomption from Place d'Italie, in the pouring rain, by way of Boulevard Saint-Germain, feeling utterly happy. Soon after that, however, he fell into a depression – perhaps not his first, and certainly not his last, but the one that came, through his memory of it, to form the ground of a whole part of his later writing. Depression is pretty much an inevitable part of a thoughtful life. You do not have to be ill to be depressed, but when you are depressed, perhaps especially in youth, you may well believe that you are ill, or mad, and in desperate need of help, or of cure.

Les Errants *tells the story of four white jazz musicians who bum around the world and end up dying in Guatemala beside Colonel Arbenz. There's a trumpeter, a saxophonist, a drummer, and a bass. One of them is called Doug Watkins [. . .] The technical terms came from Jacques Lederer: tempo, riff, chorus, high-hat, etc. Each one lets the music take him and dreams of what is torturing him – one of them of a woman, Gloria, a transposition of Leila, night[1] [. . .]*

Les Errants *began: "Tomorrow I shall be dead". Then the hero remembered that as a child, when he got to the end of the road he lived in, he would imagine that he had as many kilometres left to travel as the number of his house (at the bottom of Rue de l'Assomption: 18 km to get to number 18) and would begin a race that he obviously won.*   [FP 57, 17]

Much of *Les Errants* was composed during the Christmas holidays of 1955, in a café (*stripped pine, big bay windows, beer and kirsch*) in an Austrian winter sports resort. It was typed up in Paris, presumably in January 1956, not at the Bienenfelds', but in the student room that Michel Rigout (a childhood friend from Rue de l'Assomption) now had near Place d'Italie. Few people ever read it. Duvignaud criticised the vagueness of his pupil's first attempt at fiction and gave him a solid piece of advice: "When you talk about a thing, you have to describe it so that the reader can see it or at least imagine what it looks like." Jacques Lederer objected to the gratuitous use in *Les Errants* of musical terms that he had provided. Philippe Guérinat was perhaps the only other person who read it straightaway. It was not submitted to a publisher. Very soon Perec himself could not bear to reread his own first stab at sustained writing. In the end, he lost *Les Errants*, probably when he lost a clutch of early works, but he never forgot that he had written it. Like so many fragments of Georges Perec's life, it is "inscribed" into *Life A User's Manual* (as "*The Wanderers*, by George Bretzlee", *see* pp. 5–6), and it was also the subject of a large part of one of the lectures Perec gave in Australia in 1981, comprising his choicest example of how *not* to write.

After some months Perec posted a copy of his first novel to his cousin Henri Chavranski (by then a civil servant on secondment in Morocco), half hoping and half fearing that it would be confiscated by customs; he was glad to be rid of it but just as glad, later on, to

---

[1] *Leila* means night in both Arabic and Hebrew. Perec probably picked it up as a nickname for a girl from his Tunisian friends at Etampes, but he may also have remembered the lullaby sung around kibbutz campfires: "*Ha-leila, ba-leila . . .*"

hear that it had reached its destination. *Les Errants* had enormous significance for him, he wrote to Henri. It was the manifestation of his will to write, proof that he was a writer, and, despite the faults that were only too obvious to him now (poor characterisation, a lack of unity, childishness, clichés borrowed from Dos Passos and Flaubert), a book that he had wanted to write, and had written, and by that token *a magical promise for the future . . .*

In the spring of 1956, around the time of his twentieth birthday, Georges Perec became depressed about his writing, about his future, about his laziness, about his past, about his loneliness: in a word, depressed. Ten years later he would turn back to the earlier experience and write about it in the form of a novel, which he called *A Man Asleep.* But he also wrote about it at the time, in letters to all his friends and mentors, appealing to them for help.[1]

From a Marxist point of view, I am an unproductive being, an undesirable; from my own point of view I am a failure [. . .] I am ugly. Once I had a degree of charm, but it did me no good; I had a certain smile, but it proved of little use; I had some culture – but Mozart Joyce Flaubert Greco have no need of me. I've not got the facile talent of Minou Drouet or Françoise Sagan, nor the genius of Stendhal, nor the craft of Flaubert, nor the brilliance of Barbey d'Aurevilly, nor Gide's profundity, nor Malraux's elevation, nor Hemingway's heart – I've got more talent than Bernard Buffet and Antoine Blondin, but that's because they haven't got any at all. I am a bad son and a poor historian. Where will I find hope?

My subject? Where to find, each night, enough hope to want to go on living the next day.
> *Superficial cause: loneliness.*
> *Deep cause: impotence.*
> *First cause: lack of self-confidence.*
> *Hidden cause: lack of tenderness.*

And I don't know what to do any more. I've managed to overcome the shadow of that helmeted soldier who kept guard at the foot of my bed every night for two years and who made me scream as soon

[1] The following paragraphs alternate between two letters, written by Perec to different correspondents in April 1956.

*as I caught sight of him. I've managed to overcome the fear of my
death and my anxiety about my future life; and my heartaches. And
I have never known what, for me, is the main thing, because I was
deprived of it by my mother's death: tenderness.*

*I guess loneliness is the cause of it all, but I can see that my loneliness
exists only because I have created it – it is the outermost symptom
of what I can only call my impotence. Yes, impotence – to live, to
love, to give something of myself to others . . .*
    *I have sought for so long, so often thought I had found, so often
failed. I've no more strength to look, no strength to wait. I don't
want to risk a fiasco, and I know that what I will find will almost
necessarily be a fiasco. I am waiting for a miracle. And slowly going
mad.*

*I want to be a man, I want to re-create in me my part of humanity.
I reject mediocrity – and I sink into it. Every night enough hope
enough hope to live? Where is hope? For me it means finding
someone whom I can help to live . . .*

On a trip to Trouville with Jacques Lederer in May 1956, Georges
declared that he had "abdicated" (from life?) and went to buy himself
a pistol. He did not pull the trigger; he cannot have known how to
load a gun properly. The theatrical flourish was for his pal. Writing
to his teacher Jean Duvignaud, Perec suggested a less dramatic escape:

*I don't know where I am anymore. No one else is likely to know . . .
[. . .] How can I succeed? Recover my self-confidence? Perhaps, as
a last resort, I'll go back to see Madame Dolto, the doctor who
treated me several times a few years ago, though I'm not sure I will.*

In fact, Perec did not return to Françoise Dolto for more psychotherapy, but instead began psychoanalysis with Michel de M'Uzan,
who had also been treating Jacques for some time. The problem for
which Perec sought help explicitly was his lack of self-confidence.
He had set out to be a writer, but he did not know what he could
write about, and he did not know yet whether he could write at all.
Flaubert, Perec wrote in his letter to Jean Duvignaud, had felt the
same kind of impotence at much the same age, but by then he had
already written the first drafts of *Sentimental Education* and the first

Temptation of Saint Anthony! I've only written Les Errants. *I'm not a genius, that's clear,* he concluded.

Perec's youthful ambition was not to be just a writer, a hack, a competent producer of copy. Like Victor Hugo, he wanted to be either a genius or nothing: *Etre Châteaubriand ou rien!*: the steaks were high, Perec punned a couple of years later, in a different mood. His depression sprang from many sources, but the acute form that it took in 1956 corresponded in large part to the impossible demands Perec made on himself.

His constant refrain was *I am a bad son.* His analyst may have asked him whose son he thought he was. Had he read *Hamlet?* There was not only Freud's essay on Hamlet and Oedipus to understand, but also a recent and brilliant book on Hamlet by Jean Paris,[1] one of Duvignaud's coeditors at *Théâtre populaire.* One evening when he was rather drunk, Perec took the one photograph he had of his father out of its leather frame and tried to scrawl on the back of it, in French, "There is something rotten in the state of Denmark" [*W* 26]. What was it that the "bad son" thought rotten in the state of France? His father's ghost? His uncle "Claudius"? Or himself, Hamlet-Oedipus-Georges?

The analysis began sometime before mid-June 1956 and continued for the best part of a year. Three times a week Perec would walk by one or another of his meticulously mapped-out itineraries, either by way of Montparnasse or by way of Place d'Italie, to Villa Seurat, where de M'Uzan had his consulting rooms in a house in which Henry Miller had lived with Anaïs Nin. The fees for his treatment came out of his orphan's pension, accumulated by his aunt Esther. There was no higher priority in Perec's life in 1956 than "Dem" (or "Demdem"), whose sessions structured his weeks, the rest being filled in by flippers and by films. On 14 June, for example, Georges was one of the few guests at the marriage of his old English teacher Huguette to Antonio Angel Cristobal Marcello de la Santissima Trinidad Moralès Macias, a colleague of hers at the Collège Geoffroy-Saint-Hilaire at Etampes, but he did not attend the wedding luncheon that followed because, he said, he had an unbreakable appointment – with his analyst.

To begin with, Perec thought he was getting on quite well on the couch, and even found some of the sessions fun. *But what a bloody*

[1] Jean Paris, *Hamlet ou le personnage du fils* (Paris: Le Seuil, 1953).

hotchpotch there is in my head! I now realise that most of my thoughts follow mental processes that are completely distorted.

Perec's anguish was compounded by poverty – not destitution, since he had his bed and board at Rue de l'Assomption, but a young man's empty purse. He could not afford the books, the records, and the journals he wanted, could not go to concerts or have the bean-feasts, the beer, and the cigarettes that he ached for; nor did he have enough small change for the pinball machines or the entrance tickets to art galleries, museums, or jazz clubs. His uncle David probably gave him a sensible allowance, but there must have been a yawning chasm between David's idea of the necessary and Perec's need for the superfluous. To bridge the gap, Perec took on a dozen different odd jobs in 1956 and 1957, but he still had to borrow from his friends. By the summer of 1956 he had debts of twenty-two thousand francs. So when Esther agreed to give him thirty thousand francs to attend a festival in Marseille organised by Jean Duvignaud, Georges fixed it up with Philippe to spend a fortnight on a shoestring at La Payre, the Guérinat home at Jaunay-Clan, near Poitiers. Perec confessed years later that he had not used the funds solely to pay off his debts. *With the money my parents gave me, we bought masses of West Coast records.*[1] The two jazz-buffs spent their whole time at Jaunay-Clan playing the 78-rpm gramophone and designing sleeves for their very best collectors' pieces, signed with their joint, palindromic initials, GPPG.

Perec returned to Paris from Poitiers by train. From the main line, the whole town of Etampes can be seen, and Georges shed a tear as his old school swept past: *I am a complete idiot, but that's the effect it has on me.* Paris was deserted, or almost, but Jacques was there, and the two boys set off on his Lambretta for a beanfeast in a country res-taurant (*It cost us 3,700 francs!*), before it was time for Perec to present himself at Blévy penniless, exhausted and delighted with his very profitable attendance at an intellectual gathering in Marseille. At Blévy he had to cram for his resit examination in modern history, having failed it in June. *So far so good on the Marseille front,* he reported to Philippe. *My aunt hasn't changed. But as I am up in my room all day long and spend evenings playing bridge, trouble looms at mealtimes only.*

It must have been in the autumn of that year that the combined influence of his aunt Esther, Michel de M'Uzan, and William Shake-

---

[1] Georges Perec, "Je me souviens du jazz", *Jazz-Magazine* no. 272 (February 1979), p. 33.

speare led Perec to stand beside his father's grave. It was on 1 November, the conventional time for paying respects to the dead in France. Dressed in an ill-fitting suit lent to him by one of his cousins, Perec took the train to Nogent-sur-Seine to see for the first time the wooden cross in the military corner of the municipal cemetery marked PEREC ICEK JUDKO E.V. 3716.

> *Finding my father's grave, seeing the words PEREC ICEK JUDKO followed by a regimental number, stencilled on the wooden cross and still perfectly legible, gave me a feeling that is hard to describe. The most enduring impression was that I was playing a role, acting in a private play: fifteen years after, the son comes to meditate on his father's grave.* [W 37–38]

Hamlet-Georges at Yorick's graveside; Hamlet-Georges on the ramparts, meeting his father's ghost: the Shakespearean reminiscences in this artful reconstruction of a visit that certainly took place must be attributed to the writerly Perec of 1974, but perhaps they were not entirely absent from the feelings of the "neurotic" twenty-year-old. What burden of guilt, what responsibility did Perec-Oedipus feel then for his father slaughtered in war? What did he know of his father, anyway? In response to questions such as these, Perec sat down to write two short biographies of his father and mother. They are printed in boldface, with all their allegedly original errors, in chapter 8 of *W or The Memory of Childhood*.[1] Perec had begun to explore the material which would always remain fundamental to his life in words, because it was fundamental to his identity. *The idea of writing the story of my past,* he said, *arose almost at the same time as the idea of writing* [W 26]. It is now possible to suggest a more precise sequence: the idea of writing about his own past arose a year and a half after Perec decided to be a writer. Perec's childhood autobiography, though it was not published until 1975, is less a work of early middle age than it is the final achievement of a project first planted in 1956. For

---

[1] The inserted texts in *W or The Memory of Childhood* have been thought to date from 1959–60 because Perec states they were written *fifteen years earlier* than the main text, published in 1975. However, the first substantial draft of the "childhood memory" was composed in the summer of 1970 and then abandoned for several years. Fifteen years before the date of first composition takes us back to 1955–56. It seems probable that these first biographies of Perec's parents date from the time of his psychoanalysis, and that when Perec came back to his autobiography, in 1974, he omitted (perhaps consciously) to alter the existing reference to *fifteen years earlier.*

Perec, from this point on, and despite his many subsequent evasions, masquerades and double covers, writing *was* autobiography. Like psychoanalysis, autobiography involves the transformation of memory into narrative; but the two processes, like two parallel lines, never quite cross over in Perec's life and work. The tension between self-analysis through writing and the "analysis" provided by the talking cure – a tension that is made almost explicit in Perec's later work – has its point of departure here, where de M'Uzan, Jean Paris, Shakespeare, and Icek's grave met a young writer still diffident about the vocation he wished to be his.

When Perec decided to be a writer, he did not fool himself that he knew what he had to write about. He did not decide to become a writer because he had great truths to announce. Duvignaud did not urge him to be a writer of a particular kind, to enroll as an apprentice in a particular school. What Perec got from Duvignaud was only the knowledge that he needed no other permission to write than his own free will. *The notion of permission is terribly important to a writer*, Perec commented when reminiscing publicly in Australia on the turning point in his life. To a friend in Paris, he said that it was his psychoanalyst who had given him "permission" to be a writer. Between the two of them, from 1954 to 1956, Duvignaud and de M'Uzan set Perec free to follow his bent – to write, and to write about what was freely his: himself, his past, and his own world. What was wrong with *Les Errants*, in Perec's more mature view, was that it dealt with subjects he knew only from the outside (jazz) and from newspapers (Guatemala). But what was good about it, as Duvignaud is reported to have said, was that he had actually written it.

Perec tore up and threw away hundreds if not thousands of the pages that he wrote in the first years of his writing life. One of the relatively few juvenile pieces that have been kept (in this case, because a copy was sent to a friend) shows a strong reaction to the lesson of *Les Errants*, that one should not write about things one does not grasp firsthand. Written in the autumn of 1956, "Le Fou" ("The Madman") deals with what Perec manifestly thought he now understood in the season of his psychoanalysis. One of its epigraphs is taken from the third of Descartes' *Metaphysical Speculations*, "The Existence of God", which Perec had probably studied under Duvignaud in his *classe de philo:*

I will now shut my eyes, stop my ears, and withdraw all my senses. I will eliminate from my thoughts all images of bodily things, or rather, since that is hardly possible, I will regard all such images as vacuous, false and worthless. I will converse with myself and scrutinise myself more deeply; and in this way I will attempt to achieve, little by little, a more intimate knowledge of myself.[1]

Perec's fourteen-page typescript purports to have beeen edited by a psychoanalyst at the Hôpital Saint-Anne, named "M" (for "Dem"?), from papers left by an anonymous, long-term, and now deceased inmate who believed he was in the asylum in order to carry out research into mental processes under M's direction. Perec's first pages are a pastiche of Joyce, representing the jumbled stream of a madman's consciousness; the sections that follow switch into the lucid madness of scientific reporting. The ultimate fruit of the subject's "research" into the seven hundred factors that bear on the formation of an instantaneous thought (denoted by the symbol X) is a set of aphorisms:

Readers will kindly note their poetic strength and metaphysical lucidity:

> *Look at stars*
> *MY (freedom)*
> *Rage for life, thunder of war, surname (sic)*
> *Where does the extra-ordinary end?*
> *WHO is to blame?*
> *[. . .]*
> *You MUST live BY night THE sun kills (those were his*
last words).

It can be easily guessed that "Le Fou" was written by a well-read youngster both fascinated and terrified by the possibility that he, too, was mad. It should probably be put into the category of "panic texts" which Perec created a year or two later for other abandoned efforts at writing. However, "Le Fou" is also the seed from which Perec's later novel *A Man Asleep* was to grow. *A Man Asleep* is not itself about madness, but its single premise is what Descartes proposes in the passage used as the epigraph of "Le Fou" – that one must empty the mind of all contingent knowledge in order to find out what is

[1] René Descartes, *Meditations on First Philosophy*, trans. John Cootingham. (Cambridge: Cambridge University Press, 1986), p. 24.

true. What Descartes found inside his head was "a very clear proof that God indeed exists". Perec found nothing of the sort.

Sources used include letters from Georges Perec to Henri Chavranski (16 June 1957), Jean Duvignaud (April 1956), Philippe Guérinat (June and August 1956), Jacques Lederer (15 February 1956), and Huguette Moralès (probably April 1956) and information from Michel de M'Uzan, Jean Duvignaud, Philippe Guérinat, Jacques Lederer, and Nicole Doukhan.

Page 1 of "Les Barques" is *PAP* 18, with an introduction by Ewa Pawlikowska.

"Le Fou" is in the possession of Philippe Guérinat.

CHAPTER 16

Music, Art, and Good Advice

1956–1957

In January 1956, Georges Perec, who had not yet completely dropped out of his history degree, typed out and sent to a very small number of friends (for he had very few) an invitation to a "concert of recorded music" at 18 Rue de l'Assomption. It was music that none of them could have heard before in France: Schönberg's *Verklärte Nacht* and *Pierrot lunaire*, and Alban Berg's *Wozzeck* and Violin Concerto *In Memory of an Angel*. The records had been brought back from New York by David and Esther, at Lili's request, and the party (and the musical culture) was more hers than Perec's. Duvignaud was half expected but did not turn up. However, the whole evening would return roughly twenty years later:

> *The building was virtually empty* [. . .] *Madame de Beaumont had been invited to be honorary president at the Alban Berg Festival held in Berlin to commemorate the 90th anniversary of the composer's birth, the 40th anniversary of his death (and of the* Concerto in Memory of an Angel*) and the 50th anniversary of the world première of Wozzeck*   [*L* 499]

The original "concert" in the Bienenfeld lounge probably prompted Perec to read Georg Büchner's *Woyzeck*, from which Berg's libretto is drawn, and from which Perec took the second epigraph (beneath Descartes) of "Le Fou".

Lili had befriended a Yugoslav student of Descartes's philosophy, and through that connection a whole brilliant bunch from Belgrade made Rue de l'Assomption a regular port of call. Stojan Čelić and Mladen Srbinović, young artists with established reputations in Yugoslavia, first visited in late 1955. At his first meal in the Bienenfeld flat, Čelić met a shy young man who talked (when spoken to) about Albinoni and Claude Lévi-Strauss but gave no hint of literary genius. Srbinović became a closer friend. Lili took him to see the sights of Paris, out to Chartres, and on to Blévy for the weekend. Georges came along, too, and held his own in conversations on aesthetics, de Staël, and Johann Sebastian Bach.

Zoran Petrović, another artist, came to Paris in November 1956 and, following the advice of Lili's friend Radmila, made himself known at the hospitable and international Bienenfeld flat. Conversation with Petrović was accomplished largely through sketches and gestures, since he had little French, and not much English either. His pen-and-ink series *Mašina* ("Machine"), was on show at the "Galerie Yougoslave", housed in what was then called the Palais Berlitz, and Perec went more than once to see Petrović's expressionist grotesques, halfway between living and mechanical things. It was probably on one of these visits to the exhibition that Perec first set eyes on the woman of his dreams, an art student with blond hair and fine features, considerably older than he was, and accompanied by the handsome Serbian art historian Žarko Vidović.

Žarko soon told Georges the story of his life. Born in the Bosnian capital, Sarajevo, in 1920, he had been brought up as an Orthodox Christian and had became a good club skier and middle-distance runner. He had trained around the streets of Sarajevo in the late 1930s by pretending to chase his dog, a dog he had taught to stay just ahead of him. As the lights went out over Europe, Žarko guessed that he might soon need to run in earnest. In 1939 he enrolled in the medical faculty at Zagreb, in Croatia, and joined the Communist party. When Croatia joined the Axis, in February 1941, he was arrested and imprisoned in the old international fairground in Belgrade, the *staroe šajmišto*. Most Serbian inmates were in transit towards the death camps of Poland, but Žarko persuaded his interrogators that he was not a Serbian Communist, only a Bosnian Muslim. He was deported to a slave labour camp in northern Norway. He escaped, crossed into neutral Sweden, and spent the winter in a farmer's shed, reading the only book at hand, the Bible. Žarko knew it well in Serbo-Croat and thus taught himself what he thought was Swedish. In the spring he applied for a king's scholarship, and despite his thick Serbian accent and a syntax and vocabulary unused since the sixteenth century, he so impressed his interviewers that he was awarded a bursary forthwith. He spent the remainder of the war as a student of art history. In 1945 he returned to Yugoslavia – and was incarcerated again in the fairground buildings at Novi Beograd. Stalin's army regarded returnees from the West as enemy agents. Žarko was finally freed in 1947.

He returned to art history, wrote a thesis on the sculptor Mestrović, and began teaching at the University of Sarajevo. In 1956 he won an essay contest set by the French government. The prize was a year of self-directed study in Paris. He spent the year turning his thesis on Mestrović into a book[1] and began work on a biography of a nine-teenth-century Serbian poet and politician, Njegoš. He enjoyed his evening talks with the young Frenchman who tagged along with his group. "Georges was good at listening," he remembers. "He could have made a good teacher."

There were a dozen Yugoslavs in the group, and the Soviet invasion of Hungary in October 1956 divided them acutely. Some thought that Tito should send the Yugoslav army to fight on the Hungarian side; others accepted the Soviet action. They all read Sartre's article on the subject in *Les Temps modernes* ("Modern Times"), "Fantômes de Staline" ("Stalin's Ghosts"), and argued about it. Which side was young Perec on? He took a firm pro-Soviet line, Žarko recalls, and declared that terror was *necessary for the victory of a human idea*. Perec later joked about his "post-Budapest Communism," but at the time it struck a victim of Stalin as not amusing at all. Žarko was at first shocked by, and then condescending about Perec's politics, which seemed to him to correspond to a French fashion. He decided that there was no more point in arguing with the French about politics than there was in debating taste in clothes. What he talked about most with his dreamy disciple that year was literature, art, and philosophy combined.

Perec had read a lot already and spoke of James Joyce, André Gide, and John Dos Passos. But he had not yet read Tolstoy. What, Žarko exclaimed, not Tolstoy? But *War and Peace* was the greatest book of modern times! Perec's Serbian tutor explained how Tolstoy had brought together the epic qualities of Homer and the realism of Balzac, how his great panorama of social, intellectual, and emotional life in nineteenth-century Russia must be the model on which a new literature would be built. The art of the modern world would be neither socialist nor modernist, Žarko asserted, his eyes blazing, but critical, realist, epic, and spiritual at the same time. Perec lapped it

---

[1] Ž. Vidović, *Mestrović i savremi sukob skulptora s arkhitektom.* (Sarajevo: Veselin Maslesa, 1961). [BN 16 V.10058]

all up, and two Vidović key words became his own slogans for many years. Up to the publication of *Things,* and perhaps long after, Perec's definition of literature would centre on the concepts of the *real* and the *epic.* To Jacques Lederer, Perec confided that he now knew what his real task would be: to write *War and Peace.*

Perec did many odd jobs when he was a student, in order to earn enough for the superfluities that are essential to any young man with an appetite, whether for culture or for less abstract fare. He applied for a job as librarian at the Royaumont Centre in the summer of 1956 (to succeed Alain Robbe-Grillet) but was turned down. Duvignaud asked Jean Paris to help Perec out: Paris edited the "Aesthetics and Philosophy" section of the *Bulletin signalétique du CNRS,* a journal giving abstracts of recent academic work, and was a regular employer of students who could write résumés on literary subjects. Paris was happy to recruit Perec for his team. The work was paid by the piece, and poorly, but it gave access to a world of scholarship, and provided a training in bibliography, to which Perec would remain attached all his life. Abstracting was a job that he would come back to – with his wife Paulette, in the early 1960s, to supplement meagre incomes – and which he handed on, in his great novel, to Elzbieta Orlowska, "*la belle Polonaise*", Bartlebooth's favourite neighbour at 11 Rue Simon-Crubellier.

Not long after his first meeting with the Yugoslav group, in the weeks following Budapest and the Suez campaign, Perec wrote a pastiche of André Gide's first published work, *Paludes* ("Marshlands"), and called it "Manderre". He dedicated it to Zoran Petrović but did not tell the dedicatee himself, who could hardly have read it in French in any case. Georges gave the top copy to his secret inamorata, Milka Čanak, the companion of Žarko Vidović.

"Manderre" consists of thirty brief sections, some less than a page long. Its title is a mystery (perhaps it is a pun on the German *Der Mann*) as is the character it names, a flamboyant, evanescent playboy whose arrivals and departures, seductions and challenges are the subject of dialogues between the first-person narrator and other, barely delineated figures.

"Manderre" is more than a *futile souvenir,* as Perec called it in his covering letter to Milka; it is an exercise in writing like André Gide. The silences it creates are more elaborate than those of "Les Barques"; but what they are meant to convey is unclear. Perec's language in "Manderre" is rhythmical and elegant, in what was already an old-fashioned way. It is clearly the work of a gifted writer, the fruit of a tree with its roots buried in wilful obscurity.

At the end of the year Perec moved out of Rue de l'Assomption. Did he have an angry break with his family, or was it something agreed on, either with disquiet or with relief, as the proper step for a youngster to make at that age? Some of Perec's friends refer to his leaving home as a *rupture* with his family, while others are certain that Esther went on supporting him financially after he left home.

The move took place in the coldest days of December, made even harder in Europe by the closure of the Suez Canal, which interrupted the normal supply of heating oil. Žarko helped Georges to carry his cases, and they picked their way over icy pavements to number 203 Rue Saint-Honoré, in the first arrondissement, almost opposite the church of Saint-Roch, whose great bells chimed every hour of the day and night. Perec had left home at last, for a room of his own. But still he did not tell Žarko that he was a writer.

He found another job, this one as a part-time clerical assistant in a library specialising in the performing arts. Perec's task was to snip theatre reviews from the daily and weekly press, paste them onto buff sheets that were then clipped into heavy board binders, index the cuttings under the names of the author, the theatre, the director, and the actors, and then have them checked, before they were added to the Rondel Collection. Years later, a bibliographer mentioned in passing to the famous writer Georges Perec that the Rondel files on Sartre's plays in the 1950s were impressively complete. *Yes, I know,* Perec said. *I compiled them.*

For his services from 10:00 A.M. to 1:00 P.M. five days a week, Perec was paid 13,000 old francs per month – that is to say about £10 or $28 in 1957 values.[1] It probably went on drink, and on flippers, and on films. In any case it cannot have gone very far.

Perec also translated horoscopes from English into French in the first winter of his new life. That work was extremely well paid, and when the fees came in, he spent the money straightaway on posh nosh from Gargantua, the swankest delicatessen in Rue Saint-Honoré. Perec's appetite for flippers, jazz, Joyce and twelve-tone music did not diminish his appetite for (often quite bizarre) food. He

---

[1] FP 88,1,16 (drafts of *A Man Asleep*) gives different hours of work, and pay of 23,655 francs per month at the Rondel Collection in 1957.

had a passion for steak tartare – half beef, half horse, minced fine with onions, bound with raw egg, flavoured with pepper, salt and capers, and left uncooked. For a while he yearned for whale, and when he had money in hand he would insist on taking Philippe on long treks to find the rare places in Paris that served up steak-sized slices of lesser Moby Dicks.

Perec stopped reviewing for *Nouvelle Nrf* at the end of 1955, by which time Duvignaud had also ceased to contribute to the journal. In October 1956 Perec presented himself at Les Editions de Minuit and offered to review a book about Israel for *Les Lettres nouvelles*. The proposal was turned down, but Perec found his way into *Les Lettres nouvelles* all the same, becoming a regular at the Thursday-afternoon open house held in the office of Maurice Nadeau, the journal's director. The author of the first history of French surrealism and of essays on Flaubert, Nadeau was a rare bird amongst publishers. A lover of good writing and a writer himself, he was open to new work, to new writers, and to writing from abroad. He had, for example, brought Malcolm Lowry into French. For a young man in Perec's position and with his hesitant but global ambitions, Nadeau was a beacon of hope.

The first service Nadeau did for the blushing youngster who said he wanted to write was to let him review books of his own choosing for *Les Lettres nouvelles*. Perec's wish to write on Ivo Andrić's *A Bridge on the Drina* cannot have been unconnected to his Yugoslav friendships and the Balkan history he had learnt at Henri-IV. But Andrić's saga-novel had already acquired an international audience and was being widely read in France. Perec was puzzled by Andrić's linked episodes set on the bridge at Višegrad: they did not really add up to a novel, he said, or to a history book, nor, despite appearances, did they constitute a collection of connected short stories. *A Bridge on the Drina*, he wrote, brought a huge cast of characters to life *with surprising vividness*, but as to its writing (Perec uses Roland Barthes's term *écriture*), Andrić's blockbuster was quite out of date.

Politically, *A Bridge on the Drina* met with Perec's approval. Every one of the characters whose lives bring them onto the bridge, from the peasant whose execution lasts twenty-four hours to the girl who throws herself off the parapet to avoid an arranged marriage, from Ali Hodja the traditionalist to Yelisei the old man – indeed, each member of Andrić's cast, Perec felt, *bears witness to an age of which we can see the contradictions. The little world of Višegrad is a world that calls for change. And this book calls for a revolution.*[1]

Perec's other essay, on *Les Juifs et les Nations* by Jacques Nantet, was similarly pitched: Israel was a bastion of the Western powers in the Middle East, he asserted, and only incidentally a Jewish national home. The conflict between Arabs and Jews was *not remotely atavistic and could perfectly well have been settled many times over* already, if only America had ceased to supply arms. Nantet failed to be clear enough about the real roles of the superpowers, or about the opportunism of the Balfour declaration, the reviewer claimed. In these remarks, Perec was reproducing the PCF line. There *was* no PCF line to follow on the Suez adventure (which was barely over) but Perec knew how to hedge his bets: *It is important to realise that the Jewish State is not solely responsible, and that its aggression against Egypt is the result of a crisis initiated and fomented by France and Britain.*[2] The Yugoslavs who heard Perec hold forth on these and similar topics in Paris cafés assumed that he was speaking for the PCF, which had, in their view, fallen a long way behind the more advanced thinking of Tito.

In the winter of 1956–57 Perec acquired tiny toeholds in two other camps. He was introduced to the circle of *Les Temps modernes,* Sartre's monthly (perhaps through Bianca's friendship with Simone de Beauvoir), and was able to bring back to his Yugoslav comrades advance copies of the French translation of *Irodalmi Uység,* the only reliable chronicle of events in Budapest.[3] He also attended meetings of the group responsible for a new and unconventional intellectual quarterly called *Arguments.* Its editors were Edgar Morin, a sociologist and writer (at that time) on American cinema; Roland Barthes; and Jean Duvignaud, Perec's pilot still. None of them was in the PCF, and they gathered around them a remarkable team of radical left-wingers, many from Eastern Europe, who had "survived the Stalinist shipwreck":[4] François Fejtö, Bramko Mikašinović, Fougeyrollas, and

---

[1] Georges Perec, review of Andrić, *Les Lettres nouvelles,* no. 45 (January 1957), pp. 134–135.

[2] Georges Perec, review of Nantet, *Les Lettres nouvelles,* no. 45 (January 1957), p. 139.

[3] I have found no evidence of Perec's having written for *Les Temps modernes* in 1956–57, although some people remain convinced that he did do some work for the monthly, or at least tried to.

[4] The phrase is Fejtö's.

other young Frenchmen such as Jacques Delors, Alain Trutat, and Georges Perec. The last went along to the meetings, but did not say very much. He listened instead.

Arguments was independent of political parties and devoted its issues to specific themes or problems. It did not have any "line" to promote other than argument. It was a remarkable venture from the start, and came to an end in 1962 in a no less remarkable way. The journal had a good circulation, but its editors had by then acquired other avocations; instead of allowing *Arguments* to settle into an institution, Barthes, Morin and Duvignaud chose to close it down.[1]

Perec never published in *Arguments*. In fact, he wrote no more reviews at all. He slid into a depression again and was unable to work well or even to keep commitments or meet deadlines. He did not show much of his misery to his Yugoslav friends, however. He would go round to Žarko's place, whistle the signature tune of Radio Kossúth (the free radio of Budapest) to call him down, and take him off to Le Select or Le Bonaparte for an evening of talk and drink. (If you got a seat on the terrace of Le Bonaparte, Perec said, and craned your neck a bit, you might even see Sartre puffing his pipe at the window opposite. But Perec's Yugoslav friends never did catch a glimpse of the philosopher at his mother's flat.) Perec did not say what else was happening in his life. Other members of the Yugoslav circle sitting round the same tables could see that the young man was in love with Milka Čanak. They warned Žarko, but the athletic scholar dismissed it as silly gossip: Georges was Žarko's friend and disciple, and he was there to listen to Žarko's ideas. He had more reason to be wary of his Yugoslav colleagues than of the intelligent ugly duckling who sat dreamily listening to stories of Serbia, Sweden, and Tolstoy.

Žarko was a member of *Zlatni Rez,* a circle of non-Marxist Serbian thinkers, artists, architects, historians, and musicians who sought, in the decade after 1948, to renew Serbia's traditional cultural links with the West. *Zlatni Rez* is Serbo-Croat for "the golden section", called *le nombre d'or,* "the golden number", in French – the infinitely recurring decimal expression that you get if you divide the length of one side of the Parthenon by that of the other. Since the time of the Greeks, metaphysical, spiritual, and esoteric meanings have been attributed to the golden section; it goes without saying that any group taking

[1] *Arguments* is available in facsimile reprint (Paris: Privat, 1983) in 2 volumes.

that phrase for its name must be concerned with tradition, and with rules and constraints. *Zlatni Rez* aimed to preserve and renew Serbia's own ancient and Christian artistic inheritance. It saw art as the only real defence against totalitarianism, but it was not just any kind of art that was meant: the group's motto was the German proverb, *Willkür ist keine Freiheit,* ("Licence is not liberty"). It was Vidović who first exposed Perec to the notion that the freedom to create was the fruit of tradition, and of constraint.

The freedom Perec had in his little student quarters at 203 Rue Saint-Honoré, however, was limited by less creative and quite irksome constraints. The room was in an attic, up six flights of stairs; Jacques Lederer once climbed up, found his pal out, and left a note saying he would never again go to such exhausting lengths to visit Perec's hideous and filthy nest. Once, Amor Fezzani came up with his girlfriend Paulette Petras, and Georges took them on a tour of the roof. But no one else dropped in, and, aside from the Yugoslavs, who could go on talking half the night, Perec's social circle was fast shrinking to nothing. Three times a week he would traipse over to Villa Seurat to see Dem, and he went at least that often to the cinema – sometimes to see Woody Woodpecker or Tex Avery cartoons. For a while he got paid to write reader's reports on American pulp fiction, and was amazed to discover that the French publishers gave him a bigger fee than Grasset paid Clara Malraux to advise them on difficult literary works. He spent some of his money getting into the Club Saint-Germain to hear the Jazz Messengers, Miles Davis, Al Levitt, and Barney Wilen (who wore an impressive silk-lined tuxedo), but these brief pleasures and excitements, and the cheap sweet liqueurs from the local Prisunic, bought with Michel Rigout, barely slowed down his inexorable depression. In stolen moments he confided to Milka – *mila Milka, "Milka la douce"* – that his ambition was to write, and that he feared he was not up to it. He never dared to call on her at her flat in Rue Racine, to take her out, to tell her that he loved her. What chance would he have had with this gentle, scholarly older woman? Georges kept his feelings bottled up: it was *the period of maximum inhibition.* When Milka asked him what he had done that day, he sometimes replied that he had spent it thinking about what she had said the night before. He seemed to her to be a boy in a dream, a young man half asleep. As winter turned to spring, past the anniversary of his first great depression, Perec could take no more of his loneliness, of the struggle just to get by on his own, of the mess he was making of what was supposed to be the best year of his life. He caved in. In June he wrote to his cousin Henri:

> *After dropping my studies and my family, I ended up dropping everything; I didn't even want to write any more: for three months I scrawled hundreds of pages without managing to get anything right. [. . .] So I cut my losses on that, and on everything else as well, and even, worst of all, on the articles and reviews I was supposed to do. At the end of May I was so fed up with my rabbit hutch, so sick of sandwiches and hot dogs, that I came back to 18 Rue de l'Assomption! That didn't help matters much, either!*

Perec also wrote to Maurice Nadeau, the editor of *Les Lettres nouvelles*, to explain what he had not quite dared to tell him to his face:

> *I want to write, but I encounter unmanageable blocks, and over the past six months I have been unable to finish any one of the texts I have begun.*

He had thought of stopping writing altogether, but he did not think that he could,

> *for despite my failures, despite the atmosphere of scorn and utter incomprehension that surrounds me in my family, I believe I can write, or at any rate I know that writing is for me the only means of reconciling myself to the world, the only way I can be happy or even just live.*

Nadeau wrote back and Perec hung on to the reply all his life.

> Don't apologise for having sent me your letter [. . .] Nobody finds it easy to write, and I am, moreover, quite sure that those who have seen none of the difficulty can never go very far in expressing themselves. They can have honourable careers nonetheless. That is not what is in your mind, and I am sincerely glad for you.

Nadeau told Perec of the advice he himself had got, at much the same age, from his teacher, and he handed on the lesson:

> [My teacher] simply advised me not to force myself to express what, in view of my age, I could not be certain of truly possessing (you think you are original but it is just a stage of your own development, shared with many others in whose work you are steeped), but instead to frequent great works

and great authors. [After] some years of such company, which by no means prevents you from taking up your pen from time to time, a kind of osmosis occurs, by means of which things become clearer and one's self by the same token. To sum up, I think that in order to find yourself in the end you must assimilate a great deal, and before rejecting anything you must absorb a great deal, too.

It was not original advice, but that did not make it less good. Most important, it was not advice to be original. Perec had read *The Counterfeiters* and must have had his interest in copies and fakes whetted by exhibitions. He had certainly begun to read the great masters, and had already tried a "remake" of Gide's *Paludes*. In response to Nadeau's wise counsel, he would now read even more widely, more voraciously, and with an eye to the craft he had yet to learn. The oeuvre of Georges Perec, in all of its many parts, from *Things* to "*53 Days*", eventually vindicated Nadeau's confidence, beyond anything he could have expected, in the "osmosis . . . by means of which things become clearer, and one's self by the same token".

The letter from Georges Perec to Maurice Nadeau is published in Maurice Nadeau, *Grâces leur soient rendues* (Paris: Albin Michel, 1990), pp. 430–432 and Nadeau's reply is published in *CGP IV* 67–68.

Perec's reminiscences of Rue Saint-Honoré are to be found in FP 57, 5, FP 57, 28, FP 57, 83, and FP 57, 127.

Other sources include letters from Georges Perec to Bernard Quilliet (6 January [1956]) and Henri Chavranski (16 June 1957); a letter from Editions de Minuit to "Geroges Perrec'h" [FP 31,1,35d]; and the recollections of Ela Bienenfeld, Philippe Guérinat, Ambassador Bramko Mikašinović, François Fejtö, Professor Žarko Vidović, and of those of Perec's Yugoslav friends whom I met in Belgrade alongside, and with the help of, Professor Vidović: Milka Čanak-Medić, Stojan Čelić, Zoran Petrović, Mladen Srbinović, and Ljubomir Tadić.

CHAPTER 17

Real Life

1957

Georges Perec reached the age of legal majority in March 1957. Military service was required at twenty, but students enrolled at universities were entitled to defer it until the completion of their first degree. By the spring of 1957, Perec had long ceased to be a student in practice and he decided to cease being one on paper as well. He had to accept the almost universal obligation of twenty-seven months in the French army (recently raised from twenty-four), unless he could find a way out of it. Exceptions were rare: at that time, the well-off were occasionally able to purchase medical exemptions; a very few had exemptions awarded on technical grounds; still others were genuinely unfit for service. But France needed comprehensive military conscription to keep Algeria French, and so the loop-holes were being tightened by the day.

The son of a parent who has died "in the service of France", when he comes to do his military service, is allowed to decline a posting to an active war zone, while one who has lost both his parents "in the service of France" is exempted from all military obligations. Georges Perec qualified for the lesser release since his father, though Polish, had died on active service in the foreign legion. He would be able to avoid Algeria, at least. But did he qualify for the second and larger exemption? Had his mother, Cécile, also died "in the service of France"?

For years he had evaded most of the issues raised by his mother's short life and unspeakable death. Now it was time for him to get a grip on them.

The first question that had to be answered was whether Cécile was administratively dead or whether she had only disappeared, officially speaking. Years before, when Esther and David had begun to tackle these matters on Jojo's behalf, they had been given first provisional documents and then a missing person's certificate for Cécile. It was not a death certificate. It was called an *acte de disparition* (illustration 12).

The "certificate of disappearance" stated in the small print that if the person had gone missing either on active service or as a prisoner of war, a political deportee, member of the Free French forces, or the like, *was of French nationality*, and was still missing five years after the date of issue, then the certificate could be exchanged for a death certificate. But as Cécile had not been French, she remained, from an administrative point of view, insufficiently dead for her death to be legally certified.

The Germans had deported Resistance fighters and political opponents as well as Jews. Some deported *résistants* had been Jewish, and some deported Jews had been political opponents; for simplicity's sake, the French treated death in deportation, irrespective of the "reason" for that deportation, as death in the service of France. This equivalence, however, which might otherwise have exempted all doubly orphaned male children of wartime deportees (the majority of whom were Jewish) from serving in the French army at the time of the Algerian War, applied only to deportees of French nationality. Since a large proportion of the Jews deported from France between 1941 and 1944 were immigrants who had not been naturalised, the majority of doubly orphaned male survivors of the *shoah* had to serve in the French army. The logic of Vichy left its trace in the administration of postwar France.

There was no death certificate for Cécile because she had not been French. Because she had not been French, she could not have died in the service of France. Because Cécile had not been French, her son, who was, would have to do military service in the French army. The ironical thing, which could have been foreseen long before, was that if Cécile had been French at the time of her death, then her son would have been excused from his army service. He had been declared French at birth (or, rather, five months after he was born), but how French was he? The wafer-thin difference between being plain French, and "French by declaration", meant a prospective gap of twenty-seven months in Perec's career.

When he turned twenty-one, Perec sought reparations due to him from the West German government. His aunt Esther may well have been the driving force, but the signature on all the documents was Perec's own. He must have spent much of March, April, and May 1957 collecting the papers: his birth certificate, his attendance certificates from his old schools and from university, his father's death certificate, and his parents' marriage certificate, as well as the documents about Cécile that Esther had already obtained. He signed a power of attorney to a German law firm and made an oath before witnesses following a precise legal wording in German: "Ich bin Volljude im Sinn der Hitlergesetze", "I am a full Jew within the meaning of the Hitler laws".

The papers submitted on 29 May 1957 with the application for a retrospective orphan's pension under the *Bundesentschädigungsgesetz* (Federal Reparations Law) made Perec's position in French civil society abundantly clear. At the time of his mother's deportation, her official status had been that of a refugee (the word *Polish* had no legal meaning between 1939 and 1945). His own status is described correctly as *Français par déclaration* and glossed as *fils d'immigrés*. It was probably the lawyer handling his reparations claim who informed Perec that there was no way he could avoid military service.

The German court case reached a successful conclusion in February 1959, and Perec was awarded compensation of around one million old francs. The German money would pay for his first flat in the Latin Quarter. In the meantime, parallel and related steps were taken on the French side, resulting, first, in the issue of a "special" death certificate for Cécile, in October 1958, and then, in November 1959, in a decree stating that "had she been of French nationality", Perec's mother would have been entitled to the qualification "died in the service of France". Perec was released immediately from the remainder of his military service, though by that time he had only four more months to do.

The twin decisions made by Georges Perec just after his twenty-first birthday were practical ones, appropriate to administrative circumstance: he happened to turn twenty-one just as the Federal Reparations Law (passed in August 1956) came into force; the process of applying for a capital endowment was all the more straightforward for him because the law firm which handled such matters was Victor Borten, the same firm the Bienenfelds had used for their naturalisations in 1927. It was also Perec's misfortune to come of military age before Alain Resnais's documentary on Auschwitz, *Night and Fog*, fractured France's voluntary amnesia about the Final Solution and the position of its survivors. Perec went into the army in 1957 because he had no real alternative.

However, it has to be said that Perec did not go into the army under protest. In principle he could have gone back to his history books, scraped through his examinations, and deferred the whole business for a year, or for two. He could have asked David Bienenfeld to find a complaisant doctor friend to sign a medical certificate for him. But he did not. He did not relish the prospect of army life, but military service was nonetheless something that he *decided* to accept. Perhaps he imagined that it would make him less of a "bad son", since he would be following his father's example. Moreover, he had recently returned to Rue de l'Assomption, having made a mess of his first attempt at leaving home. David must have wondered whether his ward was growing up into a man or a homing pigeon. Military service was a godsend for a youngster in Perec's situation, at least from one angle: it would get him away from Rue de l'Assomption.

Politics came into it, too, of course. Perec spoke at length to Bianca about the anguish he felt at the conflict between his fear of soldiering and his conscience. He did not want to be a soldier, he said, but how could he justify taking steps to avoid the draft? What moral right did he have to escape the fate of his comrades? Was there not something shabby about exempting oneself from the common plight? He knew how opposed Bianca was to the presence and the actions of the French army in Algeria; he also knew that his questions, sincere though they were, gave voice to the current doctrine of the Communist party. The party came to support Algerian independence only a short time before it was granted by de Gaulle, in 1962; in 1957 the PCF held that Algeria was not yet ready for nationhood. Although it criticised the actions of the government and army, it did not back the FLN, and it took as stern a line as did the authorities on draft dodging and desertion from the ranks. The duty of the militant, according to Lenin, was to militate in the army if that was where History landed him. The party remained the conscience of the left, and its influence over young men – whether or not they were members either of it or of its student organisation, the UEC – was inescapable. If Georges had played his cards patiently, or cleverly, or corruptly, he would not have endeared himself to his friends on the left. Although they, too, regarded the Algerian War as a political, human, and national disaster, they would have treated spurious medical or technical exemption as plain desertion.

Sitting in a duty hut some months later, in a godforsaken hole in southwestern France, Perec put the matter in a letter to Jacques Lederer, as was his frequent custom, back-to-front. He penned a counterfactual paragraph for a right-wing biographer to insert, at some future date, into the brief life of Conscript Perec G.:

Quite the opposite of Jules Roy, Georges Perec moved from a firm left-wing position, through a grave crisis of conscience, to an ardent desire to save France, and so joined the parachute troops . . .

Conscription was organised by calendar year, and so Perec had six months to fill between his decision in May and the selection exercises at the Fort of Vincennes in December. In the meantime, there was another matter to attend to. Where would Milka be? There was his answer: he too would go to Belgrade!

Sources include Perec's application for West German reparation payments, consulted at the Landesrentenbehörde Nordrhein-Westfalen (Düsseldorf); a letter from Perec to Jacques Lederer, from Pau [?20] April 1958; and other information from Henri Chavranski, Serge Klarsfeld, Bianca Lamblin, and François Maspéro.

CHAPTER 18

Sarajevo Incident

1957

My 'cure' began the day I caught the train to Belgrade, Perec asserted twelve months after the event, in a letter to Jacques Lederer. What was the malady? "Neurosis", overwhelming shyness, inhibition, writer's block. And the cure?

Perec got to Sarajevo by train, straight from Paris, whence Žarko Vidović had only recently returned to his old job as docent, to his old flat and his wife. Madame Vidović took umbrage at the close friendship between her husband and his French disciple and threw the pair of them out. Perec had barely two days in the capital of Bosnia to sleep off the journey and to visit the Sarajevo Incident Museum.

The museum stands on the site where Gavrilo Princip, a member of the Young Bosnia group, shot Archduke Ferdinand of Austria on 28 June 1914. Because he did it with a weapon supplied by the Serbian Black Hand, otherwise known as Ujedinenje ili Smrt ("Unity or Death"), the Austrians put the blame on the Serbian government and treated the assassination as a *casus belli*. Perec had covered the Sarajevo incident in his Balkan history course at Lycée Henri-IV and he must have been familiar with the background and consequences of Princip's nearly-bungled shot. Žarko introduced him to Vaso Cubrilović, the sole surviving member of the Young Bosnia group, who was still living in Sarajevo, but the man said nothing.

Homeless in Sarajevo, Žarko took Perec up to Belgrade. Where could the young Frenchman stay? Fortunately, Mladen Srbinović, a painter who had frequented Rue de l'Assomption, had room in his studio–cum–flat, in the historic centre of the town. Mladen had been expecting an August of uninterrupted work, but he took Perec in, if somewhat grudgingly. He was anxious about what the youngster might get up to alone amongst his paint pots and wet canvases, so he took Perec along when he went out to give lithography classes at the Academy of Fine Art's summer school. Perec would do as a model. His curly black hair, flap ears, heavy nose, and hollow cheeks made him a good Srbinović subject. Mladen did a line drawing, then showed his class how to elaborate it into a portrait as seen through a broken mirror. He did not aim to portray Perec as Franz Kafka, but he came to be retrospectively proud of his prescient eye.[1] For his part, Perec was delighted: *Mladen's done my portrait – now I'm famous!* he wrote to Jacques. In France he had seen himself as an ugly duckling, but in Serbia, intense Jewish looks were something of an artistic craze. Only a handful of Belgrade's own Jews had survived.

Srbinović asked a friend of his wife's family to find a companion of the right age for his unexpected houseguest, and a rendezvous was arranged in the Engineers' Club, which had the best and cheapest bar in Belgrade. Perec found himself paired up with a great bear of a man who had a doctorate in Turkish and spoke fluent Russian, English, German and French. Even in the Balkans his linguistic achievements were deemed unusual, and he was nicknamed Ciga (pronounced "Tziga"), the Serbian word for "Gypsy" – just as Perec's name spelt "peretz" in Yugoslav eyes, meaning "pretzel" in a city well-supplied with Hungarian bakers, which prompted witty linguists like Ciga to retranslate Perec into French as *petit pain* ("bread roll").

Ciga held his liquor well. Perec matched his consumption of *vinjak*, a rather rougher brandy than Rémy Martin, and soon passed out cold. Ciga hoisted him over his shoulder like a half-empty sack of coal and took him back to his own flat, from which Perec was too ill to emerge for three days. Srbinović heard what had happened at the Engineers' Club, and was fearful that the young Frenchman might vomit on his half-dry paintings if it happened again. When the two boozers groped their way blindly back into the studio flat after their next binge, they found the inner doors locked, save that of the bathroom. "Gypsy" and "Pretzel" slept it off in the bathtub, together.

Georges was not a real drinker, Ciga thought; his liver was not up to *vinjak*. He surmised that Perec drank because drinking was what tough young men were supposed to do. What he did not guess, and what Perec never told him, was that he was also drowning his sorrows, in the way that less tough young men sometimes do.

---

[1] Ela Bienenfeld does not think the portrait (photograph 19) a particularly good likeness: Perec's cheeks were not nearly so hollow as they appear in the Srbinović portrait. The resemblance with Kafka, she says, is a fantasy that comes from elsewhere.

One day Perec plucked up his courage and called at Milka's flat. He made a vigorous declaration of his passionate love, which took Milka quite by surprise. She had not imagined the violent feelings that were hidden behind Perec's hesitant exterior. She let him down as gently as she could. Was he too young? he wondered. Too ugly? Too poor? Or was it all Žarko's fault? *I am strongly inclined to kill that man Jarko* [sic] *who is getting on my nerves,* Georges wrote in one of his long letter-reports to Jacques.

Perec's own "Sarajevo incident" took place in Belgrade, when the young man confronted his Archduke in Café Kolorać and asked him to step outside. He put up his fists, and said: *For the love of Milka! May the best man win!*

Žarko was floored. So this was why the scruffy youngster had tagged along behind him in Paris and tracked him to Sarajevo and Belgrade! Not to listen to his ideas, but to catch up with a skirt! He took Georges's clenched fist in his larger hand and pushed it down.

"This is not a civilised way to sort out a problem," he said. *There are times when it is matters more to be a man than to be civilised!* Perec retorted. Remembering Corneille's heroes who had bored him at school, he explained to the philosopher that it was a question of honour, and that when honour was at stake, fighting was called for between civilised men. Žarko held Perec's fist tight and led him back to Milka's flat. *L'homme révolté* did not have much choice but to listen. On no account, Milka said, may you two fight over me. She was leaving the next day for the country, to excavate Roman remains. Later, Milka Čanak wrote the standard work on the art and architecture of the buried city of Gamzigrad. She never saw Perec again.

He made it up with Žarko and went back with him to Sarajevo and then on to the Adriatic coast. He would have liked to travel down-river to Višegrad, *where there's that famous bridge,* but he went only to a hard-currency resort of the Club Méditerranée type – a less magical place, no doubt, than that part of the Adriatic coast which the main characters of one of Perec's later fictions view from a yacht:

> the pink palaces of Pirano, the grand hotels of Portoroz, Diocletian's ruins at Spalato, the myriad Dalmatian islands, Ragusa, which had become Dubrovnik a few years before, and the wild contours of the Boka-Kotorska and Montenegro.
>
> It was during this unforgettable journey that one evening, facing the crenellated walls of Rovigno, Valène declared to [Marguerite

Winckler] *that he loved her, and obtained in reply only an ineffable smile.*   [*L* 246]

Perec's letters from Yugoslavia bubble with jokes, puns, boasts, and ideas. He was commissioned to write a piece on French policy in Algeria for *Pregled*. Žarko translated it, but it was not published: "Muslims were not as popular in Yugoslavia then as they have become nowadays," he explains. Perec also thought of a novel (presumably set at Etampes, *see* p. 103) to be called *Les Enfants de Guinette* ("The Children of Guinette"), and sketched out an outrageously cloak-and-daggerish melodrama called *Les Amis parfaits* ("The Perfect Friends") for his perfect friend Jacques [*CGP IV* 53–55]. He also talked at length to his Yugoslav friends about another project, a part-historical romance with a title that would mark its origin quite precisely. This book, his first book, which he was determined to get published, would be called *L'Attentat de Sarajevo* ("The Sarajevo Incident"). Ciga listened to Perec's plans over glasses of slivovitz in the Engineers' Club bar and meals of *čevapčiči* in the restaurant at Kalemegdan. It sounded to him like a remake of Hesse's *Glass Bead Game*, and he said so, but that did not make Perec read Hesse. He had just started *War and Peace*, so he wrote to Jacques, *and in Russian, scout's honour.*

Perec's high spirits did not desert him when he got back to his maid's room at Rue de l'Assomption. He persuaded a friend from his old school at Etampes, now a trained shorthand typist, to act as amanuensis, and he dictated his novel to her, improvising as he went along, just as Stendhal had composed *The Charterhouse of Parma*, in fifty-three days flat. Perec's creation went swimmingly. When Ciga himself got to Paris, towards the end of October, Perec insisted that he read the typescript on his arrival, straightaway, overnight. Pretzel was so pressing that Ciga conceded and sat up to read Perec's first masterpiece in a dingy bedroom in the cheapest hotel he could find. He was no more impressed by the finished product than he had been by the plans laid in Belgrade. The book was choppy by design; chapters alternated between a narrative of Balkan history and a tale of romance. It was the sort of thing Andrić did, Ciga thought, but with passages that sounded more like Françoise Sagan trying to impersonate Jean-Paul Sartre. By the time the cafés opened for breakfast, Ciga had finished Perec's second first novel, and he thought, all in all, that it was tripe.

The harsh judgment of an outsize orientalist did not stop Perec from submitting his novel to Le Seuil and Julliard. Le Seuil sent *L'Attentat de Sarajevo* out for a report from Jean Paris, whose criticisms, Georges boasted later, made him blush with pride. Maurice Nadeau, who had now moved with Les Lettres nouvelles to Julliard, talked to Perec about the book. What a pity it had been done in such a rush, he said to the fledgling writer. Taking that into account, it was not bad, not bad at all, but it was not yet ripe. In the end, Le Seuil took the same view. Perec considered rewriting it, but he preferred to let it lie for the time being, wanting to get his teeth into something fresh. The oddest thing, he confessed with apparent modesty, was that everyone seemed to believe him capable of writing something worthwhile – everyone except himself. He seems to have forgotten Ciga.

Extracts from *L'Attentat de Sarajevo*, by Georges Perec

I met Branko for the first time in Paris some evening or other in November. At the Dôme, I believe, or the Select, at any rate in one of those cafés in Montparnasse which foreigners seem to like so much. [. . .] Branko was ugly. To tell the truth, he looked like Popeye the Sailor Man, especially when he began to ponder, for then he put on a grimace that emphasised most disagreeably the shape of his chin, which looked like an upturned boot. You couldn't take him anywhere. He would talk in the street, gesticulate wildly, then sit down in a café and call the waiter "my dear sir", whilst leering at girls at the next table. His French was quite passable but dotted with tiny errors that became quite unbearable within fifteen minutes. He was certainly very intelligent. The trouble was, he thought he was a genius. I can't remember in what context he once said to me that he wasn't far beneath Hegel: "You'll see, one day." His secret ambition, I do believe, was to be Jesus Christ.

Revenge may be sweet; but is it literature?

When I think of Branko today, I seem to have rather ambiguous feelings. And I am not a little surprised to remember that there was a time when I felt a great deal of friendship for him, a time when he was important to me. But I remember that period so badly, as if I wanted to bury it, rub it out, as if it signified danger, as if it were liable to explain to some extent what happened after. Is that poss-

ible? No, all that happened took place because I fell in love with Mila.

Today, today, I really think there are some questions I would do well not to ask, ever. For then I might have to answer them.

The narrator follows Mila to Belgrade (but wonders whether he is really following Branko) and lodges with a painter called Streten, on Knez Mihajlova. Streten (a conflation of Čelić and Srbinović, with the former's looks and the latter's address) acts as the young man's worldly-wise adviser. He takes him to see the Jewish cemetery and explains that it is a good place to be alone: solitude, Perec the narrator says, is the most valuable lesson he learnt in Belgrade.

The narrative tracks the unsatisfactory and awkward triangular relationship of Mila, Branko and the narrator day by day, until the young man says to Streten, "I give up".

"That's wise"

[. . .]

*   "I'm off to Skopje tomorrow."*

"Sarajevo would be better," said he.

I looked at him quizzically.

"Sarajevo?"

"It's pretty."

"No, not Sarajevo. Maybe Dubrovnik."

"That's right, Dubrovnik. Interesting town. Folklore, history, sea, cliffs."

I burst out laughing. "I'll go to Višegrad. I'll throw myself off the bridge, into the majestic Drina, like the fair Fata, daughter of Avgada, who wanted to escape from an arranged marriage."

The bottle of raki was emptying, slowly but surely.

"Women just aren't real chaps."

The sentence was a bit difficult for Streten. He raised his eyebrows.

"Oh, Streten, my Streten, ya sam danas veliki drugi, a bitchou soutra veliki prvi, mojda, za Milou."

Now Streten burst out laughing. "Who taught you that?"

"Nobody. I worked it out myself, step by step."

The incident-plot is also first given in Serbo-Croat, when, in one of a series of drunken toasts, the narrator raises his glass and mutters: "*Branko smrt*".

The narrator does not leave. He continues to pursue his beloved with acute and imaginative sensitivity, hemmed in by the hideous, domineering Branko – who himself suddenly has to depart. There follows a fortnight's idyll, in which the hero gets his girl, who is disturbed by long, powerful letters from the crucified philosopher in Sarajevo. The letters trouble the narrator too, and he decides to accept the man's invitation to visit him in his native habitat, and there to finish him off.

The narrative is told retrospectively, and apart from the few passages in dialogue, it is more a contemplation of the ambiguities of a past affair than a straightforward love story. Although Perec's cynicism about himself is almost alarming, the text is more interesting than Ciga granted – perhaps because Ciga appears in it, under his own name. The last part is the least satisfactory. The narrator meets Branko's angry wife, Anna, and slips a pistol into her bag. He summons Mila to a meal at the Evropeiski Hotel, opposite the Sarajevo bridge. He invites Branko and Anna, too, and plans to provoke such a row that the pistol will be reached for and pointed in the right direction . . . But the tale stops short of a murder planned but not executed by the narrator on the site of the Sarajevo incident of 28 June 1914.

Perec had the "love story" typed out first and then dictated a narrative of the 1914 Sarajevo incident to his secretary, using a transcript of the trial of Princip and his accomplices published in French translation by Albert Mousset.[1] Next he cut up the historical section and shuffled pages from it between pages of the love story. The result is a work that is formally similar not to *The Naked Lunch* but rather to *W or The Memory of Childhood*.[2]

Perec might well have revised *L'Attentat de Sarajevo* and got it published had he not had military service hanging over him in a few weeks' time. He might have come to regret it, however, had he entered French literature eight years before *Things*. The book is at bottom a settling of scores; its qualities of language, self-doubt, analysis, and design are not matched by adequate plot construction, and

[1] A. Mousset, *Un Drame historique. L'Attentat de Sarajevo. Documents inédits et texte intégral des sténogrammes du procès.* (Paris, Payot, 1930). The inventory of Perec's own book collection made by Eric Beaumatin and Catherine Binet contains this item. Another copy is AL 8º 67,249.

[2] The pages of the historical part are numbered sequentially from the end of the love story. Consequently the typescript begins with a page numbered 113.

the last pages leave the reader more than a little perplexed. The novel's implied argument that the resolution of a mildly homoerotic love-hate relationship with an intellectual father figure can be compared to an act of political terrorism is not entirely convincing. *L'Attentat de Sarajevo* is a remarkable achievement nonetheless. Perec's trip to Yugoslavia had unblocked his energy, allowing him to write fluently and fast immediately upon his return; he was right to say in retrospect that his self-invented cure had begun the day he took the train to Belgrade.

The autumn months of 1957 were an interlude for Perec, between his first self-assertion and the challenge of basic training. And what an interlude! He dropped his psychoanalysis, he wrote a novel at top speed, he met and talked to real publishers. He went out a lot, to the cinema and to some of the most exciting jazz bars in Europe, squeezing every last drop of culture out of his final weeks as a civilian. And at last he had a girlfriend.

At Le Tournon, a café where tables were laid out for chess and where expatriates often came in for a drink – among them Chester Himes, Richard Wright, and a tall Nigerian called Slim, whom Georges befriended – Lili introduced her cousin to a young colleague from the market-research firm where she was at that time employed. Dominique was a live wire, with dark hair and dark eyes, as tiny as Slim was tall and, like Georges, the French child of Polish Jews. Georges and Dominique began to go out together. On their own, or with the few chums Georges had – Jacques, Nour, Philippe – they went to the Caméléon, to hear Art Blakey and the Jazz Messengers, or to the Mars-Club, in Rue d'Estienne, just off the Champs-Elysées, next door to the most lavish of Paris's PX stores, where duty-free goods were sold to U.S. military personnel. The Mars-Club was best late at night, after the shows, when American jazzmen on tour would drop in to relax, to let their hair down, to "bull" the night away.[1] Chili con carne was an effective substitute for sleep, and the youngsters raved on into the small hours with their American friends, moved by the music to moments of ecstasy. On one occasion, the Harlem Globetrotters, in town for a basketball game, descended on the club in a fleet of pink Cadillacs. They took Georges and Dominique for a ride up and down the deserted Champs-Elysées as dawn broke.

[1] Georges Perec, "Je me souviens du jazz", *Jazz Magazine*, no. 272 (February 1979), pp. 30–34.

It is a mystery how Georges even managed to pay the door-money at the Mars-Club. Like all of his crowd, he did a little trading on the black market, reselling cigarettes and whisky that friendly Americans bought for him at the PX. He must have had an allowance of sorts from David Bienenfeld, and he earned something from his odd jobs, but of course he was always short of money, as anyone would be who went very often to nightclubs on or off the Champs-Elysées. He could not pay Noëlla Menut properly for typing *L'Attentat de Sarajevo*, so he took her to see *Around the World in Eighty Days* instead. When he wanted to take Dominique out for dinner – her first proper dinner-date, and no doubt his as well – he had to sell several volumes of his collection of Pléïades. Later on, he had to sell Jacques his glass-fronted "Oscar" bookcase, too.

Dominique enjoyed Georges's company and felt very fond of the lonely, still rather provincial lad. He was not terribly funny, except when he had had a bit to drink and was under the influence of jazz. What would she do if he made any advances? She did not find him attractive, especially as he would not have his warts seen to, nor his teeth mended. Georges talked to Dominique of Stendhal's *Armance,* and of *La bella estate* ("Beautiful Summer") by Cesare Pavese, which had just appeared in French. Later Dominique realised that both of these works dealt with impotence, and that Perec may have been trying to lay clues, or to engage her sympathy. At all events, Georges Perec was not a very forward suitor. Dominique once found him staring into the mirror in the lounge of her parents' flat, muttering at his own reflection, in a kind of English: *I yam ergly, I yam ergly, I yam ergly* . . .

Perec saw Ciga nearly every day during his six-week stay in Paris, from late October to mid-December 1957. Ciga was appalled by the rampant Americanism of French life, and especially that of young intellectuals such as Perec. Despite holding firm views on neo-colonialist imperialism, Perec took his friend from socialist Yugoslavia for a drink at the Granada, a bar decorated like a Laundromat, with pinball machines and jukeboxes blaring out Frankie Lane. *Les Cahiers du Cinéma* decreed that *My Darling Clementine* and *Gunfight at the O.K. Corral* were great works of film art; Perec toed the line, to Ciga's amazement. But Ciga saw through his close-cropped hair in a flash: the crew-cut was worn solely to make him look even more like a GI. "They were all just phony French-American kids," Ciga recalls. "They hoodwinked nobody but themselves."

Ciga found Paris youth quite bizarre, with its culture heroes from Hollywood and its politics delivered daily by the Ost-West Express. Perec, for his part, disapproved of Ciga's private enterprise. It was immoral, he said, to risk giving diners food poisoning by reselling second-rate caviar out of a suitcase. When he took Ciga to see one of the city's late-night sights – prostitutes coming into Le Pied de Cochon, at Les Halles, after their work was done – he was shocked by the Yugoslav's suggestion that they go over and chat. He was closer to his bourgeois background than he liked to admit.

At Rue de l'Assomption, Perec showed Ciga how to make steak tartare from meat bought at the *boucherie chevaline*; he also took him along to his girlfriend's family home in Montmartre. It was like stepping back two hundred years, into a vanished eastern Europe, Ciga thought. Amidst the heavy old furniture, over heavy *haimische* meals, Ciga chatted in a mixture of Russian and Polish with Dominique's father. The old man didn't call him Ciga. Because the Serbian was a huge man, father Frischer called him "titch", "little lad", or "sonny boy" – in Polish, of course. It could also have been Russian or Serbo-Croat, though, since the word that he used was: *synok* (сынок). Perec, who had suppressed all memory of the Polish he must have known as a child, heard the sound in French and thought Frischer had said *sinoque*, meaning "nutcase" or "bonkers" in slang. Ha! Perhaps that *was* the right word for Ciga, and for all his crazy, talented, self-obsessed and impecunious Serbian friends. Perec did not manage to place the Pan-European pun for another twenty years, and when he finally found the right spot for it, he covered his own tracks with almost impenetrably contorted branches. Irrespective of the sentimental connections that Perec's telling of the tale may suggest to sharp-eyed readers, the surname of Albert Cinoc, dissected at length in chapter 60 of *Life A User's Manual*, is just the Polish pet name of a Serbian whose real name neither Perec nor Monsieur Frischer were ever quite sure of pronouncing correctly. "Synok"'s real name is Voijin Čolak-Antić in Latin characters; after careers in film and merchant banking, he became a Serbo-Croat newsreader for the BBC World Service.

Perec sent a copy of *L'Attentat de Sarajevo* to Mladen Srbinović in Belgrade, with apologies for not having entered in all the corrections he had made on the top copy. He was now starting a different project, "Vertige de Minuit" ("Midnight Vertigo"), which may have been the draft title of a text that has survived as "La Procession. Phantasme" ("The Procession. Phantasm"), dated 19 November 1957 [FP 48, 9, 3, 1; partly reproduced in *PAP* 22–23]. Onto a stage set of fearsome complexity (requiring an exploding cathedral), literary fantasies from wild Gothic, Romantic, Symbolist and Surrealist shores process and then exit, leaving a Beckettian wasteland at the end. Like "Manderre", written twelve months before, "La Procession" is an exercise, but unlike "Manderre" it shows a writer in full flow, displaying all his cultural wares. Perec must have felt, on the night that he wrote it, that his period of inhibition was over, that his analysis had put him in touch with his imagination, that his Serbian summer had got him over his block – in short, that he was set fair to be a writer, and a great one. In French? Maybe; maybe not. He put sentences in English in all his letters to Yugoslavia, and bits of Serbo-Croat in his fiction; he signed himself off to Philippe Guérinat in Spanish gleaned from Lowry (*Salud y pesetas*), and asked Jacques to get hold of some money for him in Hebrew-cum-Yiddish (*kessef*). The closer Perec got to being a plain soldier in the French army, the more he played at being something else. He knew that as a linguist he could never be more than knee-high to Ciga, but he tried.

Perec learnt through an indiscretion that Frischer's *sinoque* had made a date to see Dominique on his own. The two young men were slightly drunk at the time, on Rémy Martin laced with Aspro. It was a winter's evening. Perec pounced on Ciga like a cat, like a child whose toy had been taken. They quarrelled on the steps leading down to a metro station, exchanged violent insults, and parted. Years later Ciga asked Dominique if he should try to see Georges Perec in Paris once more. No, she said. "He won't speak to you again."

Based mainly on letters from Georges Perec to Milka Čanak, from Paris (June 1957); to Jacques Lederer, from Belgrade (August 1957) and Sarajevo (26 August 1957); to Bernard Quilliet (September 1957); and to Philippe Guérinat (autumn 1957); and on the reminiscences of Milka Čanak-Medić, Voijin Čolak-Antić, Dominique Frischer, Philippe Guérinat, Jacques Lederer, Mladen Srbinović, and Žarko Vidović.

Other details from FP 57, 3 and from Ela Bienenfeld and Richard Gibson.

The uncorrected typescript of *L'Attentat de Sarajevo* is in the possession of Mladen Srbinović.

CHAPTER 19

Parachutist Perec G.

1958

Georges Perec went to the Fort of Vincennes on 10 and 11 December 1957 for military selection. He was found to be medically and technically fit for service as a son of immigrants, "French by declaration". The little scar on his upper lip was recorded as his only distinguishing feature [*W* 108].

Conscripts were normally asked which service they wished to join. Whatever Perec may have replied, the result was the XVIIIe Régiment de Chasseurs Parachutistes, a branch of the French infantry that only teenage Rambos sought to join. The selectors at Vincennes found Perec not just fit for service but fit for service in the parachute troops. Perec mentions having been a parachutist very seldom in his autobiographical writing and once even ascribes this implausible episode to military chance [*W* 55]. However, at a meeting of contributors to Duvignaud's quarterly, *Arguments*, in January 1959, during which the tape recorder was left on by mistake beyond the conclusion of the formal proceedings, Perec explained that he had *volunteered* to be a parachutist, *because I had the impression I would experience something new* [*Jsn* 42].

Perec did and did not volunteer. He was probably not put into the XVIIIe RCP at his own request, but once conscripted, he could have chosen (in theory) to be a nonjumping infantryman. But like tens of thousands of other young men at that time, he was told to *sign here* beneath a scrappy typed statement of willingness to jump. The paperwork was done to respect the universal principle that parachuting must be a voluntary activity, but in practice, in France, during the war in Algeria, conscripts were given no option.[1]

Perec gave a gloomy party in his maid's room at Rue de l'Assomption to say farewell to his friends. There was barely more than bread

[1] See J.-F. Steiner, "Fabrication d'un parachutiste", *Les Temps modernes*, no. 188 (January 1962), pp. 939–951.

and sardines to eat. Georges did not say that he had had to "volunteer" for the parachute troops; he seemed shocked by the fate that had befallen him, and they all thought it horrendous. Poor Georges! A wandering Jew, an unacademic intellectual, a budding writer with biceps no bigger than two peas, was about to be thrust into the company of wolves who would have liked to take over the republic and who were, at that very moment, burning and bombing Algeria into submission. It was alarming. It was tragic. It was ridiculous.

Perec had applied for exemption from Algeria at the time of his selection, and he knew it would be granted automatically because his father had died "in the service of France". He would not have to jump into the Sahara. There would be ordeal enough in France.

Perec reported to his unit on 7 January 1958, at Idron Camp, on the outskirts of Pau, in the southwestern corner of France, not far from the Pyrenees. For the next eight freezing weeks he was made to run, crawl, jump and clamber over obstacles; carry stones from one end of the camp to the other and then back again; brush out the huts, clean the latrines, muck in with his hutmates, to do press-ups and bunnyhops. He nearly died for lack of blood sugar. *Send me chocolate! Send me sweetened condensed milk!* he scrawled in his first letters home. He got fitter. He even came to have a grudging respect for the brutes who gave him a hand when he was near to collapse. His exemption from Algeria came through officially in mid-February, but he found the ceremony painful:

> *I am in despair. My exemption from Algeria was pronounced officially at midday today* [22 February 1958]. *I am the executioner. The adjutant who announced it called the whole company together (300 men) and read out aloud: "In accordance with the law of . . . exemption from Algeria is granted to Georges Perec, father died for France."*

Whose executioner was he? His comrades'? Or his father's? He went off into town that evening to get as drunk as he possibly could.

Weapons training was as hard as physical jerks. He made a mess of dismantling and oiling and reassembling the hardware and could never remember which of the guns was which: MAS 36, MAS 47, MAT 49, and so forth.

Then came survival training: nights under canvas, dummy battles, long marches without maps. Georges got lost for hours on one of the sorties; when he finally made it back to camp, every muscle in his body ached. He was shattered, and just a little bit proud.

After eight weeks there were tests. Perec came top in the written paper and got a prize of cigarettes and cake. It is not clear why he did not get into the officer training corps. Some say that he was debarred because of his exemption from Algeria. Perec himself said that he had *called it quits* after passing the *tests paras* at huge effort. The last and most gruelling of these required him to run fifteen hundred metres in nine minutes and then, after thirty minutes' rest, to jog eight kilometres cross-country in an hour, with pack and arms. He was groggy with the effort, dribbling, sweating, blind, and mindless, and grateful for the help of a sergeant who carried his knapsack and rifle for him, held out towels wet with snow, and talked him through it, shouting at him to run, to walk, to breathe in, breathe out, keep his head up. He finished just inside the time. He wanted never to do anything like it again. When joggers came out onto the streets of Paris in the 1970s, Perec was one of many ex-conscripts who thought them utterly mad.

After passing the parachuting physical in March, Perec did a six-week training stint as a medical orderly at the nearby camp of Pau-Le Hameau. He learned to give injections by practising on a friend, who practised on him, reciprocity encouraging the rapid acquisition of skill. He did guard duty on wards where malarial patients lay delirious in their cots. At the end of Perec's training, his CO entered in his passbook the comment "adequate medical orderly after 4 ½ months".

Perec did his parachute training in April and May 1958, at BETAP, the oldest flying school in the world, set up by Wilbur Wright in 1909 and taken over by the French air force not long after. It occupies one end of the runway of what is now the civilian airport of Pau-Pyrénées, and adjoins the vast barracks of the Camp d'Astra, where Perec was billetted.

The first week at BETAP was spent on "simulators", scaffolds equipped with harnesses so arranged as to cause the novice jumper to land from about fifty feet with the same terminal velocity he would have if he jumped from far higher with a parachute on. Perec said over drinks and dinners later on in his life that he had been terrified of the simulator. At the time, however, he boasted in writing that it was a piece of cake: *rather pleasant, actually.*

Airborne training started on Monday, 5 May 1958. The night before, Georges tried to conjure his fear by writing out the next day's schedule, from reveille to *"Exit exit exit!"* followed by *"Splaat!!!"*. In retrospect, he described his first experience of jumping as an ordeal of anticipation.

> *There's a huge noise of planes taxiing around the apron. It's an extremely long-drawn-out expectation [. . .] We're just waiting, nothing else, we have a cigarette, have a pee, because you always pee at such moments [. . .] then suddenly an order comes, it's called "Line up". We all run to the line, stand to attention [. . .] Until we're told to put on the gear, we're not afraid because it's still not certain that we will jump. From the moment we begin to gear up, we're certain that we will have to go.*   [Jsn 35]

You come to a moment of existential truth, Perec continued, talking to his *Arguments* friends, a moment when you realise that you have to put your trust in alien things: a piece of cable, a roll of silk, a few ropes and leather straps. You have to assume your situation not in principle but in practice, on the spot. Somehow you find that you are standing in the rattling fuselage of an aircraft flying at four hundred metres, you are "clipped on" to the safety cable, and you are being given a final inspection. The siren goes, and the men in front of you begin to disappear. As you come up to the wind-blast from the open tailgate, your mind goes numb, you have no feelings save the desire to be done with it, to be free of the weight on your back, to be out of your crippling position, out of the overcrowded, flying tin can. You need to believe it will all work; you have no choice but to have faith, and so you jump, and float to the ground beneath a spectacular canopy of white silk. Parachuting, Georges wrote to Jacques, is an ineffable joy.

Parachute training taught Perec obligatory optimism. Optimism alone allows you to do something new, with consequences you cannot imagine in advance. Whether it was a challenge genuinely chosen or a challenge imposed upon him, Perec overcame the terror of falling and completed his parachute training honourably. He jumped six times in the space of a few days and was promptly awarded his licence, number BP 140602, on Saturday, 10 May 1958.

Later on, it was thought that Perec had managed to jump only with the help of a tranquilliser obtained from a chemist in Pau – a relative of the *chocolatier* in Avenue Mozart, around the corner from Rue de l'Assomption, whose address Lili had forwarded to him. Perec does not mention any tranquillisers in the (uncensored, unsupervised) letters he wrote from Pau, but he did come to feel embarrassed about having been a *para*, and he encouraged friends and family to see him as a sensitive weakling. He was certainly fibbing when he convinced one of his later Left Bank friends that he had had a bad fall with a half-opened parachute. Some conscripts did die at BETAP, and Perec recorded each fatal accident in his letters, usually as a spoonerism (*aujourd'hui un char à putes s'est mis en short*). However, the worst that happened to Parachutist Perec G. was that he missed his landing-ground on jump number three and had his lead-lines begin to twist on jump number four. He panicked for a split second, then followed the proper procedure for untwisting the lines, got his parachute to open perfectly, and made a first-class landing, his face beaming with joy. He was a normal young man and not immune to the macho atmosphere of the regiment. From Saturday, 10 May 1958, he wore the wing emblem on his red beret and on his tunic. On Sunday he went into town to celebrate and saw *Monsieur Hulot's Holiday*, by Jacques Tati, at the cinema.

Perec became a *para* at a dramatic moment in the history of France. After the loss of Indochina in the early 1950s and the Suez debacle in 1956, the army was deeply embroiled in Algeria and prepared to use any methods to avoid another humiliation. Perec was shocked by Henri Alleg's "La Question", a report on torture published in a banned issue of *Force ouvrière*, a copy of which he obtained in Pau in March 1958. By the end of that month civil war was on the horizon. The army was no longer under complete government control; in Algeria the generals were taking the law into their own hands. What would Perec do if it came to the crunch? *Emigrate, perhaps; or join in with the under-dogs*, he wrote in a letter to Jacques Lederer.

The crisis came in May. On the Tuesday after Perec qualified as a parachute trooper, French Algeria, backed by the parachute regiments, declared independence. On Thursday, 15 May, Perec's unit was put on alert. Perec correctly assumed that his regiment was being prepared to support not the government but pro-Gaullist insurgents. *If it's civil war, I'll desert*, he wrote that day. *I would rather die a civilian than a soldier.*

Soon the crowds in Algiers began to chant, "les paras à Paris!" Georges wrote to Jacques, *I may be coming up to Paris – by special train and in battle dress. Exciting, isn't it?* [1] His unit was moved first to Toulouse, where Perec, with a six-week training course as a para-

---

[1] The underscored words are in English in the original.

medic, found himself responsible for the health of 150 men at Clairfont Barracks. He went for a ride around town in a jeep, and a girl smiled at him: she fancied his red beret, his battle dress, the insignia shining on his chest. *My life is like an adventure film,* Perec boasted to Jacques. The next day, parachute units in Corsica declared the island to have seceded from metropolitan France. Perec learnt of this ludicrous turn of events on 26 May. What were his own commanders going to do? On 27 May they transferred him to Quartier Niel, in the centre of Toulouse, to join an already huge mass of other soldiers. *Major disturbances are expected tonight and tomorrow,* he scribbled to Jacques.

Charles de Gaulle had prior information about what the Toulouse parachute regiments planned to do on the night of 27–28 May. Anxious to take over by legal methods and not by way of a putsch, de Gaulle alone could stop it from happening. At 12:30 P.M. on 27 May, a few minutes before Perec's unit got to the centre of Toulouse to join the other troops being assembled by their generals for a military takeover of France, de Gaulle issued a statement to the press:

> Any action, wherever it may come from, which would disturb public order risks producing the gravest consequences. Whilst making allowances for circumstances, I cannot approve of any such action [. . .] I expect the land, sea, and air forces to maintain the strictest discipline under the command of their chiefs.[1]

The warning worked. Civil war was averted in the nick of time, and de Gaulle's accession to power was ensured. Perec had had a walk-on part in the greatest piece of political theatre in modern France. By 5 June the alert was over, troops were stood down, and Perec was back in his barracks, listening to de Gaulle's address on the radio. *Heigh-ho for the Fifth Republic!*

For the rest of 1958 Perec served as the regimental quartermaster's typist-secretary. Frustration, boredom, and isolation came to replace aching muscles and physical fear as the main attributes of military life. His new clerkly existence also gave him access to a typewriter, which he used to write even more and longer letters to his friends.

[1] Charles de Gaulle, *Discours et messages* (Paris, Plon, 1970), volume III, p. 11.

Perec had been writing almost daily letters since he had first got to Idron Camp, and even in the toughest period of basic training, he wrote about his future writing, and also simply wrote. He dreamed up banner headlines for the reviews of his next novel – "*Better than Céline!*" – and listed the riches that would accrue: vacations in Palm Beach, a lecture tour of the States, a yacht, skiing holidays, and treatment by the very best psychoanalyst. Things English and American figure frequently in Perec's letters. Has Jacques got hold of Lawrence Durrell's *Justine*? he asks. Has he yet read Lowry? Sartre's *Nausea* strikes Conscript Perec as excessively intellectual and already old-fashioned, whereas Faulkner's *Go Down, Moses* (read in English) gives him *an extraordinary sensation of discovering a new language, a kind of writing close to what I am aiming for, a necessity in words and approach.*

Stendhal, Gide, Joyce, and Brecht remained reference points in the first six months of Perec's military life, as did Thelonius Monk. Music on the camp radio reconciled Perec to his plight: Bach filled his eyes with tears of joy, and alone in his hut, he put Vivaldi on to play. After June 1958 Perec's reading list exploded: he gulped down Victor Hugo, more Sartre, Simone Weil, Giraudoux's *Electre* (which he thought marvellous), Mauriac (*idiotic*), and Baudelaire; *War and Peace* (again); the first half of Conrad's *Typhoon;* and a couple of Graham Greenes, Bradbury's *Fahrenheit 451*, and a San-Antonio – and all that by mid-August! From then on he planned to march through Dostoyevski, Kafka's *Diaries*, Ponge, Michaux, Svevo, Krlja, Borges, Swift, the *Mémorial de Sainte-Hélène* (*why not?*), Proust, Goethe, Goldstein, Gobineau, *and so on*. In September he added Pasternak, Musil, Henry James, and Virginia Woolf to his 1959 new reading list, and put under the heading of books that needed rereading the Bible, *War and Peace*, *The Red and The Black*, *Lucien Leuwen*, *Ulysses,* and most of Flaubert. His appetite had no bounds.

Because of the political situation, Perec had little leave before June 1958 – just a few short weekends in Pau, seeing friends of Philippe Guérinat's, or going to the cinema, or to the local art gallery, which was free for soldiers. Its holdings included some major works: a Saint Francis by El Greco, *which rooted me to the ground*, and a splendid Degas narrative painting, *Le Bureau des Cotons* ("The Cotton Office"), intended for a Manchester trader. Perec did not forget the Degas and later put it in the original list of paintings to be distributed throughout the text of *Life A User's Manual*. For another one of his short leaves, Perec acquired a "Dream Factory" (otherwise known as an Indicateur

Chaix, a French railway timetable) and made a dash via Toulouse to Cahors, to see his old friend from primary school Michel Rigout – a round trip of seven hundred kilometres in forty-eight hours. Once de Gaulle had taken power, the barrack regime was less constraining, and Perec was able to spend more time away from Pau. In June he had nine days in Paris, during which he planned to visit every one of his old haunts – the Caméléon, the Club Saint-Germain, the Mars-Club, La Bûcherie, and Harry's New York Bar in Rue Daunou. A men-only party was arranged with Nour, Philippe and Jacques. The plan was for them all to drink themselves silly and then make their entrance at the offices of Les Lettres nouvelles, with Perec in full battle dress, to scare the wits out of Maurice Nadeau.

On the night of the Algiers putsch, when France was on the brink of civil war, Dominique had rushed to PCF headquarters to join the vigil. In the small hours she began to talk to a dark and bespectacled young man whom she had seen before at student meetings. When Perec got back to Paris at the end of June and took his girlfriend out, she wanted to talk about politics, about the meetings she had been to, about the men she had met. There was a new gulf between them, and Georges handled it by pretending to be asleep, by being rude, sentimental, provocative, and finally by getting very drunk. He reported the comical scene in a letter to Philippe:

> I'm in the lounge. She comes in all sweetness and light. Sits next to me. Silent scene à la Hemingway. Then all of a sudden:
> "Bloody hell I'm legless!"
> There follows a lecture in comparative psychology whence it emerges that I have been utterly erroneous in loving her.
> "Well, it is obvious, isn't it?"
> Whereupon and notwithstanding I abandon her delicious chubby paw, become upstanding and exit with dignity, attempting not to damage the furniture. I have not spoken to her since.

A little later, in July, on weekend leave, Perec went back to Toulouse and picked up a prostitute. The experience itself was paltry, he wrote, but its significance was enormous. He had already overcome his fear of death, his fear of flying, his fear of falling; now he had overcome his fear of failing. It was time to celebrate the birth of the real Georges Perec, homme de bien, homme de lettres, homme de gauche, homme tout court. This epistolary trumpet blast was probably intended to be sung loud and flat, to the tune of the children's marching song, "L'Homme de Cromagnon".

A fortnight after that, Perec spent a weekend with Bianca Lamblin and her daughters, Marianne and Sylvia, at the spa town of La Bourboule, in the Massif Central. Bianca had never seen her cousin looking so well. He had broadened out, he stood straighter than before, and he had lost his adolescent flabbiness. It was in the quiet town of La Bourboule that Perec got the worst fright of his military life. He wore his uniform to stride along to the local barber's to get shaved. The barber could not but notice the wing emblem on the tunic of his suntanned customer, and such was the *para*paranoia at that time that he began to quake with fear (or anger). His trembling hand slowly brought the open razor under Perec's chin and down towards his throat, and the conscript suddenly grasped that the barber was about to slit it, if not out of revenge, then with an uncontrollable jerk. He was weak in the knees when he stood up from that barber's chair.

On his return to camp, Perec acted on a suggestion made by Jean Duvignaud and called on Henri Lefèbvre at his house at Navarrenx, a picturesque fortified town some fifty kilometres southwest of Pau. Lefèbvre, a vigorous sixty-year-old with an undiminished reputation as a bon vivant and Don Juan, was an eminent Marxist philosopher, teacher and social critic. He had recently been expelled from the PCF for publishing a French translation of Khrushchev's "secret" report to the Twentieth Congress of the CPSU (the report on Stalin's crimes). For many years more, the French Communist party would refuse to treat the Khrushchev report as genuine. Lefèbvre was branded a *gauchiste* or "left deviationist" and soon became the guru both of nonsectarian groups such as *Arguments* and of semiclandestine *groupuscules* which would achieve notoriety in 1968.

In 1958 the first (theoretical) part of Lefèbvre's *Critique de la vie quotidienne* ("Critique of Daily Life") had just appeared, and the philosopher was working on the second volume, which in its philosophical and roundabout way touches on the same social themes as Perec's own later writing. *Things* is not just a fictional recreation of Lefèbvre's *Critique*, but a theoretical philosopher might easily believe that it was. Lefèbvre and his companion, Evelyne Chastel, were happy to have Duvignaud's ex-pupil and *poulain* as an occasional houseguest at the Maison Darraq at Navarrenx. The moment he got there – usually after hitchhiking from the railhead at Orthez – Perec would settle into the little bedroom overlooking the main street of the town and get down to writing. Lefèbvre hardly saw him, save at meals. The table conversation was heady and brilliant (*alienation, music, fiction*, Perec reported to Jacques), but the soldier-writer mostly kept his own counsel. Lefèbvre thought Perec the most enigmatic young man he had ever met, and never knew whether he meant his sparse remarks to be taken seriously or not.

Perec's time at Pau was a period of growth and progress on every front, including his conception and practice of writing. Despite being exhausted by physical training, despite the excitement of parachute jumping and the drama of the politics in which he was an involuntary actor, despite the humiliations and servitudes of conscript life, Perec found the time and the energy to keep on thinking about what writing should be – and to keep on writing. A few weeks after arriving at Idron Camp, he copied out a quotation from Roger Judrin: "For years I imitated others before resembling myself", and added that he had begun to understand that sentence in a new way: *I am beginning to know who I am and what my life will be.*

His ideas, at this stage of his life, owed a lot to Žarko Vidović. Art was epitomised by the prehistoric bison on the cave wall at Lascaux: *Creation is first of all an explosion*, Perec asserted. Writing, however, had to be more than "the bison", the release of energy in creation. It had to be based on clear-headedness and on good faith, so as to give *the sincerest reflection of the writer's personality*, the achievement of which was writing's real aim. Writing was not a substitute for psychotherapy, he declared wisely, nor was psychotherapy a prerequisite for good writing. Action had greater power to heal than words, he wrote to Jacques, and he clearly counted his military service, and especially his parachute training, as healing experiences. *You can leave pathology behind you if you want*, he boasted; it was as easy as jumping out of a plane.

The project Perec worked on throughout 1958 had been started towards the end of 1957, whilst *L'Attentat de Sarajevo* was still being read for Le Seuil by Jean Paris. It was, to begin with, a skein of different stories, one of which might have been called *La Cassette* ("The Casket"), then *Le Coffre* ("The Trunk"), brought together under a collective title that may also have served for an earlier story, *La Nuit* ("Night"), which itself subsumed and also spawned other texts or fragments including *Les Amis parfaits*, *Les Enfants de Jéricho* ("The Children of Jericho"), and others. In May 1958, when Elie

Wiesel's *Night* was first published (in French), Perec conceded defeat: the titles were identical, and, he claimed later, *the two approaches were almost the same . . .* Not long after, Perec's writing project had settled down: all the post-Sarajevo texts and titles had been absorbed into a novel called *Gaspard*, Perec's third "first book". By September, thanks perhaps to his quiet weekends at Navarrenx, he had got to page 120.

The narrative of *Gaspard* – or of one part of it, at least – was to be the story of a craftsman who attempts to make a perfect copy of an inlaid and carved wooden box but slowly loses himself *in the meanders of his phantasms, in the detail of his copy.* Twenty years later the *topos* recurs in *Life A User's Manual*, in association with another (or perhaps the same) character called Gaspard and a chest he has carved with minute and intricate scenes from Jules Verne [L 25–26]. The craftsman's chest is more than a story; it is, so to speak, a "material theme" or magical object in Perec's work. The writer summarised its meaning curtly in February 1958, when it first occurred to him, between bouts of basic training. What it had to do with, he said to Jacques, was *Falsification; or substitution (don't try to understand).*

The 1958 project soon became a composite work, a structure organising different kinds of texts and stories. In the most elaborate of the diagrams that Perec posted to Jacques Lederer, he planned four distinct works (*La Rencontre* ("The Meeting"), *Les Amis parfaits*, *La Cassette,* and *La Nuit*) around a central core, labelled *Les Dieux* ("The Gods"), with the relations between the parts expressed by a web of lines and arrows. The five themes, he wrote, would destroy each other and still produce coherence: *Paradoxes and chaos whose demiurge I am.* He liked the phrase and repeated it at the head of his letter, as his *definition of creation on 3 June 1958.*

In another version of the plan, the fivefold construction was explained in terms of five literary models: one part of *Gaspard* was to be a twin narrative, like René de Obaldia's *Tamerlan des coeurs*; the second would have the form of an inquisition, like Horace McCoy's *They Shoot Horses, Don't They?*; the third would be a detective story; the fourth, an internal monologue modelled on part 3 of *Ulysses*; and the fifth, the diary of an investigation, would be like Michel Butor's "Manchester novel", *L'Emploi du temps.*

A little later the five-part plan was replaced by a binary structure. *Gaspard* was to be a novel containing within it the story of an "I" who was writing the book. In the first half, the "narrating I" pulls along the tale narrated; in the second half, the fiction becomes the dominant, pulling the "writer's journal" along in its wake. The parts were to hinge on a fulcrum or "watershed" or "cleavage" that, Perec pointed out to Jacques, was not without similarity to the three blank pages in the middle of *L'Attentat de Sarajevo*.[1]

The double design of the *Gaspard* plan announced a characteristic feature of Perec's later work. The idea of a two-part text of which one part "undoes" or deconstructs the other is realised in its most complex form in the autobiographical fiction *W or The Memory of Childhood* (1969–75). The idea of a "reversible text" reached its most rigorous realisation in "9691 Edna d'Nilou", Perec's "Great Palindrome" of 1969 – a text hinging on three points, to each side of which stretch different stories made of the same letters in reverse order. If Perec's "palindromic ambition" had its roots in Pau, its ultimate fruit was the story of Percival Bartlebooth, in *Life A User's Manual* (1969–78), whose life is divided into two opposing halves: he gives twenty years to painting watercolours and to having them made into jigsaw puzzles, and the following twenty to putting the puzzles back together again, regluing them, separating the watercolours from their backing, and then dipping the sheets in detergent, so that all that remains is blank Whatman art paper. *"53 Days"* (1981–82) is also a work in two parts, of which the second was intended to undo what had been set up in the first. In the space of a few months of military service, Georges Perec hit on a device that he was to spend the next twenty years developing into both an oeuvre and a whole conception of literature.

Perec yearned to get out of Pau and back to Paris. He requested transfer to the Ier Régiment du Train (or First Transport Regiment), which was stationed at Vincennes and in which Jacques was now serving. He wished, or so he said in the florid language of French bureaucratic bidding, to pursue his theoretical and practical studies of the English language – which it was not feasible to do in Pau – *so as to resolve the possible future problem of* [his] *reinsertion into civilian life*. The application was made on 19 August; the reply was a long time coming.

Gaspard had by now acquired a firmer structure: 4 parts, 16 chapters, 64 "subchapters", 256 paragraphs. It was this *strict order* that

---

[1] The cut-up numbering of the pages of the carbon-copy typescript makes it impossible to know where the blank pages would have fallen in the top copy.

would allow the author to digress without losing his thread, or his time: every page he wrote would have a place within the overall plan. Perec hoped to finish by December, to get the book accepted by Le Seuil or by Gallimard, and then to spend 1959 on corrections and revisions. He would use the royalties the following year, on his release from the army, to live in London or New York. In the autumn of 1958, he even started writing his letters in English; it confused Jean Paris, who did not realise for a while that it was Perec who was writing to him.

Gaspard is the French name of the first of the Three Magi, and an infrequent but real French first name as well. Its best-known literary use is in the title of Aloysius Bertrand's collection of prose poems, Gaspard de la Nuit (1842), which impressed Baudelaire and is some- times held to be an anticipation of surrealism. But the principal echo of the name Gaspard for Georges Perec lay in Verlaine's poem "Gaspard Hauser chante" (see pp. 108–109), an imaginary recreation of the case of Caspar Hauser.

On 11 August 1958, Perec wrote to Philippe Guérinat with a request:

> I need info on 1) Carbon 14; 2) the width of the streets on the edges of Parc de Monceau; 3) the effect of sulphuric acid on reinforced concrete; 4) air-guns (construction, parts [for compression], veloc- ity), pneumatic drills; 5) comparative resistance of sandstone and clay – the presence and distribution of these materials in the subsoil of Paris (geological strata, etc.).
>
> Also need a book on the law and court procedure (look in the Que sais-je? series [. . .])
> – and Verlaine's poem "La Chanson de Gaspard Hauser"
> – information on the aforementioned Gaspard Hauser (if possible, a bibliography).

Had Philippe used an old encyclopaedia[1] he would have found some- thing like this for his pal:

> HAUSER, KASPAR, a German youth whose life was remark- able from the circumstances of apparently inexplicable mys-

---

[1] Catherine Binet, in "La Commande: Projet d'un voyage à W", provides much the same information from the Larousse encyclopaedia. It is not known whether Philippe Guérinat or Georges Perec were familiar at that time with the novel, Caspar Hauser, by Jakob Wasserman (1873–1934).

tery in which it was involved. He appeared on the streets of
Nuremberg on 26 May 1828 . . . He showed a repugnance
to all food except bread and water, was seemingly ignorant
of outward objects, wrote his name as Kaspar Hauser, and
said that he wished to be an officer, like his father. For some
time he was detained in prison as a vagrant, and was then
handed over to a school-master, Professor Daumer, who
undertook to be his guardian . . . On 17 October 1829, he
was found to have received a wound in the forehead, which
he said had been inflicted on him by a man with a blackened
face . . . He was visited by Earl Stanhope, who became so
interested in his case that he sent him to Ansbach in 1832 to
be educated under a certain Dr Meyer. Interest in his strange
case was revived by his receiving a deep wound on his left
breast, on 14 December 1833, and dying from it 3 or 4 days
after. He affirmed that the wound was the work of a stranger,
but many believed it to be the work of his own hand . . .
The affair created a great sensation, and produced a long
literary agitation.[1]

Whatever it was that Philippe posted to Pau, it helped Perec with his
work, which was moving forward at speed. On 3 September,
Georges wrote to his friend:

Dear Phil:
  Here is the current if not the final epigraph to Gaspard
  No I did not want freedom. Only a way out; to right, to
  left, no matter where: I had no other request; and if the way
  out should be merely an illusion, the request being a small
  one, the illusion would be no greater. On, on! Anything but
  that standing still with arms upraised, pressed up against the
  side of a crate.
                          Franz Kafka, A Report for an Academy[2]

To Jacques Lederer, Perec explained in a striking phrase that his new
first book was *the novel of unsonliness: I have suffered so much from being*

[1] *Encyclopaedia Britannica,* Eleventh Edition (New York: Encyclopedia Britannica Inc, 1910), vol. 13, p. 70.
[2] To translate Perec's French Kafka, I have used Franz Kafka, *Stories 1904–
1924,* trans. J. A. Underwood (London and Sydney: MacDonald, 1981), p. 223.

the son *that my first work can only be the total destruction of all that engendered me*.

There is no trace in Perec's papers of the first *Gaspard* of 1958, but, apart from *Le Condottiere* (1960), the novel which brought Perec's first Gaspard cycle to its conclusion, there are a few tantalising fragments that cast some light on what the writer may have meant by *the novel of unsonliness*. One is the autobiography of Gaspard Winckler, a lad from Belleville, trained as a carpenter but now grown into a pickpocket who plans to make his first million by kidnapping "Regis D.". His father died in 1940; his mother had an affair with an officer before disappearing to Germany in 1945 [FP 119, 21, 16]. In another, closely related third-person version, Gaspard dreams of becoming the greatest criminal the world has ever seen, *the king of forgers, the prince of crooks, the Arsène Lupin of the twentieth century* [FP 119, 21,19]. A third fragment makes the author-character identification even closer, for in it Gaspard's mother disappears in a Gestapo raid from Rue de l'Ermitage, just round the corner from Rue Vilin [FP 119, 21, 21]. *Gaspard* the lost book and Gaspard the character are clearly related to Perec's Belleville background and seem to be attempts on his part to shuffle aside a complex skein of guilty and hostile feelings about his mother and father, and, most of all, about himself – an orphan turned crook, a false carpenter, a gifted forger. Far from being buried beneath layers of forgetting, as the reader of Perec's later work might well believe, the *shoah* was very much part of Perec's awareness and of the image he had of himself in 1958. He wrote to Jacques Lederer that his will and his need to write derived from his absent relationship to his first family. Writing would not alleviate the pain, for *there are wounds too deep ever to heal over entirely*. But the triple gap *between what we were, what we are, and what we could have been without the war* was what drove him, and Jacques, too, *to assert ourselves before others, to create, and to write*.

What Perec thought he and Jacques would have been without the war is unclear, and his attribution of his creative energy to the gaps between what is, what was, and what might have been remains interestingly ambiguous. After all, without the war Perec might have become a barrow boy, like his grandfather Aaron, or a rabbi, as David Peretz might have wished. Equally, he might have grown up to be a writer. Orphanage alone cannot explain Perec's career.

In September 1958 Perec took several days leave at La Payre, the Guérinat home near Poitiers. Philippe brought down a typewriter and some of Perec's drafts from his room at Rue de l'Assomption. Jacques Lederer came, too, and the three of them went out for a memorable meal at a restaurant at Langeais, the mere memory of which brought tears to Perec's eyes in later weeks when he was faced with his military potage. But the main aim of the weekend was to get *Gaspard* together. Progress was made, but it left Perec feeling low: *I don't know what I want to say any more*, he wrote when he was back in camp. What he had written now seemed graceless and inadequate. He had wanted to write *the self-conscious, self-willed book of my own " absolution"*. If *Gaspard* did not come out right or was not even finished by April 1960 (when he expected to return to civilian life), Perec declared, he would give up writing for good. Henri Lefèbvre had got him started on anthropology, and he read a couple of volumes of Marcel Mauss with some interest. Duvignaud encouraged him to enroll for a degree in sociology, and for a while Perec thought he might do so. But the doubting moment passed, Perec started writing again, and any thoughts of an academic future evaporated. It is unlikely that he ever read any more Marcel Mauss, since he went on quoting all his life (see, for example, *PC* 109, 145) the same passages from the volumes he read in 1958.

Perec's letters from Pau, full of jokes, puns, plans, disquisitions on art and music, lamentations on women (*they just aren't real chaps,* another Perecquian refrain), and essays on life and on literature, are like lava bubbling in a volcano that is close to eruption. Some of the main structures of his life and writing were already hardening into rock. There was no question of his following either of the merely fashionable trends in contemporary French literature: he viewed "committed literature" as old hat, and refused to take seriously the work of the "new novelist" Alain Robbe-Grillet – Robbe-Grillet was not a writer but a laboratory technician, he assured Jacques. *Gaspard* was going to have a real hero *in the Arsène Lupin sense of the term*, and Perec did not care a fig that it put him *automatically out of the bounds of contemporary literary fashion (Reverzy, Butor, Camus)*. He had already decided that Camus was of no importance, and that he had read all the Malraux he would ever need. Perec was going to follow his own path, not the paths laid down by fashion. He thought he knew now what he had to write about. Like the narrator of *L'Attentat de Sarajevo*, Gaspard was himself, only more so. He was not the only young writer to use autobiography as the material of fiction, or to use fiction as a means of self-definition and self-defence. Perec would never seek originality for its own sake; he would never really seek anything but himself.

Based on Perec's military record, which was consulted at the Caserne de Reuilly, Paris; on the numerous letters Perec wrote during his time at Pau to Jacques Lederer, Philippe Guérinat, Jean Duvignaud, and François Wahl; and on the recollections of Ela Bienenfeld, Dominique Frischer, Philippe Guérinat, Bianca Lamblin, Jacques Lederer, and Henri Lefèbvre.

CHAPTER 20

Coherence and Paul Klee

1959

Friday, 21 November 1958, was a red-letter day for Conscript 11478 Perec G. His transfer from the XVIIIe RCP stationed at Pau came through, signed by a lieutenant colonel, authorising him to leave next morning for Paris. As he watched Pau slip away behind the windows of his compartment, Perec had no reason to believe that he would ever see the place again. Sunday was no doubt given over to sleeping in late in his own bed at Rue de l'Assomption and to savouring his favourite morning snack, café au lait and buttered bread. On Monday Georges was to report to his new posting. Although he was officially attached to the Ier Régiment du Train at Vincennes, he had the good fortune to be given a clerical job at QGAC, the army's administrative HQ, located in the war ministry building, in Rue Saint-Dominique. The street had been the heart of the aristocratic quarter in Balzac's day; it was only a few minutes away from Saint-Germain-des-Prés, the smarter end of the Left Bank, where there were publishers' offices in profusion. It would be hard to imagine a handier location for a novice writer's military service.

All Perec had to do to discharge his duties was to work through a five-day week of typing and filing and general office duties for a Lieutenant Molitor. He did not even have to live in barracks! For a few weeks he lived at home, at Rue de l'Assomption, and then, on 7 January 1959, he moved into Philippe Guérinat's old room at 217 Rue Saint-Honoré, a few doors down from his own former attic at number 203. His aunt Esther paid the rent. Philippe had just begun his military service and was stationed to begin with at Poitiers, then at Castres, before being sent to fight in Algeria. In spite of his poverty, Georges was lucky, relatively speaking. His office job may have been irksome, and military discipline hard to bear, but he now had some real compensations. The moment his duties were done each day, he could step out of the ministry building, dressed in his embarrassing uniform and red beret, walk down Rue Saint-Dominique, go over the Solférino Bridge into the Tuileries gardens and saunter past the statue of Eblé, the least famous of Napoleon's generals, or alternatively, using the Pont-Royal, pass through the Place du Carrousel, then cross Rue de Rivoli, and reach his perch in ten minutes at the most. He would reemerge metamorphosed, wearing (perhaps) a broad-striped red and green pullover, tight trousers, and shoes as unlike military boots as could be managed; and in such or similar informal evening attire, he would head for one or another of his regular haunts to drink with his friends and discuss the major issues of the day, from food to philosophy to film. *Ach! Quand même allez, c'était la belle vie pour les militaires!* [QPV 14].

Perec had strong but ambivalent feelings towards two women at the beginning of his time at the Ministry of War. He took Dominique Frischer out on a few occasions – once to Harry's New York Bar at 5, Rue Daunou, where he got her to scribble a message to Philippe on a Harry's Bar postcard with its printed information for GIs arriving in the city: "Just tell the taxi driver: Sank Roo Doe Noo". And then there was Marceline Loridan, a redhead of striking independence and vitality who had survived several years as a child deportee. Which did he love? Which loved him? Marceline declined his advances. He decided he loved Dominique, but she infuriated him as well. She preferred the man she had met at PCF headquarters the previous May. *Obviously I lost on both fronts. A farcical scene.* Perec went to watch Woody Woodpecker instead.

There followed a romance with Jeannette Simon, a girl Perec had known at Etampes. They went out together for a while and one day came back to the room in Rue Saint-Honoré. They undressed and lay on the bed. Years later, Perec recorded this episode with sober precision. Jeannette offered herself to him, but he pushed her away; because she did not try to escape from his grasp, he explained to himself, she was not able to draw him on. The recollection of this fiasco persuaded the thirty-six-year-old Perec that, far from being a new problem of early middle age, his self-thwarting "system of defence" had in fact been in place since his teens.

Dominique Frischer's new boyfriend smoked a pipe and wore glasses and rather smart clothes, for, as a tailor's son, he could tell well-cut jackets from cheap ready-mades. He and Perec had misgivings about each other at first, but these were soon set aside, or at least buried at sufficient depth to allow each to find in the other an intellectual companion and a real friend. They became inseparable mates and introduced each other to their respective social sets. Roger Kleman's was far wider than Perec's; in losing Dominique, Georges gained a world of new acquaintances, some of whom became lasting members of his family of friends.

Perec and Roger both knew the Frischers' Romanian lodger, from whom they perhaps acquired their attachment to smart shoes. The Romanian had learned from Balzac that in Paris the road to riches lay in the conquest of women. Though very poor, he invested every sou he could muster in the apparel of seduction, and kept, in his tiny box room, dozens of handmade shirts, masses of fine underwear, and perhaps fifteen pairs of smart leather shoes. Perec and Kleman also came to see footwear as a marker of life's stations, whose true way led from mere moccasins to shoes made by Weston (Georges's uncle David had given him his first, treasured pair), from there to Church's, and then, by way of Buntings, to the ultimate elegance of Lobbs, leather brogues handmade by English craftsmen, so exclusive that they could (and still can) be bought only in a single boutique, on Boulevard Saint-Germain.

Kleman had been a teenage member of the Jeunesses Républicaines, the Communist youth movement, and was now a stalwart of UEC, the union of Communist students. He had read Marx and could hold forth equally well on Kant and Hegel. He drew Perec into questions he had never really confronted before, questions of first principles, aims, and methods, and made him see the need for coherence, for arguments that hung together, the need for thinking in wholes. They called it, without the slightest ironical intent, a totalitarian approach. With his intellect, his culture, his dialectical skills, with his booming voice and his air of authority, Kleman cut a striking figure on the café seminar scene. He was a thinker, a teacher, and could be a leader of men.

In his first few weeks back in Paris, Perec pressed ahead at full speed with his novel. Despite spending his days as a pen-pusher and his evenings drinking, talking and going to the cinema, he managed to put the greater part of his energy into finishing *Gaspard* – in three weeks, according to his later memory of the room where he did it. On 11 February 1959, he wrote to François Wahl, at Le Seuil, to say that the completed novel would be ready on Saturday next and would be 353 or 359 pages long. Luc Estang, a senior editor, read the typescript first and summoned Perec for an interview; after which he turned the book down. The author agreed that the tone, the style, and the whole approach of his work were not pleasing, but in less than a month he was in touch with the publisher once again, with plans for rewriting the novel entirely. He proposed to submit the new version in three or four months' time. It would have a new title, in English, taken from the Bible, as Perec said (and from William Faulkner, though he did not say that): *As I Lay Dying*.

Only the characters would remain from the text Le Seuil had seen: Gaspard, Rufus, Madera, Jérôme, Geneviève, Mila, Nicolas, Otto. The plot would be much simplified and would consist of only four overlapping parts, dealing with four episodes in the life of Gaspard: when he leaves home and becomes a forger; when he meets Geneviève and works on the treasure at Split; when he makes a mess of a pseudo-Giotto (Gaspard being not a forger of existing paintings but a creator of false ones, like van Meegeren with his Vermeers); and when he avoids arrest by the police. The first two episodes, Perec noted, would be written retrospectively; the second two would be in the present tense. The whole book was *simply the story of a man becoming aware of the world*, and since that was a serious subject, he swore to his putative publisher that he would make as few puns as possible. He went on:

> *I have read* Moby Dick. *It is not worth writing if one is not aiming for a work of that calibre.*
>
> *I am twenty-three years old, I refuse to play around with literature, I have deliberately chosen to give one third of my life to writing, making as few concessions as possible, and at the same time I am bloody scared that it's all to no purpose, that all I undertake may be destined to be imperfect, may be a dead end, a failure . . . (And yet I am confident . . .)*

Jean Duvignaud read the 1959 *Gaspard* and spoke warmly of it to Georges Lambrichs, an editor who had recently moved from Editions de Minuit (the publishers of Beckett, Robbe-Grillet, and Butor) to head his own collection and review, *Le Chemin*, at Gallimard. At the end of April Lambrichs dropped Perec a line, asking to see the novel he had heard about from Duvignaud. After reading it, he wrote again to say that he liked the opening very much but felt there were problems later on in the text; Perec should call in at Gallimard for a chat. A solution must have been found, because while Le Seuil could offer Perec only "potential encouragement", France's foremost literary publisher, Gallimard, issued a firm contract dated 22 May 1959, for a new novel by Georges Perec entitled *Gaspard pas mort*. The soldier-writer was paid an advance of 75,000 francs against future royalties.[1] It was a tremendous coup, achieved with unusual speed. Success was at hand; no, it was in the bag!

The title had changed in the course of 1958 from *La Nuit* to *Gaspard*. The title of 1959, *Gaspard pas mort,* seems to allude to a famous telegram sent in 1891 by Zola's disciple Paul Alexis to a newspaper enquiring about the future of the French novel: NATURALISME PAS MORT. LETTRE SUIT ("Naturalism not dead. Letter follows"). It is not clear what the connection is.

When it was Roger Kleman's turn for call-up, he was luckier than Perec had been. Dominique was there to see him emerge from his selection exercise at Vincennes with a hop, skip and a jump, unable to contain his glee. He had failed the medical exam! He was unfit for service! He could now take a longer view of his prospects and ambitions. The previous year, when he was in *hypokhâgne*, the first year of preparation for the entrance examination to Normal' Sup', there had been some talk amongst the brighter boys in his class at Lycée Louis-le-grand of founding a new journal. Roger was now at the Sorbonne, reading history and earning money by doing part-time market research work. The others were all in their year of *khâgne* and, with luck, would be *normaliens* soon. It was time for them to begin to turn their classroom dreams into reality.

Their aim was to create a periodical that would dominate the coming decade as Sartre's *Les Temps modernes* had held the high ground since the war. Roger was fascinated by Sartre's manifesto and had a complete set of the review on his shelves. The new review would need to draw on more than one brain, however, even one the size of Sartre's. It would have to be the concerted effort of a team, of the leading group of the next generation's intellectuals. Perec would be part of it. The review would give voice to a carefully worked out, coherent, encyclopaedic, nonsectarian, Marxist reassessment of culture, set on a firm theoretical base. What was planned was an intellectual revolution; what was needed was the manpower to achieve it.

[1] The issue of the contract and the payment of the advance were confirmed by Robert Gallimard in 1990, from company records.

One of the first meetings took place at the Frischers' flat in Rue Bergère. About forty young men (and hardly any young women) responded to the call of Kleman and Perec and crammed into the heavily furnished lounge. The main contingent came from Lycée Louis-le-grand. Regis Debray was the son of a well-known Gaullist town councillor; Bruno Marcenac's father was a poet, a friend of Aragon and a senior PCF journalist; Jean-Pierre Sergent was already involved in the Algerian conflict, on the FLN side, and was soon to feature in Jean Rouch's documentary film on French youth, *Chroniques d'un été;* Claude Burgelin was related to the director of La Maison des Ecrivains; Marcel Benabou, a Jew from Morocco with a great gift for Latin and Greek, had a name that, like Perec's, often attracted an acute accent on the first *e;* and Jean Crubellier, a schoolmaster's son, one of the few from this glamorous set who did not go on to Normal' Sup' (he would later give his name to "Le Commandant-Crubellier", the fictional steamship of *Things,* and to the street in which *Life A User's Manual* is set). Other recruits also came to the group, sooner or later, from Kleman's network of left-wing acquaintances: Jacques Mangolte (educated at Lycée Jacques Decourt) and Pierre Getzler (from Lycée Voltaire), along with Jean-Sebastien Swarc, Le Troquer, Bruno Queysanne, Grobla, François Lebowitz, Pamart, Bataillon, Henri Peretz (a distant cousin of Perec's "by agreement" rather than by genealogical proof), and of course Perec's old friend Jacques Lederer. Many others were involved to a greater or lesser degree, for a few weeks, or a few months, or even a few years. They are now business tycoons, advertising executives, magazine editors, university professors; only Regis Debray went on to make a career in politics. What brought them all together at the dawn of the Gaullist age was the conviction that a revolution was inevitable.

The group was independent of political sponsorship, but it was laid down from the start that it would not act against the PCF. "We assert that to be anti-Communist in 1959 is to be not on the left", announces an undated draft manifesto from this early period [FP 48, 9, 3, 3, 2]. But what did it mean to be "on the left" in terms of French culture? There was little difference, bar political point scoring, between a film review in the Communist daily *L'Humanité* and one in the Gaullist *Figaro. Les Lettres françaises,* Aragon's weekly and the literary voice of the PCF, had even taken up Robbe-Grillet and Philippe Sollers, proving itself to be not just a Stalinist organ, which was explicable, but an *eclectic* one, which was far worse. What was needed in order to save culture for the left was a philosophy that could identify and make a coherent sense of the great art of the modern era. *Coherence* was the group's key word, its call sign. They were young men. They wanted all of life to cohere.

Such a project undertaken collectively risks collapse into chaos unless it is structured. By reflex, the leading members reinvented a way of working that combined representation with hierarchy. They borrowed it from Lenin, by way of the PCF, but stopped short of calling it bureaucratic centralism. It involved dividing culture into its constituent fields – jazz, film, art, drama, fiction, poetry, and so forth – and setting up working parties, under appointed conveners, that would then report back to the plenary group. The conveners convened themselves as a central committee, chaired by Kleman. Perec, as a kind of general secretary, ran the "Index", an alphabetically sorted set of large filing cards carrying personal details, a career profile, an intellectual assessment, and other comments on each member of the group, as well as on nonmembers it might be useful either to bring in or, on the contrary, to keep well away. The Index was eventually kept in a locked metal box to which only the general secretary and one other had a key. It was a working scale model of the Leninist state, but it was not the only thing that now makes ex-members declare that the group was the most bureaucratic organisation ever devised. Bibliographies, reading lists, notes on Lowry and Georg Lukács, and thoughts on Vincente Minelli, Hitchcock, Tolstoy, *Moby Dick*, and Elie Faure were all put as points, and the points put on cards, and the cards sorted into order. Perec learnt his filing-card technique from Kleman but quickly became a master in his own right. When someone enquired, a few years later, whether Perec had any aptitude as an archivist, the answer from friends was loud and clear: "Perec is an absolute virtuoso! He's the king of filing-card schemes!"

The group's internal procedures were laboriously bureaucratic, as is traditional in splinters. Every paragraph of the minutes, of the manifestos, of the articles written individually or by collectives, of the resolutions put and of the amendments proposed – every tiny element of the work and the workings of the group – constituted an administrative and therefore a political matter, on which a vote had to be taken at a meeting that had to be quorate. As for the review that was to come out of all this, it would be called *La Locomotive* – not to honour George Stephenson (the print of Stephenson's *Rocket* on the wall of Jérôme and Sylvie's ideal flat, in the opening chapter of *Things*, is there rather to honour *La Locomotive*) but because of Karl Marx's dictum, "Revolution is History's locomotive".

The group had difficulty funding the work that it planned to do. Public libraries barely existed. At the Sorbonne, the Bibliothèque Victor Cousin was antiquated and slow, and had few current periodicals. Few if any members yet had access to the Bibliothèque Nationale, which was in any case two years behind schedule in getting new works onto the shelves. Members therefore had to purchase their reading matter, but the cost of what they wanted was far beyond their means. They were reduced to standing by the magazine racks of Latin Quarter bookshops – Les Deux Masques for the theatre reviews, La Hune, PUF, and La Joie de Lire – reading every fourth page only, since they could not slit open the uncut leaves without having to pay up. It was a skip-reading skill that Perec explained in ironical detail years later [*PC* 116–117], mostly for archaeological interest, as by then few books were still being published uncut. In 1959 Perec was not amused by having to skip-read out of poverty. He wrote a begging letter to Le Seuil asking for free copies of *Esprit* and of any books about literature on Le Seuil's list. It seems that the publisher responded by sending him an order form.

Out of the forty or fifty young men and half a dozen women in the group, which was always perceived as the creation of Kleman and Perec, a smaller set emerged as a circle of friends. Perec found himself for the first time at the centre of a web of relations. Roger and Dominique were full of ideas and energy and passions for things; Pierre Getzler was quite different, a hesitant and thoughtful man set on a life devoted to art; Claude Burgelin, elegant, kind, and well-mannered, came from another world, and Marcel Benabou was an affectionate friend, ambitious, amusing, and, in his own words, *very political* at that age; Jacques Lederer also belonged to and fitted with this circle which was, as if by chance, entirely Jewish, with the exception of Burgelin, who, as the child of a protestant family, belonged to France's other historical minority. None of them was religious, though Marcel could read Hebrew. At least two of them understood Yiddish; three had lost parents in the *shoah*. All of them had a way of mocking themselves and each other that it took Claude Burgelin time to latch on to and that came to seem to him the essence of *Yiddischkeit*. The more deadpan the delivery of an explanation or doctrine, the surer you could be that a pun was in the offing. Behind every reason, the *yiddische Witz* would find the reason's reason, and the other reason behind it, and so on, until the argument went into infinite regress, and the arguers collapsed in snorts of laughter. Perec was the funniest by far, and he used humour as a means of defence. Under threat of attack, he would pretend to be hurt already, putting on such comical grimaces and appeals for sympathy that his potential opponent could not but laugh and be disarmed before the fight even began. Woody Allen has made convoluted self-mockery of this kind part of mass culture nowadays. For Claude Burgelin, the Yiddish habit of making the most serious things sound funny – of turning arguments on their head so as to see them properly, of puncturing profundity with puns – all these traditions seemed bewildering at first. But before long, of course, these traditions became the very hallmark of Perec's mode of thinking and being in the world, and in words.

When he first got back to Paris, in November 1958, Perec needed money. The army gave him only 5,000 old francs a month, a mere pittance (less than £5), and there was so much more to spend it on now than there had been in Pau. All he could afford to eat in a regular manner was subsidised tins of army rations, and they made him ill. He squared the circle by whatever means came to hand – filling in questionnaires for market-research surveys, doing résumés for the *Bulletin signalétique du CNRS*, as before – but he wanted to earn his living by his pen. That was not so easy. Le Seuil could not offer him anything by way of translation or reviewing. The editor of the series Le Temps qui court did not think much of his proposal to write a book on *les paras* – on *what paratroopers do, what they think, what they're like, what they are, especially as seen by others* . . . What Perec wanted was a publisher who would fund his living costs for six or twelve months so he could write – whether in the form of an advance, a sabbatical, or a salary. He had no chance of getting any such thing. He kept on trying to obtain such an arrangement, though, and finally managed to pull it off in 1978, in his contract with Hachette. In no country in the world is it easy to live by the pen alone. The absence in France of equivalents to Arts Council bursaries, writer-in-residence schemes, and creative-writing courses underlay many of the choices Perec made, which, in turn, and under those circumstances, under-lined his unwavering determination to write.

Perec continued to frequent the *Arguments* group, in which he was sufficiently relaxed – or drunk, on at least one occasion – to hold forth on his experience as a parachute trooper. He disliked the Thursday-evening receptions at Le Seuil (*I like alcohol very much, but I can't bear cocktails and the polite conversation that goes with them*) but did not cease to haunt Maurice Nadeau's office at Les Lettres nouvelles (henceforth referred to as LN, to distinguish it from the review of the same name, *Les Lettres nouvelles*). But in spite of now numerous contacts in French literary publishing, Perec produced only one piece that was printed in 1959, and that not even under his own name. To review the first volume of the memoirs of the dissident Yugoslav Communist leader Milovan Djilas, Tito's former associate and subsequent bête noire, Perec, for the only known time in his life, wrote under a pseudonym in *Les Lettres nouvelles*. The review of *Pays sans justice* ("Land Without Justice") appeared on page 22 of issue number 3 (dated 18 March 1959), over the just plausibly Serbian name of Serge Valène.

Perec must have written the review in late February, after he finished the 350-odd-page version of *Gaspard pas mort* – that is to say, in the week during which he heard that his claim for compensation from West Germany for the loss of his mother at the hands of Nazi murderers had been approved, and that a sum of nearly one million old francs had been awarded to him. The only survivor of the Peretz-Szulewicz family of Belleville, apart from Georges himself, was his grandmother Rose, now living, in her eightieth year, in a flat in Tel Aviv. Perhaps that is why Perec chose to adapt her name to designate himself. The sonorous and misleadingly Serbian pseudonym Serge Valène consists of the main vowels and all but two of the consonantal sounds of Rose's full maiden name, Sura Rojza Walersztejn, when it is properly said in Polish: S-R-ZH V-L-N.

Perec's more recent past was smuggled into the Djilas review in a way that could be described as cheating. The memoirs, Valène says in his concluding flourish, draw their literary value from their style, a rhythmical prose harking back to the language of Prince-Bishop Njegoš, the nineteenth-century poet-politician whose career Djilas sketches in the first few pages of his book.[1] It sounds as though Serge Valène could read Serbo-Croat. He could not, of course, but he did know a little about Njegoš, and from the very best of sources. He had listened many times to his old friend and enemy Žarko Vidović

---

[1] Georges Perec [Serge Valène, pseud.], "L'Enfance de Djilas au Montenegro", *Les Lettres nouvelles* no. 3 (18 March 1959), p. 22.

talking of the founding father of modern Serbian literature – the subject, the Yugoslav had declared, of his next important book. For political reasons, it took Vidović thirty years to get the book published, so the indirect source of Perec's 1959 article is to be found, in effect, in a biography of Njegoš that appeared only in 1989.[1]

Roger Kleman brought Perec new reading, including Musil, Hermann Broch, and Thomas Mann (again). Dominique had also enjoyed, and taught Roger to enjoy, Valéry Larbaud's strange, dandified novel of a millionaire imprisoned by his fortune, *A. O. Barnabooth* (1913). Although Perec once admitted that he had only ever read the first thirty pages of Larbaud's book, he hung on to its name, giving the last half to Percival Bartlebooth, the millionaire puzzle fiend of *Life A User's Manual*. The other half of Bartlebooth's name comes from something else Perec encountered in 1959, Herman Melville's "Bartleby", a short story about a copying clerk (or scrivener) who "prefers not to" do anything at all. It is not certain that Perec read the Melville story then, but he cannot have failed to see its name, which occurs towards the end of the review that Maurice Nadeau wrote of Jacques Mayoux's introduction to the American author, *Melville par lui-même*, a review printed on the same page of *Les Lettres nouvelles* as the article on Djilas by "Serge Valène".

Friendship, history and literature have supplied me with some of the characters of this book, Perec states in the disclaimer at the head of *Life A User's Manual*. To a considerable extent, the names of the characters and places in that book were supplied to Perec by the friends he made in Paris in the first months of 1959 (*Simon, Crubellier*), by the books that he read or read about then (*Bartle-* and *-booth*), and by the historical events of his own life (*Serge Valène*) at that time. The name of the novel's master craftsman and puzzle cutter, Gaspard Winckler, comes of course from Perec's own work if not, very distantly, from Verlaine.

Kleman taught Perec to look at paintings as well. They would go to exhibitions together, and to the Louvre, often lingering in front of Italian Renaissance works and most especially, in the seven-metre gallery, before an *unbelievably energetic portrait of a Renaissance man* [*MA* 187, *W* 109] whose face seemed endowed with the fearsome light of a man with the world in his arms. The bulging eyes of the

---

[1] Жарко Виловић, *Његош и Косовски завјет у новом вијеку* ("Njegoš and the Kosovo Question in Modern Era") (Belgrade: F. Višnević, 1989).

portrait seem to be staring straight at you whether you look at the face head-on or from the side, from the left or from the right. If you look very closely indeed, you can also see on the young man's upper lip a tiny scar, somewhat similar in shape and location to the one Perec acquired in an accident with a ski-stick in the changing room of his primary school at Villard-de-Lans. Antonello da Messina's *Portrait of a Man Known as Il Condottiere* ("The Warlord"), became a personal symbol for Perec. It figures in one way or another in nearly every one of his published works.

Kleman was given to declaring that in France there was no art history worthy of the name. Perec and Pierre Getzler were the other main members of Roger's art-history working party. They were not concerned simply with situating themselves within contemporary fashions; they were not surrealists, or modernists, or abstractionists, or defenders of the Ecole de Paris. In principle, they were for representation and against abstraction and would have wished to be thought of as being on the side of realism in art – provided that you understood that the real work of their working party was to discover what the "real" in art really was.

A work of art, Perec wrote in a "Defence of Klee" that he sent to Pierre Getzler half as a letter, half as a draft article, was *a relationship built between man and the world*. Style, manner, school, degree of abstraction – all these aspects mattered much less than a work's success in achieving the aim of art, which was to provoke in the beholder some reaction that reduced his alienation from the world, to build bridges between the self and the other. In Paul Klee's painting, or at least in the two Klee canvases that he saw and pondered in 1959 (*Ville de lagunes* and *L'Enfant au perron*), Perec found something that moved him. He came to the conclusion that Klee's paintings had to be rethought as realist works. For what, in the end, was realism? An attempt not simply to represent reality but also to enrich and heighten it, an attempt to make reality denser, and to make it *mean*.

> *Klee disturbs because he is disturbed – I recognise his anxiety and do not despise it [. . .]. (Picasso disturbs no longer, he is playing, and Buffet never disturbed anyone except art dealers). I recognise this anxiety, that is to say I know it is the ground of my own sensibility, that it underpins and nourishes it, that it explains my approach and the constant need I have for certainties: Klee appears to me as a mirror; he gives no explanations: he was afraid, he paints*

his fear, we are perhaps less afraid than he was; we look in the mirror. [. . .] It is wrong to claim that art is a refusal of anxiety [. . .] it is above all the conquest of a necessity . . . As we proceed, Klee takes his distance, together with Kafka, Lowry, and Antelme; Stendhal and Chardin, Botticelli, Ghirlandaio, and Antonello da Messina draw nearer . . .

Based on Perec's memories of 1959 as found in FP 57, 5, FP 57, 50, FP 57, 51; on letters to Georges Perec from Luc Estang and Georges Lambrichs [FP 31, 2, 17; 31,1,18, and 31,1,20]; on letters from Perec to Philippe Guérinat, Luc Estang, François Wahl, and Jean Duvignaud; and on the recollections of Marcel Benabou, France Benoît-Mayo, Claude Burgelin, Stojan Čelić, Regis Debray, Dominique Frischer, Marceline Loridan, Bruno (Mathieu) Marcenac, Michel Martens, Harry Mathews, Henri Peretz, Jean-Pierre Sergent, and others.

G. Perec, "Défense de Klee", is in the possession of Pierre Getzler. Photocopy at AGP.

CHAPTER 21

The General Line

1959–1960

The age of the consumer had barely begun, but *Arguments* was already planning a special issue on *Le Bien-Etre* ("Being Well-Off"). The new constitution of de Gaulle's Fifth Republic was drafted, but the old war in Algeria dragged on. Increasing numbers of Frenchmen were dodging the draft; some helped the FLN in mainland France, "carrying cases" for the Algerians, as the saying went. Perec and Kleman were not tempted by direct action, though they knew that one member of their group had joined the *réseau Jeanson*. The PCF still refused to condone desertion from the ranks, but 121 non-Communist intellectuals on the left gave voice to the widespread opinion that orders to shoot Algerians should be disobeyed [see *Jms* 243]. No daily newspaper would publish the statement (which Perec's mentors at *Arguments*, Duvignaud, Morin, and Barthes, had signed), and so the "appeal of the 121" was distributed by protesters who blocked railway lines and halted trains taking conscripts to Mediterranean ports.

Meanwhile, at his barracks at the Fort of Vincennes, Jacques Lederer was asked one day by a conscript whose name no one ever managed to remember if he wouldn't mind – seeing that he had a Velosolex – if he please wouldn't mind running him over. A broken arm or leg would give him a few months in hospital, by the end of which the Algerians would have won, the war would be over, and he would not have to face sandy wastes, nights under canvas and a bloody death.

Jacques raised the matter with his friends. Did they have the right to do violence to a man in order to save him from doing violence to others? The answer was clear enough: they did. Of course, it would not be easy, breaking a man's arm just like that. They would need to do it together.

Jacques brought the chap along to meet the others, and they all had dinner. The half-named conscript (he was called Kara-something:

Karakorum? Karavadjo? Karaway?) did not care for their steak tartare, and grasped almost nothing of their heated intellectual debate.
But none of that mattered. They should not refuse him their help just
because he did not belong to their crowd. However, said the group's
chief egghead, puffing his postprandial pipe (it had been an excellent
meal, followed by four brandies), and notwithstanding our desire to
do you grievous bodily harm, what you're asking for is a risk. Under
local anaesthetic you'll feel absolutely nothing. We could easily over-
reach and bust not just your armbone but your articulations, your
synovials, and your ligaments, too. No, my old fruit, Kleman concluded, it's not so easy. It would be safer to underestimate an overdose
and leave a really barmy suicide note, so that when you wake up in
hospital sheets they'll diagnose two screws loose and invalid you out
on the spot. There's nothing the army likes less than a nutcase – it's
bad for morale.

The alternative plan was agreed upon, and they set off with Kara-
thingy to find tablets of Dr Morty Kohl's Soluble Camphorated
Thanatine. They sat their oaf down in a café and dictated a suitably
paranoid suicide note, which Karapsyche signed and put into his top
pocket before downing four downers with a mug of black coffee.
They now had to find a hotel where Karasnooze could oversleep and
be found in the morning by a shrieking chambermaid. But they found
no inn with a room at that hour of the night, and Karadiddle had
already slumped into the gutter. So they hailed a cab and packed the
snoring refusenik back to barracks. Once he got there, Karamello
sniffed the night air, took a brisk constitutional, relieved his stomach
of dinner, and drinks, and the coffee and the pills, and then took a
brief nap. When reveille sounded he awoke and left for Algeria, as
per orders.

For Georges Perec, the bombshell came on Friday, 3 July 1959. His
detachment to QGAC was cancelled; he had to rejoin his regiment at
Pau forthwith. He left Paris the same day. For no reason that he knew
of, his brilliant, blossoming life in Paris was being cut off, just like
that. He had ten more months to go and he would have to spend
them in provincial Pau, in the dreary barracks of Le Hameau. And it
might be even worse. Parachutists were sent almost everywhere; he
was exempt from Algeria, thank goodness, but he could still be sent
to Morocco, or Senegal, or any one of the "DOM et TOM", the
far-flung "domains and territories" of overseas France, from Saint-
Pierre-et-Miquelon (in the St Lawrence) to the Kerguelen Islands. He

must have shed tears of anguish and frustration on the ten-hour train ride to Pau. Farewell, Rue Saint-Honoré! Goodbye, Rue Bergère! No more *Arguments,* no more *Lettres nouvelles!* He had just begun to take possession of the city, and now it was being taken from him.

Before receiving his marching orders, Perec had just seen in close sequence four films of some importance: *Senso,* by Lucchino Visconti, a sumptuous, operatic melodrama, which he loved; Howard Hawkes's *Rio Bravo,* in his view the greatest Western ever made; *Hiroshima mon amour,* directed by Alain Resnais from a script by Marguerite Duras, which had just won the Palme d'Or at Cannes; and a classic work of revolutionary film art, Sergei Eisenstein's *The Old and the New,* which was screened in Paris that summer under its other title, *La Ligne générale* ("The General Line").

Although originally commissioned as a propaganda film, *The Old and the New* is a work that transcends the particular "general line" of the CPSU in the period in which it was made (1925–29).[1] Structured like a traditional fairy tale (the peasant heroine, Marfa, overcomes three obstacles in her quest for a better life), the film is an epic account of the battle between the "old" ways of the Russian peasantry, and the "new" as represented by Fordson tractors, mechanised milking, and animal hygiene. Its most celebrated sequence transforms a cream-separator plant into a potent symbol of optimism. Close-ups of stainless steel parts seen from different angles are intercut with shots of peasant faces, at first bewildered, then suspicious, then intrigued, and finally beaming as they see cream gush forth from the spout, with the image of a crashing waterfall superimposed upon it. Eisenstein's use of montage endows the object, which is cream and also water, with a reality that is "supercharged" with meaning.[2] His recourse to blatant, accessible symbols (the water of the waterfall signifies that the milk from the machine is natural and clean) does not diminish the reality of the cream-separator but rather heightens it, giving it epic significance. Eisenstein himself likened the machine to the Holy Grail, an object inspiring both scepticism and ecstasy:

> *The Old and the New* [. . .] deals with the everyday, ordinary, but no less profound cooperation between town and

[1] See Vance Kepley, Jr, "The Evolution of Eisenstein's *The Old and the New*", *Cinema Journal,* Fall 1974, pp. 39–50.

[2] See Edgar Morin, *Le Cinéma ou l'homme imaginaire* (Paris: Minuit, 1953), p. 78, for an analysis of the cream-separator sequence in *The Old and the New.*

country, between *sovkhoz* and *kolkhoz*, between peasant and machine, between horse and tractor, as they tread their burdensome path towards the common goal. Like that path, *The Old and the New* needs to be clear, simple, and well-defined [. . .] Like that path, the film is, from start to finish, a quest – the quest for the line along which we must advance in order to make a reality of all our social aspirations.[1]

Perec thought that "La Ligne générale" would be a much better title than *La Locomotive* for the review his group was planning. It may have been Pierre Getzler who suggested it first – he had been reading Eisenstein's *Zametki Kinorezhissora* ("Notes of a Director") in French translation,[2] and lent the book to Perec, if not then, then not long after – but it seems that it was Perec who formally proposed to a meeting of the central committee that they should adopt the title, and he was mightily pleased that the proposal was adopted *nem con*. La Ligne générale, Lg for short, became the name not just of a review still unborn but of the whole movement, of the group, of the fine band of friends. *Quel Petit Vélo à guidon chromé au fond de la cour?* ("What Wee Bike with the Chromeplated Handlebars at the Back of the Yard?") (1966), Perec's uninterruptedly unserious account of the Karasomebody whose stomach failed to process Dr Morty Kohl's Camphorated Thanatine (shamelessly adapted above), is dedicated to Lg, *in memory of its finest hour on the field of glory (I mean it, I do)*. But Lg was itself a serious project, and its aims were parallel to those of Eisenstein's film: it was a quest for the *general line* that would bring to realisation all the cultural aspirations of the group's leading members, and especially those of Georges Perec.

Lg did not collapse when its general secretary was called away. Letters flowed between Pau and Paris. Perec kept in touch with Jacques, with Roger, with Pierre, with Claude, and no doubt with others, too, writing to each in intense bursts when camp life gave him the chance. Lg was in good health in the summer of 1959. *Gaspard* was not.

Gallimard had issued the contract in May for a *revised* version of the novel, to be delivered in September. It was important to publish

---

[1] Transl. from Sergei Eisenstein, *Au-delà des Etoiles* (Paris: 10/18, 1974), pp. 59–60.

[2] Sergei Eisenstein, *Réflexions d'un cinéaste* (Moscow: Foreign Language Publishing House, 1957).

new novels in the autumn, in the run-up to the circus of prizes (Goncourt, Renaudot, Médicis) that had their closing dates around the end of November. Perec had expected to spend the summer in stimulating Parisian surroundings, but he found himself instead in a Nissen hut, eight hundred kilometres from Saint-Germain-des-Prés. In such circumstances, and in the *black solitude and disgust* that they engendered, he could not write properly, or indeed at all. He appealed to Georges Lambrichs at Gallimard to pull strings to get him out of his hole, but to no avail. Had it all been a dream? He writes a book, gets a contract, founds a review with a whole heap of new friends – and wakes up in a bunk, in a barracks, in the back of beyond. *Gaspard mort*, he scrawled after a fortnight. He must have scribbled something similar to his editor, who scribbled back that he should not torture himself so: "I have confidence in your novel."

Perec accepted the fact that the *Gaspard* he had written was not yet ripe for publication. He aimed high, *a thousand times higher than a merely crazy ambition*. In the second month of his reincarceration, he reread his imperfect masterpiece. Some bits were not bad, he thought; others were weak. *It has to be simple*, he wrote to Pierre Getzler, echoing the Eisenstein line. After that, he never again mentioned a novel called *Gaspard pas mort,* except as a reference in his autobiography [*W* 108–109]. He did not abandon the project itself, however, only the title: when he returned to his Gaspard material, he called it by a new name, *Le Condottiere* ("The Warlord"), after the Renaissance portrait in the Louvre, a postcard reproduction of which he pinned above his bunk.

In the autumn another project supervened. It was to be a short story (for a collection that Lambrichs proposed but never published, under the title *Jeune Prose* ["Young Prose"]), a love story, a composite version of all Perec's experiences with women. As he described (in a letter) how he was going about his task, it struck Perec that his method of constructing a love story was *simply paranoid*. But since he had never known complete love with a woman, he was obliged to use montage to write about it, so he said.

The tale was to consist of a long discussion in Belgrade between a man and his lover, over roast boar, *čevapčiči*, and melon disdained for glass upon glass of slivovitz, Balkan apricot brandy. As their intoxication increases, a crisis grows between the lovers, and the tale turns into twin internal monologues, then broadens out into what Perec calls *cosmic depression*. Perec also meant the story to be a version of Descartes's *Discourse on Method*, but he found it hard to avoid writing a pastiche of Butor's *La Modification*. The first twenty pages were easy: *there's nothing simpler than "doing" nouveau roman,* he boasted. But he wanted then to put the machine into reverse, to make everything in the second part not absurd but necessary, so that every detail would fit into a perceptible order. He had set himself a brainteaser that he was not sure he could solve.

There are close similarities between the plan for the story, as detailed in 1959, and *L'Attentat de Sarajevo,* completed two years previously. In fact, the story was to be called *Toplicin Venać,* after the quarter of old Belgrade where Mila lives in the earlier novel, and where Milka Čanak had her flat in reality. The story itself has not been found; perhaps it was never really written.

❀

Meanwhile, in Paris, Lg was flourishing. Roger Kleman recruited a polyglot PCF member, Michel Martens, partly for his political connections and partly for his outstanding knowledge of American cinema, which Lg wanted to cover in one of its first issues. Martens was told that his membership was subject to the approval of the real leader, the brains behind the project: the general secretary himself, unfortunately detained in the provinces, in a paratroop unit. Martens, a red-head of Jewish, Austrian, and Russian descent, had a private income and a car, so his first duty was to go to Gare d'Austerlitz to pick up his leader and bring him to a meeting of the group. He could not have missed Perec in the crowd alighting from the southwest express: he was the only dark, stocky, crumpled, and unmistakably Jewish traveller adorned with an implausible red beret. The two got on well. Martens was confirmed as head of the cinema section and also became Perec's trusty, the only other person with a key to the box in which the Index was kept.

Perec was able to attend several Lg meetings in spite of his transfer back to Pau. He took leave to go to Paris for two days at the end of July 1959, then on two separate occasions in September, and then again for a few days from 31 October. At the meetings, Martens remembers, it was as if the green eye of Dr Mabuse were bearing down from above the general secretary's metal box, in which, as everyone knew, there were assessments of all present, appraisals drawn up by Perec alone . . . Was this kind of group control to be his real career, now that *Gaspard* was dead?

Some days I tell myself that I don't want to write anymore, or that
I never really had any talent, just a number of intentions that I can
fulfil much more easily by busying myself with Lg, for example.

The moment he wrote that down, he knew there was something specious about the reasoning. Behind every reason, there is always the reason's reason to be sought. What did Perec propose to achieve through Lg?

The first issue of the review would be entitled *Against Humanism,* the second *Against the Illusion of Good Conscience* (that is, against "eclecticism" and the French New Wave in the cinema); issue 3, *The Farce of Anguished Conscience,* would tackle Samuel Beckett and the merchants of gloom, and issue 4, to be ready by May 1960 and in the shops by the *rentrée,* would be Perec's own special number, *The Epic,* with draft contents to include a theoretical article (on the necessity of the epic, criteria, potential) and essays on the Western, on Eluard, on Brecht, and so forth. After that there would be an issue called *Socialist Realism* and then one entititled *Revolutionary Romanticism.*

Not all of the comrades were as committed as Perec to the review's imminent reality. He wrote to Jacques that one day the historian of Lg – *some subnado[1] who will build his career on that necrophagic enterprise –* would be obliged to describe the rift that existed between the "encyclopaedists" (Kleman, Henri Peretz, and at times Jacques himself) and the "speedsters" (Perec, Crubellier, and Sergent). The first group wanted all or nothing, preferred to make haste without speed, to chew sixty-four times before swallowing, and to put off publication until they were perfectly ready; the second wanted to get everything down on paper straightaway, to prove to themselves that they could. Unless they changed their ways, the encyclopaedists would soon be suffering from nonwriter's block!

Nulla dies sine linea, *whether you're a genius or not. We must engrave these words in letters of gold on the arachnoid recesses of the cerebral circumvolutions of our dear friend RK.*

Perec had no hope of another Paris posting. In September he heard rumours that some conscripts might be released after only twenty-four months' military service; in fact, the duration of service was

---

[1] I.e., "sub-Nadeau".

extended to thirty-two months in the last year of the war in Algeria. But in November 1959, nine months after the German courts found the circumstances of Cécile's death to be sufficiently well established to award her son substantial compensation, the French authorities finally issued the special decree stating that she "would have been entitled to the status *died for France* had she been of French nationality". Perec had just passed his CS1 examination and was soon to be promoted to corporal, with better pay and conditions, and he was due ten days' leave in mid-December. But before he left for Paris, he knew he would never have to come back to Pau-Le Hameau. Even though the authorities had put it as a hypothesis (". . . had she been of French nationality"), the decree carried an automatic meaning for a conscript whose father had also died for France: exemption. Perec's release was in the bag when he stepped onto the platform of Gare d'Austerlitz on 10 December 1959. He had done all but three weeks of two full years in one of the toughest regiments in the French army. Retrospectively, and quite officially, he need never have done a day. In a way, it could all have been foreseen. But what a relief, all the same!

One evening, at a party in Paris, Perec heard Michel Martens attack the film that had won the top prize at Cannes the previous May. He took the head of his cinema section into a corner to talk him through *Hiroshima mon amour*. Almost until dawn Georges demonstrated, argued, persuaded, and finally convinced the younger man that it was the greatest work of film art that had yet been made. Martens had lost to a man with the intellect of a grand inquisitor, he said to himself as he walked home, reflecting that what he had learnt must be in accordance with the necessarily correct general line. He would not be able to write on *Hiroshima mon amour* for *La Ligne générale*, even if he was head of the cinema section: he had changed his mind, and shown thereby that he could not be relied upon to toe the general line.

In December 1959 Perec met a girl he had known for some years through Nour and through Amor Fezzani, who had now returned to Tunisia to become a diplomat. He asked Paulette Petras out, and they went to a bar, at Mabillon. Perec recalled years later in one of his written reminiscences of the place that what they had both wanted was a coffee, but the bar served only rum and suchlike. He could not afford it and had to tell Paulette that he did not have a sou. "Don't worry," she said, "I've got some change in my bag." When they got up to leave, in the confusion of putting on their winter coats, each thought the other had put the money down. On the pavement outside, they realised that neither had, and they ran off, laughing and a little scared of being already accomplices in crime. Soon after, they decided to settle down together.

Paulette was a student at the Sorbonne. She came from a working-class background, and was as penniless as Perec had been. She came to live in the maid's room at Rue de l'Assomption, pending a more permanent arrangement. It was not an easy time. Esther was perhaps secretly disappointed that Georges had chosen a non-Jew, and David may have been sorry that he was not marrying up; or perhaps it was Paulette's plainspoken commitedness to left-wing causes, or her feminist commitment to being just plain, that caused the friction between the generations. There was no family celebration of Georges's birthday in March, which was near enough Paulette's birthday, too. The young couple just munched a sandwich together on a bench near Place des Ternes and then went to see *North by Northwest*.

Lg was now at a critical stage. Articles on Lowry, Melville, *Hiroshima mon amour* and so on were ready, and the first issue could be sent to press. The group stuck to its decision to do nothing *against* the PCF. As it was hard to know in advance what the PCF would think of Lg's plan, a delegation was sent to ask. The party's "leading intellectual", Laurent Casanova, was not personally hostile to the ideas the youngsters proposed to elaborate in a new review to be called *La Ligne générale*. But the decision had already been made by an apparatchik, Gaston Plissonnier. No rival to *Les Lettres françaises* and *La Nouvelle Critique* (respectively the party's literary and intellectual organs) would be permitted. Casanova attacked the young men from Lg, accusing them of "left deviationism" in advance, and threatened to have them expelled from the UEC if they persisted. First the big stick, then a slender carrot: if Lg renounced its own review, then its members might find their work accepted for publication in *La Nouvelle Critique*. The offer was turned down flat.

Perec and Kleman could certainly have edited a challenging new quarterly, and they might well have made an impact on French culture in 1960. The enterprise was not fundamentally flawed, only doomed by the decision to make PCF approval a condition. It is true that the review could not come out without a backer, to fund printing and distribution costs at the start. But many others have been told to publish and be damned and have gone on to make their mark. Why did Lg prefer not to publish, and to avoid the PCF's damnation? Its supplication to Casanova was naive, the outcome entirely predictable: the PCF had an obvious interest in suppressing a review that it could not control and that, if successful, could only dent the circulation of its own publications. Lg's wish for PCF approval and its abandonment of publication plans on being rebuffed have to be seen as symptoms of some kind of inner collapse, and also, very clearly, as an indication of the PCF's authority over French intellectual life.

Casanova's *non fiat* killed the review, but it did not kill the ideas of Lg or split its inner circle, which now consisted almost exclusively of Jews and *normaliens*. Members carried on reading, drafting, and debating as a collective for many years more. Perec went on summoning and attending meetings, and doing a great deal of work for them, but from the spring of 1960 he knew that no Latin Quarter bookshop would ever display on its magazine rack a new periodical (*General Editors: Georges Perec, Roger Kleman*) announcing in its title, with the arrogance of youth, that it constituted *La Ligne générale*.

Based on a letter from Georges Lambrichs to Georges Perec [FP 31,2,22]; a letter from Amor Fezzani to Philippe Guérinat; letters from Perec to Jean Duvignaud, Pierre Getzler and Jacques Lederer; Perec's reminiscences of Mabillon [FP 57, 14] and of Place des Ternes [FP 57, 26]; and the recollections of Marcel Benabou, Claude Burgelin, Michel Martens, Henri Peretz, Dominique Frischer, Pierre Getzler, and others.

CHAPTER 22

Who *Was* Gaspard Winckler?

When the PCF put its buffer in front of *La Ligne générale*, formerly *La Locomotive*, it deflected Perec's energy back into *Gaspard*, which he now rewrote, shortened radically, and renamed *Le Condottiere*. It had been a long haul. On Thursday, 25 August 1960, at Druyes-les-belles-fontaines, where Paulette's mother lived, Perec completed the final version of the story he had been working on for nearly three years, and after putting his signature after the last sentence of the 157-page typescript, he thumped out on the old Underwood *endendendendend* across a whole line along with a serious warning to his editor: *YOU'LL HAVE TO PAY ME ABSOLUTELY MASSES TO MAKE ME START OVER AGAIN.*

Le Condottiere is the story of Gaspard Winckler, told twice over, first in simultaneous narration and then retrospectively, in the form of a confession to Streten, the Serbian painter who was first introduced in *L'Attentat de Sarajevo*. Perec may have envisaged linking the two novels through reappearing characters, in the manner of Balzac, but it is also possible that the reuse of the name meant that the old Sarajevo plot had been killed off and was now buried.

The novel begins with Gaspard Winckler dragging the corpse of his paymaster, Anatole Madera, whose throat he has just slit, down the staircase of the millionaire's French country seat at Dampierre. *Madera was heavy* are the first words of the text. Madera's factotum, Otto Schnabel, comes upon the scene, forcing Gaspard to barricade himself in his basement studio-laboratory. How can the criminal escape? He decides to dig a tunnel from the laboratory into the grounds (whence Perec's request, in the summer of 1958, that Philippe Guérinat do some research for him on the composition of the subsoil, on pneumatic drills, and so on: Gaspard's tunnel must have been first dug in the very earliest versions of this tale). As he digs, Gaspard reflects on his failure. He had approached the greatest challenge of his career – in retrospect, his only real challenge – with all the resources that an infinitely wealthy patron could provide, and with all the technical gifts of the world's greatest, still-undiscovered art faker: himself. He had used wood of the right period, with genuine wormholes; he had concocted a *gesso duro* of the correct chemical composition; he had fabricated the right paints and colours; and he had applied to the finished image a varnish that cunningly simulated the *craquelure* and patina of age. What he had aimed for was not a copy of an existing portrait by Antonello da Messina but a *new* picture that would be both an Antonello *and his own*. Despite the seven months of seclusion he had devoted to this single counterfeit portrait, Winckler had muffed it. His work may have had all the technical qualities of a genuine Antonello, but even a moderately sensitive eye could see that it lacked the one thing that made an Antonello unmistakable: it lacked life. He was not a real painter. He could have killed himself; instead, he had taken a razor to the throat of his manipulator. There is just a shade of Camus's *The Outsider* about Gaspard's lack of remorse, and perhaps a vaguer tinge of Gide's once-fashionable doctrine of the *acte gratuit*.

The tunnel is ready; Otto is still waiting outside the laboratory door, like an implacable and patient Alsatian. He must have heard the noise of tunnelling and is no doubt ready to rush round and grab the forger when he makes his break. Gaspard telephones the local exchange from his lab and asks the operator to test the line to the house. When the telephone rings, Otto will dash in the other direction to answer it, enabling Gaspard to make his escape into the garden, onto the road, and far away.

Dampierre, the name of the place where the twin crimes of forgery and murder are committed, is the name of a real stately home to the west of Paris, but it is also the name of a tiny village down the road from the Bienenfelds' weekend home at Blévy. It is used again by Perec in *La Boutique obscure* ("The Darkshop"), a book of dream transcriptions published in 1973, to replace the name of a different country house. In *Le Condottiere*, it seems to link Perec's fantasy of art and crime to the house at Blévy, where the writer himself had played at painting in his teens.

The second part of the novel, which is almost exactly the same length as the first, is cast as a long conversation in Belgrade between Winckler and Streten, in the role of father confessor. Winckler now paints in words the portrait of a young forger whose long-suppressed ambition it was to rival and to surpass the greatest artists – all but one of whose works he could easily reproduce – so as to be able to say: *I, too, am a painter*. (Perec himself later faked a Correggio of exactly that name, *Anch'io son' pittore* [*UCDA* 65].) Winckler's early life echoes Perec's own in a vague but significant way – he had been sent as a child to an Alpine resort for safety during the war, adopted by a mentor who exploited his gifts, and cut off from his parents, who had fled to America and with whom he had had no further contact. Winckler had been educated in Geneva and New York, obtaining qualifications that allowed him to hold a part-time job as a restorer of works of art, to serve as a cover for his real career as an art forger, first as assistant and then as successor to the great Jérôme Quentin. His patron, Rufus Koenig, sold the products of the secret atelier in Gstaad through his own gallery in Geneva. Behind Rufus stood Madera, the ultimate master of the fake-art ring, whom Winckler had met only when the crucial challenge was laid before him: to fake a painting that would sell for 150 million francs. Winckler had chosen to invent an Antonello partly for technical reasons, but it is gradually made clear that the technical side was no more than a convenient excuse. What really inspired him was the look in the eye of the man in the portrait known as *Il Condottiere*, a look of calm brutality and boundless self-confidence that would forever crush all who, by looking, were looked at – that is, unless that uniquely energetic visage could be simulated, and thus mastered, like everything else, by the patient application of the faker's technique.

For twelve years (the traditional length of a Renaissance painter's apprenticeship) Winckler had led a charmed life, with all the money he wanted. He had taken breaks in luxury hotels when he felt like it, travelled first-class or by air taxi when it suited him. His hundreds of more or less interesting forgeries (many of them very similar to items that Perec probably saw in the exhibition of fakes at the Grand-Palais in 1955) had earned him a handsome living, but Winckler had come to realise that they stopped him from ever being himself.

> *It's not that I ever felt guilty . . . no, it wasn't that at all . . . I've never had a bad conscience because I was making fakes . . . Between a counterfeit Chardin and a genuine Vieira da Silva, I would take the Chardin option any day . . . If I had been a real painter, I don't think I would have done anything remotely good enough to be accepted . . . I had been convinced of that for ages . . . but that wasn't the issue . . . What I was doing had no meaning, but that's not what mattered . . . I don't know how to put it . . . What I was doing could not lead anywhere else . . . I had no chance of escaping*

. . . All that was left to me was to go through the history of art. Every painter, engraver, sculptor . . . In alphabetical order . . . do you see? Antonello, Bellini, Corot, Degas, Ernst, Flémalle, Goya . . . etc . . . you see? Like kids who amuse themselves by finding a writer, a painter, a musician, a capital, a river, and a country that begin with the same letter . . . There you are. I was reduced to carrying on with a brainless game. [*Le Condottiere*, ff. 97–98]

One of the forgery jobs that Winckler refers to repeatedly in his self-portrait is his fabrication of a hoard of gold and silver medals and jewels, which he had made in a secret workshop set up in the very vaults of Diocletian's palace at Split. This underground adventure seems to announce his later escape from Dampierre by tunnel (or rather, in the novel's back-to-front structure, to echo it, adding a psychological note to the forger's bizarre means of escape). But the episode also casts a strange light on the barely fictional Mila, the only woman who had ever really mattered in Winckler's life, and who, like Streten, is taken over from *L'Attentat de Sarajevo*, where she stands for the real-life Milka Čanak, *mila Milka*, an expert on classical antiquities. It is almost as if Perec were trying to tell Milka that the treasure she had studied at Gamzigrad might also have been made by Gaspard, *his* Gaspard – that is to say, by Perec himself.

Perec's later reference to *Le Condottiere* as *the first more or less complete novel that I managed to write* [*W* 108] is borne out by the typescript, only recently rediscovered. The novel of 1960 is an ambitious fictionalised reflection on the relationship between the true and the false, between the artist and the world. A good deal of art-historical research went into it. As in *L'Attentat de Sarajevo*, Perec pastes in material from other sources, but now he does so more effectively. Winckler's explanations of painterly technique owe much to standard works, and the career of his mentor, Jérôme, as well as his own, is a plausible amalgam of the biographies of famous modern fakers such as Hans van Meegeren, Joni Icilio, and Alceo Dossena. These "foreign bodies" are fictionally plausible in the mouth of the forger and art historian Winckler, and do not give themselves away. (There is no reason to suppose, for example, that Winckler could not quote from Vasari in Italian, as he does on folios 133–134, even if Perec himself had little knowledge of that language.) As Winckler's confession proceeds, however, it turns by degrees into an essay on the meaning of art, an essay of the sort Perec might have penned, with Roger Kleman, perhaps, or with Pierre Getzler, for *La Ligne générale*. *Le Condottiere* focusses increasingly on the one Antonello portrait that Perec had seen (for it is the only one in France), which gives the novel its name.

> *Why should one want the Condottiere? Who was the Condottiere? The painting of a triumph, or painting triumphant? Who had structured it all, made it all perceptible?* Antonellus Messinæus me pinxit. *And there he is, pinned to the panel, labelled, defined, finally brought within bounds, with his strength, his serenity, his certainty, his impassibility. What was art, if not this approach, this manner of defining an era, explaining and transcending it at the same time, explaining it by transcending, transcending it by explaining? That identical movement. Beginning we know not where, perhaps in the mere requirement of coherence, and ending in a complete, brutal, decisive mastery of the world . . . [. . .] Is that art? The revelation of rigour, order, and necessity? Why should that concern him? How did that justify him? What you did at Split . . .*
>
> [*Le Condottiere*, ff. 138–139]

Gaspard Winckler's monologue ends with an explanation of what had led him to murder Anatole Madera, and a last, obsessively detailed account of the act of slitting the rich man's throat. *I had the courage, yes, the courage to be done with him. I regret nothing!*

Perec adds an epilogue, as he was to do in most of his later novels.

> *The Condottiere is forever still. Inexpugnable, terrifying in his palpable perfection, he stares at the world with the cold eyes of a judge. You allowed yourself to be mesmerised by that glance, whereas you should have mastered it, explained it, overcome it, pinned it down on your panel.* Antonellus Messinæus me pinxit. *The Condottiere is not human. He knows neither struggle nor action. Beneath glass, in a red velvet surround, he has, once and for all, ceased to live. He breathes no more. He suffers no more. His mind is blank. You sought to reach him, and at first you believed that reaching him was what mattered. But the only thing that mattered was the movement you made towards him, that mere movement, the forward thrust of the body, the movement of your mind, of your will, of your effort. What you will reach will be elsewhere, after years and years of trial and creation, of fumbling, of exhaustion, starting over for the tenth, for the twentieth, for the hundredth time in search of your own truth, in search of your own experience, in*

search of your own life. The mastery of the world. Ghirlandaio,
Memling, Cranach, Chardin, Poussin. The masters of the world.
You will get there only at the end of a wearisome long march, just
like that team of climbers [. . .] who on a July dawn in 1939
reached, near the Jungfrau, a horizon they had long sought, and,
beyond the fatigue they felt and the joyous splendour of the sunrise,
were flooded by the radiant discovery of the other side of the moun-
tain, of the parting of the waters . . .

The Condottiere does not exist. But a man called Antonello da
Messina does. And like him you will go towards the world, seeking
order and coherence. Seeking truth and liberty. In this accessible
transcendence lies your epoch and your aspiration, your certainty
and your experience, your lucidity and your triumph.

[*Le Condottiere*, ff. 155–156]

Those of Perec's first readers who remember *Le Condottiere* admit to
having been baffled by it. Part thriller, part art history, and part essay,
it corresponds to no known genre and crosses the boundary between
high theory and low plotting in a way that only the founders of La
Ligne générale could have imagined at that time. On reading it now,
one finds it hard to suspend the fascination of hindsight, for *Le Condottiere* appears to resolve the later mystery of the revenge of Gaspard
Winckler (it is a different Gaspard Winckler, of course, but also, in a
sense, the same one) on Percival Bartlebooth, in *Life A User's Manual*.
It is even harder not to read into the epilogue an alarmingly prescient
announcement of the arduous path that Perec himself was to follow
thereafter. Without the illumination of hindsight, *Le Condottiere*'s first
readers can hardly be blamed for thinking the novel pretentious,
puzzling, perhaps even incomprehensible. Perec's first real work bore
little obvious relation either to conventional story-telling or to what
was considered avant-garde fiction in 1960.

All the same, *Le Condottiere* was Perec's laboratory of new techniques. The text alternates among first, second, and third persons,
bending the otherwise rigid rules of narrative. It is the first accomplished instance of Perec's mirror-story form, where one part
"throws back" meanings onto the other. It uses genuine erudition to
substantiate a story of faking, as if to presage Perec's later use of fake
erudition to decorate an art which he had then mastered. In 1960 no
one could have been aware of the potential that these strange devices
held, but despite the obscurity of its technical interest and its not

always convincing pastiches of Faulkner and Joyce, Perec's first complete novel was then and will ever remain a powerful, intellectually challenging, and emotionally disturbing work.

In *Le Condottiere*, the minuscule difference between *faking* and *making* is presented as the central issue of Gaspard Winckler's artistic life and by extension of all art. More recently, the gurus of postmodernism have denied that such a difference exists. Despite his present reputation as a postmodern master, Perec knew in 1960 that his creative project might release energies and grasp realities that were not simulacra at all, even if they could be approached only through the metaphor of the fake, or represented only through the techniques of the counterfeiter. The first Gaspard Winckler is a false orphan; because he is merely a forger, he is also a false image of Georges Perec. Winckler is a figure of Perec's anxiety, not of his ambition.

The disturbing element in all this is the text's suggestion of the author's involvement in the shabby drama of Winckler's failure. For where else could Winckler have got his rock-bottom self-esteem, where else could he have learnt the two-edged envy of artists greater than he, what else could have led him to find satisfaction of a sort in a bloody, alphabetic revenge? The murder of "A. M." (Madera's initials do not coincide with Antonello's just by chance) is, so to speak, a parallel primal scene, the originating fiction, wrapping up in a single package of art and crime that deeply buried resentment which would henceforth propel Perec forward through his extraordinary writing career, towards the last shimmering page of *Life A User's Manual*, with its chilling reversal.

The only known text of *Le Condottiere* (a carbon copy typescript) was kindly given to me by Alain Guérin.

The standard works which Perec used for his art-historical information probably included Alexandre Ziloty, *La Découverte de Jan Van Eyck et l'évolution du procédé de la peinture à l'huile du Moyen Age jusqu'à nos jours* (Paris: Floury, 1941) and Jean Rudel, *Technique de la peinture* (Paris: Que Sais-je?, 1950); contemporary works on forgery which he may well have consulted include Sonia Cole, *Faux Crânes et Faux Tableaux* (Paris: Hachette, 1958) and Guy Isnard, *Faux et Imitations dans l'art* (Paris: Fayard, 1959).

This chapter incorporates suggestions and information kindly provided by Pierre Getzler, Patrizia Molteni and Claude Burgelin.

georges perec

le condottière

roman

paris
navarrenx
druyes-les-belles-fontaines

1957-1960

pour jacques lederer

comme beaucoup d'autres, j'ai
fait ma descente aux enfers;
et comme quelques uns, j'en
suis plus ou moins ressorti

michel leiris - l'age d'homme

et premièrement je rappellerai
dans ma mémoire les choses que
j'ai ci-devant tenues pour vra-
ies, comme les ayant reçues par
les sens, et sur quels fonde-
ments ma créance était appuyée;
en après j'examinerai les rai-
sons qui m'ont obligé depuis à
les révoquer en doute; et enfin
je considérerai ce que j'en dois
maintenant croire

descartes

CHAPTER 23

Rue de Quatrefages

1960

Georges and Paulette set up their first home in the spring of 1960, in a flat that was not rented but bought, in Perec's name. Home ownership was less common in Paris then than it is now; amongst Latin Quarter loafers with high ideas and low incomes, it was almost unheard-of. Few of Perec's friends, if they had fantasised about spending their first million, would have thought of putting it into bricks and mortar: buying property smacked of compromise with bourgeois values. That explains why Perec played little part, and Paulette none at all, in finding and buying the flat; Aunt Esther did it all.

Esther had always wanted to "put a roof over the head" of her brother's son, and the windfall from West Germany allowed her to do just that. When talking to his friends, Perec was studiously vague about how he had come by his flat. It was none of their business, to be sure, but he was not averse to allowing them to believe that his eyrie had been thrust upon him by his "bourgeois" aunt and uncle.

Number 5 Rue de Quatrefages was an ideal address. The street is a quiet backwater in the heart of the Latin Quarter, a few minutes' walk from the Sorbonne, from the cinemas and bookshops of Boulevard Saint-Germain, and a stone's throw from the one open space in that part of the city, the Jardin des Plantes. Number 5 stands on the site of the old city prison, Sainte-Pélagie, where many famous writers had "done time" in the nineteenth century, and faces the splendid Paris mosque. The building itself is an L-shaped block, with the shorter arm facing onto the street. Georges Perec's perch was at the back of the longer arm. To reach the staircase, you pass through a dimly lit corridor under the street-facing side of the building and then enter a rectangular courtyard. It is not the anonymous cobbled or concreted space one might expect, but a patchwork of tiny garden plots laid out in a curious way. There are two tall trees, patches of lawn, bits of flowerbed, minuscule fences and tiny crooked paths leading to the three stairwell entrances, and, hidden under some overgrown laurel bushes, plaster busts, possibly of Greek demigods. The garden-yard of number 5 is so odd that it makes you laugh, and then smile, for it really is quite charming. It is one of those hidden crannies in central Paris where you can regularly hear birds singing.

The flat that Georges Perec bought with his money from Germany and with the practical help of his aunt Esther was on the top floor, under the eaves, at the back of the building. It was just as quaint as the courtyard it overlooked. It was a real find, but it was tiny, comprising just a three-cornered entrance hall, a triangular kitchenette, and a room bisected by a low beam. Two dormer windows were set into the sloping roof that formed both ceiling and wall on one side of the main and only real room in the place. To start off with, Georges and Paulette had little furniture, but even that was not easy to fit in. From one visit to the next, friends would find tables, chairs, and boxes in different places, shifted around in an attempt to discover the least inefficient way of using what was little more than thirty-five square yards. On the low beam on which all save Dominique banged their heads, Georges pinned a sheet of passport-sized photographs of all his friends' faces; on the wall he hung the mariner's chart that Bianca had given him in 1945, entitled *Carte particulière de la mer Méditerranée faicte par moy François Ollive à Marseille en l'année 1664,* and a reproduction, from the National Gallery in London, of *Saint Jerome in his Study* by Antonello da Messina, which shows the patron saint of translators at work in a wooden scriptorium that looks prophetically like a set of 1960s whitewood furniture modules from an ideal-home exhibition.[1]

Georges and Paulette did not abandon their friends or change their way of life after they acquired and moved into the flat. They would leave the key in the door so that people could drop in, take a beer from the fridge, and play a game of patience whilst waiting for others to call. They were no less part of the crowd for living together as man and wife; they made Rue de Quatrefages a base for the whole bunch. Their living together would be unstuffy, open and free. The real problem was that everything *else* had to be paid for.

On the first day of the new decade, 1 January 1960, the new franc replaced the old at a conversion rate of 100 to 1, with a hefty devaluation that was masked by the issue of new banknotes with lower

[1] The reproduction was a gift from Pierre Getzler. It is described in detail on pages 117–118 of *Espèces d'espaces*, a work dedicated to Getzler.

numbers on them. It was the symbolic inauguration of a kind of French renaissance. Over the following months came the launch of the world's most luxurious transatlantic liner, *Le France*, the explosion of the first French atomic device, and the opening of the first stretch of French motorway, from Paris to Orly Airport. Domestic deep-freeze machines became available, and the first Astérix cartoon album appeared. The new symbols of national wealth compensated for the Americanisation of daily life. Quixotic press campaigns were conducted by the conservative left, attacking television, comic books, and Livres de Poche, the first low-priced paperback reprints. But amongst the hundreds and thousands of things new and old that were now offered in shop windows and advertised in *L'Express* (an imitation of *Time* magazine), there were plenty that even left-wing intellectuals found tempting – far more, in any case, than Georges and Paulette or any of their friends could afford. They felt hemmed in. *They would have liked to be rich* [*T* 27].

There was no question of Georges's getting a proper job whilst Paulette completed her degree – not because he had no qualifications, but because he already had a career. He was a writer. He wore his status with modest and persuasive conviction. Not one of his friends doubted that Perec was a writer; it was merely a contingent fact that he was for the moment an unpublished one. It was only a matter of time, but in the interval Perec needed a means of survival. Many of the people he knew – from his cousin Lili to his old friends Philippe, Jacques, Marceline, Dominique, and Roger – had worked at different levels of the hierarchy of what was called market research. The work came in short, relatively well-paid bursts. It required no long-term commitment. It was an ideal way of keeping the wolf from the door.

Market research provides information about consumer preferences and motivations, on which companies can then base their production, marketing, and advertising strategies. The discipline came to France from America in the 1950s, with all its philosophical underpinning, its methodology, its notions of mass psychology, and its statistical finesses. The French took over the methods of American market research lock, stock, and barrel, and much of its jargon, too: English words such as *pool* (of investigators), *briefing*, *brainstorming*, and even *open-ended* (often misunderstood as "open and closed", *ouvert-fermé*) became French words around 1960. With his knowledge of English, Perec was at ease with the jargon. One of his first jobs in 1960 was to compile an annotated bibliography in French of American writing on directive and nondirective interviewing techniques [FP 74].

The lowest level of work in market research consists of accosting consumers of a specified type and asking them a set sequence of questions, ticking the Yes, No and Don't Know boxes on the form as appropriate. *Do you like ready-made mashed potato? If so, why? Because it's light? Because it's creamy? Because it's easy to make?* [T 37–38]. Filling in these kinds of questionnaires was a common enough way for students to supplement their allowances. However, it could be embarrassing to hang around school gates waiting to interrogate young mothers, and it proved much easier to ask people one knew already, or even to ask good friends to pretend they were young mothers, or middle managers, or retired ticket inspectors. In the end it was most efficient of all to imagine oneself in all these roles. Georges Perec taught Régis Debray how to get through up to three hundred instant alter egos in a night.

The second type of contract work generated by 1960s market research was the transcription of tape-recorded interviews with selected consumers. Perec did transcription work for Michel Jousse, under contract to the cosmetics firm L'Oréal and to Philips, makers of tape recorders and electrical appliances. Instead of boiling down digressive tapes to a set of main points, as others did, Perec scripted the mumbling, the pauses, and the unfinished sentences and even added stage instructions for gestures and grimaces in his subdramatic scenes between interviewer and interviewee. His transcriptions were unique.

The people who did the interviewing in the field went by the pompous name of *psychosociologues,* a new word signifying no particular expertise in sociology, nor in psychology, nor even in psychosociology, whatever that might be. "Psychosociologists" were just hired interviewers who worked in teams, applying the techniques of open-ended interviewing to allegedly significant samples of consumer target groups, seeking thereby to uncover the hidden structures of purchasing preferences. It is not difficult to get people to reveal almost anything once you have learnt the trick of steering them with well-placed *Hms?* and arched eyebrows. Sometimes the interviewers would take down the conversations with pencil and paper, but by 1960 tape recording was the norm. Cassette recorders had not yet been invented; market researchers had to hump to the four corners of France heavy Bakelite open-reel machines.

The market-research milieu was predominantly left-wing, and

attitudinal surveys done in the service of advertising were not unrelated to the concerns of Marxist sociology. In his *Critique de la vie quotidienne*, Henri Lefèbvre had sought to apply an old idea inherited from Hegel to the modern world of consumer capitalism: in an affluent society, or one that was fast becoming affluent, Lefèbvre argued, people came to define themselves as consumers: their lives, at the mundane and everyday level, were constructed according to the list of things they purchased, or wished to purchase, until in the end they were themselves no more than items on the list, mere *things* in the circuit of economic exchange. Volume one of Lefèbvre's *Critique* had appeared in 1958. In 1960, he was still at work on volume two, which was intended to support the broad denunciation of reification with examples and case studies from contemporary life. Lefèbvre set up a *"Groupe d'étude de la vie quotidienne"* and assigned his students various research projects on aspects of France's new love affair with things. What he asked them to do was often parallel to the kind of work being done professionally by market-research organisations such as IRES or IFOP, France's oldest established mass-observation company. Hearing that the industrial subdivision of the market-research branch of the latter (IFOP-ETMAR) was about to undertake a full-scale attitudinal survey of a mining community prior to the probable closure of iron-ore mines in Normandy, Lefèbvre introduced one of his protégés to the survey's director, Yvon Eizler,[1] and got him taken on to the interviewing team. Lefèbvre may have been helping out a young man in need of a job, but he was also placing Georges Perec as his informant inside a project whose results were supposed to be confidential to the mining company, the Société Métallurgique de Normandie.

The team of ten or or twelve freshly minted *psychosociologues* assembled for an American-style briefing in the offices of IFOP-ETMAR early in January 1960. Each had to present himself to his new colleagues. Amongst them was Pierre Bessis, who had done a postgraduate thesis on Hegel and then his military service before getting involved in market research; an elegant, if rather hesitant young man whose name was Denis Buffard; and a sloppily dressed, crew-cut youngster with warts and wide ears, who said, with quiet dignity, that he had studied history and sociology, was a writer, and was called Georges Perec.

[1] In some places Perec spells the name *Heisler*.

They all set off together for Caen by train, lugging tape recorders, clipboards, notepads and their working briefs. They lived in hotels but never saw much of each other, since they were out "in the field" at most mealtimes: their "targets" were working miners and their families, who had to be interviewed at home. In each household visited, the interviewer had to down an appropriate number of glasses of *calva*, the local apple brandy; not to do so would have been unfriendly. Pierre Bessis suffered terribly in trying to steer conversations nondirectively through what was, by the second or third interview each evening, an alcoholic haze. Perec said he liked it, quite a lot.

After ten freezing days in the still war-damaged city of Caen, Perec and Buffard were kept on in Paris by ETMAR to analyse and write up the results. They worked together at a desk in an office in the ninth arrondissement, beneath a slogan pinned to the wall: "Chassez le naturel, il revient au galop." When they were finished, Perec asked Buffard to come with him to present the data to Lefèbvre. Buffard declined (out of bashfulness, it seems), and so there is no retrievable record of what Perec said to the "daily-life study group" – nor, of course, of the survey report itself, which went in strict confidence to the board of the SMN.

Some time later, probably in the summer of 1961, Perec and Buffard teamed up again on a tape-recorded, nondirective interviewing campaign. It took them to the prosperous farming area of the department of Oise. They were based at Montdidier and descended on the village of Rollot to investigate the underlying structure of the agricultural mind. The big issues of the day, in Buffard's memory of that campaign, were the Common Agricultural Policy, which had just been invented, and the controversy over intensive versus free-range livestock farming.

Georges Perec's direct experience of market research, acquired principally in the first nine months of 1960, during his first experience of quasi-married life and alongside his activity in La Ligne générale, was not insignificant, but it fell a long way short of turning him into a professional sociologist, psychologist, or *psychosociologue*. He gained much more knowledge of the milieu, of its methods and its techniques, from his friends, at second hand. In several cases these potboiling adventures of youth evolved into adult careers, in public relations (Bessis), in market research (Buffard), or in advertising (Kleman and Lederer). Dominique Frischer also worked in market research until she thought of applying nondirective interviewing techniques to the customers of French psychoanalysis and made a name for herself with a book based on the results.[1] From those friends, from three of his early mentors – Duvignaud, Morin, and Lefèbvre and from his own brief sampling of practical sociology in the form of market surveying, Perec gleaned some of the ideas and attitudes that underpin the sociological dimension of his later work: for example, the idea that life can be grasped at the level of the things that people want, and acquire, and put on their shelves; or the realisation that the every-dayness of objects does not deprive them of meaning, or of passion; or the more technical lesson of constructed silence, which says that you learn far more by not asking questions directly.

Only one piece by Perec appeared in print in 1960. It was a substantial review of *Hiroshima mon amour*, written in collaboration with his "pseudo-cousin" Henri Peretz and published anonymously in *La Nouvelle Critique*, the review Kleman had turned down on behalf of Lg.[2] The prestige accorded to *Hiroshima mon amour* by the whole group at that time, Henri Peretz explains, came not at all from the fact that the script was by Marguerite Duras (indeed, she is barely mentioned in the essay that Peretz and Perec wrote). Rather, the film was taken seriously because it was directed by Alain Resnais, who had also made *Night and Fog*, the first (and government-funded) documentary on Auschwitz, withdrawn from the 1957 Cannes Festival at the request of West Germany. The commentary of *Night and Fog* was by Jean Cayrol, a poet who had been deported during the war, though not to an extermination camp. The words that accompany Resnais's images of corpses being bulldozed into mass graves in that film are consciously echoed in Perec's later works.

Hiroshima mon amour has two plots. One of these involves a love affair between a Japanese architect-politician and a French actress playing in a peace-propaganda film being shot on location at Hiroshima after the war; the other is the story of a girl who is seduced by a German soldier at Nevers, then imprisoned by her own family at the Liberation, and finally allowed to escape (by bicycle) to Paris. Both female roles are played by Emmanuelle Riva, but the first-time viewer realises only gradually that the two characters are the same. Resnais does not mark the earlier story as a flashback: it does not

---

[1] Dominique Frischer, *Les Analysés parlent* (Paris: Stock, 1973).

[2] [Georges Perec and Henri Peretz], "La Perpétuelle Reconquête", *La Nouvelle Critique*, May 1960, pp. 77–87.

precede but rather runs parallel to the Hiroshima tale. No wonder the film appealed to the author of *L'Attentat de Sarajevo*! Resnais's editing gives accomplished form to Perec's own intuition that meaning might emerge from alternation. *Hiroshima mon amour* deals with the task of facing up to horror, not simply in Nevers and in Hiroshima but in the parallels and the gaps between the two; simultaneously, it is an essay in film on the nature of memory, cast throughout in a kind of present tense.

Hiroshima mon amour was a beacon of hope for Georges Perec. It proved that it was possible to confront both horror and memory and to produce from the otherwise ungraspable concerns that were already his own a total vision, in which *reality is unveiled in its true dimensions, in a world of relationships where at first everything seems incoherent but where little by little connections are made*. It is the sort of statement used by the setters of examination papers. It would make a good essay-question on Alain Resnais's film; but it would serve just as well as an invitation to discuss the later work of Georges Perec.

Despite their concertina budgets, Georges, Paulette, and their network of friends led a jolly, carefree life in 1960. Paris belonged to them, with its films, its bookshops, its galleries, its flea markets and antique dealers' shop windows. They ate together, played cards for hours on end (bridge, poker, or a simpler, interminable game called *le barbu*), and spent whole nights on Monopoly and Scrabble. Money earned in a lump from a market-research contract would be spent straightaway, on posh food or on wine, at the flea market or at the jumble sales organised by the good ladies of the English colony, at Saint George's Church Hall. "We were outrageous snobs," one of the group now recalls with a laugh. As soon as he could afford it, Roger bought himself a pair of smart English shoes. Perec followed suit. One day Pierre Getzler too would be shod in Westons. They all searched for coherence in ideas, in art, and in the vague, still-unexplored area of everyday life. They tried to imagine forms that might allow a vision of modern life in which Eisenstein, Stendhal, *Saint Jerome*, Paul Klee, Howard Hawkes, and leather brogues would all have a place. It would take a life's work.

Based on the recollections of Mireille Archinard, Pierre Bessis, Ela Bienenfeld, Denis Buffard, Regis Debray, Dominique Frischer, Pierre Getzler, Michel Jousse, Henri Lefèbvre, Henri Peretz, and others.

CHAPTER 24

Sfax

October 1960–June 1961

They were all young in 1960, but for many of them – friends from
Etampes, from Lg, from market research – it was time to settle down:
Dominique was pregnant; Roger would shortly have to start earning
a real living; Jacques's military service would soon be over, and he
would get a job and a flat with Mireille, Jean Crubellier's old girlfriend; they would be married before the end of the year. Noureddine
Mechri decided go back to Tunisia, to a job virtually designed for
him by his old classmate Ridha Jemmali, at the newly established
state film-production company, SATPEC. Jean Duvignaud, Perec's
teacher and pilot from Etampes to *Arguments* and Gallimard, was also
leaving, to take up a chair in sociology at the University of Tunis.
In the summer of 1960 Georges and Paulette saw Henri Chavranski,
back from his secondment in Morocco. He spoke of his disappointment with life in North Africa, of the cultural as well as material
poverty of Rabat and Marrakesh, of the highly perishable appeal
of exotic scenery. With the authority of convictions unsullied by
experience, Paulette and Georges firmly told Henri that he was turning into a closet colonialist.

Paulette had a temporary job at the Louvre that summer, as a
catalogue assistant. A colleague mentioned that there were teaching
posts available in Tunisia even for candidates with incomplete qualifications. Georges agreed that she should apply; the decision was
reached quickly, without argument or a great deal of thought. The
application was put in late but it was nonetheless successful. In
Tunisia, where life was cheap, one salary would be enough for two.
Perec would go with her, and get on with his work.

Le Condottiere had been typed up in four copies, one of which was
now with Gallimard, with another couple in circulation amongst
Perec's friends. Jacques Lederer, Claude Burgelin, Jean Crubellier,
and Jean Duvignaud each had it in front of them for a while, and no
doubt many others did, too. *Le Condottiere* was the only really com-

plete thing any of the young bunch had yet managed to produce, and they were all proud of it for that reason, if for no other. It was manifest proof that all their talk, their comradeship, their way of life, could result in something more than hot air. They kept their embarrassment to themselves. Claude Burgelin admits that even he did not understand then what Perec's famous forger was doing in a tunnel. Roger Kleman prefers not to say what he thought of Perec's art history, but there is no hint that he or anyone else was bowled over by the long-awaited creation.

Paulette received a Tunisian residence permit with her appointment to a teaching post. Perec, however, had no right of residence in his own name. He could enter the country as an accompanying spouse, but first he and Paulette would have to marry. It was something of a formality. On 28 September he wrote to Philippe Guérinat:

> Dear Phil
>   1) *We should be off to Tunisia by the end of October.*
>   2) *We're getting married around 20 Oct.*
>   3) *My book's been accepted.*

The first two assertions turned out to be true; the third did not. Lambrichs's letter of rejection, dated 3 October 1960, must have reached Perec at Rue de Quatrefages. He could not accept what Lambrichs was saying and wrote back to query his meaning. It was not until Perec was in Tunisia that things became absolutely clear to him.

Georges and Paulette tied the knot officially on 22 October 1960, at the *mairie* of the fifth arrondissement. The event was as unceremonial as the *faire-part de mariage* that Perec had sent to his old friend Phil. Esther and David were not informed; Lili did not attend.

A problem arose when the time came to fill in Perec's profession. He was a writer, that was obvious, but the pettifogging deputy assistant mayor who was conducting the proceedings that Saturday morning insisted on checking the official list of permitted professions to see if Perec's self-description was there. It turned out that *écrivain* ("writer") was not on the list. So what would it be? Perec settled for *homme de lettres*, "man of letters".

The following Saturday there was another marriage, this one between Pierre Getzler and Denise Roubaud, a teacher and translator of English, whose brother Jacques Roubaud was a professional mathematician. The newly-wed Perecs met the newly-wed Getzlers in a café later that rainy afternoon. They handed over the keys of Rue de Quatrefages to Pierre and Denise, and went on to the Gare de Lyon to board the night train for Marseille, whence they would sail, the next day, for the coast of Africa.

They knew before they left that Paulette had been posted not to Tunis but to the second city, Sfax, halfway to the Libyan border. They probably did not realise just how long it would take to cover the three hundred kilometres from Tunis to Sfax by train, by bus, or by car – a whole sweltering day, or a long and sticky night. When one gets there, there is not that much to see. The old Arab city, the medina, is a walled fortress that looks spectacular from a distance, but strikes Europeans who enter it as disturbing and alien. The French town is laid out on a grid on flat land between the station and the port, forever covered in desert dust and in potash from the mines at Gafsa, which is loose-loaded onto freighters day and night in the docks. The town centre is a single roundabout at the junction of Avenue Hedi-Chaker, named after the father of Perec's classmate from Etampes, and Avenue Habib Bourguiba, which leads triumphantly to the railway station, the fairest prospect that a Dr Johnson would have espied in the place. Its main feature of interest is a small museum on the ground floor of the town hall, containing a few entrancing mosaics from Roman villas excavated nearby. Opposite the town hall stood the Hotel Mabrouk, and on the other corner of the town centre square there was a café, then called Café de la Régence, now Café de la Paix. There were a few cinemas and not much else, save some sprawling, dirty, semi-industrial suburbs with shacks and houses that look to untutored European eyes like permanent building sites.

By mid-November, Georges and Paulette had moved into a flat that was the antipodes of Rue de Quatrefages. In a modern concrete block in Rue Larbi Zarouk (or Al-Arbi Zarruk) they rented three vast, square rooms with bare plaster walls and high ceilings. They had been accustomed to a cramped little nest; now they had an echo-chamber. They were only a few yards from the fishing harbour, a raw concrete basin that came alive every morning with fishermen in multicoloured boats selling their catches of sardine and squid. Their proximity to the docks also meant, however, that the smell of potash was overpowering whenever the wind blew in its prevailing direction.

They did what they could to make a homely space out of one of the rooms, with a bit of carpet, orange-box furniture, and shelves for their books, and they carefully stuck up once again the sheet of pass-port photographs of all their friends. Whilst Paulette saw to her classes at the Collège Technique, teaching French literature to bewildered Tunisians, Georges settled into a routine of reading and writing. He was not much taken with his exotic surroundings. *Yes, there are palm trees*, he wrote to Jacques.

> *And so what? White, wide streets, little shrines, street-sellers, min-arets, and so on and so forth. It's sunny. All that's entirely uninter-esting. What's most important for me, here, is still French culture and the French novel since the Liberation. My card index is as big as that. Do you see? No, a bit bigger still. Cards, cards, cards. Enough filing cards to make Roro blush.*[1]

Georges spent his mornings wading through the postwar French novel. He read the *hussards*, the "anticommitted" writers of the 1950s, Blondin, Weber and Nourissier. He read the "new novelists", Claude Simon, Robbe-Grillet (*The Labyrinth*), and Michel Butor, whom he put in a quite different category; and he read a whole variety of modern authors, from Kateb Yacine to Michel Zeraffa, including his old schoolmaster M. Poirier (writing as Julien Gracq), Roger Vail-land, Henri Thomas, Castillo, Gamarra, and Guilloux.

Perec wrote a good deal in Sfax, but none of it was published and not much of it has survived. He drafted an article on Claude Simon, perhaps for Lg, in which he attacked the retreat into art for art's sake. Simon's aesthetic despair, Perec said, was *fashionable nihilism*, an attribute of that part of the bourgeoisie which thinks of itself as left-wing but which has lost its faith in communism. Simon made him wonder whether there was any real difference between right-wing and left-wing fiction, or at least between what passed for either one in those days.[2]

Perec took a much kinder view of *John Perkins*, by Henri Thomas, winner of the 1960 Médicis Prize. Thomas, Perec maintained, pro-vided an accurate and objective depiction of the contradictions of the American way of life, in a novel that was also in part autobiographi-

---

[1] "Roro" was Roger Kleman. The whole bunch kept their "babynames" amongst themselves in adult life: Perec was still "Jojo", Henri Peretz "Riri", and so on.

[2] Georges Perec, "Situation du roman français contemporain". Unpublished typescript dated 18 January 1961 [FP 119, 13].

cal. In his overview of Thomas's oeuvre, Perec stressed that it formed a single entity, and he surmised that all of the novels gave Thomas a way of putting his own life into words.[1] Perec seems to have been talking here as much about his own intentions in literature as about the subject of his review. What he valued in Thomas corresponded to the ambitions he nourished on his own behalf: realism, irony, coherence, and self-depiction.

It was a year of emptinesses: an empty flat, a city empty of friends, an empty future. The rejection of *Le Condottiere* was a big blow, though Perec put a brave face on it: *I read somewhere that the same thing happened to Sivoir de Beaumone and to Sartrimself*, he joked in a letter to Jacques. He would come back to the book in ten years' time, he said, and then turn it into a masterpiece, or else he would wait in his grave until some faithful scholar unearthed it in an old box that had once belonged to Jacques. But when the idea arose of his seeking the help if not of "Sartrimself" then of Bianca's friend Simone de Beauvoir, Perec instructed Jacques most urgently to take his copy straight round to the Lamblins' flat. *It's the only chance to get zebuk published. A slim one, to boot.* Two months later he reported back. "Civoire de Beaumone" had read *Le Condottiere*: she had not liked it, but had stopped short of telling Bianca that her cousin should abandon writing altogether. It is not at all surprising that Beauvoir was not enthusiastic about an early Perec novel; neither did she enjoy *Life A User's Manual* when it appeared, in 1978. It would be hard indeed to find a French writer with less Perecquian affinity than she.

Meanwhile, in the sweaty gloom of Sfax, Perec was trying to write *the story of a chap on a stove, he gets hot, he says to himself that God exists and so he does, too:* yet another workout on René Descartes, whose unbroken presence in Perec's mind from the moment he decided to be a writer in his *classe de philo* is marked by the epigraphs in *Le Fou* (1956) and *Le Condottiere* (1960) and plain to see in the accounts given to friends of *La Nuit* (1958) and *Toplicin Venać* (1959). The novel of 1961 was entitled *J'avance masqué*, a translation of *Larvatus prodeo*, Descartes's motto, which Roland Barthes likewise plundered, as in his 1959 review of Raymond Queneau's *Zazie in the Metro*: "[Queneau] dons the mask of literature but points it out at the same

[1] Georges Perec, "*John Perkins*, de Henri Thomas". Unpublished typescript [FP 119, 17].

time. That is a very difficult thing to do."[1] Perec's Cartesian project rapidly elided with another planned novel about a proof corrector, originally dubbed *Le Pêcheur de perles* ("The Pearl Fisher"), after an opera by Bizet. By February 1961 the two books had become one, and there was at least a detailed plot summary for *J'avance masqué*, if not a more than half-finished draft. Its hero was not a pearl fisher but a pearl trader (just like Perec's uncle David), working in the Philippines, on the island of Palawan. The novel was to have (once again) a double structure: a story about the advance of Communist insurgents on the estate where the pearl trader lives would be overlaid on the pearl trader's attempts to write about his own life.

> In *J'avance masqué, the narrator tells his life story at least three times, the three tellings being equally false ("a written confession is always untruthful": I was full of Svevo at the time) but perhaps significantly different from each other.*   [*Jsn* 10–11]

Why Palawan? Because it was both the poorest and the most Americanised place in the world, Perec told Jacques. But there was another reason, too: Denise Getzler was translating the biography of Ramon Magsaysay, the president of the Philippines from 1953 to 1957, and could send Georges the background information he needed. *It's quite like* Le Condottiere, *but a suppler and subtler version of it,* Perec admitted. It was also quite like *L'Attentat de Sarajevo*:

> I must get my subject right at last: a book that puts itself into question, that denies itself, a hypocritical book, a book that cheats but works nonetheless [. . .] and then I'll move on to a different register.

Perec completed *J'avance masqué* and submitted it to Gallimard before he returned to France for the summer of 1961. Lambrichs acknowledged receipt and had the novel read, as was normal at Gallimard, by three members of the firm's reading panel. Their confidential reports are apparently still in the firm's files: Perec's novel was turned down, and the typescript of it has long since disappeared.

In Sfax, the Perecs hardly mixed with the expatriate set, and saw little of Georges's Tunisian pals from Etampes. Paulette's old boyfriend, Amor Fezzani, was now a consular official in Benghazi, and

---

[1] Roland Barthes, "Zazie et la littérature" (1959), reprinted in *Essais critiques* (Paris: Le Seuil, 1964), pp. 125–131.

M'hammed Chaker, with his dozens of cousins, was far too important to hobnob with French intellectuals who had not made it. The
Perecs bumped into Jemmali in a bookshop in Tunis: he was a big
shot as well, in the Ministry of Information. Nour was at work on
his film about the Jews of Djerba when he was not at the SATPEC
studios at Gammarth. Of all Perec's Tunisian classmates, the only
one mentioned in his few known letters from Sfax is Abd-el Kader
Zghal, who was in contact with Jean Duvignaud.

Duvignaud took up his post in Tunis in January 1961 and rented a
house at Carthage. Perec went to see him more than once and was
talked into doing academic work again. He enrolled in Duvignaud's
department, began to read Gurvitch (*what a pain!*), and sent in an
essay. "Dear Georges", his professor replied. "Your essay is brilliant
and potty [. . .]. There are two solutions: either you rewrite your
essay as an academic piece of work, or you do me another one. Title:
'The Concept of Social Class'."

Duvignaud's own work that year was an interdisciplinary study of
life in an Arab village and he frequently passed through Sfax on his
way to and from the place.[1] Once he took Perec back with him for
a short stay with the Hensons, a wealthy Anglo-American society
couple who divided their time between Florence and a house by the
sea at Hammamet. In the well-watered microclimate of the bay, Dar
Henson was a magical place. The house itself comprises a discreet
clutter of small buildings of different shapes, connected by pathways,
arcades and bowers. The interiors are treasure stores of curios and
works of art both ancient and modern: but it is the gardens that make
the place unique. Crisscrossed by paths and little canals, designed
around Greek and Roman columns, arches, busts, and statuettes,
the Hensons' garden, their life's work, is a perfect private world of
subtropical luxuriance. It has been described in print by some of the
writers who were guests of the Hensons at different times.[2] Perec's
own description of it, in *Things* [*T* 117–118], where it figures as an
oriental paradise visited by Jérôme and Sylvie, is not overwritten.
Dar Henson really is a dream.

[1] The work resulted in an important book: Jean Duvignaud, *Chebika. Mutation
dans un village du Maghreb* (Paris: Gallimard/ New York: Pantheon Books, 1968).

[2] See for example Catherine Hermary-Vieille, *Le Jardin des Henderson* (Paris:
Gallimard, 1988); Michel Tournier, *Le Vent Paraclet* (Paris: Gallimard, 1977),
p. 260, and "Cinq Jours, Cinquante ans . . . à Hammamet", in *Petites Proses*
(Paris: Folio, 1986), pp. 38–52.

Perec also travelled to other parts of Tunisia. Paulette went along when she had no classes and when they could get a lift or some other form of transport, for they had no car, and neither of them ever learnt to drive. They visited the desert, and they saw the Algerian border [*EsEs* 100]. They also went to Kairouan, where Paul Klee had stayed in 1914 with August Macke and his friend Moilliet, and where he had done some of his most celebrated canvases.

Memories of tourist sites must have seemed paltry by-products of a whole year spent in exile for the purpose of writing. On the main front, the period in Sfax was disastrous: *Le Condottiere* turned down to start with and *J'avance masqué* rejected at the end. But Perec did bring back a few scraps of value from his year in the sun.

The first was an encounter with Michel Butor. Perec read with care and made notes on *L'Emploi du temps,* Butor's first novel, which is set in "Bleston", a thinly disguised Manchester – quite as exotic a location as Sfax in French eyes. Perec insisted that Jacques Lederer send him Butor's theoretical essay, "Le Roman comme recherche" ("The Novel as Experiment"),[1] and after receiving it, he thought about it at length. The essay argues that stories connect us to reality: story-telling is part of our everyday lives, part of the world we con-struct for ourselves. The novel, however, is the workshop or labora-tory of storytelling forms. The whole point of the genre is to renew the ways in which we tell stories about ourselves and the world. That does not disconnect the novel from reality; rather, it means that *formal invention* is at the heart of what novelists do. In later years Perec would refer to Butor as the source of his personal conception of literature as a jigsaw puzzle with a blank piece in it, the blank piece being the writer's work in progress [*PAP* 36]. Butor does not actually use the metaphor of the puzzle in the article in question, but Perec's decoration remains faithful to Butor's main point.

The second Sfaxian scrap is a loose sheet dated 3 May 1961, contain-ing notes for an attack on *L'Express.* One of the projects set up by Lg was an analysis of the ideology of that perfidiously attractive publication. Paulette had taken on the task of deconstructing the image of the "modern woman" (successful, well dressed, simul-taneously maternal, ambitious, and seductive) as presented in the "tips" given in the women's column, "Madame Express". It was a

[1] Reprinted in Michel Butor, *Essais sur le roman* (Paris: Gallimard, 1975), pp. 7–14.

project that would live on and eventually provide the explicit material for one chapter of *Things*.

Perec kept in touch with his friends in Paris, and a small group also came to visit him, taking time out from an official exchange between Normal' Sup' and the Ecole Normale Supérieure de Tunis. Claude Burgelin and Marcel Benabou (and perhaps also other *normaliens*) made the long overnight bus trip to Sfax to see what their old pal was up to. They found him not up to much – distant, disconsolate, and depressed. They wandered round the town together, had a drink at a bar, and chatted. Perec was stuck. He was near the muddy bottom.

When the school year came to an end in the last days of June, the Perecs returned to France for the holidays. Pierre and Denise Getzler had left Rue de Quatrefages for a larger flat, more suitable for Pierre's work as a painter, in Rue de l'Ermitage, in the twentieth arrondissement, just round the corner from what was left of Rue Vilin. The Perecs' Latin Quarter cabin had been relet to Regis Debray, who, though he had regulation quarters at Rue d'Ulm, needed a place to be with his girlfriend. Georges and Paulette rented a house near Saumur with Roger and Dominique, for their first real holiday. The house turned out to be not very grand, equipped with rather more crucifixes than kitchen utensils. They ate and they slept, they drank and they talked, and they tried to get back to their old comradely ways. But neither Roger nor Dominique enjoyed eating and drinking in quite the way the Perecs did. They played games, in particular a French version of pick-up-sticks, a test of dexterity, patience, and elementary calculation. With his "crablike hands", Perec proved unbeatable. He played the game intensely, even obsessively, and as he always won, he began to get on the others' nerves. Roger Kleman had always been quick to take offence, but on this occasion it was Dominique who boiled over first. Her flash of temper spilled into a larger row, a slanging match in which old resentments came out of their bottles. It was not long before Georges and Roger made it up, but their wives never really got over the insults they hurled at each other.

The Perecs next descended on Philippe Guérinat. He had just finished his military service in Algeria, and the experience had affected him deeply. He had met a schoolteacher, Anne, whom he would soon marry, and for the time being the two of them were living in a suburban villa that belonged to Anne's parents. Philippe was looking for a job and a career; Georges and Paulette were not. To Anne it seemed as if they were set fair to become parasites, and she, as the only wage earner amongst them at that time, was alarmed. Paulette defended Georges's right to live as a writer, if necessary at the expense of others. Anne threw the Perecs out.

In July 1961 a quarrel of a different order broke out in Tunisia. Demonstrators paraded noisily in front of the last significant vestige of French colonial rule, the military base at Bizerta, on the Mediterranean coast northwest of Tunis. The soldiers inside reacted with stupid brutality and wrought murderous vengeance on the demonstrators and on the surrounding area. There was an international outcry. The United States lodged an official protest at the heavy hand of the French. Ambassadors were recalled, from Paris and from Tunis. Franco-Tunisian relations went into deep freeze, and cooperation treaties were put on ice. It became uncomfortable to be a French national in Tunisia. The Perecs were in France at the time, and in no danger from Tunisian reprisals for the Bizerta incident, but Paulette's contract, which had been expected to run for two years, was not renewed. They now had no job between them. The Perecs were back home, and they were beached.

Unattributed quotations in this chapter are from letters from Georges Perec to Jean Duvignaud, Philippe Guérinat and Jacques Lederer. Other information is taken from letters from Jean Duvignaud and Georges Lambrichs to Perec [FP 31,3,33], from letters from Perec to Pierre Getzler, and from the recollections of Marcel Benabou, Claude Burgelin, Henri Chavranski, Regis Debray, Jean Duvignaud, His Excellency M'hammed Chaker, Dominique Frischer, Robert Gallimard, Pierre Getzler, Anne and Philippe Guérinat, and Bianca Lamblin.

CHAPTER 25

Perec in the Lab

1961–1978

France Benoît, the girlfriend of Regis Debray, and hence the Perecs' tenant at Rue de Quatrefages, ran into her cousin André Hugelin at a family gathering in the summer of 1961. Hugelin was still in his thirties and already a medical professor, in charge of his own research unit at the Hôpital Sainte-Anne. He asked France if she knew of anyone who might be suitable for a new post that had just been awarded to his unit by the CNRS, the scientific research funding council. It was not exactly a secretary that he was looking for, though an ambitious and bright typist might be able to work her way into the job. What Hugelin was after was someone to fill the post of *documentaliste*, or scientific archivist. The job called for library skills, or at least a notion of information-retrieval techniques. France put in a word for her landlord, who was, she knew, quite desperate for work. Hugelin was sceptical. The man France was describing was no more than a stranded Left Bank intellectual, with no grounding in science, no education to speak of, and no vocational training, not even a typist's diploma. This Perec did not sound at all like the sort of person he had in mind for his lab. But France protested: Perec was a virtuoso when it came to filing and sorting! There was nothing he didn't know about information retrieval! He was the king of filing-card schemes! She must have been eloquent; in the end André Hugelin agreed that she could tell her landlord to call him.

France Benoît reported all of this to Perec, and he made the call. He spoke on the telephone so timidly and with such a high-pitched voice that Hugelin thought it was a woman enquiring about the vacant post. He began to answer, "Alors, chère mademoiselle . . .". Perec interrupted, *Je ne suis pas UNE documentaliste, Monsieur le professeur, je suis UN documentaliste. Voilà.*

Hugelin thought he should at least interview the candidate. The young man who came into his office at the appointed time looked awful. He was not dressed properly, not by lab standards, and he

appeared to be unwashed as well as sloppy. When he grinned diffidently, he bared blackened front teeth. Perec had no qualifications he
could prove beyond the baccalaureate: why not? Hugelin asked.
Because of my bad relationship with my uncle, he remembers Perec's
replying. What made him want a job as an archivist cum secretary?
Because he was a writer. It seemed odd. But the candidate was intelligent, to a high degree; he was keen, not just to get a job but to
involve himself in information analysis, storage, and retrieval. He
said he knew English well, which would be useful, since Hugelin's
own knowledge of the language was poor. Most important, he was
available there and then, and if an appointment were not made soon,
the post might be lost. So Professor Hugelin set aside his reservations
and appointed Georges Perec on the spot to the job that was to be
his for nearly two decades, that of *documentaliste,* graded for official
purposes as *Technicien IIIB.* He would start on 1 October 1961. Even
after his scale had been readjusted to that of *Technicien IIB* (when he
was able to prove that he had passed *propédeutique*) Perec's salary was
not much different from what a typist or a primary-school teacher
was paid.

Hugelin's research unit, officially CNRS Laboratoire Associé 38,
or LA 38 for short, was a province of the empire established by Paul
Dell, the rough-mannered buccaneer of French neurophysiology. At
the end of the war Dell had gone to the United States; when he
returned to France in the 1950s, the country was still extremely poor,
but contract work from the U.S. Air Force and funding from Marshall Aid programmes had enabled him nonetheless to set up his own
research laboratory devoted to the physiology of the brain stem. In
the 1960s, Dell's scientific enterprise spanned several distinct subfields. One of his assistants, Suzanne Tyc (later Tyc-Dumont),
specialised in the physiology of eye movement. Another member of
the team, Marthe Bonvallet, worked on the central nervous system
or CNS (in French, SNC), studying in particular cats' brains, a brace
of which she dissected every week. Henry Gautier, a medical doctor,
concentrated on human breathing but allowed himself to digress into
such respiratory curiosities as feline purring.[1] As for the laboratory's
primary focus and Dell's own specialism, the neurophysiology of
sleep and wakefulness, that was being carried forward by the rising

---

[1] J. E. Remmers and H. Gautier, "Neural and mechanical mechanisms of
feline purring", *Respir. Physiol.* 16 (1972), pp. 351–361.

star of the group, André Hugelin. By definition, no one knew which of these (or other) overlapping areas would come up with the first real breakthrough, but the common goal of the whole team was clear: they were to make a leap forward in the understanding of how the nervous system actually functioned in the head and win the Nobel Prize for it.

In October 1961 Perec became a staff member of the Laboratoire de neurophysiologie médicale (over which Paul Dell held sway for several more years) in a unit that was exclusively funded by the CNRS, not by outside contract work. Between 1961 and the mid-1970s, Hugelin's LA 38 grew just like Topsy: at its peak, it had a staff of around seventy-five, from medical doctors to scientific researchers, technicians, photographers, engineers, cat minders, secretaries, and typists, right down to one archivist cum information officer, who also happened to be a famous writer. In the serious world of medical research, that made not a whisker of difference.

Perec's statutory duties were to work forty hours a week, with thirty days' paid holiday a year. Hugelin was not an unreasonable *patron*, and he agreed from the start that Perec would be free to work the hours that suited him, provided that the job got done and the terms of appointment were respected overall. Some of the unit's work involved live animals and experiments in real time, so the premises were lit and the doors open round the clock. It was not unusual, in the 1960s, for his colleagues to find Georges Perec crouched over his typewriter late at night, with a Gitane or a Celtique burning in the ashtray beside him. No one in the lab recalls seeing him there at eight in the morning, however: Perec was not an early riser until much later in his life.

Perec's job was to organise the information contained in the unit's research library so that people could get out of it anything that might concern their current work. The unit subscribed to about thirty general and specialised scientific journals, but it lacked an indexing system for locating what was in them. Perec set about designing such an index, for a highly technical field about which he knew exactly nothing. It would have to be capable of answering very specific questions, typically along the lines of, What work has been published, by whom, in which countries, about ᵗhis part of the brain, using that technique and relating to such and such a hypothesis? The system also had to be a relatively open one, able to serve present and future research specialisms equally well. The first problem was one of categorisation: How could the field most usefully be divided up? How many different categories would be needed, and what were they? It is just the sort of quandary faced by the editors of cookery books. Should the index include entries for *lemon flavouring* and *garlic* as as well as for *soups* (cold) and perhaps *tomatoes* (ways of using), to allow the reader to access *gazpacho* under four rather than only two of its features? In a cookery book, of course, one can always flick through until one finds the relevant illustration, recipe title, or ingredient. In a research laboratory, in contrast, the sheer number of possible locations and the impenetrability to most scientists of work outside their own specialism rule out browsing as an information-retrieval device. There has to be a system that works, or else everyone wastes their time.

Dividing the field into its constituent categories was only the first part of the exercise. Next came the related problem of hierarchising the categories chosen. For instance, should an article reporting experiments on the hypothalamus of cats be indexed under "CAT: brain (hypothalamus)", or under "HYPOTHALAMUS, cat", or under "BRAIN: hypothalamus (feline)"? What is the least time-consuming way of linking, in a stack of say ten thousand articles, all those that contain references to both the hypothalamus and to cats? And this is but a trivial instance of the more general problem. The shortest line between two points is a straight one, but what is the shortest line connecting x points dotted randomly around n-dimensional space? (Before large computers came into general use, no one knew how to calculate with certainty the shortest route joining all 50 state capitals of the U.S.A., in merely two-dimensional space, and a large cash prize was offered – by a company with a vested, cable-laying interest in the matter – to anyone who could discover a formula that would demonstrably produce the right answer.) Someone mentioned to Perec that there was a branch of modern mathematics which tackled the general area of nonlinear solutions, called graph theory. Perec read his way into the field through the work of a distinguished mathematician who happened to be French, Claude Berge.[1] He could have had no idea at the time that Berge had recently joined a discreet little

[1] Claude Berge, *Théorie des Graphes et ses applications* (Paris: Dunod, 1958). Published in English under the title *Graph Theory and Its Applications* (New York: Methuen & Wiley, 1961).

group that called itself the *Ouvroir de littérature potentielle* ("Workshop for Potential Literature"), or OuLiPo.

Perec could have had no inkling either of the mathematics involved in graph theory. Jacques Roubaud, Pierre Getzler's brother-in-law, got to know Perec well around 1966 and recalls that he had no more mathematical knowledge than the average twelve-year-old. In 1961, however, Perec found something in graph theory that fascinated him, and he kept trying to tell his friends about it. *How many terms are there*, he would ask as a riddle, *between* ruban ("ribbon") *and* cadeau ("present")? The question would stump most people for a moment or two. *Aha! Just one!* Georges would interrupt with glee: *faveur* (a word meaning both "hair-ribbon" and "favour"). This was supposed to be an example of graph theory, as was the oft-repeated "fact" that between any two persons A and B chosen at random – let's say, the barman over there and the president of the Republic – there has to be a pathway connecting them through no more than two intermediate points (so that, for example, the barman's [A's] window-cleaner [1] would be the second cousin of the president's [B's] chauffeur [2]).

As part of his information-gathering tasks, Perec also set about reassessing the unit's sources of scientific knowledge. To supplement the journals under subscription and to afford a window on the wider world of scientific publishing, Hugelin used the abstracts in the *Bulletin signalétique*, published in French by the CNRS. Perec had first-hand experience of how the *Bulletin* was put together (on the arts side) and was sceptical of its value. He went to a talk about the handling of scientific information given by Eugene Garfield at the American Center, and came back convinced that *Current Contents* would provide a more reliable input into the system he was about to set up. In the end, Perec insisted on the change, and was given free rein. His *patron* was impressed with the scientific patter that his scruffy *documentaliste* had already acquired; the intensity of his interest in information management was striking. Hugelin congratulated himself on having made a good appointment.

The system could not be made to work with the sort of filing cards that Roger Kleman had taught Perec to use. It was no longer a matter of sorting things alphabetically, or chronologically, or by genre or theme; it all had to be organised every which way at once. Perec must have looked long and hard in specialised stationery catalogues before finding what he wanted: a card system called Flambo. Measuring 200 by 215 millimetres, Flambo cards have twenty-one numbered divisions printed along the top edge, with twin slits cut beneath each division so plastic tags can be inserted. Let us say tags of seven different colours are used. The Flambo system does not give just 147 (or 7 x 21) different combinations, nor even 168 (8 x 21) if the absence of any tag at all is counted as significant. It gives 8^{21} separate specifications, 8 to the twenty-first power, which is a very large number indeed. If the problems of categorisation and hierarchising are solved competently for the field in question, Flambo allows rapid and detailed interrogation of a database of considerable size. It might become impracticable beyond fifty thousand entries, given the physical dimensions of filing-cabinet drawers, but such a number would represent many years' output of articles in neurophysiology.

In consultation with the scientists in the unit and especially with his one real friend amongst them, Henry Gautier, Perec established the twenty-one field divisions and the colour-coding of the tags. He presented the projected system to Hugelin and was told to go ahead with it. On each card he would type the bibliographic reference for one article; then he would insert the appropriate tags into the relevant slots and put the card into the permanent file drawer. It no longer mattered what order the cards were in; instead of searching for a thematic heading or section of the index, one would look for, let us say, slots 7 RED and 9 GREEN, the "keys", perhaps, for RESPIRATION and CAT, and HYPOTHALAMUS and EXPERIMENTAL. As long as the cards were stacked in a line, their order was irrelevant to the search. The literary researcher's fear of dropping his index box and having to sort his filing cards into order all over again was a nightmare of the past.

Perec was expected to put away about four thousand Flambo cards a year, and he did. In practical terms, that involved scanning maybe a hundred highly technical articles or résumés every week, then typing up a reference for each and tagging the card under its key words. It was not a purely mechanical job; an elementary grasp of the contents was a sine qua non, for a Flambo system was no different from a computer: if you put garbage in, you got garbage out. In fact, Perec's information system was much admired, and word of it got around to other research laboratories. Emissaries would drop in for a chat, so it seemed, but while there they would also have a look at the cards, and the coding sheet. It is said that several similar systems were set up elsewhere in the following years.

Perec's virtuoso performance with the Flambo cards did not make him an equal among scientists, for he had no doctorate, nor even a first degree, and could only ever be a *Technicien IIB*. In French it is much trickier than it is in English to sidestep marks of social and professional hierarchy, since the language itself contains grammatical signs of status relations that are difficult to avoid in even the shortest conversation. It is neither natural nor correct to say just "Hullo" in French; one says "Hullo, darling", "Sir", "Mr Professor", "Smith", "Tracy", or "Mrs Mop", as the situation demands. Nor can one say "How are you?" without first deciding whether to use the singular and familiar form *tu,* or the plural, usually more formal *vous,* for the "you". The rules of usage are not absolutely uniform; there are specific variations for particular social and professional contexts. Because CNRS LA 38 was a unit staffed in part by medical doctors who rank higher than doctors of science, "hospital rules" applied. In the medical world, male colleagues address each other by their surname only (so "Bonjour, Gautier"); female scientists are addressed by male colleagues of equal rank as Madame (or Mademoiselle) followed by their surname; and nonacademic female staff are called by their forename, preceded by *Mademoiselle* (or *Madame*) when spoken to by their superiors. Relations between members of different generations or rank are signalled by the use of *vous.* "Comment allez-vous, Mademoiselle Yolande?" may seem to mean no more and no less than "How are you, Tracy?" but in fact it says many things about both Yolande and the person speaking to her that the plain English words do not communicate. In a medical environment, "Bien. Et comment vas-tu, Gautier?" would not be just a cheeky rejoinder to such a greeting; it would be a revolution.

Perec stuck out like a sore thumb in the conventional language system of the lab. He was not a woman and therefore could not be called "Madame Georges", according to the formula used for other staff of equivalent rank; nor could he be called "Monsieur Georges", as that would have made him sound like a janitor. Only the professors themselves were entitled to have the honorific appellation *Monsieur* coupled to their surname and then only when being addressed by a member of the lower ranks. For lack of a real alternative, then, Georges Perec was assimilated in this one respect to the status of scientific colleague, and was called simply "Perec" by the research team and by Hugelin. He wore a white coat at his typewriter, just to rub it in, for he was not in any other sense a ranking member. Hugelin could never have said *tu* to him; if Gautier used the familiar form, it was only because he became a real friend. To tease Henry for his lofty status, Perec never called him anything other than "Gautier" – even when he went skiing with him, or flying in his two-seater aeroplane.

On the one hand, Hugelin was not an illiberal, conventional or over-bearing boss by normal standards: he never enquired where Perec was when he was not in the lab, never made him apply for leave for his various absences abroad, never pressured him to go onto a part-time contract, and always turned a benign blind eye on his other activities, which might well have been considered improper by another *patron*, since Perec's standard contract as a full-time employee of the science research council explicitly forbade him to undertake other gainful employment. On the other hand, Hugelin gave Perec little sign of recognition and never thought of trying to get him promoted. (In principle, it was for Perec to request his own upgrading, but without a higher qualification, he would have stood little chance of success.) Perec came to resent the reserved, distant and condescending professor. He may even have hated Hugelin, and the whole hypocritical unit, whose members depended on his work for all their scientific information and even had him type up their applications for promotion to higher ranks and larger salaries, whilst they treated him as an oddity and paid him a pittance. Perec clearly enjoyed his work, perhaps even loved it obsessively, but he had no love for the lab itself.

In 1965 Hugelin's unit moved from its premises in Rue des Saints-Pères, and from the Hôpital Sainte-Anne, to new and much larger accommodation in the first purpose-built teaching hospital in Paris. Its new letterhead read:

UNIVERSITE DE PARIS – FACULTE DE MEDECINE

CENTRE HOSPITALIER ET UNIVERSITAIRE SAINT-ANTOINE

LABORATOIRE DE PHYSIOLOGIE

27, RUE CHALIGNY
PARIS-XII

An information-storage-and-retrieval scheme even grander than Flambo could now be envisaged. Perec researched the alternatives and came up with Peekaboo, a system of cards with number-coded locations around all four sides that could be hole-punched using a mechanical, number-driven device. Each hole position would indicate the presence (punched) or absence (not punched) of a key word in the article indexed by the card. The user operated the system by placing a stack of cards in front of a light source and shuffling them until all the required key positions showed light shining through. Unlike Flambo, Peekaboo was not a hierarchised system but rather what would nowadays be called a random access database. It allowed for even greater specificity in searches, since the cards afforded a far higher number of slot combinations than Flambo.

Perec worked out the larger "thesaurus" of key terms for the new system and then convened and chaired a meeting of the whole scientific team to amend, refine, and confirm his proposals. The meeting was a resounding success and Peekaboo went ahead. In time it comprised a grand total of a hundred thousand cards, every one of them typed up, coded, and hole-punched by Georges Perec, who was, though few really grasped the point, simultaneously one of Europe's most prolific experimental writers. Just as he was first setting up Peekaboo, he happened to win an important literary prize. Ah well, said people in the lab, this year we didn't get the Nobel; the Renaudot Prize will have to do.

Perec got his own back, both in the lab and outside, in writing. One of his tasks, in addition to information handling (which he got through in rather less than forty hours a week), was to compile bibliographies for the articles that the researchers in LA 38 wanted to publish. His work was never acknowledged in print, and thus it will never be possible to establish an exhaustive bibliography of the work of Georges Perec, which ought to include these modest, scholarly, but not insignificant appendices. One item that can be included is the bibliography of André Hugelin's 1967 treatment of electrocortical activity connected to states of sleep and wakefulness, for it is no less a part of Perec's oeuvre than the index of *Life A User's Manual*.[1] If proof were needed, one has only to read the opening pages of *A Man Asleep,* which constitute a "translation" in subjective terms of the process that Hugelin's thesis describes with electrochemical objectivity: what happens between the eyelid, the retina and the cerebral cortex as one falls asleep.

[1] André Hugelin, *Les Activités électrocorticales et les états de veille et de sommeil.* (Paris: CNRS LA 38, 1967).

Perec extorted occasional bibliographic quid pro quos for his work. Though he never flaunted his writerly fame in the lab, he did slip a card coded up for his novel *Things* into the Flambo system and, in the bibliography of one of Gautier's publications, he inserted a reference to an article entitled "Attention and Respiration", published in *Konink. Akad. Wetenschap. Amsterdam Proc. Sect. Sci* 1 (1899): 121–138, by a Dutch scientist called Caspar Winckler.[1] He played other tricks, too, on the world of neurophysiological research. Gautier's telephone rang one day; it was a long-distance call from a colleague in an American lab with an urgent, frantic enquiry: Who was this chap *Lévêque* referenced in his latest publication? Where did he work? What else had he done? Gautier was baffled, and then he checked. Light dawned. Perec had replaced the name of a distinguished scientist called Bishop with his own silly translation (*évêque* is French for bishop), just for fun – and to give Gautier's rivals palpitations over the appearance of a new and unknown research team.

For André Hugelin, Perec hardly ever typed anything straight the first time off. He would always put in his own red herrings, puns, irreverent asides, fancy layouts, and subversions of every imaginable kind. It was a waste of time, of course, but it amused him. Hugelin saw no point in correcting Perec's first-draft derisions. Do it again, Perec, he would say, and this time do it properly. Why should he say please?

To get promoted to senior positions in the French scientific establishment, one has to put in not just an application but a whole dossier, including a narrative account of one's own career and intellectual development. It is a tiresome sort of thing to compose. When Suzanne Tyc-Dumont gave Perec her first draft to type, she got back a text incorporating numerous emendations by the typist, such as a specially concocted epigraph in English that was even more French than her own, studiously "improved" verb endings in the past historic tense (usually reserved for formal narrative), and bizarre fluctuations between the scientific and street-corner registers of French, which had surely not been there in the original draft.

On other occasions, Perec embellished otherwise undistinguished reports of laboratory experiments with quite special layouts:

[1] Henry Gautier, "Effets comparés de stimulations respiratoires spécifiques de l'activité mentale sur la forme du spirogramme de l'homme", *J Physiol. Paris.* 1 (1969), pp. 31–44.

260 GEORGES PEREC · A LIFE IN WORDS

ouais this work shows that the direct electrical stimulation

of the cells that had previously responded to eye stretch

pruscle moduces a monosynaptic reflex recorded from the

IIInerve. This demonstration implies the method descr

ibed by Lorento de Ne (1939) for analyzing the ocul

o-motor circuit Il is based upon a classical ele

ctrophysiolophysiolophysiolophysiological manip

ulation that Reine-Chaud (40) had also used f

or his demonstration of the monosynaptic n

ature of the spinic myotatal reflex. The

features of the cocosynaptic reflex re

corded from the IIInerve are similar

to the characteristics of the mass

eter myotatex reflic. They both

behave similarly. Contradicto

ry tb these last date is th

e general belief that no

reflex organization ex

ists in the eye musc

les (McCough & Adl

er, 1932; Whitte

ridge, 1960; R

obinson, 197

1). Failur

e to dem

onstra

te a

fu

II HYPOTHESES ET SYNTHESES§

> *"The one who thinks that one will one day elucidate the sophisticated intrication of the nervous machinery, is fouring himself a finger in the eye until the elbow"*
>
> John Carew ECCLES

A l'époque où j'entra au laboratoire de Paul DELL, l'hypothèse déjà ancienne, d'une formation nerveuse centrale responsable de la vieille, avait été confirmée, quelques années auparavant, par une expérience désormais classique de MORUZZI et MAGOUILLE (1949): la stimulation électrique de n'importe quoi partiquement n'importe où entre le bulbe et l'hypothalamus provoque une réaction d'éveil electrographicocortique.[1]

Three kinds of play ran through Perec's subversions of his colleagues' attempts to write up their work. The first was a schoolboyish taste for puns, spoonerisms, misspellings, mispronunciations, and other primary distortions of written language. The second, just as significant to an understanding Perec's more public work, was the interpenetration of English and French. About three quarters of the typing Perec did in the lab, representing perhaps a fifth or a quarter of all the typing he did overall, was in English – or to be more precise, in that ineradicably Gallic pseudo-English in which French scientists publish. Perec's games with English involved making the scientists' garbled syntax so much worse that even they would have to get the point. He inserted French words apparently at random and applied to written English spelling distortions that represented the sound of atrocious French accents, often compounded by spoonerisms and metatheses. In his diabolical joke-typist persona, Perec murdered the English language, but his aggression was directed as much towards the unfunny ghastliness of scientific pseudo-English as towards the language itself, which he knew well and could bend quite effectively to his own humour. The third thread in Perec's bad-boy behaviour

[1] From Suzanne Tyc-Dumont, "Titres et Travaux". Draft typescript.

at the keyboard was his delight in making creative use of the typewriter, and especially in using incremental indentation to compose diamond-shaped, E-shaped, triangular, V-shaped, or diagonal slab-shaped texts. Since all of these exercises were done at the expense of Perec's free time (he knew he would have to do them all over again "properly"), he must have loved typing for its own sake, as if he wanted to be able to say, like Jules Michelet, that before *writing* books he *composed* them, in the material sense.[1] He loved the actual machines, for their feel, their various clatterings, and the different scripts they could produce. His first faithful servant was a manual Underwood, on which he worked at home throughout the 1960s. He commemorated its eventual demise by casting it as a musical instrument in the last of the plays that he wrote for German radio. For sequence 16 of *Konzertstück für Sprecher und Orchester*, entitled *Sonate für ältere Schreibmaschine* ("Sonata for an Ageing Typewriter"), the composer/performer was instructed to use only an Underwood Four Million model. Tryouts were performed on Perec's own machine in Paris; the German radio station found an identical one in Saarbrücken for the final recording of the play.

The Underwood was replaced by a secondhand electric IBM golf-ball machine, of the kind that Perec had used at the lab for years, purchased from a shop in Rue de Rennes. The novels that Perec wrote in the 1960s contain churlish references to the authoritative look of evenly spaced IBM typescripts (see, for instance, *T* 84), which he associated during that period with the hierarchical atmosphere of Hugelin's lab; once he had an IBM at home, however, he saw golf-ball type rather differently. On occasions Perec would put in the Greek character set when typing notes in French to his friends, producing a relatively transparent kind of modern macaronic. It was on the IBM, also, that he wrote the final version of *Life A User's Manual*.

The third special typewriter in Perec's life was the Olivetti ET 221 that he was allowed to use during his stay in Australia in 1981. It opened up the magical world of daisy wheels and page memories for him. When he got back he boasted to his German translator, Eugen Helmle, a constant improver of his own office gadgetry, that he had used a typewriter more magnificent than any of Eugen's toys. Well, as a matter of fact, Eugen admitted with a blush, I've had an Olivetti

---

[1] See Jules Michelet, *Le Peuple* (1846) (Paris: Flammarion, 1974).

ET 221 myself for some while now. Perec was distinctly downcast at the news.

Did he type well? Superbly, according to Suzanne Tyc-Dumont, faster and more accurately than a trained typist. Gautier agrees that he typed fast, but remembers that he used only some of his fingers, and did not work like a trained typist at all. Hugelin, for his part, thought that Perec was a hamfisted joker who made countless involuntary keyboard mistakes.

Perec appropriated the literature of CNS research only once as unmodified material in his own work. *Fonctionnement du système nerveux dans la tête* ("The Functioning of the Nervous System in the Head") is a radio play that he wrote in 1972 for Cologne Radio. It bears a formal resemblance to Perec's early works, in that it comprises two separate texts; in performance, these are spoken simultaneously but kept discrete by the use of stereo sound. Track One is an academic lecture on how a visual message travels from eye to brain, which Perec cobbled together from snippets of articles written by the staff of the lab and by other authorities on the subject. Track Two, which is fragmentary at the beginning but grows in quantity and volume as the play proceeds, consists of the subjective responses of the brain to the visual stimulus whose route the learned lecturer is describing. That stimulus turns out to be a mythical tableau inside the lecturer's head: Freud's "primal scene" itself, the sight of parents copulating.[1]

If the radio play is the only example of direct transposition of the work of LA 38, lab life nonetheless figures in one way or another in most of Perec's literary publications, from a genuine technical reference to experiments with cats in *W or The Memory of Childhood* (page 77) to the tale of elaborate professorial skulduggery in kidney research in *Life A User's Manual* (pages 474–480). Perec invited all of his lab colleagues to the first performance on stage of his hilarious bureaucratic tragedy, *L'Augmentation* ("The Increment" or [for American readers] "The Rise"), which presents the infuriatingly repetitive and finally self-defeating attempts of a nameless little cog in a great organisational machine to obtain an additional increment or pay-rise from his boss. The point seems to have struck home, judging from reports that the performance "did not endear Perec to his colleagues". But

---

[1] Georges Perec, "Fonctionnement du système nerveux dans la tête", *Cause commune* 3 (1972), pp. 42–55.

Perec's ultimate riposte to André Hugelin, his magnificent retaliation for years of humble service to bizarre scientific pursuits, was an apparently serious scientific article of Perec's own, written in what might seem in French scientists' eyes to be English and entitled "Experimental Demonstration of the Tomatotopic Organization in the Soprano (*Cantatrix sopranica* L.)". It was composed as a contribution to a specially-bound volume of articles by members of LA 38 presented to Marthe Bonvallet on her retirement in 1974. For many years ever-fainter photocopies of Perec's typescript circulated from hand to hand around the world of neurophysiology. A copy found its way to a lab in New Zealand and at international conferences, small groups of attenders sometimes still gather at the back of the bar-room to listen as someone reads out Perec's account of the electrochemical coordinates of soprani subjected to regulated tomatic pelting. For years it was just about the most-heard-of and least findable non-publication of LA 38 of the CNRS, as if Perec the champion of information retrieval were also making a point by the way he put his work into the underground circuit: who needed Flambo, Peekaboo or, God forbid, a data-processing machine for an article people actually wanted to read?

"Experimental Demonstration" [*CSL* 13–33] can gravely compromise one's composure, especially if one begins by taking it seriously. At a meeting of the CNRS biochemistry commission, it is said, the chairman glanced at a photocopy of Perec's spoof that had been slipped (by mistake?) into the pile of papers in front of him. He scanned the first page, began to redden, then spluttered and had to hold on to the sides of his seat. "Experimental Demonstration" precipitated the only recorded instance of a CNRS commission granting itself an adjournment for laughter.

In the article Perec experimentally demonstrates the neural routes or pathways (usually written *passe-ouais* in Perec's other role, as joker-typist) that lead to YR (the "yelling reaction") in sopranos pelted with common tomatoes, "tomato rungisia vulgaris". (The choice of prima donnas for vivisection is a dig at Gautier, Perec's only real pal in the lab, who was, and is, amongst other things, an opera buff.) The techniques applied to the 107 specimens provided by the Conservatoire National de Musique (mean weight: 101 kilograms) are those used by Suzanne Tyc-Dumont and Marthe Bonvallet on cats:

Halothane anasthesia was utilized during the course of tracheotomy, fixation in the Horsley-Clarke, and major operative procedures. 5% procaine was injected into skin margins and pressure points. [. . .] Spinal cord transections were performed at L^3/T^2 levels, thus eliminating blood pressure variations and adrenaline secretion induced by tomato throwing (Giscard d'Estaing, 1974). The fact that the animals were not suffering from pain was shown by their constant smiling throughout the experiments. [CSL 16–17]

The article's bibliography is a minefield of puns, only some of which can be understood by monoglot French speakers. It is an Anglo-French "cod" bibliography, a constellation of classroom jokes so elaborate, so unremitting, and so well aimed (since in every reference there is something relating to real science) that it almost transforms silliness into an art form. Entries for Marks & Spencer and Wait & See are transparent enough to English readers, whilst the listing for Timeo (W.), Danaos (I.) & Dona Ferentes (H. E. W.), authors of an article on "Brain cutting and cooking", requires a bit of classical knowledge, and that for Donen (S.) & Kelly (G.), responsible for "Singing in the Brain", appeals to movie fans. The only fishy thing about the entry for the real neurologists McCulloch, Pitts, and Levin is that Perec has them publishing in *Proc. Leap & Frog Ass.* Finally, a little mathematical knowledge is necessary for an understanding of the dig in the last reference:

Zyszytrakyczywsz-Sekrâwszkiwcz, I. The Monte-Carlo theorem as a use in locating brain and other sites. J. math. Vivisec. 27, 134–143, 1974.

Illumination is provided by the dream which the avenging murderer, Sven Ericsson, recounts in a letter to Madame de Beaumont, on page 146 of *Life A User's Manual:*

Standing beside a huge blackboard covered in equations, a mathematician was concluding his demonstration, in front of a turbulent audience, that the celebrated "Monte Carlo theorem" was generalisable [. . .]: a roulette player placing his stake on a random number had just as much chance of winning as a martingale player systematically doubling his stake on the same number on each loss in order to recoup eventually.

In 1975 there was a fire at Hôpital Saint-Antoine which did extensive damage, and LA 38 had to be evacuated from its premises in Rue Chaligny. Stopgap accommodation during rebuilding was found for Hugelin's unit at the CNRS campus at Gif-sur-Yvette, in the southern suburbs, almost at the end of the line to Saint-Rémy. The unit never really got over this disaster: Suzanne Tyc-Dumont took her research off to Marseille, technicians left and could not be replaced, and the operation moved into a lower gear. Perec, for his part, found himself a contraflow commuter from central Paris. He hated it. He tried to use the forty-minute stints on the train to do minor work, such as composing crossword puzzles, or making up exercises or games, but the crowded and bumpy carriages were not conducive to invention, and he resented the wasted time. His position at the lab had also changed by then. He was the virtuoso of manual information-retrieval systems, but every other leading lab in the field was now using computers. Peekaboo had become old-fashioned – not yet old enough to be a historical monument but too outdated to be mentioned to visiting professors from America, even if it did work. Perec was asked if he would like to retrain as computer data-base operator. He thought about it. He was nearly forty and in the throes of creating what must be his masterpiece, his long-planned, meticulously prepared omnium-gatherum, *Life A User's Manual;* he did not want to learn new tricks now, and frankly, he was intimidated by computers. He said no. Hugelin suggested that he ought to resign, but he could not: his CNRS salary, miserable though it may have been, was his only truly regular income. He had a tenured post as a *documentaliste*, not as a computer man; Hugelin could not sack him. It was an awkward, irksome stalemate.

Ten years earlier, when Perec won a substantial sum of money with the Renaudot Prize for *Things*, his lab colleagues had wondered why he bothered to carry on with his lowly job in a medical research unit. To one or two of them Perec explained his position: he wanted the freedom to be a writer, most certainly, but he was equally determined to remain free *as* a writer. It seemed at that time too dangerous for him to depend on writing alone for his livelihood. It would put unpredictable, unliterary constraints on what he wrote; he might become just a hack, which was not his ambition at all. So despite his overall aim to be a writer and nothing but, he resisted the temptation to go freelance. It seemed a reasonable bargain to give up forty hours a week to medical science in return for the licence to write his own work, in his own way.

By the mid-seventies, however, Perec's feelings had shifted on that score. *Why should I, who work on words, not be paid as a researcher?* he asked his colleagues in front of a journalist who had come out to Gif-sur-Yvette to investigate the pay and conditions of scientific researchers. *You*, he said to the scientists whose information he handled, *you undertake experiments so as to produce articles, and so do I. So you can see why I'm jealous!*[1]

But the CNRS would not pay him a salary just to write, so he continued to search for a publisher who might. After several disappointments, Perec at last obtained an arrangement whereby he was assured of being paid advances on royalties in monthly instalments, in imitation of a salary. He acted slowly, and with some trepidation, but in September 1978 he finally made the break with the CNRS and resigned from what was by now a redundant post. Flambo and Peekaboo were put out with the rubbish. Perec became a writer full-time.

Based on the recollections of Mireille Archinard, Marie-Claude de Brunhoff, Philippe Drogoz, Henry Gautier, Eugen Helmle, Geneviève Horcholle-Bossavit, André Hugelin, Marie-Claude Lavallard-Rousseau, Michel Martens, Harry Mathews, France Mayo, Jacques Roubaud, Suzanne Tyc-Dumont, and on archival information kindly provided by the secretarial staff of LA 38.

Biblio. Gestion de fichier bibliographique. (Paris: CHU Saint-Antoine, 1989), compiled by J.-F. Vibert, is dedicated to Georges Perec, whose bibliographic work constitutes the source of the computerised bibliography to which this handbook is the current user's manual.

[1] Quoted in Bruno Frappat, "Le Métier de chercheur", *Le Monde*, 13 October 1976.

CHAPTER 26

Partisans

1962

When the Perecs came back from Tunisia in the summer of 1961, they found a country divided and once again on the brink of civil war. In April de Gaulle had outflanked "a mere squad of generals" – Salan, Jouhaux, Challe, and Zeller [*Jms* 217] – who attempted a putsch to keep Algeria French. Now France was believed to be moving towards a settlement of sorts, though no one knew what the president's real plans were. Extremists in Algeria and in France took to terrorism, both to intimidate the FLN and also to discourage the government from taking any conciliatory action. The OAS relegated the building of the Berlin Wall to the second page of the French newspapers in August by committing almost daily *plasticages* in Paris. On 8 September OAS members tried to gun down de Gaulle on his way to Villacoublay Aerodrome. Subsequent demonstrations against *Algérie française* were broken up by riot police, with unheard-of violence. In a single night of protest, on 17 October, 11,538 arrests were made, at least two hundred Algerians died, and several hundred others disappeared.[1] Nobody trusted the forces of order any more. Nobody knew for certain whether the army was obeying the government or vice versa. Housewives stocked up with sugar in kilos, bottles of cooking oil, tins of tuna, coffee, and condensed milk. Squads of helmeted security policemen in shiny black waterproof capes and service boots patrolled up and down Boulevard Sebastopol, where many Algerian immigrant workers lived. It was a tense and violent time, one that left its mark on Georges Perec and all his friends.

The Latin Quarter was in ferment, and in disarray. The PCF, which commanded more than twenty per cent of the popular vote, had great prestige among intellectuals, but still it gave no moral support to

---

[1] The "Night of 17 October" remained an almost secret scandal for almost thirty years. It was first commemorated publicly on 17 October 1990.

young men unwilling to face thirty-two months' service in an army whose chief objective was to suppress a national liberation movement in Algeria. Could Marxism be combined with democracy to generate a revolutionary solution to the problems confronting French society? Splinter groups debated the issue in the corridors and study rooms of the Sorbonne and Normal' Sup', torn between the need for coherence (the watchword of Lg and of the new "thinking master" at ENS, Louis Althusser) and the practical complexity of the Algerian question. But there was really only one place where such ideas could be explored outside of the grip of the PCF, and that was a quite remarkable bookshop, La Joie de Lire ("The Joy of Reading"), which was owned and run by François Maspéro and Jeanne Bercier, in premises in Rue Saint-Séverin, almost backing on to Perec's old social headquarters in Rue de la Bûcherie.

La Joie de Lire stocked an unusually wide range of contemporary literature, including much-talked-about but rarely displayed works by Boris Vian, Raymond Queneau and Frederick Prokosch. Perec was an assiduous standing reader at the shop, which was run on convivial rather than strictly commercial lines, and he may have had a soft spot for Jeanne Bercier, who often stood at the under-used cash desk. He and his friends from La Ligne générale would not have thought of buying books anywhere else, not just because La Joie de Lire provided access to the literature that interested them, but because it gave tangible form to their political view of the world.

Maspéro's treasure store offered customers a unique selection of books, tracts and pamphlets on what were then called colonial issues, many of them put out by revolutionary liberation movements in the "three continents" of the Bandung declaration (Latin America, Africa, and Asia). It was in La Joie de Lire that the *gauchistes* to the left of the hidebound PCF could find out about Castro and Che Guevara, about the Vietminh, the FLN, and the GPRA. The shop became so well known as a nest of revolutionaries that many people wanted it closed down. In the eyes of the right, and even of the merely timid middle classes, La Joie de Lire was a sinister place; for Left Bank left-wingers, it was almost a second home.

La Joie de Lire was not a front window for any political party, and therefore it was an easy target. In the brutal circumstances of 1961–62, another man might have chased the *gauchistes* away and got on with the business of selling books, but Maspéro invited them in and got them to organise, launch, and write a new review. It was to be a partisan review by design, speaking for Marxism but not following the rigid line of the PCF. Vercors (the pseudonymous author of *The Silence of the Sea*, the classic novel of wartime resistance) penned the manifesto which preceded articles by Danilo Dolci and Yevgeny Yevtushenko in issue number 1 of *Partisans*:

> We support . . . the Algerian revolution. We support it within a vaster context of which it is but one element: the emergence of the Third World. We believe that our era, and probably the whole of the second half of this century, will be dominated by this gigantic phenomenon inaugurated in China.

"*Partisans* was our only outlet," says Marcel Benabou, speaking for all his friends at Normal' Sup' and his comrades from La Ligne générale. Other periodicals were too far to the right, or impossible to break into, or controlled directly by the PCF (like *La Nouvelle Critique*), or by its front organisations (like *Clarté*). But who controlled *Partisans*? Although Maspéro was its publisher, editorial policy was made by the youngsters who turned up at the meetings in the back office of La Joie de Lire. These were informal, often noisy and chaotic occasions. It took Maspéro some time to grasp that behind the individuals making shorter or longer speeches, either with fluency (as Regis Debray) or with stuttering timidity (as Jacques Rancière), stood splinter groups locked in combat in the corridors of Rue d'Ulm or in the caucuses of the UEC. Perec was older than the others; he had done his military service, had seen North Africa, and was not from Normal' Sup'. He seemed to put points that were genuinely his own. Maspéro asked him to come onto the editorial board; he cannot now remember what reason Perec gave for declining.

Some of the *Partisans* group turned out to be Trotskyists of one kind or another; some were placemen for the UEC or the PCF (which practised entryism as skilfully as did its opponents); and some, though they kept it secret from Maspéro, were "old boys" from Lg, which had begun to meet again as a discussion group now that the Perecs were back from Tunisia, and now that there was a *Partisans* to publish some of its members' work.

Regis Debray asked two friends to review an orthodox introduction to Marxism for *Partisans*, and to use the opportunity to mark the journal's nonallegiance to the PCF line. The acidic review appeared over the signature of "Georges Burnacs", a name that simultaneously masked and designated its two authors, Claude BURgelin and Bruno MarceNAC, with a nod to the Hungarian philosopher Georg LukáCS, whose more interesting works had only just appeared in French.[1] Burnacs runs through Perec's whole oeuvre like a red thread loosely tying together his *Partisans* and his Lg days. Perec twice turned him into a carpet seller, Marcel-Emile Burnachs, whose sign-card is one of those contemplated in a typesetter's shop window, first by the unnamed "you" of *A Man Asleep* [*MA* 166], and then again by Grégoire Simpson in chapter 52 of *Life A User's Manual* [*L* 238]. In *"53 Days"*, Marcel Benabou's career as a Latinist, his forename, and the forename of Burnacs's originator Claude Burgelin are all woven into Marcellus Claudius Burnachus, a Roman soldier who becomes a North African king. But Perec was by no means the sole retrospective proprietor of the "Burnacs" sign. In fact, Benabou was the first to borrow it, "like a circus nose", when he wrote for *Les Temps modernes* in 1964–66. Later he slyly suggested "Martin Burnacs" as a possible pseudonym for the narrator of his literary memoir, *Pourquoi je n'ai écrit aucun de mes livres* ("Why I Wrote None of My Books"). François Maspéro also appropriated the name, along with the intellectual hero of its inventors, for *The Fig Tree*, in which his half-fictional characters refer to a Hungarian philosopher by the name of Laszlo Burnács. A full life of the Protean Burnacs has yet to be written.

The intense young men of 1961–62 who squatted in La Joie de Lire to talk for hours about China, Cuba, and Algeria may have indulged in factional fighting among themselves, but they were mostly loyal to Maspéro's enterprise, and to the man himself. Some of them became self-appointed night sentries at the bookshop, to protect it from OAS saboteurs. Once, they witnessed the bombing of an Algerian night-club on the opposite side of Rue Saint-Séverin and noted down the number-plate of the car that sped away. Such was the gulf between French youth and the police at that time that reporting the crime was a tricky moral issue for the guards. Would they be "collaborators" if they rang the police? Or would they be even more guilty if they did not? After long debate they decided, with reluctance, that they had to report the incident and the number-plate, though they knew their action would probably put the bookshop at the top of the OAS hit list, since the police force, if not hand in glove with the extremists,

[1] Georges Burnacs, "M. Martinet ou le marxisme d'un autre temps", *Partisans* 9 (March 1963), pp. 192–194.

was certainly infiltrated by *Algérie française*. Maspéro insisted that the night watches cease; he did not want anyone killed when plastic explosive blew in his shop windows. La Joie de Lire was bombed a fortnight later. Someone took a potshot at Maspéro in broad daylight, from behind, in the street; he was injured quite seriously but eventually recovered.

In their first year back in Paris after their Tunisian adventure, Georges and Paulette could not but be involved in street politics. They took part in demonstrations against the OAS, against police brutality, and against de Gaulle, who had declared a state of emergency and was ruling by decree under special powers conferred on him by Article 16 of the new constitution. The demonstrations were terrifying. At one, near Place d'Italie, Paulette tripped over a moped parked in the central reservation and came near to being beaten by members of the CRS, the paramilitary riot police, who carried huge wooden nightsticks ironically known as *bidules* ("thingummies"). A protest march on 8 February was baton-charged by police; demonstrators were clubbed into the narrow entrance of Charonne metro station, where eight of them were crushed to death. A few days later, when Bianca Lamblin joined the hundred-thousand-strong procession behind the victims' funeral cortege, she caught sight of Georges in the crowd, looking pale, his lips pursed, his hands linked with his comrades'. This was the only time in his life that Perec was an active political militant. At that moment of history, there was no other choice: one could not abandon one's comrades, or allow one's country to be hijacked by terrorist violence. Of course Georges and Paulette marched, and militated, and held banners aloft. They were not deserters.

The winter of 1961–62, which turned Paris into the front line of a futile and corrupting colonial war, left many young people unable thereafter to regard policemen as human beings. The death throes of French Algeria laid the foundations for the pitched battles of May 1968 between "French youth" and the French police, battles that would put the Left Bank in the international limelight once again. But the violence of 1961 was self-evidently pointless. The war was ending. In March 1962 de Gaulle signed the Evian agreements, giving Algeria its independence and closing a long, nasty chapter in French history. The Algerian war had held a generation together in opposition to it. Its end left many twenty-five-year-olds stranded; there would never again be a cause to mobilise them all as one man.

In the fearful months preceding the peace, Georges began his new job as a research librarian, read his way into graph theory, wrote for *Partisans,* attended meetings of Lg, and somehow also found time to see films old and new, to chat with friends, to play Scrabble and to think up fresh ideas for novels and film scripts, now that *J'avance masqué* had met the same fate as *L'Attentat de Sarajevo, Gaspard pas mort,* and *Le Condottiere.* One night, after seeing a second-rate gangster movie with Michel Martens (who, following a long stay in Prague and Moscow, had torn up his party card and now described himself as an unemployed scriptwriter), Perec pulled up a chair in a café and began to talk. Surely he and Martens could invent a better holdup, he mused, than the one they had just seen. Why not come up with a *modern* swindle that they could turn into a best-seller or a blockbuster film? It was a matter of lateral thinking, he said: if they chose two unrelated areas that they knew something about, and put them together, then they could subvert their conjunction into a perfect and bloodless crime.

Perec and Martens dreamt up a plot that was almost plausible. Graph theory says (or at least, Perec *said* it says) that one can get from any A to any B by way of no more than two intermediate points. Let us say, for instance, that you and your friends want to get to a spot marked X, which represents a large treasure that can be stolen without risk. Nondirective interviews throw up masses of information irrelevant to the enquiry in progress; if you steer them just slightly, interviewees will tell you – incidentally of course – about their possessions and those of their neighbours. So if you were to set up a large-scale attitudinal survey of the upper-middle-class population of a provincial town, tape-record the interviews, and transcribe them, you could analyse them not only in terms of the needs of the unsuspecting bank or insurance company that commissioned the survey, but also with an eye to discovering the worthwhile object of a holdup. Clever cross-referencing (perhaps helped by a Flambo system) would easily identify X, whilst a different cut of the cards ought to lead you to a small-time criminal who might be persuaded to do the actual deed. The bunch of crooks imagined by Perec and Martens would not get their own hands dirty; they would be intellectuals of a sort, of the sort they themselves were, or might have been: market researchers. They would stick together in a bunch like magnets – whence the name of the film, *La Bande magnétique,* ("The Magnetic Bunch"), an allusion both to *The Wild Bunch* and to the tool of the market researcher's trade, since in French tape recordings are called *bandes magnétiques*, or "magnetic ribbons".

The script begins with five small cars assembling on a hilltop above Grenoble. The camera zooms in on the valley below to show the sleeping city, then pans to follow the motorised posse as it canters into a French Laramie to sort the place out, to get it taped, and to put it in filing-card order. Music by Elmer Bernstein. The story outline, which Martens typed up, turns market-research techniques and graph theory into the material of a derisive epic. But because it is only an outline, it is impossible to say how convincing, or how funny, the final product would have been, especially since the ending is a throwaway: either the "magnetic bunch" halts at the very brink of the crime, or the lad recruited to do the deed is redeemed by a love affair with the heroine of what by this point has turned into a pulp-novel plot. The fate of the script itself was rather more interesting: the idea was taken up again, adapted, cut down, reformulated, and rewritten three times, to emerge at last as the novel that made Georges Perec's name.

★

In 1960–61, György (Georg) Lukács arrived as the new intellectual pilot on the Left Bank. The interest of his three newly translated books – *History and Class Consciousness*, first written in 1923 and subsequently "disowned" by its author; *The Present Meaning of Critical Realism*, written in 1955; and *Critical Realism*, of 1958 – lay in their reading of modern literature. Lukács was a Marxist, but rather than using Marx to exclude from the canon everything that was not socialist, or realist, or both, he saw his political ideology as a way to make a coherent sense of great works written in Western as well as in Eastern Europe, in feudal, bourgeois, industrial and capitalist societies as well as under real existing socialism. Lukács had been minister of culture in the short-lived liberal Hungarian government of 1956 and his position as an elderly victim of Soviet repression in the ensuing period gave him moral credit amongst the *gauchistes*, who already held his intellect in high esteem. *My first model was Brecht*, Perec said to an audience of English students a few years later:

> *Brecht taught me a very important thing, the idea of distanciation.*
> *I found it taken up again by Lukács. [. . .] Through Lukács [I*
> *discovered] the absolutely indispensable notion of irony – that is*

to say, the fact that a character can perform an action or feel a feeling
in a book whilst the author remains in complete disagreement with
the character and shows how the character is making a mistake.
[. . .] That is what governed, it is what governs, my entire under-
standing of Mann [. . .] Fielding, Sterne, Diderot, Stendhal.

[PAP 33]

The Lukács of *The Present Meaning of Critical Realism* is the pretext,
the provocation, and the referenced authority for the articles Perec
wrote for *Partisans* in 1962–63.[1] The first of these was written with
Claude Burgelin, but the four pieces hang together and belong as a
whole to the collected works of Georges Perec. In one sense the set
of essays serves as a summary of the work of La Ligne générale and
of several years of collective thinking among Perec, Claude Burgelin,
Roger Kleman, Marcel Benabou, and others; but on a perhaps deeper
level the *Partisans* essays constitute an essential exposition of Georges
Perec's theoretical and ethical attitudes at the dawn of his career as a
writer.

Perec and Burgelin argue, to begin with (in oppositional and *nor-*
malien style), that since 1945 French fiction had been floundering in
a false dichotomy set up by Sartre's definition of "committed" literature. Although admirable in intention, Sartre's call for commitment
had been illusory, since he had omitted to account for the literary
dimension; necessary though it had been in 1945, the programme had
led the novel into a dead end. Sartre's opponents, who aimed to write
"uncommitted" literature, had not found a way out of it, as their
programme could be defined only as the negative of the other's positive proposals. Not even the *hussards* could write in order *not* to say
anything about the world.

The "new novel", which had arisen in the 1950s as an apparent
way out of the debate over commitment, had proved to be an even
greater sleight-of-hand. In an effort to depict the real world stripped
of the meanings that the old novelistic conventions had imposed upon
it, Robbe-Grillet had replaced ideologically loaded devices such as
character and plot with purportedly neutral and blank description.
The "new novel" claimed to present things "as they were", with no
involuntary meanings attached; all that could be known about the

[1] Perec is more likely to have drawn his concept of irony from Lukács's *Théorie*
du roman (Paris: Denoël/Gonthier, 1963).

world, Robbe-Grillet maintained, came from the surface of things.

Not so, Perec declares. Robbe-Grillet had in fact abandoned the true purpose of art in order to represent his personal obsessions. The world of *La Jalousie* was not "meaningless"; its meanings were simply of limited interest. Rational action was impossible in Robbe-Grillet's universe because the real structure of that universe consisted entirely of the author's sexual fantasies. The "existential despair" of what had passed for left-wing avant-gardism was actually, in Perec's view, a thin veil for subjective, reactionary pessimism.

More recently, critics and writers from Blanchot to Paulhan and Barthes had bemoaned the "crisis of language". Perec sweeps aside that intellectual fashion, too, as an empty trick cloaking a denial of responsibility. People had complained that words were tired and worn-out things, so caked with accreted meanings from centuries of misuse that they could no longer say anything directly, or at all. They were talking rubbish, according to Perec. There was no curse on the vocabulary; *the disease that eats words away is not inside words. The terror* [of language] *exists only for the writer. The "crisis of language" is a refusal of the real.*

Everything had to be started over, from scratch. French literary thinking since 1945 had been a wasteland of discredited ideas from which no great works could ever arise. What, then, should literature be? The term that Perec uses as the key to the future comes from Žarko Vidović, from Lg, and from Lukács: *realism*. Perec's definition of it is close to Goethe's notion of the classical: realism makes order out of the chaos of the world, or, in the language of Lg, it presents a coherent and "totalising" vision of the real. And what constitutes the real? Perec's answer to that question is similarly traditional: the real is in the first place an individual experience of the world. The aim of writing must therefore be to know and to understand the self, to relate the self to the world, and to give form to the real. *Realism* was the means by which a writer could gain mastery over the world.

Nothing in Perec's *Partisans* pieces makes him a prophet of structuralism, poststructuralism, deconstructionism, or postmodernism (whatever that is). His fundamental position in 1962–63 was not in fact very far from Sartre's. He believed, with Sartre, that literature existed to do something in the world; it was Sartre's implementation of that belief that was, in his view, inadequate. Perec remained unaffected by the ambient pessimism of the period, displaying no interest, for instance, in Beckett or Adamov. Indeed, what is most

striking in these essays, even if it is expressed with uncharacteristic
stridency, is Perec's *optimism* about the potential of language and
literature:

> *There is no epoch, no condition, no crisis that the mind cannot grasp;*
> *there is no anarchy that cannot be ordered, no situation that cannot*
> *be mastered, no phenomenon that reason and language, feeling and*
> *rationality cannot conquer. Out of the collapse of Germany came*
> Doktor Faustus; *it was on his return from a concentration camp*
> *that Robert Antelme wrote* L'Espèce humaine, *one of the finest*
> *books to the glory of mankind.*

Antelme's book is the subject of the fourth and final article of the
series. It was not a recent work, having first appeared in 1947, nor
was it part of a literary oeuvre, for Antelme never wrote anything
else. Somewhat like *Hiroshima mon amour, L'Espèce humaine* ("Human
Kind") is a fragmented narrative that switches back and forth between
the sequence of lived experience and the survivor's efforts, in the time
of writing, to comprehend the reality of his past. Antelme manages
to keep the two levels of the text distinct, and in that sense it is an
honest book; it is also an intellectual book, in that it obliges its reader
to participate in the arduous process of making sense out of history.
Its design therefore corresponded to Perec's conception of the book
he wanted to write – *a book that denies itself but works nonetheless* –
whilst its subject matter, the concentration camps of Nazi Germany,
was precisely that which Perec identified as the source of his own
anguish.

The central point of *L'Espèce humaine*, a point that Perec stresses
throughout his essay on the book, is that the more a man is deprived
of dignity, and the more he is stripped of the signs of humanity (as
in the camps, where numbers replace names, pyjamas replace clothes,
and so forth), the more he must proclaim that he belongs to human-
kind, and the more he needs to write, for writing is the the highest,
ultimate, and essential means of saying that one is a human being.

> *At the centre of* L'Espèce humaine *the will to speak and to be*
> *heard, the will to explore and to know, gives onto that unlimited*
> *confidence in language and in writing that is the basis of all literature.*

(The same thought is summarised, personalised, and put with greater
modesty and effect in *W or The Memory of Childhood*, when at the end

of a passage about his parents, Perec suggests that *writing is the memory of their death and the assertion of my life* [*W* 42].)

At the time, nobody took much notice of Perec's *Partisans* pieces. Robbe-Grillet did not read them; Perec's was not a name to be reckoned with, and he was hardly the first would-be writer to vent his frustration with the literary establishment by declaring that it had been getting it all wrong for a decade and more. Creators have to start by clearing their own space, and where else can they do it if not in their immediate environment? No left-wing intellectual of the 1960s bothered to attack Mauriac or the catholic novel. The differences between Perec's grasp of literature and that of the "new novelists", on one side, and of the proponents of "committed literature", on the other, are fundamental, but the fact that it was those pillars and not others that he first tried to shake shows that they occupied the space where he wished to construct his own monument – on rubble that would take quite a time to come tumbling down.

The essay on Antelme shifts the focus of Perec's *Partisans* pieces and transforms them, retrospectively, from abrasive undergraduate polemic into something that is close to being a coherent platform for autobiography. But why had Perec singled out *L'Espèce humaine* from the large number of remarkable books written by returnees from the camps? He could have chosen a more recent masterpiece, André Schwarz-Bart's *The Last of the Just*, which had won the Goncourt Prize in 1959, or Elie Wiesel's *Night*, of 1958, which had earlier caused him to alter the title of his own projected novel from *La Nuit* to *Gaspard*. Both of these novels, moreover, are unambiguously about the fate of the Jews, and of the Jewish survivors of the extermination camps; *L'Espèce humaine* is not. Antelme (at the time, the husband of Marguerite Duras) was a French political deportee, not a Jew. Like David Rousset, another returnee whose analysis of his experience had a profound effect on Perec's understanding of the world, Antelme gives a *political* analysis of the concentration-camp phenomenon.

Perec was in no position to become a Jewish writer – that is to say, a writer defined in part by being Jewish. It was not just that his memories of Jewish life in Belleville were tenuous in the extreme (what twenty-five-year-old has much recall of his or her life before the age of five?), or that his postwar home life at Rue de l'Assomption had been imbued with a deep dislike of religion and a palpable aspiration towards an ordinary French and middle-class identity. Left-wing culture, which Perec had espoused as a young man in an

apparent rebellion against his bourgeois "Bienenfeld background",
had reinforced the occlusion, if not the denial, of the Jewish specificity
of the Final Solution. Antelme's book did not speak to Perec about
what had actually happened to his mother, nor did it address what
the orphans of the *shoah* still had to cope with, but it was nonetheless
about the camps. *L'Espèce humaine* thus offered Perec a sideways
approach to his own pain, even as it comforted him by restating his
conviction that writing was an appropriate, ethical response.
Antelme's book was, so to speak, in the emotional and intellectual
middle distance for Perec. Elie Wiesel's must have seemed far too
close: the narrator-hero, a child prisoner at Buchenwald, sees his
father die of starvation and feels *liberated*.

The attitude of the French left toward the *shoah* is clearly reflected
in Alain Resnais' documentary, *Night and Fog*. Jean Cayrol's commentary states that millions of Jews died at Auschwitz, alongside Gypsies,
Communists and Poles, but the closing passage urges eternal vigilance
in cold-war newsreel style:

> *Who is on the lookout from this strange tower to warn us of the
> coming of new executioners? There are those of us who sincerely
> look upon the ruins today as if the old concentration-camp monster
> were dead and buried beneath them. Those who pretend to take hope
> again as the image fades, as though there were a cure for the plague
> of these camps. Those of us who pretend to believe that all this
> happened only once, at a certain time and in a certain place, and
> those who refuse to see, who do not heed the cry to the end of time.*[1]

Perec was far from the only one amongst French Jews of his generation to put his own Jewishness in the category of purely contingent
facts, and to seek to understand the world in terms of the conflict
between capital and labour. When he came to draft his autobiography
in 1970, he noted that Jewishness was the theme that he *tackled with
least spontaneity* [CGP II 167], and indeed, in the version that he
reworked in 1974 and finally published as *W or The Memory of Childhood*, the simultaneous assertion and denial of Jewishness is a fundamental if largely hidden feature of the book. For more than two
decades Antelme, Rousset, and Cayrol provided Perec with the only

---

[1] Quoted in E. Barnouw, *Documentary. A History of the Nonfiction Film* (New
York: OUP, 1974).

tools he was able to accept for understanding his own situation and constructing his life.

★

In the spring of 1962, six months after beginning his job at the lab, Perec imagined rewriting *Ulysses* and improving on it. Perec's Joycean project, entitled *Le Portulan* ("The Mariner's Chart"), presumably in commemoration of the one he owned, would follow two friends on an all-night bar-crawl around Paris as they talked of beer and of bladders, of the nature of reality, and of language. He wrote a couple of pages in that vein and then another fragment describing a demonstration, focussing on the image of a bus without destination boards, requisitioned by the forces of order as an additional Black Maria. Yet another fragment, written at much the same time and also under the title *Le Portulan*, sounds almost familiar:

> *I think I am asking a very simple question: how to use my eyes. How can I begin to see in things something other than what I have become accustomed to seeing? We must rediscover the eye of Galileo. See the living space beneath the house. Why don't we live in mud huts? Why are cigarettes not sold at the chemist's? Why do we go to museums? There are heaps and heaps of things we do that man has not done for all eternity. They seem natural to us, but they aren't. They correspond to something that we can't quite grasp, or can only grasp with difficulty, with leakages, with alibis, false excuses. "Things being what they are," we say, but things never "are what they are", there is always a margin.*

The passage harks back to the anthropology of Marcel Mauss and contains the kind of "sideways glance" that makes the later Perec quintessentially Perecquian. The approximate source of this fragment of *Le Portulan*, however, probably lies in a movement that called itself the Situationist International. Although its leader, Guy Debord, made sure that its membership would always be small (by excommunicating members one by one, until he was in fact the only one left), the Situationist International nonetheless contributed some key ideas to the intellectual ferment of the Left Bank in the 1960s. Perec may have heard of the group through Henri Lefèbvre, who had had the good and bad fortune to be Debord's teacher in the 1950s; or he may have come across one or another of its irregular publications in La Joie de Lire; or he may simply have picked up the Situationist notions that were in the air. Apart from calling for the suppression of all work, the "Situs" argued (with intentional and unparalleled personal nastiness towards their closest allies) for a renewal of the ways in which the world was seen, and they put forward two "techniques" for setting things aright: *la dérive* and *le détournement*. A *dérive* (literally a "drift" or "drifting") was an aimless, rapid perambulation intended to reconfigure the urban environment and allow the shape of things to determine situations: instead of using the city, the "drifter" allowed the city to use him or her. *Détournement* ("kidnapping", "subversion", "misuse") was the active corollary of *dérive*. The true nature of things, the Situationists held, was revealed not in the stultified, conventional, "proper" uses we make of them but only in their intentional abuse. Thus metro tunnels should be open to pedestrians, and pharmacists should deal out cigars. Plagiarism constituted the only true originality, but it was even better, in writing, to misquote, to leave out words such as not, and to insert taboo words here and there. Debord set an example by making a film that had no pictures in it at all and by publishing a book whose first edition was bound in sandpaper so as to damage any volume shelved alongside it. Everything, in a society that offered people images but not the experience of "reality", had to be seen differently, preferably upside down or with graffiti scrawled over it.

The Situationist International has been claimed as the inspiration for innumerable fads and fashions, from Edward de Bono's "lateral thinking" to the decor of the Hacienda Club in Manchester. Its influence on Perec's attitudes is more certain. He was familiar with the ideas of *dérive* and *détournement* in the early 1960s, and these notions informed his reinvention of the art of seeing as well as the art of writing: the nocturnal "drifts" of *Things*, the perambulations of *A Man Asleep*, the "sideways glance" of *Espèces d'espaces* ("Species of Spaces"), and perhaps even, to some degree, the whole puzzle theme of *Life A User's Manual* (since solving a jigsaw puzzle requires the solver to see the pieces *otherwise*) all reflect, more or less distantly, ideas that were put into circulation by situationism. But Perec was no more a prisoner of situationist contestation than he was of *Partisans*. His work as a writer was to grasp his own world as a whole – to understand, not to resolve, its contradictions.

Perec's life in 1962 had contradictions built into it. He worked as an underling in an expanding science research laboratory; he read Lukács and held forth on the future of French literature in *Partisans*;

he went to the cinema, played Scrabble, and dreamt of the perfect holdup; he tried to take on James Joyce and spent long hours playing patience, and poker, and bridge. In their tiny flat, Georges and Paulette also faced a contradiction between their income and their desires. They would have liked to be richer; they could hardly have been poorer. To make ends meet, Paulette took over Georges's old hack-job of writing résumés for the *Bulletin signalétique du CNRS*, and occasionally came into the laboratory, as did Mireille, Jacques Lederer's wife, to do clerical jobs on short-term contracts. Aunt Esther helped them out now and again, and even Uncle Léon, on a flying visit from Haifa, was good for a few hundred francs. For the Perecs, life was a struggle, one that Michel Martens, with his private income, did not have to fight, and that Roger and Dominique were beginning to win. They had taken almost proper jobs in advertising and market research respectively, and were earning enough to begin acquiring the things they wanted; soon they would have a car. Would they then still be *intellectuals*? What made an intellectual different from a bourgeois? How did one define the class to which their whole group of friends belonged – the "magnetic bunch", consisting of Georges and Paulette, Jacques and Mireille, Pierre and Denise Getzler, Jean Crubellier and Marie-Noelle Thibault, and all their other card-playing, film-going pals, including Babette Mangolte, Denis Buffard, Bruno Marcenac, Claude Burgelin and Marcel Benabou? Perec addressed the question when he sat down to write his essay on the "Concept of Social Class" which was eighteen months overdue:

> We are all dressed in the same way, namely, for the men, cord trousers, a coloured shirt (a sports shirt) with a tie (usually knitted), a tweed jacket – virtually obligatory, a direct import or bought in situ – we have a cigarette forever between our lips or in our hands, and a specific way of holding it, using it, flourishing it: this morning Friday 21 September [1962] I met two identical specimens and a good dozen presenting only minor variations . . .   [FP 89,3,7]

The left-wing intellectual was by definition young, Perec reflected – with the exception of *a few sad clowns like Lefèbvre or Adamov*. Young intellectuals into older bourgeois must grow, however, as the values of "left-wing intellectuals" were in reality the values of the bourgeoisie. *There is no art of living that is not bourgeois, and there's nothing I can do about that.* The only difference was that intellectuals were poor, so they scraped by on cheap restaurants, flea markets, and jumble sales, and thought it a virtue. Sooner or later – by the time one turned thirty, at any rate – decisions had to be made: whether to have no money at all, and to become slowly *un vieux con d'intellectuel*, (not an enticing prospect), or to have lots of it, and at once:

> *From there comes our quasi-perpetual desires to stage holdups, to stumble on a few million on the pavement, to inherit, to make Germany pay, straightaway and for ever, to win the Goncourt Prize, etc.*

Unattributed quotations are from Claude Burgelin and Georges Perec, "Le nouveau roman et le refus du réel", *Partisans* 3 (February 1962), pp. 108–118; Georges Perec, "Pour une littérature réaliste", *Partisans* 4 (April 1962), p. 130; "Engagement ou crise du langage", *Partisans* 7 (November 1962), p. 180; "Robert Antelme ou la vérité de la littérature", *Partisans* 8 (January 1963), p. 133.

Other written sources include Georges Perec and Michel Martens, outline for *La Bande magnétique*, in possession of Michel Martens; and FP 119, 21; 119, 27; 119, 28 (fragments entitled *Le Portulan*).

This chapter also draws on recollections and observations provided by Marcel Benabou, Claude Burgelin, Emile Coupferman, Henry Gautier, Bianca Lamblin, Michel Martens, François Maspéro, Babette Mangolte, Alain Robbe-Grillet, and others.

CHAPTER 27

The Great Adventure

1963

The commission of an intelligent crime took hold of Perec's imagination as the subject of a novel that might get him into print at last and perhaps win the Goncourt Prize. Crime was a fantasy built into market research work, where interviewers routinely went into people's homes, won their trust and made them reveal things they normally kept close to their chests – a modus operandi also used by confidence tricksters. The device of a magnificent sting would also serve fairly well both to express and to undermine the aspiration of all of Perec's friends, which was, essentially, to have the means to live well without being seen to compromise oneself. Burgelin and Benabou were on the gruelling but relatively brief track to the *agrégation*, which would provide each with an income guaranteed for life; Roger and Dominique were advancing rapidly in their fields. Perec's great adventure was writing, his prize the Goncourt. His crime-story novel, which would also re-create and represent his own world, was to be called *La Grande Aventure*.

In 1963 Perec wrote a few further pieces for Maspéro's *Partisans*: a bland report on the Sixth Congress of the UEC,[1] a maliciously gleeful review of Bruce Morisette's book on Robbe-Grillet, and a hatchet job on Kingsley Amis's study of science-fiction. That summer, he and some of his friends went to see Maspéro, to tell him that as they were all members of La Ligne générale, they would no longer be able to contribute to *Partisans*, which had been taken over by a Trotskyist faction. It was the first time Maspéro had heard of Lg. He was surprised and saddened.[2] He had always seen the chain-smoking, smiling ex-para as the only one of the bunch with a bit of maturity and sense,

[1] He might have attended on a press card; but it is more probable that he was considered a member.

[2] This account reproduces Maspéro's recollection. Benabou has no memory of such a meeting.

a man who spoke his own mind, without a platform, a man you could talk to about the ordinary things in life as well as high politics and grand vistas. All of that was undoubtedly true of Perec, yet it was also true that he had kept a more perfect cover in *Partisans* than any of the other clandestine emissaries from the factions of Normal' Sup'. La Ligne générale *was* Perec's personal platform, and he had always been able to speak for it without ceasing to speak for himself.

In the summer of 1963 Perec did not quite close the door behind him on La Joie de Lire, but he ceased to leaf through books in Rue Saint-Séverin quite so often, and he stopped publishing theory and criticism altogether. La Ligne générale would go on, as would Perec's marriage, his job at the lab, his nights playing cards and his parties at Rue de Quatrefages, his thirst for films, his need for books, his lack of money, and his yearning for refinement. His own great adventure was beginning afresh, in a square-ruled foolscap notepad used sideways-on, in landscape fashion, on the cover of which he had written, in his neatest large handwriting, *La Grande Aventure*.

The "landscape manuscript" is dated May 1962 – July 1963 on the title page, but most of its paragraphs were penned between January and March 1963. *La Grande Aventure* (henceforth referred to as *GA2*, its ancestor, *La Bande magnétique,* being *GA1*) begins with a "Chapter 0" – *which isn't one,* said Perec, *hence its title* – and describes, with savage derision, the history, structure, aims, techniques, and results of the market-research industry. It presents a team, or bunch, or "magnetic band" of seven market researchers, with fictional names, fictional social origins, and all the conventional attributes of fictional characters. One of the group, the pipe-smoking Michel, is acknowledged as the leader; as the story proper begins, the others respond to his summons to a beanfeast. After the meal, and the brandy, Michel lays out the situation to the assembled twenty-five-year-olds. They are not getting younger, and they want to enjoy the world before they are old. Instead of grinding on in their precarious ways, they should raise themselves above the crowd – by using their intelligence, their friendship, their skills, and their courage to pull off the greatest holdup of modern times. Which is where the manuscript now stops. Seven neat page stubs suggest that a craft knife was used to excise the outline of the adventure itself.

The landscape manuscript is the earliest material evidence that we have of Perec's working methods. Right-hand (recto) pages are used for the text, in which paragraphs are clearly separated and dated.

Facing (verso) pages are used for comments, forward notes, rewriting instructions, calculations of dates, and spelling corrections. The annotated calendar sellotaped to the inside front cover of the notepad suggests that Perec attached some importance to the exact chronology of the missing story of the sting. In the facing-page notes, the author questions himself on the technical problems of his novel. Should it be cast in first or third person? Should the story commence before or after the detailed exposition of market research? Should the background be briefer? How about printing the "boring" material in italics, to mark it off from the narrative proper? Should the individual characters be given more flesh and blood, or left as anonymous members of the group? The manuscript looks not at all like the work of a tousle-haired poet visited by the muse on a moonlit night, but more like an annotated research report. It seeks to be a technically self-aware organisation of knowledge about a particular world – a world Perec knew well by way of his friends and by dint of his own experience, but in which he was less an actor than an oblique and ironical observer.

Inside the back cover of the notepad is a scrawl (*see opposite*) bearing little relation to the much neater manuscript that precedes it. It looks like a set of thoughts prompted by a rereading of the excised adventure story. The line striking out the words *How to get money* may be a trace of the day that Perec cut away the seven sheets that probably held the outline of the holdup itself; it must have been done around the time that news broke of the "greatest crime of modern times", which is what French newspapers called the theft of a shipment of registered mail from the Glasgow-to-London overnight express in mid-August 1963. It is possible that the Great Train Robbery reinforced Perec's wish to write a novel about a crime; but it is much more likely that it prompted him to push his plan forward in a different direction.

Elsewhere, Perec noted down what he read during August, a slack month in the lab as in most domains of French life: Lewis Carroll's *Alice in Wonderland*, Herman Hesse's *The Glass Bead Game* (at last), Roger Vailland, Paul Nizan, Lampedusa's *The Leopard*, Verne's *Twenty Thousand Leagues under the Sea* (certainly not his first reading of it), Fielding's *Joseph Andrews*, Nabokov's *Lolita,* Tolstoy, and bits of Jorge Semprun and even Simone de Beauvoir.

Perec began the new academic year with new intentions. Having already written literary theory for *Partisans*, he now decided that he

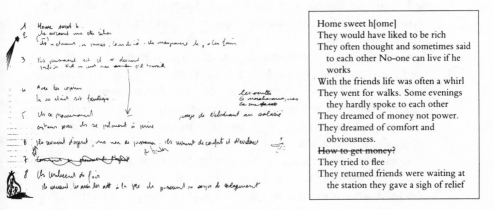

Home sweet h[ome]
They would have liked to be rich
They often thought and sometimes said
    to each other No-one can live if he
    works
With the friends life was often a whirl
They went for walks. Some evenings
    they hardly spoke to each other
They dreamed of money not power.
They dreamed of comfort and
    obviousness.
How to get money?
They tried to flee
They returned friends were waiting at
    the station they gave a sigh of relief

ought to learn some. He enrolled at the Sorbonne so as to be able to attend the lectures on the sociology of literature, given every Tuesday by Lucien Goldmann, a disciple of Lukács and the leading French advocate of critical realism. It was Perec's aim to obtain a Diplôme d'Etudes supérieures (DES) and to that end he drafted a proposal that autumn and submitted it to Goldmann. Every Thursday afternoon at five Perec also attended seminars given by Roland Barthes at the Ecole Pratique de Hautes Etudes (EPHE), located at that time on Staircase E in the main building of the Sorbonne.[1] It promised to be the most academic year Perec had had since Duvignaud's class at Collège Geoffroy-Saint-Hilaire. Between his job at the medical faculty in Rue des Saints-Pères, his classes at the Sorbonne, and meetings of Lg in Rue d'Ulm – or lunch in the refectory of ENS with Claude, or Marcel, or Jacques Joly, or (occasionally) Balibar, Duroux, and Rancière – Perec's life now turned in a circle largely described by the central institutions of learning.

Perec was twenty-seven, and dramatically underqualified for his talents and age. He had flunked every academic opportunity since his baccalaureate. At Henri-IV he had worked on strip cartoons in lieu of philosophy; at the Sorbonne he had cut most of his classes instead of gaining a degree. After he applied for transfer from the XVIIIᵉ RCP in the summer of 1958, Perec had almost allowed Duvignaud to persuade him to do a degree in sociology; but when the transfer came through, he never bothered to enrol, or to pursue the "practical

[1] See Louis-Jean Calvet, *Roland Barthes* (Paris: Flammarion, 1990), pp. 192–193.

and theoretical studies of the English language" that had been the stated grounds for his transfer request. In Tunisia he had registered at the University of Tunis but had submitted a madcap essay on Brasilia instead of a proper assignment, expecting to be awarded the credit on the nod. Perec had a long track record as an academic layabout, yet he had every gift needed to breeze through examinations: a retentive memory of uncommon power, a great facility for writing (and for writing very fast; Dominique *knew* he was a writer when she first saw his pen fly across the page), and unparalleled skill in organising knowledge, as shown by his work at the lab. Perec's academic absenteeism was slightly absurd in the context of a country obsessed with academic progression, where careers are qualification-led, and in a circle of friends the least academic of whom gained higher qualifications than he did, despite his being seen by them all as having the sharpest mind of the bunch.

When asked by his prospective employer, Hugelin, why he had nothing substantially beyond the *bac*, Perec had put it down to his bad relationship with his uncle. Even if that had been true for him at the age of eighteen, however, it could not be an excuse at twenty-seven. If the wasted years at Henri-IV and the Sorbonne had been part of a broader depression, Perec's refusal even to try to catch up after 1957 was more an expression of defiance. He was a free man. He did not want to be an academic; he was a writer, which was something else. To some extent he also wanted to be a failure, an outcast, a marginal member of the intelligentsia, free of the burdens of success. He would be nobody's son. He had taken charge of his own education and had built his own university, which he called La Ligne générale. The only examiners to whom Perec would submit were those he had chosen himself.

He could have come unstuck, and nearly did. What would Perec have become if he had not been published in time? He was well on his way to being a *raté*, a failure, by the time he left *Partisans*. There were plenty of them in the Latin Quarter, intellectuals nearing thirty who had not made it, whom you could see out of the corner of your eye, *in polo-necks and cord trousers, sitting every evening on the same café terrace in Saint-Germain or Montparnasse, scraping a living from occasional bargains and deals* [T 99], always on the lookout for a loan, or a drink.

The Perecs and their free-floating friends were riding the crest of a demographic wave and of nearly two decades of full employment.

They thought they could afford to be optimistic and believed that it was far better to be free to do everything than to settle for any one thing in particular. It was not a question of whether they could find jobs; it was a question of whether they would deign to. Babette Mangolte was flabbergasted when Paulette announced that she was going to qualify as a librarian and get a job at the Bibliothèque Nationale: it amounted to an abandonment of *disponibilité*, the cherished quality of availability. According to Marcel Benabou, "Refusing to get on, to seize opportunities, to take advantage of circumstance . . ., those were our values still. Success could only prove that we hadn't aimed high enough."[1] On the Left Bank, the Marx Brothers joined hands with Karl, in support of arrogant youngsters who declined to join any club that was so common as to let them in.

Perec did not return to formal education in 1963 in order to advance along the traditional French path of academic qualification. He had known Roland Barthes since their brief encounter at Royaumont, and Barthes let him sit in on his classes as a writer, not as a regular student. The topic was semiology, the science of signs, which was treated as a branch of linguistics, and applied in the main to the language of advertising.[2] Perec learnt the rudiments of Ferdinand de Saussure's *Course in General Linguistics* from Barthes and reused them, years later, to comic effect, in several episodes in *Life A User's Manual*.[3] He attended Barthes's seminar the following year as well, when the subject was rhetoric, the "old science" of decorative and persuasive diction, with its list of Greco-Latin terms for the different figures of speech. Paulette also attended these dry academic lectures on *inventio*, *elocutio* and *dispositio*, which Barthes enlivened, on at least one occasion, with a digression on the problem of convention and true-seemingness in the gold-leaf murder in the latest James Bond film.

Perec's proposal for a master's thesis (or DES) entitled "The Options of the French Novel in the Early 1950s" was handed in to

[1] Marcel Benabou, *Pourquoi je n'ai écrit aucun de mes livres* (Paris: Hachette, 1986), p. 62.

[2] Perec acknowledged the influence of Barthes's seminars on his writing of *Things* in "Emprunts à Flaubert", *L'Arc* 79 (1980), p. 49, but Barthes's *Mythologies* of 1957 was equally important. See Andrew Leak, "Phago-citations: Barthes, Perec and the Transformation of Literature" in *RCF*, pp. 57–75.

[3] See David Bellos, "Perec et Saussure. A Propos de *La Vie mode d'emploi*", in *PAP*, pp. 91–95.

Lucien Goldmann in October 1963. The academic preamble restates the argument of the *Partisans* pieces, which was also the argument of Lg: the conventional history of the French novel since 1945 – committed literature, then "uncommitted" literature, with the "new novel" finally providing a way out of the impasse – was inadequate. Perec proposed to study in detail the full range of novels published between 1948 and 1954 and the ways in which they had been categorised by critics of the period, in order to demonstrate the falsity of received ideas of the evolution of French literature. His envisaged method was traditional; his wish to study his material in the light of Lukács explains why he chose to submit the plan to Goldmann. What he imagined he would discover was the replacement of older masters of the modern novel (such as Roger Martin du Gard and John Dos Passos) by new literary beacons (among them Joyce, Kafka, Woolf, perhaps Paul Morand and possibly even Simenon). The king of filing cards concluded his proposal with an impressive bibliography.

Perec went to Goldmann's lectures but could not easily put his mind to academic work. An entry in his jotter, from November 1963, shows the ambivalence that he felt:

> *Last night Scrabble with LL* [Jacques and Mireille]. *Goldmann lecture – my lack of interest or rather insertion. I seem to be understanding but getting fed up with it. He didn't say anything that grabbed me. Can't see how I fit into all that. These days find myself seeing novels, and nothing but, stretching out ahead. The prospect delights and depresses me.*

Perec's projected thesis on the postwar novel was a recycling of work begun for Lg in 1959, pursued on filing cards in Sfax in 1961, and carried forward in Paris as the underpinning of the *Partisans* articles in 1962. It hardly seems surprising that he should be bored with it by 1963. He cut Goldmann's lectures after the first term and never wrote the thesis. His last shot at formal learning fizzled out.

Perec was more stimulated by what his friends were studying. *Sentimental Education* was the main set text for the *agrégation* course at Normal' Sup' in 1962–63, and Perec often listened to his friends' discussions of the work they were doing. He read Flaubert's novel again and thought about it in the light of what Lukács had said was there:

> fragments of the real . . . simply juxtaposed in all their hard-

ness, incoherence, and isolation. Flaubert gives no special importance to his novel's hero. The life of Frédéric Moreau is just as flimsy as the world around him . . . And yet this novel, despite its depressing content, is the only one that . . . has ever attained true epic objectivity and, because of that, the positivity and affirming strength of a perfectly accomplished form.[1]

Perec was never keen on all of Flaubert – he read *Madame Bovary* and *Salammbô* only once, he said later, before putting them aside. For him, Flaubert was only ever the author of *Bouvard et Pécuchet*, of the *Correspondence,* and of *Sentimental Education.*

Perec also reread *The Conspiracy,* a little-studied novel by Paul Nizan, first published in 1938 and reissued in 1962 with an afterword by Jean-Paul Sartre.[2] Perec cannot have failed to see in Nizan's novel precisely the kind of irony which Lukács analyses so well in the work of Cervantes and Thomas Mann. There was another kind of irony, too, in Perec's interest in *The Conspiracy*: its hero, Bernard Rosenthal, is a secularised Jew from the sixteenth arrondissement whose family lives not a stone's throw away from Rue de l'Assomption; moreover, he plans to launch a political periodical with a group of intellectual friends, in anticipatory plagiarism of Perec's own project with La Ligne générale. Rosenthal's group undertakes its own "great adventure", stealing military documents which they hand over to the Communist party. The friends are subsequently betrayed, arrested, and imprisoned, and one of them goes to an early grave. Apart from the coincidence, however, Nizan's novel – which is usually classified (and shelved) as the only socialist realist novel written in French – is of some importance for understanding how Perec moved from the sarcasm of *La Grande Aventure* to the irony of *Things.* Nizan portrays Rosenthal with sympathy but gives the reader the means to see his hero's self-delusions, his mistaken ideas, and his emotional limitations. Rosenthal is not exactly a modern antihero, nor exactly its opposite: he is, rather, a character moving now closer to and now further away from the narrator's position. The shifting web of relation-

---

[1] Georg Lukács, *Théorie du roman* (Paris: Denoël/Gonthier, 1963), pp. 123–124.

[2] Paul Nizan, *The Conspiracy,* trans. by Quintin Hoare (London: Verso Books, 1990).

ships that Nizan created between the reader, the narrator and the hero
was sufficiently close to what Lukács had propounded to merit Perec's
serious reflection. From a technical point of view, *The Conspiracy* must
count as a major influence on the writing of *Things*.

Few of the important elements in Perec's reeducation in his post-
Tunisian period were strictly contemporary. Lukács's ideas had been
formed in the 1920s. Nizan was a writer of the 1930s. Antelme's
L'Espèce humaine had been published in 1947. Most of the American
films Perec loved to go and see repeatedly had been made between
1940 and 1955; and the authors he reread most often, and most
intensely – amongst them, Verne, Tolstoy, and Melville – were a
good deal older than that. Perec was not out of touch with his own
time, but much of what passed for intellectual eminence on the Left
Bank in the 1960s made him want to laugh. "Derision", Marcel
Benabou recalls, "was all that could emerge from the contradiction
we lived in: refusing the idea of success, on the one hand, and jealous
of recognition, on the other."

It was the age of the media guru. In *L'Express*, in *Le Nouvel Observateur*, and even, on occasion, in *Elle*, intellectuals were put on a
par with film directors and society hostesses. Amongst the stars of
cerebration were Perec's mentors Jean Duvignaud, Edgar Morin,
Henri Lefèbvre, and Roland Barthes, as well as many others – such
as Lacan, Lévi-Strauss, Foucault, Althusser, and Marcuse – who had
passed across his horizon at one time or another, either through his
cousins' connections, or at Normal' Sup', or at the receptions that
Duvignaud sometimes took him to when he was in Paris. Perec never
allowed himself to believe that being a writer would make him a big
man, and so it seemed to him that many of the Big Thinkers of the
day, puffing pipes around well-polished round tables, were fair game.
He took a popular song about a Paris prostitute, "Nini Peau-de-
chien", and, pronouncing it only slightly differently, came up with
a new and impenetrable language: *Ninipotchien*, or Ninipotchian. It
could only be the attribute of a school of thought founded by a
philosopher called Ninipotch. Perec scribbled some notes in his jotter:

> *Ninipotch: A banker (Rufus Augustus Koenig) is looking, on behalf
> of a financial conglomerate, for a peg on which to hang a huge
> operation. Consults a young advertising psychologist who unearths
> Ninipotch. Half-consenting, N. is made the object of a subtle (retro-
> active) advertising campaign, with the help of his splinter group.*

*Systematic development, of which N. is aware: he has been taken
for a ride but – more seriously – he agrees with the image of himself
that is presented [. . .] Sartre, Lefèbvre would appear in the book,
but not Morin or [illegible] (who would be its targets).*

✝

In September 1963 Perec took up the manuscript he had abandoned
in July and began to type out a new story based on it. This third
version of *La Grande Aventure* (*GA3*) was finished on 19 October and
given to Roland Barthes on 11 December 1963. In the eight intervening weeks, Perec wrote up his thesis proposal, had a break with
friends in the country during which he listened to Bach, thought of
writing a play about Thomas Mann and a detective story halfway
between Kafka and Agatha Christie, caught up with his backlog at
the lab, and read *La Grande Aventure* aloud to some of his friends.
Should he carry on with it? Should he start all over again, with his
heroes more fleshed out, more like conventional fictional characters?
According to one of Perec's notes, Paulette felt that the characters
were too "thin"; Denis Buffard borrowed the typescript, read half of
it, came back to Rue de Quatrefages to confront the author about his
view of money, consumerism, and utopia, and ended up disagreeing
with Paulette's opinion of the novel. Perec thought Buffard was being
pigheaded, and felt depressed by such arguing. Marcel also heard
Perec read his text aloud, as did Claude and Jacques: Perec's new
work was less baffling than *Le Condottiere*, but it failed to overwhelm
them.

The characters in *GA3*, a group of young market researchers, all
have names, which are not for the most part the names of Perec's
own market-researcher friends. They dream of the ideal home; they
despise *L'Express* but read it all the same; they are flabbergasted by
their first sight of the cornucopia of the French countryside; they are
caught out politically by the end of the war in Algeria; they go to
Tunisia and come back. The main episodes correspond to the Perecs'
own recent experiences and to the brief summary inserted at the end
of *GA2*. They also correspond to the main episodes of *Things*, albeit
not in quite the same order. But *GA3* is still a development or a
recasting of *GA1*, the old *Bande magnétique*. When Jérôme and Sylvie
return from North Africa, they plan a "great adventure", using the
tools of market research. They interview a "Professor Getzler" who

reveals that his neighbour, a wealthy publisher by the name of Paul Hongre, also owns a country house at Maillebois, where he keeps his art collection. Jérôme and Sylvie go to burgle the house, but as they prepare to scale the garden wall in the middle of the night, they lose their nerve, and give up. Three days later, on 5 May 1962, in a Paris taxi, Sylvie stubs her foot on something under the seat. It is a briefcase made of green leather (or, more precisely, of shagreen, the same exotic hide as the talisman that fulfils every wish in Balzac's novel *The Wild Ass's Skin*), containing five million francs in bank notes. The youngsters take the money and leave for a trip around the world.

They travelled: it is less an echo than a lift from the penultimate chapter of *Sentimental Education*. The story jumps forward eighteen months (into the virtual present of the novel's writing, mid–October 1963), and to Belgrade, where Jérôme and Sylvie, now nearly penniless, are on the point of returning home. On the Belgrade-to-Venice express they swap reminiscences, just like Frédéric and Deslauriers at the end of Flaubert's novel. Recalling the great adventure that they planned but never pulled off, Perec's couple turn their predecessors inside out:

> "That was the happiest time we ever had," said Frédéric.
> "Yes, perhaps you're right. That was the happiest time we ever had," said Deslauriers. [Gustave Flaubert, *Sentimental Education*]

> *"That was the funniest time we ever had," said Jérôme.*
> *Sylvie didn't answer.*   [GA3]

The last meal Jérôme and Sylvie take in the Wagons-Lits dining car, with the last few francs of their found fortune, tastes, quite frankly, rather bland.

If the throwaway ending of *GA3* seems to settle scores with Flaubert, the whole work might have been intended to do the same with the Bienenfeld clan, for the house that the couple in the story plans to burgle stands in reality only a few hundred yards to the east of the country home at Blévy. It was probably not the *gentilhommière* itself on Route de Maillebois that Perec's characters do not quite dare break into: the crime that Jérôme and Sylvie fail to commit looks very much like a sideways shift of a fantasy of seizing what Perec would not inherit from the house next door. The half-autobiographical tone of this abandoned part of the plan is echoed by the story's return to the place where, in Perec's view, his own "cure" had really begun: Belgrade.

Whilst waiting for Roland Barthes to give his verdict on *La Grande Aventure*, Perec pursued other interests with roots in his past life and ramifications in his later writing. He came back to Paul Klee with the idea of doing an article, or perhaps a larger work, in collaboration with Pierre Getzler. Perec read Grohmann's standard work on the painter and made notes for Getzler; they met often, in the course of the autumn of 1963, to "talk Klee", and Perec used his regular jotter to list the questions that arose in his mind:

> *Why do we like Klee?*
> *The problem of the possibility of a coherent world directly expressed by painting. The painter must be reinserted into the work as an element that is itself contradictory.*

Perec also turned his attention to music. The great talking-point of the 1963–64 season was the first French performance of Alban Berg's *Wozzeck*, which was hailed in the Paris press as a compositional and operatic revolution. It was as if the critics had no inkling that the libretto was drawn from a work written in the 1820s, that the opera dated from the 1920s, and that Berg himself had served as a model for Adrian Leverkühn, the musical genius of Thomas Mann's *Doktor Faustus*, and also acted as Mann's musical consultant. But all this Perec knew well, from his cultural background at Rue de l'Assomption. The article he dashed off for *Clarté* in December 1963, "*Wozzeck* ou la méthode de l'apocalypse", did not really mark a return to criticism or to reviewing on Perec's part; it was more of a gleeful exposition of knowledge he had acquired from his Bienenfeld relatives (and especially from his sister-cousin Lili), which he now passed on for the benefit of parochial Parisians. Much of the material was copied straight out of Thomas Mann.

Perec's work on Klee and Berg was probably not unconnected with the attempted revival of La Ligne générale in the academic year 1963–64. Meetings were held mostly at Normal' Sup', which also provided a potential source of new members. *The* normaliens *seem – repeat, seem – to be attracted by Lg,* Perec noted, in advance of a bigger meeting planned for 12 December 1963. Perec took the chair and gave the introductory talk, which he had gone over with Kleman beforehand. Old and new members sat in a circle, like knights at a round table. Despite the overlap with the first Lg (Perec, Kleman, Lederer,

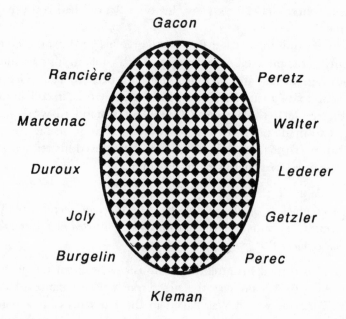

Gacon

Rancière   Peretz

Marcenac   Walter

Duroux   Lederer

Joly   Getzler

Burgelin   Perec

Kleman

Getzler, Burgelin, and Marcenac), and despite the inclusion of some of the *Partisans* team (Rancière and Walter), the main problem that the leaders faced was how to prevent the project from becoming just another Normal' Sup' seminar group. Perec sketched out a contents list for the first issues of the new review, to be called *La Ligne générale* or perhaps (with somewhat baffling irony) *La Ligne nodale*: Perec on Nizan, Getzler on art, Benabou on *Candide*,[1] Jacques Joly on Italian cinema, and an article, still unattributed, on Marxist aesthetics. Lederer was scheduled to do a piece on the filmmaker Jacques Demy, Kleman would do two on Valéry Larbaud, and "everyone" would contribute to a symposium on Alain Resnais, whose latest film, scripted by Robbe-Grillet, seemed to Lg a betrayal of the talent of the man who had made *Hiroshima mon amour*.

The plenary group met again on 10 January 1964 and Perec also lunched several times with subgroups of Lg newcomers in Latin Quarter restaurants. The *normaliens*, he grumbled, *lacked critical intelligence;* they could not see the wood for the trees, and they all ordered the same thing for lunch. He argued with Rancière as to whether the

---

[1] Not Voltaire's *Candide*, but the right-wing weekly that had usurped its title.

group's priority was to "build Marxist aesthetics" or "to foment a prerevolutionary ideology characterised by negation". On 23 January Lg met at the Klemans' flat, where members listened to Jacques Lederer's paper on film art. But the project was fizzling out. A week later Perec noted that Jacques did not want to accept the *failure, or semi-failure*, of Lg. It is not clear from Perec's notes what exactly happened, but whatever it was, it was terminal. La Ligne générale died in the days prior to 1 February 1964.

The following autumn Simone de Beauvoir, hoping to bring new blood into *Les Temps modernes,* summoned sundry *normaliens* for a discussion of the role they might play in the journal. *"La Ligne générale* will live again!" they said to themselves as they walked to the meeting together – Marcel Benabou, Henri Peretz, Regis Debray, Jacques Joly and Georges Perec. In the end, Perec did not join the team at *Les Temps modernes* and those old Lg members who did soon found themselves at odds with its editor. Beauvoir wanted the youngsters to write short notices on recent books, films and plays, whereas the youngsters themselves wanted to write proper articles. Some of these latter were accepted, and the dozen pieces signed by Marcel-Emile Burnacs, Jacques Pollak-Lederer, Henri Peretz and Roger Kleman that appeared in *Les Temps modernes* between 1964 and 1966 give an indication of the talents that might have gone into *La Ligne générale*. Lg's association with *Les Temps modernes* came to an end in 1966, whether for reasons of editorial conflict (as the youngsters who left maintained) or for political reasons (as Simone de Beauvoir saw it). By that time, however, Perec's own "great adventure" was finished, and he had won his first prize.

This chapter is drawn mainly from written sources, principally FP 31,3,6 (Perec's 1963 jotter); 31,4,1 (handout from Barthes's 1964–65 seminar); 89, 2 (carbon copy typescript of *GA3*); 89, 4 (the "landscape manuscript", or *GA2*); 119, 10 (carbon copy of DES proposal); Georges Perec, *"Wozzeck ou la méthode de l'apocalypse"*, *Clarté*, no. 53 (January 1964), pp. 51–53 (reprinted with an introduction by Vincent Bouchot in *Clarté* (new series), no. 10 [May–June 1988]); Georges Perec, reply to a survey, "Ce qu'ils pensent de Flaubert", *La Quinzaine littéraire* no. 324 (1 May 1980), and from the recollections and observations of Marcel Benabou, Pierre Bessis, Pierre Getzler, Henri Peretz, and Jürgen Ritte.

CHAPTER 28

Things

1964

It is extraordinary to note to what degree all my thoughts – repeat, all my thoughts – centre on GA: even my diploma, B's and G's lectures, discussions with friends.

Perec was still a timid ex-student and did not dare ask Roland Barthes face-to-face what he thought of his book. He knew he would have to rewrite it in any case. This time he would do it slowly and get it right at last. Perec's New Year's resolution for 1964 was to proceed patiently, like a paver relaying a path, and to perfect no more than two pages of *La Grande Aventure* each day. But he could not hold himself back. On 1 January, the first day of rewriting, he typed out all seven pages of chapter 1 of *GA4*, the description of Jérôme and Sylvie's imaginary "home sweet home".

Over the following weeks, during which he saw his uncle Léon Peretz for the last time, made his final attempt to resurrect Lg, learnt of the death of his grandmother Rose in Tel Aviv at the age of eighty-four, and held some unforgettable parties at Rue de Quatrefages (just the smell of the punch got people tipsy as they entered the tiny, crowded flat), Perec kept to his schedule. In his jotter he recorded recurrent doubts (should the first chapter be in the present? should the novel be in the first person?) as well as his progress, page by page: 13 January, *GA* 23–24; 14 January, *GA* 25–28; 15 January, *GA* 29–31. Barthes's response to *GA3* came at last, towards the end of January, when *GA4* was nearly half done:

I find your book extremely good. I believe I can sense all the novelty you expect from it: not a realism of detail, but, in the best tradition of Brecht, a realism of situation. A novel or a story about poverty inextricably bound up with the image of wealth is very beautiful, [and] very rare nowadays.

I don't know what you want to revise or add to it, but in any case, finish it quickly – and publish!

The letter must have given strength to the elbow of the ambidextrous typist at his Underwood Four Million. Despite his full-time job at the lab, Perec took barely a day's rest from writing until 22 March 1964, when he announced for posterity in the notebook that is in effect the log of *Things*: *End of GA (139) at 2:00 A.M.* Barthes had encouraged him to finish quickly and publish. He had obeyed the first part of the injunction; the second part was not up to him.

In *GA4*, the original story of a holdup or burglary recedes even further: Jérôme and Sylvie now do not even get to the brink of taking action. On their return from Tunisia, frustrated by their inadequate and unpredictable incomes in a city bursting with things to be bought, they find their marriage falling apart: *They could no longer bear each other. They hadn't managed to live together for ages.* They dream briefly of thieving a great fortune. The dream – the last trace of *La Bande magnétique* – is, in *GA4*, the main symptom of a marriage gone sour. Friends come to the rescue and find jobs for Jérôme and Sylvie in Bordeaux, to keep them afloat, and to keep them together. Perec's novel of 1964 ends with an epilogue set in the future tense:

> *They will see themselves hunting for cigarettes all across Paris, and stopping in front of antiques dealers' shop windows. They will recall their old Sfaxian days, their slow death, their almost triumphant return, and then the collapse, the stupid dreams, the fracture.*
> *"Those were the funniest times we had," Sylvie will say.*
> *Jérôme will not reply.*

Three days after finishing it, Perec delivered his typescript by hand to Georges Lambrichs at Gallimard. He rang a fortnight later: Lambrichs had not yet read it. He waited. On 20 April he rang again. Lambrichs *does not reject but does not appreciate GA*, Perec noted. The editor needed more time and would give his answer at the beginning of May. Perec rang again in due course; Lambrichs was out, so he left a message. The call was returned: Monsieur Lambrichs needed ten more days. The final answer reached Rue de Quatrefages not by telephone but on headed notepaper paper bearing the firm's standard disclaimer in small type at the bottom: "The company declines responsibility for the loss of books and manuscripts entrusted to it". The letter was dated 11 June 1964:

> Despite obvious qualities of intelligence, it seems to me . . .
> that you have lost the wager of making an entertaining or
> instructive book out of boredom. It is true that your charac-
> ters are dull, somewhat naive, without any real life. Please
> believe me, I am indeed disconcerted.

Perec had been turned down yet again, and yet again by Gallimard.
Back to square one. He did his best to take his mind off the failure.
He went to the Museum of Modern Art, then to the Café du Troca-
déro, then to the Museum of Mankind, and then to the cinema, to
see a comfortingly familiar film: *The World in his Arms* (Universal,
1952; 104 minutes), directed by Raoul Walsh, starring Gregory Peck
as a nineteenth-century Californian seal poacher and Ann Blyth as a
Russian countess. (The film involves a great race between oceangoing
yachts, a race won by Peck, seen at the wheel as the final credits roll,
gazing into the far Pacific, with Ann Blyth in his arms.) Then poker
to finish off another day, another ordinary day, like all the past days
on which no publisher had given him a contract. After a stint back
at the lab, Perec went to the office of Les Lettres nouvelles, now
owned by the publishing company Julliard, to meet Maurice Nadeau,
to whom I hand my book, almost trembling. Perec's second hope was
silent for a month. In the interval, whilst the writer waited, Henri
Peretz failed his *agrégation*, Léon Peretz died of a heart attack in Haifa,
and Perec totted up his current debts: a hundred thousand (presumably old) francs, about two months' net income.

Nadeau was not a slow reader, but like Lambrichs, he was unsure
about *La Grande Aventure.* He wanted a second opinion, so he passed
the typescript to the clever young man who had been René Julliard's
personal assistant and was now the company's troubleshooter, and, in
some unspecific way, his boss. Christian Bourgois cannot remember
what he thought of Perec's typescript, but he recalls the folder it was
in and what he took to be its author's obsession with the Great Train
Robbery of the previous year. Whatever it was that he said to Nadeau
tipped the scales. Perec's jotter for 16 July 1964 reads:

> *Nadeau.* GA *accepted, "on conditions". Howard Hawkes,* Red
> River.

Nadeau's "conditions" were that *GA4* would have to be rewritten
and part 2 recast entirely. He would not take on a novel that ended
up as a pastiche of Flaubert. Nadeau did not expect the young man

to swallow his pride and rewrite what he presumably thought was perfect already. How many aspiring authors had he not already seen, with their almost finished first novels, who lacked the wind to make the last straight!

In Perec's mind Nadeau's offer constituted a famous victory. He had been there before, in the summer of 1959, with a contract from Gallimard for *Gaspard pas mort*, but this time he did not have military service hanging over him. He was five years older now; he would make it. So the Perecs set off on a summer holiday to London, Edinburgh, Inverness, the Western Highlands, and Skye. *A Hard Day's Night* was playing in all the High Street cinemas, but they shunned it.[1] In art-movie houses, Fritz Lang's *M* was being shown, as it was in France; in fact, if the Perecs had taken along the July 1964 issue of *L'Avant-Scène Cinéma* to read on the train, they could have perused the whole script in Volker Schlöndorff's translation, as well as a strange note about the missing closing sequence of Lang's classic study of a child-murderer.[2]

When they got to the Highlands, Perec fell in love with the forests and moors. On visits abroad in later years, when his hosts would take him to some scenic spot, Perec would most often sniff the air, squint into the distance, and return to the car, saying, *Very lovely. But I prefer Scotland* . . . It may have been a play on Garance's line, in *Les Enfants du Paradis*: "C'est beau, l'Ecosse, mais c'est loin. Et moi je n'aime que Paris."[3] But it seems that it was also true, even if Perec never returned to the windswept heather or the rough sea crossing to Skye.

They were back in Paris at the end of August and soon got back to their old routines: dinner with the Klemans, dinner with Babette, with the Getzlers, with Denis Buffard; a trip to Passy to see Esther; and films, films, and more Hollywood films, at the luxurious Salle des Agriculteurs, at the well-named Cine Qua Non and the Cinémathèque, which was housed, at that time, in Rue d'Ulm. "Hollywood colonised our imaginations," says Babette Mangolte.

Somehow Perec still found time to work on *GA5*. In October he

[1] See Georges Perec, "Je me souviens du jazz", *Jazz-Magazine* no. 272 (February 1979), pp. 30–34.

[2] At least three books about Fritz Lang appeared in French in 1963–64, the most interesting of them being Francis Courtade, *Fritz Lang* (Paris: Losfeld, 1963). Pages 39–46 deal specifically with *M*.

[3] "Scotland is beautiful, but a long way away. And I love Paris alone."

left off for a week to go to Switzerland with Pierre Getzler. Their
first stop was Lausanne, to visit relatives of Perec's grandmother Rose
who had first moved to Germany, made a fortune in industry, and
slightly altered the family name to Wallerstein. (They had cousins in
the States who had anglicised the name entirely to Waller.) Perec and
Getzler also spent a day or two in Basel, where they went to the
opera to see Verdi's *Nabucco*, but the main focus of the trip was the
vast collection of paintings by Paul Klee in the artist's home town,
Bern.

In Paris, work on *GA5* proceeded on the Underwood Four Million
for the rest of the month, and then Georges and Paulette took another
break: a long weekend devoted exclusively to playing cards with
friends, in a house in Normandy, at a place called Les Petites-Dalles.
There were seven or eight of them altogether, and they kept on at
their game of *le barbu* through the night. No money was at stake, but
there was a heavy forfeit for the loser: he or she had to get up early
enough the next day to go shopping before the village store closed
down for the night.

Perec returned to Les Petites-Dalles several times in the later 1960s.
The house belonged to the parents of Babette's sister-in-law, the
Brennacs, who spent much of their time abroad. M. Brennac, like
Stendhal, was in the consular service, and he and his wife had acquired
a taste for long voyages on ocean liners. On their unhurried travels
between Europe, Africa, and Australia, the Brennacs liked to play
with jigsaw puzzles, most of which they brought back with them to
Les Petites-Dalles. Some of these were magnificent wooden puzzles,
as huge as the one glimpsed in the hallway of Xanadu, in *Citizen
Kane*. During their weekend canasta binges, one or another of the
Brennacs' and Mangoltes' houseguests would often tackle a puzzle
for a change. "We were quite clear about the distinction between
cardgames and puzzles in those days," recalls Babette. "One was a
game of chance, the other a pursuit based on skill."

Then Perec had to get back to the lab, and back to *GA5*. The
typescript was finished with speed: the last entry in Perec's log is
dated 17 November 1964. Before the end of the month, *GA5* had
been bound in a blue cardboard folder, with a title page – reading *La
Grande Aventure. Une Histoire des années soixante* – done in coloured
inks. The "great adventure", which had been the whole story in
GA1, had shrunk to the main story in *GA2* (hypothetically), to an
elaborate failure in *GA3*, to a dream of escape from a collapsing

marriage in *GA4*, and, finally, to a fantasy dismissed in two paragraphs in *GA5*. The old title was obviously inappropriate to the latest version of the novel. Even "Sartrimself" had not got it right the first time, Perec might well have reminded himself: he had called his first novel *Melencolia*, and had been turned down by Gallimard. It was only because he had accepted Gaston Gallimard's title for the book that Sartre had got *Nausea* into print at all. Should Perec leave it to Nadeau to think up a new name? Or should he find one himself? He and Paulette talked about the problem for a while. In the end it was she who came up with the answer. Towards the end of November 1964 Perec crossed out *La Grande Aventure* on the label stuck onto the cover of his blue folder, and wrote in, in blue biro, in careful capital letters, the two words that would define his first work perfectly:

LES CHOSES
("Things").

Nadeau was mildly surprised when the scruffy, crew-cut young man he had sent away to rewrite less than six months before turned up again with his novel. He thought this "second" version sharper, better written, and more publishable than the first; but it never crossed his mind that he might have a masterpiece, or a prizewinner, or a best-seller on his hands. But he had promised to publish it, and he would. The contract was signed, and *Things* was scheduled for the autumn 1965 list of new novels. If it appeared in September, along with the three other allowed to *Les Lettres nouvelles* by Julliard, it would perhaps stand a chance of making the shortlist for one of the autumn prizes. In any case it would not be worth printing more than a couple of thousand copies: Perec's first book seemed far too slim.

Based on FP 31,3,6.(Perec's jotter), FP 89,1 (*GA5*), FP 89, 7 (*GA4*), FP 31,4,8, and FP 31,4,22 (letters from Georges Lambrichs and Roland Barthes to Perec), and on the recollections and observations of Marcel Benabou, Christian Bourgois, Eugen Helmle, Georges Lambrichs, Babette Mangolte, Maurice Nadeau, and others.

In *Grâces leur soient rendues* (Paris: Albin Michel, 1990), pages 433–434, Maurice Nadeau gives a slightly different account of the decision to publish *Things*.

Appendix to Chapter 28

The Track of Things

GA1	?1961–1962	La Bande magnétique	synopsis typed by Michel Martens
GA2	May 1962–July 1963	La Grande Aventure, roman	incomplete ms
GA3	to 19 October 1963	La Grande Aventure	typescript, 117 pages
GA4	January–March 1964	La Grande Aventure. Une Histoire des années soixante	typescript, 139 pages
GA5	to November 1964	Les Choses. Une Histoire des années soixante	typescript, 159 pages
T	September 1965	Les Choses. Une histoire des années soixante	published book

CHAPTER 29

First Prize

1965

Perec's first published book can also be seen, in one sense, as the last chapter of his autobiography. With only a few exceptions, all that he wrote after *Things* draws on material from earlier periods of his life. It is as if, like Percival Bartlebooth in *Life A User's Manual*, he spent a long time learning to look, and learning to represent what he saw; he would spend the rest of his life like Gaspard Winckler, cutting snapshots of memory into thousands of puzzle pieces.

Things is not autobiographical in any ordinary sense, but it is obviously made up of disconnected and reassembled fragments of personal and shared experience. It is Perec's own work and life, but it also contains a great deal that comes from elsewhere. The title came from Paulette – and no doubt, too, from Jean-Paul Sartre, whose outrageously inauthentic childhood autobiography had appeared in the autumn of 1964, under the title *Words*, to which *Things* seems a pointed rejoinder. Perec's book is dedicated (like *GA3*, *GA4* and *GA5*) to Denis Buffard, his first market-research colleague and friend. The earlier versions had had an epigraph from Saint-Just that sounds almost like Flaubert – "Happiness is a new idea in Europe" – which thus inscribes indirectly Perec's pals at Normal' Sup'. The later versions carry an epigraph from Malcolm Lowry's *Under the Volcano*, in memory of one of Perec's articles in *Partisans*,[1] where he uses the same passage in the same way, except that in *Things*, the quotation is given in English:

> Incalculable are the benefits civilization has brought us, incommensurable the productive powers of all classes of riches originated by the inventions and discoveries of science. Inconceivable the marvellous creations of the human sex in order to make men more happy, more free and more perfect.

[1] Georges Perec, "L'Univers de la science-fiction", *Partisans* 10 (May 1963), p. 118.

Without parallel the crystalline and fecund fountain of the new life which still remains closed to the thirsty lips of the people who follow in their griping and bestial tasks.[1]

Few of Perec's French readers grasp that it is not proper English at all but rather Lowry's word-for-word translation of a parody of Homer that is translated simultaneously by one of his characters, the Consul, as he listens to a radio broadcast in Mexican Spanish. This confusion of tongues is also marked and hidden in the two sentences from Karl Marx with which Perec's novel ends. The quotation itself is from Marx's first published article, "Über die neuste preußische Zensurinstruktion" (1842), but Perec had come across it neither in Marx nor in German. He knew the passage because it is quoted at the end of an essay on film montage by Sergei Eisenstein, in a volume Pierre Getzler had once lent him, the volume that probably gave Perec and Getzler the idea of renaming *La Locomotive La Ligne générale*. The envoi of *Things* is thus an inscription of Pierre Getzler, of Sergei Eisenstein, of the whole group and the set of ideas that made Lg. In fact, it is not really Marx at all: it is a retranslation into French of a Russian translation, differing significantly from the relevant sentences as they appear in Marx's complete works, translated directly.[2] But the motto is nonetheless one to which Perec remained ever faithful:

> *The means is as much part of the truth as the result. The quest for truth must itself be true; the true quest is the unfurling of a truth whose different parts combine in the result.*   [T 126]

Between the completion of GA5, in November 1964, and its publication as *Things* the following September, Perec designed a new information-retrieval system on Peekaboo cards for CNRS LA 38. There was no question of his going freelance just because his novel had been accepted. His contract with Julliard committed him to offer his next five novels to the same firm, but it is not certain that he even got an advance out of it. Money worries persisted and put strains on his comradely but never passionate marriage. Perec's studentlike life at

[1] Malcolm Lowry, *Under the Volcano* (Harmondsworth: Penguin, 1962), pp. 371–372.

[2] For further details see David Bellos, "'Le Moyen fait partie de la vérité . . .'", *Journal of the Institute of Romance Studies 1* (1992), pp. 325–331.

Rue de Quatrefages went on as before, with nights spent at cards, drinking in bars, and at impromptu parties around a bowl of *salade niçoise* with friends from overlapping circles of former *normaliens*, market researchers, indolent scriptwriters, trainee film directors, novice teachers, and unrecognised artists of every ilk, left-wing intellectuals to a man. Perec never drank alone, but he liked drinking very much. When friends were at hand, he rarely said no to a jar. He drew the line at whisky, but if vodka was on offer – at the Klemans', for instance – or Armagnac brandy, or the historic calvados brewed by Gautier's forebears, Perec would sup with alacrity, and sometimes to excess. Martens (that rare bird in the Latin Quarter, a teetotaller *with* a car) often brought him home in comical, uproarious, and sometimes paralytic states. Alcohol made Perec funnier at first, but it could also turn him mawkish. Between the sparkle of the glass and the gloom of the finished litre, Perec's inhibitions about talking to women lifted. He could be a charmer; he could let fly quite pointed remarks; he could even be cutting before the evening was out.

As *Things* went through copyediting, final polishing, and proof stages, Perec continued to attend Roland Barthes's Thursday-afternoon classes on rhetoric. When the course ended, he took the jargon he had learnt, looked back on Lg, and dashed off a high-spirited spoof mocking both rhetoric and political action with such comic verve that it rises above offence even to the staunchest defender of either faith. *Quel Petit Vélo à guidon chromé au fond de la cour?* is as unstrictly autobiographical as *Things*. It contains affectionate digs at Jacques Lederer and his moped; a character said to be the spitting image of Roger Kleman; a dinner party that is a satire on similar evenings at Rue de Quatrefages; and swipes at Lg's culture heroes, from "Lukasse" to "Héliphore" (Elie Faure, the art historian), to "Hégueule", the name of a German philosopher misspelt to rhyme with *dégueule*, or vomit. The book's index lists the rhetorical devices used in the text – anacoluthon, anadiplosis, anaphora, Anglicism, annomination, antanaclasis, antiphrase, antithesis ("Here and there"), and so on – but the main device employed called for the wholesale borrowing of a style invented by Raymond Queneau and made popular by *Zazie in the Metro*. It has no real equivalent in English. It is a "second-order" comic language made up of wobbly spellings (born? borne? bear? bare?), names that are never quite consistent (Karawho? Karawhat?), grammar with yawning chasms (where Henri was brung up? broughted up? upbringed?), and a magical mixture of registers, where high style, low style, poetic diction, Parisian slang, and even bits of standard French all jostle together. *Zazie* exhausts the potential of the device it invents; Perec's imitation is a clever comic pastiche and tremendous fun for a page or two. But why did he go on to make a whole book of his game with Queneau-speak? *Because that is the way I write naturally*, he said, in a note probably drafted in anticipation of an interview. It was his natural inclination, he continued; it represented *what is most contrary to my idea of* littérature, which should perhaps be pronounced in English, in this instance, as "litritcha".

Quel Petit Vélo may be a long joke, but it makes a pretty short book. Perec knew that Nadeau would not necessarily accept it as one of the five "next books" that he was due to deliver. He turned immediately to a different autobiographical exercise, the story of the day he ran away from home as a boy. *Les Lieux d'une fugue* ("Runaway Places") [*Jsn* 15–31] is sober to the point of dryness, constrained, almost repressed. It is a beautiful story, but when it was finished it was even tinier than *Quel Petit Vélo*. As it could not possibly be considered a book, Perec put it away in his bottom drawer, where it stayed for ten years. He needed a project of greater substance if he was to keep his contract with Nadeau, and with himself. He wanted to be a book-a-year man.

Things was not the great work of Perec's dreams. At a mere ninety-six printed pages in the Lettres nouvelles edition, it seemed only a minor triumph to its author. He would rather have produced 850, 1,200 or even 3,000 pages:

> *My literary ambition goes so far as to make me imagine that one day I will write a* Magic Mountain*, a* Joseph Andrews *or* Remembrance of Things Past.

It was not for lack of persistence that his novel had ended up being so slim; on the contrary, what Perec had learnt from the three years it took him to decompose *La Grande Aventure* into *Things* must have been dismaying for an admirer and would-be companion of Herman Melville and Thomas Mann.

Perec mistrusted imagination and believed he had none. Most of his early works, from *Les Errants* to *J'avance masqué*, were set in places he had never been (New York, Guatemala, Palawan) and plotted around specialisms he did not have (carpentry, musicianship, pearl-trading, art forgery). None of these fictions had been published; perhaps none of them was then truly publishable. *Things* was the end result of an entirely different process. From its first joky start in *La Bande magnétique*, it had been built exclusively from "things" Perec had seen with his own eyes. It was not imagination that had provided this material, nor inspiration, but rather observation and reflection, feeling and rationality. These had given him a book that would be published. He put his achievement down not to genius but to technique.

The technique that had led Perec from *La Bande magnétique* to *Things* was somewhat alarming to him. Authors of copious fictions generally start with a scene or a story outline that they then develop in successive drafts, adding descriptions and new characters that set off subplots and digressions, and ultimately the dense web that we recognise as a novel. Perec had done the exact opposite. He had started with a full-blown adventure story and then whittled it away, saving almost nothing of its narrative or its characters, only some of its particular forms of words. Each version from *GA2* to *GA5* represented a different kind of destruction of the original. There was no special method or principle involved; Perec simply found out that that was his direction. He was a craftsman of sentences, not a juggler of plots and characters. Still, the process seemed to lead inexorably towards a book with everything cut away from it, with nothing in it at all save an exquisite vanishing point. *Les Lieux d'une fugue*, at a mere fifteen pages, had almost got him there already. But Perec had no wish for his writing to disappear; it had hardly begun.

In the course of his rewriting, Perec had had increasing recourse to Flaubert. At the start, in the throwaway endings of *GA3* and *GA4*, the allusions to *Sentimental Education* are not far from being derisions of a sacred cow. In *GA5* the technique of inscription is more general-ised. The final text contains more than a dozen lifts from *Sentimental Education*, some very small – such as the name of the paddle-steamer depicted on a print in Jérôme and Sylvie's dream home [*T* 21] – and others as long as a brief paragraph (one of which [*T* 73] is reused in this book, on page 268 above). Years later Perec would say that he had never really understood why he indulged in systematic borrowing in *Things*. He suggested that *it was probably an appropriation, a wanting-to-be-Flaubert . . .*[1] Yet the device is also emblematic of Perec's whole approach to literature and to the world. Lifting sen-tences from a great writer is an act of defiance; it creates a challenge

[1] Georges Perec, "Emprunts à Flaubert", *L'Arc* 79 (1980), p. 50.

for the reader; and yet it is an expression of modesty as well. Why should a writer not work like a carpenter, building a finished object from pieces prepared for him beforehand?

Perec's "wanting-to-be-Flaubert" influenced his entire conception of the problems of writing. The author of *Sentimental Education* would spend days at a stretch on a single page; in repeatedly reducing his text to its bare essentials, Perec was imitating a master hailed by both Lukács and Barthes as the founder of the modern era. His intense absorption in Flaubert during this period produced a style that recalls that of *Sentimental Education*: three adjectives to a noun, three nouns to a list, three legs to a sentence. Because Flaubert is widely read by French students, both at school and at university, *Things* therefore struck its first readers as an already classical text.

Most readers find *Things* as sad as *Sentimental Education*. Around the time that he was completing the final draft, Perec thought of collaborating with Denise Getzler on an essay about another sad story, one that would provide him with a self-image more probing than that of Flaubert's Frédéric Moreau. Bartleby, the protagonist of Herman Melville's short story by the same name (known in French as "Bartleby l'écrivain"), is a copying clerk in a Wall Street law firm. Little by little he encrusts himself in his employer's office, and little by little he stops writing, stops taking orders, until, with quite impenetrable firmness, he "prefers not to" do anything at all save stare out of the window at the blank wall on the other side of the street. Perec set down his thoughts on Melville's story:

> There are some works, usually amongst those we love the most, that end badly, in which something comes to an end, expires. Throughout the book there is an adventure, movement, pursuit, meetings: people who don't know each other come into contact, they walk alongside each other, love each other, change. Then it all stops. It's the end. Someone dies, or disappears. There's no sequel. We feel a gap [. . .] I would prefer works to end in plenitude. But I don't know any that do. There is perhaps War and Peace. But is that plenitude? For a long time I thought it was, but Paulette finished it this summer and felt above all the melancholy of it, and it seems to me she is not wrong.
>
> Even the final chorus of the Messiah is not plenitude. Or rather, it might be that plenitude itself soon turns into melancholy . . . but that takes us a long way from Bartleby.

In the end Bartleby has to be sent to an asylum. His employer discovers that prior to working for him, the strange, catatonic scrivener had been assigned to the dead letter office. "Dead letters! does it not sound like dead men? . . . Ah, Bartleby! Ah, humanity!" he cries.[1]

Perec's *Bartleby* fragment ends with doodle of the lawyer's last words in a kind of French phonetic transcription, along with the scrivener's name, copied out, and then recopied as in a mirror, with the left-right inversion characteristic of some of Perec's most interesting mistakes.[2]

Over the following years, in interviews, lectures, and in a draft article on "how I wrote *Things*" [FP 89,3], Perec's constant refrain was that craft, not inspiration, lay at the root of his work. It was fashionable at that time to minimise the role of the "subject"; according to Barthes, misquoting Nietzsche, "the author is dead". Perec was not unaware of current intellectual fashions, but in *Things*, as in all his work, he was driven by deeper and more personal concerns. The writing of *Things*, precisely because it had been so influenced by Flaubert, had put him on the same track as Bartleby, and he knew where that might lead him: back to depression, to impotence, to isolation in the attic room of number 203, Rue Saint-Honoré. If he needed to write in order to exist, then he needed to write about what had stopped him from writing in order to conjure it, to face up to it, to make sense of it, to fulfil the function of literature as he had himself defined it in his *Partisans* articles.

In August 1965 Georges and Paulette went on holiday with Pierre and Denise Getzler. Having explored the northwestern edge of Europe the previous year, they chose to go to the other extreme, to a rented house at Capo Vaticano, on the tip of Italy's toe. Perec brought a long book to read (in the shade, the sun being bad for his skin), Proust's *Remembrance of Things Past*. The novel begins with an elaborate narration of the experience of falling asleep. Now that was something Georges knew about! He had spent four years logging articles on the cessation of wakefulness; he was the bibliographer of France's leading expert on sleep! And here he was, on holiday, reading

---

[1] Herman Melville, *Billy Budd Sailor and Other Stories*, ed. Harold Beaver (London: Penguin Books, 1967), p. 99.

[2] The doodle, and the whole fragment, is reproduced in *Littératures* no. 7 (Spring 1983), pp. 61–67.

Proust's sensitive, scientifically dubious observations on the same subject. It must have seemed like a joke. He made notes on Proust, as he did on most of what he read. One sentence must have struck him as being particularly splendid: "Un homme qui dort tient en cercle autour de lui le fil des heures, l'ordre des années et des mondes."[1] Bartleby the scrivener defeats a New York law practice by preferring to do nothing; Proust asserts that a man asleep is master of the world. Once again, a place was being sketched for Perec's writing between other books. The twin calls to inactivity, in Melville and in Proust, provided the space in which he would confront and overcome the memory of his depression.

The Perecs and the Getzlers returned to Paris in time for the launch of *Things* on 1 September. There was no public-relations circus set up to promote the book. Perec was unknown, and Julliard, his publisher, had changed hands in the months since his contract was signed. The new owners had already disposed of the unprofitable Lettres nouvelles series, its associated bi-monthly review, and its founder-director, Maurice Nadeau, who for the time being was unemployed. On the billiard table of the book world, the tiny ball of *Things* fell by ricochet into the pocket of young Christian Bourgois, who kept his eye on a novel that he had first seen in an early draft. It was aimed at his own generation, and even at his own style of living, for he was one of the happy few who had all the things coveted by Jérôme and Sylvie. *Things* began to sell rather more quickly than expected. It was given a boost by a sensible, unsolicited, and favourable review in *Le Nouvel Observateur*, which could hardly have resisted a book that pilloried its rival, *L'Express*. *Things* had made a good start, but there were no further reviews of it for the rest of September. Bourgois decided to print a modest second run of just a thousand copies. *Things* sold out once again. Perec's novel was making its way not by media promotion but by word of mouth.

In the first week of October Bourgois attended the Frankfurt Book Fair, the regular market for trading foreign rights. He gave a copy of *Things* to the literary director of Stahlberg Verlag, who was known to be a discriminating buyer. The publisher read Perec's novel and

---

[1] "When a man is asleep, he has in a circle around him the chain of the hours, the sequence of the years, the order of the heavenly bodies" (Marcel Proust, *Remembrance of Things Past*, trans. C K Scott Moncrieff and Terence Kilmartin, vol. 1, *Swann's Way* [London: Penguin Books, 1983], p. 5).

passed it on to a translator, Eugen Helmle, for a second opinion. Helmle read it on the train home from Frankfurt to Saarbrücken. He was impressed by the language, the craft, and the wit of Perec's text, and immediately informed Herr Heller at Stahlberg Verlag that *Things* was worth acquiring; he added that he would like to translate it. Heller was a man of action. He had been in charge of book publishing in Paris from 1940 to 1944, as censor under the German occupation, and in that capacity had been acquainted with Raymond Queneau, then the executive secretary at Gallimard; he was rumoured to have given special protection to some of France's greatest writers. He bought the German-language rights to *Things* forthwith, in early October 1965.

There is not a whisper of it in any of the articles that followed in the French press, but the Frankfurt episode cannot have been without influence on the subsequent course of events. Not everyone claimed to like Perec's novel, but everyone began to talk about it.

Le Nouvel Observateur published a second review of *Things* on 6 October. It was an unusual thing to do, and the article itself – by François Nourissier, a well-known writer and journalist – was designed to start a controversy. Nourissier declared that *Things* was badly written, and its story weak, but he asserted that it was an important book nonetheless: it was a document on contemporary youth, an event in the history of ideas, even if it had no place in French literature. Christine Arnothy took the bait in *Le Parisien Libéré*, on 12 October. Perec's originality, she wrote, lay in the fact that he had written a non-novel, the novel of a sociologist or social worker. Now *Le Monde* contributed to the discussion with a quite substantial essay on Perec and *Things* by Raymond Jean, who had read *Partisans* and understood where Perec stood on "the problems of the modern novel". Replying to Nourissier and to Arnothy, Jean presented *Things* as a novel that incorporated a social document but was also a significant work of art. The dispute was a bit artificial, but it was good for sales. Bourgois printed a third run, and then a fourth, in cautious stages.

Some of Perec's readers were hurt by *Things*. It described their lives, their attitudes, their tastes, and their fantasies, and not altogether kindly. Perec did not attack them head-on but rather used a sly and chilling irony to undermine them all and to ridicule their world – which was his world, too.

Impatience, thought Jérôme and Sylvie, is a twentieth-century vir-
tue. At twenty, when they saw, or thought they saw, what life
could be, the sum of bliss it held, the endless conquests it allowed,
etc., they realised they would not have the strength to wait. Like
anyone else, they could have made it; but all they wanted was to
have it made. That is probably the sense in which they were what
is commonly called intellectuals.   [*T* 65]

There were others who also thought they saw what *Things* was getting at. Kate Manheim, the French-American companion of Jean-
Pierre Sergent, one of the earliest members of Lg, knew the
market-research crowd and at once caught the allusion in Jérôme's
passion for expensive English shoes: that was Roger Kleman all over.
Jean-Pierre had had a job with *L'Express*, and it had made him physi-
cally ill. Hadn't he quipped that even if it wasn't a *left-wing* rag, it
was certainly a *sinister* one? There was the same quip, in *Things*! [*T*
47] Jacques Joly's friends at Normal' Sup' had teased him about his
enthusiasm for clashing colours in Hollywood films; now here he
was in Perec's novel, scorned as one of *those infantile people who throw*
all critical sense to the winds [. . .] *if the pale red of Cyd Charisse's dress*
is made to clash with the darker red of Robert Taylor's sofa [*T* 56]. Once
one has been shown one or two of these nods and winks, one can
easily lose the ability to read *Things* as fiction, or as literature; every
sentence begins to look like another score settled. A little biographical
knowledge can be a dangerously coruscating thing.

However, from our later perspective, as the 1960s fade from active
memory, it may be illuminating to know that almost everything in
Things comes from *somewhere*, and that all the attitudes expressed by
Jérôme and Sylvie and their friends were first expressed by acquaintances of Georges Perec. For if *Things* is not quite a document in the
sense that Nourissier used the term, it stands as a textual inscription
of the discourse of a particular group. At parties at Rue de Quatrefages
and at meetings of Lg at Normal' Sup', they really did say that
Marienbad was "just a load of crap".

The readers to whom *Things* spoke with greatest effect, the audience that Perec's novel was creating for itself, consisted of young
people in the middle distance, close enough to feel themselves
recognised by the writer but not so close as to think they could guess
the identities behind Perec's barely delineated characters. A young
man in Grenoble, for instance, who was neither a market researcher

nor anything much else at the time beyond a student and film lover, saw in *Things* an enthralling, dismaying, affectionate, and uncannily sharp depiction of his own life; and there were thousands more like him, all over France, who came to hear of Perec's novel and then bought it, read it, argued about it with friends, and learnt something about the world, and perhaps about themselves.

Things says nothing directly about the inner lives of Jérôme and Sylvie. Unlike a copious and prying novelist of the school of Jane Austen or Charles Dickens, Perec gives us no access to his characters' crosstalk: they form an indivisible group, a collective, a common experience of life and culture. As for love, sexual desire, or even flirtation – elements present in the lives of any group of real twenty-five-year-olds – *Things* is totally silent. But despite its insubstantial plot and its avoidance of psychologising omniscience, *Things* is emphatically not a "new novel" written by a socially observant Robbe-Grillet, and it relates to what had already been dubbed the school of *chosisme* only insofar as it turns it inside out.

The unprecedented wattage of the light that Perec throws onto the things Jérôme and Sylvie desire leaves their world without a core. They have no passion that they can espouse with a clear heart.

> *In the past men fought in their millions, and millions still do fight, for their crust of bread. Jérôme and Sylvie did not quite believe that you could go into battle for a chesterfield settee.* ·[T 77]

In this they are not wrong. But they are caught between their passion for higher standards of living, and their awareness that that is no passion at all. Their emotional lives hang on an unresolved contradiction. Either they are attached to an unworthy ideal, or they are simply youngsters without much inside them. What Perec does in his novel is to put a hook into what many young people fear most about themselves, which is that they lack substance. *Things* does not speak directly of depression; but it creates *by design* an emotion of bewildered guilt, a bottomless melancholy that is both Perec's and the reader's. The emotions that Perec does not mention leave gaps in the text so carefully shaped that the reader can hardly avoid filling them in.

By the end of October 1965, Perec's novel was making waves. The prizes were in the offing; might *Things* get short-listed for one of them? Bruno Marcenac talked up his friend when dining at home in Paris, and his father, the literary editor of the PCF daily, agreed to have Perec round some evening when Aragon could come too. Bruno kept on beating the drum: Perec was a real writer, and on the right side; *L'Humanité* should wake up and take notice of something new. *Combat*, the daily newspaper of the non-communist left, got in first, with a careful reader's report that demonstrated how well Perec had identified what was wrong with modern France. His novel should be useful, the reviewer thought, in helping the country to advance more than halfway towards a new society. Jean Marcenac weighed in with his review five days later, in *L'Humanité*. He differed from his colleague at *Combat*. *Things* was to be praised, he said, for offering neither facile pessimism nor simple solutions to the malaise it described. But it was not a sociological novel in Communist eyes, nor was it realist in the proper (that is, socialist) sense, and for that reason, the quotation from Karl Marx at the end of the book was not entirely appropriate. Marcenac put up an alternative quotation from Lenin to show the young writer where he had gone astray.

These two measured accolades in the left-wing press were equivalent to the starter's gun in the race for the Goncourt, the Médicis and the Renaudot. Although no reviews of it appeared in *Le Figaro* or *L'Aurore*, *Things* was definitely out on the track. Had it not been handpicked by Maurice Nadeau, that poor man, so cruelly treated by the barons of French publishing?

The Goncourt was announced first; it went to Jacques Borel, for a huge doorstop of a novel, *L'Adoration*. The Médicis is rarely given for a first novel, so Perec was not really in the running for it. But he had been short-listed for the Renaudot Prize, which is traditionally awarded to new writers (and often ends up sinking them). The panel's final decision was due to be announced before noon on 21 November. At his school in Amiens, Bruno Marcenac informed his pupils that he would be listening to the one-o'clock news on the radio. If a certain person had won a certain prize, then afternoon classes would be cancelled, and the boys should go and read *Things*. At lunchtime he tuned in to France-Inter. Yes! Georges had made it! The Prix Théophraste-Renaudot 1965 – worth a small fortune, he imagined – had been won by the author of the shortest novel of the year, Georges Perec! Bruno dashed to the station and boarded the first Paris express. On arrival at the Gare du Nord, he telephoned Marcel Benabou from a callbox. No, Marcel said, it was not a hoax, it was true, Georges had got the Renaudot. So where was the party? Bruno asked. *Chez Castel*, Marcel said.

Castel's was a glamorous and high-priced nightclub cum restaurant with a reputation for *grande cuisine* and stylish entertainment. Later that night it opened its doors to an implausible crowd. The host was the golden boy of French publishing, Christian Bourgois, accompanied by his beautiful and highborn wife, Jacqueline de Guitaut. The guest of honour was a tipsy little imp of a man who was not even wearing a tie. Behind him came a mixed bag of ageing students and flashy dressers. There were Denise and Pierre Getzler, who would not have put on a tie if you had paid him; Bruno Marcenac, now a provincial schoolmaster; and Jacques Lederer, with Mireille and her jolly but hardly refined laugh. Next came Denis Buffard, the novel's dedicatee, and Paulette, and Roger in his best shoes, and Dominique, and then Henri Peretz the philosopher, Michel Martens the unbeatable cardsharper, as well as Noureddine Mechri, in Paris on business for SATPEC. A fine crew! the manager thought. He had a quiet word in Bourgois's ear: "Do you realise, sir, what sort of people these are? Some of them may even be *Communists!*"

It had not been Bourgois's idea, nor Jacqueline's, to bring Perec's Left Bank crowd into nouveau-riche surroundings. When news of the prize first broke, before lunch, Jacqueline de Guitaut had come down to the Julliard office to join in the first impromptu celebration. As she entered the room, she was struck dumb at the sight of a dark-haired man with darting, greenish eyes, who she knew straightaway must be the author. Her eyes met Perec's. They did not fall in love, or if they did, it was only in a fleeting and friendly way. Jacqueline thought she had been bewitched. Perec's diffident and penetrating gaze had something diabolical about it, like the look of a genie, or a dybbuk. She felt as if she had met a modern Mephisto.

She asked Perec where he would like to hold his celebration binge. Smiling a shy, embarrassed smile, he answered that he would like – if he please might – he would like to go to a place he had heard of, and which was said to have the best entertainment in Paris, a place called *Chez Castel*. Did she know it? The idea seemed outrageous to Jacqueline, and so she replied, returning his smile, "But of course, I'll book it for the night." Perec did not sound at all like a social climber; he seemed more like a child trying out the magic ring he had been given for a day and a night.

Perec drank himself silly in the opulent setting of Castel's. His boozing did not make him happy or gay, however. He had come to the end of a long road: ten years of work, ten years of writing, ten years of not quite daring to believe that he would ever make it. He had built his own family of affection and friendship amongst people still on the fringes. Was this to be his family still? Great victories can be even sadder than repeated, accustomed defeats. The witty devil, the crafty Mephisto, the artist, the intellectual, the husband, the pal – all of these sank beneath an ocean of wine chez Castel.

A few weeks later an even grander party took place at Hôtel Matignon, the prime minister's official residence. Georges Pompidou had invited the crew and cast of *Viva Maria!* to lunch, to celebrate the film's completion and its first private screening in Paris. They were all there: the two superstars of the cast, Brigitte Bardot and Jeanne Moreau, the director, Louis Malle, the scriptwriter, Jean-Paul Rappeneau, and the many others who had been involved in making the movie. The conversation turned to a book that was in the news. Pompidou, an *agrégé* and former teacher of French, liked to keep abreast of new literature; he butted into the conversation about *Things*.

"Tell me," he asked the cast of *Viva Maria!*, "this man Perec, does anyone know what he does for a living?"

Someone piped up from farther down the table, "I believe he works for the CNRS, Prime Minister."

"Aha!" Georges Pompidou quipped. "I had a feeling he wasn't too busy with *things*."

This chapter draws on the recollections and observations of Marcel Benabou, Christian Bourgois, Alain Corneau, Henry Gautier, Jacqueline de Guitaut, Eugen Helmle, Jacques Joly, Kate Manheim, Bruno Marcenac, Michel Martens, Bernard Mirabel, Henri Peretz, Jean-Paul Rappeneau, Jean-Pierre Sergent, and others.

PART II
1965–1975

That is how it is with great works of art. If only you do not try to utter what is unutterable, then nothing gets lost. But the unutterable will be – unutterably – contained in what has been uttered.

Ludwig Wittgenstein, letter to Paul Engelman

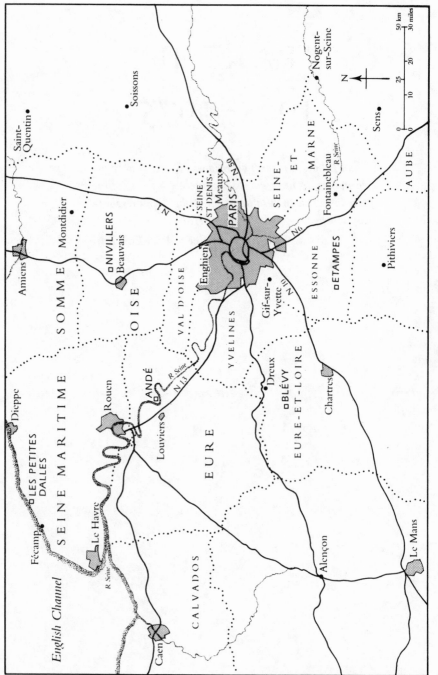

Ile-de-France

CHAPTER 30

Without a Tie

1965–1966

On 21 November 1965, the Renaudot Prize put *Things* in the limelight and made Georges Perec a national celebrity if not quite a household name. The crew-cut, cord-trousered author – not yet thirty, but
looking rather less old even than that – did not rush out to buy a silk
tie and dark glasses. In place of a public relations person in period
costume (that is, a miniskirt and beehive hair), he appointed his thir-
teen-year-old goddaughter Sylvia his mascot and bag carrier for signing sessions and book fairs. He was not duped by the razzmatazz. It
was not that he felt guilty about winning the prize; but he knew that
the path of a young prizewinner was fraught with danger. Like his
friends, he mistrusted success. *A book that sells well is always suspect,*
he warned himself when interviewed by Marcel Benabou and Bruno
Marcenac.[1]

At the same time, publicity made it possible for him to talk through
interviewers to many more thousands of readers. Perec met the press
willingly, had his photograph taken a hundred times, spoke on radio
and performed on French television. If he was not swept off his feet
by the glamour, neither did he shun public appearances. His celebrity
even earned him a trip to Brussels by Trans-Europ-Express, but he
overdid it on Dutch courage on that occasion, and the tape of his
performance on RTB is now kept under lock and key.

A best-seller may best be defined as a book which attracts more
readers than its publisher has predicted. Sales of *Things* exceeded
expectations weeks before the Renaudot put it onto the official best-
seller lists, so on that score, at least, there was nothing "suspect"
about the novel's success. However, it is received wisdom that great

---

[1] M. Benabou, B. Marcenac, "Georges Perec s'explique", *Les Lettres françaises*
N° 1108 (2 December 1965), pp. 14–15. Text corrected by Perec. Translated
as "Georges Perec Owns Up", in *Review of Contemporary Fiction* XIII. 1 (Spring
1993), pp. 17–20.

works of literature take decades to achieve recognition. Could *Things* be an exception to that iron rule? Perec must have wondered. Or was it just a flash in the pan, a merely topical (and therefore ephemeral) thing? Alternatively, were the sales of his slim volume only proof that it had been misunderstood?

The portrait that Perec paints of his own generation is an intentionally ambiguous one. Half critical, half sympathetic, *Things* ends with a prospect that is both firmly optimistic (for Jérôme and Sylvie will now have the means to acquire the things they want) and infinitely sad (for the feast that awaits them in adulthood promises to be *quite simply tasteless*). Few of Perec's first readers could be satisfied with such fundamental indecision, and most of them provided their own conclusion: either *Things* was a critique of modern society and justified standing aside from it; or *Things* was an attack on consumerism and justified taking revolutionary action or voting for the PCF; or *Things* was a hymn to the beauty of the modern world and justified earning lots of money in market research. The framework of reading was provided by politics in part because Perec's novel met its first public at a time when the left–right battles endemic to French culture had risen to fever pitch in a presidential election campaign.

"Georges Perec faces the onslaught of fame without a tie," *Le Figaro* explained to its readers, "as if to prove that winning the Renaudot Prize will not change his attitude toward things."[1] The paper's literary supplement filled in the details: a polo-neck sweater, a tweed jacket, and cord trousers. He must be young, he must be Left Bank, and he must be left-wing to dress that way for a celebrity interview.[2] It was not untrue. Perec could hardly object if his readers attached importance to the social meaning of clothes, since his characters did so, too. His novel was automatically draped with the same cord-trousered significance, which made it easier to read, or not to.

Perec did his best to counteract simple-minded readings of *Things*, and he spoke to the press as if he were addressing his readers directly. Yes, he agreed, *Things* contained lots of autobiographical detail. Yes, the world of *Things* was a sad one, mostly. No, he did not know the

[1] Jacques Jaubert, "Georges Perec en face des choses", *Le Figaro,* 23 November 1965.

[2] Jean Chalon, interview with Georges Perec in *Le Figaro littéraire,* 25 November 1965. Even more detail of Perec's (and of Paulette's) clothing is given in Régis Saint-Hélier, "Georges Perec", *Femmes d'aujourd'hui,* 24 February 1966.

1. *Above:* From left to right: Rose and Léon Peretz, Bianca, David and Esther Bienenfeld. Paris, 1925

2. *Right:* David and Esther Bienenfeld, with David's cousin Norbert, Vienna, 1921

3. David Bienenfeld,
Bahrain, 1927

4. Jacques Bienenfeld,
La Baule, 1929

5. The Bienenfeld families in Paris around 1930. Standing in the rear, from right to left: David Bienenfeld, Esther Bienenfeld, Berthe Chavranski, and Icek Judko Perec

6. Esther Bienenfeld,
Lublin, 1921

7. Georges Perec with his mother,
Paris, 1939. This photograph is
described on page 50 of *W or
The Memory of Childhood*

8. Icek Judko Perec in Foreign Legion uniform. This photograph is described on page 27 of *W or The Memory of Childhood*

9. *Above:* Georges Perec on the balcony of Les Frimas, Villard-de-Lans, 1942

10. *Above right:* David and Esther Bienenfeld on the balcony of Les Frimas

11. *Right:* Bianca and Ela Bienenfeld, Villard-de-Lans, 1944. The rock shown is the one described on page 78 of *W or The Memory of Childhood*

MINISTÈRE
DES
ANCIENS COMBATTANTS
ET
VICTIMES DE GUERRE

SERVICE DE L'ETAT-CIVIL
37, RUE DE BELLECHASSE
PARIS (7°)

RÉPUBLIQUE FRANÇAISE

M. 8 bis.

Paris, le 19 AOUT 1947

ACTE DE DISPARITION

LE MINISTRE DES ANCIENS COMBATTANTS
ET VICTIMES DE GUERRE,

Vu l'article 88 du Code Civil (Ord. du 30 Octobre 1945) ;
Vu le dossier de l'intéressé désigné ci-après : 52.645

DÉCIDE :

la disparition de PEREC née SZULEWICZ Cyrla

né le 20 Aout 1913 à VARSOVIE (Pologne)

dans les conditions indiquées ci-après :

- Arrêtée le 17 Janvier 1943 à PARIS
- Internée à DRANCY
- Déportée le 11 Février 1943 en direction d'AUSCHWITZ
(Pologne)

La famille peut, par simple lettre adressée au Procureur de la République du
domicile du disparu, sans ministère d'avoué et sans frais, demander :

— soit un jugement déclaratif d'absence en application de la loi du
22 Septembre 1942 validée et modifiée par l'Ordonnance d'Alger du
5 Avril 1944.

A l'expiration d'un délai de 5 ans partant du jour de la disparition, le
jugement déclaratif d'absence peut être transformé en jugement déclaratif
de décès par application de l'Ordonnance du 5 Avril 1944 ci-dessus.

— soit un jugement déclaratif de décès en application de la loi du 30 Avril
1946, si le disparu est de nationalité française et appartient à l'une des
catégories suivantes : Mobilisé, Prisonnier de Guerre, Réfugié, Déporté ou
Interné politique, Membre des Forces Françaises libres ou des Forces
Françaises de l'Intérieur, Requis du Service du Travail obligatoire ou
Réfractaire.

D'autre part, à tout moment l'acte de disparition peut être transformé par la
Direction de l'Etat-Civil en acte de décès si les précisions nécessaires sont fournies.

Pour le Ministre des Anciens Combattants
et Victimes de Guerre :
Par délégation le Directeur de l'Etat-Civil et des Recherches

P.O. Le Chef du Bureau
de l'Etat-Civil Déportés

N° 13.463/58 CT
"NE VARIETUR"

EXPERT TRADUCTEUR JURÉ
près le
Tribunal civil
de la Seine
34, Avenue Hoche
PARIS - 8°
Victor BORTEN

X. 725.000 - NOV.

12.

13. Georges Perec in a school pageant, Rue des Bauches, 1945

14. David and Esther Bienenfeld with Georges Perec, around 1951

15. Class IIIB at Collège Geoffroy-Saint-Hilaire, 1950–51. Georges Perec is second from the right in the second row from the top. Philippe Guérinat is on his right

16. The *classe de philosophie* at Collège Geoffroy-Saint-Hilaire, 1953–54. Georges Perec is in the back row, furthest to the left. Jacques Lederer is in the middle row, third from the right, and Noureddine Mechri fourth from the left

17. Georges Perec at Etampes in 1954

18. *Right:* Georges Perec at the wedding of Huguette and Antonio Moralès, Paris, June 1956

19. Mladen Srbinović, portrait of Georges Perec. Lithograph, first state.
Belgrade, August 1957

20. Georges Perec, certified parachutist, Pau, May 1958

21. Antonello da Messina, *Le Condottiere* *(Musée du Louvre)*

22. *Left:* Perec and carnation, early 1960s. Perec thought that this photograph made him look like Franz Kafka

23. *Below:* Georges Perec looking out of the window at Rue de Quatrefages in 1965. *(Copyright © 1993 Babette Mangolte, all rights of reproduction reserved)*

24. Paulette and Georges Perec at Rue des Quatrefages in 1965
(Copyright © 1993 Babette Mangolte, all rights of reproduction reserved)

25. The Underwood Four Million

answers to the problems of that world; he had only tried to put the questions correctly. He pointed out without prompting that he had appropriated whole sentences from Flaubert.[1] He steered interviewers away from the view of *Things* as a work of sociology, maintaining that it was not an essay on the evils of consumer society. He had to be quite firm: *People who imagine I have denounced consumer society have not understood a thing about my book.* It made barely a whisker of difference. Reporting on the prize-winning French novels of 1965, an anonymous reviewer for the *Times Literary Supplement* confidently described the shortest of them as "an indictment of Gaullist Consumer Society".[2] He was only repeating what the French press had long before declared to be self-evidently true.

An identikit image of Perec the prizewinner was put together at great speed without much regard for what the author himself had to say about his aims and methods. He was a former pupil of Jean Duvignaud; Duvignaud was a well-known sociologist; and so Perec must be a sociologist, too. *Things* contained a good deal of description, as did the novels of Robbe-Grillet; thus Perec must be a "new novelist" as well. Perec's characters were duped by consumer society; the PCF described consumerism as a capitalist sleight-of-hand; so Perec must be anticapitalist to match.

This simple kit suited the needs of the left to a tee. At last someone had proved that "advanced artistic practice" could go hand in hand with an "objectively correct" understanding of the capitalist world. The People's Republics clambered on board. Translations of *Things* were put in hand in every member state of the Warsaw Pact. An edition in French with notes in Russian was soon brought out for the use of Soviet students; for years thereafter, in schools and universities throughout the USSR, language learners would approach the French conditional and future tenses through the first and last chapters of *Things*.

Only one voice was raised against the reading of *Things* as an indictment of capitalism in consumerist clothing, that of Annie Leclerc. Her review is in parts an intelligent and subtle one. She shows that Perec does not stand unambiguously outside of his story, that he is himself implicated in his characters' tawdry dreams, that he shares in some measure the passions, the fears, and the bad faith of

---

[1] See, for example, *Le Soir* (Brussels), 2 December 1965.
[2] "Father Frustrations", *Times Literary Supplement*, 25 February 1966, p. 147.

Jérôme and Sylvie. Perec had managed to draw his readers into this attractive, repulsive world of inauthentic desires, she observed, and it dawned on her that she too could feel tempted by such dreams. *Things*, she asserted quite correctly, was not a denunciation of consumerism. *But it should be!* she insisted. Since it failed to provide a "coherent analysis" of the root of the evil, its descriptions were on a par with pornography and its attention to detail amounted to masturbatory ogling. Perec failed to answer the questions that his novel raised, and his invocation of Karl Marx at the end of the text was only camouflage, masking the absence of true "critical thought" in the work. Althusserians do not hold him guiltless who taketh Marx's name in vain![1]

Marcel Benabou was outraged by Leclerc's review, which he saw in typescript. What could the remnants of Lg do to stop Perec from being stabbed in the back pages of *Les Temps modernes*? They tried to get Leclerc's politico-moralistic diatribe withdrawn, or rewritten, but to no avail. Simone de Beauvoir allowed them only to reply. The rejoinder, penned in great haste by Henri Peretz, ran after Leclerc's piece in the December 1965 issue of Sartre's review.[2]

The prize, the ensuing celebrity and the political appropriation that went with it all had numerous consequences for the course of Perec's life and works. However, two sensitive readings of *Things* prior to the announcement of the Renaudot Prize also proved significant. In September or October 1965 Perec was contacted by Jean Mailland, a film director and Latin Quarter neighbour whose path must have crossed Perec's many times at La Joie de Lire or at the market in Rue Monge. Mailland had made *Hamida*, a feature film about the Algerian war, partly at the DEFA studios in East Berlin and partly on location in Tunisia, where Noureddine Mechri, in his SATPEC role, had been the producer, and from whom he heard about Nour's best friend, Georges Perec. As a result, Mailland was one of the earliest readers of *Things*, a book that seemed to speak directly to him: it was about his own generation, it was set in his own *quartier*, and in Tunisia, which he now knew well. What was more, he also knew the novelist's best friend. He knocked on the door of Rue de Quatrefages, intro-

[1] A. Leclerc, "*Les Choses*: Un Combat Malheureux", *Les Temps Modernes* XXI (December 1965), pp. 1134–1137.

[2] Henri Peretz, "*Les Choses* (suite)", *Les Temps modernes* XXI (December 1965), pp. 1138–1139.

duced himself, and asked Perec if his next film could be a screen adaptation of *Things*.

Not long after, a letter from Germany fell into Perec's mailbox. The German translator needed clarification of some difficult words and the references for the quotations from Marx and Flaubert. Perec replied to Eugen Helmle with a neat list of the thirteen "grafts" from *Sentimental Education*,[1] but he was unable to help very much with the Marx. He thought he recalled seeing the sentence in Eisenstein.[2]

Helmle asked to meet his new author on one of his visits to Paris, in a café on the Champs-Elysées. He would be with René de Obaldia, who knew Perec from Royaumont days and would be able to introduce them to each other. Perec arrived at the appointed time, came over to their table, shook Obaldia's hand, and gave a stiff nod to acknowledge the German translator. Obaldia then took his leave.

Alone with Helmle, Perec blushed and began to explain. He had not intended personal offence by his formal greeting, he said, but his mother had died at Auschwitz and he had never yet touched the hand of a German. He was sorry. Helmle was moved, and told Georges his own tale.

He was from Saarland. Did Georges know the recent history of that bone of Franco-German contention? Helmle had been born there when the Saar was still administered by France under the League of Nations mandate. His village had become German in 1935 when the Saar voted to join the Reich, and ten years of his childhood had been spent under the Nazi regime. He had been kicked out of school before he was sixteen because he scored marks of 6 in sport (the lowest mark possible: in German reckoning, 1 is top). By the end of the war Helmle was an apprentice pastrycook with only elementary-school certificates to his name. In 1945 Saarland had become French once again. Helmle got a job in Paris, in a pâtisserie in Rue Saint-Denis, where he improved his already fluent French. He returned to his village, Neuweiler, and with the encouragement of his old school-friend Ludwig Harig, he started to translate. The two of them tackled Raymond Queneau's *Exercices de style*, publishing parts of their

[1] The list given by Perec in "Emprunts à Flaubert", *L'Arc* no. 79 (1980), pp. 49–50, is less complete.

[2] This explains why the *envoi* of G Perec, *Die Dinge* (Karlsruhe: Stahlberg Verlag, 1966), is attributed not to Marx but to Eisenstein. See David Bellos, "'Le Moyen fait partie de la vérité . . .' The languages of Georges Perec's *Les Choses*", *Journal of the Institute of Romance Studies* 1 (1992), pp. 325–331.

translation in *Augenblick*, an avant-garde review edited by Max
Bense, the leading figure in the "Stuttgart school". Saarland had
begun a gradual return to German identity in the 1950s, a process
that was only completed in 1960, when Saarland became the seventeenth *Land* of the Federal Republic. In 1966, when this meeting took
place, Eugen Helmle had spent more of his life under French than
under German rule, without ever having moved for more than a brief
period from the place of his birth, near Saarbrücken.

Perec must have been reassured, if not by this history lesson then
by the fact that the hand he should have shaken belonged to a man
who had been punished for failing physical education. He was also
impressed that Helmle had translated Queneau and even met him,
and he gave the translator a copy of his own little homage to France's
least stuffy poet and polymath. *Quel Petit Vélo à guidon chromé au fond
de la cour?* would not be easy to translate, Perec acknowledged, but
since Helmle had managed *Zazie* . . .

"Would you like to visit Saarbrücken?" Helmle asked.

It took some courage for Perec to say yes to Germany, even to a
part of Germany that had long been French.

Well, yes, when I can, he replied.

🍁

At the lunchtime office party that Julliard had given on 21 November
1965 to celebrate Perec's implausible prize, the still-bewildered author
fell into conversation with Maurice Pons, whose novel *Les Saisons*
had appeared alongside *Things* in that autumn's Lettres Nouvelles
list. Perec seemed to be at a loose end as the party wound down, and
he walked with Pons to Gare Saint-Lazare. The prize was all very
well, Perec said, but it wouldn't solve his problems just like that. It
was hard enough to find the time to write, and it was just impossible
to find the space in his tiny flat. Now he was a prizewinner, he would
have journalists and photographers to contend with as well.

"Why don't you come to stay at the Moulin d'Andé?" Pons suggested. "That's where I live, in the country, a couple of hours away.
There's plenty of room. We like to have people to stay, to get on
with their work and to get a breath of fresh air." Perec was interested;
it must have sounded like a godsend to him.

There were several hours left before dinner at Castel's, and Perec
walked over to the Latin Quarter to bring his good tidings to La Joie
de Lire. Maspéro was delighted to see him, for they had hardly spoken

since Lg's departure from *Partisans*. Perec would now have quite a lot of money coming in, what with the prize and the royalties that would be sure to follow, and maybe film rights, too. Seven lean years before, Perec had fantasised about spending his first literary fortune on a holiday in America, a yacht, winter sports, and the very best psychoanalyst. What would he do now, Maspéro asked, with his newfound wealth? *I'll get on with my work, as a writer,* Perec said.

He said the same into the tape recorders and microphones that were thrust under his nose over the following days and weeks. Paulette sat alongside him for some of the longer interviews. He corrected (mis)leading questions: No, he was not the youngest-ever winner of the Renaudot; no, he could not afford to go freelance. He would not resign from the CNRS and Paulette would not leave the Bibliothèque Nationale. *A writer must earn his living outside literature, that's essential.* But wouldn't they splash out on all the things Jérôme and Sylvie yearned for? No, they would not. Writing *Things* had distanced him from his earlier appetites and desensitised him to material objects; he had reached a state of indifference, so to speak. In any case, the craving for luxuries had only been one part of himself.[1] So what would he do with all that money? With a smile that may have been weary, if it was not downright impish, Perec gave *L'Express* what it had been fishing for: *Why, everything I ever dreamt of . . . I'll have my flat done up, at long last.*[2]

Fame did not spoil Georges Perec, nor did it cause him to desert his old friends. He did not have his flat done up, and he carried on holding parties for the crowd at Rue de Quatrefages. He took his friends out for meals in restaurants and spent nights playing cards with them. He was still shy, with a twinkling eye, always bubbling on the verge of a pun, repressing the laughter that would spoil the as yet unuttered joke. Now that he had the means to be lavish, he footed bills for bottles, and meals, and treats. He seemed quite unaltered by what had happened to him. Perec's example contradicted an iron rule of intellectual life – that all success corrupts, and that a great success corrupts greatly – and gave rise to contradictory feelings of affection

[1] A. Ghuislaine, "Poésie et vérité de l'objet", *Le Soir* (Brussels), 14–15 December 1965. The late A. Ghuislaine quotes in this article from an (unlocated) letter from Perec: *My book, from a certain point of view, is nothing other than a piece of work on adjectives and qualifiers.*

[2] *L'Express* N⁰ 754 (29 November 1965), p. 89.

and of annoyance amongst his friends. They were sincerely delighted not to have lost him to the stratosphere of beautiful women, influential publishers and socialite littérateurs to which he now had access – but what was he trying to prove by disregarding first principles? That he was some kind of a saint? Meanwhile, Maurice Nadeau had found a new perch in the publishing world. *Things* would stay with Julliard, but the "five next novels" which Perec was obliged to offer were now due to be offered to Denoël, which had taken over the forward commitments of the Lettres Nouvelles collection together with its editorial director. Nadeau had reservations about *Quel Petit Vélo à guidon chromé au fond de la cour?*, but since the work was finished, and since its author was a rising star, he published it in February 1966, before the last of the magazine features about the winner of the 1965 Renaudot Prize had been quite forgotten.

Quel Petit Vélo was a public-relations disaster. Perec's long joke about Jacques's moped could not be read as a sequel to *Things*. Where was the sociologist? the "new novelist"? the critic of consumer society? Literary journalists were baffled and fell silent. Instead of writing *Things II*, Perec had gone astray and thrown away his breakthrough. There must have been a misunderstanding. Left-wing papers dropped Perec like a wormy apple; the right, which had never backed him in the first place, had no trouble ignoring his latest effort. The press file for Perec's second book, which was published a mere twelve weeks after the award of the Renaudot Prize, contains just a handful of clippings: from *Les Echos*, from *Le Canard enchaîné*, from *Le Figaro*, and from *Le Parisien libéré*.[1] There was nothing in *Le Monde* or *Le Nouvel Observateur*, let alone *L'Express*. Apart from a sour interview in *Le Figaro littéraire*, in which he asserted that he had abandoned Flaubert for San-Antonio,[2] Perec got almost no coverage in the press for his witty homage to Lg and to Raymond Queneau. The public eye had opened on *Things*, seen something simple, and then shut again. Perec's second decade of obscurity began six months after the first one ended.

It would not have been worth it for him to buy a new tie.

---

[1] These remarks are based on the cuttings file assembled by AGP, which may not be complete. The reviews collected are all favourable, and one – from *Le Canard enchaîné* - is enthusiastic.

[2] Claudine Jardin "Georges Perec", *Le Figaro littéraire*, 28 February 1966.

Based on the recollections of Marcel Benabou, Eugen Helmle, Sylvia Lamblin-Richardson, Jean Mailland, Kate Manheim, François Maspéro, René de Obaldia, Henri Peretz, Maurice Pons, and Jacques Roubaud. A copy of the first letter from Perec to Helmle (January 1966) was supplied by AGP.

CHAPTER 31

Return to Sfax

1966

Perec liked the man who wanted to make a film version of *Things*. Jean Mailland took no time at all to find a producer, called Max Bonnafont, who put some start-up money into the project, and SATPEC at once agreed to coproduce. Jean Mailland asked an old friend from Lyon, Raymond Bellour, to join him and Perec on the scriptwriting team. They were set up and ready to go when they met for their first working session over an expensive breakfast at Les Deux Magots.

"What I see in *Things*," Mailland said to Perec, "is masks. What I want you to do now is tell me what lies behind them. Tell me everything!"

There was barely any interaction between the unnamed protagonists of *Things*, Mailland explained. A film needed flesh-and-blood characters with their own names, their own clothes, their own accents and words – people who had or could have relationships and adventures and affairs. Perec was open to Mailland's ideas. Although he had seen an almost infinite number of films, he had no fixed ideas about how his novel should be translated to the screen. He was unassuming in the first working sessions and agreed easily that what was needed was a completely new invention. The text was all there was, he declared: he had no prior story to reveal behind the "masks" of his novel. But as he had no imagination (so he said), they would have to reconstitute Jérôme and Sylvie's social set in real life and then observe it before they could draft the script. The writers persuaded the producer that dinner parties would have to be part of their preparatory work on the film, and they got an advance on their expenses from him. They then cast around among the people they knew and selected couples to carry out a real-life replay of *Things*. The three codirectors intended to make the adaptation an experiment in conviviality as well as an experimental film; "happenings" were all the rage at the time. They were really rather wicked, Jean Mailland concedes.

They borrowed André Glucksman's flat (which he shared with

Jean-Jacques Brochier, another *Lyonnais*) for the biggest of their parties. Few of the invited guests knew why they were there. The memories of Perec's Latin Quarter friends about the writer's generosity after his Renaudot Prize cannot all be put down to Max Bonnafont's expense account, but some of them probably can. Not all of the guests realised that the older men who threw in comments and caustic remarks from time to time were Henri Lefèbvre and Louis Althusser. The wickedness worked: one of the dinner parties turned out to be an exact replica of the party scene in *Things*. Perec made notes.

Perec, Bellour and Mailland put together a cast list, a chronology (leading up to October 1966, when they hoped the film might actually appear), and a story outline. The film would differ from the novel in that far more of the action would take place in Tunisia, Jérôme and Sylvie would have affairs, and the focus would be as much on the young people's intimate lives as on their relationship to things. Jean-Louis Trintignant agreed to play the role of Jérôme, and Marie Laforêt that of Sylvie.[1] Perec invented a new character, Jean Vergnaud (an older teacher of French in Sfax, with an unfinished thesis on the Inquisition) for the actor Jean Bouise, while Mailland dreamt up the role of Pepi (a German starlet) for Anna Prucnal, whom he had met the previous year in East Berlin. The cast list also included a character called Nour, "the perfect image of the post-independence colonial", who was equally at home and equally at sea in two cultures, and another called Gaspard, "an ultra-Jérôme, and Jérôme's best friend . . . Agoraphobic and misanthropic, Gaspard has an inimitable manner of living in absentia."

They set off in the first days of March 1966, by air, for Tunis,[2] where journalists were waiting for the celebrity writer to arrive:

> He seems ill at ease wherever he is, and likes sports jackets and polo-neck sweaters.[3] He orders a strong coffee and drinks it in one gulp. He talks quietly but a smile always hovers over his lips: he is the winner of this year's Renaudot Prize, the author of *Things*, Georges Perec.[4]

[1] Claudine Jardin "Georges Perec", *Le Figaro littéraire*, 28 February 1966.

[2] *Le Monde*, 3 March 1966 (news item).

[3] Ironically, the accompanying photograph shows Perec in white collar and dark tie.

[4] Press cutting dated 5 March 1966, unidentified newspaper published in Tunis.

They met the real Nour (who was at that time "more like Lowry's consul than the 'perfect ex-colonial'," Mailland recalls), hired a car, and drove to Sfax, where they put up in large and comfortable rooms at the Hôtel des Oliviers, off Avenue Hedi-Chaker. The lives of French teachers overseas interested Mailland and he wanted to understand what sort of people they were before scripting Jérôme and Sylvie into Sfax. So with his two coauthors he set up more "happenings", in the form of elaborate parties charged to the production budget.

They went to Hammamet to look at Dar Henson, where a major sequence of the film would be shot, and to attend a reception at Dar Sebastien, the adjoining estate, used then as now as a cultural centre, where Perec was to be awarded a Tunisian literary prize. Perec chatted afterwards with one of the judges from Paris, Roger Grenier, who was aware how Perec's name would be pronounced in languages other than French. Was he related to Isaak Leib Peretz, the Yiddish playwright? Grenier asked. He knew a former actress in the Warsaw Jewish theatre who had often performed in Peretz's classic pageant *At Night on the Old Market*.[1] Well yes, Perec replied, Isaak Leib was my grandfather's uncle. Did Perec then know the Peretz story called "Bontsha the Silent"? Grenier enquired.[2] It was oddly parallel to Melville's "Bartleby". Unfortunately, he had lost his only copy of the French; could Perec help him find another?

In Sfax, the writing team invited sundry teachers, French expatriates, and *coopérants* to lavish *kemias* well provided with wine and Tunisian fig liqueur. They observed the behaviour that they had done their best to provoke and spent their days turning the "preparatory text" into a shooting script. The ninety-seven-page scenario that came out of the teamwork both is and is not part of Perec's oeuvre: it would probably be pointless to try to extract from it what is Mailland's, what is Bellour's and what is Perec's. All the same, it does have several distinctly Perecquian features. Most of the sequences are short, and

[1] Perec later obtained and hung on to a programme (in Yiddish and Polish) of a 1973 production of *At Night on the Old Market* by the Panstwowy Teatr Zydowsky (FP 48, 5,10).

[2] Isaak Leib Peretz, "Bontsha the Silent", transl. Hilda Abel, in Peretz, *Selected Stories* , ed. Irving Howe and Eliezer Greenberg (New York: Schocken Books, 1974), pp. 70–77. See also J. Joffen, *The Jewish Mystic in Kafka* (Bern: Peter Lang, 1987) for a discussion of the influence of "Bontzye Shweig" on Kafka's story "The Silence of the Sirens".

the film's overall design is based on the interweaving, by means of montage, of twin tales of life in Paris and life in Sfax. The "reference text" for the film's structure is clearly Resnais's *Hiroshima mon amour*, but the ideas of twin and fragmented narratives also go back to Perec's earliest texts – *L'Attentat de Sarajevo* and *Gaspard pas mort*. Like them, the film script of *Les Choses* anticipates the double structure of *W or The Memory of Childhood*.

At the parties in Sfax, Bellour could see that Perec did not find it easy to relate to women, particularly attractive ones. Drink helped him to quell his natural timidity, but he did not hold his liquor well and he would tip from jollity into drunkenness with surprising speed. After one particularly wicked party that ended in a ferocious "truth game", Bellour went off to the hotel with a pretty girl. Perec and Mailland got even drunker together, and eventually went on a rampage around the bars and restaurants of the town, bawling their heads off and pulling tablecloths out from under diners' plates. They ended up in the early hours back at the hotel, where they were looked after by the pretty girl, who may well have been the innocent cause of it all. Perec's behaviour was not that of a happily married young man.

Sfax, Tunis, Paris: Perec was back in mid-March. The script was to be typed up professionally and then submitted to the Commission d'avances sur recettes, or CAR, a government body that provides start-up funds for films with artistic merit. In the meantime there was lab work to catch up on, a new novel to pursue (now that *Quel Petit Vélo* was out of the way) and amongst other things a copy of "Bontsha the Silent" to find and send to Roger Grenier.

Based on the recollections of Raymond Bellour, Roger Grenier and Jean Mailland, and on documents kindly provided by Jean Mailland:

Raymond Bellour, Jean Mailland, Georges Perec, "Les Choses": Travail préparatoire. Scénario, adaptation et dialogue. Cyclostyled typescript, February 1966, 49 pages.

Raymond Bellour, Jean Mailland, Georges Perec, "Les Choses". Un film en couleurs d'après le livre de Georges Perec. Cyclostyled typescript, before May 1966, 97 pages.

CHAPTER 32

Paradise

1966

"Do you have time to write?" Perec was asked by a Belgian journalist in December 1965. "Or is it a struggle for you to get away from the daily grind?"

I don't write every day, Perec replied, *except in my jotter. I write three of four times a year. Not in Paris. Elsewhere.*[1]

"Elsewhere" was a place quite out of this world, a writer's retreat in an old water mill on the Seine, in the gentle Kentish countryside of lower Normandy. When Perec's fellow-novelist, Maurice Pons, had first mentioned the place to him, he made it sound like paradise. When Perec took up the invitation and went to Andé, he found a setting, a style of living, and a community that must have seemed not far short of sheer heaven.

The half-timbered mill was part of an estate given by the founder-owner of the Vérigoud soft-drinks firm to his only daughter, Suzanne, as a wedding present. When her marriage came to an end, she moved into the mill with her three children and Pons, her lover. Little by little she transformed the estate from a quaint toy into something like an open home, or a country-house commune – at all events, something quite unique.

Suzanne and Maurice had no real plan laid down in advance; they were not seeking to set up a model village or a *phalanstère* in the manner of nineteenth-century French utopians. The mill community just grew up around them. The first people to use Andé as a retreat were the architects and planners of the nearby new town of Val de Reuil. Then came friends from the film world, notably François Truffaut, whose first full-length feature, *Les Mistons*, was based on a story by Pons. Truffaut was enchanted by the Norman buildings and the waterside setting of the estate, with its private island and its densely wooded slopes. He shot much of *The Four Hundred Blows* –

---

[1] Interview with Adrien Jans, *Le Soir* (Brussels), 2 December 1965.

his next film, and the one that, along with Resnais's *Hiroshima mon amour* and Godard's *Breathless,* launched the "new wave" in 1959 – on location there, and used the buildings again for his most famous work, *Jules and Jim.* If you can take your eyes off Oskar Werner and Jeanne Moreau in the final sequence of the latter film, when they drive into the water in a silent suicide pact, you can see, in the building that forms the background, the window of the room that Georges Perec would come to live and write in for most of his weekends throughout the second half of the 1960s.

Maurice had long since ceased to be Suzanne's lover, but he remained her faithful companion and a pillar of the Andé community. The estate belonged to her, of course, and she ruled over its floating population with the smiling grace of a statuesque and libertarian suzeraine. There were no rules except those of communal living. In the 1960s, before rebuilding and extension expanded it to its present capacity, the mill could sleep only about fifteen people, and much of the time – outside of weekends and holiday periods – there were fewer guests than that. But whether the complement for dinner was a bare handful or a whole crowd, everyone was expected to lend a hand with the cooking and the clearing away. "Don't go in empty-handed!" was the unchanging after-dinner refrain.

Nobody applied to become a "friend" of the Moulin d'Andé, and residents normally paid a modest charge for their room. Suzanne and Maurice built their community informally and according to their own changing personal and cultural tastes. Georges Perec came into the circle at a time when the mill's film years were giving way to its writerly period, and a little while before a certain fascination with exotic political figures took hold of it, as it took hold of much of French intellectual life. There were no clear-cut policy decisions about what sort of people should be invited to stay, just successive waves of interest which, as they lapped onto the shore of the mill, washed up artists, writers, creators and thinkers of different kinds. Some of those who used the Moulin d'Andé did so for only a brief interlude in their lives; others have been "regulars" for many decades. For Perec, the Moulin was a precious boon for about five years, from the season of *Things* in 1965–66, until 1970 or thereabouts.

In the first phase of his "Moulin period" Perec spent numerous weekends and some longer intervals – over Easter, for instance, and a long week in September 1966 – in his room at Andé, looking out over the stream that flows back into the Seine. It was always the same room, the *chambre Jeanne d'Arc*, situated directly over the grinding-wheel room which Suzanne had converted with drapes and cushions into an Ottoman lounge. In his later Andé years – from 1968, or perhaps even earlier – Perec divided his time on a weekly basis between writing in the country and working in Paris. He would arrive on Thursdays at the railway station at Saint-Pierre-du-Vauvray (on the main line from Paris-Saint-Lazare to Le Havre), where he would be met, most often by Maurice. First his mop of hair would appear as he climbed the steps from the subway under the tracks, then his smiling eyes, and then his great grin of relief, as if to say, Home again. On the Tuesday following, Maurice would drive him back to the station, less than two kilometres from the mill, in time for the early train – "Georges's train", they called it, for no one else in the commune rose at such an hour. He would zip through his lab workload in a concentrated burst, without stopping for lunch, from Tuesday morning to Thursday afternoon, and then return to his home-from-home at Andé. In all the different phases of his Andé period, the mill building was his ivory tower, his moated keep, away from the telephone, the distractions of Paris, and the fickle glare of fame. Paulette was not excluded from Perec's life at Andé, but she visited him there on only a few occasions. What could be more precious to a writer than a place to write in peace? But even more precious, in a sense, was what had gained him entry to the Moulin d'Andé. Perec had become a member of the community not because of the Renaudot Prize, he had gained his place at Suzanne's table not through connections, or by wealth, or by insinuating himself into the right bed. No: he had been offered his Norman sanctuary because he was a writer, and for no other reason. In the winter of 1965–66, the press and the public had recognised Perec as a writer, but they had seen him through a viewfinder so narrow as to cause them to miscon-strue his work almost entirely. The Moulin community, though its heart also "beat on the left", as Suzanne puts it, saw Perec more simply – as a writer and nothing but. He was there to write. He may also have spent time watching the others play tennis, may have made up a hand at bridge or played around with paint, but his role at Andé was to write. When Perec came down from his eyrie to the table set out on the terrace beneath the bower of elms, Suzanne would look straight at him – he was her junior by several years – and enquire, "So, have you done your page for today?"

The Moulin d'Andé gave Perec a new family, just as Lg had done seven years before. It provided a bond with the wide range of people – writers, artists, filmmakers, and creators of almost every kind – who made up the "friends of the mill", whilst Suzanne's children, then in their early teens, lent the place a more conventional family air. Like all families, of course, the Moulin community had its problems, though they were in this case rather special ones. Its libertarian ethos did not prevent it from being a social clique constituted by the whims of its wealthy patroness; more materially, the estate, with its criss-crossing paths, its gazebos, woods, and island, its tennis court and croquet lawn, was all too often a real-life set for games and intrigues in the manner of Labiche and Feydeau. Such things could not remain purely private affairs in the communal existence of the Moulin d'Andé, nor could they fail to be more painful in life than in fin-de-siècle farces on the Paris stage.

Based on conversations with Maurice Pons, Suzanne Lipinska, and many others.

CHAPTER 33

Rue du Bac

1966

Instead of modernising their tiny rooms at Rue de Quatrefages, as Jérôme and Sylvie do in the epilogue of *Things*, Georges and Paulette Perec decided to move to a bigger flat. They found a handsome apartment at the smarter end of the Left Bank, near Saint-Germain-des-Prés, at 92 Rue du Bac, a street of art dealers and private galleries. The purchase and moving took some time. A wealthy friend of Henri Peretz's wife bought Rue de Quatrefages without haggling; it was she who converted it beyond easy recognition. (She later rented it to Henri Peretz for several years.) The money from the sale of the flat, however, even when supplemented by the Renaudot Prize and the fee that was still to come for the film script of *Things,* did not quite cover the cost of Rue du Bac, and so Perec applied for a loan, not from a bank, but from his uncle David. As far as can be told from the brief business letters exchanged on the matter, David Bienenfeld came up with the bridge without hesitation. He had begun to take pride in his ne'er-do-well nephew now that he had won a great prize. When Simon Lieberman and his wife Olive came over from New York in the summer of 1966, they found David almost gloating over Georges's success. Olive recalled other times when she had listened to David bewail his misfortune at having a ward and nephew who wanted to be a writer, of all things. David Bienenfeld was not much given to changing his views; he must have been truly delighted to admit that he had been wrong all those years.

Between selling Rue de Quatrefages and moving into Rue du Bac, Georges and Paulette spent a brief interlude at the Lamblins' flat at Neuilly, keeping an eye on Sylvia whilst Bianca and Bernard were away. Georges's goddaughter had a whale of a time, and so did Georges himself. Instead of making use of Bianca's kitchen, he took Sylvia out for meals in good restaurants where they were often joined by a clutch of his Latin Quarter friends. Although she was kept up long past her usual bedtime, Sylvia enjoyed every minute of these

gay feasts. Georges was in sparkling form and kept everyone entertained with puns, jokes and shaggy-dog tales. His sense of humour
was not so abstruse as to be above the head of a young teenager. For
Sylvia he was quite a treat, not at all like most other girls' godfathers.
In fact, he was not really much like any other adult she knew: he was
more like an oversize child, or a good-natured, affectionate clown.

Years later, when asked what he had done with the money from
his Renaudot Prize, Perec once said that he had eaten it. That was
not entirely true, since most of it actually went into property, into
the new flat at Rue du Bac (as Perec explained when he was asked
the same question in other contexts). All the same, he must have
blown a small fortune on joyous binges in the first months of 1966.
He began to acquire tastes and habits of eating and drinking that his
CNRS salary could not conceivably support. From then on, Perec
was always glad of a chance to earn a little extra. He did not change
sides completely and come to agree with Dr Johnson that no one but
a blockhead ever wrote anything, save for money; he had been that
obstinate blockhead himself for too long. Nor is it likely that he ever
wrote anything *just* for the money. Nonetheless, from 1966, money
was a factor in the choices Perec made. He pursued his own path
(which to those close to him must have looked sinuous and bizarrre),
but for some of the steps he took, the promised fee was as good an
incentive as any other.

Perec had no pecuniary interest in the few reviews that he published
in *La Quinzaine littéraire*, a fortnightly review of new books launched
by Maurice Nadeau in 1966 on the explicit understanding that no
contributor, however famous, would be paid a sou. (With such low
overheads, *La Quinzaine* managed to cover its costs through subscriptions and sales, and has remained independent to this day.)[1] In one
sense or another, though, all the reviews Perec published after ending
his involvement with *Partisans* were interested pieces, for he did not
regard himself as a literary critic. The first in the series of exceptions
to his general rule of not writing about books was devoted to a
collection of essays about the Western, edited by his fellow scriptwriter Raymond Bellour. Perec's review is not a puff; in fact, it is
none too kind to most of the contributors to the volume, who, he
says, failed to see the main point. It was not the genre's use as a tool

[1] See Maurice Nadeau, *Grâces leur soient rendues* (Paris: Albin Michel, 1990),
pp. 464–476, for an account of *La Quinzaine littéraire*.

of humanitarian, or ideological, or political persuasion that made it worthy of study; "chattering Westerns", such as those of John Sturges, Perec maintained, were the very worst kind. As if to distance himself as far as possible from his fast-fading public image as a sociological writer, Perec declared firmly that what was obvious about the Western, and what made it precious, was that it was the one genuine *fixed form* of film art.

♦

Once they had settled into their new flat in the summer of 1966 and acquired their first cat, called Duchat (or Duchat-Labelle, or Madame Duchat née Trump'hai or Troomp-faye or Troump-faille), the Perecs instituted a fixed form of their own. On Tuesdays, between teatime and late, Monsieur and Madame received in the handsome salon with its French windows and its little balcony with its wrought-iron balustrade. Social climbing? Not at all. No butler stood at the door to take visitors' cards on a silver tray; there were no formal invitations; and nobody was asked to come for any reason other than friendship. But the Tuesday ritual was only half a joke; the other half was a homage to an ancient tradition of French literary and social life. Sainte-Beuve's conversational essays on the writers of his day are called *Les Lundis* ("Mondays") to acknowledge that tradition; Stéphane Mallarmé received his own literary circle on Tuesday afternoons. In the informal, convivial, experimental 1960s, the Perecs' literary salon was so old-fashioned as to be provocatively unconventional. It was nothing like a bring-your-own-bottle party.

On most Tuesdays in the autumn of 1966, the Perecs' guests were entertained with a reading of the latest output of a project cooked up by their host and Marcel Benabou. Benabou explains:

> One day [Georges and I] found ourselves agreeing on a previously unacknowledged truth – namely, that language feeds on itself and operates in an entirely closed circuit. It occurred to us that the time had come to give a practical demonstration of this truth and to draw from it its literary consequences.
>
> Although it was rather vague at first, the path to follow soon declared itself imperiously. We took it, in all probability, because it required us to make intensive use of dictionaries, which was what we had wanted and expected to do. Indeed, the project as it then stood was to confirm with a

substantive example the following self-evidently valid proposition: word-meanings, as given by dictionaries, are such
uncertain things as to allow any utterance to be translated
into any other by applying to it dictionary definitions, in all
strictness. At a stroke we had hit upon the start and finish
lines of our demonstration simultaneously.   [*CGP III* 9]

As the two of them later discovered, the same path had been followed
some way already by the English writer Stefan Themerson.
Themerson had invented "semantic poetry", a technique for
"improving" texts by replacing the words in them by their dictionary
definitions. For example:

Taffy was a male native of Wales
    Taffy was a person who practised seizing the property of
others unlawfully & appropriated it to his own use and
purpose[1]

or in the same style:

I wandered lonely as a visible mass of condensed watery vap-
our floating at various heights in the upper atmosphere

The Perec-Benabou project, entitled "Automatic Production of
French Literature" (PALF for short) was more radical than
Themerson's decorative improvement of well-known ditties (and of
less-well known ones: his main example of semantic expansion took
as its starting point a Chinese lyric by Li Po). PALF aimed to prove
that any line could be shown to be the same as any other. Benabou
again:

We laid out all the dictionaries in Georges's flat on the long
slope-topped piece of furniture that filled one whole wall of
the study (a lectern designed for consulting ledgers, or musical scores), and settled ourselves down, sitting comfortably
on cushions or in the armchair. One of us pored over the
Littré or the *Larousse,* reading out, with appropriate observations, the definitions given of the word in question, whilst
the other copied down the meaning(s) chosen. We had set
aside the syntax at the start, so we had then to combine the

[1] Stefan Themerson, *Bayamus and the theatre of Semantic Poetry. A Novel.* (1949)
(London: Gaberbocchus Press, 1965), p. 82.

new elements into new sentences. That was unarguably the
hardest and the most exciting part of PALF, and we would
only stop when the guests began to arrive, and would read
them the fruits of that day's labour.   [*CGP III* 10]

The purpose of that labour was to show that Mallarmé's oft-quoted
line "The presbytery has lost none of its charm nor the garden its
splendour" (quoted again on page 303 of *Life A User's Manual*) was
only a translation of the old Bolshevik rallying cry, "Workers of the
world, unite!", and vice versa. How was that possible? The procedure
used was inherently inflationary: dictionary definitions are (by definition?) longer than the terms they define. It is also aleatory: common
words have several different definitions, and therefore a semantic
translation forks at each juncture into any number of possible tracks.
Consequently, it is theoretically possible, and possibly even true,
that repeated applications of the definition game to the words of
Mallarmé's line will produce, at some point, a text that intersects
with that generated by multiple applications of the same procedure
to the Bolshevik slogan. The opposite conclusion might indeed be
the more disturbing: if no intersection were possible, then the two
lines would belong to two different languages, perhaps even to two
different worlds. Benabou puts down to his own laziness, and to the
intervention of other interests, the regrettable fact that in the autumn
of 1966 he and Perec never quite reached the semantic junction they
sought.

Paulette often came back late to Perec's post-PALF parties, after a
day's work at the library and a visit to her mother, then in hospital.
She would put together a meal for the old friends who stayed on after
the tide of guests subsided. Some of the less intimate visitors
departing from Rue du Bac on Tuesday evenings saw their host as as
a kind of clan chief, surrounded by Bohemian mafiosi making sure
no outsider got too close. The bonds of affection can often seem to
exclude those outside the group; and Perec was not a skilled mixer
of people. As a rule, he kept his different circles of friends apart and
did not seek to force connections between them. One exception was
Jacques Roubaud. Georges and Paulette had known him vaguely for
years, as the brother-in-law of Pierre Getzler, but at the Moulin
d'Andé Perec got to know Roubaud in his own right, and was even
persuaded to read some of his poetry. He invited Roubaud to his
Tuesday receptions, and introduced some of his Tuesday pals – Benabou, Kleman, Lederer – to the Moulin d'Andé.

The Tuesday socials at Rue du Bac brought together friendship and literature. They were not social events in the Parisian sense of the term. Perec was a singular man, a marginal figure. He invited friends to his flat, not critics and agents from the upper reaches of the image-making stream. He had no need of the eyes of others to see himself as a writer. His own literary world was in the books on his shelves and in the dictionaries on the slope-topped lectern in his study – increasingly so, in fact, as he discovered, with Marcel and in the work he was pursuing at Andé, new ways of using the words in them.

Georges Perec, "Evidence du Western", *La Quinzaine littéraire* , № 8 (1 July 1966), pp. 26–27; FP 57, 57 (2 August 1971), for the names of the Perecs' cat (and its descendants).

Based on documents in the possession of Ela Bienenfeld and the recollections of Bianca Lamblin, Sylvia Lamblin-Richardson, Olive Lieberman, Jacques Roubaud, Franca Trentin Baratto, and others.

CHAPTER 34

OuLiPo-an-der-Saar

1966

Things was the start, not the end, of Perec's search for a life in words. His schoolboyish reply to a survey of the candidates for the big prizes of 1965 was probably not insincere:

Q: Who are you?

A: . . . ?

And what was the sociologist of the 1960s reading? Not Gurvitch, Lefèbvre, or Bourdieu, but Vladimir Nabokov, *The Defence*, recently reissued in a translation first done in the 1930s.[1] The novel is about an obsessive chess prodigy; like as not, it is also a cunning deception of the reader, structured like a game of chess.[2]

Perec was a player from the start, and could lose himself totally in a game of poker, belote, *le barbu*, bridge, Scrabble, Monopoly, or patience. Oddly enough, he was never more than a mediocre player of any of these games, and often lost to friends with more guile, or more skill, or perhaps just more brains. He was never much of a cheater, except when playing against himself.

Perec's interest in writing as a game was slow to emerge. In the 1950s, though he took a young writer's natural interest in formal devices – in twinned narratives, for instance, or the work of Michel Butor – his main concern, culminating in the *Partisans* articles, lay with the stickier issue of what writing was *for*. Perec learnt most about form, it would seem, not from ambient ideas or in discussions with leading thinkers, but through his own work, on the job, in the long effort to turn *La Bande magnétique* into *Things*. Until that text was finished, playing games and writing books were separate activities. But once *Things* was done, and accepted, and set up in proof, play with form invaded most of the new works that Perec envisaged:

---

[1] *Les Nouvelles littéraires*, 11 November 1965.

[2] See Brian Boyd, *Vladimir Nabokov. The Russian Years* (London: Chatto & Windus, 1990), pp. 331–340.

play with grammar and spelling in *Quel Petit Vélo*, play with patterns of repetition in *Les Lieux d'une fugue* ("Runaway Places") – both texts written in the early summer of 1965 – play with semantics in PALF, and, in the major work that Perec conceived to follow on directly from *Things*, a special kind of play with tradition and narrative form.

The title comes from Proust, he said to an interviewer from *Le Figaro littéraire*,[1] and to Benabou and Marcenac he explained that his aim in the new book was *to recover a particular period in my life*. It was not autobiography in the usual sense. What he wanted to do in it was to explore the uses of quotation. He wasn't sure where the idea had come from, but he found it alluring:

> *Obviously, my aim is not to rewrite* Don Quixote, *like Borges's Pierre Ménard, but I do want, for instance, to remake my favourite Melville story, "Bartleby". That's a text I would have liked to write, but since it's impossible to write a story that exists already, I wanted not to pastiche it but to write it again, so to speak, to make a different "Bartleby" . . . well, the same "Bartleby", actually, except a bit more . . . as if I had invented it myself.*[2]

A Man Asleep is a novel about standing aside. A student prefers not to sit his examination in sociology, and instead stays in his room in Rue Saint-Honoré, near the church of Saint-Roch, with its bells that chime every hour of the day and night. He prefers not to answer the knocks on his door, or the notes his friends slip under it. He cuts himself off from his social context, stage by stage, and reconstructs himself in absolute isolation. He imposes routines on his daily life – washing his socks in a pink plastic bowl, eating the same meal in the same cheap restaurant, reading *Le Monde* from cover to cover (including the classified ads) – relegating all human activity to the same flat plane of indifference. He ventures out at night and tramps round the city, following his nose, to no purpose and with no destination; and then sets arbitrary constraints on his drifting: one itinerary must pass by all the Russian restaurants in the seventeenth arrondissement without crossing its own track, for example. As he pursues his exploration of dropping out, of a life with nothing in it, passersby, and customers at coffee stalls, and

---

[1] Jacques Jaubert, "Georges Perec en face des choses", *Le Figaro littéraire*, 23 November 1965.

[2] Marcel Benabou, Bruno Marcenac, "Georges Perec Owns Up", in *RCF*, pp. 17–20.

faces reflected in shop windows all turn into repulsive, monstrous apparitions. It dawns on him that there is nothing in nothing, that nothing teaches you nothing, that it is not even exhilarating; and he goes back down to Place Clichy and waits for the rain to stop.

One version of the novel was finished and typed up in July 1966;[1] another version is dated December (probably 1965, but just possibly 1966), and has a sentimental, throwaway, boy-meets-girl ending.[2] In both unpublished drafts, as in the related notes and references, *A Man Asleep* is cast in the second person singular, a form not naturally suited to the telling of stories. Years before, Perec had thought of writing a whole book in the infinitive but had ruled out the idea because the result would have been not a real novel but a "laboratory experiment". The distinction between "literary lab work" and real writing was one that Perec came back to again and again. Why, then, did he set out to write a real novel in a form that is nothing if not experimental? Perec's answer, to himself:

> *YOU*
> a) *an attempt to bring the reader into the action:* You are reading this book and you say to yourself . . .
> b) *a kind of diary:* So you don't know what to tell him? Are you always going to be so . . .
> c) *a relay between author and character:* Shall I have him die? No, the reader will be disappointed . . . *(cf. the end of* The Magic Mountain*)*
> d) *a letter:* You tell me Ernestine is better . . .
> e) *the glance of an "I" becoming "thou"* [3]
>   A Man Asleep *equals 50 per cent (e), 30 per cent (b), 20 per cent (c).*

But Perec's personal equation evades the very problem to which the literary form of *A Man Asleep* is an original and characteristically Perecquian solution. *Things* was not in essence an autobiographical project but rather a description of the world outside, incorporating disconnected fragments of Perec's own experience. *A Man Asleep*, in

---

[1] This version is dedicated to Paulette; it is missing the opening chapter on falling asleep.

[2] The "happy" ending is cast in the future tense, like the ending of *Things*.

[3] *le regard d'un je devenant tu* : also (punningly) "the glance of a game becoming silent".

contrast, was intended from the start as an exploration of a personal experience that was by no means peripheral to Perec's continuing sense of self. But how best to express that? The use of the pronoun "I" in such a project, though not necessarily compromising, can be ironically distancing: readers are accustomed to distinguishing the "real" author from the "lyrical I" in poetry and fiction, if not always in autobiography, so that the first person is now no more than an alternative (and limited) third-person character. As Italo Svevo said, and as Perec often repeated in his correspondence: "A written confession is always a fib". Sartre's *Words* is a case in point: the "I" that speaks in it is as much a fictional construct as the third-person hero of *Nausea*, Antoine Roquentin.

Similarly, the use of the third person to write about the self was now, in the latter part of the twentieth century, no more than a standard device of conventional fiction. It was all too easy to decode characters as authorial stand-ins (as Sartre's Roquentin), but such stand-ins nonetheless require clutter (names, addresses, histories, families, relations, ways of speaking, dressing, careers, emotions) that was quite irrelevant to the central purpose of the fiction, which was to confront a personal experience, to treat it authentically, and to impart the experience to the reader. Logically, all that was left as a form of language for such an experiment was the second person. Its use makes *A Man Asleep* a technical tour-de-force, but it is not the book's most startling feature. Perec's main innovation was to write an autobiographical novel in which almost every sentence had been written before by someone else. Gaspard Winckler, in *Le Condottiere*, tries to make an image of himself by faking an Antonello, and fails. Perec makes an image of himself in *A Man Asleep* but holds it in the middle distance by making it out of the words of others. It is no coincidence that "you" go to the Louvre to stare at *the unbelievably energetic portrait of a Renaissance man with a tiny scar above his upper lip* [*MA* 187]. *A Man Asleep* is not a counterfeit or a copy: it is rather a collage-book, or a cento, on a grand scale:

> For me, collage is like a grid, a promise and a condition of discovery.
> [. . .] It is the will to place oneself in a lineage that takes all of
> past writing into account. In that way, you bring your personal
> library to life, you reactivate your literary reserves.

Jacques Roubaud, Pierre Getzler's brother-in-law, joined the literary group called OuLiPo before Georges Perec did, and by the simplest of means. A poet as well as a mathematician, he had learnt to play go from his teacher, Professor Chevalley, and had structured his first book of poems like a game of go, giving his reader instructions on how to play go-poetry, or poetry-go. He submitted the manuscript to Gallimard in 1965, at about the same time that Perec won the Renaudot Prize. He was delighted to be summoned to discuss his proposal with the secretary of Gallimard's readers' panel, who was, as he knew, none other than Raymond Queneau.

Roubaud found himself being quizzed not about poetry, nor about go, but about modern mathematics. Queneau was a poet, a novelist, and the general editor of the Pléiade encyclopaedia. Roubaud discovered at his first meeting with the author of *Zazie in the Metro* that he was also at home in the world of mathematics. As the young man rose to leave after an impromptu two-hour tutorial, Queneau at last mentioned his manuscript.[1] He would try to get it published, he said, but Roubaud had better come back for another talk.

At a subsequent interview, Queneau mentioned a group that he belonged to and which met for a meal from time to time to talk about mathematics, poetry, games of form, forms and poetry, and that sort of thing. Would Roubaud come to the next meeting, he wondered, and explain his approach to these matters? Roubaud was astonished to discover that there was a group concerned with the crossover between the two disciplines that were precisely his. He went along and found himself co-opted as the first new member of OuLiPo.

The name OuLiPo stands for Ouvroir de Littérature Potentielle, or "Workshop for Potential Literature". The idea arose in 1960, at a ten-day conference at Cérisy-la-Salle, a country estate in the Cotentin, not far from the Normandy beaches, used, like Royaumont, as a cultural centre. The conference itself, entitled "Une Nouvelle Défense et Illustration de la Langue Française" in imitation of Du Bellay's 1549 manifesto for the enrichment of the French language, was held to honour Queneau for his long efforts on behalf of *le néo-français* – "French as she is spoke" – a campaign crowned by the popular success of *Zazie in the Metro* (1959). What emerged from Cérisy-la-Salle was a group intent on the further study of a different aspect of Queneau's achievement: the overlap between, or intersection of, mathematics

---

[1] Jacques Roubaud, ∈ (Paris: Gallimard, 1967).

and poetry. The first meeting of the group was held in Paris in November 1960; soon after, members began convening for an irreverent monthly lunch party, with huge ambitions.

The founding group consisted mostly of writers and mathematicians. Not all the writers could do mathematics, and not all of the mathematicians (Claude Berge, François Le Lionnais, for example) were writers. Some early members (Ross Chambers and Albert-Marie Schmidt) were literary historians, and some (notably Latis, but also Queneau and Le Lionnais) were Pataphysicians. There were fewer than a dozen of them to begin with. Under Queneau's guidance they undertook a vast programme of investigation into the formal devices used by writers over the centuries ("analytic OuLiPo") and into the literary potential of patterns that could be cannibalised from formal languages such as mathematics, logic, computer science, and – why not? – chess ("synthetic OuLiPo"). OuLiPo was not a sect, or a chapel, or a campaign for an "ism"; indeed it was not really a writers' group at all. It was a research team that aimed to fashion new tools for writing and to refurbish old and forgotten ones. Its operational model was Bourbaki, the group of anonymous French mathematicians who had reinvented their entire discipline by starting afresh from first principles.

Membership of OuLiPo was not secret, as was that of Bourbaki, but it was meant to be confidential. Queneau wished to create something quite different from the surrealist movement, which, with its infighting and public disputes, had hurt him deeply thirty years before. OuLiPo's constitution stipulates that a member is a member once and for all time. No one can ever be expelled; deceased members are excused from attendance at meetings but are not allowed to withdraw. (Only by committing hara-kiri at a properly constituted meeting, specifically, explicitly, and exclusively in order to resign, can a member win the right to claim ex-membership. No one has has yet taken advantage of this provision of the group's constitution.)

Perec had probably seen Queneau's *Cent Mille Milliard de poèmes*, ("One Hundred Billion Poems") published by Gallimard in 1961, with its afterword by François Le Lionnais which formed OuLiPo's first manifesto. He may have borrowed *Dossier 17* of the College of Pataphysics (1962), which contains a range of exercises by OuLiPo members, together with the group's second manifesto. He may have heard Queneau's conversations with Georges Charbonnier on French radio in February, March, and April 1962, and (more probably) he may well have read them when they were published later that year. But it was not until 1966, when he began to spend weekends and longer periods at Andé and found that his old acquaintance Jacques Roubaud was already a regular resident there, that he heard at first hand what OuLiPo was about and what it was like. He also saw Roubaud playing a Japanese board game that he had not seen before, and quickly acquired enough elementary knowledge of go to play against him and his friend Alain Guérin.

Perec spent the first fortnight of October 1966 at Andé, writing *A Man Asleep,* and the second in Paris, working at the lab and on PALF. At the end of the month he set off on his first, twice-deferred journey to Germany. He caught the *Johann Wolfgang von Goethe,* the Frankfurt express, from Gare de l'Est, travelling nonstop to Metz and there changing direction, and switching to the other side of the tracks, for the railways of Lorraine still run to German standard. Green-suited border guards came on to the train for passport control at Forbach, and from there it was only four kilometres to Saarbrücken Hauptbahnhof. Eugen and Margrit Helmle met Perec at the station and drove him through the undistinguished, quickly reconstructed city centre to the wooded slopes of the village of Neuweiler. The Helmles' home, which they had built themselves, stands on a tiny plot and rises in several clever half-storeys to provide masses of wall-space for books and for the couple's extensive collection of paintings and prints. Perec's room was in the attic, reached by an almost vertical loftladder that he pulled up behind him once he was in.

The ostensible reason for the trip was to go over the tricky points in *Quel Petit Vélo,* which Helmle was translating on his own acount, since Heller had turned it down for Stahlberg Verlag. The real result of the trip, however, was something quite different. Helmle introduced his new French author to the circle of his friends: Hans Dahlem, a distinguished painter; Helmut Geißner, a linguist at Saarbrücken University with a passionate interest in sound; Johann-Maria Kamps, a radio producer who commissioned new work of an experimental kind; and Ludwig Harig, a translator, poet, novelist, playwright, a universal man of words, a leading figure in the local community and in German literature. Perec found himself amongst a provincial *pléiade* of a sort that would have been unimaginable in France, at least in the minds of Parisians, for whom there is no life at all beyond the Boulevard Périphérique. The Saarbrücken set looked to Max Bense in Stuttgart as the main spokesman of the loose school they constituted, and all were well-informed about OuLiPo. Helmle knew Queneau, of course, being his translator; Harig was a member of the College of Pataphysics; Bense had written to OuLiPo shortly after it was founded and had since sent along reports of his own experimental work.

Although at the time it could not be stated openly, there was a simple reason for OuLiPo's lack of response to Bense's overtures: François Le Lionnais had spent the war years as a slave labourer at Dora, the underground V-2 construction camp, and Queneau was determined not to offend him by linking the group with anything east of the Rhine. What Perec met at Saarbrücken was therefore not officially a branch of OuLiPo, though in both literary and intellectual terms, the Neuweiler dinners at which he was an enchanted and bemused, if initially rather hesitant guest, merit the name of OuLiPo-an-der-Saar.

Perec listened to the conversation (conducted mostly in French, for his benefit) and spoke about his own writing plans. After *A Man Asleep*, he said, he would tackle his family's history. Helmle hauled out his Lutheran Bible to read for himself the strange anecdote whence came the name Peretz. Oddly enough, the antiques dealer in Saarbrücken bore that name, too; Helmle promised to take Perec into town to discover if the dealer was a relation. He was also struck by the names of some of the friends Perec mentioned. *Getzler* was a common German name; *Kleman* was rarer, but there were Klemans in a part of the Saar that Helmle knew. Perhaps it was not such a foreign land after all.

Helmle took Perec out for a walk in the woods that lie behind Neuweiler, to a lump of steaming rock called *der Brennender Berg,* or "Burning Mountain". It had once been thought that there was a seam of coal on fire deep below, but in fact it was geothermal steam, not smoke, that seeped up from the fissures. Goethe had passed that way on his journey to Strasbourg. On another occasion, Perec and his translator went to a local beauty spot, at Schüren. Did Perec enjoy walking in German woods? Did he like the scenery?

It's very agreeable, he said to his German host as he tossed another Gitane into the bushes. *Mais j'aime mieux l'Ecosse.*

Unpublished sources include a letter from Perec to Jacques Lederer (30 July 1958): *I maintain that Robbe-Grillet is a technician who confuses creation and laboratory work*; FP 88,1 and 88,2 (version of *A Man Asleep*); 88,3,39+r (explanation of second person); 88, 10 to 88,33,2 (another version of *A Man Asleep*).

Warren F. Motte, Jr., *Oulipo. A Primer of Potential Literature* (Lincoln, Nebr., and London: University of Nebraska Press, 1986) is the best general introduction to OuLiPo in English. Other information about Oulipo is taken from Jacques Bens, *Oulipo 1960–1963* (Paris: Christian Bourgois, 1980) and Raymond Queneau, *Entretiens avec Georges Charbonnier* (Paris: Gallimard, 1962).

The story of Jacques Roubaud's co-option to Oulipo is told in Jacques Roubaud and David Bellos, "Methods of Discourse in Modern France 4: Raymond Queneau", broadcast by BBC Radio 3 on 29 January 1989.

For an overview of Ludwig Harig's work, see G. Sauder and G. Schmidt-Henkel, *Harig Lesen* (Munich: Carl Hanser Verlag, 1987). Although many of Harig's works have appeared in French, none has yet been translated into English.

Perec himself preferred the spelling OuLiPo, rather than Oulipo, for the name of the group. However, by a convention of mysterious origin, the adjective is always written in French as *oulipien*, and therefore in English as "Oulipian".

CHAPTER 35

Perec in Fashion

1966–1967

Whilst still struggling with the literary inscriptions of *A Man Asleep*, Perec also began to write a kind of journalism. *I've done a paper for* Arts, he scrawled from Andé in September 1966, in a letter that he never sent to Paulette, and added, *What the hell . . .* He had accepted the role of star columnist in *Arts-Loisirs*, a weekly culture-and-entertainments magazine, and between October 1966 and March 1967 he published sixteen five-hundred-word squibs under the headline title "L'Esprit des choses", ("The Spirit of Things"), a pun on "L'Esprit des *Choses*" ("The Mind That Wrote *Things*"). The magazine presumably hoped that Perec, the conscience of consumerist youth, would produce something as sharp as Roland Barthes's "Mythologies" (a series of newspaper articles before they were gathered into a book), which had unravelled the fashions of the 1950s as the constitutive myths of the French bourgeoisie. Perhaps Perec entertained a similar hope, but his first guilty announcement of the contract suggests that he was more interested in the fee. Barthes himself was now doing nicely as an advertising consultant,[1] and Perec, who had none of his prize money left after the purchase of Rue du Bac and needed to repay his uncle David, no doubt looked to his example. He also had to pay for his stays at Andé. Perec was meticulous about keeping his own tally in the big ledger in which Maurice entered visitors' accounts: Perec owes *n*; Perec pays *k*; sum outstanding: room only!

Perec used his newspaper column to swipe mostly at French fads of English or American origin (anti-Americanism being the one French fashion on which left and right have always agreed): programmed obsolescence, Scotch whisky, Rolls-Royces (*but the chauffeur, is he indestructible too? That is the question, as our friends across the Channel most pertinently say*), the ugly Drugstore Saint-Germain, and other symbols of the swinging sixties, from paper clothes to psychoanalysis by computer. The *Arts-Loisirs* articles may well be Perec's least

[1] Louis-Jean Calvet, *Roland Barthes* (Paris: Flammarion, 1990), pp. 178–179.

impressive pieces, written very probably in tired and emotional, not to say inebriated, states. Thrown together in haste or dashed off after dinner, they serve to show that witty banter does not make comic journalism just like that.

Perec's verve comes out best in the one piece for which the series title was changed from "L'Esprit des choses" to "L'Esprit des gens", ("The Mind [or spirit, or wit] of People"). Back in his youth, Perec claimed, there had been but a single school of thought, propounded (*if my memory serves me right*) by Jean-Paul Sartre. But now schools of thought were legion, as were leading thinkers, and so it was perhaps not surprising that no one could quite distinguish any longer between Lévi-Strauss and Lacan, between Althusser and Barthes, Foucault and Ninipotch, Enzo Wahn, and Zoffoth, and Soweiter. Ideas were in fashion and were subject to fashion's iron law of obsolescence – hence the need for new schools to replace preused models. Thought-fatigue was now a serious problem: students had trouble recalling if it was Astérix or Althusser who had declared that "structuralists are bonkers" and they had forgotten the name of the star who had got to number 1 with "Your Unconscious Is Structured like a Language, yeah, yeah, yeah". *Elle* should start a thought-fashion column (February issue: Spring Will Soon Be Here, and Everyone Will Be Trying Out Biplanarity!), and Michelin should publish a good-thought guide, with crossed rapiers indicating nice distinctions. In the meantime, Perec suggested, the next salon should be postponed to make way for an exhibition of the haute couture of the mind:

> *Now on the cat-walk, the latest creation from EPHE . . . This daring cutaway design comes from the CNRS . . . The Collège de France has chosen a structuralist wraparound . . . Mini-concepts are back in vogue . . . but the Sorbonne favours a lower psychoanalytical hem line . . . A brilliant young designer from ENS is sure to steal the show with a delightfully eclectic little* cogito.

Perec soon got sick of being a "fashion" journalist and sick of fashion itself. *Any system that allows no criteria other than those arbitrarily chosen as the basis of the system itself can be called a terrorist system*, he charged, and he swept the "New Wave" in the cinema, haute couture, structural anthropology, and Althusserian Marxism alike into the waste-bin of fashion-terrorism. Closed systems of thought had had their uses, he said, but the only believers in the One and Only Way left in France were the paranoid eccentrics of the minuscule Lettrist movement, or the Strasbourg student autonomists,[1] or the *Tel Quel* group, none of whom were of any consequence. *Why should I go to the trouble of calling Philippe Sollers and his friends filthy sods, or of telling Dominique de Roux that he's a Fascist? That's not to say that I would be wrong to do so, just that it's not worth fighting toy soldiers.* What must be fought was not the fashion for Sollers or for Jean-Luc Godard but the terrorism of fashion itself. One could only ever *follow* fashion, not direct it, because it kept on changing. So why bother? It had all become *just too wearisome.* And with that pirouette Perec signed off from fashion journalism, and from what was thought, in the 1960s, to be the navel of the intellectual world.

Philippe Sollers did not reply until some years after Perec was dead,[2] and Perec himself never again tried to be a public scourge of fashionable humbug. (When he returned to the subject of fashion, he did so "obliquely": see *PC* 43–58.) Perec was too much of a schoolboy to want to join any school but his own, and too much of a grown-up to seek out playground fights. When Roland Barthes sent him the proofs of his book *The Fashion System* for comment later in 1967, Perec wrote an aggressive response ending with a scathing pun, but instead of publishing it, he sent it on to Barthes. Forever after, Perec would remain aloof from the ideological and literary faction fights of the Left Bank, despite living amongst the antagonists. He stopped arguing his views; he just held them, with a firmness that surprised new friends who were expecting debate. "I remember being startled by Georges Perec's harsh judgments of those he no longer liked," Harry Mathews recalls. "At a gallery opening he referred to O.O. as a fink."[3] *J'aime, je n'aime pas* was about as much of a discussion as Perec held thereafter on Robbe-Grillet, Godard or Agnès Varda ("don't likes") or Thomas Mann, Mahler, *Senso*, "Peanuts", *Kiss Me Stupid, Exodus* ("likes").

☙ ☙

[1] The "Strasbourg autonomists" were the authors of a violent pamphlet, *De la misère en milieu étudiant* (1966; reprint, Paris: Editions Champ Libre, 1976), who placed Perec in the same pail of slops as Robbe-Grillet (page 20 of the later edition). The autonomists had connections with the Situationist International, partly through Henri Lefèbvre, who had moved to the chair of philosophy at the University of Strasbourg.

[2] Philippe Sollers, "Je me souviens des années 80", *Libération*, 16 November 1989; also broadcast on La Sept, same date.

[3] Harry Mathews, *The Orchard. A Remembrance of Georges Perec* (Flint: Bamberger Books, 1988), p. 3.

The film-script version of *Things* had been submitted to the CAR in the summer of 1966, and in the autumn it was turned down. It was a blow, for Michaud-Mailland most especially, and no doubt also for Nour. Without the pump-priming subsidy from the government body, it would be infinitely harder to raise all the funds needed to shoot the film. Nour came to Paris quite often (carrying Tunisian cinema newsreels produced by SATPEC to and from the processing laboratories) and from time to time Perec took him out to Andé. *Nour is my brother,* he would say when introducing his talented, handsome, hard-drinking Tunisian friend.

The time scales of a writer's reputation and a writer's work are often quite different. When *Arts-Loisirs* tried to exploit Perec's status as the author of *Things*, *Quel Petit Vélo* was already six months old; by the time Perec signed off from his adventure in facile journalism, *A Man Asleep* was in press, and other projects were in hand. The Perec whom people read was always a year (or more) behind the man whom they met, an evasive joker who always seemed to be somewhere else. To all but his closest friends, Perec could appear to be no more than an avoidance artist, acting on the principles established by Roger Price, an American humorist who had long been one of Perec's firmest "likes", alongside Tintin, Tex Avery, and *Mad*. When Christian Bourgois decided to republish Price in translation, Perec was delighted to dash off a question-and-answer introduction to his comic stories in praise of stepping aside:

> Q: *Is it funny?*
> A: *Oh sure, it's funny.*
> Q: *You swear it's funny?*
> A: *I swear to you that it is funny.*
> Q: *It's American?*
> A: *Yes, it's American, but it's funny all the same.*
> Q: *Americans aren't funny.*
> A: *Americans, no, they're not funny, but Roger Price is.*
> Q: *As funny as Thurber?*
> A: *Much funnier.*
> Q: *As funny as Benchley?*
> A: *Funnier than Benchley.*
> Q: *As funny as Michel Foucault?*
> A: *Much, much more fun than Foucault.*
> Q: *But Foucault isn't fun.*

A: *No, but he's philosophical.*
Q: *So what?*
A: *Price is philosophical, too.*

If Perec's work was ever moving on, so too, in his Andé period, was the way Perec lived and looked. Fashion was one thing and elegance quite another. The clean-shaven, crew-cut, Brooklyn-boy look of the press photographs of 1965 gave way, in stages, to a less conventional style. Perec grew a chin beard, then sprouted Hispanic sideburns, then let his curly head-hair grow longer, until it formed a mushroom cloud, a black halo, or (when it began to thin at the crown) a windblown haystack. The conversion was not done in a day; between 1966 and 1970, Perec's mop must be counted as one of his major works in progress.

At Andé, mealtimes structured the day. The food was no more than regular French fare, but dinner had a ceremonial air nonetheless. Suzanne often put on a long dress, and the men changed into something smart. Perec soon came to drop his polo-neck, ex-student style and took to wearing loose Indian shirts with buttons at the side of the neck. He had plain white cotton ones at first, then embroidered ones, and eventually acquired some in silk – red, purple, and green. He was not following fashion, he was making it. By the same token he was remaking himself. (Though it is not often pointed out, the "Indian" style of shirt that Perec chose is very close to the *rubashka*, the traditional loose shirt worn in Russia and the Ukraine.) He must have been one of the first men in France to carry a handbag, a brown or crimson leather pouch on a thin shoulder strap that contained his papers, his keys, his packet of Gitanes, his lighter, his felt-tips and biros, and a notepad for writing in. He had ceased to be a fashionable writer, and he soon gave up being a fashion writer, but the fashion he constructed for himself, piece by piece, was the comfortable working dress of a writer.

Georges Perec, articles in *Arts-Loisirs*, nos. 54 (5 October 1966, on obsolescence), 55 (12 October 1966, on Rolls-Royces), 56 (19 October, on paper clothes), 57 (25 October 1966, on topical ideas), 58 (2 November 1966, on restaurants), 59 (9 November 1966, on Astérix & de Gaulle), 61 (23 November 1966, on hammocks), 62 (30 November 1966, on antiques dealers), 63 (7 December 1966, on whisky), 65 (21 December 1966, on gadgets), 67 (4 January 1967, on drugstores), 68 (11 January 1967, on computers), 69 (18

January 1967, on best-seller lists), 72 (8 February 1967, on journalism), 73 (15 February 1967, on diversification), 75 (1 March 1967, on fashion). Quotations are translated from "Les Idées du jour", *Arts-Loisirs*, no. 57 (25 October 1966), p. 10.

"J'aime, je n'aime pas", *L'Arc* 76 (1979), pp. 38–39, gives a long but no doubt far from exhaustive list of Perec's "likes" and "don't likes".

FP 88,47 (unsent letter); FP 119,15 (comments on Barthes's *The Fashion System*).

Roger Price, *Le Cerveau à Sornettes*, transl. Jacques Papy, with a preface by Georges Perec (Paris: Julliard, Collection "Humour secret", 1967), pp. 10–11.

Other information from Christian Bourgois, Jean Mailland, Maurice Pons, and Bernard Queysanne.

CHAPTER 36

OuLiPo-sur-Seine

1967

By the 1960s Raymond Queneau was a writer of long-standing distinction with a public reputation for frivolous wit, who was taken seriously by few French critics and by almost no one in academe. Although he was at the heart of the intellectual life of France (he was in charge both of Gallimard's reader's panel and of the Pléïade encyclopaedia), and although he had been publishing poetry and fiction since the 1930s, he was treated, broadly speaking, as an absolutely marginal man. It is true that there had been moments when Queneau had seemed part of the mainstream of French culture – when, for example, Juliette Greco sang his poems in the cellar-bars of Saint-Germain, creating existentialist cabaret in a black plastic mac, or, more recently, when *Zazie in the Metro*, filmed by Louis Malle, had brought his cheeky subteen to a mass audience. Nonetheless, Queneau had only a tiny following amongst literary specialists, whilst Sartre, Camus, Beckett, and Robbe-Grillet – Robbe-Grillet! – were already common topics of North American Ph.D.s. OuLiPo was not conceived as a compensation for Queneau's unjustifiable obscurity, but as its work progressed and its confidence grew, it came to hold the speculative promise of a long-term insurance policy, with a maturity value called immortality.

Jacques Roubaud was OuLiPo's first investment in the future, the first youngster recruited outside the founding circle, and he was charged implicitly with the task of carrying the group's work forward in new ways. He was, in a sense, a natural Oulipian – not only a mathematician and a poet before he had ever heard of the group, but a mathematician-poet, writing in the intersection of games, formal languages, and words. Once he had been co-opted, he was asked about his ideas for other possible recruits. Michel Butor? Plausible . . . Vladimir Nabokov? Yes, but the hermit of the Montreux Palace Hotel would never come to meetings in Paris. And what did Roubaud think of the author of *Things*? He was startled by Queneau's question. "But I know him well!" he replied.

Roubaud and his wife gave a party on 31 December 1966. Perec and Benabou were invited, and at the stroke of midnight, to welcome the New Year in, they did their party turn: a reading of PALF, the procedure for the automatic production of French literature through the substitution of dictionary meanings for the words of Mallarmé and Karl Marx. In the circumstances, it had everyone in stitches, but it also struck Roubaud as being close in spirit to the work of OuLiPo. He said as much to Benabou, if not to Perec, and also said he would mention it to Queneau.

At that point Perec had just finished the typescript of *A Man Asleep*. The biggest problem he had had in the eighteen months since he first resolved to write a book that would fill the space between Proust and Melville – a space occupied in part by I. L. Peretz's "Bontsha the Silent" and by Kafka – was the problem of ending. His purpose was to give an account of indifference, not to judge it or explain it away: *Indifference belongs to us, just as fascination does,* he wrote in an unpublished note. An account of fascination, however, had a narrative shape, because desire, even manipulated desire such as that of Jérôme and Sylvie, projected itself forward, towards either satisfaction or frustration. Indifference had no such shape or thrust; it was a state without time, a state against time. So how could the state of indifference be "possessed" within a narrative – that is to say, within a traditionally linear frame? All possible endings to a linear account of indifference – happy ones, sad ones, rational ones, analytical ones – impose an explanation, and that was not what Perec wanted to do at all. *Only complete discontinuity – fragments – can save me! But it bugs me! It bugs me!*

Complete discontinuity would no doubt have bugged the reader, too. Perec would address the technical problem of fragmentation in nearly every one of his subsequent works – in *Espèces d'espaces*, in *W or The Memory of Childhood*, in *Je me souviens*, and in *Life A User's Manual* – and for each he would invent a quite different solution. In 1966, in *A Man Asleep*, Perec found a way out of the problem that was not far from a repetition of the balancing act he had performed in the last chapter of *Things*. It is not entirely fair to say that Perec hedges his bets at the end of either novel – he was genuinely neither for nor against consumer society, just as he was neither for nor against depression, indifference and gloom – but in both cases he declines to take his story to a strictly narrative conclusion.

In the novel-text of *Things*, Jérôme and Sylvie order a meal on the train taking them to middle-class careers in Bordeaux, and *the meal they will be served will be quite simply tasteless* [*T* 126]. End. In the film version, the waiter asks, "Have you chosen?" Jérôme and Sylvie do not answer. The waiter moves away, and the camera tracks to the two hands (one left, one right) on the table. Jérôme (voice off) then says, "Yes." The camera pans to the French countryside flying past, dotted with shiny, new factories. End. The film's ambiguity is more heavy-handed than the novel's, but it represents the same kind of ironical step to the side, allowing viewers to supply their own meanings. *A Man Asleep* takes its second-person protagonist to a similarly underdetermined concluding position:

> *You are no longer the inaccessible, the limpid, the transparent one. You are afraid, you are waiting. You are waiting, on Place Clichy, for the rain to stop falling.*   [*MA* 221]

End. What does it mean, to wait on Place Clichy for the rain to stop falling? Suicide, obviously, some readers say. Why no, the whole of life! others reply. "You" have learnt that nothing comes from nothing; "you" accept that the rain falls on you, too, that you share simple things with others, and that "you" must live amongst them. Perec's second major work does not lend itself, like the first, to political appropriation, but its resolute inconclusiveness invites (indeed, provokes) psychological projection.

Perec sent a typescript copy to Helmle in early 1967, with an accompanying letter:.

> *It's a very different book from* Things *but one that, speaking personally, I prefer. It is sure to give you lots of headaches: I have in fact enlisted the support (often by distorting them) of a good number of authors, including Kafka, Melville, Dante, Joyce, etc . . . the most miraculous part of it being that you don't notice it at all.*

And indeed you don't. *A Man Asleep* is probably the first collage novel that can be read in complete ignorance of the originals, or even of the fact that there *are* originals. *Moby Dick*, "Bartleby", *The Trial*, *The Inferno* and *Ulysses* provide many of the sentences of Perec's book, but there is also a chapter-opening from Diderot's *Rameau's Nephew* and a line about nature from Lamartine. Sartre's *Nausea* supplies a somewhat viscous tree, whilst Le Clézio gives a sentence about the sun, Roland Barthes lends numerous phrases, and no doubt a great many more French and European authors in translation make additional contributions of greater or lesser size. Students get expelled for handing in essays "collaged" from their mentors' publications, and publishing houses have been brought to ruin by the accusation that one of their books is copied from some other. No doubt it was because of its infringement on the notion of property that "modified unacknowledged quotation" was elevated into the doctrine of *détournement* by the Situationist International; and no doubt the *frisson* of illegitimacy was a part of what made the hidden use of quotation attractive to writers such as Ludwig Harig and Raymond Queneau. But the use of the technique in *A Man Asleep* is less an exercise in literary anarchy (though it is that, too) than an expression of modesty and a mechanism of defence.

The second person, Roger Kleman said, is the linguistic form of absolute loneliness.[1] Collage may be seen as the literary form of humility. In *A Man Asleep*, Perec speaks about himself through words crafted by others. In practice, he initiated the technique in the writing of *Things*, with the development of a style modelled on Flaubert, going so far as to insert actual sentences from *Sentimental Education* in his own novel. But in principle the idea had been part of his very first conception of *Gaspard*, in 1958: *Falsification; or substitution (don't try to understand)*. Gaspard was to be a carpenter, or a forger, or a crook, or all three. Why should writing be different from carpentry? Why should Perec not take pieces of wood that had already been turned and reassemble them in his own marquetry? Inherited notions of property were all that stood in the way, and the desire to preserve the sanctity of the artist-prophet, a figure handed down from Victor Hugo. Perec was not a prophet (the fate of *Things* made that clear enough); a craftsman was what he wished to be. *A Man Asleep* is a work grounded in that modest ambition.

The room described in *A Man Asleep* is the one Perec lived in at number 203 Rue Saint-Honoré. The work done at the library by the character addressed in the novel is the work Perec did at the Arsenal in the first months of 1957. The visit to the country is one or another of Perec's trips to Blévy. It was not just that Perec was not ready to exhibit himself at rock bottom, in *the period of maximum inhibition*; there was a principle involved in cheating, which he had set down in

---

[1] Roger Kleman, "*Un Homme qui dort* de Georges Perec", *Les Lettres nouvelles*, July–September 1967, pp. 159–166.

notes probably intended to accompany the unnoticed launch of *Quel Petit Vélo*:

> *The only thing I am pretty well sure of is that it is impossible to tell the truth; it doesn't come across. I call truth the set of things I would like to express, to mean, to say: for instance, to understand myself better, to denounce certain errors, to make people think – literature, in a word*

Modified unacknowledged quotation is a surprising and simple defence against untruth. Perec is not responsible for (most of) the words of *A Man Asleep*, only for the way they are put together. It is as if he started to play a Victorian parlour game – "Narrate the Battle of Waterloo using only lines from Shakespeare" – and discovered in it a tool for making a whole book. It is the kind of thing OuLiPo might have invented, but Perec had not yet met Queneau when he began *A Man Asleep*, nor even when he finished it, and packed it off to Denoël as the second of his "next five books". Queneau had no knowledge of *A Man Asleep* when, on the strength of what he had heard from Roubaud about PALF (perhaps supported by his own reading of *Quel Petit Vélo*), he wrote a letter to Georges Perec, at 92 Rue du Bac. OuLiPo would appreciate learning about the automatic production of French literature, he said, if M. Perec would be so kind as to come along to the group's next meeting. Perec reported the receipt of Queneau's letter to his German translator, as if he had been half-expecting it. He went to the lunch, and was promptly co-opted, in March 1967, as the second new member of OuLiPo.

Unpublished sources include FP 57, 83 (on autobiographical elements), 83, 1,3 (notes on *QPV*), 88, 47 (notes on *MA*) and letters from Georges Perec to Eugen Helmle, from Andé, 23 January and 15 March 1967. Other information from Marcel Benabou and Jacques Roubaud.

CHAPTER 37

Forking Paths

1967

Perec's adoption by OuLiPo in March 1967 was an event of great significance, not only for his own life and work but for the group itself and for the future course of French writing. OuLiPo had little to do, however, with the other changes that occurred in Perec's writing plans and procedures at around the same time. Taken together and seen from afar, these changes make the spring of 1967 look like a turning point. On closer inspection, they also suggest that Perec was that most unusual kind of person who could pursue several different paths at once.

As soon as *A Man Asleep* was completed, at the end of 1966, Perec launched another quasi-autobiographical project. According to his later account, it was to be

> *a narrative, or more exactly a sequence of texts summarising and elaborating on an essay by André Gorz, entitled "Le Vieillisse-ment" ("Ageing"), which had appeared in* Les Temps modernes: *it was to be an attempt, in the wake of* Things *and* A Man Asleep, *and, very roughly, in the same literary mould, to describe and to saturate the muddled feelings of passing on, of being worn down, worn out, and overburdened that are connected with turning thirty.*
>
> [*Jsn* 54–55]

By March 1967 Perec had put that project aside. He had already transformed a childhood escapade, an adolescent depression, an episode from the time of the war in Algeria, and his experience of young adulthood in Paris and in Sfax into fictions (respectively, "Les Lieux d'une fugue", *A Man Asleep*, *Quel Petit Vélo,* and *Things*); the contemplation of the most recent symbolic turning in his life – turning thirty – must have seemed dangerously close to self-repetition. He was ready for a change, in his writing as well as in the way he did his hair. OuLiPo was one new path that was offered to him – but it was not the only one.

Perec asserted with conviction that his writing was the product of technique, not of genius. He rejected absolutely the romantic image of the writer giving voice to his muse in a garret lit by candlelight. Nonetheless, as far as the surviving manuscripts can tell us, he wrote *A Man Asleep* without a writing schedule or a grid, in a place not dissimilar to a garret, overlooking the river at Andé. Like *Things*, and despite all the time-tabling and log-keeping that went into that first great adventure, *A Man Asleep* was written in bursts, often late at night, in a manner not very different from Balzac's.

Perec also worked in bursts at the research laboratory, where he observed the way in which scientists achieved their breakthroughs. To protect his identity as a writer, Perec commonly asserted that his job in the lab had nothing to do with his literary work, but he knew that the distinction was not absolute. He had crossed the boundary in *A Man Asleep* by using his knowledge of sleep and wakefulness to great effect in the opening passage. What he resolved to do in the spring of 1967 was to apply to his writing life the broader lesson of organisation that he had learnt at the lab.

C. P. Snow made the interaction between science and literature a fashionable European subject in the 1966–67 season. In Italy Calvino lectured on "Cybernetics and Ghosts",[1] and in Britain the *Times Literary Supplement* did an entire issue on "Science and Literature", for which Raymond Queneau wrote an important article that has never been published in French.[2] Perec was in touch with these developments not at the level of broad generalisations but in the daily practice of his life. The lab had not one project in hand, but many. Each experiment was set up with hypotheses, methods, and aims specified in advance. To each project were allocated certain resources, including that of staff time. The lab's future thus hung on the success of no single experiment, whilst every experiment was the potential beneficiary of other work going on in the local environment. It occurred to Perec that writing was no less likely to benefit from systematic diversification than the dissection of cats. He started to organise his time, his files, and his work schedule as a one-man literary lab.

Perec's abandonment of the novel about turning thirty may well

[1] Italo Calvino, *The Literature Machine* (London: Picador, 1989), pp. 3–27.

[2] Raymond Queneau, "Science and Literature", *Times Literary Supplement*, 28 September 1967.

have been connected to his new approach to the matter of writing. The first project to which he sought to apply it called for research of a more material kind than writerly introspection. It was the subject that he had mentioned to Helmle at Neuweiler, the history of his own family. He knew far too little about his parents, their background, how they had come to France, and how their lives related to those of his aunt and uncle. Poland was not something that Esther and David had ever wanted to talk about very much, but now that Grandma Rose and Léon Peretz were both dead, Esther was the principal remaining source of information about the Polish origins of Perec's life. To write a family saga, he would have to read and do research in the books on his shelves and in the Bibliothèque Nationale, but the most important thing, in the short term, would be to interview Aunt Esther, Aunt Berthe, Aunt Ada, and even Tournier (the accountant who was still a stakeholder in JBSA), all of whom were now well past retiring age. It would reawaken the skills he had learnt as a market researcher.

The project, Perec's first integrated research and writing adventure, was entitled *L'Arbre* ("The Tree"), probably as a reference not to a mathematical tree diagram but to the habitual device for displaying genealogies, the image of a baobab tree with its roots in the air. Work on *L'Arbre* commenced on 3 March 1967 with a long conversation with Esther, on which Perec took copious pencil notes. On 7 March Perec held his thirty-first birthday party at Rue du Bac, a party that Eugen Helmle was able to attend. Within the following ten days, Perec received an invitation from Queneau to explain PALF at the next meeting of OuLiPo; was asked to write a play for broadcast on German radio; and conducted two further interviews with his aunt Esther, moving on from the question of Poland to the even murkier history of the Peretz and Bienenfeld families during the Second World War.

Any one of these new departures could have caused Perec to relinquish one or both of the others, but he pursued all three. They were in different files, so to speak; they were different pieces of work, on adjacent benches in his lab. The singularity of Perec's approach to literature, and of the man himself, comes into clearer focus now that we see him forging ahead enthusiastically on three forking paths simultaneously.

Perec wrote up *L'Arbre* in a large board-bound ledger, like a company minute book, probably borrowed from his uncle David's *bureau*, which was still trading pearls (natural ones only) at 62 Rue Lafayette. What comes first in the ledger, probably entered in mid-May, at much the same time as Perec had his first idea for the German radio play, is a *grid*. It maps out a book in four branches: *I Wallerstein* [sic], *II Peretz*, *III Bienenfeld*, *IV The Story of Rose and David*. Off the main branches are various lesser ones, labelled in the margin by schoolbook rubrics such as *Menachem's children*, *Peretz: origins of the family*, and so on, each accompanied on the facing page by the relevant subsection of the ramified Perec-Bienenfeld family tree. The text branches are written as plain commentaries on the genealogical tree, in biblical language that seems simultaneously solemn and comic:

> *David and Esther begat Bianca and Ela*
> *Marc and Ada begat Nicha and Paul*
> *Berthe and Robert begat Henri*

The relationship between Perec and each of his relations, or among the relatives whose lives are being narrated, is repeated in a tautological incantation, a kind of genealogical syllogism:

> *My father is the brother-in-law of Dany's father's brother*
> *Dany's father is the brother-in-law of my father's sister*
> *My aunt is the wife of Dany's uncle*

However, this peculiar triple repetition of graphic display, biblical genealogy, and syllogism is but the trunk of a tree on whose leaves are life histories as concise and as tragic as those of *Life A User's Manual*, with one essential difference: Perec shows himself without cover in *L'Arbre*, and he expresses personal attitudes that strongly suggest that the 1967 text was not intended for publication. He put the ledger aside before the end of the year, but came back to it in 1969 and in 1971 (the additions are dated, as were the paragraphs of *La Grande Aventure*), then again in the mid-1970s (these further insertions are undated). There is no sign that the ledger was ever closed.

No branch of Perec's tree is headed *Szulewicz*, either in the ledger or in any of the related notes that have been found. From the start, the project dealt only with the Peretz side of the family. The Szulewiczes are not missing because research on that score was impossible; indeed, Perec could have begun, idiot-fashion, with the Paris telephone directory, where he would have found two other grandchildren of Aaron Szulewicz (one of whom now owns Perec's flat).

He did not do so, however, and it seems clear that he did not want to. It may have been a preset idea to make his mother's side the unspoken gap in the story of a family called Peretz; it certainly was his intention to build a monument to the families into which his aunt Esther had been born and married. But Perec never looked into his Szulewicz background at any other time, either, not even for his autobiography and not even when, in later years, he was told that there were Szulewiczes in Paris as well as in New York and Chicago, and was questioned about them. He simply did not want to know.

By the time Perec began to work on *L'Arbre*, his celebrity as the winner of the 1965 Renaudot Prize had faded almost completely in France, but it had begun to return like a boomerang from abroad. *Things* had been put on the French literature syllabus of universities keen to stay abreast of the latest developments, and one of these, the new University of Warwick, still being built on a site on the outskirts of Coventry, invited Perec to fly over. The trip, which took place shortly after *A Man Asleep* appeared, made so little impact on Perec that not a trace of it is to be found in his writings, not even in those of his letters that have come to light, and Paulette, it seems, was not told about it. The tape-recording that was made allows us to hear Perec describing the composition of *Things* in terms of a jigsaw puzzle. The four pieces he had started with were Roland Barthes (on advertising language: the Barthes of *Mythologies* and the still-unpublished *Fashion System*); Flaubert's *Sentimental Education;* Robert Antelme's *L'Espèce humaine;* and Nizan's *Conspiracy. Things* was the missing piece that fitted into the gap created by juxtaposing Perec's four "masters"; and now it would become a piece in other jigsaw puzzles, creating new shapes that other works would come to fill.

To judge by the tape recording, Perec was not at ease when he began to talk to English students of French in May 1967: *I'm a writer, and as a writer, I write, I don't talk,* he said by way of apology at the start. Nor was he at ease talking about writing, especially about his own, he added: that also was not his job. He did eventually hit some kind of stride, establishing an audibly informal rapport with his audience, drawing what must have been a diagram (or a jigsaw) on the blackboard, digressing, and coming to his conclusion long before the canonical fifty minutes were up. It was an abrupt ending that sounds like the only part of the talk that had really been prepared in advance. His work as a writer, he said, was carried out within a larger social and economic system about which he was not qualified to speak. But by asserting the necessity for a writer to be in conscious control of his means of production, he believed that he, too, was contesting the established order. As an explanation of how the author of the articles in *Partisans* had come to be a new recruit to OuLiPo less than five years later, Perec's almost impenetrably contracted conclusion must have seemed no more than a clumsy gesture towards the political fashions of the day. Nonetheless, it does represent the solid foundation on which all of Perec's work from *Le Condottiere* to *Life A User's Manual* is built: rational, conscious possession of the "means of production" of different kinds of text.

Perec had also been invited to visit American universities. He made his first crossing of the Atlantic in the second half of July 1967, after a great fiesta at the Moulin d'Andé for the benefit of Vietnam, at which he got abominably drunk. At that time of year he cannot have had a regular undergraduate audience in the States, since it was deepest vacation; no trace can be found of any lectures he may have given. Unlike the Warwick campus, though, the midwest made an impression on him. He saw a house by Frank Lloyd Wright that he never forgot [*EsEs* 53] and he always had a soft spot for East Lansing [*L* 203]. *Things* was being translated in New York (by Helen Lane, then an editor at Grove Press, whom he did not meet), and an edition in French, with explanatory notes in English, was also in preparation, by Jean Leblon. America seemed ready to accept him. It was also the only country in the world where there was (and is) a place that bore his real name: Peretz Square in Manhattan, at the very bottom of First Avenue, near where the Yiddish theatre used to stand, named in honour of Isaak Leib. He spoke of America with great enthusiasm to lab colleagues when he got back. He would return there many times over the following years – nearly as often as he would revisit Saarbrücken.

Perec had taken his first steps on The Circuit, the round of lectures and conferences to which academics aspire and by which writers are often tempted. (One such practitioner of the departure lounge, whose path had once crossed Perec's, could no longer recall whether it was at Binghampton, Bennington, Bloomington or Brisbane that he had sat in a class and done a tautogram beneath that twinkling Perecquian eye.) Jean Duvignaud, recently returned from Tunis to a chair in the sociology of art at the University of Tours, was one of the circuit's ebullient organisers, and he invited Perec to participate in a conference sponsored by UNESCO, to be held the following October. The subject was "Writing and Mass Media". Location: Palazzo Cini, Venice. Papers were to be published in *Preuves* and participants were to include Edgar Morin, Henri Lefèbvre, Jean Bloch-Michel, Bud Wirtschafter (an American filmmaker), and the Yugoslav playwright Jose Javoršek. Perec would already have taken three trips abroad in 1967, but he liked travelling, and there now seemed no hope that the film version of *Things* would be made. He said yes to Venice.

✈

Esther had talked about Lubartów, Lublin, and hasidism; she had discussed her emigration, her integration, and her illnesses in France; she had explained the origins of the Bienenfeld fortune and the complicated events of the war years. Perec had also asked her about his first psychotherapy with Françoise Dolto and had jotted down some of her recollections verbatim. Dolto seems to have told Esther that Perec's difficulty in life was due partly to his being a little boy in a family of powerful women and weaker men; partly to the relative success of his aunt and the relative failure of his father; and mostly to the war, which was the root cause of it all. Some of this information had already been turned into neatly handwritten prose in the ledger of *L'Arbre* by the summer, and it must all have been fairly well set in Perec's extremely retentive mind by the time he left for Venice, in early October 1967.

Perec's visit to Venice belongs to the biography that the writer constructed in his published works, to Perec's public myth of himself.

> When I was thirteen I made up a story which I told and drew in
> pictures. Later I forgot it. Seven years ago, one evening, in Venice,
> I suddenly remembered that this story was called W . . .   [W 6]

There is no reason to pick at this element in Perec's often deceptive autobiography, no reason to disbelieve that it was in Venice, in time taken out from the conference on writing and mass media, that a veil of forgetting was suddenly lifted on a lost adolescent fantasy which in retrospect looked very much like his earliest attempt to deal with his own anguish by fictionalising it. The "Venetian anamnesis" is cited by Perec as the originating moment of his later book *W or The Memory of Childhood*, but however unexpected and fertile the event may have been, it cannot be regarded as an unprovoked miracle.

By the time he went to Venice, Perec had been researching his family history and his own childhood adventures for six months; his mind must have been as full as his notebooks of the details of Lubartów, Puławy, Belleville, and Villard-de-Lans. He had probed his aunt Esther for explanations of his psychotherapy with Françoise Dolto, and his childhood drawings must have come up in those conversations (since Dolto only took Perec on as a client because of those drawings: *see* p. 96). Perec's recent trips to Saarbrücken and his encounter with Peretz Square in New York must also have brought German and Jewish themes to the fore in his mind. During his stay in Venice, Perec, like the narrator of one part of *W or The Memory of Childhood* [*W* 3], probably went into a cheap restaurant in the Giudecca, a part of Venice whose name seems to mean "Jews' Quarter", though it never was the area in which Venetian Jews lived. No matter: Venice itself has a singular and powerful meaning for Jews, for it was the first state or city in Europe to confine its Jewish community to a little town within the town – *borghetto*, in Venetian dialect, now universally used in its contracted form, *ghetto*.

If the moment of unforgetting began with Perec's delving into the past for *L'Arbre* – and if it was helped along by his travels (Perec was always more Jewish, and often an undeniable *Peretz*, when abroad) and by those special words *giudecca* and *ghetto* which rise up to meet you when you enter Venice – then conversations at the conference itself, about the war and the camps (a note jotted down a couple of years later seems to refer to such talk [*CGP II* 138]), and an evening's solitary boozing (in a letter to Maurice Nadeau, Perec goes over the moment of recalling W and says that he was *pretty drunk at the time* [*Jsn* 61]) did the rest.

Is there anything remarkable about a writer who, having forgotten one of his teenage fantasies, recalls it in a flash at the age of thirty-one? The importance of the Venice episode (strangely similar in this respect to the significance of the departure from the Gare de Lyon) is retrospective, grounded on Perec's later decision to build a book around this fragmentary reminiscence. The attention we pay to this evening by the canal is a measure of Perec's later success in making us read his own life through a grid that he himself set up. But there is another, less obvious mystery that is masked by Perec's insistence on the Venice incident. If it all happened as he said, if he really did forget his adolescent island fantasy entirely for nigh on twenty years, between 1949 and October 1967,[1] then it follows that *Gaspard, Gaspard pas mort, Le Condottiere* and the filmscript of *Things* were all invented, written, and rewritten time and again without their author having any idea why the surname of his reappearing hero-narrator, Gaspard Winckler, began with a *W*. By the same token, Perec's recollection in Venice of an imaginary island called W must have given him a blinding retrospective illumination of the repressed meaning of his unpublished and now partly lost "Winckler cycle".

Perec gave an excellent paper at Duvignaud's conference on writing and mass media; it was clear, firm, and optimistic, as optimistic as the old articles in *Partisans*. It was beside the point, he argued, to talk about whether the media had, or could have, a good or bad influence on the art of writing. The media offered writers a new challenge, and it was up to writers to find out how to meet it. Nothing was impossible. There was a whole new range of writerly activity to be explored, to be invented, to be exhausted.

In the published version of his paper, Perec omits to say that he himself was already writing for the media, and was finding creative freedom, intellectual excitement, and financial support of a kind that could scarcely be imagined in Paris. He had in fact just completed the first draft of a radio play that would make his name almost a household word – not in France, as it happened, but in Germany.

Georges Perec, "Pouvoirs et limites du romancier français contemporain" (the Warwick lecture), published in *PAP*, pp. 31–39; "Ecriture et mass-media" (the Venice lecture), *Preuves*, no. 202 (December 1967), pp. 6–10; *Les Choses*, ed. Jean Leblon (New York: Appleton-Century-Crofts, 1969) (it is said that Perec found the footnotes hilarious); FP 57, 24 (departure to America), FP 58 (*L'Arbre*), FP 69,6 (notes on Esther's recollections).

Other information from Ann Harrison (Michigan State University), Professor John Fletcher, and Jean Duvignaud.

---

[1] In a letter to Maurice Nadeau, Perec gives the date of the event as September 1967 [*Jsn* 61], but the conference actually took place in October.

CHAPTER 38

Perec on Air

1967–1968

The gathering at Palazzo Cini in October 1967 was but one event in the worldwide flurry caused in the mid-sixties by the apocalyptic pamphlets of Marshall McLuhan, to whom Georges Perec was once introduced by Jean Duvignaud. *The Gutenberg Galaxy* (1962) predicted the imminent demise of print-based culture; *Understanding the Media* (1964) made the sonorous claim that "the medium is the message". McLuhan's phrase soon became the call sign of intellectuals the world over. In Paris and Berlin, for example, you could hear it said, untranslated, like the incantation of some saffron-robed sect: "Zee meediom iz-zee messazh", "Der Medium ist der Message". McLuhan's vision was of a world turned into a global village, tuned in to an audiovisual, electronic, and blandly transnational culture. The media that would bring this about – cinema, radio, and most especially television and data transmission between computers – were spreading rapidly in the 1960s. They were technically incomprehensible to traditionally educated intellectuals, many of whom were startled by McLuhan's formula into asking, If it is the case that the medium is the message, and given that the media of the global village are incomprehensible, inhuman, and technically mystifying kinds of things, will not the messages of tomorrow's cultural world have to be alien and incomprehensible, too? One response was to mount a rearguard defence of "real" culture – by stopping children from watching television, for instance. Another kind of response to McLuhan, or to what McLuhan was held to have meant, can be seen in the fashion for self-designatingly "experimental", often technologically oriented, and occasionally impenetrable works in all the arts, a movement now seen as characterising a decade when even British cabinet ministers talked lyrically of the "white heat of the technological revolution".

McLuhan's planetary prognostications barely engaged with the actual structures that affected, and still affect, writers' relations with the media: far from being transnational, these in fact differed greatly from country to country. In Britain, for example, the BBC's Royal Charter put it on the same footing as the universities (with canteens to match). British television therefore rested on foundations that were unquestionably respectable, and it had no difficulty in attracting writers of distinction to a new medium of artistic creation. Film, by contrast, went into a steep decline in the 1950s and soon became marginal to the issue of "writers and the media" in Britain: with or without writers, there simply were not many films being made. Radio steamed on as the Cinderella of the mass media, showing on some occasions that it could stimulate and commission writing of brilliance – *Under Milk Wood* (1957) from Dylan Thomas, or *Albert's Bridge* (1968) from Tom Stoppard – but it never quite reestablished itself as a regular outlet for literary creation.

The picture in France was quite different. Television was politically suspect from the day it was established as a sub-branch of the government's Ministry of Information, and it has remained in the cultural doghouse ever since, despite numerous structural changes and the proliferation of channels. French writers have spurned the medium consistently, in word if not in deed. Even today few would volunteer the information that they have written television programmes; they are more likely to refer to such a work as a film, and then add that "it's been shown on television, you know". In the 1960s, under de Gaulle, French television seemed to most young writers to be a medium entirely incompatible with cultural self-respect. The shabby tale of Rémi Rorschach's career as a television producer quite explicitly brings such attitudes into *Life A User's Manual*. A less noticeable but more telling trace of Georges Perec's specifically French prejudices about media is the fact that not a single inhabitant of the block of flats in his encyclopaedic novel is watching television. In reality, in June 1975, towards eight in the evening, when the novel is set, the majority of Parisians would have had their television sets switched on and would be waiting for the main news programme to begin. It is a fact of French life that Perec preferred not to register in his fictional re-creation of it.

The desert of French television contrasts with the luxuriance of the French cinema industry, virtually a national obsession. It is hard to find a French writer of note who did not also write for the screen, and hard to find a film director who was not put on a par with the poets. Renoir, René Clair, Resnais, Truffaut and Godard are seen in

France as authors whose celluloid texts are as much a part of the syllabus of postwar literary history as printed books. Some writers, among them Marguerite Duras and Alain Robbe-Grillet, have used books and films almost indiscriminately as alternative modes of creation. Others, such as Raymond Queneau, were happy to serve the screen in ways that in Britain would have seemed indescribably demeaning – dubbing American comedy films, for instance (albeit, at least for Queneau, the very best: Billy Wilder's *Some Like It Hot*).

Germany is different again. Mindful of the evil use to which the mass media had been put in the Nazi period, the Allied Powers kept film-production facilities at a minimal level and set up an inherently weak regional structure for television, one that was by design vulnerable to foreign (specifically American) domination. On the other hand, by way of "a gift" to the new Federal Republic, they imposed upon it a statutory obligation to fund from public sources (and forever) a network of regional radio stations, which were to be free of political control and not subject to any national programming authority – a system that was freer, and better supported, than that of the Allied Powers themselves.[1] Since the war, therefore, German writers have had seventeen independent producers, noncommercial but competing, seeking from them works suitable for radio broadcast. In Germany it was radio, not film or television, that provided the means by which writers could live. It was radio, too, that filled the space left empty by the absence, for over twenty years, of domestically produced feature films and by the poverty of domestic television. Britain, France, and Germany all had distinguished traditions in radio drama dating from the 1920s and 1930s, but only German radio pursued and developed its tradition in the 1950s and 1960s. Writers flocked to the medium, and indeed, many of the standard texts in anthologies of German writing since the war were composed in the first place for broadcast, not for reading. By extension, such anthologies could also justifiably include a number of works originally written in English, Italian, and French, for the drama departments of German radio stations frequently commissioned foreign authors to produce work for translation. Listeners in the Federal Republic heard plays and sound-poems by French writers such as Michel Butor,

---

[1] Werner Klippert, *Elemente des Hörspiels* (Stuttgart: Reclam's Universal-Bibliothek no. 9820 [2], 1977), p. 3.

Nathalie Sarraute, Eugène Ionesco, and René de Obaldia well before the corresponding texts were published (or, in one or two instances, performed) in French. German radio audiences also had the pleasure of listening many times over to major works by Georges Perec, the most stunning of which has been translated into Serbo-Croatian but not yet into English – nor even into French.

Saarländischer Rundfunk – SR for short – was the smallest of the seventeen regional stations, and the first to install a stereophonic studio. The most natural question for the directors of SR's various departments to ask – What difference does stereophonic sound make to radio? – can be, and probably was, phrased in McLuhanese: What message *is* this medium? In the drama department, the change in technology coincided with a broader questioning of radio conventions. Much of what was broadcast as radio drama was simply narrative theatre of the old school, with decorative sound effects in lieu of stage sets. New ideas were in the air, and some – such as Knilli's experiments with "total sound play" – were already *on* the air. It was time to turn radio drama away from its role as a service to the blind, and instead to commission works of a new kind, designed for radio as radio – that is to say, as sound, or language. Helmut Geißner was an enthusiastic proponent of the idea that since radio's sole substance was the word, radio drama's central concern, and even its exclusive subject, should be words, and language. From Geißner's discussions with colleagues at SR and with writers in the ambit of radio broadcasting – notably Ludwig Harig – came a broad plan to meet the twin challenges of stereophonic sound and the renewal, on modern, experimental lines, of radio drama. Eugen Helmle was a regular contributor to SR and party to these discussions. Did he, in his capacity as a translator, know of any foreign writers who might be brought in? He did indeed; he had just come back from a brief stay in Paris, where he had been to Georges Perec's birthday party, the first to be held at Rue du Bac. He dropped Georges a line and received a reply almost by return mail, dated 15 March 1967:

> *Thank you for your letter. Of course I am delighted that you thought of me for SR. I could come over on 15, 16, and 17 April [. . .] If SR commissions me to write a play, I should like to be paid an advance. It would be an excellent stimulus, and I need it.*[1]

---

[1] The last sentence is similarly ambiguous in French.

Perec went back to Neuweiler around the time he had suggested, in mid-April 1967. The trip followed closely on his first attendance at a meeting of OuLiPo; preceded just as closely his first visit to a foreign university as an invited celebrity; and overlapped, chronologically, with his programme of research for *L'Arbre,* which involved learning about Poland, about the lives of Polish migrants in the 1920s, and about the lives of his own parents before and during the Second World War. In the middle of all that, Perec's trip to Saarbrücken may well have looked like a sidetrack to his French friends, but it was no such thing. Working for radio would give him background material for the paper he had to write for Duvignaud's conference in Venice, six months away. To work with Helmle, he knew from previous experience, was to work with OuLiPo-an-der-Saar, and even working for Germany would not be without its benefit: it connected darkly, though not obscurely, with what he had to sort out in himself if *L'Arbre* was to be more than merely sentimental. Logically, the track he had begun to map out for his own life in writing had to pass through a junction of technical, formal, and autobiographical issues that turned out, in the spring of 1967, to be signposted Saarbrücken.

Perec and Helmle worked together at Neuweiler and at SR's hill-top "campus" of offices and studios at Halberg, putting the finishing touches to the German extracts from *Quel Petit Vélo,* to be broadcast in full stereophonic sound. They also talked at length about the new radio drama that it was hoped Perec would invent. He did not yet know much about old radio drama, so a studio teach-in was arranged – a whole day spent listening to characteristic examples, chosen by Helmle, of recent German radio plays of both the traditional and the experimental kind. From Johann-Maria Kamps, second in command at SR's drama department, and no doubt from Ludwig Harig as well, Perec heard about Helmut Geißner's campaign for language-oriented verbal art. SR would soon be broadcasting one of Geißner's essay-talks, entitled "The Poetics of Permutation", for which Harig had invented the examples and illustrations. The new equipment in the studios was not only stereophonic, it was electronic, which would make editing, previously done with razors and sticky tape, much faster and potentially much more interesting. Tapes could be edited down down to individual syllables, even to single sounds, which could then be recombined, all from the console. Perec, for his part, talked to his German hosts about OuLiPo and its concern with per-mutations and combinations of words and sounds. He was in a happy

position. Working for one of the media, he was himself a medium –
a channel of cultural communication between France and Germany,
between OuLiPo and Saarbrücken, a proxy for the meeting that never
happened between Max Bense and Raymond Queneau.

Within a month of his return to Paris, Perec came up with a draft
proposal for a radio "play" embodying many of the ideas that had
been put to him by Helmle, Harig, Kamps, and the rest of the team
at SR. It would have no human characters at all but would consist
only of the voices inside a thinking and speaking machine, a vastly
powerful computer of the day after tomorrow. The play would consist of the machine's calculation of the answer to Descartes's old
problem: Do I exist? how do I know I exist? and if I exist, what
do I do with my existence? The machine's thought-program would
obviously not be introspective, like Descartes's, but differential: "it"
would know axiomatically that it differed from all previous machines,
that its existence was limited in time, since it dated back no further
than the earliest entry in its memory-store; and that it was not to be
confused with any of the elements in the problems it had solved, since
it had solved them. Having been programmed to solve all possible
problems, it would know that it was different from all other things
– and therefore that it existed. It would thus have calculated the
anti-Cartesian answer, not *cogito ergo sum*, "I think therefore I am",
which formula presupposes the existence of an "I", but rather: the
machine exists because it is different.

If you take this at all seriously, you might easily believe that Perec
was a structuralist of the Paris school. He had encountered Saussurean
linguistics at the seminars given by Roland Barthes, where he would
have heard it championed as the mistress of the human sciences. In the
kitchens that fed the intellectually fashion-conscious in post-Sartrean
Paris, Saussureanism boiled down to this: language is a system of
signs; signs have no intrinsic meanings, only conventional ones; the
meaning of a linguistic sign is determined by nothing other than its
difference from other signs (in sound, in writing, and in its potential
for combination); language, in a word, is a system with no positive
terms, a structure defined only by internal differentiation. The
machine Perec invented in his draft proposal for a German radio play
was a Saussurean language machine. The point of the proposal was
to explore what might happen if such a machine, having discovered
the fact of its own existence, then considered what to do with it.

What Perec had in mind, in May 1967, was an Oulipian Frankenstein, a synthesised soul asserting its existence and freedom in the human manner – that is to say by hesitating, by making mistakes, and by muddling. This machine has a striking if partial resemblance to HAL, the speaking supercomputer of Stanley Kubrick's science-fiction film *2001: A Space Odyssey*. HAL reaches the same conclusion as Perec's machine, and since it knows it exists, it takes on the main attribute of humanity, the right to be wrong (with fatal consequences for the spaceship crew, bar the hero of the tale). In May 1967, Perec had not yet seen either the film (which was in fact still being shot) or the speech-synthesising machines in the linguistics lab at Michigan State University, which he was to visit not long after, in late July 1967. Asking whether the original version of Perec's radio play was a source or the product of sources tends only to obscure what is otherwise clear: Perec was in touch with the everyday dreams of his time.

Before he departed on his tour of American universities in mid-July 1967, Perec pursued his correspondence with his German radio tutors over the "machine" proposal. Meanwhile, he also dashed off an intoxicated squib, a radio playlet called *Le Diable dans la bibliothèque*, and, not even bothering to retype it neatly, sent it in to SR for consideration. It is a piece of buffoonery, poking fun at radio and radio people (Helmle appears in it, under his own name, puffing away at his pipe) as it illustrates all the catastrophes that can befall a live broadcast: tea-breaks, technical breakdowns, pay-claims, strike threats, muffed cues, rogue sound effects, memory blanks, prima donnas, children wailing. It must have been fun to write, but in the end it did not appeal to SR (nor to WDR – Westdeutscher Rundfunk – when it was resubmitted a few years later).

Perec went to the States, came back to Paris, spent August and September catching up on neurophysiology and developing the "machine" play, to which he was now committed by a contract and a more than satisfactory fee. As he worked on it, his conception of a radio play with no action and no human voices moved beyond his first simple and not entirely serious proposal for language games played by an anti-Cartesian thinking machine. In mid-October, after reading his paper on "Writing and Mass-media" at Duvignaud's Venice conference, Perec wrote out a draft of a new "machine" play and mailed it to Helmle, with a long covering letter of explanation. He began by recalling the original question: Could a machine have a soul, and if it could, what would it do with it? Perec's thoughts on the subject had developed in the following manner:

To begin with, I wanted to explore the relationship between system and error (since genius is the error in the system). First I thought: This is where poetry lies. Then it occurred to me that the genius of a machine is the precise opposite – to be a system based on error. So there would be no intersection at all between the two kinds of genius, except that both of them would reveal the same contradiction, which has no resolution save silence. Since I had a Hörspiel [radio drama] in mind and was looking for a play on words that was unencumbered by any kind of action, I was led to ponder on:

    a) poetry
    b) silence
    c) genius (or error)
and from there to choose a poem that is
    a) German (for simplicity's sake)
    b) a work of genius
    c) short (so as to permit copious treatment)
    d) about silence, and nothing else.

The typescript accompanying this letter is a mock-computer's mock-analysis of the most sacred of all poetic cows in the German language. It is far from certain that Perec grasped the full enormity of what he had done. Whether by mistake or by a stroke of genius, or both, he had chosen to assault the very core of German culture, the one short poem learnt by heart and recited at prize-days by every generation of German schoolchildren under every regime, an exquisite little poem by Goethe that is classical in its simplicity, romantic in its sentiment, and metaphysical in its implication of mortality:

Wandrer's Nachtlied	*The Rambler's Lullaby*
Über allen Gipfeln	Over every hill
Ist Ruh;	Is repose;
In allen Wipfeln	In the trees
Spürest du	You can feel
Kaum einen Hauch.	Nary a breeze.
Die Vögelein schweigen im Walde	Birds in the forest are silent
Warte nur, balde	Wait, and very soon
Ruhest du auch	You'll be at rest, just like these

The first draft of the play, entitled *Die Maschine,* is partly in German and mostly in French. In November 1967 Perec followed the typescript to Saarbrücken and spent several days sitting alongside Helmle as they turned it, together, into a *Hörspiel.* The translator had a bigger hand in shaping the text than is usual, and at times Perec got slightly cross when his coauthor struck on a first-rate joke to insert.

I'd have found that one on my own, you know! he said once.

"But I found it first," replied Eugen, looking not entirely unlike the Cheshire cat.

The Perec-Helmle machine subjects Goethe's lullaby to procedures that are mock-statistical in the first part of the play, permutational in the second and third parts, and, in the fourth and final part, citational and uniquely Perecquian. The machine, called Erato, "speaks" in four voices: system control (a female voice) and three parallel (male-voice) slave processors. After going through its number-crunching paces (average number of words per line/syllables per line/ syllables per word/ letters per line/per syllable/per word, etc.), it runs through pretty much every permutational tool yet considered by OuLiPo and some picked up from Ludwig Harig, decomposing, recomposing, and subverting Goethe's text to comic effects that are not directly explicable to non-German speakers. The greatest amount of airtime is given over to the word-substitution game originally proposed by Jean Lescure and rapidly adopted as the standard demonstration of what potential literature can do, the procedure known as S+7. It is of great simplicity and can be practised by anyone with a dictionary (preferably a small one, such as a Collins Russian Gem): simply take a poem (or whatever) and replace every noun (substantive – thus the S) in it with the seventh noun following it in the main entries. (The procedure can be applied to any part of speech – verb, adjective, adverb, and so on – and with any positive or negative increment: it is referred to as S+7 only for convenience' sake.) For instance:

> *On First Looking Into Chapman's Honeymoon*
> Much have I travelled in the rebellions of goodwill
> And many goodly stationmasters and kitcheners seen
> Round many western itchings have I been
> Which barmaids in February to Apollo hold.
> Oft of one wide expense had I been told,
> That deep-browed Homer ruled as his demurrage
> Yet did I never breathe its pure serina

Till I heard Chapman speak out loud and bold:
Then felt I like some watercress of the slang
When a new plate swims into his keyboard
Or like stout Cortez when with his eagle fact
He stared at the Pacific – and all his manias
Look'd at each other with a wild surtax –
Silent, upon a pebble in Darien.

Die Maschine concludes with a *Zitatenexplosion*, an "explosion of quotations" dredged up from the computer's multilingual memory, all related in one way or another to Goethe's theme: silence, sleep, and mortality. Stereophonic sound keeps the languages just sufficiently apart to permit overlaid translation between German, French, English, Spanish, and Japanese. The quotations, from a huge variety of sources, some no doubt suggested by Helmle and others by Harig and perhaps Roubaud, rise and fall in waves of declamation and whispering. Heine's "I know not who is speaking, nor do I know who would dare to make an end to the endless poem" seems to herald an ending. But after an instant of total silence comes a lyric by Narahisa:

tsui ni yuku	that is a road
michi to wa kanete	which some day we all travel
kikishikada	I had heard before
kino kyô to wa	yet I never expected
omawazarishi	to take it so soon myself

After which, there is hissing of words in many tongues, all meaning "peace", "silence", or "rest", maintained *for long enough that it begins to be mildly intolerable* . . . Then there is a sharp "psst!", and silence. End of *Die Maschine,* ein Hörspiel von Georges Perec. Deutsch von Eugen Helmle.

Practice makes perfect. *Die Maschine* was not Perec's first go at writing in collaboration (PALF had come a year before), nor his first use of other tongues in his writing (the epigraph of *Things* is in English), nor even quite his first attempt at a radio play (that was *Le Diable dans la bibliothèque*). All those parts of his curriculum vitae found their place in the creation of this literary equivalent of a *Meisterstück*, the demonstration-piece that apprentices must bake in order to be admitted as masters of their craft. *Die Maschine* was presented to OuLiPo, and Jean Lescure promised to talk to some people in French radio about it. Perec considered recasting the whole thing around a poem by Mallarmé, for a French audience, but in the end nothing came of it. Nevertheless, the German original established that Georges Perec was a virtuoso of potential literature: whilst still the OuLiPo's youngest and most recent recruit, he had pulled off its greatest coup to date. *Die Maschine* would soon bring rigorous formal wordplay to a mass audience, and would make it laugh.

Perec's language machine has another, two-sided significance beyond its technical cleverness. It is an assault on consecrated poetry, a derision of a literary fetish, and in that respect it was in tune with the counterculture that was seething under the lid of "bourgeois" society in 1967 and would bubble over the following May. But *Die Maschine* is also an extraordinary act of love. The sheer persistence with which the object – the poem – is taken to pieces, reassembled, and turned on its head and inside out undoes the overt aggression against poetry; the orchestration of world verse in the fourth section is itself a poetic construction, and in the end, *Die Maschine* comes near to finding poetry's "soul" in the intimation of mortality. Perec's radio play thus marks something arguably more important, in the long run, than his mastery of Oulipian tools. It was the first time since his teens that he had deigned or dared to confront poetry, and it was the first time that the theme of mortality – as opposed to the fear of ageing – was allowed to enter his work. It is therefore necessary to consider *Die Maschine* the first work of Perec's maturity. Is it only a contingent fact that it can never be included in Perec's complete works in French?

Heinz Hostnig, the senior director of SR's drama department, thought *Die Maschine* too experimental to broadcast, and the typescript lay on the desk of his deputy, Kamps, for weeks and months. It was noticed, then borrowed, and then read and promoted by Wolfgang Schenck, a producer whose main job was in educational radio. Eventually Schenck was allowed to produce it, with WDR in Cologne taking a half share in the costs. *Die Maschine* was recorded in the stereophonic studios in Saarbrücken in the second week of May 1968 and finally broadcast on 13 November following. Perec and Paulette travelled to Germany for the occasion, which turned out to be a triumph. *Die Maschine* was reviewed enthusiastically in the local and national press, and the play went into the regular repertory of all

German-language stations. It was judged almost immediately to be one of the most complete and accessible examples of the "new radio drama" that was then establishing itself as the main mass-public form of artistic experimentation in Germany. *Die Maschine* became, and will no doubt remain, an obligatory reference in all accounts of the history of acoustic art in Europe. It is the funniest by far of the foundation texts of *das neue Hörspiel*, and it was written in German by a Frenchman with a Polish and Hebrew name.

Many of Perec's French friends were led to believe (quite possibly by the writer himself) that *Die Maschine* had been done just for the money, and money certainly comes into the story of *Die Maschine* right at the start, as we have seen. But it was not just any money, the kind of money that, as the French say, "has no odour": deutschmarks must have seemed different when they were banked by a Frenchman of Jewish extraction whose father had died after defending the Marne and whose mother had been murdered at Auschwitz. He was being paid for making thousands of Germans split their sides. It would not be quite right to see Perec's radio play merely as a means of revenge, nor would it be right to put *Die Maschine* down simply to the Franco-German reconciliation symbolised by de Gaulle's state visit to Bonn and Stuttgart in 1962. All the same, Perec had made an assault on German culture, had succeeded, and had asserted his existence as a writer in a way that engaged his whole identity. The cheque from SR must have meant much more than just money to him.

One night, on a later trip to Neuweiler, Georges clambered up the stepladder to Eugen's guestroom in the loft and asked himself why and how he had got involved in German radio. He jotted down a few thoughts and left the unfinished scrap folded up in a French first edition of *Things* on the shelf. These are Perec's only known words of reflection on German radio drama:

> *The art of* Hörspiel *is virtually unknown in France. I discovered it at a point when a need for new techniques, new forms of writing was uppermost in my mind. I saw very soon that* Hörspiel *could provide solutions to some of my preoccupations with form, answers to my questions about the value, the powers and the functions of writing; that it offered solutions that I had not managed to find, at that time, in the context of experiments in fiction. The intrinsic space of radio drama – its special features of voice alternation, timing,*

the logical development of an elementary premise, the making-real of that fragile, vital relationship between language and speech – thus became a primordial axis of my work as a writer.

Based on letters from Georges Perec to Eugen Helmle, 15 March [1967], 17 May 1967, and to Eugen Helmle, Johann-Maria [Kamps], and Ludwig [Harig], 15 October [1967] and on the unpublished drafts of *Die Maschine* in the possession of Eugen Helmle.

On the history of German radio drama, see:

Helmut Geißner, "Versuch einer Poetologie der Permutation" (mit Textbeispielen von Ludwig Harig). Discussed by Klippert, p. 68. Written in August 1966, first broadcast by SR under the title of "Wenn der Hund mit der Wurst übern Spucknap springt – was ist eine Permutation?", 8 June 1967.

Bianca Marinoni, "L'Originale radiofonico in Germania", *Rivista di letterature moderne e comparate* 19 (1966).

Uwe Rosenbaum, *Das Hörspiel. Eine Bibliographie.* (Hamburg: Hans-Bredow-Institut, 1974), lists foreign writers who worked for German radio.

Klaus Schöning, *Neues Hörspiel. Essays, Analysen, Gespräche* (Frankfurt-am-Main: Suhrkamp Verlag, 1970).

Stefan Bodo Würffel, *Das Deutsche Hörspiel* (Stuttgart: Metzler, 1978).

Key examples of *das neue Hörspiel* around the time of *Die Maschine* include:

Ernst Jandl and Friederike Mayrocker, *Fünf Mann Menschen.* Winner of the 1968 War Blind Prize. Available as a cassette from Klett-Cotta Verlag, Stuttgart.

Wolf Wondratschek, *Paul oder die Zerstörung eines Hörbeispiels.* Winner of the 1969 War Blind Prize. Available as a cassette from Klett-Cotta Verlag, Stuttgart.

Wolf Wondratschek et al., *Maschine Nummer Neun* (1973).

J. J. White, "Goethe in the Machine: Georges Perec's Computer-Based Exercises with the Repertoire of 'Über allen Gipfeln'", *Publications of the English Goethe Society*, n.s.41 (1971), 103–130, is not only the first academic article in any language about *Die Maschine* (and the first in English about Perec), but a stimulating introduction to experimental thinking about literature at that time.

Radio Perec: German Checklist

Radio Dramas (Hörspiele)

Die Maschine, transl. and adapt. Eugen Helmle.

Broadcast by SR on 13 November 1968, 1 January 1969, 29 June 1975, 16 May 1982, etc.; by WDR on 5 December 1968, 25 June 1979, 29 August 1982, etc.

Translated into Serbo-Croation by Dubravko Ivacan and broadcast as *Stroj* by Radio Zagreb IIIrd Programme on 5 March 1972.

Translated into Italian by Bruno G. Chiaranti and recited at the Teatro Franco Parenti, Milan, May 1991.

German text published with an essay on radio drama by Werner Klippert (Stuttgart: Reclam's Universal-Bibliothek no. 9352, 1972).

Wucherungen (L'Augmentation), transl. Eugen Helmle.

Broadcast by SR on 12 November 1969, 9 September 1970, 16 October 1983, etc.; by WDR on 27 January 1970, 18 June 1981.

Tagstimmen (by Perec, Philippe Drogoz and Eugen Helmle)

Broadcast by SR on 28 April 1971, 29 March 1972, 9 April 1978, and 28 August 1986.

Record (not for sale) produced by SR in 1971.

Text published in *Die Funkpostille: Ein Querschnitt durch das Programm des Saarländischen Rundfunks im Sendejahr 1971* (Saarbrücken: SR, 1971).

French and German résumés in Georges Perec, *Tagstimmen/Voix de jour* (ARD – Prix Italia, 1971).

Der Mechanismus des Nervensystems im Kopf ("Fonctionnement du système nerveux dans la tête"), transl. Eugen Helmle.

Broadcast by WDR on 15 June 1972.

Konzertstück für Sprecher und Orchester (by Perec, Philippe Drogoz and Eugen Helmle).

Broadcast by SR on 18 July 1974.

Der Kartoffelkessel (La Poche Parmentier), transl. Eugen Helmle.

Broadcast by SR, Südwestfunk, and Süddeutscher Rundfunk on 15 October 1987.

Der Teufel in der Bibliothek ("Le Diable dans la Bibliothèque"), transl. Eugen Helmle.

Broadcast by Norddeutscher Rundfunk in October 1991.

Readings

Was für ein kleines Moped mit verchromter Lenkstange steht dort im Hof?
(*Quel Petit Vélo . . .*), transl. Eugen Helmle.
Read by Nestor Xaidis. Broadcast by SR on 15 June 1967.

Der Mann, der schläft (*A Man Asleep*), transl. Eugen Helmle.
Read by Heiner Schmidt and Gretl Palm. Broadcast by SR on 12 September 1968.

Begegnung in Saarbrücken.
Extracts read by Perec (in French) and Helmle (in German). Broadcast by SR on 26 June 1969.

Der Tod Helmles (extract from *La Boutique obscure*), transl. Eugen Helmle.
Broadcast by SR on 5 January 1975.

Autoren im Dialog.
Discussion and reading in French and German of *W or The Memory of Childhood*. Broadcast by SR on 12 December 1975.

Interview

Die Lösung des Rätsels. Interviews zu Thesen der Pataphysik.
Broadcast by SR on 2 November 1967.

CHAPTER 39

Writer's Block

1967–1968

Duchâteau is alleged to have repeated a remark by Niels Bohr as quoted by Theo Kahane. In response to a paper by Pauli on elementary particles, Bohr is said to have said: "We are all in agreement on the fact that your theory is mad. The question we have not settled amongst us is whether it is sufficiently mad to stand a chance of being proved correct".

Jacques Bens, *Oulipo 1960–1963*

On 13 November 1967, a shortish, broad-shouldered man with a mop of curly hair boarded the Frankfurt-Paris express at Saarbrücken, made for the dining car, took off his parka, put down his handbag, and extracted from it his packet of Gitanes, his lighter, his jotter, and a felt-tip pen. Once past the border, he would begin to count the kilometre posts, measuring the train's progress as Henri had taught him to do on his first train journey to Paris, twenty-two years before. Perhaps Perec also used the five hours of suspended time to reflect on his position. He had just spent four days in a state of verbal elation with his German colleagues, tearing Goethe to pieces. They were good people to work with, but he had been unnecessarily cruel to them, saying, straight-faced, that he knew no German beyond the three words for "beer", "cosiness", and "concentration camp". Perhaps that was what had left him feeling low, like a dog – three other words of German he could have offered with equal meaning. They come from the end of *The Trial,* when Joseph K. is stabbed in the heart. His last words are "Like a dog". Kafka explains, "as if the shame would live on after him". Not exactly survivor guilt: what survives is guilt itself.

Kafka's ending gave Perec the first idea for a new German work. His uncle David looked quite like Franz Kafka at times; he liked to think that he did too, in the portrait that Srbinović had done of him, and which now hung in Esther's bedroom at Blévy. On the train, perhaps on that return from Germany or perhaps on a later trip along the same track, Perec put down in the black jotter the title and his first thoughts for a radio play to be called *Wie ein Hund* ("Like a Dog").

Kafka's presence in *A Man Asleep* had not gone unnoticed by the more serious reviewers of the book, which had appeared the previous April but was allegedly out of print by the end of June. It had not been put up for a prize, it had not been taken on by Stahlberg Verlag, it had been bought for translation only by the Hungarians and the Dutch, and no one had even thought of film rights. The reception of *A Man Asleep* overlapped with Perec's first introduction to OuLiPo, with his trips to Saarbrücken, to Warwick, to the American Midwest, to Venice, and then to Saarbrücken again, with his work on *L'Arbre* and with the invention of the first "Machine" project. He would hardly have had time to cope with a public success on the scale of *Things* – and he did not have to. *L'Aurore* and *La Croix*, conservative papers in all respects, panned the book, while *Combat*, the left-wing daily founded by Camus, misunderstood it entirely, taking it for a revision of *The Outsider*, a book that Perec had no wish whatsoever to plunder: he had decided when he was still a *para* in Pau that he would pay no further attention to Camus. *Arts-Loisirs* gave Perec a full-page review, but that was hardly significant since he had only just ceased being a columnist on that paper. On the plus side, Roger Kleman published a good essay in *Les Lettres nouvelles*, and in *Le Nouvel Observateur* Roger Grenier wrote with enthusiasm about the book and let out in public what Perec had told him in private at Hammamet – that he was the great-great-nephew of the author of "Bontsha the Silent", Isaak Leib Peretz. In fact, Perec had just recently come across a fine hand-printed edition of Peretz's *The Golem* in a German bookstore and had made a present of it to Helmle. Somehow it was easier to pull the Jewish-Polish-orphan string in Germany. A sympathetic reaction was guaranteed, which made it seem less crushing.

A Man Asleep also provoked two sensitive and favourable essays in quarters where Perec had no particular reason to expect them. Writing in *L'Express*, Etienne Lalou likened Perec's book to Kafka's *The Metamorphosis* and grappled very well with the meaning of the second-person form of address, and in *La Quinzaine littéraire*, the novelist Bernard Pingaud devoted two full pages to Perec, comparing

his work to Rilke's *The Notebooks of Malte Laurids Brigge* and concluding that *A Man Asleep* was "the story of a disturbance – but above
all, a language that disturbs, and in which we should recognise the
hand of a real writer". That judgment must have pleased Perec rather
more than many of the encomiums he had received for the sociological acuity and critical correctness of *Things*.

He was a real writer, he did not doubt that; he was more given to
doubting whether he was anything *else* in reality. But what was he
writing now, as 1967 drew to a close? He had managed to publish a
book a year since his breakthrough, but his annual rhythm was about
to collapse. No typescript lay on his desk at Rue du Bac for Nadeau
to make into the new Perec book of 1968. *L'Arbre* was an idea, a plan
of work, a set of notes, fragments entered neatly into a ledger; it was
not yet a book, nor was it likely to be one for some time. Perec had
not got very far with *L'Age*, and was not inclined to take introspection
any further just now. *Die Maschine* was done, very nearly, but it
would not be a book, not even if Lescure could persuade French radio
to commission an adaptation. The prospects were not so brilliant. If
he allowed himself to fall too far out of the limelight for too long,
he would have a mighty struggle to get published again. Denoël was
not committed to publishing him; the obligation was the other way
round. Perec could not offer his work to any other publisher until
Denoël had either taken or turned down five novels of his beyond
Things. At the end of 1967, three books short of the five, the contract
had become academic. He had nothing to offer. *A Man Asleep* was
not reprinted.

In his own terms, Perec had hit writer's block. It was the first time
in ten years that he had not got a project time-tabled over the months
ahead, and he must have wondered, at low moments, if he had not
already written himself out. Such problems his friends would have
been glad to have! Jacques Roubaud had waited two years for the
publication of his book of poetry, entitled $\in$ ("element of": the sign
that links an element to its set in mathematics, a sign called "the sign
of belonging" in French). Pierre Getzler was still waiting for a gallery
to hang any of his canvases. Roger Kleman had not yet penned a
satisfactory page of the great book that all his friends were convinced
he had in him. What could Perec do to help the others with the greater
blocks on their work? He had already done his best for Kleman by
introducing him to the Moulin d'Andé, where he could get away
from his business worries and have some peace in which to write.

Getzler didn't need a place to work, since he had a studio in Rue de l'Ermitage, very near to Rue Vilin. What he did need was access to the art-collecting public, an access denied him by the tradesmen and "terrorists" who controlled fashion. Well, they would not control the creators, Perec and his friends said to themselves; if no one else would exhibit the works of the gentle Pierre, then Perec would, himself. He lived at the right sort of address.

In December 1967 the Perecs converted their flat in Rue du Bac into a temporary art gallery. For a week, twenty paintings and twenty pen-and-ink drawings by the unknown Getzler hung on their walls, where a trickle of friends and acquaintances came to view them. There was a cyclostyled brochure containing a list of the works on show. Not all were for sale: number 3, oil on chipboard, was the property of Mme & Mr Perec; number 14, the property of Mme Getzler; number 19, the property of Mme & Mr Kleman; number 20, the property of Mme & Mr Mangolte, and so on. The catalogue proper was preceded by presentation texts: five poems by Jacques Roubaud, essays by Alain Guérin and Roger Kleman, and a general introduction by the promoter, host, and moving spirit of the Getzler gallery project, georges perec, a text typed without capital letters, e.e. cummings-style, and entitled *chemin de pierre* ("Pierre's Way", but also "Stony Path").

The exhibition was both an act of love (for Pierre) and an act of anger (with the art establishment), and in those senses – the best senses – it was entirely amateur. Its aim was nonetheless perfectly serious: to promote an artist and a friend, against the grain. At least one distinguished art collector came to view the assembled works. Georges was honoured, and more than a little flustered, to be Raymond Queneau's host: what a coup it would have been if Queneau had bought a Getzler from the walls of his flat!

■

Not many might have diagnosed themselves as having writer's block had they found themselves in Perec's position in December 1967. Despite having to do his forty hours in the lab every week, he had had a quite remarkable year in his writing career. PALF had earned him a place in OuLiPo, to which he had taken as a duck to water. *Things* had earned him trips to Warwick and the States and, indirectly, a commission from German radio, which he had fulfilled with brilliance. But Perec had fixed his own hurdle at a punishing height. In

**ALAIN GUERIN   ROGER KLEMAN
GEORGES PEREC   JACQUES
ROUBAUD   SUR DES DESSINS
ET DES PEINTURES DE PIERRE
GETZLER   PARIS   DECEMBRE
MIL NEUF CENT SOIXANTE SEPT**

1959 he had confided to his putative publisher, François Wahl: *I have read* Moby Dick. *It is not worth writing unless one is aiming for a work of that calibre.* In 1965, he had written to himself:

> *My literary ambition goes so far as to make me imagine that one day I will write a* Magic Mountain, *a* Joseph Andrews, *or a* Remembrance of Things Past.

There is no reason to suppose that Georges Perec had mellowed into a more reasonable man by 1967. By his own yardstick, he measured himself as a pygmy still. He did not suffer from delusions of grandeur; quite the opposite. He was not a Goethe, a Melville, or a Kafka, at least not yet. Could OuLiPo teach him how to become a Perec?

No minutes have been found for the meetings of the group in 1967, so it is uncertain what contributions Perec made at the start of his apprenticeship. It is more than likely that he made very few, since he had no mathematical knowledge to speak of and no great expertise in literary history. His task, probably, was to listen, and to learn, and to try to write with the tools proposed by the more senior and learned members. He most assuredly heard Claude Berge's 1967 report to OuLiPo on a discovery made by three mathematicians working in the United States, Bose, Parker and Shrikhande, who had disproved the supposition of Euler, in the eighteenth century, that there could be no bi-square of order 10.[1] Berge suggested that this new configuration could serve as the generating device for a work of fiction. Perec needed to have the whole thing explained to him simply, and he was fortunate to have in Claude Berge a world-class mathematician who was both able and willing to give tutorials in less than mathematical language. Consider the following square:

A0	B1	C2	D3	E4
E1	A2	B3	C4	D0
D2	E3	A4	B0	C1
C3	D4	E0	A1	B2
B4	C0	D1	E2	A3

[1] The following passage is adapted from page 83 of Claude Berge and Eric Beaumatin, "Georges Perec et la combinatoire", *Cahiers Georges Perec IV*, pp. 83–96.

It is a square of five (or of order 5), each of whose twenty-five locations is occupied by a pair of elements – hence the term *bi-square*. It is also a "magic square", so called because no number-letter combination occurs more than once in the square as a whole, and each of the numbers and each of the letters occurs once, and once only, along each row of the square and down each of its columns. The bi-square distributes all of the possible combinations of the 2 x 5 elements used. The shape itself has long been associated with melancholy: the first known representation of a magic square is Albrecht Dürer's engraving *Melencolia II*.

If you imagine that each of the letters in the bi-square stands for a character, and each of the numbers for a property, or an action, or a place, then you can have twenty-five different stories made from a very simple set of ingredients. A bi-square of order 5, however, was obviously less exciting as the basis of a work of fiction than the newly discovered bi-square of 10, which would yield a hundred chapters (the square of 10), ample scope both for masking the underlying constraint and for giving rein to the wildest imagination. Georges Perec lodged Berge's demonstration in his mind, but as he was convinced that he had no imagination, he did not think he could fill out a hundred preset permutations of just 2 x 10 elements. He was more attracted to a simpler procedure that he had found mentioned several times in the cyclostyled minutes of the early meetings of OuLiPo: the lipogram.

The word lipogram comes from the Greek stem *lipo-* (or *leipo-*), meaning "to miss", and the device itself is simple enough: the idea is to write a text with one (or more) of the letters of the alphabet missing. Queneau had brought it to the attention of the group (on 13 March 1961) after coming across it in Gaston Brunet's *Poétique curieuse*, an ancient compilation of literary and linguistic oddities. It was a fully Oulipian device in advance, since its definition was absolutely rigorous, unlike the equally arbitrary but far woollier rules of the sonnet or of the three unities of classical tragedy. One cannot cheat with a lipogram: it either is or is not. In working their way through various sourcebooks for historically attested formal rules, Oulipians frequently found that their ideas had been foreshadowed by writers of past ages, and for such happy encounters they coined the term "anticipatory plagiarism". The lipogram went one better than these, however, because the first part of its name anticipated the latter part of OuLiPo's, making it as worthy of interest as the Chinese poet Li Po, who had pulled off the same trick. It was Claude Berge, again, who had remarked (on 22 February 1963) that the Oulipian interest of a lipogram was in proportion to the natural frequency of the letter(s) missed out. In French or in English, for example, a lipogram on *x* is so easy as to lack any literary potential at all. The greater the frequency of the letter omitted, the greater the potentiality of the constraint. In Spanish, the hardest and therefore the most potentially creative lipogram would be on *a*, in German probably on *r*, in English and in French, on *e*. Could anyone write a novel without the letter *e* in it? Queneau pointed out that an obscure Californian publisher, Ernest Vincent Wright, had already succeeded in doing so.[1] Perec must have read into that exchange the unspoken suggestion that the lipogram on *e* still awaited its French (and Oulipian) explorer.

It probably began as a game, alongside the other games that Perec played in 1967: bridge, poker (not often), and go. To begin with, at least, Perec hid the literary purpose of making his friends speak without using the letter *e* beneath the hilarity that their successes and failures provoked. Marie-Noëlle Thibault recalls a mad evening in a restaurant with Georges, Paulette, and Marcel Benabou, where the rule was set that they should utter nothing that would be written with an *e*. It limited the choice of dishes on the menu somewhat! If the game had been pursued to the logical extreme, considerable arithmetical skill would have been required to count the change from the bill (the numbers 2, 4, 7, 9, 11, 12, 13, 14, 15, 16, 17, 19, 21, 22, 24, 27, 29, 30 and so on being ruled out in French). Perec also played the game at parties at Rue du Bac. Michel Martens remembers his darting from one side of the room to the other to inform a chatting couple that they had done it, they had just uttered a whole sentence without an *e*! It was a kind of social joke, Georges's little obsession, a way of diverting attention and diverting himself. But by December 1967, if not earlier, the idea of meeting Queneau's implicit challenge had grown into a determination on Perec's part to overcome his writer's block. The idea was insane – sufficiently insane to stand a chance.

The lipogram was not a rewriting project like PALF or S+7, nor was it an affectionate assault on literature, like *Die Maschine*. At

---

[1] Ernest Vincent Wright, *Gadsby. A Story of Over 50,000 Words Without Using the Letter E* (Los Angeles: Wetzel Publishing Co., 1939). Copy in NYPL Rare Books Collection.

bottom the plan to write without the letter *e* was an attack on language itself. In Venice, a few weeks earlier, Perec had suddenly recalled the symbol-letter of his childhood fantasy, W. Turn a W on its side, and you get a kind of E. Round off the points and you're left with ∈, the name of Roubaud's book of poems structured like a game of go. The letter itself was completely neutral yet at the same time full of potential meanings. Then there was an old story that Perec may have only half-remembered from Paul Wegener's celebrated silent movie, a variant of the Golem that he may have heard either as a child, from his grandfather David, or more recently, from one or another of the aunts whom he had interviewed about his Polish and Jewish past. (Or he may just have read it somewhere, for it is really not terribly obscure.)[1] In this version, the clay statue that defends the Jews of Prague against the Gentiles has three Hebrew characters marked on its forehead (or written on a slip inserted into its chest) – אמת aleph, mem, tav (reading from right to left), spelling the word *emeth* ("truth"). But the secret word that when whispered in the ear of the dangerous monster will make it come alive, or calm down, has been lost. The final recourse against the random power of the Golem is to rub out the first letter on its forehead, leaving just מת mem and tav. The statue crumbles to dust, for mem and tav together spell *meth*, meaning "dead".

The letter rubbed out in the story is not a true vowel, since Hebrew does not mark vowels in its script, only the soft and harsh breathing sounds. Nonetheless, the syllable that the aleph denotes at the head of the word for "truth" has a vowel value, which value is represented in English and French by the letter *e*. It is not clear that Perec grasped it clearly in advance, but a lipogram on *e* would be an exploration of the world in which the Golem has turned to dust. Such a project proved irresistible to him. It displaced the historical and autobiographical interest of *L'Arbre*; it displaced the introspection of the abandoned book about being thirty; it displaced the literary potential of the recently remembered W. The lipogram became an obsession and an absolutely necessary book. Perec now faced difficulties that no serious writer before him had ever imposed on himself; but at

---

[1] He refers to the story ten years later, in *Récits d'Ellis Island* (page 35), as if it were common knowledge. See also Marcel Benabou, "Perec's Jewishness", *Review of Contemporary Fiction* XIII.1 (1993), pp. 78–87.

least he would no longer have to confront that banal and boring problem called writer's block.

Alain Guérin, Roger Kleman, Georges Perec, Jacques Roubaud, *Sur des dessins et des peintures de Pierre Getzler, Paris décembre mil neuf cent soixante sept.* Exhibition catalogue (typescript with dry-print cover); letter from Georges Perec to Eugen Helmle, 29 June 1967.

The reception of *A Man Asleep* in 1967: *Le Canard enchaîné*, 16 April; *Les Echos*, 28 April; Bernard Pingaud, "L'Indifférence, passion méconnue", *La Quinzaine littéraire* no. 27 (1 May); Mathieu Galey, "La Révolte en chambre", *Arts-Loisirs* no. 84 (3 May); Etienne Lalou, "Un déserteur de l'histoire", *L'Express* no. 829 (8 May); *L'Aurore*, 23 May; *Combat*, 27 May; Roger Grenier, "Le Club des Silencieux", *Le Nouvel Observateur* no. 133 (31 May); *La Croix*, 15 June; *Les Lettres nouvelles*, July–September 1967, pp. 159–166. The novel was also widely reviewed in the Swiss, Belgian and German press.

Jacques Bens, *Oulipo. 1980–1983* (Paris: Christian Bourgois, 1980), pp. 40, 198. Ernest Vincent Wright's *Gadsby* is referred to on p. 159.

Many years later, when given a copy of Gustav Meyrink's *The Golem* by Catherine Binet, Perec gave a shout of delight on finding the "emeth/meth" myth, as if he had never known it before. "But that's just what I did in *La Disparition!*" he exclaimed.

CHAPTER 40

L'Imagination au Pouvoir!

1968

Like *L'Arbre*, the lipogram-novel was, at the start, a programme of research, which Perec organised as any sensible research worker would. The problems created by the avoidance of the letter *e* may have seemed insoluble at first, but patience, organisation, and team support would eventually crack them. Perec's method – again, the method of any scientific research worker – was to assemble the material for the experiment before jumping to premature conclusions. In this instance the material consisted solely of words. Words without *e* could be found in dictionaries, of course, and Perec no doubt combed the *Littré* and the *Larousse* for them. But there were other ways also of assembling an *e*-less lexicon: in bars, on trains, on restaurant menus, for example, or even in the street considerable numbers of naturally *e*-less words and expressions can be noted (nowadays there is McDonalds, Pizza Hut, FNAC . . .). Perec was never without a jotter, and it was but a minor task for him to transcribe the day's catch into files labelled for different narrative situations (in a bar, on a train, in the street, and so on) in which specific items could be used. Patience: when the lexicon was sufficiently large, then and only then could he conduct the full experiment by learning to speak, think, and write inside a new language which is all the more constraining for consisting only of words that were also part of normal French.

> *I decided to write so many lines per hour and so many hours per day, and I did it without any plan, without a story. The narrative simply came, it just arose. I was in a state of jubilation from the start.*

The point of the experiment was not to translate into twenty-five-letter French a story that already existed, or could exist, in an alphabet of twenty-six letters. That would be to treat the constraint as a parlour game. Although it is true that in the lipogram-novel Perec explores some familiar themes – it begins, in a way, as a rewriting of *A Man Asleep*, and includes amazing translations of well-known poems – Perec's chief experimental aim was to see if *e*-less French could invent its own story and thus vindicate the potentiality not only of that constraint but of the very principle of constraint. Ernest Vincent Wright's *Gadsby* shows that such an experiment can produce a work of no literary interest whatsoever. Perec was taking a risk: if he ended up with nothing more than a *Gadsby*, what would he have done to OuLiPo?

It was safer to let non-Oulipians believe that he was engaged in a kind of literary jest, a madcap exploit halfway between the impossible and the insane. The title he chose for the novel was a self-referential joke: *La Disparition* ("The Disappearance") pushes the reader's nose into the book's design, the *disappearance* of the commonest letter of the alphabet. Perec proceeded with the project as an experiment in conviviality. *La Disparition* was not exactly composed in public, but its composition was a communal activity at the Moulin d'Andé. Perec reported to the others on his progress, read them passages, and kept them in stitches. And more than that, he got them to play lipogram with him.

For much of 1968 no one came to stay at the Moulin d'Andé without being tackled by a grinning imp of a man intent on extracting at least a sentence or two without an *e*. Perec had never really allowed himself to develop his talents as a seducer or manipulator of others, but now he learnt how to make himself irresistible in the service of words. He may have wheedled, and needled, and cast down challenges, but most of all he played the clown and drew people into his obsession by appealing to their sense of fun. Dinners beneath the elm-tree bower fell under his spell. He was the court jester, and also the king. The project progressed; it seemed that a novel really was emerging from the lunatic in the *chambre Jeanne d'Arc*. There was intoxication, even euphoria in the riverside air.

> I was in a state of jubilation from the start. I felt I was a bricklayer, like someone who puts down a brick, then cement, then a brick, and step by step makes a house.

La Disparition is the only one of Perec's major works that was written in that way. In one sense the experiment in sharing was a logical extension of the happy collaboration Perec had just had with Eugen Helmle, on *Die Maschine*; in another sense, the sharing was a safety valve for an obsession that, if pursued in solitude, might have been dangerous for anyone's grip on reality. Finally, there was also a purely practical side to Perec's method. *E*-less French is an "unnatural" language, and the technical challenge was to make it read like a natural one. What is a natural language, then? Saussure maintained that a language was a system of signs shared by a community of speakers, shaped by all and by none. To achieve at least a degree of simulated naturalness in *e*-less French, Perec needed other speaker-hearer-writers. The hidden linguistic agenda was covered by the social clowning, but as on many other occasions in Perec's life and works, one cover covered another. In the case of *La Disparition,* the double cover hid something that none of the author's closest friends could have guessed at, unless they, too, were orphans of the *shoah.* The novel's title is a slightly arch euphemism for death, but it is also something much more special: it is the term used in administrative French for persons missing and presumed dead. In his drawer at Rue du Bac, Perec still had the certificate issued in 1947 by the Ministry of War Veterans in re Perec Cyrla née Szulewicz, last seen alive at Drancy on 11 February 1943, a document headed ACTE DE DISPARITION.

E

In May 1968, when Perec was midway through *La Disparition,* the Latin Quarter exploded. Clumsy handling of student demonstrations by the police and the CRS led to barricades and pitched battles, a brief revolt that for a moment seemed set to become a revolution. The general strike that ensued stranded Perec at the Moulin d'Andé. Everyone there was on the side of the students. The cause of the young was untrammelled by established interests or ideologies; students painted the walls of the Latin Quarter with poetic, surrealist slogans, calling society "a carnivorous flower", and demanding that imagination be put in power. The whole of society must be overturned! Down with work! If you take up the cobbles, you'll find the beach underneath! Long-pent-up frustrations burst forth in the near anarchy of the second fortnight of May. The Sorbonne was occupied and became a nonstop Situationist teach-in. The black flag flew from the Odéon, where Duvignaud (amongst many others) harangued the masses from the stage. Factories were taken over by workers, and everyone talked about new forms of life that would be nonhierarchical, convivial, and free. A delegation from the Moulin drove down to Paris to join in the demos and the occupations. Perec almost certainly did not go along, though he did join a more modest delegation to Louviers, where he chatted with his companions about the historic role of the town under the Popular Front government of 1936. He kept his views on the current political scene to himself, just as, in *Life A User's Manual,* he allows only a single, glancing reference to the *great wave of intoxication and joy* of May '68 [*L* 269] which affected the lives of many of his friends profoundly.

The "events" of May 1968 came to a rapid and depressingly familiar end. Conservative forces rallied around the government; the Communist-dominated trade unions accepted a modest "new deal" on wages and conditions; workers returned to their jobs; things got back to normal. The revolt did not turn into a revolution; seen in retrospect, it was not even a real uprising. By July, students and workers alike were leaving for their usual holidays by the sea, and the worst injuries most of them suffered that summer were second-degree burns from sunbathing too long on the sand. In August Soviet tanks put down the Czechs who had tried to launch "socialism with a human face". Order reigned.

Georges Perec missed May '68, just as Balzac missed the revolution of July 1830, by being away in the country during the days of rioting and passion, when France might have changed track. Was he frightened of the upheaval? Some believe that he was too fragile within himself not to be apprehensive about such unrest, that the set of props he had constructed for himself would not have stood up to social changes. But in another sense, Perec was writing 1968 as it happened: *La Disparition* is the work that allowed his own imagination to come to power, the imagination he thought he did not have, an imagination full of the sombre violence of the students' demands for an end to work, to restrictions, to law, order, and the whole stultified mess called society. *La Disparition* is not exactly a political thriller, but like the dreams of May '68, it is a contestation of (literal) order, and a horrifying vision of what can happen when the sign of a soft breathing sound is lost.

La Disparition is about a man who disappears. His friends look for him, but one by one they disappear, too. It is a multiple whodunnit in which everything leads to disappearance, the only possible outcome when a letter has been purloined: in a world destabilised by the removal of a mere nothing, a letter shape, an empty symbol, death ensues. But the symbol is not entirely empty. Its name, pronounced *eu,* has the same sound as *eux*, "them". What has disappeared, then, from *La Disparition? E* has. "They" have – those who have the Golem to protect them no longer.

The cruelty of the content of *La Disparition* is perhaps proportionate to the mental mutilation involved in writing without *e*. That Perec managed to make it seem like a game at Andé is not the least of his achievements in the whole affair. He got the feminist-separatist Monique Wittig to provide him with one rather good paragraph [*D* 64]; Raymond Queneau came up with a passage that is a lipogram not just on *e*, but on *a* and *o* too [*D* 296]. Alain Guérin provided a mock-cryptic security report, which he dashed off not at Andé but at the Bibliothèque Nationale, on a day when Perec, dropping in to see Paulette at work, caught him there [*D* 77–78], and Maurice Pons wrote a lipogrammatic résumé of his recent novel, *Rosa* [*D* 291–294]. Fragments by many other hands are likewise integrated into *La Disparition,* including an anonymous account of the events of May in Paris [*D* 64–65], and a piece in German provided by Helmle [*D* 65–66] (which, as Perec gleefully pointed out, *had an* e *in it* in the original version).[1] Perec himself had found it hard to keep *es* from slipping into the first draft – the manuscript has four or five of them ringed, on second reading, in red, with exclamation marks in the margin. Long after the novel was finished, he had half-humorous nightmares about *es* spreading like a virus all over the text [*BO* 95], and even today the rumour persists among Perecquians that there is a solitary *e* somewhere in the published version of *La Disparition.*

The novel was completed by the end of the summer at Andé, and Perec was on top of the world. Although he was no longer living very much with Paulette, he had overcome the sticky patch of the previous winter, and, thanks to the constraint of the lipogram, he had discovered that he could invent stories as convoluted as those of the books he had loved since his childhood at Villard-de-Lans and Rue de l'Assomption – books by Dumas, Jules Verne, Jack London, Curwood. He had learnt that he was not without an imagination; it just needed to be constrained in order to be set free. That seeming paradox was in fact the fundamental hypothesis on which OuLiPo's

[1] Also part of the text are passages by Catherine David, on page 61, and Jean Pouillon, on pages 63–64; a poem by Lady Murasaki Shikibu from *Die Maschine*, page 114; a retranslation of Narahisa from *Die Maschine*, page 115; and even a paragraph from Ernest Vincent Wright, in English, on page 63.

work was based. All the same, it did not fit well with the libertarian language of May '68. Perec could only be on the sidelines of topical debates, which moved more slowly than his leapfrogging mind. That is not to suggest that he was absent from his times; on the contrary, Perec had his own singular path to follow through them, encompassing several different tracks at once.

The quotations are taken from a transcription of an interview of Georges Perec by Bernard Noël (broadcast by France-Culture on 20 February 1977) kindly supplied by AGP. Other information from the manuscript of *La Disparition*, in the possession of Suzanne Lipinska, from a letter from Georges Perec to Eugen Helmle, and from the recollections of Marcel Cuvelier, Alain Guérin, Anne Lipinska, Maurice Pons, Marie-Noëlle Thibault, and many others.

CHAPTER 41

Happiness

1968

Nineteen sixty-eight was the year of the *événements de Paris* and also the peak of the *"années* Perec" at Andé. Now habitually dressed in loose Indian shirts, Georges Perec was the star performer of Suzanne's community, a happy joker, a man in his prime. He was Suzanne's lover, and he was in love with her, head over heels. Perec's two passionate affairs – with a twenty-five-letter alphabet and with a blond, left-wing millionairess – coincided, producing euphoria at the Moulin d'Andé. Most of the community's friends came at weekends and went back to their Paris flats, to their jobs and their marriages on Sunday afternoons. The smaller group that stayed on into the week dined largely on the leftovers from Sunday lunch, and always made French toast (*pain perdu*) from the stale bread. They would stand side by side in the narrow kitchen, and Perec would cut and pass baguettes with a regular litany of puns:

> *Pain d'perdu, pain d'retrouvé*
> *A la recherche du pain perdu*
> *Pain perdu sans collier*

La Disparition, whilst it was still in progress, required an unprecedented degree of concentration, and even Perec needed distractions from the obsessive world of words without *e*. At Andé he busied himself with paint, daubing oils and gouache onto paper and then pressing leaves or treebark into it to make pleasing patterns. Ping-pong was Perec's only physical pursuit; no one ever saw him out rowing, or playing croquet, or with a tennis racquet in his hand. He was nonetheless frequently to be found at the courts, in the umpire's high chair, calling out the score in ever sillier ways: love-fifteen, *Louis-Quinze*; love-thirty, *Louis-Seize*; warning to server: *Louis XVI had his head chopped off!* He could be just as infuriating in front of the one television set at Andé. The actress Thérèse Quentin first made contact with Perec when she rolled up a magazine and used it to whack the curly mop in front of her, to stop its owner from interrupting the programme with his idiotic schoolboy jokes.

In the evenings, after dinner, they played bridge. Suzanne could rarely give her undivided attention to the cards. There were telephone calls to deal with, problems with the boiler or with the baker's delivery van, guests to book in or cross out – all the thousand and one matters that arose in this commune that was also a sort of hotel. Perec took no part in the management of the Andé estate, and he paid for his room and board like everyone else. Like everyone else, he also took his turn at cooking and clearing away, but he was not as fast or as dextrous as some of the others. In the eyes of Alberto the Argentinian, a first-rate cook, Perec was a liability within five yards of a soft-boiled egg. Perec's role, irrespective of his relationship with Suzanne, was to entertain and to write. To some, he seemed like a circus dog playing to an audience at the Moulin d'Andé, but Suzanne's daughter Anne, then a rebellious teenager, felt somehow that even a circus dog should have more of a bark, and a bite.

The other great game of '68 was go. Roubaud taught Perec, and Perec taught others. Some (amongst them Marie-Noëlle) were bitten and played with the black and white buttons for hours on end; others (such as Maurice) found it less entrancing than bridge. Go is never a short game: Japanese masters take weeks to play a championship match.

In May 1968, in the midst of *La Disparition* and of the first great love affair of his life, Perec had a dream that he noted down, and later tidied up for publication:

> *A room, with several people. In the corner there is a wooden measuring apparatus. I know I may be forced to spend several hours under it. It's a punishment rather than a real torture, but it would be extremely uncomfortable since there is nothing holding up the measuring arm and it could well squash me smaller.*
>
> *Obviously I am dreaming and I know that I am dreaming, obviously, that I am in a concentration camp. It's not really a camp, obviously, it's a camp-image, a dream-camp, a metaphor-camp, a camp that I know to be a familiar image, as if I were dreaming the same dream over and over again, as if I had never dreamt any other dream, as if I had never done anything else but dream about this camp.*
>
> *It is clear that the threat of the measuring rod suffices at first to*

concentrate in itself all the terror of the camp. Then it turns out that it isn't so awful after all. In any case I escape from the threat, which is not implemented. But it is precisely the evasion of the threat that constitutes the clearest proof of the camp: what saves me is only the torturer's indifference, his freedom to do or not to do; I am entirely at the mercy of his whim (just as I am at the mercy of this dream: I know it is only a dream, but I cannot escape from the dream).

The second sequence takes up the same themes with only minor modifications. Two characters (one of whom is very definitely me) open a wardrobe in which there are two storage spaces for the deportees' riches. By "riches" you have to understand any object capable of increasing the owner's safety or survival prospects, whether by immediate use or by exchange. The first stowage contains woollens – huge amounts of old, dull, and moth-eaten woollens. The second, which contains money, consists of a swing-top device: one of the cupboards inside the wardrobe has been hollowed out and its front flips up like a desk lid. However, this hiding place is reckoned unsafe, and I am in the process of working its mechanism so as to withdraw the money when someone comes in. It is an officer. We understand instantly that everything is, in any case, useless. Simultaneously it becomes obvious that leaving the room is the same thing as dying.

The third sequence, if I had not forgotten it almost entirely, could have given a name to this camp: Treblinka, or Terezienburg, or Katowicze. The stage performance was perhaps "Terezienburg Requiem" (Les Temps modernes, 196, no., pp. –). The moral of this erased episode seems to refer back to older dreams: You can get away (sometimes) by playing games.   [BO 1]

Not long after he had this dream, Perec took a break from his battle with the alphabet to ponder on his future path as a writer [Jsn 52]. *Moby Dick* remained the model of what he should be doing with his "accursed biro", his *maudit bic* [D 89], and he had not lost his conviction that a writer could grasp the world only by making sense of himself first. He took up once again the work he had dropped when the lipogram seized his imagination, the work about turning thirty, entitled *L'Age*. He sketched out a new structure for it that resembled the manner of Raymond Roussel, based on two sets of phonetically similar keys: *m-r* words – *amarre* ("mooring"), *amer* ("bitter"), *mire* ("target"), *mort* ("death") – and *p-r* words – *épars* ("scattered"), *épeire* ("arachnid"), *pire* ("worst"), *port* ("port"), *pur* ("pure") – to which, he warned, one should not necessarily add *mère* ("mother") or *père* ("father") [*Jsn* 55]. But what could have motivated the choice of those particular groups of consonants, if not the disappeared branches of Perec's family tree?

In 1968 Perec proposed to be both a lover and a husband. And why not? Neither partner in the marriage regarded sexual adventure as a crime. Paulette was free to come to Andé, and she did, once or twice. It was 1968, after all. Perec confided to friends that had never known joy of the sort that Suzanne gave him.

Once *La Disparition* was done, in September, Perec got down to a month of happy collaboration at the Moulin d'Andé with Jacques Roubaud and the mathematician Pierre Lusson, putting together the first French guide to the game of go. A novel by Alain Guérin had recently alerted Christian Bourgois to the existence of go (when he read Guérin's typescript, he at first took the game to be entirely fictional!) and he was happy to publish a book on the subject. Roubaud provided the Japanese background and technical knowledge of the game; Lusson, who had also been taught to play by Chevalley, supplied gambits and more technical expertise; Perec contributed the jokes and acted as scribe for the project. Perec was in top form, full of good cheer, full of himself. The book reflects his mood directly; it contains as many puns and leg-pulls as rules for playing go. But it is not an insignificant item in the oeuvres of its authors. The *Petit Traité invitant à la découverte de l'art subtil du go* ("Short Treatise Inviting Discovery of the Subtle Art of Go") puts forward an argument that must first have been Roubaud's, before it became Perec's as well – that there is only one other activity to which go can be compared: not chess (the bête noire of the book) but writing [*PTG* 41]. This was not to say that writing was only a game, but rather that go was a serious pursuit.

Perec was the prince consort beside the queen bee. Andé was a place founded on libertarian values, the ancestor of the communes that mushroomed "after May". However, the "tuned-in, turned-on" fashions of unwashed hippiedom, which the French called *baba-cool,* had no impact on Andé's older radical chic. It had always been a convivial, nonhierarchical, nonauthoritarian, left-wing place, but Woodstock it was not. If hashish was smoked, it was done privately. If people got too drunk and made real fools of themselves, they were not asked to return. In the summer, few women sunbathed topless

The Rule of Ko ["Eternity"]

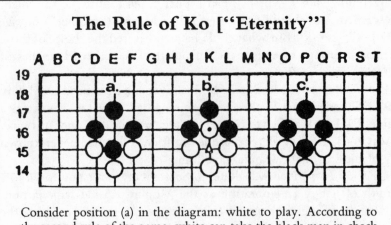

Consider position (a) in the diagram: white to play. According to the second rule of the game, white can take the black man in check (position (b)). Black can then take it back, which brings the situation back to where it was (c) after an exchange of men (one white prisoner, one black prisoner). The exchange could go on indefinitely until all the pieces are used up. The rule of KO forbids white and black to use their men in this way: after white takes KO as in position (b), black may not play in △ before another move has been made. Then white has two options: either he can play in △ ("white fills KO") or he can play elsewhere, and black may now play into △ ("black retakes KO").

on the lawns by the river. Suzanne's aim was to give artists of all kinds a place where they could get on with their work without being bothered by families, jobs, or the time-wasting confusion of the city. Relaxation was part of that, up to a point, and of course people liked playing games. But Suzanne must have wondered just what real work was going on when she saw Perec sitting at a board with black and white buttons laid out on it, when she watched him play cards late into the night, when she listened to him teasing *e*-less sentences out of every one of her guests. There was always a smile on her face, but ther may have been something anxious, insistent or even sharp in her voice when she asked him, as he came down for lunch: Well, *have you done your page for today?* Ouch!

A priest said one day that he considered that a man who spent his days and nights playing GO committed a worse crime than if he were guilty of all the Four Great Crimes and the Five Great Offences put together.   [PTG 7]

Perec was floating on a cloud of creative ease, but after finishing *La Disparition*, he was not ready to start straightaway on another large project. The *go* book was a break, as was a commission he then accepted from the Humanities Computing Centre of the CNRS, where Pierre Getzler had a part-time job as a graphics designer. His boss was Bernard Jaulin – who had lived as a boy at number 16 Rue de l'Assomption and had accompanied a neighbour called Jojo to the Wolf Cub pack at the top of Rue de Boulainvilliers. By coincidence, Getzler put the two childhood friends into contact again, and thereafter there really was not much question as to which writer to commission for the Centre's well-funded project whose appropriately Oulipian purpose was to explore the literary potential of an algorithm.

An algorithm, as defined for this experiment, is an ordered sequence of instructions written in a programming language for input into a computer, usually laid out as a flow chart for human understanding. Perec's commission was to turn into a text the flow-chart representing the steps that a lowly employee would take in order to obtain a pay rise. The plot itself is a pun, since the French word for a pay rise or increment (*augmentation*) also signifies "incrementation", the procedure used by a computer to mark its path around an algorithm. The idea was originally conceived by Jacques Perriault for the Bull computer company and then amended by Perec before he began to write out his text.

> *The problem is a simple one. It consists of a certain number of propositions that can take either yes or no for an answer, each answer having certain consequences. The concatenation of causes and effects and the choice of answers are represented by arrows that are the only syntactic connectors between the propositions. In brief, it is a tree structure, a network, a labyrinth, and the "reader" chooses ONE route amongst all the possible routes, the totality of possible routings being presented SIMULTANEOUSLY on the flow chart. [. . .] Instead of telling the story so as to leave the reader free to choose his own route,[1] I have made a LINEAR TRANSLATION of the chart – that is to say, I have followed ONE BY*

---

[1] Raymond Queneau had invented a reader-selected tree-story in "Un Conte à votre façon", *Les Lettres nouvelles*, July-September 1967), translated as "A Story As you Like It" in Warren Motte, *OuLiPo. A Primer of Potential Literature* (Lincoln: Nebraska University Press, 1986), pp. 156–158. Children (and their parents) may find in the Tracker-Book series a familiar example of tree-structure narrative.

ONE all the steps of the route chosen, going back to the start every time an arrow sent me back there; in other words, I have not allowed myself to utter a proposition before having retraced all those that precede it: the end result is a text of fifty-seven pages built entirely on redundancy.

This text, entitled "L'Art et la manière d'aborder son chef de service pour lui demander une augmentation" ("Ways and Means of Approaching Your Head of Department to Request an Increment") is written, like *A Man Asleep* (though to different effect) in the second person, and despite its length, it consists only of a single grammatical sentence. The effect of a linear translation of a step-by-step procedure that, like the real-life situation it represents, takes you back again and again to square one, is to bring in the element of time. To write out the steps over and again is a laborious and lengthy business; it can hardly fail to make the writer particularly conscious of the time that elapses between each attempt to approach the Head of Department. And it was no doubt because of this – because the lesson taught by the linear expansion of a flow chart is that time passes – that it occurred to Perec, as soon as he had finished the exercise, that the project was ideal *Hörspiel* material. He explained it to Helmle, who in turn spoke about it to Johann-Maria Kamps at SR, and over the following months Perec transformed his single-sentence second-person narrative into a sound-play for six voices, entitled *L'Augmentation* ("The Increment") and intended for performance in German.

At Andé, in the best of his years there, Perec met many fascinating people, some of whom became real friends. Maurice and Suzanne invited a number of celebrated figures from the exotic fringes of world politics to stay: Alain Geismar, one of the student leaders of May '68; Bernard Kouchner, another young man destined for a political career; the editors of *Tricontinental*, a Marxist review based in Havana and partly funded by Suzanne; and René Depestre, a Haitian intellectual who became a French poet and novelist. But Perec kept his politics to himself at Andé ("He really wasn't very interested," says Suzanne) and made new friendships mostly amongst the filmmakers who continued to come there from time to time. He got to know Alain Cavalier, and formed a solid bond with the tall and already balding Jean-Paul Rappeneau. He naturally met Maurice Pons's nephew, Bernard Queysanne (whose elder brother Bruno had been a leading light in Lg), who had just begun a film career as

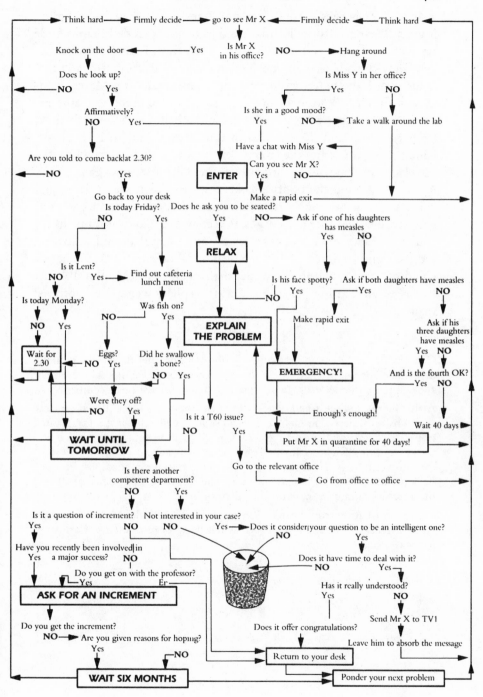

assistant to Georges Franju. Some of Perec's own crowd – including Marcel Benabou, Roger Kleman, and Jacques Lederer – became Andé regulars, and other old friends came down from Paris for the parties and fancy-dress balls that were held in the grounds from time to time.

In 1970, Babette Mangolte was the "cameraman" on Marcel Hannoun's film *Le Printemps*, and she asked the codirector, Catherine Binet, to accompany her to the midsummer ball at Le Moulin d'Andé. Catherine had read *Things*, and imagined its author to be a carrot-haired Breton wearing the tweeds and smart English shoes which the novel's main characters so ardently desire. Girls draped in gauze stood in a circle around the bonfire to keep warm, for it was a damp and chilly night at Suzanne's riverside estate. Babette introduced Catherine to her old friend Georges Perec, who looked nothing like a countrified city gent: he was dressed up in a turban and a flowing red robe embroidered with white leaf-and-branch motifs. Catherine could not find much to say to the maharajah of the Moulin d'Andé. It was an enchanting place, but the atmosphere was more contrived than gay.

Georges Perec, "L'Art et la manière d'aborder son chef de service pour lui demander une augmentation", *L'Enseignement programmé*, no. 4 (December 1968), pp. 44–68; letter to Eugen Helmle (from Andé), 14 December 1968.

Alain Guérin, *Un bon départ* (Paris: Christian Bourgois, 1967). Perec's review of this novel appeared in *La Quinzaine littéraire*, 15 March 1967; it is reprinted in part in *Christian Bourgois 1966–1986*, p. 83, and in first draft form in *Jsn* under the title "Kleber Chrome", where it is mistakenly said to be a draft for a novel by . . . Georges Perec. The same mistake is made by Philippe Lejeune, in *PAP*, p. 59, where he quotes the review as an instance of "Perec the autobiographer in search of his identity".

Other information from Jacques Roubaud, Eugen Helmle, Marcel Cuvelier, Anne Lipinska, Christian Bourgois, Michelle Georges, Alberto Carlinsky, Maurice Pons.

CHAPTER 42

Places of Safety

1968–1969

May '68 was a tremor that left institutions outwardly intact but opened up myriad fissures within them. Jacques Lederer, Perec's oldest friend, turned his back on his middle-class career, joined the Jeunesses Communistes Marxistes-Leninistes, and signed on at the SNECMA engineering works, to throw spanners into it, Maoist-fashion. Perec's goddaughter, Sylvia, a gifted mathematician who was not yet seventeen, joined an anarcho-syndicalist grouplet and brought the proletarian struggle into the Lamblin home at Neuilly. Roger Kleman left Dominique and moved to Andé, to make a real stab at writing at last. Jean Crubellier and Marie-Noëlle had also broken up; Claude Burgelin, who had gone from ENS to Harvard and then to Troyes, now found himself a junior lecturer at Lyon, sandwiched between nervous professors and vociferous student reps. The street fighting of May did not dislodge the regime, but it shifted hidden pillars that propped up families, schools, and institutions. Inhibitions of all kinds were swept away for a time. However, Perec's main observation on the impact of "the events" concerned microscopic rules of social contact:

> It was in July 1968, I think, that I had a most curious dinner with Paulette [. . .] We were next to two lads [in a restaurant] who asked us stupid questions (stupid even before I replied?) but only so as to get us to buy them a drink. Which we did. The fact that we let ourselves get drawn into conversation is presumably an instance of what people now call the fall-out from May.

"May" had kept Perec at the Moulin d'Andé (there were no trains and no petrol for two or three weeks), which was where he wanted to be in any case. In the wake of being stranded there, he made it into his real home. From the summer of 1968, it was at Andé that he had his Underwood typewriter, his works in progress, and his back papers – such of them as still existed, that is. He could not bring his whole literary archive with him because he had lost the main part of it, in *one of the most curious accidents* of his writing career.

> *For years I kept all my papers quite scrupulously. At one time they were all in a little cardboard suitcase. I sorted them and reread them periodically. I had even done index cards for each one (including very short stories) and for planned works which were never written.*[1]
> *I don't know when I threw the case or its contents away, but the fact is that I realised, either when we left Rue de Quatrefages or when we unpacked at Rue du Bac, that almost all of my works prior to 1963 (or '62) had disappeared. It is not impossible that during a major tidying operation I thought what I was throwing away was the carbons. I don't think I ever wanted to destroy those works – maybe* Les Errants, *probably* J'avance masqué *or* Gradus ad Parnassum, *but certainly not* L'Attentat de Sarajevo *or texts such as*
>
> > *"Les Barques"*
> > *"Manderre"*
> > *"La Procession"*
>
> *and especially not the various versions of* Gaspard pas mort – Le Condottiere.

There is no reason to doubt the sincerity of this note written in 1969, but the recent rediscovery of many of Perec's early works make their long disappearance seem baffling. At the time that Perec moved to Andé on a permanent basis there were carbon typescripts of the works he had *not wanted to destroy* in the hands of the very friends to whom he had given them: at the very least, "Manderre" was with Milka Čanak and *L'Attentat de Sarajevo* with Mladen Srbinović in Belgrade, and copies of *Le Condottiere* were with both Jean Crubellier and Alain Guérin. Perec's note of 1969 suggests that he had completely forgotten that he had given these copies away. His forgetting of the location but not of the existence or contents of his early works must be the bizarrest act of selective amnesia by a writer with an otherwise unusually retentive mind.[2]

Perec's settling down with *la dame du Moulin* was all very well,

---

[1] A few of these index cards were not lost, amongst them FP 119, 21, 29 (for *L'Attentat de Sarajevo*), and 119, 21, 30 (for "La Paix", "La Procession", "Le Fou", "La Tyrannie").

[2] See also David Bellos, "Perec avant Perec", *Ecritures* (Liège) 2 (1992), pp. 47–64.

Paulette might have said, but if he thought he could carry on using *her* home like a hotel . . . and she slammed the door of Rue du Bac on him. For the two or three nights that he had to spend in Paris most weeks, Perec could stay at Suzanne's flat on Ile Saint-Louis, or in a flatlet she owned near Mabillon, in Rue de l'Echaudé. It was at the latter address that he had a brief fling in November 1968 with a woman he had known for many years. It ended badly, by his own admission, for his heart was not in it. Alberto, his old kitchen-rival from the Moulin d'Andé, opened an Argentinian restaurant on the ground floor of the block in Rue de l'Echaudé: Perec was less than complimentary about the food that was served there.

Perec's position in the autumn of 1968 was less enviable than it might have seemed. He had no capital beyond the flat in Rue du Bac, in which he had invested both his endowment from the German court award and his Renaudot Prize. He now depended on Suzanne, but she was tied to her Moulin far more than to him. She admired the writer in Perec and had great affection for the man, but she had never said that she loved him alone. It was a matter as much of principle as of personal taste: exclusive passions were unreasonable, she maintained. Perec noted down another dream in November 1968:

The Trays
With a laugh that can only be called sardonic, she began to make advances towards a stranger, in front of me. I said nothing. As she persisted, I left the room in the end.

I am in my own room with A and a casual acquaintance whom I am teaching to play the game of go. He seems to understand, but then I realise that he thinks he is learning bridge. The game, in fact, consists of distributing trays *of letters (more like a kind of lotto than scrabble).* [BO 2]

Suzanne did not want Perec to leave. Why should he go away? Several of her ex-lovers had become just good friends and remained faithful to the Moulin community. But Perec was not made that way. His friend from the lab, Henry Gautier, amongst others, urged him to cut free; it was clear that the unbalanced situation was doing him no good at all. The crisis came over Christmas. Perec could take it no longer, and went so far as to ask Jacques Roubaud if he would value him less if he took his own life. No less, said Roubaud, but also no more. In the end, Perec resolved not to be a circus dog; he had to go. He did not use his uncle David's cutthroat razor (recalled years later in *Jms* 359), but moving out must have hurt almost as much as slashing his wrists.

Perec did not really have anywhere to go. He took refuge first with Jacques Lederer and then with his cousin Lili, in her flat at Saint-Cloud, in the western suburbs of Paris. Had he been right to leave the Moulin d'Andé? Yes, he told himself firmly on 5 January 1969. What was the real problem? His own weakness, he scribbled. And what could he do?

> *Wash, change, change skin (clothes, look), stop thinking, forget, stop waiting, expect nothing ever again, stop counting the hours, stop making comparisons, stop making associations, stop expecting anything (repeat), PULL SELF TOGETHER, recuperate, stay in one piece, sleep, stop having toothache, begin again, step by step, talk, judge, understand, FORGET. If I need comfort, I must tell myself: the worst is over. Be patient. Do things one by one. Stop the mind from wandering back to the Moulin d'Andé, stop wondering what she is doing, what she is thinking, what she wants.*

One of the first things he did was to finish the letter he had been trying to write to help Sylvia over her teenage crisis, which was simultaneously (and typically) a matter of high politics and a question of family relations. He spent two pages on politics, and then came to the point:

> *I believe you have more or less important decisions to make at the moment, as far as your studies and your parents are concerned. But there's no reason to lose hope, or to let yourself be dragged down. There's only one important thing in life, and that's energy: that is to say, the quantity of strength and sustained effort you can bring to bear on a single person or thing. Not your ability to change the world (that's not an aim any individual conscience can entertain, except as a historical vanishing point, or frame of thought), but your relationship to the world. "In the battle between the world and you", Kafka said, "back the world." It's a sentence that it's taken me years to understand, but I am sure, now, that it is absolutely fundamental.*

By the middle of January 1969 Paulette had relented and she let Perec move back into Rue du Bac. He apologised to Eugen Helmle for not having *much heart for real work* and promised to send him a sample of his flow-chart play before the end of the month; to Jean-Paul Rappeneau, he explained in more detail:

> *I've left the Moulin d'Andé, a haven of peace where I had peace no longer, a place of work which I thought, for years, would also be the only place of my life.*
>
> *I'm not exactly on top of things. My sense of humour has lost much of its charm and my critical faculties a good part of their splendour. I'm trying to recuperate.*

Moon shots were featured in most of the magazines that Perec could have flicked through to distract himself in January 1969. NASA planned to place on the moon, and on all the heavenly bodies to which it was sending unmanned probes, shockproof canisters of microfilmed images of life on Earth in 1968–69 together with messages of welcome, in dozens of Earth dialects, addressed to whichever superintelligent aliens might one day find them. The canisters being placed around space were known as time capsules.

Had Perec really meant to cut himself off from Suzanne forever, he would have emigrated (or so he said to himself eighteen months later) but instead his cunning unconscious invented a modest, methodical means of keeping him in Paris, too close to Andé to allow a real cure. The programme of work was a Parisian parody of NASA's bid to ensure the survival of our times in the deserts of outer space. Without the time-capsule programme, after all, future extraterrestrials might well believe that earthlings all looked like Mickey Mouse.

> *I have selected twelve places in Paris – streets, squares, and crossroads connected to important events or moments in my existence. Each month, I describe two of these places: one in situ (in a café or in the street itself), relating "what I can see" in the most neutral manner possible, listing the shops, architectural details, microevents (a fire engine going by, a lady tying up her dog before going into the charcuterie, a removal in progress, posters, people, etc.); the second I write anywhere (at home, in a café, in the office), describing the place from memory, evoking the memories that are connected to it, the people I knew there, and so on. Each text (which may come down to just a few lines or extend over five or six pages or more), once completed, is put away in an envelope that I seal with a wax*

*seal. After one year I will have described twelve places twice over,
once in memory mode, once in situ in real descriptive mode. I shall
begin over again in the same manner each year for twelve years.*

[*Jsn* 58]

Perec's twelve places all belonged to his past life, or to what, in
January 1969, he wished to believe was the past. In biographical
order, they were Rue Vilin, *the place where I began, the place that will
soon die (it won't be there twelve years from now), where I ran with a
drawing in my hand, where I was demoted (had the medal torn off);* Avenue
Junot, where the Chavranskis had lived since 1945; Rue de l'Assomption; Franklin-Roosevelt, the site of Perec's truancy; Place
d'Italie, where he had typed *Les Errants* in 1956; Place de la Contrescarpe, where his Tunisian friends had lived in 1955–57; Rue Saint-
Honoré, where he had a room of his own in 1956–57 and again in
1959; Rue de la Gaîté, near where Jacques Lederer had lived in the
1950s; Mabillon, the site of his first escapade with Paulette in 1960;
Jussieu, the metro station and *café-tabac* corner nearest to Rue de
Quatrefages; Passage Choiseul, near the Bibliothèque Nationale (he
never understood quite *why* he chose Passage Choiseul); and Ile Saint-
Louis, where Suzanne had her Paris quarters. The last was the most
recent in biographical terms, and the most important for Perec to treat
as dead, for the book that he envisaged writing out of his twelve-year
time-capsule project was to be a commemoration of *dead places that
ought to survive.*

As self-help psychotherapy, the places project was fraught with
ambiguity. Philippe Lejeune has called it "a tomb of love" [*MO* 146],
but if it was designed to bury Suzanne, it was also meant to resurrect
her. *I don't want to forget,* Perec insisted in one of the texts. *Perhaps
that is what is at the bottom of the whole book.* Twelve places times two
versions (one real, one remembered) times twelve years would make
288 envelopes in all, 288 stones heaped onto a corpse, to hide it
absolutely and to build a cairn that marked a parting of ways.

It did not work as psychotherapy, however, and perhaps it was
not really supposed to. Perec caved in and went back to Andé in the
spring – back to his old *chambre Jeanne d'Arc*, to his umpire's high
chair, to dinners laced with puns and bridge fuelled by vodka. It was
already a different milieu. Maurice had also left, and returned with a
new girlfriend, a very young journalist on *L'Express*. He was now a
member of the Commission d'Avances sur Recettes (CAR), the state

subsidy authority for new films. Suzanne had fallen in love with a young man whom Maurice had first met at meetings of the CAR.

Superficially, the events of the winter of 1968-69 brought Perec back to where he had been a year before, with a marital home at Rue du Bac and a home-from-home at Andé, but his underlying situation was far less happy than it had been in the previous spring, when the lipogram-novel had kept him in top form. Nonetheless Perec's pen began to flow again as the winter drew to a close. Whatever its first purpose may have been, the places programme now acquired a dynamic of its own. Every month Perec would spend an afternoon training himself to see and to write down precisely, exactly, what he saw, without elaboration, at "degree zero" of style. Every month, too, he would spend an hour or two summoning up his memories, for the "memory" texts were not just descriptions *from* memory but also descriptions *of* the memories attached to the various places, the memories that gave each one its place in the places project.

At first Perec called the book that he would compose twelve years hence, on reopening his sealed envelopes, *Soli loci*, punning on *soliloquy*[1] as well as on Roussel's title *Locus solus*. But if he was to trace the history of Paris itself along with the history of his own memory and his own writing, random soliloquising would not suffice: he would have to find a way of alternating the order of the "real" and the "memory" places year by year. There was not much point in having twelve descriptions of Place d'Italie in autumn, or in getting into a routine in which every March he would have to remember Rue Vilin. He recalled a device that Claude Berge had proposed to OuLiPo some time before, a sort of number-jumble that allowed paired squares to be programmed so that no combination occurred more than once in the grid as a whole (*see* p. 393). He had already had a go at thinking out an approximate (and incomplete) application of Berge's formula to a detective novel that seems vaguely based on the board game called Cluedo (*see* p. 420). This scrap, from an envelope dated 1968-69 by Perec himself, contains tantalising hints of many things to come. It is the earliest trace of a plan for a formal detective novel that would be realised only many years later in "*53 Days*"; the dog who "discovers he is related to one of the others" may presage the plan for a radio play entitled *Wie ein Hund* ("Like a Dog"); and the servant who "ponders his revenge" could well be the first step in

---

[1] The pun is closer in English; in French *soli loci/ soliloque* is an *à peu près*.

10 characters	10 situations	10 motives or clues
Grandfather	Murderer	~~Important clue~~
Grandmother	Victim	~~Reveals clue~~
Son	Detective	Has the weapon
Daughter	Witness of crime	Only appears on a photo or portrait
Son-in-law	Suspect number 1	Ever present but never speaks
Grandson	An essential clue	Knows nothing
Private secretary	Reveals important clue	Inherits a vast fortune
Childhood friend	Has the weapon	Is mistaken for another
A servant		Ponders his revenge
A dog		Discovers he is related to one of the others.

the transformation of the forger-murderer Gaspard Winckler of *Le Condottiere* into the mysteriously avenging Winckler of *Life A User's Manual*. What the scrap also suggests is that Perec was beginning to see the possibilities of applying combinatorial devices to plot-elements (character, situation and motive), whereas in all his work up to this point, including *Die Maschine*, permutational and combinatorial rules had been applied only to elements of language (letters, sounds and words). However, Perec could not now adopt Claude Berge's ten by ten grid for his places project, since there were twelve places to plot through the twelve months of the year. Perec needed a different bi-square to permute his place-time coordinates, and so he wrote to one of the joint authors of an article entitled "On Methods of Constructing Sets of Mutually Orthogonal Latin Squares Using a Computer"[1] and got a prompt reply in French from Indra Chakravarti, at Chapel Hill, North Carolina, who sent him two 12 × 12 number squares that were "mutually orthogonal", meaning that, when put together, they constitute the table as laid out on page 421.

The application of the bi-square to the places project is slightly bizarre because the two sets – represented by the numbers 1 to 12 on each side of the comma – have identical members: the "memory" places

[1] By R.C. Bose, I.M. Chakravarti and D.E. Knuth, in *Technometrics* II.4 (November 1960), pp. 507–516.

1,1	2,2	3,3	4,4	5,5	6,6	7,7	8,8	9,9	10,10	11,11	12,12
2,3	3,4	4,5	5,6	6,1	1,2	8,9	9,10	10,11	11,12	12,7	7,8
3,2	4,3	5,4	6,5	1,6	2,1	9,8	10,9	11,10	12,11	7,12	8,7
4,11	5,12	6,7	1,8	2,9	3,10	10,5	11,6	12,1	7,2	8,3	9,4
5,10	6,11	1,12	2,7	3,8	4,9	11,4	12,5	7,6	8,1	9,2	10,3
6,12	1,7	2,8	3,9	4,10	5,11	12,6	7,1	8,2	9,3	10,4	11,5
7,4	8,5	9,6	10,1	11,2	12,3	1,10	2,11	3,12	4,7	5,8	6,9
8,6	9,1	10,2	11,3	12,4	7,5	2,12	3,7	4,8	5,9	6,10	1,11
9,5	10,6	11,1	12,2	7,3	8,4	3,11	4,12	5,7	6,8	1,9	2,10
10,8	11,9	12,10	7,11	8,12	9,7	4,2	5,3	6,4	1,5	2,6	3,1
11,7	12,8	7,9	8,10	9,11	10,12	5,1	6,2	1,3	2,4	3,5	4,6
12,9	7,10	8,11	9,12	10,7	11,8	6,3	1,4	2,5	3,6	4,1	5,2

are Jussieu (1), Assomption (2), Saint-Honoré (3), Junot (4), Franklin (5), Gaîté (6), Mabillon (7), Vilin (8), Italie (9), Saint-Louis (10), Choiseul (11), and Contrescarpe (12), to the left of the comma, whilst the "real" places are Mabillon (1), Vilin (2), Italie (3), Saint-Louis (4), Choiseul (5), Contrescarpe (6), Assomption (7), Saint-Honoré (8), Jussieu (9), Franklin (10), Gaîté (11), and Junot (12), to the right of the comma. To keep track of his ambiguous digits, Perec wrote out the whole chart with the place names inserted and with the columns labelled for the months and the rows marked for the years. He ticked off the envelopes as he went along, so that if he got behind or ahead of schedule he would still know where he was in space and time. An envelope designated, say, September 1969 would always be the September 1969 envelope, despite its contents being written six months in advance or árrears.

In February 1969 Perec revisited Rue Vilin, on schedule, and wrote the first version of his memories of Rue de l'Assomption: of the crayfish expedition with Michel Rigout (see p. 90); of seeing the Yves Klein exhibition at the Galerie Allendy (see p. 119); of having to fetch his ball from the other side of the convent wall opposite number 18; of his first bedroom (see p. 90) and of the bedroom he moved into when the Lamblins moved out; of the mobile he made out of purloined car-radio antennae and a ball of wool; of the view from the kitchen window onto the balcony of the building opposite, where a jazz tympanist practised; of Lili's room, where he wrote a long letter to no one on a miserable 14 July; of meetings of Lg in the dining room; and of his first and all too platonic love for a blue-eyed classmate from Etampes.

The quality of Perec's memory was remarkable. The places programme presupposed that its inventor had memories to write down, at the very least; and the project itself served as first-rate memory training. But the visual precision, the emotional content, and the sheer scope of Perec's memory of his childhood at Rue de l'Assomption and of his student years are quite simply stunning. It is not just that he knew without having to think about it that the Italian front-runners for the 1947 Tour de France were Brambilla and Ronconi, who lost in the end to Robic; he could also remember the names of all the bars and restaurants on Place de la Contrescarpe in 1956, and the names of all his Tunisian friends in Rue Blainville, even though he had not seen any of them save Nour for nearly fifteen years. Perec's places are not empty at all, with one exception: Saint-Louis.

In February 1969 Perec travelled once again to Germany, to give a reading of his works in French at Saarbrücken University, alongside Eugen Helmle, who read the relevant passages in translation. It was part of a series entitled *Begegnung in Saarbrücken*, sponsored (and recorded for broadcast) by SR. It afforded Perec and Helmle an opportunity to discuss the arrangements for an exhibition of Pierre Getzler's paintings at a local gallery, and to get down to preparatory work on the promised sequel to *Die Maschine*, the still unwritten flow-chart radio play. Recasting the single-sentence-monologue format of the original "incrementation" exercise, Perec put the algorithm into six "logical operators", each of which was to be represented by a different radio voice: the proposition (the affirmative instructions on the flow chart: *you go to see*), the selector condition (*either he is . . . or he isn't*), the positive hypothesis (*if he is . . . then . . .*), the negative hypothesis (*if he isn't . . . then . . .*), the selection (*he isn't . . . so . . .*) and the conclusion (*you wait for a happier day to go to see your Head of Department*). The play, written in bursts in March, April, and early May 1969, consists exclusively of repeated six-part "consequence" propositions (with one deviation: the interruption of measles, speaking in its own voice, straight out of an encyclopaedia), in the course of which "you", the supplicant for a measly increment from your boss, get older, and tireder and deeper in debt. Perec humanises the repetitions by inserting tiny variations in the wording, making them all the funnier for bending the iron rule of computer logic; the outcome, which is really no outcome at all (a medal from the company for long service, and larger debts incurred in the ensuing celebration), introduces into the simple marking of time a note that is properly tragic.

Helmle translated *L'Augmentation* straightaway, and it went into production with SR as *Wucherungen*, after Perec's next visit to Saarbrücken, in September, for the opening of Pierre Getzler's exhibition at the Elitzer Gallery. The play was first broadcast on 12 November 1969. With its ironically expressionless voices, its rhythmic regularity, its almost intolerable repetitions, and its closing sadness, *Wucherungen* was as much of a new departure in *Hörspiel* technique as *Die Maschine* had been before it. The latter play was repeated by several radio stations that month as an established classic of the genre, despite its being little more than a year old.

In May 1969, before he had quite finished the radio version of *L'Augmentation*, Perec accompanied Suzanne, Maurice and Maurice's new girlfriend, Michelle Georges, to Carros, a pretty Provençal *mas* in the hills above Cannes. It was film-festival time, and Perec had his first experience of the film world's own Frankfurt Book Fair, a celluloid jamboree where million-dollar deals are done in hamburger bars whilst aspiring starlets display their wares on the pavements outside. He bumped into Rappeneau, who had at last finished the script of *Les Mariées de l'An II* and was in Cannes to finalise the business side of the film. Rappeneau had found a backer, who signed on the line well before the festival's end; the worst was over, and all that was left, he joked, not altogether unseriously, was the easy part: the actual making of the film. "Well," Perec said, "Why don't we write the next one together?"

Perec and Rappeneau devoted the remaining days of the festival to a film binge of the sort possible only at Cannes – four or five movies a day, some great, some new, some old classics, and some absolutely dreadful junk, including a pornographic version of *Romeo and Juliet*, in the midst of which an actor turned from a clumsy orgy to the camera to ask, "Just who wrote this shit?"

Rappeneau joined Perec at Carros for a brief sunlit holiday after their long hours in darkened rooms, and the two friends of Andé got down to work in Suzanne's southern retreat on what was intended to be the first Rappeneau-Perec spectacular.

The Riviera in May was perhaps what made them think of satirising the Club Méditerranée, a rapidly-growing French enterprise that offered falsely communal adventure holidays in sanitised camps in exotic locations. The film's working title was just *Le Club,* but there is no doubt which club was meant. The heroine was to be a provincial hairdresser (Catherine Deneuve, with her beehive hairdo, would have fitted the role well) who spends all her savings on a fortnight in a Caribbean island camp. Her flight is hijacked to South America, where the passengers are held hostage by Tupamaro guerrillas. The adventures that would befall the hairdresser were left to be worked out later, but she would have to be rescued – by English ecologists, Perec insisted, riding bicycles. *Ecologists* was a new word for Rappeneau, as it was for nearly everyone in 1969, and Perec explained it to him. But a *bicycle* rescue in the Amazon was pretty implausible, the director opined. Perec conceded, crossed the word out, and inserted instead *rescued by tandem.*

Le Club was meant to be a "madcap comedy" in full colour, with wonderful photography of places that Perec had not yet seen. Obviously he did not tell Rappeneau that his own mother had been a hairdresser, or that she had been taken on a long journey to a destination that she had failed to foresee. Rappeneau was somewhat bewildered by Perec's creative procedure, which consisted very largely of modifying scenes from other films he knew and liked. It was altogether colder than Rappeneau's own method of writing. Where, he asked, were the feelings?

Feelings? replied Perec. *You can put those in at the end.*

Unpublished sources used in this chapter include FP 57, 17 (18 September 1969), 57, 24 (1 January 1970), 57, 41 (2 October 1970), 57, 65 (4 September 1972); FP 41, 1, 22 (the detective story plan) and FP 72, 3, 3, 32 (the personal note written on 5 January 1969); draft notes for *Le Club* (in the possession of Jean-Paul Rappeneau); and letters from Georges Perec to Eugen Helmle, Jean-Paul Rappeneau and Sylvia Richardson-Lamblin.

The bi-square of *Lieux* is taken from *MO* 155.

Other information used was provided by Alberto Carlinsky, Michelle Georges, Suzanne Lipinska, Maurice Pons, Jean-Paul Rappeneau, and Jacques Roubaud.

CHAPTER 43

Into Reverse

1969

In der Schränke zeigt sich der Meister

Johann Wolfgang von Goethe

All Perec's cunning could not mask his misery at the Moulin d'Andé, to which he returned as to a disaster. He let his hair grow longer, he let his bad tooth turn blacker, and he let his parka get grubbier by the day. With his green eyes and forced grin, and the odd way he had of using his hands to hold his pen or his never-unlighted cigarette, Perec looked less like a writer than like Rumpelstiltskin as depicted in old German editions of Grimm. One visitor to Andé went so far as to show Perec what he meant by sketching the unappealing imp on a paper napkin. Unloved, unsuccessful, and underpaid, Perec did his best to embarrass dinner-table partners by making his plight very plain. They may have wanted to offer bland comfort and say "Oh come on, don't be silly" to the glum and sometimes tearful writer, but they could not easily do so, because the role Perec played up to was very near to the truth. He was Jewish, he had terrible teeth, and he was desperately lacking, not in sympathy but in love. For comfort, and for protection, Perec turned to the alphabet, which had given him such joy in 1968. In 1969, however, even the alphabet went into reverse.

The Andé community included several psychoanalysts and as a whole was very open to Freudian ideas. One psychiatrist who first came in 1969 (and who quickly inserted himself into the serious bridge-playing circle) stuck out like a sore thumb by disputing the validity of the "talking cure". Cyrille Koupernik thought that Perec in particular was an entirely unsuitable candidate for analysis: his defences were too active; he could bend words to his will and to his devious wit like no other. Woe betide the analyst who dared to take him on!

At Andé Perec was and would ever remain the lipogram man, and indeed, he himself regarded *La Disparition* as a work that belonged to the Moulin. He put the manuscripts (his own, as well as the passages contributed by others) into a fibreglass attaché case that he decorated with transfer lettering, and gave it to Suzanne as a souvenir. The idea of a return match – the revenge of the *e* – arose straightaway, and throughout 1969 people played at inventing sentences that contained no vowels other than *e*; Michelle Georges, for instance, offered "Estelle est très belle et préfère les esthètes". Since *e* is the commonest letter in the alphabet, a univocalic on it is less constraining than a lipogram (or than a univocalic on *a*, for example) and therefore has (in Oulipian principle) only a moderate literary potential. Perec did not proceed very far with what was first dubbed *Les Lettres d'Eve* ("Eve's Letters"), for he needed and sought alphabetic defences that were more extreme.

On Sundays he would nag those with cars to take him down to Saint-Pierre-du-Vauvray to fetch the new issue of *Le Nouvel Observateur* fresh off the Paris train, so as to have Robert Scipion's crossword to crack before lunch. Ah! Now that was a real ambition, he often said – to become such a master of words as to rival Scipion himself!

In the winter of 1968–69 Perec had made the acquaintance, through a colleague of Paulette's at the Bibliothèque Nationale, of a musician-composer named Philippe Drogoz. Drogoz had read *A Man Asleep* and had been moved by it, and he was willing to take seriously Perec's proposal for an opera. French musical notation uses the tonic sol-fa, *do ré mi fa sol la si*, out of which monosyllables can be built longer words such as *doré* (golden), *Rémi* (a man's name), and homophonous combinations such as *ciré* (oilcloth) or even little sentences such as "dort Emile assis?" (*do ré mi la si*) ("Is Emile asleep in his seat?"). The projected opera would have a libretto written in words consisting exclusively of tonic sol-fa syllables and a melodic line corresponding exactly to the musical value of the syllables sung. It was completely mad and quite exhilarating, even if it was not entirely original, since Bach had done something similar in *The Art of the Fugue*, based on B^b–A–C–B (pronounced in German musical notation as B-A-C-H). However, when the project was explained one night at a dinner in Paris to Alain Moène, a musician who might have helped to arrange a commission, it did not go down at all well, and Paulette ended up speaking her own mind in her customarily forthright way. The conversation froze, until Moène came up with a different idea for an experimental work: a science-fiction opera, based on a story by Ray Bradbury. How was he to know that Bradbury was one of the science-fiction authors whom Perec *didn't like*?

The Perec-Drogoz project, entitled *L'Art effaré* ("Art in a start" – *la ré fa rê*) was put on the back burner, since a commission from Radio-France now seemed barely plausible, but the two men became good musical friends. They would get together to listen to music on the Perecs' hi-fi, or on the tapedeck installed in Philippe's car (with acoustics of hair-tingling quality), or at La Cigale, still going strong, still playing the same old jazz. La Cigale was also where Perec took Jacqueline de Guitaut, who was now separated from Christian Bourgois, and whom he only ever called *Guitaut* (as her own father did, in mild mockery of an aristocratic tradition). She accompanied him to the opera, too, as did Gautier, his surname-only colleague at the lab, where he continued to work, in ever more concentrated bursts, for what had to pass as forty hours per week.

One of Perec's defences in the early months of 1969 was scholarship. Partly for OuLiPo and partly for himself, he decided to research and write a proper history of the lipogram, which would allow *La Disparition* to be seen in context once it appeared. The article is Perec's only straightforwardly scholarly publication. It begins with a crib from Gershon Scholem on the Kabbala and ends with a personal and Oulipian manifesto:

> *The suppression of the letter, of the typographical sign, of the basic prop, is a purer, more objective, more decisive operation* [than the suppression of words], *something like a constraint degree zero, after which everything becomes possible.*[1]

Perec's adult life had been structured so far by three self-constructed families of unconventional kinds: La Ligne générale, the Moulin d'Andé, and, to a lesser degree, OuLiPo. What was left of the first had been largely integrated into the second (Kleman, Lederer, and Benabou); but the second was now fragile, and Perec's need for the third grew in proportion. In 1969 Perec protected himself by bringing his OuLiPo pals out to Andé and by immersing himself in the world of letters to which OuLiPo had first opened his eyes.

[1] Translated by Warren Motte.

Most of the Andé regulars, however, thought Perec's approach to writing bizarre and told him so. Suzanne was not interested – cinema and politics were her current avocations – but Maurice Pons tackled Perec directly. Writing, he said, had to do with telling stories. Where was the story when you were forcing patterns out of alphabetic signs? *Look*, Perec replied, *there are two ways of getting water. You can go to the spring and bring it back in buckets; or you can lay down pipework and pumps to make it play before your eyes. It's the same water either way.*

The smallest of Perec's alphabetic fountains from this time is called *Les Horreurs de la Guerre* ("The Horrors of War"), a playlet whose dialogue consists of the names of the letters in strict alphabetical order, beginning *A, B, C, D* (*Abbé! Cédez!* ["Father! Give way!"]), with convoluted stage directions allowing the dialogue to enjoy (minimal) plausibility and sense.[1] It is a little joke, but a violent one, as was Perec's alphabet-spectacular of 1969, the "Great Palindrome", *9691 Edna D'nilu.*

"First find a word that doth silence proclaim,/And backwards and forwards is always the same" goes the riddle (answer: MUM), but the difficulty arises when you try to find sentences, not just words, that can be read left to right *and* right to left. Perec already held the world record in the lipogram event; he had a parachute licence as well, and was on track to rival NASA with his time-capsule project. To be worth doing – to be truly *potential* – a palindrome would have to be longer than anything contemplated in mere jest. The constraint tightens not in arithmetical proportion to the length, but rather geometrically, logarithmically, exponentially, or perhaps even asymptotically, for every letter that is added to a text that must be readable both forwards and in reverse forces a reconfiguration of the whole.

Perec's Great Palindrome [*Clô* 45–53] is about 500 words long in each direction, and it earned its author a place in the *Guinness Book of World Records* from 1983 on. It is not a "perfect" palindrome – that is to say, a text that is the same in both directions, such as "Madam I'm Adam" – but rather a "twin" palindrome, meaning that it gives different readings (by way of different word divisions and punctuation) in each of its two extensions. For that reason,

---

[1] *Les Horreurs de la Guerre* was submitted to ORTF in 1969 but was not accepted for performance as a radio play.

the five-hundred-word text is given twice in the finished version, once in left-right orientation and once in right-left (or vice versa). In the original typescript the two extrapolations (*which deny each other,* like the first *Gaspard* that Perec dreamt of writing, in his barracks at Pau) are separated by a blank page bearing only three points – so-called points of suspension – just as the two parts of *W or The Memory of Childhood* would be separated, a few years later, by a blank page bearing a nonalphabetic typographical sign.

> *These . . . do not constitute a poem in themselves; they are the centre of the void, the gap between two texts that mirror each other. [. . .] It is to that extent only that their poetic virtue seems to me to be certain.*[1]

The Great Palindrome must have been the very hardest of texts to write, and it is undeniably difficult to read. Knowledge of the constraint disarms critical faculties; when you know that it is a monster palindrome, you tend to see nothing but its palindromic design. At Manchester, in 1989, doctored photocopies and unsigned handwritten versions were given to students and teachers of French who were asked, respectively, to use it for the exercise of *explication de texte* and to mark it as an essay. Perec's palindrome barely made sense to the readers. Some teachers took it for the work of an incompetent student, while others suspected that they had been treated to a surrealist text produced by "automatic writing". Those with psychiatric interests identified the author as an adolescent in a dangerously paranoid state; those who had not forgotten the swinging sixties wondered whether it was LSD or marijuana that had generated the disconnected images of the text. Readers seem to project their own positive and negative fantasies onto Perec's palindrome, as they do onto other difficult, obscure and unattributed works. But it is perhaps not now simply a matter of projection if we glimpse anger, cruelty, and self-mutilation in some of the jagged images of Perec's reversible text. Here are the first and last 115 characters, with plain prose translations following:

[1] Georges Perec, "Points de suspension", *Roy Rogers* (New York), Winter 1974, p. 37. In *OCR* 101–106, the points are replaced by asterisks.

TRACELINEGALPALINDROMEN EIGEBAGATELLEDIRAHERCULE LEBRUTREPENTIRCETECRIT NEPERECLARCLUPESETROPLIS AVICEVERSAPERTECERISED	DESIRECETREPASREVECIVASIL PORTESEPULCRALCEREPENTIR CETECRITNEPERTURBELELUCRE HARIDELLETAGABEGIENEMORD NILAPLAGENILECART
Trace l'inégal palindrome. Neige. *Bagatelle, dira Hercule. Le brut* *repentir, cet écrit né Perec. L'arc lu* *pèse trop, lis à vice-versa.* *Perte. Cerise d. . .*	*Désire ce trépas rêvé: Ci va! S'il* *porte, sépulcral, ce repentir, cet* *écrit ne perturbe le lucre:* *Haridelle, ta gabegie ne mord ni la* *plage ni l'écart*

"Trace the uneven palidrome. Snow. A trifle, says Hercules. Unadorned repentance, this piece born [of] Perec. [If] the bow of reading is too heavy, read back-to-front.

Loss. Cherry . . ."

"Desire this dreamt-of death: Here goes! If it bears, entombed, this repentance, this writing bears not on lucre. Strumpet, your trickery has no bite on range or space!"

La Disparition came out in the spring of 1969. It was not well received. Long-standing friends of Perec's were baffled and irritated by it; Roland Barthes refused to read it; Le Nouvel Observateur did not review it. News of it spread by word of mouth and by recommendation amongst writers of the literary avant-garde rather than by critical notice. Maurice Roche explained what La Disparition was to an American writer friend, Harry Mathews, who recalls the very moment:

> I sat down in a corner by myself and put my hands over my eyes, tormented by the question, Why would any writer wish to inflict on himself the linguistic equivalent of Oedipal blinding and castration? I didn't yet have the sense to experience either admiration or jealousy.

One reader wrote to Perec care of Les Lettres Nouvelles to ask him to what extent Roussel had been his master. Perec replied:

It is [. . .] undeniable that Roussel and Jules Verne are my masters, and it is probable that imagination obeys stricter rules than are usually supposed. It seems that, for me, the choice of a formal constraint (what you call a convention) has the effect of liberating my imagination by putting into the background the habitual concern for realism that to some degree clutters up the modern novel, and allows me to rediscover the archetypes of the adventure story – multiple and mysterious births, filiations, inheritances, aquatic monsters, curses that hang over characters, and so on.

Things continued to clock up tens of thousands for Julliard, but sales of Perec's Denoël books were slow. Only the regular trickle of letters from keen readers, so Perec said to friends at Andé, persuaded Nadeau to keep him on. His fans were thin on the ground, spread far and wide. The enquiry about Roussel had been posted from Sfax; another letter, attached to an offprint of a review of *A Man Asleep* by Michel Rybalka, came from Rochester, New York. Perec met his few faithful readers whenever possible and some of them, including Rybalka, became regular friends.

Bourgois made more of a buzz in the early summer of 1969 about the *Petit Traité*, the book on go, than Denoël did about *La Disparition*. A press party was held at a Paris bookshop that sold chess sets, backgammon boards, and go-bans. It was run by a Greek called Thanasekos, whom Perec promptly dubbed *la mort en kilt* ("Tartan Death"), *thanas* being not quite Greek for "death", and *ekos* being (approximately) *Ecosse*. *L'Express* sent a photographer down to Andé with André Bercoff, who interviewed Perec, Roubaud, and Pierre Lusson; another roll of Perec alone was shot in Paris. As for *La Disparition*, the longest review published was an attempt to drive a blunt nail into Perec's coffin:

> Alas! I fear that Georges Perec, justifiably encouraged in 1965 but flattered and worshipped prematurely, has forced his inspiration and his talent somewhat, and especially his spontaneity. [. . .] Obviously, he can't change his spots entirely: he was the first writer of *contestation*, and he has to continue contesting. [. . .] The student riots? It's already been done, with photographs. The Vietnam war? He's a sociologist, not a scoop journalist. The plight of small traders? Not his subject, not his readers' subject, either. The troubles in French farming? He hasn't got a clue. So he has had to find his

material [. . .] in the murkiest of all recent politico-criminal
scandals.[1] To establish his distance and to set a stylistic register, he has used not the mannerism of the "new novel" but
a subtly jarring language, combining psychological reportage
with fragmented psychological notations.

La Disparition is a raw, violent, and facile fiction. A man
disappears: Anton Voyl. Another man disappears: the Moroccan lawyer Ibn Abbou. The police have made enquiries, are
continuing to make enquiries, will go on making enquiries.
But the friends of the two victims gather on a private estate,
at Agincourt, to conduct their own investigation. And then
it all begins to read more like a pulp novel than a criminal
enquiry. All the same – and you must have guessed this –
Georges Perec is too crafty to supply any conclusion for the
twin investigations. The mystery remains entire, but the
novel is finished; that is the contemporary form of "literary"
detective fiction (as in Robbe-Grillet, though in a different
style). Perec carries it off perfectly, in a book that is captivating and dramatic, but that gives off a strong whiff of
artifice.[2]

Those in the know could only view the article as Perec's greatest
triumph to date: a professional reader *simply had not noticed* the lack
of *es* in *La Disparition*. Perec had pulled off his challenge to the alphabet and to the French language. What did it matter if most of the
print run remained unsold?

In less than four years, Perec's public image had shifted from that
of a social critic, a Flaubertian stylist and sociologist with Robbe-
Grilletian tendencies, into that of an unrivalled and probably quite
potty master of letters. The new persona was as incomplete as the
old one. Perec kept quiet about his career as a German radio playwright. When he gave a copy of *L'Augmentation* to Marcel Cuvelier,
a distinguished director of Ionesco's plays, saying, *This might interest*

---

[1] That is to say, the Ben Barka affair. Mehdi Ben Barka, a Moroccan trade-
union leader, "disappeared" from the pavement outside the Drugstore Saint-
Germain in October 1965 and, despite presidential promises and unending
imbroglios, no trace of him was ever found again.

[2] René-Marill Albérès, "Drôles de Drames", *Les Nouvelles littéraires*, 22 May
1969. Albérès's references to Perec should be treated with care; elsewhere, he
attributes *A Man Asleep* to Jean-Claude Hémery and in several places confuses it
with *Things*.

you, all he added by way of explanation was that the play had been written for radio, never mentioning that it had been written for *German* radio. Perec even pretended to Suzanne's paramour, Regis Henrion, that he knew nothing at all about Germany, and prodded him with questions about Hegel and Goethe. Perec was much more forthcoming about his time capsules, though not everyone to whom he described the project grasped that the most important part of it was the transcription of memories of childhood and adolescence. In 1969 Perec presented himself as a man of formulas, of defences, of alphabetic constraints in prose. He did not attempt to compete with his fellow-Oulipian Jacques Roubaud, who was engaged at that time in rule-governed poetic adventures, amongst them, the creation with Octavio Paz, Eduardo Sanguinetti, and Charles Tomlinson, of a multilingual European renga, or chain-poem.

Artur Adamov, the absurdist playwright whom Perec had dismissed long before as *an intellectual idiot*, spent the summer of 1969 at the Moulin d'Andé. His most recent play also had an alphabetic title: *M le Modéré* ("M the Moderate"), an answer to Fritz Lang's film *M* (or *Dein Mörder sieht dich an* ["Your Murderer is Looking at You"]), called *M le Maudit* ("M the Accursed") in French. It is not likely that Perec read it.

Georges Perec, "J'aime, je n'aime pas", *L'Arc* no. 76 (1979), p. 39 (Ray Bradbury); "Histoire du lipogramme", *Les Lettres nouvelles*, June 1969, pp. 15–30, reprinted as "History of the Lipogram" in Warren F. Motte, Jr., *Oulipo. A Primer of Potential Literature* (London and Lincoln: Nebraska University Press, 1986), pp. 97–108; "Les Horreurs de la guerre", *Union des écrivains*, no. 1 (1969), reprinted in *OCR* 111–114.

Letter from Georges Perec to Bernard Mirabel, 10 June 1969; FP57, 30 (28 March 1970).

Michel Rybalka, review of *A Man Asleep*, *French Review* no. 41 (February 1968), p. 586–587.

Reception of *La Disparition*: *L'Express*, 28 April 1969; *Les Echos*, 9 May; *Les Lettres françaises*, 4 June; *Le Figaro littéraire*, 9 June; and the Albérès review quoted above.

Roubaud et al.'s *Renga* was written in April 1969 and published in French in 1971 by Gallimard, and in an English version (by Charles Tomlinson) in 1972 by George Braziller, New York. The press file of Artur Adamov's *M le Modéré* is AL 4° Sw 2367.

Tony Augarde, *The Oxford Book of Word Games* (Oxford and New York: Oxford University Press, 1986), p. 129, gives English examples of "alphabetic dramas". Susan Glover's unpublished B.A. thesis (University of Manchester, 1989) describes the palindrome-reading experiment.

Other information used in this chapter was supplied by Marcel Cuvelier, Philippe Drogoz, Jean-Pierre Garcette, Michelle Georges, Jacqueline de Guitaut, Regis Henrion, Cyrille Koupernik, Suzanne Lipinska, Harry Mathews, Maurice Pons and Jacques Roubaud.

CHAPTER 44

The Constraint of Time

1969

Quite apart from his anguish at Andé, Perec felt profoundly liberated by the constraints he now imposed on his writing, and his creative confidence grew in the spring and summer of 1969. Winter crises had by now become almost as regular for Perec (1956–57, 1961–62, 1964–65, 1967–68, 1968–69) as the budding of trees in May; his seasonal mood swings make his writing look in retrospect like the fruit of nature's own rhythm.

Because alphabetic constraints affect the basic, individually mean-ingless building-blocks of writing, they can function as defences against emotion. If pushed to the limit, however, as in the lipogram and the palindrome, they may go into reverse, or through the look-ing-glass. They did precisely that in Perec's case, forcing out of him things he would not have easily admitted to having – things like imagination, anger, cruelty, and poetic genius. Perec's radio work with Helmle had acquainted him in technical ways with another kind of constraint not unrelated to poetry: the constraint of timing, and of time. In the course of writing *L'Augmentation* for translation, in April or May 1969, Perec realised that time could also be taken as a quasi-Oulipian device. The passage of time is the theme of *L'Augmentation*, not its constitutive form (except insofar as time is constitutive of any play in performance), and time's passing was intended to be a constituent of the book that was to come out of the 12 x 12 places project; it seems quite logical (again, with hindsight) that Perec should therefore think that he might also *use* time, instead of just suffering it, as a literary constraint.

Berthe Chavranski, Henri's mother, who had looked after Jojo for a whole year at Villard-de-Lans, fell ill with cancer and passed away within a month, on 5 April 1969, at her nephew Paul Bienenfeld's clinic, Les Abeilles ("The Bees", after *Bienenfeld*, German for "field of bees"). Perec attended the funeral at Pantin on 8 April and met many relatives and friends of the family whom he had not seen for years. On 21 April he wrote up the event as his "memory text" for Avenue Junot, due that month.

> *Someone called Todd or Tot told me that he remembered my "having read, at Villard, on 30 August 1945, over someone's shoulder, the newspaper headline of the capitulation of Japan". The way this memory was put left me puzzled: how can you read over someone's shoulder at the age of nine? In my mind, I was running back to Berthe's villa, holding* Les Allobroges *in my hand and yelling that it was victory, or peace.*

The time-capsule project, now called *Lieux*, brought Perec back once a month to his memories, mostly of adolescence and young manhood, but also, in the case of Rue Vilin, Avenue Junot, and Rue de l'Assomption, of childhood. Whether or not *Lieux* had been begun to elicit autobiography (in a sense, it had been conceived to do the opposite, to bury it), autobiography emerged in the spring of 1969 as a dominant trend in Perec's planning, and at one moment, at least, *the only kind of writing possible* [*MO* 162]. To take stock of where he was in the evolution of a career that, from a publishing point of view, had started well and gone downhill ever since, Perec wrote a long letter to his mentor, editor, and somewhat distant friend, Maurice Nadeau. It is a remarkable essay of what might be called prospective autobibliography, posted just fourteen days before man first set foot on the moon.

After explaining how he had used his time since finishing *La Disparition*, Perec asserted that he was now on his way towards *something more ambitious:*

> *The Book, whether it be a* Remembrance of Things Past *or a* Règle du jeu *(I should probably say that ironically, but on the other hand, insofar as* La Disparition *has got me over my block and allowed me to progress, it's now or never that I can envisage without too much trepidation a project of major dimension.)*
>
> [*Jsn* 57–58]

"The Book" was to be a *vast autobiographical ensemble* in four parts, of which the last would span the time it would take to write the other three, since it would be *Lieux*, the product of the time-capsule programme, to be written only after 1980. Perec's major work in the 1970s would therefore consist of part 1, his family history (*L'Arbre*), part 2, *Lieux où j'ai dormi*, ("Places I Have Slept In") – *a kind of catalogue of my bedrooms, the meticulous description of which (including the memories attached to them) will sketch out a kind of vesperal autobiography* – and part 3, an adventure novel.

> *[This last] comes out of a childhood memory, or, to be more precise, out of a fantasy that I developed at length around the age of twelve or thirteen, during my first psychotherapy. I had forgotten it completely; it came back to me one evening in Venice, in September 1967, when I was fairly drunk, but the idea of turning it into a novel didn't arise until much later. The book is called*
>
> W
>
> *W is an island, somewhere off Tierra del Fuego. It is inhabited by a race of athletes wearing white track suits emblazoned with a big black W. That's about all I can remember. But I know that I told the story of W a great deal (in drawings and speech) and that today I can, in telling W, tell the story of my childhood.*
>
> [*Jsn* 61–62]

Perec proposed to write this third book first, and to write it *in time*, as a fortnightly serial for *La Quinzaine littéraire*. He explained to the no doubt bemused Nadeau that he wanted time to play the same role for *W* that the absence of *e* had played for *La Disparition* [*Jsn* 65]. He still found writing difficult, he complained; he needed a spur, a stimulus, a constraint to get him going. He surmised that once he had started, he might not need the time constraint for the rest of the book.

The day after he wrote this nine-page letter to Nadeau, Perec got down to work on PALF with Marcel Benabou [*CGP III* 22]. Over the following weeks (interrupted by two radio interviews, neither of them about *La Disparition*) he sketched out various narrative tracks to get a narrator or a hero to an island off South America [*CGP II* 125–131]. Should his character travel Jules Verne-style, by hot-air balloon? Or by yacht, à la Raymond Roussel? Should there be a shipwreck off Cape Horn? Or should the story begin more simply, with a history of the island community? As he had said in his letter to Nadeau, there were many possible points of departure, but none of them seemed quite right. Perec fell back onto his original idea of serial publication. It was a risk, but the pressure would make it easier for him to get into stride: he was like a tightrope walker who stumbled only when on flat ground.

Georges and Paulette now finally agreed to split up, and in the summer of 1969, Perec set about finding a new flat. When he inspected an artist's studio in the twelfth arrondissement that had been recommended by Alberto, he took along his "business adviser", a chain-smoking, wrinkle-faced lady with an Eastern European accent. Esther played up to her designated role for Alberto, at least, tapping the clapboard walls with her knuckles and exclaiming, "No, no, no! Put your money into bricks and mortar instead!"

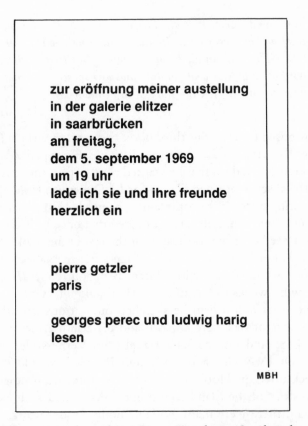

zur eröffnung meiner austellung
in der galerie elitzer
in saarbrücken
am freitag,
dem 5. september 1969
um 19 uhr
lade ich sie und ihre freunde
herzlich ein

pierre getzler
paris

georges perec und ludwig harig
lesen

MBH

In September 1969, after taking Pierre Getzler to Saarbrücken, Perec made a longer trip to Carros, where, on or before 17 September, he had a most curious dream involving a dinner outing with initially faceless friends. In the car one of the friends turns round to speak to the dreamer in the back seat, revealing himself to be the poet Jean

Cayrol, whom Perec respected greatly, not least as the author of the script of Alain Resnais's film *Night and Fog*. In the ensuing dream-narrative, Perec talks to Cayrol about his "first book", which the poet was supposed to have read for Le Seuil (which he may have done in reality, alongside Jean Paris). Dream-Cayrol says that he remembers it but was more impressed by another story called "The Father" – a text which dream-Perec cannot at first recall, but which *then suddenly appears to me to be the only text I have ever written*.

This dream – which Perec did not include in *La Boutique obscure* ("The Darkshop") even though he had already begun to keep the dream-log that would eventually produce that uniquely fascinating book – may be the key to one of the more puzzling "mistakes" in Perec's published work. The "first book" referred to in it – the first one submitted to a publisher, at any rate, and submitted to Le Seuil specifically – must be *L'Attentat de Sarajevo*, which ends rather clumsily, with the narrator attempting to get Anna to shoot her faithless and opinionated husband, Branko, with a revolver he has planted in her handbag (*see* p. 179). At the time of his "first book" dream, Perec was putting together the first instalment of his serial for *La Quinzaine littéraire*; the mid-October issue would go to press before the end of September. The serial version of *W* begins just like the later book version, *W or The Memory of Childhood*, but the trailer for it on the cover page of *La Quinzaine* is decorated with a symbol that leads readers to expect a quite different kind of tale from the one Perec had begun to write. The symbol belongs – it is obvious only now – to *L'Attentat de Sarajevo*:

From October to December Perec kept to the routine of serial publication, writing a chapter a fortnight, never getting ahead of the flow of real time or behind it, despite being burdened with the lab (as ever), and with house hunting, which got him down. He had to dash over to Saarbrücken again in October for the recording of *Wucherungen*, and came up with some ideas for *Wie ein Hund* on the way back; Marcel Cuvelier's proposal to put *L'Augmentation* on stage in French, at the Gaîté-Montparnasse, must also have absorbed some of Perec's enthusiasm and energy.

Perec's German activities slipped into the serial *W* almost as self-quotations. The story begins in Germany, *near the Luxembourg border*

– in other words the Saar – and the Otto Apfelstahl whom the narrator has to meet at the Berghof Hotel is named in part for Stahlberg Verlag, the publishers of *Things*. The tone of the story's beginning owes much to Jules Verne but even more Georges Perec's own early works, since the narrator has taken the name of Gaspard Winckler, now said to be the *real name* of an autistic child lost at sea off Cape Horn.

The nature, origin and treatment of infantile autism were much in the news in the autumn of 1969, when Bruno Bettelheim's *The Empty Fortress* appeared in French translation.[1] Bettelheim's own experience of absolute deprivation at Dachau and Buchenwald was the basis for his later work with emotionally deprived children in Chicago. He argued that autistic behaviour was most often a defence against a grief so acute that it could not be grieved in any other way, and he was particularly eloquent on the special plight of the orphans of the *shoah*. They had never had a chance to grieve their parents' death properly, because, by the time it had become an established fact, it was already many years old. Grieving that has no beginning can have no end; children deprived of their parents' deaths often retreat into the "empty fortress" of their hearts, where they have no real memories, only infinite guilt. Perec may or may not have read *The Empty Fortress* in November 1969, but there can be no doubt that Bettelheim's much-publicised subject-matter, arguments and title affected the course of his major and obliquely autobiographical work in progress.

That autumn Perec also invented a new alphabet game for *Les Cahiers du Moulin*, a projected Andé journal that never got off the ground. The idea was to take a consonant, put each of the five vowel-sounds after it (thus: *Ba-bé-bi-bo-bu, Ca-cé-ci-co-cu,* and so on), and then invent a situation or story in which the sound-string (just) makes sense. Perec was pleased with the result, which he entitled *Petit Abécédaire illustré* ("Little Illustrated ABC"), and did not want to put it back in his bottom drawer when *Les Cahiers du Moulin* failed to materialise. He made a stencil of it and ran off a hundred copies, which he folded into booklets and gave out to friends and acquaintances as New Year's gifts. The method of distribution was quite informal. Perec would always have a few copies in his bag and, when

---

[1] Bruno Bettelheim, *La Forteresse vide*, transl. Roland Humery (Paris: Gallimard, 1969). Originally published in English as *The Empty Fortress* (New York: The Free Press, 1967).

he bumped into a friend on Boulevard Saint-Michel or in a café, he would say, *Hang on a tick, I've got something here*, and pull out a numbered copy of his "Abécédaire illustré". Every year thereafter, with only a few exceptions, he produced a New Year's gift (sometimes a little late) of the same general kind: alphabetic gamelets, brainteasers, sequences of (very approximate) thematic puns (the more approximate, the better, in fact). These annual exercises in contorted verbal humour were also exercises in practical bookmaking, through which Perec acquired the interests and skills that would lead him in later years to have some of his own books made by hand.

By the end of 1969, the Perecs had found two smaller flats, one for each of them. Once again Perec turned to his uncle David for a loan to help him over the move, for two Left Bank flats, however small, cost more than one in Rue du Bac. In the midst of those transactions – and, almost foreseeably, in mid-December – Perec ran into a crisis. *W* was off track. It did not become apparent to the reader of *La Quinzaine littéraire* until the mid-January issue, but the break in the tale was not just unmistakable, it was foregrounded with quite unpalatable bluntness. Beneath an altered logo, the traditional paragraph about "the story so far" read as follows:

> There was no story so far. Forget what you have read: it was a different tale, at most a prologue, or a memory so distant that what follows cannot fail to submerge it. For it is now that it all begins, now that he sets off on his search.[1]

The "new" story is set in W, but none of the devices Perec had toyed with the previous summer (a balloon, a yacht) is used to get the story from Europe to South America. Why South America, anyway? The location of W in Tierra del Fuego was part of the core memory that Perec had supposedly recovered in Venice, and it was precisely its identification as a memory of childhood that gave *W* its place in the "vast autobiographical ensemble" to which he intended to devote the next twelve years of his life. *I have forgotten what reasons I had at the age of twelve for choosing Tierra del Fuego as the site of W*, Perec wrote in 1974 [*W* 164], but it would be naive to take any of his words in the book version of *W* as the unadorned truth. Tierra del Fuego, "Land of Fire" in Spanish, is called Terre de Feu in French. *Feu* does

---

[1] *La Quinzaine littéraire*, no. 87.

not only mean "fire", however. As a child, perhaps at school, Jojo
must have been asked about his father. It would not have been polite
for teachers to refer to him as *ton père*; rather, out of respect for the
dead, a speaker of formal French in the 1950s would have asked the
little boy about his *late* father, *feu ton père*. Thus those islands near
Cape Horn are, in the mind of a French-speaking child, the "Lands
of the Dead".

Perec did not design the first break in his most important work to
date. The fracture of serial *W* between episodes 6 and 7 was more of
a minor breakdown, precipitated perhaps by the difficulty of writing
to fortnightly deadlines, perhaps by Bettelheim, or perhaps, more
prosaically, by the difficult business Perec had in hand, the business
of breaking up his own home.

The Perecs were just separating, not getting divorced. It was to be
a fresh start, not a running sore, and so they held a party to mark the
occasion. Everyone was invited to Rue du Bac for the "house-
cooling" on 27 January 1970, and about ninety people came. Philippe
Drogoz was in a miserable mood himself and remembers it as a glum
night of drinking. Members of the older generation such as Lefèbvre
and Duvignaud did not think there was much to celebrate, and left
early. Suzanne, Maurice, and a delegation from Andé dropped by, as
did a group from the lab, the playwright Romain Weingarten, the
novelist Maurice Roche, and most of the old members of La Ligne
générale who were still in circulation. Jean Mailland stayed on until
late, when something like a truth game was played. Although they
planned to remain good friends and comrades, Georges and Paulette
(she in particular) were not as unembittered as they liked to appear.

Marcel Cuvelier's production of *L'Augmentation* opened at the Gaîté
Theatre, in Montparnasse, on 26 February 1970. Perec had been to
rehearsals, and was happy to let things proceed. *I like what Cuvelier's
done with it*, he wrote to Helmle. *I think it comes over very well indeed.*
For actors Perec's play is diabolical. Written for radio, it has no body
movements and no exits or entrances to serve as cues. Even worse,
it consists of material that is repeated over and over with only minor
variations. If an actor muffs a line or gets a variation out of place, the
only way for the company to recover is to go round the loop again
to return eventually to where the error occurred. It could go on for
ever! Cuvelier drilled his small cast to perfection, and kept the play
to its radio time of sixty minutes. Since that was too short for the
main evening performance, *L'Augmentation* was put on as a theatrical

hors d'oeuvre at 6:30 P.M., allowing a ninety-minute meal-break before the nine-o'clock performance of *A Day in the Death of Joe Egg*.

Before the dress rehearsal, Perec gave five francs to a beggar who accosted him. *As if a good deed could determine the play's success!* he exclaimed in a note put into one of the envelopes of *Lieux*. In the foyer André Hugelin and Suzanne, Aunt Esther and Jean-Paul Rappeneau, and cousin Lili and Romain Weingarten all came together (for the first and probably the only time in their lives) to make a most curious Perecquian crowd.

Helmle came from Saarbrücken for the first public night, and Perec took him, along with the cast and crew, back to Ile Saint-Louis for a party at Suzanne's flat. Perec wore Esther's old marmot coat, recently retailored to fit him approximately. With his fur coat, his handbag, and his Afro hair that no bonnet could now hide, Perec in winter looked utterly unique. Maurice Roche's friend, Harry Mathews, who first met Perec around this time, thought he resembled a faun, a dormouse, or a newborn bear.[1]

At the cast party Perec beamed. He did not seek the limelight, but nor was he averse to a little glory. He seemed to take an almost sensual pleasure in his opulent, if borrowed, surroundings – for Suzanne's duplex was grander than even the grandest dreams of Jérôme and Sylvie. Perec took to refinement with natural ease, unburdened by the chips of envy that weighed on other leftish shoulders. He had, for example, acquired a genuine attachment to the brass fittings and plush curtains of Le Bar du Pont-Royal, around the corner from Rue du Bac, a few yards from Gallimard's headquarters. Perec was a regular at the "BPR", where Francis the barman allowed him (quite exceptionally) to eat and drink on tick; he enjoyed bewildering his impecunious Latin Quarter friends by making appointments to meet them in the hushed luxury of a place designed to reassure publishing executives that they, too, belonged to the *grande bourgeoisie*.

Most critics were not unkind to *L'Augmentation*. *Le Figaro* gave the production plenty of coverage; *Les Lettres françaises* gave a good account of the subject and published an interview with the author; *L'Aurore* was favourable, as were *Combat* and *La Croix*. Perec also spoke on radio about the play. There were but two blots on the critical landscape: *Le Nouvel Observateur* did not review it, and *France-Soir* panned it. "An exercise in nullity", the critic for the latter

[1] Harry Mathews, *The Orchard* (Flint, MI: Bamberger Books, 1988), p. 28.

declared. "Grotesque . . . flat-footed . . . pretentious . . . Mr Perec's
ideas about the relations between staff and their employers come from
the 1880s."[1] Of course he was wrong: Perec's knowledge of the
relations between himself and his employer, the CNRS, was bang up
to date. The unfairness of it hurt him, as it hurt the play, which
closed after only four weeks. It left Perec feeling battered and angry.
His next memory text (allegedly relating to Avenue Junot) must have
seemed as good a place as any to vent his spleen, since it would be
put in an envelope and sealed for ten years.

He was angry with Roland Barthes, whose refusal to read *La Disparition* made him feel like a clown, with no right to aspire to being a
Roussel or a Queneau, and even less a Leiris: *Leiris will never read me.*
Perec's rare moment of anger is barely distinguishable from self-
hatred; he tells himself that he is an envious and nasty fool, that what
keeps him awake at night is jealousy of Sollers, of Le Clézio, even of
Jacques Roubaud. *I cannot stand being scorned or ignored, nor failing,
obviously; I was better off before (before* Things*); at least I kept up the
fight; I had fantastic luck; and now?*

Perec knew even whilst he was scribbling his jealousy text that it
was no more than an unfaithful quotation from Thomas Mann (from
Die Schwere Stunde ["The Difficult Hour"], in which a half-imaginary
Schiller curses Goethe for finding everything so easy). His ability
to be angry, self-accusing, sincere, and self-aware simultaneously is
admirable, if a little alarming.

It was whilst *L'Augmentation* was still running that Perec moved into
his new Paris quarters, a two-room flat in fashionable Rue de Seine
that had been redecorated and furnished in a style recommended by
Suzanne. (Paulette moved to Rue des Boulangers, not far from the
Jardin des Plantes.) As he now had to repay the loan from his uncle
David, Perec was in need of cash. However, with a run that lasted
only four weeks, *L'Augmentation* earned him very little, and he was
paid nothing at all for the serial version of *W*, as it was running in
Nadeau's *Quinzaine*; and he would have been lucky to earn one more
franc from *La Disparition* than the sum total of *e*s he had put in it.
Perec thought of doing another film script for Jean-Paul Rappeneau
(the draft, apparently an adaptation of a story by Arthur Schnitzler,

---

[1] Jean Dutourd, review of *L'Augmentation*, *France-Soir*, 4 March 1970.

was entitled *Les Grandes Eaux* ["Floodwaters" or "Washouts"]), but he put the typescript and the covering letter, penned on the day of his house-cooling party, into his bottom drawer.

Soon after moving to Rue de Seine, however, Perec encountered Med Hondo, a radio producer and writer from Mauritius, who had a different kind of money-spinner to offer him: a comic radio serial for the broadcasting service of the Ivory Coast, sponsored by the Eveready electrical battery firm. Perec jumped at the chance and used it to have as much fun as he could whilst also earning a very decent fee. The first episode of *Les Extraordinaires Aventures de Monsieur Eveready* ("The Extraordinary Adventures of Mr Eveready") was broadcast by Radio-Abidjan on 15 April 1970, and every day thereafter (except Sundays) until 31 October Ivorians were treated to a 15-minute stint of lunatic adventures featuring "Mr Eveready", a bright spark who tackles every obstacle by throwing light onto it with his battery-powered torch. Perec's script stumbled only once, when a battery runs flat and – o horror! – the boy-hero Antoine (unashamedly modelled on Hergé's sexless teenager Tintin) strikes a match. But once he was in his stride, Perec's imagination took flight on the back of Dumas, Jules Verne, strip cartoons, and the works of Georges Perec. In *Eveready* Perec reused names and whole passages as well as themes from his earlier and concurrent works: episode 54, for example, begins with the first line of *L'Augmentation*; in episode 59 Antoine and the professor set off for New York on board the *Commandant-Crubellier*, the same ship that bears Jérôme and Sylvie to Tunis in *Things*; episode 142 is set in Azincourt, where Augustus B. Clifford (from *La Disparition*) is still in residence. Perec pasted in personal memories, too (parachuting, in episode 102), and collaged work in progress (Hugh Canterel and Geoffrey Barton in *Eveready* 145 must be related to Hugh Barton in serial *W*, second instalment). The "extraordinary adventures" also take the small cast to places that Perec had seen with his own eyes: a hotel at the corner of Lexington and Ninety-Sixth Street in New York, a conference centre in Venice, and the kingdom of Oulipia.

It is hard to imagine what Ivorians listening to Radio-Abidjan would have made of Perec's in-jokes. One of the first exclamations that is heard in Oulipo-speak (in episode 47) is *Esartunilapo li va hé!*, a nonsense string consisting (at the start) of the nine commonest letters of the French alphabet, in rank order (ESARTUNIL). The language of Mr Eveready's Oulipia (a kingdom in constant conflict with neighbouring Flasterland, where they speak double-Dutch) contains expressions such as *Niégoche* (as in Njegoš, the Serbian poet-prince and the subject of Žarko Vidović's research) and *Radom* (the name of a small town in Poland, not far from Lubartów), and insults made of the names of Perec's friends from ENS and the Moulin d'Andé: *Pouillou! Badiou! Binabou! Dourou! Balibar!* Old favourites such as Professor Burnachs and future characters such as Gromeck are also featured, as is a tunnel that leads back to *Le Condottiere*.

The recordings of *Eveready* were done in Paris with a very small cast and hilariously amateur sound-effects. In later years, when coming back to his flat after a night out, Perec would often put on one of the Abidjan tapes and start chuckling even before the jingle gave way to one or another of his old jokes.

Perec needed the money from Radio-Abidjan for perfectly mundane reasons, but he spent at least part of it, by decision, on sampling better cuisine than Andé normally offered. At Andé, meanwhile, now that Alberto had gone back to Argentina, Perec took his turns in the kitchen again. Philippe Drogoz was amazed, and amused, on one of his few visits to Andé, to see Perec in an apron, directing the use of communal pots and pans.

Perec wrote *Eveready* at the same time as the second half of serial *W*. He produced *W* fortnightly, never before time, and with increasing reluctance, while he turned out *Eveready* in facile bursts. As a rule, Perec did not like to type up the latter on the IBM golf-ball machine in the lab. He used CNRS facilities for his "big" works, which he believed were entitled to research support just like scientific experiments, but *Eveready* clearly had no claim on public resources. He therefore spent many evenings at the Bienenfeld *bureau*, still at 62 Rue Lafayette, where Lili, who was now helping to run the JBSA, also helped Perec to type *Eveready* on the company machine. *Eveready* was business, even if it *was* an Oulipian mixture of *The Adventures of Tintin*, *The Goon Show*, and *Round The Horne*.

W was a more serious work by far, but Perec enjoyed writing it far less. After changing track in January, he wrote slow, obsessive, and ponderous descriptions of his island community founded on the Olympic ideal. With each episode he found it harder to stop the shadow of the concentration camps from becoming too dense. There was no story; Perec's readers, who had been first misled by the pistol symbol advertising episode 1 and then misled further by six episodes unrelated to what was now following on, could not see where his sport-camp description was really going. There were letters of complaint and Nadeau told Perec that it was not going well. It is unlikely that Perec did not know it himself. Breakdown loomed yet again, but so did the 1970 film festival at Cannes, whither Perec set off, in the first days of May, for a different kind of break.

Georges Perec. "Petite histoire d'un texte source", in Italo Calvino, *Piccolo sillabario illustrato* (Paris: La Bibliothèque oulipienne no. 6, 1977).

FP 57,7 (21 April 1969, the memory of Villard), 57, 17 (18 September 1969, the "Cayrol dream"), 57, 26 (includes a list of guests at the "house-cooling"), 57, 30 (28 March 1970, anger), 57, 33 (25 June 1970, first night of *L'Augmentation*), 119, 31 (text of *Eveready*).

Letter from Georges Perec to Eugen Helmle, 16 February 1970.

Reception of *L'Augmentation*: in *Le Figaro*, advance notice on 16 February, 1970; Perec's own description of the play (later printed on the back cover of *Théâtre I*, in 1980) together with his acknowledgment of the roles played by Jacques Perriault, Eugen Helmle and Johann-Maria Kamps in its invention, on 21 February; photographs of the cast and director on 23 February; and favourable reviews by Claude Baignères on 4 March and by Jacques Lemarchand (in *Le Figaro littéraire*) on 6 March. In *Les Lettres françaises*, interview (by Colette Godard) and review stressing the play's pathos, on 25 February; *L'Aurore* on 4 March, *Combat* on 10 March, *La Croix* on 22 March are all more or less favourable. Robert Kanters, in *L'Express* on 16 March, thought the play too long. Perec also had a five-minute slot in the radio magazine programme *Une Semaine à Paris*, broadcast on France-Culture on 8 March, and all of thirty minutes on *Les Matinées de France Culture* broadcast on 27 March, too late to save the play.

This chapter is also partly based on the recollections of Ela Bienenfeld, Catherine Binet, Alberto Carlinsky, Philippe Drogoz, Jean Duvignaud, Eugen Helmle, Jean Mailland, Francis Moaty, Maurice Nadeau and Jacques Roubaud.

CHAPTER 45

I Remember

1970

Sometime in the first part of 1970, perhaps when he called at *La Quinzaine littéraire* with another instalment of *W*, Perec was given a copy of the proofs of the French translation of *The Conversions*, by Harry Mathews, due to appear in the Lettres Nouvelles collection later that year. Perec read it and was entranced. He knew how much fan mail could mean to a writer, so he wrote to Mathews straight-away. Mathews recalls:

> I answered his letter, and we soon arranged a meeting, which took place in the Bar du Pont-Royal, an agreeable place much frequented by writers and publishers. We drank together, and went on to have dinner, and I thus entered into the most exhilarating, hilarious, intense, and satisfying relationship I have ever known with a man, and doubtless will ever know.[1]

Harry Mathews had read nothing by Perec, but he lied to him and said: "Je n'ai lu de toi que *Les Choses*" ("All I've read of yours is *Things*").[2] He knew of Perec's reputation through Maurice Roche and was predisposed to find the man at the BPR witty, clever, and audacious. The real Perec did indeed turn out to be funny. He drank five neat glasses of Wyborowka at the Bar du Pont-Royal and then took Mathews for dinner at the Chope d'Orsay, where they both got even drunker on wine.[3] Beneath his gaiety, Perec was in despair.

> Georges Perec wore a comic goatee that made him look like a silly scientist in the comics. His complexion was rough and peppered with warts. When I first met him he used to speak with one hand in front of his mouth to hide his disreputable

---

[1] Harry Mathews, "Autobiography", in *The Way Home. Collected Longer Prose* (London: Atlas Press, 1989), p. 139.

[2] Harry Mathews, *The Orchard* (Flint, MI: Bamberger Press, 1988), p. 1

[3] Ibid., p. 7

teeth. Wiry hair swelled about his head like a disintegrating bird's nest . . .

When we met in 1970, our lives were at an ebb, professionally and privately. Georges was more obviously depressed; I maintained an air of confidence as though my life depended on it. In admitting his suffering, Georges was the wiser.[1]

Perec's life was painful enough, and his problem with *W* was no trivial matter, either. The challenge he had set himself was to tell the story of his childhood by retelling his childhood story of an Olympic island. By May 1970, when he went to Carros for the film festival, it was not clear that he had pulled it off, or that he ever could. The serial written for *La Quinzaine littéraire* was no more like his childhood fantasy than his fantasy was like his childhood [*W* 7]. However, the project was supposed to be the third leg of his four-part "autobiographical ensemble". In 1969 and 1970, *Lieux* caused him to dredge up a great number of real childhood memories, to add to the information he had gathered for *L'Arbre*. Now, as Perec sat on the train going south along the same tracks on which he had travelled north with his cousin Henri twenty-four years before, it occurred to him that the story of W and the story of his childhood had to be brought together, and he jotted down the following plan:

CARROS MAY 1970	ON THE TRAIN
W or the Memory of childhood	
1: W for Robert Antelme	
2: for E	
3: for S	
3 Venice the Congress	
J. Bloch-Michel spoke about the Resistance	
A first memory: drawings of unmasted boats	
life without moorings: block	
The Plan	
memory returns	
Its formulation?	
The serial	

[1] Harry Mathews, "Autobiography", in *The Way Home. Collected Longer Prose* (London: Atlas Press, 1989), p. 140.

The first effect of this long-prepared conjunction was to bring writing to a halt. There was no instalment ready for the mid-May issue of *La Quinzaine*, and instalment 16 – the cruel chapter on organised rape, chapter 28 of *W or The Memory of Childhood* – did not appear until June. Perec had sketched out a triple structure: the first part, dedicated to the author of *L'Espèce humaine*, the one book about concentration camps that for Perec was fundamental, would be the story of W; the second part, dedicated to "E", probably Esther, was unspecified but would presumably correspond to the new second half of the title, the "Memory of Childhood"; and the third part, dedicated to Suzanne, would be concerned, as the notes labelled "3" indicate, with how the book itself had been written. That was a lesson that had already emerged from the "places" project: the insertion of time into writing put "metalanguage" – writing about writing – into the foreground. At Carros Perec did not manage to launch into the three-part book he had just invented:

> *I can play patience for hours instead of writing* W.
>
> *I am trying to specify the mechanisms of this kind of block – what fascinates me about it (not about patience but about the fact that I can wait for hours without writing).*
>
> *A whole chapter of the future* W *ought to be devoted to the difficulties I have had in writing the story.* [MO 118]

It may have been at Carros, or shortly after his stay there, that Perec wrote out a more elaborate plan for the new book. At any rate, something happened in May that got the serial going again, to the extent that what with the ten days he spent each month on *Eveready*, he now had no time at all to work on his projected next radio play, *Wie ein Hund*. Perec wrote ahead of himself in June and early July, and the nineteenth and final episode of *W* appeared in the August issue of *La Quinzaine*.

The plan that had perhaps got Perec's parable on the move again is laid out on page 451.[1] Column A lists the nineteen instalments of the serial that were published in *La Quinzaine*. Columns B and C are fractured by the same line that separates the first six "Gaspard Winckler" instalments of the serial from the exploration of the island of W. Column B contains in summary form many of the recollections that Perec had already written out for *Lieux* and hidden away in sealed

---

[1] *MO* 150 is a photographic reproduction of the original.

A: W	B: M of C	C: Intertext
1 Prologue	2 My birth	3 The irrecuperable
4 The letter	5 My father	6 Old texts 1
7 Otto A.	8 The Peretzes	9 Old texts 2
10 Gaspard 1	11 My mother	12 Photos 1
13 Gaspard 2	14 The Szulewiczes	15 Photos 2
16 The mission	17 Childhood in Paris	18 Venice
19 W 1	20 Departure	21 Psychotherapy
22 The villages	23 Villard 1	24 Drawings
25 The heats	26 Collège Turenne 1	27 Interpretations
28 Victories	29 Collège Turenne 2	30 The break
31 Names	32 From Villard to Lans	33 Difficulties in writing
34 Defeats	35 At Villard	36 Letter to Nadeau
37 Spartakiads	38 The end of the war	39 Notes
40 Women	41 Return to Paris	42 Sport
43 Atlantiads	44 Discoveries	45 Drawings 2
46 Children	47 Running away	48 Ψ analysis
49 Novices	50 Dolto and W	51 Writing
52 Officials and pack-mules	53 At my father's grave	54 Osmosis
55 The world of W	56 ?	57 *Mise en place, mise en page*

envelopes. Column C outlines the story of the book's writing to date, and it this account of the difficulty of creation that "belongs" to Suzanne. In calling it the intertext, Perec borrowed a modish term from literary theory, but his intended meaning had little to do with common notions of "intertextuality". The third section or series would link the first two, like a "metafiction" or, more plainly, a commentary on how the book came to be.

The original flap copy of *W or The Memory of Childhood* states,

> *In this book there are two texts which simply alternate: you might almost believe they had nothing in common, but they are in fact inextricably bound up with each other, as though neither could exist on its own, as though it was only their coming together, the distant light they cast on each other, that could make apparent what is never quite said in the one, never quite said in the other, but said only in their fragile overlapping.*[1]

Whatever interpretations are put on Perec's pointer towards a "third book" in the "fragile overlapping" of his two texts, it is clear what the "third book" was planned to be at the beginning: the history of the book's own composition, much of which is in fact included, mostly by means of digressions, in the "memory" chapters of the published text.

At the end of July Perec went with Paulette for a weekend with Marie-Noëlle Thibault and her family at Annecy. It was an excuse to spend some of the *Eveready* money on fine food, for the Thibaults lived within striking distance of one of the most celebrated restaurants in Europe, chez le Père Bise, at Tailloires, a lakeside dream patronised by presidents and princes. The luxury of the Thibault family's house also plunged Perec into reflections on his own disinheritance:

> *The floor tiles of the W.C. would by themselves suffice to root one's existence, to justify a memory, to found a whole tradition – and it's not just a game of words [. . .] that makes wandering my principal subject* (Les Errants, *the title of my first book, the unmasted boats, etc.), wandering and its opposite, the search for places.*

The pretext for this piece of self-pity was, precisely, the "places" programme, which required a memory of Rue Vilin in that month. Perec proceeded to go over his memory of the first Hebrew letter he

---

[1] Printed after the title page in the British and American editions.

had deciphered as a child, a vignette he had explored at some length the year before, in the first Rue Vilin memory envelope. In 1969, Perec remembered a shape that looked quite like a **ת**, or tav, the last letter of the Hebrew alphabet, with its legs the wrong way round:

The shape recalled in 1970 is still much the same

In 1969 Perec could not remember whether the letter was called a daleth, a gimmel or a yod (it is none of these); in 1970 he speculated that he had wanted to call it a yod to pun on *youd* (*Jud*, the Yiddish word for "Jew").

The "memory of Vilin" gives way to a day-dream of a somewhat different kind.

> *The war has happened, and twenty years have passed (they have wiped everything out, obviously) and one day, quite by chance, my train stops at Saint-Pierre-du-Vauvray. I get off (I recall that I used to come often in times past), I think I even recognise the station, and the way . . . I get to the Moulin; it is lived in by strangers who are polite, hardly hostile, indifferent, they don't know. No one remembers S., or her children, or anything.*

Perec had already written the last instalment of *W* and had appended to it the following convoluted announcement:

> *I should like to thank Maurice Nadeau and* La Quinzaine littéraire *for having made room for this enterprise, and for having thereby shared its risks with me. I would like the journal and its readers to know that by entering on that irreversible path with me they have allowed me to progress in what is for me a difficult exploration of a project now sufficiently advanced to make fortnightly publication no longer necessary, and to permit me to go so far as to announce the*

forthcoming development of these texts under the title W *or* The Memory of Childhood, *to appear next year.*

He got down to work on it the day after the August issue of *La Quinzaine* appeared. Committing himself publicly was not a wise thing to do; he got stuck on his fourth post-*Things* book before he even began:

> *Where to begin? Almost despairing of an answer, I ended up finding a photograph album in my files, from which I took out the seven oldest. I examined them at length, even enlarging some of the details with a weaver's glass, and then I went to watch athletics on the television.*

The fresh notebook in which Perec down jotted this account of the first steps in the writing of his autobiography, as well as descriptions of the seven photographs themselves (the same ones that are described in the final text of *W or The Memory of Childhood*), was not used again until 7 September. In the intervening weeks Perec worked on PALF with Marcel Benabou [*CGP III* 64–84], dashed off more episodes of *Eveready* (whose plot was now firmly engaged in the struggle between Oulipia and Flasterland), played table-tennis, watched television, and sat in the umpire's high chair at Andé, where he got to know Stella Baruk, a mathematician who was a useful addition to the bridge-playing fraternity. *Our names are the same*, he told her, misapplying entirely a curiosity that Benabou had come across in his academic work (a reference to late Latin transcriptions of Hebrew *Barukh* as Barek, Berek, and Perec, on lumps of stone, somewhere in the Middle East). In September Perec joined Suzanne, Maurice, and Michelle Georges at Carros again and tried to get back to autobiography. The first new section due to be written, chapter 2 of the fifty-seven-part plan, was headed "My birth".

> *I was born on 7.3.36. How many dozens, how many hundreds of times have I written that sentence? I've no idea. I know that I started early on, well before the plan to write an autobiography took shape. I turned it into the material of a bad novel called* J'avance masqué *and of a story that was equally lousy (and was moreover just a poor reworking of the preceding one) called* Gradus ad Parnassum.
> *It can be noticed that such a sentence is complete, forms a whole.*
> *It is difficult to imagine a text beginning:*

I was born
On the other hand you can stop as soon as the date is given:
I was born on 7 March 1936. Full stop.
Which is what I have been doing for several months! It's also
what I have been doing for thirty-four and a half years, to the
day!
Usually, you go on. It's a fine start, which calls for more
details, lots of details, a whole story.
I was born on 25 December 0000. My father, so they say, was
a carpenter. Shortly after my birth, the Gentiles became less
gentle, and we had to flee to Egypt. That is how I learnt I
was Jewish, and in those dramatic circumstances lies the origin
of my firm decision not to remain so. The rest is history.

[*Jsn* 9–10]

Humour was only half a way out of the difficulty. Research was also needed, and Carros was hardly conducive to that. The question was not Why should I go on?, nor even Why am I not managing to go on?, Perec noted, but simply How to go on? He picked up books (amongst them Marcia Davenport's autobiography and the *Diary of Anne Frank*); he looked at articles on behaviour in the concentration camps, which he had had photocopied for him through the lab; he lit a cigarette, wandered around the rim of the pool without really meaning to go for a swim, played patience, twanged the strings of the grand piano, reread a bit of an old newspaper, had a shave, had a beer, wasted time, and wasted it most subtly (as he wrote, in a Talmudic pirouette) by writing out a list of all the ways in which he was wasting time, as in this sentence. Well, he continued as he wrote to himself, most authors of autobiographies gave some details about their parents and about the circumstances surrounding their birth. He would have to look a few things up. For a long time he had thought that Hitler had invaded Poland on 7 March 1936, but he had been wrong either about the date or about the country. *Sudetenland, Anschluss, or Danzig, or Saarland – I know all this history very badly, even though it was vital for me,* he confessed. In Paris, later that month, he spent a few hours at the Bibliothèque Nationale, copying out some of the headlines in French newspapers for 7 and 8 March 1936. He learnt that his birth had coincided with the Paris premiere of Charlie Chaplin's *Modern Times*, a film whose significance was such that Jean-Paul Sartre had named his postwar periodical, *Les Temps modernes*, after it. Perec *didn't like* Charlie Chaplin.

I am perhaps backing off from a task of daunting size: from
unravelling the skein once again right to the end, from shutting
myself up for I don't know how many weeks, months or years
(twelve years, if I stick to the rule laid down for Lieux*) in the closed*
world of my memories, from chewing that cud until I'm gorged, or
sick with it.   [Jsn 14]

On 7 September he wrote out another summary of his memories of
his father, of his mother, of Rue Vilin, of Villard, up to his return to
Gare de Lyon in 1945. He did not use the notebook again for a
fortnight.

On 19 September 1970 Perec wrote another brief life of his father,
the text described on page 41 of *W or The Memory of Childhood* as
rather less good than the biography written *fifteen years earlier*. Better
or worse, it is more digressive than the early text printed in bold on
pages 27–29 of Perec's published autobiography[1] and it tails off into
a comparison between Perec's father and Franz Kafka.

Isie Perec and Franz Kafka are two Central European Jews; they
are roughly the same age.[2] *Franz Kafka was probably better dressed.*
    They have a similar expression on their lips, a similar smile, a
similar way of looking. On the other hand their hair is different.
                                                        [CGP II 169]

It was with these thoughts about family resemblances that *W or The*
Memory of Childhood came, for the time being at least, to a stop.

On 7 September he wrote out another summary of his memories of

Four weeks later Perec boarded the now familiar train from Gare de
l'Est to Saarbrücken, where he was picked up at the station by Ludwig
Harig, in the role of chauffeur, and Eugen Helmle, who, like Perec,
could not drive a car. Their destination was Hof, a small town in
Germany at the dead centre of continental Europe, and in 1970 a dead
end, up against the Iron Curtain. Claus Henneberg, a local man of
letters whose Verlag für Neue Literatur had just brought out *Quel*
Petit Vélo in Helmle's translation, was seeking to wake Hof from its
provincial slumber with a "Festival of New Literature", and his

---

[1] No material trace of this earlier text has been found in Perec's papers. See
p. 153 above on the probable date of its composition, and also pp. 545–555
below.

[2] The same age on the photographs that Perec had to hand.

French author was to be the star of the show. Perec sat on the platform, with Ludwig Harig to his left and Eugen Helmle on his right (or perhaps it was the other way round: Perec still could not tell one hand from the other). Just like a prisoner, he joked, between two Gestapo agents. East of the Rhine, Perec enjoyed taking wit to the brink of bad taste. Happily, Ludwig and Eugen both had a sturdy sense of humour.

At Hof Perec went to see the obligatory sight, the view from a local hill-top tavern which embraced *something that was West Germany, something that was East Germany and something that was Czechoslovakia: a single dull and gloomy expanse, as it happened, with a few copses in it* [*EsEs* 100]. Before leaving, Perec left his mark in Henneberg's visitors' book (*see* p. 458).

Helmle and Harig must have spoken to Perec about his radio work. Where had he got to with the long-promised *Wie ein Hund*? He was having problems with it, he admitted, problems of form. Harig may have suggested he look at some of Heißenbüttel's work for a pattern of permutation to use for a collage of Kafka texts. He and Helmle also spoke of the latest thinking on radio drama. At the time of *Die Maschine,* the drama department at SR had sought to redefine *Hörspiel* as "language drama", on the grounds that language was radio's particular and exclusive medium. On reflection, however, everyone agreed that that had been a specious argument, since language in the broad sense was the medium of all forms of verbal art, from lyric poetry to lipograms. The new dramaturge at SR, Werner Klippert (Johann-Maria Kamps had moved to WDR, in Cologne), held that radio drama's specific material was *voice*. That made better sense, and SR was now looking to writers to invent *ein Theater der Stimme*, a "theatre of voice". Perec was interested. He had had nothing new on German radio for nearly a year, since *Wucherungen*, in November 1969. *Le Diable dans la bibliothèque* was unlikely to be broadcast in the near future: WDR was no more taken with it than SR had been. *Wie ein Hund* might use voices, but its main idea had nothing to do with "voice drama", and in any case it was stuck, much like his autobiography. The idea for Perec's third major German work had its origins in the discussion at Hof, and in the car, about voice.

On the Saarbrücken–Paris express on 18 October, Perec wrote out a vague plan – *seven voices, seven works, seven series of animals* – under the heading *Wie ein Hund,* and then he doodled some puns. He had no real inspiration for his Kafka piece. Back in Paris, his thoughts

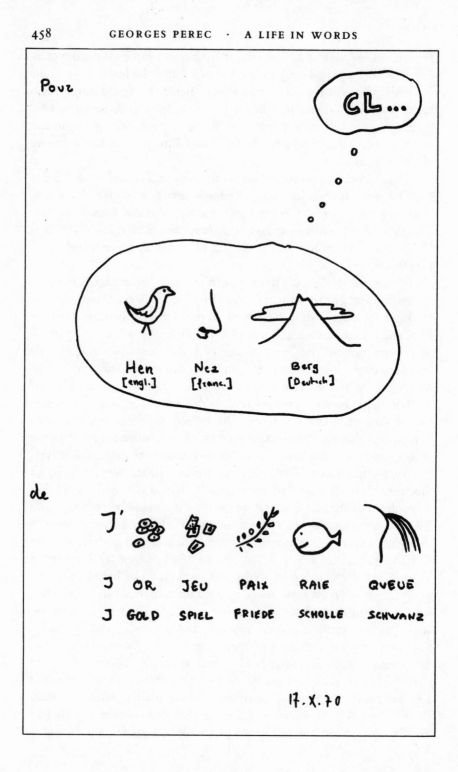

turned to the voice play for SR. Philippe Drogoz had just put the *Petit Abécédaire illustré* to music, off his own bat, and Perec was quite delighted with the gift. He asked Drogoz if he would like to collaborate with him on a new German radio play, for a fee. Yes, indeed! said the composer. *Tagstimmen* ("Day Voices"), was invented, proposed to SR, and accepted before the year was out.

Perec had several other projects more or less vaguely in mind in the autumn of 1970 (he wanted to make *an implausible film of A Man Asleep*, for example), but the announcement he had made in the August issue of *La Quinzaine* committed him to writing *W or The Memory of Childhood*. That had been more than a literary mistake. He was unable to make much progress on anything at all, for his life was falling apart.

> *I am not sad, it's more serious than that. I have hit a limit, a wall. How can I manage henceforth? For years I lived as best I could in lopsided places of safety that protected me from people, [. . .] getting drunk now and again so as to pour my heart out, and for the rest of the time in a rut made by lab work, heel-kicking, and mad (inconstant) hopes. Desire failing to find its point of application. Then I found it. I was swallowed up. Cannot live without her anymore.*

In a quite extraordinary leap, Perec moves on almost without transition from this frightening admission of dependence to the first hint of the great work to come, which seems, at this point, to have been already invented long before:

> *It was in January 1969, when I had just left the Moulin d'Andé, that the idea of Lieux took shape: a peg to hang on to, a false idea. Later on, I said to P. that I had described (or was about to describe) Passage Choiseul. P. took it amiss: it was one of her places. But arcades don't belong to anybody [. . .] You can buy jigsaw puzzles in arcades (I think I did so once with J.R. and straightaway constructed the synopsis of Bartlebooth) as well as cards [. . .] I am going to buy cards and jigsaws. The time has come to live Bartlebooth – not in an attic in Rue Saint-Honoré, but in the cosy cabin of Rue de Seine.*

Those were terrible times. Rue de Seine may have been a comfortable, well-lit cabin, with tasteful, 1960s decorations – a glass-topped "designer" writing desk, a decent hi-fi, a purple pineapple bedside lamp – but it was still a cabin, not a home. The corner of Boulevard Saint-Germain was often full of police vans at night, with *gardes mobiles* in helmets and shields chatting to plain-clothes colleagues at La Pergola. At the Saint-Claude, on the opposite side of the street, the waiters were not polite; once Perec got the impression that they did not want to serve him. *Because I am a Jew?* he wondered. Rue de Seine did not even have a telephone. His home was Andé, and that was even worse.

When he was at the Moulin, he would have fits of panic at night and would call Maurice to come and help him. Drunk, in a fever, in despair, Perec was a sorry sight. He would go back to Paris, find a telephone, and ring up Andé, insisting that he be put through to Suzanne, whatever the hour. On one occasion, he forced Gautier to drive him back to Andé before dawn. Perec was not exactly a wanderer in those closing months of the year; he was more like a yoyo on a string, going back and forth between Gare Saint-Lazare and Saint-Pierre-du-Vauvray.

In the daytime at Andé he played bridge with intensity and obsession, did crosswords, and worked a bit on his radio plays. There were some moments of relief, such as a day trip with Maurice, Suzanne, and Michelle to the Normandy coast to see a film shoot. Then, too, there was Harry.

Perec and Mathews made a comical pair: one squat, the other tall, one who wore his hair in a haystack, the other elegantly barbered. One worked in a lab for a pittance; the other had a private income. The handsome New Yorker attracted women in droves, whilst the black-toothed Parisian had a problem on that score. Harry had parents, he had children, he had a degree, he had a house, he could drive. From the point of view of a French-born orphan of Polish Jews with a broken marriage, no children, and no satisfactory place of his own, Harry was a being from outer space – or off a library shelf, from the section marked ROUSSEL (Raymond), or the pages of Larbaud's *A. O. Barnabooth*. But it was far from being a one-way affair. Harry had grown up in a city teeming with dark-haired, intense, and intelligent Jews of foreign origin, whom he had always suspected with mild envy of having greater inborn powers of creation than well-brought-up WASPs. Perec and Mathews each thought the other more fortunate by far, and they fell into a solid and unaffected friendship when they recognised that they both found writing impossibly hard.

It was from Harry that Perec first heard about Joe Brainard's memory exercise, recently published in New York – a whole book consisting of sentences beginning "I remember". The idea of it appealed to a writer with two memory projects in hand (the autobiography, and the time-capsule programme), and Perec took to playing "I remember" straightaway. He got people at Andé to join in. The rules that he gave for the game were that the memory had to be one that other people might also have, and it had to be of something that was no longer present. (*I'd like to put in "I remember Vidal Sassoon"*, Perec said to Michelle Georges, *but I can't because he's still going.*) These were not in fact the rules by which Joe Brainard had played, but Perec had not yet seen his book. Mathews may have come up with them himself, but they may also have been chosen by Perec as appropriate for playing "I remember" not as a writing exercise but as a kind of parlour game.

Mathews lived for most of the year in a house that he owned in the French Alps, not far from Lans-en-Vercors, just beneath the tree line to the east of the road that leads to Villard. Jojo had tramped down the same road, in the other direction, one summer's day in 1944 [*W* 128], and he must have had the house that was now Harry's in view for hours on end. Of course he accepted his friend's invitation to visit, and he went down to the Alps, his mind still not made up about Andé, in December 1970. He brought a record along as a present. Shortly after, he sent Harry a postcard from Morocco, to say thanks. Since there is no evidence that he actually went to Morocco, it seems likely that the card was probably the first of the epistolary pranks that Perec played on the man he came to think of as "dear Harry" and to address in silly phonetic spelling as *Dirari*.

Perec offered to translate Mathews's second novel, *Tlooth*, even before he had read it. *Tlooth* is not an easy book for a non-native reader of English. Mathews helped at the start, providing explanations, in French, of part of the book's structure, its puns, the rules of baseball, and other exotica. Perec took the book with him when he left Lans on 24 December to catch the train at Grenoble. The carriages were packed tight with people rushing to Paris for Christmas parties; amongst them was a once-famous, now-forgotten French writer determined to make that night's event at Andé his last.

Georges Perec, "J'aime, je n'aime pas", *L'Arc*, no.76 (1979), p. 39 (Chaplin).

FP 57, 34 (8 June 1970), 57, 37 (21 July 1970), 57, 43 (10 October 1970), 57, 91 (17 October 1972), 116, 5.

From WDR archives: readers' reports on *Le Diable dans la bibliothèque* dated 27 January and 3 February 1970. One is guarded in its judgment, the other not: "uninteresting".

Some of the material relating to the genesis of *W or The Memory of Childhood*, some of the material quoted from FP 57 and in particular the material dealing with the "Hebrew letter" has been published by Philippe Lejeune in *CGP II* and (with revisions) in *MO*, to which all subsequent studies, including this one, are indebted.

Other information from Eugen Helmle, Claus Henneberg, Harry Mathews, Marie-Noëlle Thibault, Michelle Georges, Maurice Pons, Henry Gautier, and Philippe Drogoz.

CHAPTER 46

Like a Dog

1970–April 1971

QUENEAU: In Stuttgart, they can do all the work they want to with computers. So, they feed in Kafka's vocabulary, and then get Kafka out of it. [. . .] The trouble is, Max Bense selects the sentences he wants from the output. So, so . . .
LATIS: So that wouldn't prove that he was a Jew.
DUCHATEAU: It wouldn't prove that he wasn't.

Jacques Bens, *Oulipo 1960–1963*

Another man might have taken a lace handkerchief from his cuff, dabbed at his eye and turned away from what had become a dangerous liaison. What memories remain of Perec's final departure from the Moulin d'Andé suggest that he left more like a dog. Maurice helped him bring down his typewriter and his boxes of papers from the *chambre Jeanne d'Arc* to the car. It was not a dignified departure.

Perec was not thrown out of Andé; on the contrary, Suzanne would have liked him to stay, and indeed, he had every material reason for doing so. He had no real home to go to; Rue de Seine would only ever serve as a perch. Andé was where his routines were, where he had met most of his friends, where he had partners for bridge, poker, and go, a television to watch on occasions, and a log fire to keep him warm. More prosaically, Andé gave him clean sheets and regular meals. He had seen it coming for months, if not years, and had even spelt it out on 25 April 1970:

Useless Addendum to the History of My Life

I measure my dependence on her; I think that is what shatters me most [. . .] I am shit and I deserve to have that happen to me [. . .] I cannot stand silence, indifference. Objectively, I do not know what to do: to look once again for the soul mate (soul mother, rather), a protectress, a bosom

Leaving Andé may have been a disaster for Perec in one sense, but it served an inner and imperious necessity. His pride was at stake, to be sure, and that was no trivial matter, but the issue went far deeper, to the very principle of life. He had become a worm, and an invalid to boot. He was taken to a doctor, who gave him pills to help with his nerves (on 28 December 1970), but he would have to find another way of being a man.

Work alone could not fill the gap left in Perec's life by his break from Andé. He took to dropping in, unannounced, on Stella Baruk, and from one impromptu dinner date at Le Balzar to another, he turned the conversation to the many compatible sides of their personalities. It was not long before he proposed – to be a father to Stella's two children, and to be her lover to boot. The offer was not unappealing to her. Perec was engaging, amusing, and both needful and deserving of love. They made plans to go on holiday together for part of the summer. But Stella soon had to confess to herself and to her shy suitor that the greater plan was built on sand. Perec's distress had propelled him towards her, and she wisely chose to avoid being a substitute for Suzanne. They talked it over in July and agreed that it would be better to remain just good friends.

The fracture of 1970–71 is marked clearly in *La Boutique obscure*, the book of dream-transcriptions that Perec published in 1973. Dream number 37 is dated December 1970; it is followed by three "foreign bodies", dreams supposedly dreamed by one "J.L.", dated 1966, 1968, and 1972, respectively. Perec's own dreams are taken up again in chronological sequence with dream number 41, dated January 1971. And what a sequence it is! There are no less than twenty-eight dreams related from the first four months of 1971 (compared with only forty for the preceding two and a half years), including some of the longest and most elaborate dream-form novelettes in the whole book. But it is perhaps the shortest of Perec's winter dreams that point most acutely towards the direction of this curious form of autobiography:

Number 46   *January 1971*

Concentration Camps in the Snow;

or,

Winter Sports at the Camp

Only one image remains, that of someone with shoes perhaps made of very hard snow or ice, irresistibly suggestive of a hockey puck.

Number 49   *February 1971*

M/W

In a book I am translating, I find two sentences; the first ends in "wrecking their neck", the second in "making their naked", a slang expression for stripping.

The time-capsule programme also served as a repository for Perec's dissection of his own plight, in which past and present were likewise intertwined. Into the envelope for March he slipped a timetable for 13 February 1971, a day on which he told himself to get down to composing crosswords and to rewriting *Le Condottiere*, ten years on from its last refusal by Simone de Beauvoir, just as he had promised he would. But he had lost the original text, and his musings on "*Condo bis*", begun on 6 February and pursued on 14 and again on 17 February, are more like "memory texts" than the draft of a new novel.

The finest memory text of the whole time-capsule exercise was written on 13 March, allegedly as a recollection of Rue Saint-Honoré. It is a tense and moving description of Perec's first, flawed affair with a girl, in 1959, and also a reflection on his continuing difficulties with women. He was still lumbered with the inhibitions and the "system" that had wrecked that early affair almost before it began, he reflected. Into the same envelope Perec inserted a passionate, intoxicated letter to Michel Leiris. He had just bought another copy of *Nuits sans nuits* and had reread *La Règle du jeu* many times; he wanted to meet Leiris, to talk to him, and – in a sense – to *be* him, which is presumably why he never sent the letter.

OuLiPo gave the often despairing Perec regular monthly support through the best times and the worst. Out of deference to the age and ill health of the group's cofounder, members now went to Boulogne (the Paris suburb, not the port) to eat, drink, and work around the dining table of François Le Lionnais. The three younger members – Marcel Benabou had now joined Roubaud and Perec – gasped at the size of the contribution they were expected to make to the cost, and for months they suspected that the admirable grandmaster and noble ex-deportee had become a grubbing miser in his old age. When they realised that Le Lionnais was only charging what his housekeeper charged him, the slight frost between the junior and senior Oulipians melted away.

For years OuLiPo had been planning to publish a first volume of its collective work, not in Paris, but in London, with Jonathan Cape. The idea had arisen through Queneau's contacts with Stefan Themerson,[1] the inventor of "semantic poetry", but it had never got very far. It really was time now, Queneau said, to bring the "Cape dossier" back to life. Perec was put in charge of the project, which had no title yet beyond its self-evident identification as the *dossier Ex-Cape*. At the same time, he was pursuing a parallel track that might bring new blood to the group.

> *Paris, 4 January 1971*
> *Dear Harry*
> *I've managed to carry on with* Tlooth *on my own, and I've got without too much trouble to the soirée at the Palazzo Zen; then I ran into a leg-over episode and lost the thread entirely, but I think we'll be able to get on fairly fast when we work together again.*

It is not surprising that, despite his serviceable English, Perec "lost the thread" of the passage:

> Unpleasant Stella crossed my path. Dismayed at even greet-ing her, I tried to escape by speaking crudely. "Stella, I need to get laid." She said "Let's go," and took my arm. Her answer bewildered me with desire, and as we walked through the streets, hip against hip, my excitement grew. She ceemed exsited too, by her red cheeks and quick breath. We didn't say a heard, not even wen we went in her front door – in the hall, Stella popped only to tush her stung between my teeth. Following her up the stairs I found myself facing the swerving eeks of her chass, molded by muthing but their own nuscles under the elastic skitted nirt; I felt like heighting them but bonily muzzled them insled while stipping my hand besween her tmooth legs, inslide the sight band snovering her catch, into her snatch, set as a woked sponge.[2]

---

[1] This is perhaps the origin of the erroneous claim made in *Libération* (R. Rumney, "La Mort de Stefan Themerson", 10–11 September 1988, p. 28) that Themerson was the only English member of OuLiPo.

[2] Harry Mathews, *Tlooth* (1966; reprint, Manchester and New York: Carcanet, 1987), p. 118.

The interchange of initial consonants in Mathews's "blue movie scenario" is not random but subject to incremental plotting. When Perec finally grasped how it worked, he must have felt vindicated in his supposition that Mathews had long been an Oulipian without knowing it. He would have to introduce him to the group.

An extract of the minutes of the 119th meeting of OuLiPo, held at Boulogne-sur-Seine on 12 January 1971, indicates the following:

> Present: Le Lionnais, Perec, Arnaud, Etienne, Braffort
> Action: Perec, documentation [Ex-] Cape
> Erudition: Perec, phonological translation
> Miscellaneous: next guest of honour: Mathews?

Harry would also have to meet Perec's wider circle of friends. He met Stella Baruk and Paulette; he met Philippe Drogoz and many of Perec's other, older friends. Some of them took to Harry immediately, while others wondered what Perec was up to, consorting with an American *rentier*. *Tlooth* was light-years from *Partisans*, yet less than a decade away from it in real time. The warmth that the two men brought to each other was not understood on the spot.

In the cold, gloomy months of his first winter without Andé, Perec worked most intensely not *as* a translator, but *with* one, on *Tagstimmen*. The first sketch had been done in December 1970, and the project was further developed in patches of work and in correspondence in January and February 1971. The logistics of the voice play were more complex than those of Perec's previous ventures in radio, not only because there were now three coauthors (Perec, Helmle and Drogoz) but also because music requires more rehearsal and more complicated recording arrangements than simple speech. Perec took charge of the scheduling and organised the timetables of Helmle's visit to Paris and his own trip with Drogoz to Saarbrücken. *Tagstimmen* does not really have an original manuscript, nor can it ever be translated conventionally. It exists in a Germano–musical composite form, which Perec described thus:

> *Tagstimmen does not tell a story in any ordinary sense. It is a narrative continuum, made from very simple basic material, which attempts to exploit to the limit the phonetic possibilities of language and the musical potential of the human voice.*
> *The basic material consists of proverbs, fixed phrases, and count-*

ing rhymes, used in such a way as to incorporate the greatest possible number of types of speech and forms of voice, of tonality, etc. The whole work could be summarised as telling (or rather suggesting) a day in the life of a man in a city, and, in a barely less symbolic way, the life of a man. The following table shows the play's structure, roughly:

Day	Life	Speech Types
Waking	Birth	Cries and stutters, murmurs, whispers, etc.
Morning	Childhood	Counting rhymes, recitations, information bubbles
Noon	Youth	Hullaballoo, slogans, speeches, chanting, sermons
Afternoon	Maturity?	Internal monologue, narration
Evening	Maturity!	Song
Sunset	Old age	Repetition, monologue, chant
Night	Death	Silence[1]

Performers and studios were booked in Saarbrücken from 15 to 26 March 1971. Perec and Drogoz would stay with the Helmles at Neuweiler for the duration, but they decided to go there by car so as to have their own transport for journeys to and from the studios at Halberg. On the appointed day Drogoz drove round to Rue de Seine to collect Perec. He parked the Volkswagen, went up staircase A, and rang the bell. An ashen-faced Perec opened the door, avoiding eye contact with Drogoz, who saw straightaway, and with horror, the bandages on the writer's wrists.

It's all right now, Perec said. *I've been a bit of a fool. It's nothing, really.*

Drogoz led him by the arm to the corner chemist. The razor-slits were not infected, and would heal up soon enough; no special treatment was required, just clean bandages.

During their long drive east, Perec talked about *Tagstimmen* most of the way but slipped in a few casual remarks about his "suicide". No, of course it hadn't been a real suicide attempt. No, he hadn't wanted to die, and he certainly didn't want to die now. How had he ended up with slit wrists, then? asked Drogoz. Well, he hadn't really been drunk, just pleasantly light-headed, in a mood not of gloom but

---

[1] The German text says: *Silence (Scream)*.

of exhilaration. It had struck him that it would be interesting *just to see*. *I did it just to see*: he had said that before, long before, to "explain" to Bianca why he had covered Bernard Lamblin's eyes whilst he was driving (*see* pp. 115–116). In March 1971 Perec wanted very much to make Drogoz believe that he had done nothing worse than play a boyish prank on himself. He knew he had been very foolish, and he knew he had been lucky. He had slit both wrists with an old cutthroat razor whilst standing under a hot shower. As soon as the blood had started to gush, the water had made it swirl around and seem like a flood; the visible volume of it had brought him to his senses. He had staunched the haemorrhages in the standard way, with a tourniquet on each upper arm, and then sterilised and bandaged the actual cuts. Drogoz tried to keep the conversation on a matter-of-fact plane. Did he realise he could have died? Had he any conception? Perec said he was very sorry. He had been very foolish. He wouldn't do it again. Not to worry.

The bandaged wounds could hardly be hidden from Helmle, and Perec retold the story, making light of it now that the narrative was well run in. Drogoz found a moment to take Helmle aside. It wasn't as trivial as Perec had made it seem, he informed the translator; he could easily have killed himself. Helmle also surmised that it must have been a close shave with death if hamfisted Perec had managed to tie two tourniquets on his own arms. From that time on Perec and Helmle dropped the *vous* form of address and said and wrote *tu* to each other.

Tagstimmen was rehearsed, adjusted, rerehearsed, and recorded with the speaker and the singers, then edited and mixed over the following ten days. There were the usual problems attendant on any ambitious enterprise involving more than a dozen people; they were surmounted, and the "voice drama" went on air one month later, on 28 April 1971. It was a triumph. Once again, Perec's name was attached to a reinvention of the *Hörspiel*. *Tagstimmen* was selected as the German national entry for the Italia Prize 1971, an unusual honour for a writing team that was two thirds French.[1] SR made it into a record to distribute to its staff as a New Year's present for 1972, and printed the German-language text in its yearbook. Naturally enough, SR also offered the Perec-Drogoz-Helmle consortium whatever resources it wanted for its next radio play.

---

[1] They did not win; in the end, no prize was awarded in 1971.

By March 1971 Perec was already at least a year late with the work he had promised to Johann-Maria Kamps at WDR. In doing *Tagstimmen* before *Wie ein Hund*, he broke a promise to, if not a contract with, the man who had helped him get started on *Die Maschine*. Like a boy caught with sweets in his hand, Perec was detained in Helmle's study until he wrote an explanation of his behaviour. There were two sets of reasons for his delay, Perec wrote to Kamps.

> *The first is personal: in the course of the last year I have had to make great upheavals in my living and working conditions, I have moved back to Paris, I have had to reacclimatise to new modes of living and of survival; in a word, I have not done much work, not only for lack of time but because confidence and persistence just haven't been forthcoming. It is in these somewhat tormented circumstances (following on from a long period of happiness and fertility) that the plan for* Wie ein Hund *has grown, developed, matured, and taken on the essential quality that it did not quite have at the start: it is no longer merely a commissioned work but something profoundly anchored in an inner necessity. But as the plan has become ever more personal, difficulties of a quite different order have arisen – namely difficulties that are strictly literary.*
>
> *The point of departure for* Wie ein Hund *is both extremely simple and extremely ambitious: it is an effort to penetrate the very core of Kafka's language and, by identifying certain constants and certain constraints in it, to follow the path of an idea (that is to say, of a set of words) inside the author's "head". It is not exactly a work of criticism, even if contemporary criticism often operates in that manner, but it is, quite precisely, an attempt at* appropriation.
>
> Je, *"Ich" ("I") put myself in Kafka's place and I reconstruct the very mechanism of his writing. The plan is not ridiculous in itself since the material exists (the works of Kafka) and since it has today become obvious to me that the choices I have made, the samples and sections I have performed on the Kafka corpus around a central theme (animals) and some very simple cognate themes (theatre, spatial orientation, Sundays, food), are significant, are relevant – that is, they can allow me to construct a* model *of Kafka's oeuvre, can give a* true reading *of Kafka (I'm not saying the only true reading, I am saying a* true reading *amongst all possible true readings, though it is a particular, angled reading that is simultaneously a decipherment*

of my relationship to Kafka and of my relationship to writing and a revelation of that spectacular and subterranean mechanism which is writing – the f/act of writing). [. . .]

It's only a matter of MONTAGE (of ordering), but montage is so essential in this case that I was at fault in believing that an arbitrary choice of a very rigorous structure – that of the renga[1] – would be efficient. In advance it seemed a safe bet that the combination Kafka+renga would work, but independently of the fact that I wasn't much "inspired" last year, I think it is not true. The renga is a form of collective improvisation under strong constraints supported by a tradition with no equivalent nowadays (not even in Japan!).

He had done additional unsatisfactory trials with "vertical permutations" borrowed from Heißenbüttel, and had yet to find the device that would allow him to write *Wie ein Hund*. Kamps should not expect to see it on his desk for two years at least. Two years! Perhaps Perec really meant *never*.

Perec's "Kafka problem" was not quite as separate from the difficulties in his personal life as this letter makes it seem. According to Jacques Roubaud, the three writers who provided Perec with a self-image were "Kafka, Kafka, and Franz Kafka". In 1957 Mladen Srbinović had done a portrait of Perec that Perec thought made him look like Kafka; in 1964 Getzler had taken a photograph of him in a way which Perec thought did the same. Perec often studied his copy of *Kafka par lui-même*, an illustrated introduction to the writer and his work. After flicking through the pages on 19 September 1970, he had noted:

I don't know when I first knew that my father looked like F. K. Three photographs in K par lui-même (pp. 46, 149, 160) convince me afresh each time, but it's years since I last saw a portrait of my father. [CGP II 168–169]

---

[1] "The ground rules of the renga ('connected or linked poems' or otherwise 'a chain of poems') are simple: unequal sections (links) of three lines (5–7–5 syllables) and two lines (7–7) are prepared (or improvised) successively by two or several poets, the poem thus composed presenting the following feature: any given link of the renga must form a poem along with that which precedes it and this poem must be different from that which it forms with the link which follows." (Jacques Roubaud, in Octavio Paz et al., *Renga,* [New York: George Braziller, 1972], p. 31).

Perec's self-identification with Kafka remained a powerful fantasy throughout his life, and it casts a shadow even over his identification of kith and kin. Izie does not look at all like Kafka on the photograph of him that Perec possessed, the photograph of his father in French military uniform (illustration 8). In the very poor photograph of him at the age of twenty-one (illustration 5) which Esther must have kept, since it was found again by Bianca Lamblin, there is at least something that could count as a likeness, except that it is not so much to Kafka as to Georges Perec. There are no other known photographs of Izie.

Wie ein Hund was intended to be Perec's own *Kafka par lui-même* and, by the same token, a sort of *Moi par Kafka même* – which title could also serve, in effect, as a definition of *A Man Asleep*. If Perec never returned to his projected rewriting of Kafka in German, it was partly because the idea of translating *A Man Asleep* to the screen, which had first occurred to him some months before, began to take off within a few days of his deferring *Wie ein Hund* for two years. On 31 March 1971 Perec posted a letter written on paper made in Germany, and probably taken from the desk in Helmle's study, to Maurice Pons's nephew, the young assistant film director Bernard Queysanne:

> Dear Bernard
> 1) *Have you read* A Man Asleep?
> 2) *Do you think a film can be made of it? (I do.)*
> 3) *Would you like to make a film of it?*

In the same post he sent a reminder in comic kitchen-German to "Herr Dr Professor Heinrich Walter" (that is, Henry Gautier, at the lab) to remind him that they were due to meet (*pour fressen und ripaillieren usw*) on the day of his return.

Perec and Drogoz drove back with handsome cheques in their wallets, but not before Perec spent a good part of his fee on a new hi-fi, far cheaper in Saarbrücken than it would have been in France. Drogoz did not dare smuggle it through customs, so a German employee of the radio station drove it through in his German-registered car and transferred it to the Drogoz Volkswagen at Sarreguemines, where the long-haired and jeans-clad Frenchmen put up for the night in the best hotel in town. As Perec later told the story to Helmle,

Next morning, instead of taking the main road to Metz, I persuaded Philippe to take a side road towards Nancy. Philippe agreed, because Nancy is much prettier to drive through than Metz. It added a few miles to our route, but it was early, and it was a beautiful day. And above all I wanted to go through the village of Saint-Jean-Rohrbach, since I had learnt the previous night that it was the home of General Eblé, whose exemplary life, as you know, I've been wanting to write for ages. [1]

We went through Saint-Jean-Rohrbach. There's a little statue of the general himself. I bought a postcard. And a few kilometres down the road, we were stopped by the Customs Squad!!! They didn't notice Philippe's radio, but my hi-fi got the treatment. It wasted several hours and cost me 1,000 francs (new ones!!), which is to say that the set has now cost me 2,000 francs whilst being worth only 1,400 in France. That's life.

I hope Tagstimmen *will be rebroadcast by lots of stations so I can recoup something from fate's cruel blow, and that the life of General Eblé, when I've written it, will be a best-seller!* [2]

The good humour, the jokes, the brilliant work on *Tagstimmen*, and the renewal of Perec's interest in the cinema did not mean that ten days in Germany had cured him of his despair. His suicide attempt, if perhaps something less than a sincere effort to end his life, was certainly an appeal for the affection of friends. In Paris, in early April, he took Jacques Lederer, his oldest confidant, out to dinner at the Chope d'Orsay. By chance, Harry Mathews was eating there as well. Perec went over to greet his American pal. Mathews recalls,

When he came over, he pulled up his left sleeve to reveal two parallel razor cuts. He looked like a schoolboy showing a bad report card to his parents. [3]

---

[1] Jean-Baptiste Eblé (1758–1812), an artillery specialist and hero of the Beresina. See Girod de l'Ain, *Les Grands Artilleurs. Le Général Eblé* (Paris, 1893).

[2] FP 41,1,1 is a single folded piece of listing paper marked FORTRAN DOS 16. 1.1968, containing the only known draft of *La Vie du général Eblé d'après des documents inédits*. It consists of five pencil drawings in inked rectangles – the size of large postage stamps – with decorative hand-written legends, reminiscent (as an idea, not in execution) of the postage-stamp stories of Donald Evans (see Bruce Chatwin, *What Am I Doing Here?* [London: Picador, 1990], pp. 263–268).

[3] Harry Mathews, *The Orchard* (Flint, MI: Bamberger Books, 1988), p. 8.

Harry took one look at the scars and then glared at Perec, like he was a dog. His only words were "Get some help, Georges, or get lost!"

Unpublished sources used for this chapter include FP 57, 41 ("Useless Addendum"), 57, 50 (13 March 1971), 119, 30 (*Condottiere bis*).

Letters from Georges Perec to Johann-Maria Kamps, from Neuweiler, 26 March 1971 (WDR archives, Cologne), Bernard Queysanne, Henry Gautier, and Eugen Helmle (from Paris, 19 April 1971).

ARD-Prix Italia 1971: Tagstimmen/Voix de jour, the Franco-German booklet produced to assist the judges of the main international prize for radio drama. The French text is by Georges Perec, in collaboration with Eugen Helmle.

Other information from the recollections of Stella Baruk, Philippe Drogoz, Eugen Helmle, Harry Mathews, and Maurice Pons.

CHAPTER 47

A Year in Splinters

1971–1972

I've got nothing against moving around, quite the contrary.
Why not privilege dispersion?
Georges Perec, *Espèces d'Espaces*

Harry's stone wall was not what first suggested psychoanalysis to Perec, but it must have helped to prod him into action. From his past work with Dolto and de M'Uzan, he knew that the process would be long, and from his Andé acquaintances he knew that it would be expensive. He went to see Jean-Bertrand Pontalis for an assessment interview in early May, was taken on, and had his first session the same day.

> *Psychoanalysis is really not at all like the advertisements for cures for baldness: there wasn't a "before" and an "after". There was a present of analysis, a "here and now", which began, went on, and drew to an end. I could just as well write "which took four years to begin" or "which went on ending for four years". There was no beginning and no end: long before that first session, the analysis had already begun, if only in the slow decision to undertake an analysis and in the choice of an analyst; long after the last session, the analysis continues, if only in this solitary duplication that mimics its persistence and plodding. The tense of the analysis was a stuckness in time, a time balloon: for four years there was an everydayness of analysis, a routine – little marks in a diary, work strung out through the fabric of the sessions, their regular recurrence, their rhythm.*
>
> *In the first place analysis was just that, a particular way of separating days – days on and days off – and on days on, something resembling a fold, a retreat, a warp: in the layering of hours, a suspended, alien moment, a kind of halt, a pause in the day's flow.*
>
> [PC 62–63]

What Perec does not say in the essay from which this passage is taken is that he stopped writing when he went into analysis – or, to be more precise, he stopped writing for himself, and instead dispersed his talent in a dozen collaborations of every imaginable kind. Every one of the sole-author works that Perec had in progress in 1971 – *L'Age*, *L'Arbre*, *W or The Memory of Childhood*, the history of his bedrooms, the univocalic on *e*, even the game of "I Remember" – seems to have been shelved. Perec's irregular transcription of his dreams and his monthly description and recollection of his Parisian "places" were just about the only writing habits that survived the rupture of May 1971, no doubt because they were orderly routines, not demanding imaginative projects. Perec had trained himself to wake up in middream; he kept a notepad and a felt-tip pen at his bedside table wherever he slept, and he was able to to wake, jot down an image, a note, or a narrative capsule, and go straight back to sleep again. He took his dream memories along to his sessions with Pontalis, as the sign-posts marking out Freud's "royal road to the unconscious". Pontalis, however, was sceptical:

One of my patients – let's call him Stéphane – dictated to me, in a sense, what I suggested elsewhere when referring to analysands who make you wonder, when you listen to them, whether they really experienced their dreams or whether they dreamt them on purpose as dreams and, in the end, in order to recount them. These are the "dream-makers". In Stéphane's case, I realised after a while that I wasn't "buying" the dreams he offered. Obviously, I had good reasons for my doubts: if I wasn't buying them, it was because the dreams lacked body, found an evident place in a superficial kind of language, were unpunctuated by silences and were lacking in the expression of affects, as if anguish dissolved itself in the saying and made itself felt only in the tension of the session. The dreams were, so to speak, deposited, checked off, and dealt with by Sté-phane like texts to be deciphered, like a letter certainly written in a foreign tongue but not posted in a far-off place, and bearing no specific address. Maybe he even dreamt them in the way he composed crosswords, or played patience, or solved jigsaw puzzles [. . .] or devoted himself to games of writing. It could be said of Stéphane and those like him that they are waking sleep-walkers.[1]

Awake or asleep, in a dream or just deep in thought, Perec could often be seen walking the streets of Paris in his post-Andé years. He knew the city like the back of his hand, even if, as he claimed, he could not tell which of his hands was which. Perec's cherished problem with laterality did not impinge on his command of urban space. Whilst other harassed Parisians scuttled down one-way streets in the unending search for parking spaces, Perec usually got to his rendezvous early, or at the latest on time. He would get there by metro, or by bus, or on foot, along routes fully mastered by very few even amongst expert *piétons de Paris*. When acquaintances came across the sauntering writer, he inevitably donned a mask of casual gaiety and always had time for a drink and a chat. But when Perec did not know he was being observed, his body language often told a less sanguine story. His straggly hair and Russian shirt made him visible from afar, as striking as a figure from Chagall, but his downcast gaze, sagging, asymmetric shoulders, and leaden tread were those of a lonely and sorrowful soul painted implausibly into the busy sidewalk scene.

In effect, Perec came alive for others in these difficult years, and it was for others that he now used his pen. Like a mirror image of Melville's Bartleby, he *preferred to* write whatever he was asked to do. From his return to Paris with bandaged wrists at the end of March 1971, Perec ceased to aspire to being a book-a-year man and instead took on at least one new writing project *per month*. An overview of his life and work in this period of anxious diversification can only be given in fragments.

A libretto

The main response of the French authorities to the seismic shock of May 1968 was to introduce institutional reforms in schools, universities, and the broadcasting system. The ORTF set up the Atelier de création radiophonique (ACR) as a self-governing department

---

[1] Jean-Bertrand Pontalis, "A Partir du contre-transfert: le mort et le vif entrelacés", *Nouvelle Revue de Psychanalyse*, no. 12 (Autumn 1975), pp. 81–82. Pontalis has declined to contradict the widespread assumption that "Stéphane" is Georges Perec.

charged with the task of bringing artistic innovation to the hidebound
world of French radio. Its prime mover was Alain Trutat, who knew
Perec vaguely from the *Arguments* days, in the 1950s. As a radio man,
Trutat had heard of *Die Maschine*, and he had had the French stage
production of *L'Augmentation* recorded for possible use by the ACR.
In 1971 he put a proposal to their author, and on 19 April Perec
reported a new commission to his radio prefect, Eugen Helmle:

> *I've had a little commission from Alain Trutat for a micro-opera
> with a musician by the name of Bruno Gillet. It's called* Diminu-
> endo in Grey,[1] *and it'll be performed at the Paris Biennale in
> September* [1971]. *It's a dialogue of roughly twenty minutes dwin-
> dling into silence, between a man and woman who have had an
> affair. So ist das Leben!*

An adaptation

If Perec never wrote anything just for the money, money nonetheless
sometimes served as both carrot and stick. In 1971 he was in particular
need of additional income, since his sessions with Pontalis could not
possibly be funded out of his salary as a *Technicien IIB*. By reputation,
at least, cinema promises the largest financial rewards for a scrivener,
larger than those offered by radio or theatre and certainly much
larger, page for page, than those produced by even a successful book.
Perec had been a consumer of movies in vast quantities ever since
his teens, but apart from what he may have learnt from the failed
adaptations of *Things* and his sketchy start on *Le Club* with Jean-Paul
Rappeneau, he had no notion of how to actually go about making a
film himself. Still, he was set on the idea, so he turned to some of
the young film makers he had met at the Moulin d'Andé. They had
the technical knowledge and were registered with the Centre National
de la Cinématographie (CNC), the prerequisite for a successful application for a subsidy from the CAR.[2] He had asked Bernard Queysanne if he would like to make a film of *A Man Asleep*; he soon got a
positive reply.

They began by trying to turn Perec's static second-person text into

---

[1] The work's final title was just *Diminuendo*.

[2] Except for adaptations of works by the applicant, that is. Perec was technically entitled to apply on his own behalf for a film of a novel he had written.

a conventional screen narrative, but it was an impossible task, and they soon gave up. Why not just leave the text as it is, one or the other of them asked, and have it read as a voice-over? They did not want to make another "neo-realist" movie like Ermanno Olmi's *Il Posto* ("The Job") but rather envisaged something closer to the fragmented technique of *Hiroshima mon amour*, with material not far distant from that of another black-and-white film they both admired just as much, Alain Jessua's *La Vie à l'envers* (1964; the English title is "Life Upside Down"), a slow, entrancing, terrifying portrayal of schizophrenia as seen from the inside. In the film version of *A Man Asleep*,[1] the visual images of a lonely young man in his room, washing his socks in a (pink?) plastic bowl, playing pinball, looking at his reflection in shop windows, exploring the odder corners of Paris, and so forth, would be edited out of phase with the voice-over text, to keep the viewer puzzled by the relationship between word and image, and also to say something more in the gap between the two. That would mean cutting out the self-analytical sections of the text, since the film's sole character must not seem to be talking to himself. Once they had agreed on those principles, Queysanne and Perec worked up the outline and the shooting text very quickly. Maurice Pons was a member of the CAR and thus the obvious person for them to consult on the layout of their application as well as the politics of their whole approach. Perec was more than reluctant to set foot on Suzanne's estate again, but for the sake of the film, and Bernard, he consented to go back to Andé to see Maurice. He drank like a fish throughout the entire time he was there.

The selection panel met in June. Jean Lescure, a fellow Oulipian, is said to have tipped the scales by exclaiming, "This is a film that we have to support! It will make Marguerite Duras look as jolly as Laurel and Hardy!" The CAR decided to award Perec and Queysanne a pump-priming "advance on receipts" of fifteen million francs. Had they been new francs, the subsidy would have got the film off to a flying start; unfortunately, they were old ones, and the advance was the smallest that it was in the committee's power to make, worth not much more than twelve thousand pounds in the money of that time.

---

[1] Harry Mathews translated the text of the film for an English-language version, which was released in 1974 as *A Man in a Dream*. To avoid confusion, I refer to Perec's film by the title under which the original novel was published (fifteen years later) in Britain and America.

The would-be directors needed to attract a producer who was prepared to finance almost the whole cost of their project. Producers of that kind were thin on the ground.

Two scripts

Self-adaptation was but one possible form of writing for the screen; Perec also offered himself as a scriptwriter to directors with their own ideas for films. The first to collaborate with him in this way was Jean-François Adam, for *Les Oiseaux dans la Nuit* ("Birds in the Night").[1] The two of them *worked like brutes on it*, Perec wrote to Helmle, *a bit like when we made* Tagstimmen. Some weeks later he reported, *I've just about finished my film scripts. The first, which I counted on to earn several million francs,*[2] *has already gone for a burton, but* – so ist das Leben!

Perec was in contact, too, with another "friend and relation" from the Moulin d'Andé, Jean-Pierre Prévost, the companion of Suzanne's daughter, Christine, the apple of her mother's eye and her spitting image.[3] Prévost's idea was to adapt and transform a news story known as the Cestas affair: a divorced father had hung on to his children after his legally permitted "weekend access", barricaded his remote country cottage, flown the black flag alongside the tricolour from the chimney stack, and challenged the authorities to recover the children by force. Having declared that he would shoot anything that moved, he proceeded to do so, killing one policeman and badly injuring another. The police, instructed to use all necessary force to overcome the "madman of Cestas", stormed the cottage, using an armoured car and a whole panoply of military hardware. Inside, they found two children shot dead by their father, who had also blown his own brains out.[4]

[1] *Les Oiseaux dans la Nuit* is probably an early version of the film eventually made by Jean-François Adam under the title *Retour à la Bien-Aimée*. Perec is credited as one of the four scriptwriters of the latter film.

[2] Only a few thousand pounds sterling, since Perec meant old francs. The French have not ceased even now to add two orders of magnitude to significant sums of money, at least in conversation.

[3] Perec had actually played a small part in Prévost's first film, *Jupiter*, shot at the Moulin d'Andé in the summer of 1970. *Jupiter* was never released but it is possible that a copy of the film still exists.

[4] See *Le Monde*, 13 February 1969; *Le Nouvel Observateur*, 24 February 1969; *Paris-Match*, 1 March 1969, etc.

For most of July, Perec and Prévost (accompanied for part of the time by a cigar-smoking ladyfriend nicknamed Bonaparte, with whom Perec had a brief affair) worked on the project in Harry Mathews's house in the Vercors. The finished filmscript, entitled *Malédiction!*, has little more than countryside, carnage and copious weaponry in common with the original story. The central character is a former deserter from the French army, called Joseph (or Maxime) Bertin. He has taken over a disused branch-line station building and lives as a rural scavenger with his Algerian wife Mona, their two boys, and Mona's sixteen-year-old sister Marine. When the police come to evict them, they make racist remarks about Mona, provoking a fight with Joseph who ends up shooting the policeman, and also, in a tragic error, his own wife. The rest of the film follows the conventional form of a manhunt, set in the French "Wild West" of the Cévennes. In one sequence, Joseph shoots his brother Henri in his study, beneath a reproduction of Ingres's *Portrait of Monsieur Bertin*; in another, he guns down a CRS marksman. When Marine eventually finds him holed up in a forest hut, he takes her for Mona and leads his substitute wife through spectacular countryside to a hilltop fortress formerly used by the Resistance. It is still stocked with air-dropped crates of corned beef, dried milk, machineguns and hand-grenades. Marine refuses to play the role of her sister any longer, and Joseph, now manifestly deranged, slowly strangles her as dozens of trucks, half-tracks, armoured cars, fire engines and mobile ladders surround the place. An "epitaph or epigraph" from Alfred Jarry's *Ubu Roi* is superimposed on the final carnage, seen from far above: *Then I shall kill everybody and go away.*

It is obviously impossible to judge how much of *Malédiction!* was Prévost's and how much was Perec's. However, some of the apparently minor details of the script, such as the place-name Saint-Chély-d'Apcher and the little boys' dream of desert adventures, as well as the imagination of extravagant police violence, find later echoes in *Life A User's Manual*, *W or The Memory of Childhood*, and *La Boutique obscure*. In general, however, *Malédiction!* reads more like the script of a blood-and-guts movie by Sam Peckinpah than a story from the pen of Georges Perec. The CAR did not like it enough to give it a subsidy. (Committee members may have been unwilling to approve a script that presents French police as clumsy and trigger-happy racists.) At all events, the project was abandoned and Perec never mentioned *Malédiction!* again.[1]

A Play

On his return from Lans-en-Vercors at the end of July 1971, Perec spent a fortnight in Paris, interrupted by a weekend at Blévy, and he dropped into the lab now and again (*mainly to use the telephone*, he wrote to Harry – for there was still none at Rue de Seine) at times when he hoped his summer zeal would be noticed by his boss, André Hugelin. Chakravarti's pitiless bi-square demanded an August memory text for Ile Saint-Louis:

> *I am not suffering, not waiting, I nourish almost no illusion, I can't reach any serenity in my memory. The recollection of it no longer even moves me, but it is still this absence of feeling that gets at me the most.*
>
> *Unique object, lost object: perhaps I'll begin to write again, to fabulate, to construct in order to put off.* [. . .]
>
> *Perhaps the analysis will tell me what I was seeking beyond it . . .*

Any hopes that Perec may have had of film-work's providing a path to financial salvation had proved vain, with two defeats and one useless victory so far, and not a penny to put in the bank. The stage, too, offered opportunities for earning money: Sartre's notoriously bulging pockets, for example, were stuffed not so much with royalties from his books as with the receipts from the theatres that produced his plays. The "well-made play" was no more Perec's bent than rhyming poetry, but perhaps he could find something that he *could* do for the stage.

He was quite aware that he was dispersing his intellectual energy in too many directions at once. He needed to work, but did he need to work in that way? He tried to explain to Stella Baruk, who was resting on Ile de Ré:

> *Saturday 7 August* [1971]
> *Dearest Snoozer*
>   [. . .] *Work keeps three great evils at bay – I always forget what a couple of them are, but it must be true anyway. At any rate,*

---

[1] Prévost eventually made a different film from similar material, called *L'Homme du fleuve* (1974). The latter script was partly written by Regis Henrion.

I'm madly eager to work, mad in the sense that I actually work rather little, less from laziness than from dissipation. By dissipation I mean both that I am dissipated outside of work (drinking, for example) and, what's worse, dissipated in my work: doing fifteen things at once, instead of finishing any one of them properly! The two phenomena have been going on each as long as the other, and perhaps there's a correlation between them. Should I drink less so as to dissipate myself less? Or will I only ever work effectively if I stop drinking? Or will I only ever drink less if I work more?

I shall let time bring in its wake a solution to such minor problems (for they are minor). Nulla dies sine linea, *whether you're a genius or not (Stendhal's motto: there are plenty worse!).*

Perec popped down to see Bernard Queysanne at the country house he was sharing that summer with the film-director Robert Enrico. Whilst there he picked up a copy of Shakespeare, leafed through *Hamlet* in French, and found something in it with which to start constructing a piece of theatre, that strange milieu in which people talk to each other whilst pretending that the room they are in has four walls instead of only three. On his return to Paris, Perec set about organising the holiday that he and Stella had planned to take together, which they saw no reason to abandon just because they had called off their envisaged affair.

They met at Angoulême station on 20 August and pushed off in Stella's "choo-choo" car (a Renault 4, or *petit monstre*) on a gentle route through the Dordogne to the Minervois, where they stayed with Pierre and Denise Getzler at the Roubaud family's country home, La Tuilerie de Saint-Félix. Up in the attic was a dusty stack of old and curious books, among them an antiquated potato grower's vademecum, which Perec seized upon with glee. He copied out pages of recondite details about the varieties, yields, cooking methods, and diseases of the divine tuber, which was made popular in France not by Sir Walter Raleigh, of course, but by Parmentier, after whom *hâchis Parmentier*, the French version of shepherd's pie, is named. Perec's unorthodox and passably aggressive new play, entitled *La Poche Parmentier* (literally "The Parmentier Bulge", to be understood as a salient in a potato campaign or alternatively as a spud-shaped warp in time) began to emerge from the implausible conjunction of *Hamlet* and a dog-eared growers' manual.

At Saint-Félix Perec renewed his acquaintance with Duchat, out of

Duduche, by Duchat I, the first of Perec's feline friends at Rue du Bac. Stella was a cat lover too, and, in honour of his holiday with her, Perec put her favourite cat, Felice, in *La Poche Parmentier* [*Th* 85]. Thereafter Perec inserted cat-winks to his human friends in nearly all his books – from Lady Piccolo in *Life A User's Manual* (to say hallo to Philippe Drogoz), to Ursule Boulou in *Un Cabinet d'Amateur* (a nod to later friends, the Brunhoffs).

Stella drove on, with Perec beside her, from Saint-Félix to Albi, whose cathedral, consecrated to Saint Cecilia, reminded Perec that his mother had taken the name of the patron saint of musicians [*W* 39]. They went on together in an arc through the Cévennes before heading north again back to Paris. The trip lasted no more than ten days, but from it came Perec's only play specifically conceived for performance on stage.

In *La Poche Parmentier*, five people are imprisoned in a room with three walls, with sacks of potatoes to peel. They talk. They talk about potatoes, of course, and they talk about what might lie outside the room, what it might have been before (an inn, a grand mansion, a country house), and what might have caused them to be shut up in it. Their words include long quotations from *Hamlet*, act 5, scene 2, from an agricultural handbook, from a nineteenth-century farce of wooden banality – *La Station Champbaudet*, by Labiche and Marc-Michel – and perhaps from other sources, too. In the back-panel copy that he wrote for the volume in which it was eventually published, Perec described *La Poche Parmentier* as a play on theatrical illusion. Just as significantly, it is also a barely disguised evocation of the Moulin d'Andé, a country-house prison where all the guests, however celebrated, "peel potatoes" and live, like the characters of Sartre's *Huis Clos,* in permanent sight of the Other. Perec's apparently flippant and aleatory manner of composing the play turns out, in retrospect, to have been a form of psychological defence. The ruse may have worked only too well: it is difficult to take the moments of cribbed pathos in *La Poche Parmentier* as self-expression, and it was some years before a theatre director thought the play worth putting on stage.

A Hörspiel

Perec's fourth radio play, *Fonctionnement du système nerveux dans la tête*, was first mooted in March 1971. It was to be a collage, like the stage play invented a few months later, as well as a confrontation with the lab. It would describe the "functioning of the nervous system in the head" by splicing together extracts from scientific articles on the brain stem, all taken straight out of CNRS LA 38; and at the same time it would narrate what was "really" happening in the "head" of the scientist delivering the paper – a replay of the "primal scene" identified by Freud as the fundamental trauma of early childhood (*see* p. 263). Like *L' Attentat de Sarajevo*, the palindrome of 1969, and many of Perec's other works, *Fonctionnement* exploits the idea of twin tracks that converge but do not quite meet at the end. Kamps was not certain that the formula would work on radio, even if stereophony were used to keep the two texts apart, and he expressed his concerns in a letter – and in German. Perec pretended to panic:

> *Dear Eugen* [Helmle]
> *I got your postcards and a letter from Johann-Maria Kamps that I had a devil of time trying to understand: I think he agrees more or less with all that I told him; he queries whether the overlay of voices in* Mechanismus des Nervensystems im Kopf *isn't going to make it difficult to understand . . .*

Perec's German was not really that bad, and the résumé of Kamps's views that he gave to Helmle shows that he had understood the letter perfectly well. He answered Kamps's objections by asserting that the two strands of the play would be clearly separated: the lecture would be a continuous stream of sound, whereas the fantasy would be *a fragmented text that imposes itself in a sense through the other speech: as if you were hearing a text and, beneath it, an internal monologue.*

Perec wrote the play in French, largely from English-language sources, but it was intended from the start to be performed in German. He advised Helmle to cull his German neurophysiological vocabulary from O. Creutzfeld and H. Akimoto, "Konvergenz und gegenseitige Beeinflußung von Impulsen aus der Retina und den unspezifischen Thalamuskernen an einzelne Neuronen des optischen Cortex", *Z.f.d.ges. Neurol.*, no. 196 (1958), pp. 520–538 – just to remind his translator that he also worked for forty hours a week, and that Peekaboo was in good shape, thank you.

Mechanismus was not actually written until the autumn of 1971. What with three film scripts, a stage play and two months spent away from the typewriter, Perec had no choice but to make WDR wait. By November, however, SR was getting impatient, too: where was the new radio play by the *Tagstimmen* team, to which unlimited resources had been promised the previous March? Helmle nagged Perec whilst reassuring Jochen Senf ("Mr Mustard", Werner Klippert's deputy at SR) that something truly splendid was on its way.

The Tale of the Bi-Square, the Orchestra and the Superannuated Musical Writing Machine

The first idea came from Philippe Drogoz. He wrote to Perec on 1 August 1971 with two vague plans. One was for a sort of "Hearse-Peel" (that is, *Hörspiel*) consisting of an internal monologue overlaid on a "real" conversation not necessarily connected to it – a design not at all distant from that of the still-unwritten *Fonctionnement du système nerveux dans la tête*. Drogoz's second idea came from Bach, who had likened polyphony to a conversation between many voices, all present throughout but taking turns to speak. What he suggested for the radio play was a musical "conversation piece" set in real-life situations where two or more sound-tracks normally occur.

Perec could not reply until after he had returned from Saint-Félix and settled back into his lab routine, which allowed him to polish off his twin-track brain-stem radio play fairly quickly. By November he had written up a draft along the lines suggested by Drogoz, an ironical "Theme and Variations for Narrator and Orchestra", which he sent (in French) to Helmle, who then reported on it to SR. This new work, the translator said reassuringly, would be a sequel to *Tagstimmen*, exploiting, in the place of voices, the varieties of instrumental music that form the aural environment. The thread on which the variations were to be strung was a journalist's enquiry into the role of music in everyday urban life, from a blind busker's violin to a jukebox, from a concert heard on a taxi-driver's radio to the concert's actual performance, stopping on the way for a visit to a one-man band who trips on the stairs when coming to answer the door. There would be seventeen variations, each with a different musical form as well as a different narrative pretext. Why seventeen? According to Drogoz, "It was a fashionable number. A nice prime. Everyone wanted to use it that year."

Helmle's long report was not yet the script itself, but a month later he reminded SR that the project was well under way. Perec and

Drogoz intended to take the radio station's generous offer literally: their first draft called for two violins, a viola, a cello, a double-bass, a flute, an oboe, a clarinet, a piccolo, a French horn, a trumpet, a cornet, timpani, and a tuba, and they would probably also need an electric guitar, a bandonion and a *Frequenz-Generator*, whatever that was.

In Paris the two pals worked sporadically but intensely on the project, which grew ever more complex. By early February 1972 they had found the key for their joint work, now called *Concertstück für Sprecher und Orchester* [sic]. It was *a little more elaborate* than what had first been contemplated, Perec admitted to Helmle, but it would come complete with a colour-coded chart of its musical and narrative composition. The coding represents the musical and narrative "colour" of each of the seventeen variations, as determined by four variables (length of sequence, expression, tempo, and "dynamic"), each with two possible values (short/long, emotional/neutral, slow/fast, piano/forte). The French abbreviations used produce an unpronounceable exotic language; a "long", "emotional", "slow" and "piano" sequence, for example, is coded LERP. In handwritten drafts of *Konzertstück* Perec even introduced a "Professor Corsppeeggree" to give a lecture on the dialects of Polyphonesia, beginning, "*Cnelp lerf lerf frec prel plec cnelf celp Boro lerp . . .*". "Polyphonesian" is undoubtedly a reminiscence of the language of Oulipia, created for the "extraordinary adventures" of Mr Eveready some eighteen months before, but Perec's irreverent musical extravaganza also bears a more central relationship to the work of OuLiPo, and to the fictional extravaganza that Perec would soon announce to his colleagues, under the provisional title *La Vie, Mode d'emploi*.

OuLiPo invented formal tools for writing, and the tests for its tools tested one tool at a time. For that reason, all of Perec's previous Oulipian works had been formally "simplex"; even *La Disparition*, which is much longer than anything produced by the group up to that time, exploits and exhausts one constraint, and one only. *Konzertstück* is the first formal "multiplex" in Perec's oeuvre, and in the work of OuLiPo, though, it is far from being the first formal multiplex in the history of literature. Harry Mathews had explained to Perec (up to a point) how he had constructed the musico-dental misadventure in prose that he had named *Tlooth*: by using a *set* of rules that generated multiple features in each chapter.

Each of the seventeen sequences of *Konzertstück* has two predetermined musical forms: one for the verbal structure and another for the music itself. Sequence 11 ("In the Restaurant"), for example, is a gypsy chaconne as far as the musical sound is concerned, but its story takes the form of a sonata. The Perec-Drogoz demonstration of the presence of music in everyday life goes beyond "programme" illustration, embedding in its trivial narratives (all ending in misadventure) the properties of canonical musical forms. The medium is, in this instance, the message, and the underlying message is the possibility of form's overlaying form. The plan for *Konzertstück*, rather more than its realisation, contains the core idea that would permit Perec to design his later masterpiece. It gave him his first inkling of the vast potential of multiplex constraint.

To find a means of distributing the different musical shapes around the thirty-four slots (two each for the seventeen episodes), Perec went back to the key that Claude Berge had first proposed to OuLiPo years before, the one that he had already adapted as a simplex device to structure *Lieux:* the Graeco-Latin bi-square of order 10. Precisely how the truncated bi-square included in the *Konzertstück* file (*see* p. 489) relates to the distribution of elements in the finished play will be for others to determine, but Drogoz has no doubt that it controls the placing of elements and vectors in the colour-coded chart sent to Helmle in February 1972, which has been miraculously preserved in the archives of SR.

Klippert's deputy, Jochen Senf, was not much impressed by the text he received in February, and he wrote a long letter to Perec pointing out all the difficulties in the hugely expensive proposal. Perec replied on 14 March 1972, assuring "Mr Mustard" that he had misunderstood the true nature of the programme, that it was in fact *animated by the somewhat irreverent wish to desacralise music . . . (just as the point of* Die Maschine *was to desacralise* Uber allen Wipfeln *[sic]).* That must count as Perec's gravest error in Franco-German relations: the wish to desacralise Goethe is one thing, but music is altogether more sacred – and more German. Meanwhile, as the exchange of letters continued, Drogoz composed the score and had performance copies made in Paris. The completed dossier – now calling for a symphony orchestra, a massed choir, and a performing typewriter – reached Saarbrücken in May. Then nothing happened.

If "Mr Mustard" had doubts about the musical good taste of *Konzertstück für Sprecher und Orchester*, he had even more of a problem with its production. New orchestral music was the responsibility of

	1	2	3	4	5	6	7	8	9	10
pour 1	1_1	7_8	6_9	5_0	0_2	9_4	8_6	2_3	3_5	4_7
−2	8_7	2_1	1_8	7_9	6_0	0_3	9_5	3_4	4_6	
−3	9_6	8_1	3_3	2_8	1_9	7_0	0_4	4_5	5_7	
−4	0_5	9_7	8_2	4_4	3_8	2_9	1_0			
−5	2_0	0_6	9_1	8_3	5_5	4_9				
−6	4_9	3_0	0_7	9_2	8_4	6_6				
−7	6_8	5_9	4_0	0_1	9_3					
−8	3_2	4_3	5_4							
−9	5_3	6_4								
−10	7_4									

dans la séquence 1 le personnage 1
dit la phrase 1 en 1ère place
le personnage 2 dit la phrase 7 en place 8 ..

Somme : impaire : phrase positive
          paire : neg ou inter.
Différence : pair : enchaînée
          impair : libre

the music department, quite separate from the *Hörspielabteilung*. The dossier began to yellow. Finally, fifteen months later, in October 1973, a summit meeting was set up at SR's Halberg headquarters to sort out the internal boundary dispute. The head of the drama division, the head of the music division, the composer, the translator, and the others in attendance (not including the author, who was in Tunisia at the time) agreed in the end to go ahead with *Konzertstück*. The recording was scheduled for the following May; eight studio days would have to be booked, given the number of musicians involved. It was further resolved that the author's wishes concerning episode 16, the "Sonata for an Ageing Typewriter", would be respected, and that SR would somehow find an Underwood Four Million in Saarbrücken, so as to produce the correct clang-click-ding.

The summit meeting resulted in cheques' being sent to Perec and Drogoz, two years after they had first begun the work together. In the course of the following winter they practised the sonata on the old Underwood in Paris. Perec now had an IBM electric golf-ball machine, so it did not matter too much if the rehearsals wrecked his old typewriter, which they did, though not quite irreversibly. It had been Perec's friend, companion, and unfailing prop for two decades; he was not necessarily doing violence to it when he added an implausible coda to its career and turned it into a musical writing machine.[1]

Konzertstück was broadcast in stereo by SR and WDR on 18 July 1974. It was not made into a record or a cassette, it was not well reviewed, and it was never repeated on air. It had cost SR's drama department much more than it was supposed to, and it had caused a minor crisis in interdepartmental relations. But if *Konzertstück* turned out to be Perec's last German radio play, it was due not so much to its production problems as to the fact that by the time of its broadcast, the different approach that Perec had taken in 1971 had finally had its effect. He had not become a playwright or a highly paid French cinema hack; he was about to emerge once again as a writer of books.

A new periodical

Recollections of Perec's gloomy appearance in the early 1970s are inseparable from the recollected air of the times, thick with the fallout

---

[1] Drogoz later lent it to Paulette and had it properly repaired when she returned it to him. It is still in (approximate) working order.

from the explosion of May 1968. The intellectual landscape of the Left Bank seemed to many to have been laid to waste: the heroic slogan of the great demonstrations – *Etudiants! Ouvriers! Même combat!* – now had a bitter ring, as the PCF had regained control of the main trade unions and was keeping all "innovators" at bay. The banners that had optimistically proclaimed *Ce n'est qu'un début* seemed to have come true, albeit ironically: May '68 had been but the beginning of the end of ideology. The radical intellectual heart of the country, lying between Les Deux Magots and the Jardin des Plantes, had become isolated from society as a whole, and the "forces of order" now maintained a high and visible profile in the Latin Quarter. At ENS and at the Sorbonne, splinter groups formed and were dissolved, leaving barely a ripple on the surface of things. By 1972 what remained of the Situationist International had resolved to commit organisational hara-kiri: "Operation Dissolution was intended as one of the principal contributions of I.S. to the revolutionary movement . . . May hostilities continue."[1] A number of intelligent youngsters who had "done" May '68 observed the desolate scene, drew their own conclusions, and went into business, or journalism, or advertising. The older generation of intellectuals, for whom 1968 had represented an unexpected culmination of earlier hopes, were more often stranded. Some, like Roger Kleman and Jacques Lederer, left their careers; others, like Babette Mangolte, emigrated to the States; but most stayed on, beached by the tide of history on what now seemed a barren shore.

Perec and Kleman had by now fallen out, and the long-drawn-out wake of May '68 caused other rifts to open up in Perec's social life. The sharpest quarrel that he had was with Alain Guérin, whose attack in *L'Humanité* on the youngsters who had led the demonstrations outraged him, as it did many others.[2]

Fifteen years earlier, Jean Duvignaud, Edgar Morin, and Roland Barthes had launched *Arguments* to assert the possibility of dialogue and intellectual debate in circumstances that had seemed just as blocked between the right and the conservative left. Duvignaud returned to his old barricade in the winter of 1971–72 with a new

---

[1] Jean-François Martos, *Histoire de l'Internationale situationniste* (Paris: Lebovici, 1989), pp. 275–276.

[2] The dispute explains why Guérin himself forgot for twenty years that he had a copy of *Le Condottiere*.

review, *Cause commune* ("Common Cause"). His two principal collaborators in this venture were Paul Virilio, an architect and writer who led the Ecole Spéciale d'Architecture, and his old pupil and protégé, Georges Perec.

Cause commune was published by Denoël in association with the Swiss firm Gonthier. The following were its professed aims:

> To grasp at the root and to question the ideas and beliefs on which the workings of our "civilisations" and "culture" are based, and to undertake an anthropology of contemporary mankind;
>
> To elicit the bases of a new critical position so as to constitute a modern political theory free of the suffocation of outdated prejudices and traditional humanism;
>
> To undertake an investigation of everyday life at every level, right down to the recesses and basements that are normally ignored or suppressed;
>
> To analyse the objects offered up to satisfy our desires – works of art, cultural objects, consumer goods – in relation to our lives and to the realities of our social existence
>
> To restore the free discussion of attitudes and ideas, outside of sectarianism, ideologies, and schools of thought.

Like its predecessor, *Arguments*, *Cause commune* had no party-political allegiance; it was intended to be a vehicle for the "turbulent left", and it was organised and run at convivial meetings of an editorial board that was open to all with contributions to make. In practice, those who took part in the discussions or submitted pieces for publication were linked to one of the three core editors, and most were drawn in out of loyalty to Jean Duvignaud. *Cause commune* was not a faction defined by a particular set of ideas; it was in obeisance to none of the current masters of French thought (Lacan, Foucault, Lévi-Strauss, Sartre, and Roland Barthes are barely mentioned in its pages). Because it rejected any doctrinal definition of its membership and aims, it could only comprise a clique of people who could refer to the editor as *mon ami Duvignaud*. Henri Lefèbvre was the only other contributor with an established reputation as an essayist, and Marshall McLuhan the only guru whom the whole team respected. Much of the review was written by Duvignaud himself, though Virilio also contributed frequently. Occasional collaborators ranged from the not-yet-famous novelist Pascal Lainé to young scholars in a variety of fields, from German studies to mathematics, all sharing, at least to some degree, the conviction that they were survivors of a catastrophe:

> French society is falling apart, our culture is in dissolution, our institutions are hollow: we don't even need to call ourselves nihilists anymore because we are living inside nihilism.[1]

Perec used *Cause commune* to publish work in progress[2] and the French text of his latest German radio play.[3] He attended all the editorial meetings, Paul Virilio recalls, and paid attention, with his head cocked to one side, but it was not hard to guess that behind his dreamy gaze a hidden world was spinning. In the years following the publication of *Things*, Perec had been reluctant to accept his simplified public image as a sociologist and critic of contemporary society. By 1972, however, he was no longer trammelled by that distorting image, or indeed by any image at all, which left him free to return to an area of thought and writing, and a set of ambitions, that had been his since the 1950s. Some of Perec's earlier pieces in *Cause commune* give an idea of what *La Locomotive* and *La Ligne générale* might have been like had they appeared. The "political Perec" of 1955–65 had not simply been superseded by OuLiPo, by Andé, by German radio, by marriage, passion, separation, despair, and analysis. In politics, at least, Perec had hardly grown up at all.

Issue number 1 of *Cause commune* (May 1972) featured an essay by Jean Duvignaud called "Subversion", a symposium on "Le Gauchisme et après?" ("Leftism, and then what?"), and a "Self-Portrait" by Georges Perec, whose subtitle, "Les Gnocchis de l'automne" ("Autumn Pasta"), was comprehensible only to those who had heard Alain Guérin's riddle on the Greek adage *gnoti se auton* ("know thyself").

> *Writing protects me. I proceed beneath fortifications of words and sentences, of cleverly ordered paragraphs, of cunningly programmed chapters. I am not without ingenuity.*

---

[1] Manifesto over the signature "C.C.", to which Perec presumably gave his assent.

[2] "Six Rêves", a fragment of *La Boutique obscure*, in issue number 2.

[3] "Fonctionnement du système nerveux dans la tête", in issue number 3.

Do I still need to be protected? What if my shield should turn into a shackle?

One day I will have to start using words to unmask my reality, and to unmask the real that lies beyond my own singular questioning of it. That is probably how I can best formulate my task at present, even if I know (and that "even if" is not the limit of my task but more like a guarantee of its reality) that it can never be quite completed until the day when, once and for all time, the Poet is expelled from the City, the day when workers take over the ivory tower, when artists burn their smocks, the day when we are at last able – without laughing, without feeling once more that we are being derisive, or playacting, or being heroic – when we are able to take up a spade or a pick, a road hammer or a trowel. Not that that will mean we have advanced very much (for things certainly won't be measured in that way anymore) but our world will at last have begun to be free.   [Jsn 73–74]

Perec reviewed Stanley Kubrick's film *A Clockwork Orange* in issue number 3. What he saw in this version of Anthony Burgess's novel (disowned by the author) was not a parody but a representation of a society based on violence, a *real image of our world as it is:*

Violence is the only institution, the only currency, the only value recognised by mankind . . . All that has been said about the concentration camps must be repeated here . . . violence is the only truth of capital, its sole instrument, its sole recourse . . . All that we know about the camps does not seem to have sufficed to make the truth obvious . . . that the camps are not and never were an exception, a sickness, a blemish, a scandal, a monstrosity, but rather the only truth and the only coherent response of capitalism.

Such paranoid delusions were not at all rare amongst French left-wingers, and Perec's perception of the housing estate at Thamesmead as an image of Auschwitz and of capitalist society should not be attributed overmuch to his personal background. *Cause commune* reveals the paradox of Perec's political position. Not all of the friends that Perec made after the collapse of Lg knew that he had any particular political views, even if his bearing and manner suggested a man of the leftish fringe. Suzanne had thought that he "really wasn't very interested" in politics at all, whilst another close friend puts it more bluntly: "Perec's politics? Zero!"

A performance

The near success of *Tagstimmen* in the 1971 Italia Prize competition once again brought Perec's name to the attention of Alain Trutat, the head of the ACR. It was odd, if not absurd, that a French radio playwright of European distinction had never been heard on French radio; Trutat proposed to make amends on a grand scale, with a whole evening of *Audioperec*, on 5 March 1972, as a thirty-sixth birthday present for a man born in '36. The main items included were *L'Augmentation* in its 1970 recording, enhanced by a "sound commentary" by Philippe Drogoz; *Diminuendo*, Bruno Gillet's "micro-opera" with a libretto by Perec, recorded at its premiere the previous autumn; and *Tagstimmen*, as broadcast on German radio in 1971. Spliced in between these three works were three others: a recorded discussion centred on a reading of selected texts by the members of OuLiPo; a performance of Perec's first alphabetic year-end gift to friends, the *Petit Abécédaire illustré*, which had been set to music as witty and delightful as the text itself by Philippe Drogoz; and Perec's one and only actual musical composition, recorded at its one and only rehearsal-cum-performance by the Groupe d'Etudes et de Réalisations Musicales, or GERM, and conducted, in joyful confusion, by the composer-author himself. The score that Perec gave to the instrumentalists to guide them was bizarre, even for an experimental group (*see* p. 496). Each row (numbered 1, 2, 3, and 4) is performed by a different random group of instruments. The piece is thirty units in length (a to z plus A to D), and each unit might best be realised in about ten seconds. Relative pitch is indicated by the vertical position of the symbols inside each row, whilst volume is signalled by their relative size. Black and white are used to represent contrasting timbre – that is, pizzicato versus bow for stringed instruments, open versus closed for winds, and so on. The six symbols themselves are to be interpreted thus:

The musical phrase chosen by each group as its "quotation" has to be repeated each time the quotation symbol appears, but beyond that

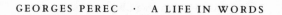

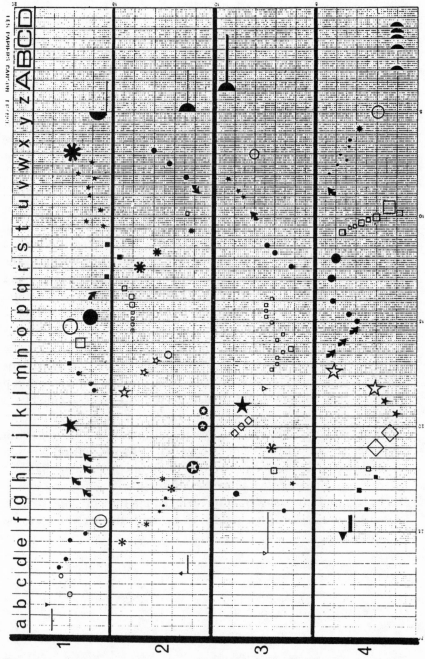

© P.O.L. 1985 (Proceedings of the Colloque Perec at the Centre Culturel International de Cérisy-La-Salle, 1984)

the musicians may realise the score in any way they please within the rules already laid down. The score – which must be the maddest and most entertaining use ever made of those assortments of stickers sold by newsagents to schoolchildren, who personalise their homework folders with them – is allegedly a fugue. Its performance is aleatory (*aléatoire*), which explains why Perec suggested that it should be played at a party to be held in western France, in the small town of Thouars: to hear the music, *allez à Thouars*. The ghastly pun was not put into practice; Perec's *Souvenir d'un voyage à Thouars* ("Souvenir of a journey to Thouars", where he himself had never been) was instead performed and recorded in the ORTF studios in Paris.

A novelette

Cause commune was no more Perec's main commitment in 1972 than were any of his other activities, whether in radio, in music, in film, or in translation, in France or in Germany. His only firm principle, it seems, was to be committed elsewhere. Although he wrote no "big" books of his own, he did commit a little one, which was quickly published: *Les Revenentes* ("The Revenents"), the "retern of the *e*", from which all vowels are banned save the one dispensed with in *La Disparition*. Originally envisaged as *Les Lettres d'Eve* as early as 1969, the univocalic was finally put together over the Easter holidays which Perec spent at Blévy, in the company of Sylvia Lamblin and her future husband, James Richardson. It must have been convenient for him to have an Englishman on hand, for the story the novel tells with ribald *e*s was inspired by the family legend of how they had all just missed becoming American thirty years previously (*see* p. 54). In the darkest days of the war, David Bienenfeld had entrusted those jewels that belonged to him, rather than to the JBSA, to the firm's commercial traveller, who smuggled them over the demarcation line and then took them further south to Marseille, where it was possible, in practice, to embark for neutral Spain, and thence to the New World. The traveller was a notorious homosexual; once in Marseille, the story went, he organised a transvestite orgy and bedecked his party companions with the pearl necklaces he had brought along. Foreseeably, they ran off before changing back into male attire, and the Bienenfelds' real fortune was never seen again.

Apart from *Mechanismus des Nervensystems im Kopf*, *Les Revenentes* is the only one of Perec's works to deal directly with sex – and sex, in *Les Revenentes*, takes every imaginable form, from masturbation to buggery, fellatio, cunnilingus, and bestial copulations in fancy dress. It tells an implausible tale of the theft of a fortune in pearls during an extravagant bisexual orgy, and it seems to be absolutely different from everything else that Perec ever wrote. What prompted this discreet and never vulgar man, who preferred on almost all other occasions to hide his characters' erotic activities, like his own, beneath a veil of propriety, to spill out sexual fantasies that are closer to de Sade than to Stendhal? French has more than a sufficiency of sexual vocabulary spelled with *es* only (*fesses, sexe, lèvre, membre,* and *pénétrer* come immediately to mind), but that cannot account for it entirely. In *La Disparition* the rules of spelling and grammar are respected almost entirely despite the absence of the letter *e*, but *Les Revenentes* is less a reciprocal than an opposite type of exercise. It takes *liberties* with language; it is not an experiment in univocalism but rather an exploration of *how far you can go* with foreign words, misspellings and crazy accentuation whilst keeping your reader's attention.[1] The impropriety of the characters' behaviour matches the impropriety of Perec's French, and the linguistic fog that the atrocious spelling casts over scenes of stage-managed multiple orgasms raises the erotic temperature as effectively as the veil of metatheses thrown by Harry Mathews over the "blue-movie scenario" of *Tlooth*, which novel Perec had now at last dismembered and reassembled in French.

A Compendium

At the very first OuLiPo meeting after his departure from Andé, Perec had put *Ex-Cape* on the agenda again. Turning a decade's work into a publishable volume would require a good deal of fastidious action, especially since no real minutes had been kept since 1963. But help was soon at hand.

Paul Fournel was just eighteen when he first saw Perec on television, as the winner of the 1965 Renaudot prize. Since then he had gained a degree in French literature at Saint-Etienne, taught at Princeton and Boulder, and then settled in Paris to write a master's thesis on Queneau. He organised an OuLiPo exhibition at his faculty on 4 March

---

[1] See Bernard Magné, "*Les Revenentes:* de l'effervescence entre lengge et texte", in *Pérécollages 1980–1988* (Toulouse: Presses universitaires du Mirail, 1989), pp. 175–192.

1971, which Le Lionnais urged all his fellow Oulipians to attend, and his thesis pleased Queneau. He was still far too junior to be considered for full membership, but the group had many other uses for the energy, intelligence, and devotion of Fournel. He was therefore appointed to the Oulipian post of "slave" and allowed to attend the monthly meetings. Queneau passed the thesis on to Nadeau, who agreed to publish it straightaway: P. Fournel, *Clés pour la littérature potentielle*; ("Keys for Potential Literature") marks the first emergence of OuLiPo as a subject of academic exploration, and its official publication date – 7 March 1972 – marked Georges Perec's thirty-sixth birthday.

The slave's regular task was to keep proper minutes, in alternation with Marcel Benabou, and to circulate them. One or the other of them must have typed up the account of the meeting on 27 August 1971, which Perec read on his return from Saint-Félix in Stella's "choo-choo" car. The argument over the aims and purpose of the OuLiPo that broke out at that meeting was not entirely new, but Jacques Bens expressed his frustration, this time, in a particularly pointed way:

> I am fed up with structures that produce three little snippets of verse. Is it possible to find an Oulipian structure that would allow someone to write an eight-hundred-page novel? Until we've answered that question, all we'll have done is improve on a few parlour games.

Fournel was Perec's "slave" in "Operation Augias", the dusting and sorting of François Le Lionnais's collection of books. Le Lionnais never wrote very much, but he was more than a gifted mathematician with a wide literary culture. He was also a skilful conjurer, an acknowledged expert on legerdemain, and a world authority on chess problems. Le Lionnais seemed to know something about everything, and inspired awe in younger men like Fournel and Perec.

They took several days just to dust and sort the books in Le Lionnais's bedroom – mostly popular novels and general literature – and make a start on the hall, which was crammed full with books about chess. A projected second operation, "Augias II", which would have led them into the other rooms in the house, never came to pass.

For Fournel, the author of *La Disparition* was OuLiPo made flesh, "the incarnation of all our dreams and ambitions as writers". It was an honour as well as an opportunity for him to assist Perec in the editing – at last! – of *Ex-Cape*.

Queneau was in control of the volume and had the final word on the selection of material, its organisation, and the content of the "continuity" texts. That led to no friction at all among Fournel, Perec and the author of *Zazie*: as Fournel remarks, "Trailers don't argue with their tractor unit".

OuLiPo. Créations, Re-Créations, Récréations appeared in 1973. Queneau had persuaded François Erval to publish this unusual book in the Idées collection, a mass-market paperback series restricted to reprints of works first published in the French equivalent of hardback editions. From that point on, Oulipianism ceased to be the preserve of a Parisian clique, even if OuLiPo itself remained a private circle. It was through this book – masterminded by Queneau, put together by Perec, and kept tidy by Paul Fournel – that thousands of readers first encountered constraint and potentiality, first experienced the exhilaration of combining words and numbers, and first realised that writing could once again be fun.

Georges Perec, "L'Orange est proche", *Cause commune*, no. 3 (October 1972), p. 1.

Unpublished sources for this chapter include FP 57, 69 (3 November 1971, on commencement of analysis); FP 91, 5, 1, and 91, 12, 4, 1–3 (correspondence related to *Konzertstück*); letters from Georges Perec to Stella Baruk, Eugen Helmle, and Harry Mathews; and documents relating to *Konzertstück* from the archives of SR.

This chapter also draws on the recollections of Stella Baruk, Claude Burgelin, Jean Duvignaud, Philippe Drogoz, Paul Fournel, Alain Guérin, Pierre Getzler, Eugen Helmle, Pascal Lainé, Francis Moaty, Jean-Michel Palmier, Jean-Pierre Prévost, Bernard Queysanne, James Richardson, Wolfgang Schenck, Staša Stanojević, Alain Trutat, and Paul Virilio.

Les Revenentes has been put into English by Ian Monk, under the title *Perec: The Exeter Text. Jewels, secrets & sex*.

CHAPTER 48

Avenue de Ségur

1972

> People don't think enough about stairs
> Georges Perec, *Espèces d'espaces*

When Perec bought his two-room flat in Rue de Seine, in January 1970, it was to serve as the pied-à-terre of a newborn bachelor with permanent quarters elsewhere, at Andé. It was really not much more than a large studio, and it never became a working home. When he lost his place in the country twelve months later, he had to make do without a study. In 1971–72, he did most of his writing somewhere else; his dispersion was thus a matter as much of finding space as of finding potentially lucrative collaborations. Lans-en-Vercors was the venue for *Malédiction!*, Neuweiler for *Tagstimmen* and *Konzertstück*, Saint-Félix for the potato play, and Blévy for *Les Revenentes*. As none of these projects brought in much money, Perec seemed to be stuck with his housing problem.

He was on comradely terms with Paulette and often went over to her flat for a meal, sometimes unannounced and sometimes carting his laundry. The Perecs still had many friends in common, one of whom moved into a rented flat in an agreeable, old-fashioned block not far from UNESCO in the early months of 1972. Perec soon heard from Paulette, who had it from her friend Francis Moaty, that another flat was vacant in the same house. Perec did his sums. It was unusual to become a tenant again when you owned your own place, but Rue de Seine was a smarter address, and ought to be able to produce an income sufficient to cover the rent of a larger flat further away from the heart of Saint-Germain. In June 1972, Jean-François Adam moved into Rue de Seine, and Perec settled himself into his new rooms at number 85, Avenue de Ségur, third floor front.

It was the last house in the street, standing at the corner of Boulevard Garibaldi, right across from the elevated metro line number 6 (Nation-Etoile), whose trains did not yet have rubber wheels. All day long, from dawn until after midnight, the old rolling stock would rattle and screech right past the front window, at third-floor height.

The six-storey house was owned by a Madame Reyrolle, who, together with other members of her family, occupied the two top-most floors. She had a weakness for artists and was delighted to count a prizewinning author amongst her tenants. What she offered was convenient but far from grand. The flat had a tiny entrance hall and a kitchenette with a bathroom right next to it, fed by an extension pipe from the sink. The living room was of a decent size, but the main advantage was that there were two other small rooms as well – a bedroom and, at last, a room that could be used for writing, and for nothing else.

Perec used the kitchen only for his start-of-day coffee ritual: he would make a jug of filter coffee, drink a cup, and pour the rest into a thermos flask, which he kept beside him to fuel his work until dinner. He rarely stopped for lunch, though he was not averse to popping down for an *express* and chat at the corner café; for dinner he would most often eat out, with friends, with Paulette, or in one of the decent restaurants with which the Left Bank was still plentifully supplied. He had a special liking for Le Balzar, in Rue des Ecoles, and for Le Buisson Ardent, round the corner from his first home in Rue de Quatrefages, but he also dined out in many other places that year and thereafter, and there is hardly a restaurant of any antiquity in Paris nowadays that does not have at least one waiter who remembers a good customer from years ago called Perec. Monsieur Georges? Yes, of course, sir! I remember him well.

Francis Moaty had the fourth-floor flat immediately above Perec's, and he had a telephone, a rare treasure in Paris before the end of the 1970s. He had got it installed because he worked for a graphic arts company and had a boss who was prepared to pull strings for his staff. Perec had no chance of getting a line in his own name for several years, but he needed a telephone, desperately. Moaty agreed to have an extension fitted, with a long lead trailing down the stairs. When the phone rang *chez Perec,* it also rang *chez Moaty,* and vice versa. The two of them got to know each other quite well.

Perec found redecoration a stressful bore. Paulette came over to help him move in, and did the painting and wallpapering too. Perec was not utterly incompetent with his hands; in fact, he was probably far less clumsy than he pretended to be. He assembled the bookshelves from a kit and set them up very well. He had his priorities.

Rue de Seine had been bought during Suzanne's reign, and it was thus a physical reminder of a lost love. The move to Avenue de Ségur put more distance between Perec and Andé, and in time his injured heart began to recover. In July 1972, writing his programmed memory of Ile Saint-Louis, he still felt *nostalgia and spite* about the place. He added:

> But I feel I am getting away from it even if I am not yet mobilised by other places, faces or passions. There's even the beginning of a convalescence, perhaps, at last, the real beginning.

In August Perec dreamt the last of the dreams that he would include in *La Boutique obscure*. It was not just that he was now sleeping in a bedroom shaken for all but four hours of the night by passing trains on the overground metro line; nor can the closure of Perec's dreambook be explained solely by the course of his psychoanalysis, in which he

> ended up admitting that these dreams had not been experienced in order to be dreams, but were dreamt to be written, and that they were not the royal road that I thought they would be, but tortuous paths taking me ever further away from self-recognition. [PC 70]

There is no reason to think that the date above dream number 124, which corresponds to the date of the slaughter of thirteen Israeli athletes at the Munich Olympics, was "arranged" for publication. The transcription itself returns Perec to themes that he was always reluctant to write about explicitly, those of Jewishness and oppression:

> The cloth merchant held a credit from my father and decided to denounce him to the S.S., and, at the same time as my father, his own son (or just an employee), who had been found carrying clandestine newspapers.
>
> It's much more muddled than that. But that's what it was.
>
> The S.S. come to arrest us. They have black uniforms and very tight-fitting, spherical helmets, like masks. They prepare to arrest the boss as well, but he points to me, takes my chin in his hand, and shows the little scar I have beneath it.
>
> We cross the city.
>
> If only we could go and drink a coffee. It looks so easy, but it is impossible. Moreover, the casino is shut, or closed to Jews. All the same, there is a light shining from inside.

We retrace our steps. We pass by the cloth merchant's again. It's a shop on a corner: neo-Gothic architecture (turrets, machicolated doorway). It looks spanking. We watch with justified bitterness.

We get to the station.

Disorder.

I know what we're in for. I have no hope. Get it over with. Or else, a miracle . . . one day, learn to survive?

My father dips his left boot into the icy water of a pool. He's trying to reanimate an old wound and perhaps get invalided out. But everyone watches him with indifference.

We are put in a room reserved for monsters. Two children, amputated above the knee, a boy and a girl, naked, writhe like worms. Myself, I have become a baby snake (or was it a fish?).

It is after a long sea journey that we shall get to the camp.

Our warders, torturers with degenerate faces, some pale, some ruddy, some cruel, some stupid, are graced with absurdly named functions: "(Worm?) Disinfection Operative", "Conversational Attaché (to conservation?)".

Soon their faces are framed with garlands, streaks, vignettes; it becomes an album that I leaf through, a memorial volume, as pretty as a theatre programme, with advertisements at the end . . .

I am back in this city. There is a great memorial ceremony. I attend, sickened, shocked, and, in the end, moved.

I get to the middle of a crowd. There is a party. Lots of records scattered around, I look for one to put on the turntable of a little record player. I burst into tears. J.L. reproaches me for doing so.

I am a little child. On the edge of the road, I stop a driver and ask him to dare, for me, to ask the gardener of the great orchard for my ball, which had gone over the wall (and, as I note this, the real memory returns: in 1947, at Rue de l'Assomption, I played with a ball against the wall of the convent directly opposite our block of flats).   [BO 124]

Raymond Queneau was provoked by *La Boutique obscure* into composing dream narratives, to demonstrate to himself that the dream-quality of Perec's texts was a rhetorical feature and not necessarily the product of actual dreaming.[1] Others may be more sus-

---

[1] Raymond Queneau's exercise, "Des Récits de rêve à foison" is described by Jacques Jouet in *Raymond Queneau: Qui êtes-vous?* (Lyon: La Manufacture, 1988), p. 18.

picious of the essay by Roger Bastide that closes the volume, in which he argues that Perec is the model of the modern Western dreamer, whose unconscious no longer erupts with repressed sexuality but is instead riven by fears of violence and authority. "What is there to be found in the obscurity of this book?" Jacques Roubaud asked.

> Obviously not a personal memoir, because anecdotic reality has been twice covered over: by the dream's own dissimulations and by the work of recovery in writing, the two intermingled processes each working on its own account towards ends that are in considerable disharmony with any biographical basso profundo.[1]

There is no doubt that there is a biographical "basso profundo" reverberating through La Boutique obscure, however, and no question that the publication of the book was an *act* in its author's manipulation of his own life. Perec's decision to draw a line after dream number 124 is the clearest signal that he could give *to himself* that he really had separated from Andé:

> La Boutique obscure *is an autobiographical text in a very precise sense: it tells the story of a separation. These dreams tell that story in a completely buried manner [. . .] That was part of the book's design; it arose as a refusal of psychoanalysis – that is to say, I did not take my dreams to my analyst but stole them so as to put them in a book. There was an aggressive relationship that comes across in* La Boutique obscure.[2]

It was an act that he half-regretted later on, he said to Lili, because the dreams were not sufficiently worked over. Doubtless he was eager to get the fourth of the five post-*Things* books that he owed to Denoël into print, to get nearer to the point where he could begin to make his own terms with publishers. But he was certainly just as eager to declare that his greatest nightmare, the long process of casting off Suzanne and Andé, was over, and that he was returning to concerns with deeper historical roots. He still telephoned Suzanne's daughter from time to time, and he was still very much involved in competing with the film-world of the Moulin d'Andé, but the cure

---

[1] Jacques Roubaud, "Les Rêves écrivent", La Quinzaine littéraire, no. 166 (16 June 1973).

[2] "En dialogue avec l'époque: Patrice Fardeau s'entretient avec Georges Perec", France nouvelle, 16 April 1979.

– not the psychoanalytic cure, not the self-invented time-capsule cure, but perhaps only the cure of passing time and moving houses – was beginning to work. At Avenue de Ségur a different passion was burrowing its way into the light.

The translation of *Tlooth* had been done mostly in 1971. Extracts appeared in *Les Lettres nouvelles* in September 1972, after more than one postponement, for the last pages of the text had been dealt with and typed up as long ago as May or June of that year. The outstanding problem was the title. Marc Adrian, the German translator of Mathews's novel, had a relatively easy job: *Zlahn* does just about the same thing with palatal occlusion that *Tlooth* does in English. But in French? In March Perec had suggested a voiceless filling of the French word for "filling": *Plombh*, or *Plohmb*. In September he was still doodling with *Dlent*, *Blouche*, *Balbouth*, *Balbousse*, *Balblouch*, *Maldlouch*, *Dlentité*. French *Tlooth* stayed in untitled limbo for the rest of 1972, and for the whole of 1973, and on into 1974, when Nadeau was finally able to have it set in type. The author was in New York just then; Perec rang him and gently, tactfully, and firmly persuaded him to accept the title that he and Nadeau's assistant, Geneviève Serreau, were convinced was the best: *Les Verts Champs de moutarde de l'Afghanistan* ("The Green Mustard Fields of Afghanistan").

Perec was not without occasional girlfriends after his separation from Paulette and his divorce from Andé, but none amongst them cast a lasting spell. At times he would joke with his men friends that he was waiting for a film-star to make time in her schedule to pass through Paris now and again, rush to him, make love, and fly off (first class). Perec's discretion about his actual love affairs (all of them very brief) does not mean that his heart beat only for writing, but it is true that he did not invest a great deal of himself in his relationships with women in his first post-Andé years. Nor did he yet have the courage, despite Harry's literary and personal encouragement, to get his tleeth seen to.

Sources include FP 57, 85 (3 July 1972) and 57, 89 (20 September 1972); a letter from Georges Perec to Harry Mathews, 14 March 1972; and the recollections of Ela Bienenfeld, Philippe Drogoz, Christine Lipinska, Harry Mathews, and Francis Moaty.

CHAPTER 49

Rue Simon-Crubellier

1972

In the autumn of 1972 the archaeologist who lived in the flat opposite Perec's at 85 Avenue de Ségur left rather suddenly. Perec asked Paulette to consider moving in and letting out Rue des Boulangers to tenants, as he had done with Rue de Seine. She declined, and the flat went to Philippe Drogoz, Perec's "chronic collaborator" since *L'Art effaré*. Madame Reyrolle was content for her staircase to be graced by another artist, one with shoulder-length hair, a rich baritone voice, and a laugh like a rusty hinge.

Before Drogoz moved in, Perec took a short break away, in New York. It did not count as a holiday, but neither is it clear exactly what business he was on. He stayed for some of the time with an old acquaintance, Kate Manheim (formerly a market researcher in France, now the star of the Ontological Hysteric Theater company), in her Greenwich loft. He renewed contact with Babette Mangolte, who was making a film of Henry James's *What Maisie Knew*. And he spent a day with Guitaut, who had given herself a twelve-month Manhattan sabbatical, and walked with her for miles, from the Guggenheim to the Frick Collection and down to Little Italy, looking, and laughing, in excellent spirits. Perec and Guitaut ended up at the southern tip of Manhattan, at the ferry pier, whence you can glimpse Ellis Island.

On 8 November 1972 the guest of honour at the meeting of OuLiPo sketched out a plan for a formal detective novel involving four characters and twelve crimes, to be called *The Mystery of the Haunted House*. There was some discussion, following Italo Calvino's proposal, of "remarkable numbers", one of Le Lionnais's many pet subjects, and Queneau commented on the literary potential of "false coincidences", coincidences that are in fact no such thing.

The meeting then moved on to the next main heading of the

agenda, "Creation". Georges Perec described what he imagined as "FLL's perfect cup of tea":

> *A plan for a novel in semantic Oulipian mode:*
>> *Knight's tour on a ten-square board*
>> *Latin bi-square of order 10*
>> *false* dixain
>> *description of a painting: a house with the façade removed.*
>> *Ten floors, ten rooms per floor*

The "knight's tour" problem to which Perec refers in his outline is the fastidious conundrum set by the chess piece called the knight (the "horseman" in French), which leaps two squares in any direction and then one further square at a ninety-degree angle to its first direction of move. Getting such a quirky jumper to land once only on each of the sixty-four squares on a standard eight-by-eight chessboard can take a month of Sundays, the worst of it being that there is more than one possible solution. The sideways lurch of the knight was Vladimir Nabokov's preferred image for his own writing procedures. *The Real Life of Sebastian Knight* (1939) – the first book that Nabokov wrote in English, whilst he was still living in France – was one of Perec's favourite pseudo-biographies of a writer.

> In those last and saddest years of his life Sebastian wrote *The Doubtful Asphodel*, which is his unquestionable masterpiece . . . The theme of the book is simple: a man is dying: you feel him sinking throughout the book; his thought and his memories pervade the whole with greater or lesser distinction (like the swell and fall of uneven breathing). . . . A man is dying, and he is the hero of the tale; but whereas the lives of other people in the book seem perfectly realistic (or at least realistic in a Knightian sense), the reader is kept ignorant as to who the dying man is. . . . The man is the book; the book itself is heaving and dying, and drawing up a ghostly knee. . . . They are, these lives, but commentaries to the main subject. We follow the gentle old chess player Schwarz, who sits down on a chair in a room in a house, to teach an orphan boy the moves of the knight. . . . The lovely tall primadonna steps in her haste into a puddle and her silver shoes are ruined. . . . Professor Nussbaum, a Swiss scientist, shoots his young mistress and himself dead in a hotelroom at

half past three in the morning. . . . Sebastian Knight had always liked juggling with themes, making them clash or blending them cunningly. . . . In *The Doubtful Asphodel*, his method has attained perfection. It is not the parts that matter, it is their combination.[1]

What would Perec's parts be? Everything, obviously. Everything OuLiPo had given him, to make his novel Le Lionnais's "perfect cup of tea"; everything that life, travel, art, and literature had given him, to make it a fitting realisation of the *vast ensemble* that he had promised Nadeau some three years previously.

Perec never commented in writing on the role played by Nabokov in the invention of *Life A User's Manual*, but he provided a host of clues about his other sources, both before and after the novel was written.

> *The sources of my plan are several. One of them is a drawing by Saul Steinberg, which appeared in* The Art of Living *(London: Hamish Hamilton, 1952) and which depicts a lodging house* [in New York] *(you can tell it is a lodging house because beside the front door is a notice saying No Vacancy) with part of its façade removed so that you can see inside maybe twenty-three rooms (I say "maybe" because there are some hints of other rooms behind them). Just making a list – which can't even claim to be exhaustive – of the furniture and actions represented is a quite vertiginous enterprise.*
>
> [*EsEs* 58]

✈

In Munich, meanwhile, *L'Augmentation* went on stage as *Die Gehaltserhöhung* ("The Pay Award"), a more socially eloquent title than the formal *Wucherungen*. Annette Spola, the director, produced it for the Theater am Sozialamt not as ironic anti-theatre *à la* Ionesco but as agitprop farce in the manner of Dario Fo. The actors paraded, and clowned, and spoke to each other whilst wearing absurd costumes and striking comic poses, making the point that bureaucracy crushes us all and must be subverted. Perec's well-crafted language-machine bore this re-creation very well, and the whole was closer in

[1] Vladimir Nabokov, *The Real Life of Sebastian Knight* (London: Penguin Books, 1964), pp. 146–147.

Saul Steinberg, "The Art of Living" (1949)

spirit to the re-politicised Perec of *Cause commune* than a purely formal presentation would have been.

"First forty-five performances already sold out", claimed the TamS press release in November 1972. "A wow like Queneau's *Autobus S*".[1] The Munich success attracted the interest of theatre directors all over Germany. In February 1973 *Die Gehaltserhöhung* opened in a rival production directed by Kurt-Achim Köweker, in repertory at the Studio-Souterrain in Wiesbaden. Simultaneously, and whilst it was still playing to packed houses in Munich, Jens Scholkmann staged Perec's play at the Zimmertheater in Münster. Annette Spola's original production eventually closed, only to be revived during the Studio Theatre Week in Munich in June 1973.

Perec thus became a German playwright as well as a celebrated innovator of radio drama (the script of *Die Maschine*, considered a classic of its genre, was now available in the yellow pocket-book series published by Reclam). What was more, he was being credited with the invention of a new kind of dramatic social criticism, the enunciation of whose name calls for a careful swallow and a clearing of the throat:

Abteilungsleiteraufsuchsaktionstheater.

♩

Occasion: 2 December 1972, at 85, Avenue de Ségur, third floor, a record party, to listen to Wagner – *all* of Wagner. From 10:30 A.M. until whenever. *Present*: Georges Perec (host, record-changer), Harry Mathews, Philippe Drogoz, Sylvia Lamblin, James Richardson. *Comments*: Concert abandoned at 5:30 P.M., with twenty sides (*Siegfried, Götterdämmerung*) left to hear. *Anyway,* Perec confessed, *I don't think we could have stood it* [*MO* 220].

The dizzying prospects of "FLL's perfect cup of tea", if not the sound of seven solid hours of Wagner, were whirling around Perec's head when Philippe Drogoz moved into the flat opposite his at Avenue de Ségur. Neither Francis Moaty nor Perec had yet celebrated their respective arrivals in the proper style, and Philippe's seemed an excel-

---

[1] The stage version of *Exercices de style*, translated by Helmle and Harig.

lent pretext for a triplicate housewarming. On 9 December 1972 the friends of all three poured into the house, climbed up the stairs, and milled around on the two floors to be warmed. There was dancing aloft, in Francis's flat; in Philippe's, on the third floor, a group formed in a circle on chairs and cushions to discuss the great issues of the day; over the landing, *chez Georges*, the main supply of drink was meted out. At the party's peak there were maybe 150 people on hand – old friends, new friends, friends of friends, amongst them mathematicians, painters, writers and musicians, librarians and neurophysiologists, people in advertising, people in journalism, people who still went to the Moulin d'Andé and people who had never heard of the place, film directors, putative producers, actors, and university teachers. The revelry spilled out of the three flats and onto the stairs, where neighbours perforce joined the chattering throng, and everyone stood and talked, holding glasses and cigarettes, and snack-laden cardboard plates, and one by one they all began to sit on the steps. The last of them did not leave until five in the morning, to the sound of the first metro train of the day. When the three hosts awoke, sometime towards dusk, they had a long night's work ahead of them clearing up. Where else would Perec have found all of the following?

Several odd shoes, a long white sock, a pair of tights, a top hat, a false nose, cardboard plates in piles, or crumpled, or lying singly, laden with left-overs – tops of radishes, heads of sardines, slightly gnawed lumps of bread, chicken bones, cheese rinds, crimped paper boats that have been used for petits fours *and chocolates, cigarette butts, paper napkins, cardboard cups; [. . .] various empty bottles and an almost entire pat of butter in which several cigarettes have been neatly crushed; [. . .] a whole assortment of small triangular trays with various morsels still in them: green olives, roast nuts, salty biscuits, prawn crackers; [. . .] a barrel of Côtes-du-Rhône on its own stand, beneath which floorcloths, a few yards of kitchen towel that has capriciously loosed itself from its dispenser, and a whole collection of glasses and cups, some of them still half-full, are spread; [. . .] here and there [. . .] lumps of sugar, liqueur glasses, forks, knives, a cake-slice, coffee spoons, beer cans, Coca-Cola bottles, almost untouched bottles of gin, port, Armagnac, Marie-Brizard, Cointreau,* crème de banane, *hairpins, innumerable receptacles used as ashtrays and overflowing with carbonised matchsticks, cigarette ash, pipe ash, butts with and without lipstick*

stain, date stones, walnut, almond, and peanut shells, apple cores,
orange and tangerine peel; [. . .] *a bowl of gooey mayonnaise*
[. . .] *in an armchair;* [. . .] *dried-out cucumbers, aubergines,*
and mangoes and a remnant of a lettuce gone sour [. . .] *near the*
top of the bookcase, [. . .] *and the remains of an elaborate party*
cake – a huge meringue in the shape of a squirrel – [. . .] *between*
two folds in one of the carpets.   [L 132]

Perec finished off 1972 with a holiday in Tunisia – his first real holiday, so he said, in eighteen months. From Sfax, he sent a postcard
to Harry.

▨

Life A User's Manual was not simply thought up in the autumn of
1972, even if the OuLiPo minute of 8 November is the first firm trace
of its design. Many of the fragments of life that Perec would eventually incorporate into his masterpiece come from long before 1972: the
theme of travelling, for instance, was already present in his first, lost
novel, *Les Errants*; the name of the street in which *Life A User's Manual*
would be set is made from those of two friends of the 1950s, Jeannette
Simon and Jean Crubellier; two of the novel's main characters, Serge
Valène and Gaspard Winckler, also have names first invented before
1960. Perec could have been thinking about the fictional uses of Paul
Klee, jigsaw puzzles, and Steinberg since the early 1960s, and, as we
have seen, he had something called "the Bartlebooth synopsis" in his
mind since 1969, if not earlier (*see* p. 459). What was it that allowed
these and many other pieces to begin to assemble themselves into a
hugely ambitious plan in 1972? The closing of Perec's dreambook in
August and the healing of the wounds of Andé were no doubt necessary prerequisites; Perec's perception of the potential of "multiplexed" constraints, gained from translating Mathews and from
Konzertstück, must also have played some part; but some of the
writer's friends remain convinced that the vital catalyst was 85
Avenue de Ségur itself. Like many other houses in Paris, Madame
Reyrolle's block had a concierge, cats, a staircase and two façades of
regular windows with white-painted double shutters. Seen from the
corner cafe on the other side of the street, number 85 resembles a
beehive. Through the eyes of Nabokov's defensive prodigy Luzhin,
however, it could be taken for an outsize chessboard.

The formal plot presented to OuLiPo on 8 November may seem

impenetrably abstract, but Perec's many subsequent explanations make his design for *Life A User's Manual* crystal-clear. The basic figure is a 10 x 10 grid, an oversize chessboard. It had to be 10 x 10 to honour OuLiPo, for it was the recently discovered Graeco-Latin bi-square *of order 10* that Claude Berge had set as a challenge. Perec proposed to map the grid onto a Steinbergian apartment house with its façade removed, thus:

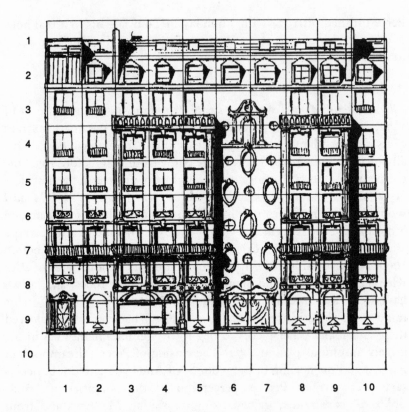

He would meet Jacques Bens's challenge as well, by writing an eight-hundred-page monster-book that described each of the one hundred grid locations, or spaces, or rooms, in order. But what order? It would not do to plod predictably along the rows or down the columns of the table. Perec's Nabokovian answer was to use knight's-tour order – for which an original solution was required, since no one had ever bothered to plot the knight's tour on anything other than an eight-by-eight-square chessboard. The solution he found, "gropingly", by himself, was this:

	1	2	3	4	5	6	7	8	9	0
1	59	84	15	10	57	48	7	52	45	54
2	98	11	58	83	16	9	46	55	6	51
3	85	60	97	14	47	56	49	8	53	44
4	12	99	82	87	96	17	28	43	50	5
5	61	86	13	18	27	80	95	4	41	30
6	100	71	26	81	88	♞	42	29	94	3
7	25	62	89	70	19	36	79	2	31	40
8	72	65	20	23	90	69	34	37	78	93
9	63	24	67	74	35	22	91	76	39	32
0	66	73	64	21	68	75	38	33	92	77

The Knight's Tour solution. *The tour begins on square 6,6*

An orthogonal bi-square can now be mapped directly on to the block of flats, and for each grid location (that is, each room and chapter) it gives a unique pair of numbers, out of two sets only from 0 to 9, or twenty "elements" in all. Perec knew what he was doing in this domain already, since he had been using a bi-square of order 12 to pattern his visits and memories of places in Paris for nearly three years now, and had had a go at overlaying a bi-square of order 10 on a musical structure in *Konzertstück* earlier that year. However, an eight-hundred-page novel based on the exhaustive recombination of just two sets of ten elements could prove to be more than a little tedious. Harry Mathews had used many different "generators" for each of the chapters in *Tlooth* and *The Conversions*. The most elegant solution for Perec, because it was the simplest, would be to use the bi-square device over and over again. In the end, he employed twenty-one bi-squares, each comprising two lists of ten "elements", giving forty-two lists in all, with 420 "things" to distribute, forty-two to a box (and never the same forty-two twice). With so much of its material predetermined – the place of each chapter in the novel's sequence, the place of each room described in the block of flats, and forty-two different things to say about every room – surely the book would just write itself.

Perec did not use the same bi-square twenty-one times over. Queneau had studied the mathematics of permutation in the poetic form called the sestina and had worked out from it a formula that can be generalised to accommodate permutations of different sizes. The formula, called a quenina after its inventor, produces sestina-like structures out of five-, six-, eleven-, fourteen- and eighteen-line stanzas, or indeed out of any list of elements that can be treated as a sequence. Perec checked with Berge and found that applying Queneau's formula to a bi-square of order 10 would require some finessing, which meant that the sequence of twenty-one rejumbled ten-by-ten squares would follow the rules of a "false" *dixain*, or "pseudo-quenina". The underlying number-order of the contents of the one hundred chapters would thus be invisible to the readerly eye and probably to the author too, once he turned the handle of his great narration machine.

All of this is contained in the nutshell announcement made to OuLiPo on 8 November 1972. Further twists would be incorporated into the formal plotting before Perec actually began to write, but at this point, he had the basic design in place and much of the material in mind. He could keep a folder for each chapter, accumulate things to put in it, and distribute elements appropriately by means of his diabolical multiplex jumble device. He had picked up the gauntlets thrown by Berge, Bens, Queneau, and Le Lionnais, and he was nearly ready to brew his Oulipian cup of tea. He knew what it would take. He had explained it to Sylvia already, at one of the lowest points in his life, in a letter written on 2 January 1969:

> *There's only one important thing in life, and that's energy: that is to say, the quantity of strength and sustained effort you can bring to bear on a single person or thing.* [. . .] *"In the battle between the world and you", Kafka said, "back the world".*

Georges Perec, "Quatre figures pour *La Vie mode d'emploi*", *L'Arc* no. 76 (1979), pp. 50–54, also in *Atlas* 387–393. For further illumination of the combinatorial structure of *Life A User's Manual*, see Bernard Magné, "Cinquième Figure pour *La Vie mode d'emploi*", in *CGP I* 173–177, and Claude Berge and Eric Beaumatin, "Georges Perec et la combinatoire", *CGP IV* 83–96.

The reception of *L'Augmentation* on the German stage: *Münchener Abendzeitung*, 7 November 1972; Arnim Eichholz in *Münchner Merkur* and *Süddeutsche Zeitung*, both 9 November 1972; *Aachener Volkszeitung*, 16 November 1972; *Westfälische Nachrichten*, and *Münstersche Zeitung*, both 5 February 1973; *Wiesbadener Tagblatt*, and *Wiesbadener Kurier*, both 10 February 1973; *Frankfurter Rundschau*, 14 February 1973; and *Kieler Nachrichten*, 15 June 1973.

On the quenina, see *Atlas* 243–244; Jacques Roubaud, "Mathematics in the Method of Raymond Queneau", in Warren F. Motte, Jr., *Oulipo. A Primer of Potential Literature* ((London and Lincoln: Nebraska University Press, 1986), pp. 79–96, in particular paragraph 8. The numerate may refer to Raymond Queneau, "Note complémentaire sur la sextine", *Subsidia Pataphysica* no. 1 (1965).

The Art of Living, by Saul Steinberg (1949), is reproduced from a copy provided by the artist. The original has been lost.

Other sources include the archives of OuLiPo, letters from Georges Perec to Eugen Helmle, Sylvia Lamblin, and Harry Mathews, and the recollections of Jacqueline de Guitaut, Kate Manheim, Babette Mangolte, Francis Moaty, Philippe Drogoz, and Bernard Queysanne.

CHAPTER 50

On Location

1973

Meanwhile, Perec's analysis continued. He brought Pontalis not only his "overdreamt dreams" but also his time-capsule project and perhaps his "I remember" game as well.

> It was Pierre G. who made me see what the passion for places can sometimes mean. Childhood memories, Pierre used to say, were just not his thing. No point hunting for them. He didn't grumble about the emptiness, the bottomless gap at the origins of memory, nor did he turn it into a reason for believing vaingloriously that he was in some sense self-engendered. All he could do was take it on board as a fact . . .
>
> In fact his memory was immense, able to accept – no, to register – all kinds of information: telephone numbers, the name of a supporting actor in a B movie, of a horse that won at Longchamps, of a junior minister at the Department of the Environment, or the address of a restaurant in the department of Yonne that serves leek salad well worth the journey, or the shelf-mark of a tome he had had occasion to consult at the Bibliothèque Nationale, or the precise location of a statue in a square in the eighteenth arrondissement . . . Pierre's memory was like an inexhaustible bank of data in random array, like an unprogrammed and facetious computer . . .
>
> Sometimes, however, his memory would fix on something, and that was where it went astray. It would visit and explore particular places, determined to grasp them, to capture them like a patient camera, or to seize them like a bailiff. Pierre described to me the streets where he had lived, the rooms he had slept in, the design of the wallpaper, the exact size of the bed, the shape of the door-knob . . .[1]

---

[1] Jean-Bertrand Pontalis, *L'Amour des commencements* (Paris: Gallimard, 1986), pp. 165–166. Pontalis has not contradicted the general assumption that Pierre G., who bears Perec's palindromic initials, is the writer.

Lieux lost its impetus after the summer of 1972. The programme was nominally respected, but with increasing delay; descriptions and memories grew thinner, and the bimonthly envelopes holding them shrank accordingly, from 320 x 230 mm in March 1972, so Philippe Lejeune tells us, to 250 x 175 mm later on in the year [*MO* 174]. Perhaps Perec's scaling down of a project that he still talked about with enthusiasm to his friends and acquaintances stemmed from his lessening need to bury Ile Saint-Louis beneath a heap of other places, or perhaps it was simply that descriptions done now four times in a row had become boring; but it seems equally likely that his passion for filling in all the boxes in his twelve-by-twelve bi-square was undermined by the greater potential of what he had now decided to do with a multiplexed ten-by-ten grid, and by the greater number of hiding places it offered for "rooms he had slept in, the design of the wallpaper, the exact size of the bed". *Lieux* finally petered out in the summer of 1973 [*MO* 199], though retrospectively, Perec would declare that he had only taken a sabbatical [*EsEs* 73].

From January 1973, in fact, Perec was more concerned with locations of a different sort, for he and Bernard Queysanne had just about put together the resources required to turn *A Man Asleep* into a film. No doubt they would have started filming sooner had they found financial backing, but none of the production companies they had approached in 1971 was inclined to invest in a film with no dialogue, no characters, no plot, no box-office stars – with nothing, in fact, that might make it a viable proposition. Despite their setbacks, Perec and Queysanne were determined to use the money awarded them in June 1971 before the twelve-month time limit ran out. Nour came to the rescue: SATPEC would provide editing studios and processing laboratories in return for a fifty per cent stake in the production. That offer enabled Perec and Queysanne to obtain a six-month extension of the CAR subsidy, up to the end of 1972. Beyond that point they would have to start shooting, or lose the money for good. The French film producer Pierre Neurisse agreed to distribute the film once it was made, on the strict condition that its budget remained within the limit set by the CAR. It was far from obvious that a feature-length film *could* be made for only fifteen million old francs, but Perec and Queysanne decided to take Neurisse's closed purse as a challenge. There was a measure of leftish bravado in their decision to make the film on those terms; however, there was nothing haphazard in the way they went about the task.

Queysanne showed Perec how to go about preparing a film: how to survey and then select locations, how to list them and sort them into a practical order; how to identify the props that would be needed and divide them into things to be bought, things to be borrowed, things already to hand (example: a postcard reproduction of Antonello da Messina's *Le Condottiere*), things to be asked for (example: from Nestlé, a magnum instant coffee tin, circa 1956), and things that have to be accepted (in place of the BEA poster on the wall of the room in Rue Saint-Honoré, an advertisement for Air Tunisia). The filmmaker's craft is essentially a practical one, an acquired expertise in the ordering of times and places, in the collection and disposition of people, equipment, sets, and things – from beds and plastic bowls to tripods and teaspoons. Perec worked alongside Queysanne, watching, listening to, and learning from him, not allowing his deeper reflections to puncture the fun of their cooperative pursuit.

As a filmmaker, Queysanne was accustomed to being part of a team. Perec was a rare bird amongst writers in that he had already enjoyed several different and successful types of collaboration (on *La Disparition*, the book on go, the German radio plays, and PALF, a fragment of which was about to appear in *Change*, the review that Jacques Roubaud [and others] hoped would outshine Philippe Sollers's *Tel Quel*). The arrangement between the two directors of *A Man Asleep* was as effective as it was simple: Queysanne held sway over the filming and Perec over the text, but the whole project would be done by the two of them working together. Neither was in charge, and yet both were; each had the right to veto the other's ideas.

A Man Asleep is a film made under constraint – the constraint of an unprecedentedly tiny budget. It affected every aspect of their work. Perec could not take leave from the lab to make a film that would earn him nothing, so the shooting had to fit around his regular job. It was done at weekends, or in the very early hours of the morning, in forty-one separate shoots between the beginning of March and the end of July 1973. They were in no great rush to complete a sequence on any particular occasion, and under no pressure to compromise on a take in order to meet a producer's deadline; they could wait for the sun to go in, or for the rain to stop falling. They invented their own "special effects". For a sequence in which the film's single character turns into his reduplicated double, they asked a wall-mirror wholesaler to let them film in his stockroom. For the examination that the "sleeping man" misses, they did not need to pay extras; Paul Virilio, Perec's coeditor at *Cause commune*, lent a classroom full of real examinees at the Ecole Spéciale d'Architecture. For the cinema scene they rounded up friends to make up a crowd: the usherette, barely visible, is Kate Manheim, and one of the heads seen from behind belongs to Babette Mangolte, on one of her brief returns from New York.

Before shooting began, during the weeks of intensive preparation, Perec's work for *Cause commune* took a significant turn. The paranoid outrage of the early political pieces was replaced by a more modest but no less radical way of looking at things. The new buzzword of Anglo-American anthropology had perhaps been tossed around at meetings of the editorial board, but what Perec proposed, in an article published in February 1973, was as much the fruit of his work with Queysanne as a French reinvention of ethnomethodology.

The media provide us with news, Perec wrote, but news is, by definition, an account of the unusual, the extraordinary, the exotic.

> *Where is the rest of it, the rest of our lives, the rest of what really happens? How can we give an account of what goes on every day and goes on going on from day to day – the banal, everyday, obvious, common, ordinary, infraordinary, habitual background noise of living? How do we approach it, how can we describe it?* [inf 10–11]

The difficulty in looking critically at what is utterly ordinary lies in the fact that its very ordinariness makes it invisible. Learning to see the world that surrounds us as an object of critical understanding, Perec suggests, could be tantamount to reinventing anthropology – an anthropology *that will talk about us, that will elicit from us what we have for so long stolen from others: not exotics but endotics* [inf 12].

The proposal for a "new endotics" is not at all far from the ideas that Perec had gleaned from Marcel Mauss in the 1950s, and it makes sense of some of the writing projects that had been in his mind, and in his files, for several years:

> *What we must question is bricks, concrete, glass, our table manners, our utensils, our tools, our timetables, our rhythms of living. Question whatever seems to have ceased to surprise you forever. We are alive, to be sure; we breathe, no doubt about it; we walk, we open doors, we go down stairs, we sit at tables to eat, we lie down in a bed to sleep. How? Where? When? Why?*
> *Describe the street you live in. Describe another. Compare.*

Make a list of the contents of your pockets, of your handbag. Query the origin, the use, and the future of every one of the objects you find.

Interrogate your teaspoons.

What's under your wallpaper?

How many movements do you have to make to dial a telephone number? Why?

Why can you not buy cigarettes at the chemist's? Why not?

It matters little to me that these questions are fragmentary, barely indicative of a method, at the most a pointer to a project. It matters a great deal that these questions should seem trivial and futile. That is precisely what makes them at least as essential, if not more so, than so many other questions by means of which we have tried in vain to tune into our truth.   [*inf* 12–13]

All of Perec's subsequent writing is to some degree a prosecution of the aims that he first formulated in February 1973. At a stroke, the "invention of endotics" gives Perec's early career, from La Ligne générale to *Things*, an obvious retrospective coherence, and joins it, in a leap that leaves out most of the Andé misadventure, to the works he published thereafter.

The first of the new works undertaken alongside the preparation of *A Man Asleep* and the "invention of endotics" was – like almost everything Perec would write henceforth – the realisation of something begun long before. On 21 January he took a fresh, unused leather-bound ledger (of the sort his uncle used to record purchases and sales of pearls at the *bureau*) and wrote on the cover page: *Choses* ("Things").

Years before, in trying to describe how he had first started writing *Things*, Perec had recalled the first flood of fragments and sentences that had started it all off, sentences such as:

One day Michel wanted to be immensely rich
or:
   There were seven of us
or:
   There were seven of them
or:
   I remember . . .

or:
Michel didn't remember very well . . .[1]

The title page of the ledger opened in January 1973 reads: *1973. Choses communes. Espèces d'espaces*. "*Choses communes*" ("Common Objects") links *Things* (*Les Choses*) to *Cause commune* by way of a Franco-Italian pun, *cose comuni*, which sounds like *cause commune* pronounced with an Italian accent but in fact means "common objects", or *choses communes*. On 21 January Perec entered the first of his own written *I remembers* in the ledger. Over the next five months he would add 154 more recollections of "common things" – *almost forgotten, inessential, commonplace memories, shared if not by all then at least by very many* [*Jms* p. 119; *MO* 242–244].

On location Perec did not play the role of the fretting man of letters but instead assumed the persona that had always suited him better, that of clown. When Bernard turned on the ignition of the mini-moke to drive his codirector and his equipment off for the day's shooting, Perec would (almost always) scream *aie!!!* as if he had just had his finger smashed in the (nonexistent) car door. When he had had a drink or two and was feeling mawkish, he would recall, with a crocodile tear in his eye, how he had chopped off the finger of one of his dear cousins in the Negev when he slammed a car door in anger. Perec allowed his interlocutors to understand that this was why, though a Jew, he was anti-Zionist and could not bear the idea of ever going back to Israel. For Bernard, it merely explained why Georges was forever carrying on with his silly car-door joke.

The only practical role that a hamfisted imp could be safely asked to play on a shooting location was that of clapperboard man – the minion who scribbles the name and number of the take on a clapperboard that is then filmed as the first frame, to label the sequence for subsequent editing. Instead of a conventional chalkboard with a zebra-stripe clapper, Perec used a spiral-bound writing-pad on which he could let his puns run free: on any given take, *Un Homme qui dort* might be transmogrified into *Hom ki dort*, *Un Homme Cukor*, *Une Pomme qui dort*, *Un Homme au bras d'or,* or *Little Big Man Sleeping*.

Shooting began on 4 March. In the preceding four months, Perec had invented, out of ideas, projects, drafts, and knowledge garnered over a lifetime of writing, not only the main principles of *Life A User's Manual* but also the concept of the "infra-ordinary", *Je me*

[1] FP 89, 3 (probably 1965).

souviens, and *Espèces d'espaces*, whilst not ceasing even for a week to be an employee of the CNRS, an assiduous analysand, and the convivial codirector of his own semiautobiographical feature film. But there were old scores for him to settle still, most particularly the embarrassment of a book announced in August 1970 that had sunk without trace in the autumn of that year, as he himself nearly had. He no longer even possessed a complete run of the episodes published in *La Quinzaine littéraire*. On 7.3.73 Perec turned thirty-seven; it was as if the calendar itself were trying to remind him with a palindrome that something was missing. On 8 March 1973 he wrote to his publisher:

> *Dear Maurice Nadeau*
> *I am soon going to go back to W and finish it: I've been feeling the need to do so for three years but only very recently has the possibility emerged.*[1]

It is possible, even likely, that Perec's analysis with Pontalis, alongside the publication of his dreambook and the healing of the wounds of Andé, had prompted the reemergence of *W*, but there was at least one other factor involved. David Bienenfeld had fallen ill with stomach cancer and would not last long. The imminent disappearance of the authority-figure of Perec's childhood, who had in all probability made the refugee *forget* what he had left behind in Belleville, must have played a role in rescuing Perec's autobiography from the limbo of abandoned works. Perec may have wanted to get the story done in time for his uncle David; alternatively, he may have felt that he would soon be free to write it for himself. Before taking up *W* once again, Perec polished off "Quinze variations discrètes sur un poème connu" ("Fifteen discreet variations on a well-known poem"). Step by step, the "well-known poem" is transformed, much like Goethe's lyric in *Die Maschine*, into something quite unrecognisable. However, the pretext of Perec's 1973 exercise lies quite near the first roots of Gaspard Winckler, for the poem transformed and mocked is Verlaine's "Gaspard Hauser chante" – as if, by rewriting it, Perec could at last shed the lyric of the unloved orphan.

> *O vous tous, ma peine est profonde*
> *Priez pour le pauvre gars*

[1] Translated from a photographic reproduction of the original in Maurice Nadeau, *Grâces leur soient rendues* (Paris: Albin Michel, 1990).

("Everyone, hear my deep pain/ And pray for the poor wee chap")

[*Atlas* 157]

Tutorial
> *Observe a street [. . .] Make an effort. Take your time.*
> *Note down the place: a café terrace near the Rue du Bac–*
> *Boulevard Saint-Germain junction.*
> *time: 7 in the evening*
> *date: 15 May 1973*
> *weather: fine*
> *Note down what you can see. Anything notable that happens.*
> *Do we know how to see what is notable? Is there anything we are*
> *struck by?*
> *Nothing strikes us. We do not know how to see.*
> *We'll have to go about it more quietly, almost idiot-fashion.*
> *Force ourselves to write down what is of no interest whatsoever,*
> *what is absolutely obvious, commonplace, dull.*   [*EsEs* 70]

Meanwhile, filming continued, in leisurely fashion but not without rigorous organisation. Jacques Lederer became Queysanne's assistant director for the interior sequences. Acquaintances from the film world and from *Cause commune* dropped in on location. The novelist and biographer Dominique Desanti found herself being subjected to a strange quiz: what did she know about *Les Allobroges*? About its editor? Had she been married? Had she been happy?

"Ah, that's not a simple question."

Yes it is, said Perec. *Did she love her husband and her lover at the same time?*

Did Dominique Desanti remember François Billoux? Yes indeed, but Perec should not think he was a hero. In 1945, she asserted most emphatically, Billoux had been just a very grey man on the PCF's Central Committee.

But people came to hear him in Grenoble from all the villages for miles around!

There were other open-air conversations in the summer of 1973, including one on the relative merits of Stendhal, Balzac, and Dumas.

Why should he read *The Three Musketeers*, Perec asked, when he knew what happened in *Twenty Years After*? But why should I read *Twenty Years After*, his sparring partner retorted, when I've no wish to know that Athos, Porthos, and d'Artagnan grow old?

Staša Stanojević, a Yugoslav acquaintance from the Moulin d'Andé whose own film, *Le Journal d'un suicidé* ("Diary of a Suicide"), had been released the previous year, also came to see Queysanne and Perec on location. Through Stanojević, Perec sent greetings to a long-forgotten friend in Belgrade, the painter Stojan Čelić. Some time later, Stanojević invited Perec to a party in a grand apartment in Rue Vineuse, in the sixteenth arrondissement. Perec turned up with Barbara Keseljević, another *Yougoslave de Paris*, who (on that occasion at least) seemed more preoccupied with hashish than with him. The flat in Rue Vineuse belonged to Stanojević's companion, a striking young woman with a warm laugh and large, hazel eyes. It was not the first time that Perec had met her. She was called Catherine Binet.

Based in part on the recollections of Ela Bienenfeld, Catherine Binet, Dominique Desanti, Bernard Queysanne, and Staša Stanojević.

CHAPTER 51

Esartuniloc

1973

Perec was on the move for much of 1973. In April, as the author of *Die Gehaltserhöhung* and *Die Maschine* (broadcast by Radio Zagreb in Serbo-Croat translation), he was the guest of the Second International Conference of Theatre Critics and Theatrologists at Sterijino Pozorje, in the Hungarian-speaking city of Novi Sad, in Yugoslavia.[1] On the way back he stopped over in Belgrade but did not renew contact with Žarko Vidović, nor with Milka Čanak, nor even with his first portraitist, Mladen Srbinović. However, he did telephone Stojan Čelić, whom he had last seen in Paris in 1959 but who had had news of him more recently through Staša Stanojević. Perec sounded lost and more than a little drunk. Čelić ended up scouring Belgrade for him and eventually found him in the street, almost in the gutter. He took the forlorn writer back to his flat and put him to bed. The next day, after jotting down his programmed and overdue "memory place" (Franklin-Roosevelt) on headed notepaper from Hotel Trdava-Varadin, Novi Sad, Perec talked enthusiastically to Čelić about his writing plans. As for his private life, he hinted, things were not so rosy. He had lost his heart to some girl in Novi Sad, for approximately twelve hours, and he was still recuperating from the briefest and most platonic of his affairs!

Perec had been renting Avenue de Ségur for a year, but he continued to keep an eye open for opportunities to rationalise his housing position. In the early summer of 1973 he found a three-room apartment with a kitchen, a telephone, and a tiny, private courtyard garden

---

[1] Sterijino Pozorje is an annual theatre festival in the manner of Avignon or Edinburgh, named after Jovan Sterija Popović (1806–56), a Serbian poet and playwright. The title of the 1973 conference was "The Theatre as Collective Act". The sessions were not recorded and the proceedings not published. According to Katarina Čiric-Petrović, of the International Cooperation Department, Sterijino Pozorje, Novi Sad, Perec did not give a paper but nonetheless took "a lively part in the discussions".

on the mezzanine floor at number 13 Rue Linné. The flat was in poor condition and located in a part of the Latin Quarter that was less smart than Rue de Seine, so Perec could just about afford it. He made no secret of his need for money. He was happy to script a six-minute official documentary on an overseas students' hostel for Queysanne (in the middle of shooting *A Man Asleep*), for a five-hundred-franc fee.[1] He was also delighted to accept Paul Virilio's commission of an essay for a new series, L'Espace critique, to be published by Galilée, which happened to have its offices at number 9 Rue Linné; he was not embarrassed to explain that he needed as large an advance on royalties as he could decently be given, to pay back the overdraft he had incurred for the deposit on his new flat.

Lieux and *Je me souviens* were both abandoned at about the time Perec paid his deposit on Rue Linné. The essay for Virilio, which he had already pondered for several months (the title, *Espèces d'espaces* ["Species of Spaces"], goes back at least to January 1973), was now a matter of contract and had to be put at the head of Perec's writing agenda; the filming of *A Man Asleep* also took up a great deal of time throughout 1973. Perec pretended to pursue *Lieux* between March and September by smuggling all twelve locations into the film [*EsEs* 77; see also *W* 47] – insisting, for instance, that Queysanne shoot a close-up of a hand putting a ticket into an automatic ticket-perforating machine on a bus parked at the bus stop at Place d'Italie, to get that month's "Italie" done – but he did it as much out of self-derision as out of persistence. In fact, the making of the film displaced both of Perec's memory exercises in subtler ways.

Queysanne was in charge of the practical side, and it was he who hunted for locations. For the closing sequence, in which the "man asleep" comes down to Place Clichy, to wait for the rain to stop falling, Queysanne proposed to use not Montmartre but the junction of Rue du Transvaal and Rue Olivier Metra, in the twentieth arrondissement. There was enough room there to park a truck undisturbed, and it was one of the few street-level places left that offered an almost unbroken panoramic view of the city. When the two directors went to inspect the location, Perec gave no particular sign of recognition, but merely said, yes, fine, that would do very well. Queysanne went

---

[1] *Le FIAP* (Foyer International d'Accueil de Paris) was produced by Pathé for the French Foreign Ministry; it was released in 1974.

to book the equipment needed to film a full "pan". It would be available on 24 July 1973.

David Bienenfeld died in July 1973, and the funeral was arranged for the afternoon of the twenty-fourth. Perec was not sure he would be able to attend, since the booking of the equipment for filming the final sequence of *A Man Asleep* could not be changed. He looked pale and drawn when he got to the cemetery, but he made it just in time to pay his last respects to a man whom he had admired, and detested, and to whom he owed his life. He came to the ceremony direct from location, which was also, ironically, where he had begun: Rue Vilin.

The 540-degree pan and tracking shots that form the closing sequence of *A Man Asleep* were filmed on the twenty-fifth day of shooting, 24 July 1973, from a rotating camera platform mounted on the back of a truck parked at the top of the steps that lead down to Rue Vilin. During the take a little boy, a five-year-old scamp, scuttled across the street, apparently straight out of number 24, which was then still standing. It was not until Queysanne read *W or The Memory of Childhood* that he understood that Rue Vilin was where Perec had spent the first years of his life; nor did Bernard Zitzerman, the camera-man, hear Perec make any reference to the meaning that the street held for him. Perec could not possibly have planted the little boy in Rue Vilin, yet the coincidence seems to put him in his own picture, *as if [. . .] in passing [. . .] as if it were only supposed to be a signature to be read by initiates* [L 226], just as Serge Valène would have liked to put himself into the unpainted canvas of 11 Rue Simon-Crubellier.

La Boutique obscure, Perec's book of the dreams he dreamt between May 1968 and August 1972, appeared in the summer of 1973. It was his first "real" book in four years, since *La Disparition*, and it was the first of his books to contain an intricate and deceptive index.[1] It was well received in the press, earning the enthusiastic support of Claude Mauriac and the interest of Bertrand Poirot-Delpech, who would remain *Le Monde*'s regular literary columnist for nearly two decades more. These professional readers responded to the originality, the modesty, and the captivating fascination of Perec's dream-book, which convinced them that there was a major literary talent lurking in the obscurity of a marginal Left Bank life. In *Le Nouvel Observateur*, Catherine David described the author as a man "taking cover behind

[1] *Lieux* was intended to have an index also. On Perec's "index obsession", see Philippe Lejeune, in *La Mémoire et l'oblique*, p. 201.

his talent as behind the crenellations of a domino castle", but obfuscation was not Perec's real intention in *La Boutique obscure*. The published book[1], as Philippe Lejeune points out [*MO* 52], reproduces Perec's original handwritten transcriptions much as they were. Names of real people are hardly veiled by the initials used,[2] and the book's two typographical devices – paired solidi to indicate "voluntary omissions" and split lines for twin-track dreams – are infrequently applied. However, the name Dampierre, which seems almost always to stand for the Moulin d'Andé in the dreams (or in their transcriptions), has longer roots in Perec's life and works. It is the name of a village very near to Blévy, and it is also (and not coincidentally) the name of an important fictional site in *Le Condottiere* (*see* p. 225). In both appearances, Dampierre (like Maillebois, in one draft of *La Grande Aventure* [*see* p. 294]) is connected with probably resented wealth and with some kind of real or imagined offence.

Perec later confided to his cousin Ela that he wished he had done more to transform his dream-transcriptions. *La Boutique obscure* is thus the only work which Perec is known to have regretted publishing. Unlike his other books, of course, it had its roots not in a literary project but in a personal routine which was itself part of a development that led to the decision to undertake a course of psychoanalysis. Perec's rather abrupt release of *La Boutique obscure* before the analysis had run its course makes its publication seem less like a literary decision than an act of dumping.

A Man Asleep was coproduced by SATPEC, and the processing, editing and mixing were done at the Gammarth studios, in a magical sea-cliff setting shared only by a few ambassadorial residences. Queysanne rented a house at La Marsa, another suburb of Tunis, from mid-September 1973. Perec joined him there for much of the autumn but dashed back to Paris more than once at short notice: he could not do without his regular dose of Pontalis, as he told Queysanne, but he also had business to attend to in the drawn-out process of acquiring

---

[1] Two sets of dreams were published in periodicals prior to Perec's decision to make a book from his dreams: "Quatre Rêves particulièrement influencés par le cinéma", *Nouvelle Revue française* no. 226 (October 1971), pp. 147–152; and "Six Rêves", *Cause commune* no. 2 (June 1972), pp. 49–52.

[2] P. and J.L. need no elucidation. Z. is a transparent replacement for S. at a time when Roland Barthes's study of Balzac's *Sarrasine*, entitled *S/Z* (Paris: Le Seuil, 1970), was at the height of its fame. The connection is made explicit in any case in dream number 21.

Rue Linné, and now and then he simply had to put in an appearance at the lab.

Philippe Drogoz and his American companion, Eugénie Kuffler, went to Gammarth, too, to compose the sound track music, which was created by synthesizer. They took their time. Perec and Queysanne may have shot the film in an atmosphere of amateur camaraderie, but they were not making an amateur movie. Every detail of the film's triple track – image, voice, and music – had to be coordinated perfectly, for the design of the film (as distinct from that of the book, though not of other books that Perec would write soon after) was to establish a *gap* between text and image, a contradiction between what was said and what was seen, right up to the final sequence (Rue Vilin for Place Clichy) where the two coincide, and where electronic organ pipes and angel voices impose their own lyrical meaning on the work.

The film team lived and worked in the suburbs, but they had a regular rendezvous point in the centre of town, in the lobby of the Hotel Africa, in Avenue Habib Bourguiba. It is said to resemble the Grianta Hilton in "*53 Days*" in much the same way that 85 Avenue de Ségur is said to resemble 11 Rue Simon-Crubellier; but it is also like many other subtropical grand hotels, from Bahrain to Bastia, where Perec stayed on various occasions before tackling his "literary thriller" in the lush environs of Queensland. But there is another, more curious connection between the Tunisian autumn of 1973 and Perec's Australian mystery. During the work on *A Man Asleep*, Philippe and Eugénie had a souvenir photograph taken of themselves beneath a false caravan route-sign saying "Timbuktoo 52 Days", a similar sign to the one described at some length on pages 22–23 of "*53 Days*".[1]

On one of his returns to Paris from the film studios near the site of Carthage, Perec followed the advice of Babette Mangolte and went to the Recamier Theatre to see an American troupe acting out *Classical Therapy*, a dramatic happening not unlike those made famous by the Living Theatre. The leading lady appeared on stage quite naked. Perec was struck as by thunder and fell in love in a flash. He wrote an ecstatic review whose title tells almost the whole story: "O images, vous suffisez à mon bonheur" ("O Images, You Suffice for My

[1] Despite this pre-inception of the theme, the postcard showing the sign "Timbuktoo 52 Days" that Perec intended to use as the jacket illustration of "*53 Days*" was given to him years later by Gérard Zingg. See below, p. 710.

Happiness").[1] He went to a cast party – chili con carne again, just like old times! – and ended up having an affair with an American dream. She was beautiful, she was talented, she was provocative and sentimental. Yes! Georges declared to Harry Mathews, who had recently introduced him to hashish, he would give it all up, pack his bags, and move to New York to be with her! Why couldn't he become an English writer? What would Harry do if he had the chance of a woman like her?

Well, said Harry, with his greater knowledge of the daughters of Eve, I wouldn't do anything like that. He warned Perec sternly: he was sure to take a fall. Shortly thereafter, the affair collapsed, and Perec was briefly desolate. It is not impossible that it was this disappointment that made him look towards alphabetic defences again.

First, though, there was the book to do for Paul Virilio. *Espèces d'espaces* was largely written, at least in first draft, in the course of 1973; other parts and paragraphs were added the following year, and the book finally came out in covers with a wrap-around illustration of a mariner's chart[2] in September 1974. For many readers *Espèces d'espaces* is the quintessential Perec, the most perfect distillation of his intellect, humour, character, and style. It consists of short chapters on different "species of spaces", as its title states and as was required by the series as a whole, which was devoted to reflective essays on "spatial" issues. The spaces that Perec selected for his essays are, in order, the page, the bed, the room, the flat, the block, the street, the *quartier*, the city, the countryside, the country, Europe, the world, and space – as if the entire universe were a cone resting on the single point of the written word. Much of what he says about these species of spaces is radically obvious and obviously childish, but that is the point of endotics: to look *without any pretensions* at the world that lies around you. It is not as easy as it seems.

Perec's approach to space is minimalist, modest, and personal. He offers no generalisations, only observations of the kind anyone might make (if he or she had thought of them first – but that is precisely the point), and thereby invents a uniquely democratic literary style.

---

[1] *La Quinzaine littéraire*, 1 October 1973.

[2] But not the *portulan* from Rue de l'Assomption, which Perec had now rehung on the wall of his study at Rue Linné. The original cover of *Espèces d'espaces* is a detail from a sixteenth-century map of the coast of Guinea, oriented to put east, not north, at the top of the page.

By the same token, *Espèces d'espaces* is an autobiographical work. In talking about the meaning of his own spaces and places, Perec mentions a sufficient number of dated locations to allow the construction of a skeletal postwar biography, from his childhood at Rue de l'Assomption and his visit to Israel at the age of sixteen, to his summer in Cornwall in 1954 and his journeys to Saarbrücken and Hof. There are references, too, to his unwritten works (such as the history of the rooms in which he has slept) and his major works in progress, *Lieux* (still) and *Life A User's Manual* (though the title has not yet lost its comma and figures here as *La Vie, mode d'emploi*). The childish simplicity of the syntax, the openness of mind, and the impish plausibility of Perec's perceptions make the authenticity of *Espèces d'espaces* unquestionable. Pontalis seems to have taken the view that it was when his client's computer-like mind fixed on particular places that it went astray; *Espèces d'espaces* may be seen as an aggressive reply in advance to that comment. Perec's text does mislead the reader in one respect, but the deception is calculated:

> *I haven't got much to say about the countryside: the countryside doesn't exist, it is an illusion. [. . .] However, like everyone else, I have been to the countryside several times in my life (the last time, if my memory serves me right, was in February 1973: it was very cold). Moreover, I like the countryside (I also like the city, I've said so already, I'm not hard to please). I like being in the country: you eat farmhouse bread, you breathe better, you sometimes see animals that you practically never see in the city, there are fires in the hearth, you play Scrabble and other minor parlour games.*
>
> [*EsEs* 93]

This is something of an understatement of the truth! Perec had been to the country hundreds of times and had in fact lived there for a good part of his life. Villard-de-Lans, Nivillers, South Godstone, Blévy, Rock, Saumur, Skye, Capo Vaticano, Schüren, Carros, Kerkennah, Lans-en-Vercors, and Saint-Félix are all "in the country", but perhaps they do not count since Perec only went to those places for holidays. Andé, Perec's home-from-home for the better part of five years, is a more flagrant, and patently voluntary, omission. It was there, "in the country", that Perec had written *A Man Asleep*, *La*

Disparition, the Great Palindrome, *L'Augmentation,* and much else. The piece of the jigsaw-puzzle put under the tablecloth by Perec's minimalising digs at the countryside in *Espèces d'espaces* is the creator's own kibbutz, called the Moulin d'Andé.

Very soon after his last departure from his Norman retreat, Perec had found another countryside hole to hide in for long weekends of relaxation and writing. From about 1971 he went on perhaps a dozen different occasions to Saint-Dié-sur-Loire, to a house rented by his friend Jacqueline de Guitaut. On warm autumn weekends they would take the old bicycles out of the shed and pedal along country lanes to the banks of the Loire, and sometimes see well-dressed hunters swishing through the roadside woods in pursuit of wild boar.

"There goes your musketeer, Countess!" was Perec's ritual reminder of Guitaut's elevated ancestry – and of the name of d'Artagnan's valet, in *The Three Musketeers.*

"Sod off, Jew-boy!", his co-cyclist would robustly and affectionately retort.

🍁

L'Art effaré, the Perec-Drogoz collaboration on a tonic sol-fa opera, came back onto the agenda at Avenue de Ségur and again in Tunis in 1973. The creators adopted a rule to use only five of the seven notes of the octave, *do, re, mi, la,* and *si,* which instantly transformed the opera's title into a visible exception, since it contains a *fa.* Perec typed out all the permutations and combinations of the five regular syllables on the left-hand edges of a voluminous stack of filing cards, and then he worked through them, noting down in fine red felt-tip any "semanticisations" that occurred to him. He and Drogoz then worked up the beginning of a story (an island story, as it happens) and the first bars of the music.[1]

Harry Mathews had been taken aback at first by Perec's resistance to the idea of poetry. He tried to convince his friend to give it a try, arguing that poetry was the one kind of writing in which constrictions of form were customarily observed; Perec should, he said, suspend his misplaced objections to "inspiration", stop declaring that he feared nothing more than facing a sheet of paper with the intention of pro-

---

[1] Published as "L'Art effaré: Ouverture", *Le Fou parle* nos. 21–22 (1982), pp. 1–3.

ducing poetry, and just get down to it, using a suitably constrictive, Oulipian prop. In the autumn of 1973 Perec took a prop that he knew well as a crossword-puzzle player, the frequency list of the letters of the alphabet. In French it begins with *e*, of course, and continues with *s, a, r, t, u, n, i, l, o* and *c*. By definition, the commonest letters of the alphabet, taken together, permit the largest number of anagrams, and Perec invented out of that very simple principle a kind of writing that had never previously been attempted.

By means of ingenious word-splitting and the use of fragmented syntax, obsolete vocabulary, and obscurity (as in Perec's palindromes), the letters *esartuniloc* could be rearranged in a very large number of ways, some of which might count as poetry. In November 1973, Perec produced four hundred such rearrangements of the eleven commonest letters, and found he could make some kind of sense out of the material. The exploit looks easy when first explained, but actually making it work is as staggeringly difficult as composing straight off in four-part harmony. There is nothing mechanical about it. The four hundred anagrams of the eleven letters used by Perec represent only 0.001 per cent of all possible arrangements, since $11!$ $= 39,916,800$.

Perec fixed on the number eleven as the figure of his letter-based poetry for a simple technical reason: there is no word in the French language which contains all of the first twelve letters in the frequency list, used once only, but there is one, and only one, that is an anagram of the first eleven: *ulcérations*. Despite this, the number eleven also clearly carried a commemorative significance for Perec (his mother was deported from Drancy on 11 February 1943) and it recurs in his subsequent poetry and fiction in many places where it has no technical necessity – notably in the address of the block of flats in *Life A User's Manual*, 11 Rue Simon-Crubellier.

The constraint that Perec first explored in the autumn of 1973 has a triple technical definition. It is, first, simply anagrammatical, involving rearrangements of a given set of letters. Second, it is heterogrammatical, since each anagram-set must contain *all* of the given letters, and no letter may be used a second time until the whole set has been exhausted. For that reason the poems constructed are also isogrammatical, that is to say they consist of lines of exactly equal letter-length. This is the beginning of Perec's first "esartuniloc" poem, itself entitled *Ulcérations*, given in letter-box form and in its poetic transcription:

COEURALINST	Coeur à l'instinct saoûl,
INCTSAOULRE	Reclus à trône inutile,
CLUSATRONEI	Corsaire coulant secourant l'isolé
NUTILECORSA	Crains-tu la course intruse?
IRECOULANTS	
ECOURANTLIS	*O recluse with your useless throne*
OLECRAINSTU	*and the drunken instinct of your heart,*
LACOURSEINT	*Sinking pirate saving the man alone,*
RUSE	*Do you fear the intruded race?*

Perec's first sustained attempt at poetry, written between editing film in Tunis, mixing sound in Paris, doing lab work, buying a flat, and carrying out a dozen other activities, was typed up onto a stencil and run off in perhaps a hundred copies to form his New Year's gift-booklet for 1974.[1] It immediately spawned its own subversion or extension: if poetry could be achieved from the isograms of *esartun-iloc*, why not consider the potential of the other fifteen letters of the alphabet? They could not all be let in at once – that would turn Perec into Victor Hugo! – but they could be taken one by one. Perec stuck with the number 11 and experimented with using the first ten (*esartunilo*) plus each of the other letters of the alphabet in turn, to make sixteen series in all (+*b*, +*c*, +*d*, +*f*, +*g*, +*h*, +*j*, +*k*, +*m*, +*p*, +*q*, +*v*, +*w*, +*x*, +*y*, and +*z*). If there were eleven poems in each series (*Ulcérations* now being, retrospectively, a variant +*c* series of the more ambitious project), that would make 176 poems in all. In a further symmetrical constraint, each poem was to consist of eleven "lines" – that is to say, each would be an elevenfold heterogram of its letter-set, 121 characters in length. He did a baker's half-dozen of these *Alphabets* in January 1974. Maybe it was then that he said, half jokingly, half seriously, to Drogoz: *It's too hard! I'm giving up! I'll abandon all constraint!* He did give it up, in fact, at least in this particu-

---

[1] This first and now unobtainable "edition" shows both the "letter-grid" and the "poetic transcription", as does the second and equally unobtainable printing (Paris: La Bibliothèque oulipienne, 1974). In *La Clôture et autres poèmes* (Paris: Hachette, 1980) a number of variants are introduced and the letter-grid is dropped. It is reinstated in Oulipo, *La Bibliothèque oulipienne*, vol. 1 (Paris: Editions Ramsay, 1987), pp. 11–15.

larly arduous form, for many months. He did not try out another series until *W or The Memory of Childhood* was almost finished, in October 1974, and then dabbled only sporadically at heterogrammatic poetry for several months more. But in the course of the summer of 1975, as *Lieux* petered out for the second and last time, heterogrammatic poetry came to fill its place at once. Perec's poetry can therefore be counted not only as the "output" of his involvement with OuLiPo, of his ability to listen to Harry Mathews, and of his technical expertise as a setter of crossword puzzles, but also as the next-but-one staging post on his obliquely autobiographical track.

Unpublished sources include FP 57, 97 (29 April 1973) and a letter from Georges Perec to Paul Virilio (13 June 1973).

The reviews of *La Boutique obscure* are to be found in *Le Monde,* 14 June 1973; *Le Figaro,* 18 August 1973; *Le Nouvel Observateur* no. 461 (10 September 1973).

Full technical descriptions of *Ulcérations* and of all Perec's subsequent heterogrammatical poetry are given by Bernard Magné and Mireille Ribière in *Cahiers Georges Perec* 5 (Paris: Editions du Limon, 1992).

Other information was kindly provided by Ela Bienenfeld, Stojan Čelić, Philippe Drogoz, Jacqueline de Guitaut, Harry Mathews, Bernard Queysanne, Paul Virilio, and Bernard Zitzerman.

CHAPTER 52

M/W

1974

It was during their work on the film of *A Man Asleep* that Perec told Queysanne about his next book, which would be called *W*. It was, he said, the most difficult thing he had ever set out to write. One day he let slip that he had found *le truc* – the trick, the device, or the mechanism – that would make the rest of it plain sailing, but he never really said what it was.

A Man Asleep was finished in December 1973. Before the first screening at the Antégor, for a chosen audience of friends, Perec spent the whole day with Queysanne, in a state of superagitated anxiety. All he could do was pun on the film's title in an effort to conjure the fate that might await it: *A Man Asleep – in a Cinema Seat; Let Sleeping Men Lie; Sleepers Creepers*; and so on. The showing turned out to be a moving experience. Many of the spectators were in tears at the end, as were both codirectors. The audience responded to the ponderous, insistent repetition of the symptoms of depression, to the film's exploration of an almost unknown black-and-white Paris (the opposite of the Parisian theme park that most films set there now show), and to the tangled emotions of the closing sequence, in which Drogoz's lyrical theme rises over whirling images of Belleville-for-Clichy whilst Ludmila Mikael reads in a flat, inexpressive voice the ambiguous last lines of Perec's text. The directors admitted outright that they had made a film of the sort that neither of them would normally go to see – both of them preferred "Hollywood" to "art" movies – but now that they had seen it properly, they, too, were moved to tears. They were moved most of all by the sight of their friends crying. They had made a film! And it worked! They had met Neurisse's challenge, and the challenge of the screen.

Would he now abandon literature for the cinema? Nadeau asked Perec in the foyer of the Antégor. Not at all, not at all, he replied to his publisher, to whom he owed, in principle, two more novels. Alain Trutat came to another one of the showings. Queysanne noticed, with disquiet, that he kept his eyes shut throughout; but when the lights came up, Trutat bought the sound track for the ACR.[1]

Unlike the novel, the film version of *A Man Asleep* has a mathematical construction. After the prologue (part 0, so to speak) there are six sections, which Perec and Queysanne called, for ease of reference in the shooting and editing, Rupture, Apprenticeship, Happiness, Anguish, Monsters, and Return. The six sections are interchangeable in the sense that the *same* objects, places, and movements are shown in each, but they are all filmed from different angles and edited into different order, in line with the permutations of the sestina. The text and the music are similarly organised in six-part permutations, and then edited and mixed so that the words are out of phase with the image except at apparently random moments, the last of which – the closing sequence – is not random at all but endowed with an overwhelming sense of necessity.

The private viewings continued into January 1974, in the normal course of film promotion, with invited audiences of friends, critics, and opinion makers. Although reactions were overwhelmingly favourable, no cinema chain would release *A Man Asleep*; it was too experimental, they all said, too demanding, and too gloomy.

Perec and Queysanne were angry about meeting a brick wall at the end of their journey. Were they to be punished for having made a feature film on a £12,000 budget? As they traipsed from distributor to manager, almost exploding with rage, they swapped insults about the *shopkeepers* who were strangling French cinema. But on 21 March 1974, the Jean Vigo Prize committee met and voted unanimously to make the 1974 award, for the best film of the season by a new director, to Queysanne and Perec, for *A Man Asleep*. The prize itself turned out not to be worth very much, but the honour was considerable. Now the film just had to have a commercial release. At last a tiny studio cinema in the Latin Quarter agreed to take it on. *A Man Asleep* ran at Le Seine from 24 March to 8 October 1974 – rather longer than many a commercial epic at larger venues. The receipts were sufficient to repay the CAR advance in full and reimburse Neurisse and SATPEC.

[1] It was broadcast on 26 March 1974 as *186260374010*, representing the programme's ACR series number, 186, the date of broadcast, and the name of Philippe Drogoz's and Eugénie Kuffler's experimental music group, Ensemble 010.

There were stranger things to come. Queysanne was informed that the film was on the short-list for the French selection for the international film festival at Cannes in May. He was then told that it had been selected. Later he was notified in writing that it was no longer selected. Queysanne took it to Cannes nonetheless (and had posters printed calling it a "Cannes Official Selection 1974"), and it was shown "*hors concours*" on 11 and 13 May. *A Man Asleep* then began the global round of film festivals, some of them attended by one or the other of the two directors. It was screened in June at Toulon, Karlovy Vary, and Los Angeles (in an English-language version, the text translated by Harry Mathews and read by Shelley Duvall); in August at Edinburgh, where it was presented by Queysanne; in October at Thonon-les-Bains (Queysanne and Perec both attended) and Turin (Queysanne alone); in November, at the new international film festival set up by Nour at Carthage, as a way to get his pal to Tunisia again and give him another prize; and finally (for that year) at the London Film Festival, where Perec made the introductory presentation and Queysanne arranged a celebration dinner in a Soho restaurant with the star of his next film,[1] Jane Birkin, the companion of Serge Gainsbourg. Jane Birkin told Perec that he looked just like Professor Branestawm in the comics she had read as a child.

In the eleven months between the first showing of *A Man Asleep* at the Antégor and its presentation at the BFI, in November 1974, Perec wrote *W or The Memory of Childhood*. He did no "time-capsule" texts during most of that period, very few "I remember"'s [*MO* 244], and only a handful of "alphabet" poems.[2] It is true that he put the finishing touches to *Espèces d'espaces* (which was published that autumn) and that he also flew to Nice to attend rehearsals of his "potato play", *La Poche Parmentier* (which lasted but a few performances and was

---

[1] *La Nuit transfigurée*, shot in November 1975 and later renamed *Diable au coeur*.

[2] *Alphabets* (Paris: Galilée, 1976), numbers 6, 10, 14, 19, 20, 22, 23, 24, 26, and 28 were all done in January and February, before *A Man Asleep* won the Jean Vigo Prize. For a full chronology of *Alphabets*, see Mireille Ribière, "*Alphabets* déchiffré", in *Cahiers Georges Perec 5* (Paris: Editions du Limon, 1992), pp. 137–138.

promptly forgotten),[1] but the main part of Perec's energy outside of the lab and his sessions with Pontalis went into the promotion of *A Man Asleep* and the composition of his childhood autobiography.

The Renaudot Prize had taught Perec that celebrity was a mixed blessing, and he did not want the Vigo Prize to annex him to a new New Wave (God forbid!), to psychoanalytic cinema, or to whatever else journalists might find expedient. But a film is a film and needs the media, and Queysanne had a career to establish. The two codirectors therefore plotted the campaign with care. They would keep it simple. They would stick to four themes, four catchwords, and place them in every interview they gave, whether separately or together. The film's subject would be a *radical refusal*; the young man in it would have made an *existential choice*; the directors would have sought to give their film a *musical structure,* which would be glossed as *symphonic*. All of the many pieces on *A Man Asleep* that appeared in French newspapers in 1974 do indeed present the work as a film essay about a young man's radical refusal of life, an existential choice not to be confused with depression or mental illness, a film that the directors had sought to structure musically, or to endow, as it were, with a symphonic construction. "Reception studies" are fraught with pitfalls!

A special screening of *A Man Asleep* was held in March 1974 at Tours, for the inmates and staff of the psychiatric hospitals of La Borde, Freschines, and La Chesnaie. A journalist interviewed "Georges Perec" after the showing. In fact, only Queysanne was there, and because he did not take to the atmosphere of the ensuing discussion, he left well before the end. Unless an unknown bearded joker did an impromptu impersonation of Perec-as-director, it must be assumed that the journalist culled his material (which contains the three main points of the general line – *radical refusal, existential choice,* and *musical structure*) from published sources. The codirectors' plan to manage the media had succeeded to the extent that their physical presence at "interviews" was now irrelevant.

Spectators at Tours and elsewhere asked why the voice-over was

---

[1] Michel Cournot did a flippant piece about it for *Le Monde* (22 April 1974), but like Perec's other plays, *La Poche Parmentier* received its first serious attention in the German-speaking world, though in this case it was not until some years after his death. It was first performed on radio as *Der Kartoffelkessel* (broadcast by SR on 15 October 1987) and on stage as *Die Kartoffelkammer* (at the Stadttheater Luzern, 1988).

read by a woman, not a man. The decision to use the voice of Ludmila Mikael had been made early on, for a simple reason. The speaker of the "you" in Perec's second-person novel is not identical to the person to whom "you" is said, but as neither is identified, the novel-text hovers in a paradoxical and moving ambiguity. The same effect could not be achieved on screen by the same means, however, since the film *shows* a young man (played by Jacques Spiesser). A male voice-over would be heard automatically as the internal monologue of the screen-character and would thus reduce the work to only one of its potential meanings. Perec had suggested using a child's voice. Queysanne had vetoed the idea. Or the quavery voice of a really old man? Obviously not. Only a woman's voice could mark the nonequivalence of speaker and spoken-to. Because the voice-over of *A Man Asleep* is spoken by a female voice, and because the character on the screen is a young man, every viewer understands without having to reflect that the character is not talking directly to himself, and also, just as clearly, that the narrator is not speaking to herself. There were some dotty resolutions put forward for the voice-paradox set up by the film – that the speaking voice was "the mother" (proposed by the psychiatric staff at the Tours discussion) or "conscience", since *conscience* is a feminine noun in French (proposed by an English discussant at the BFI). For Queysanne, for Perec, all there was to say was that it was the *voice of the film*.

Perec's analysis with Pontalis continued throughout 1974.

> *I had to speak. That's what I was there for. [. . .] The other, behind me, said nothing. At every session I waited for him to speak. I was sure that he was keeping something from me, something that he knew far more about than he was prepared to admit, something that was nonetheless in his mind. [. . .] From then on mistrust set in and enveloped my words as well as his silence: it became a tiresome game of reflections, images returning their Moëbius garlands to infinity, dreams too good to have been dreamt. Where was the truth? Where was the untruth? [. . .] When I tried to speak, to say something of myself, to come to grips with the clown inside me who juggled so cleverly with my story and conjured with such brilliance as to mystify himself, I felt immediately as if I was starting again on the same puzzle, as if, by going through all the possible combi-*

nations of pieces, one by one, I might one day find the image I was after.

Simultaneously something resembling a memory breakdown set in. I began to be afraid of forgetting, as though, unless I made a note of everything, I would be unable to hold on to any part of passing life. Every evening, with great scrupulousness, with obsessive conscientiousness, I made entries in a kind of log. It was the opposite of a "personal" diary; I only entered in it "objective" things that had happened to me: time of waking, timetable, journeys, purchases, progress in work (measured in lines or in pages), people met or just seen, details of the evening meal I had eaten in this or that restaurant, books read, records listened to, films seen, etc.
                                                                    [PC 68–69]

Perec's "fear of forgetting" coincided with the writing of *W or The Memory of Childhood*, which was framed in time by the time-capsule project and by *Je me souviens*, both of which were begun previously and picked up again once the childhood autobiography was done.

I kept a log. I noted all my meals, and it produced a result that was both monstrous and really quite curious. It was an absolutely compulsive procedure! the fear of forgetting! I kept this log, I noted down nothing but events, no thoughts at all, just facts of the sort "I ate a leg of lamb and I drank a bottle of Gigondas" [. . .] and at the same time there was an element that I suppose you have to call derision.   [Jsn 87–88]

W or The Memory of Childhood was written at the same time, but not out of the same compulsion. Indeed, the work that Perec did for that book may well have been the cause of the "compulsive procedure" that produced the "monstrous" "Tentative d'inventaire des aliments liquides et solides que j'ai ingurgités au cours de l'année 1974" [*inf* 97–106]. The childhood memories that Perec added to the story of W, first published as a serial in *La Quinzaine littéraire* five years earlier, had all been written down already, in more or less detailed form, most of them several times over, in the sealed envelopes of the time-capsule programme. Despite this, writing the autobiography was a chore, a burden, a responsibility he would be glad to have done with, Perec told a lab colleague with whom he had a brief liaison in 1974. In all of Perec's writing career he referred to no other work in quite such a gloomy way, not even the personal projects that he had not managed to complete, such as *L'Arbre* and *Wie ein Hund*. That is only the first oddity about a thirty-seven-chapter book that Perec reinvented, after two false starts, the day after he turned thirty-seven, on 7.3.73.

After the death of David Bienenfeld in July 1973, Esther's health declined. She kept all her wits, but she had lung cancer, and she became very frail. Bianca was concerned that her mother be not left alone in her last years, perhaps her last months, and urged Perec to spend some time with his aunt at Blévy. He had been an assiduous visitor when he needed Esther's help for *L'Arbre*; Bianca thought he should now repay a little of what he owed her. Perec went to Blévy for part of the Easter break in 1974, overlapping with Bianca, and returned for a longer stay in August, when Ela and other friends and relations of the family were also there. It was in the Bienenfeld country home, with its garden and orchard, that *W or The Memory of Childhood* was finally put together. It is likely that Perec either guessed or feared that it would be the last of his works that his aunt would be able to read

In the spring of 1974, Rue Linné was at last inhabitable. Since buying it with the proceeds from Rue de Seine, Perec had had the floorboards renewed, a bathroom installed, and central heating put in, thanks to a loan from Ela. Thanks to Harry Mathews, he managed to repaint the walls without calling in a decorator (Harry was *much* taller). But there is more to moving flat than simply renovating and painting. Kitting out Rue Linné must have seemed an infinite task, and it got Perec down. He picked himself up with a list of *infinitives*:

> *Clean check try change sort sign wait imagine invent invest decide*
> *yield bend hunch cover equip bare split turn reverse beat mumble*
> *rush knead align protect mask mess strip cut plug hide release operate*
> *install twiddle grout break thread filter shake heap iron smooth shore*
> *up drive in dowel hook put away saw fix pin mark note work out*
> *climb mark off master see survey lean-as-hard-as-you-can prime sand*
> *paint scrub rub down connect climb wobble straddle lose recover*
> *fumble fritter (banana) brush apply sealant bare hide apply sealant*
> *straighten come and go buff up leave-to-dry admire bedazzle worry*
> *learn-to-be-patient get-on-with-it appreciate add up intercalate seal*

nail screw bolt sew squat perch bite nails centre get there wash wash
out work out count smile support subtract multiply cool heels sketch
buy acquire receive fetch unparcel unwrap line frame set observe
consider dream hang drill wipe off plaster dust camp enlarge raise
procure sit lean prop-yourself-up-against-the-wall rinse uncork com-
plete sort sweep sigh whistle-while-you-work lick get keen on rip
out stick up glue swear insist trace sand brush paint drill plug in
switch on fuse solder bend unpick sharpen aim fritter (banana) dilute
hold up shake-before-use file be-over-the-moon-about tweak ruin
scrub off dust operate pulverise balance check lick stamp empty crush
sketch explain shrug-your-shoulders slot in divide walk-up-and-
down have hung watch clock bring together bring closer match bleach
gloss over fill insulate reckon pin put away whitewash hang do-it-
again intercalate spread out wash hunt for come in take a breath
     settle down
     reside
     live.   [*EsEs* 50–51]

The work that Perec did on the text of *W or The Memory of Childhood* in the year of his memory-obsession and of his redecorating hassle was not unlike that done by a craftsman or a joiner. He had to to file down, join together, and adjust texts, some of of them previously published and others as good as written. The three-part plan of 1970 (*see* p. 451) was abandoned. There were probably several reasons for this change, but preponderant amongst them was the fact that Perec had dedicated the third 1970 series (called the Intertext) to Suzanne, and now wished to suppress it: he had put Andé behind him and slammed the door. A second reason for reverting to a two-part structure was precisely that: in so doing he would *revert* to the underlying conceit of all his early works, from *L'Attentat de Sarajevo* to *Le Condottiere*.

The *W* of 1970 had been Perec's nth reworking of the "Gaspard" theme; in 1971, he had not managed to get *Le Condottiere bis* off the ground, no doubt in part because the engine (the text of 1960) was missing. The *W* of 1973–74 can in one sense be seen as the long-deferred fulfilment of Perec's early ambitions (interrupted by *Things* and by his Oulipian period) to write the "Gaspard" book, which he had defined in a letter to Jacques Lederer in 1960 as *a book that puts itself into question, that denies itself, a hypocritical book, a book that cheats but works nonetheless.*

If there is cheating in *W or The Memory of Childhood*, it is not in the text of the serial published in 1969–70. The changes made to that part of the book are few: the Wincklers' yacht, formerly named *Lysander* (an allusion to Roussel), becomes *Sylvander* (an allusion to Harry Mathews); one or two place-names are altered; there are occasional very minor stylistic amendments; and the divisions between the original episodes are shifted a little so that the last part of episode 19 becomes chapter 37 of the book and is at one and the same time the nineteenth of the "W" series and the nineteenth of the "memory" chapters. Beyond that, the 1969–70 serial is simply pasted in and italicised. Perec's carpenter's work was to file down and dowel in his memories of childhood.

The memories that constitute the interleaved chapters of *W or The Memory of Childhood* correspond to the headings of the second column of the three-part plan of 1970, minus draft chapter 47, the story of Perec's "runaway day", still a typescript in the writer's bottom drawer. His reworking of the material in 1974 did not consist in adding anything of substance, only in honing, adjusting and taking away. If Perec's psychoanalysis was helping him to take possession of his past, what he found there was not reflected in the explicit text of *W or The Memory of Childhood*.

Perec's published "memory of childhood" is riddled with errors. Of course, autobiography is a notoriously unreliable genre as far as facts are concerned, and recollections of childhood are especially prone to involuntary distortions of detail. On the other hand, Perec had a phenomenal memory for detail and professional skill in information handling; he knew how to look things up at the Bibliothèque Nationale and in the encyclopaedias he had just sorted and put on his brand-new shelves at Rue Linné. Some of his errors are sufficiently flagrant to jump off the page even for readers without Perec's library skills. Did he perhaps make so many mistakes on purpose, in order to humanise himself, since, as everyone knows, to err is to be human?

For example, Perec had his own vague memory of the day when he heard of the defeat of Japan. In 1969, he had been reminded of it by a chance encounter at the funeral of Berthe Chavranski:

> *Someone called Todd or Tot told me that he remembered my "having read, at Villard, on 30 August 1945, over someone's shoulder, the*

newspaper headline of the capitulation of Japan". The way this
memory was put left me puzzled: how can you read over someone's
shoulder at the age of nine? In my mind, I was running back to
Berthe's villa, holding Les Allobroges *in my hand and yelling that*
it was victory, or peace.

Since Perec had written this down, and since he also knew Alain
Resnais's film *Hiroshima mon amour* almost by heart (the date of the
explosion of the first atomic bomb which precipitated Japan's capitulation is repeated a dozen times in the dialogue), it has to be assumed
that the following passage from *W or The Memory of Childhood* contains an intentionally erroneous date:

> *I often went to the square to fetch the newspaper. [. . .] One day*
> *in May 1945 I found the square again packed with people. [. . .]*
> *I ran home through the streets [. . .] yelling for all I was worth,*
> *"Japan has capitulated!"*   [*W* 150]

The error is *like* the mistakes which we make in our memories of
childhood, but it is not one of them. May 1945 is, instead, the date
of the fall of Berlin; and Germany, which is mentioned explicitly
only once in the text, and Berlin, which is not mentioned at all, are
near the heart of Perec's deceptive memory machine.

A similar kind of mistake, only made to be found out, undermines
and transforms one of the central pillars of Perec's construction, his
departure from Occupied Paris to the ZNO. He writes that his
mother bought him a comic to read on the long train-ride south and
mentions twice that its cover bore an image of Charlie Chaplin [*W*
26, 54]. Chaplin is mentioned in two other contexts in the book: once
by transcription from the newspapers published on 7 and 8 March
1936, as the maker of *Modern Times* [*W* 21]; and once in connection
with *The Great Dictator* [*W* 77], a film which was banned throughout
Nazi-occupied Europe and that renders the memory of the comic
bought at the Gare de Lyon an almost certain fabrication.[1] However,
the error-trap is made visible in what Perec chooses to say about the
film:

> Charlie Chaplin, *in* The Great Dictator, *replaced the swastika*
> *with a figure that was identical* [to it] *in terms of its segments,*
> *having the shape of a pair of overlapping Xs (✖)*

---

[1] See Lejeune, *La Mémoire et l'oblique*, pp. 82–83, and also pp. 57–59 above.

In fact, the insignia of Chaplin's "Adenoid Hynkel" is not as Perec represents it. It consists not of overlapping but of superposed X's:

X

X

The degree of precision involved in this error, which could alert the reader to the tragically flimsy nature of the thread of memory represented by the Chaplin comic and, by extension, the entire memory of the Gare de Lyon, makes it difficult to accept as a careless slip.

In fact, almost every assertion in the memory chapters of *W or The Memory of Childhood* asks to be questioned, and the answer in most cases is that the memory, whether first consigned to the sealed envelopes of *Lieux* or lying in Perec's drawer of official documents, has been altered, reworked, decorated or, more plainly, falsified. It is worth remembering Perec's first intuition of his "Gaspard" book, noted down in a hut during basic training in 1958: *falsification; or substitution. Don't try to understand.*

Many of the "falsifications and substitutions" of the memory chapters of *W or The Memory of Childhood* have been "corrected" in the earlier chapters of this biography, which now serve as a circuitous introduction to an understanding of Perec's bizarre and moving achievement as an autobiographer. The "mistakes" pointed out include basic statements of personal history, such as *My father's sister and her husband adopted me* [*W* 6] (had they done so, Perec would not have been exempt from military service in Algeria), and the assertions about names on pages 35–36: *Baruch* is not from the same root as *Peretz*, nor is it related to *Beretz*; Perec's aunt's name was Chaja Esther, not Esther Chaja; her brother was called Lejzor, not Eliezer; between 1896 and 1909, Lubartów did not become Polish and then Russian again; the Russians never wrote either *c* or *tz*, since they wrote in Cyrillic. The concatenation and concentration of errors around an issue of acute importance – Perec's own Jewish name – cannot be a coincidence. Perec could have consulted numerous documents in his possession or in the possession of his close relatives about the history of his name, just as he could easily have checked Hebrew roots with Marcel Benabou. In the end, however, it does not matter whether Perec did or did not check his facts before getting them wrong, as the whole dynamic of the writing of *W or The Memory of Childhood* lay precisely in falsification, in producing *a book that cheats but works nonetheless.*

Why cheat when the story was harsh enough as it was? Few of Perec's errors can be called lies. He does not actually say that he wore the yellow star, he just hints that he may have worn it, suggesting that he is to be pitied the more for having suppressed the memory. He does not say that his name was mangled by anti-Semitic registrars' clerks in the Pale of Settlement, he just lets the reader surmise as much. There are other, similar omissions as well: he does not say that the Vercors was the site of thousands of parachute drops, he just plants *unreal* parachutes around the text. He does not say that he cannot remember his mother, but he surrounds his memory of her – recovered through photographs, through writing, and through a misplaced and imaginary account of his departure from the Gare de Lyon – with such a fog (the first epigraph, from Raymond Queneau's verse narrative of psychoanalysis, *Chêne et Chien* ("Oak and Dog") begins, "That mindless mist where shadows swirl") that it would not be difficult to miss the point entirely. In a later interview, Perec said:

> All of this autobiographical work was organised around a single memory which, for me, was profoundly obscured, deeply buried and, in a sense, denied.   [*Jsn* 83]

W or The Memory of Childhood is organised in a material sense around a single page, page 61, which separates Part One from Part Two, along the same fracture-line that appeared in December 1969 in the writing of the serial. It is left blank but for a mysterious typographical signifier:

(. . .)

Round brackets normally signify that what is inside them does not belong to the structure of what is outside (as in a digression, an expansion, or a reference). Three dots (called points of suspension in French) can be used to indicate an unfinished sentence . . . but three dots in round brackets constitute the conventional sign that something has been omitted from a textual quotation. The centrepoint of *W or The Memory of Childhood* does not say that there is nothing there; in Perec's words, *I am not writing to say that I have nothing to say* [*W* 42]. To put it less obscurely than Perec wished to, page 61 indicates typographically: *I'm not telling*. Or at least not that simply.

At Blévy, in August 1974, Perec lodged not in the "little bedroom" where he had read detective fiction as a boy but in Esther's large room on the first floor. (Esther herself had moved down to the ground-floor lounge, to have easier access to the garden.) He worked at a table covered with a cloth embroidered long before by Grandma Rose, beneath Mladen Srbinović's portrait of himself, brought back from Belgrade in 1957.[1] Ela picked up some of the loose typescript sheets on which her brother-cousin was working and took them down to read to her mother, who sat wrapped in a rug in the shade, facing the apple orchard that goes down to the brook. Ela was struck by the beauty of Georges's writing. She had always believed in him, even when her parents did not; but as she read aloud from the almost-final text of *W or The Memory of Childhood*, she felt that he had crossed a sort of bridge and become a writer in a new and different sense. For Esther, the "childhood memory" of 1974 may have seemed a vindication of her long effort to set *dos Kind* on the road to self-realisation.

❄

In working on *W or the Memory of Childhood* in the spring and summer of 1974, Perec sought to tie together the two parts of the work by matching words, phrases, and names in the memory chapters with words, phrases, and names in the already-written island story. His intent – inherited from the "Gaspard" project and in keeping with his long-standing palindromic ambition – was to make the two sides of the text echo and undermine each other.[2]

There is no way of stating what it is that Perec is not saying at the centrepoint of *W or The Memory of Childhood*. The writer's radical self-constraint and craftsmanship – developed as much in the "infraor-dinary" observation texts done for *Cause commune* and for *Lieux* as in his more expansive and analytical memory pieces – allows the reader to project his or her own pathology into the textually desig-nated empty place. This is not to say that the interpretation of Perec's autobiography is in any sense a free-for-all. The author's hand is

[1] The first state of this lithograph is reproduced as illustration 19. The second state, which hung at Blévy, is darker, and decorated with Perec's name as seen through a broken mirror.

[2] The intricate verbal "stitching" of the two texts is analysed by Bernard Magné in "Les Sutures dans *W ou le souvenir d'enfance*", *Cahiers Georges Perec II*, pp. 39–55. However, it is worth remembering that Perec did not count his autobiography as an Oulipian work and never reported on its progress to minuted meetings of OuLiPo.

dictatorial and uses subtle forms of coercion that are extremely hard to resist.

You don't attack concentration-camp literature, Perec had remarked at the start of his essay on Robert Antelme (*see.* pp. 277–279), and *W or The Memory of Childhood* uses that bunker twice over, in the island story, and in the memories of childhood, which need only to mention Auschwitz once to put the author in a place of almost impenetrable safety. The cover is required for at least two divergent reasons. The first is to protect Perec from that most awkward of themes for him, his relationship to Jewishness; the second is to draw the reader into the emotion that Perec wished to share.

Like many half-assimilated, secularised French Jews, Perec was uneasy about asserting that he was Jewish in any real sense, but equally unwilling to deny it. He negotiated this personal, national minefield in his childhood autobiography by at once asserting and denying his Jewishness, in statements that are all *textually constructed* – or, to put it less tactfully, wrong.

The falsifications are not all hard to pin down. Chapter 37, for example, consists in large part of a slightly abridged quotation from David Rousset's study of the concentration-camp system. In its original role as the closing paragraph of the serial published in *La Quinzaine littéraire*, it performed a straightforward function, that of bringing the society of W into equivalence with the real concentration camps of Nazi Germany. But the reader of *W or The Memory of Childhood*, when he gets to chapter 37, knows that the author's mother "died in the camps" and is inclined, if not invited, to read the passage from Rousset with reference to that tragedy. In fact, Rousset is talking about something admittedly horrible but of a significantly different kind. Here is his sentence unabridged, with Perec's omissions in bold:

> The structure of punishment camps **for Aryans, such as Neue-Bremm, near Saarbrücken**, is determined by two fundamental policies: no work but "sport" and derisory feeding . . .[1]

Rousset's book, like the vast majority of such studies published in France before the 1970s, hardly deals with the extermination of the

---

[1] David Rousset, *L'Univers concentrationnaire* (1945; reprint, Paris: Editions de Minuit, 1965), p. 48.

Jews. The passage used by Perec to bring his twin tales together only *seems* to put the death of his mother in its context.

The mirror-image of Perec's Jewishness was his conversion to Catholicism at Villard-de-Lans, and that event, too, is displaced – from October to midsummer 1943 – in order to deny any connection that the reader might make between that event and the transfer of the area from non-anti-Semitic Italian to anti-Semitic German occupation. We also know that Perec either had forgotten or chose to hide the fact that his father's name was given as André on his certificate of baptism; this allows him to proceed with the very delicate weaving of the letters *X* and *W* into the text, and blinds the reader into not asking the obvious question: not Why did Perec think that his father was called André? but Why had he forgotten that his father was also called Izie? The answer – that he had been told to forget that he was Jewish, for his own safety – is stated nowhere in the text, but it is implied on almost every page by the author's oblique insistence on memory gaps.

The falsification that has been most studied by French scholars is Perec's alleged first memory of childhood, his recollection of being congratulated for deciphering a letter in a Yiddish newspaper.[1] In the memories of Rue Vilin that were sealed away in the envelopes of *Lieux,* there were in fact other memories that were certainly no later in date and quite possibly earlier than this one (*see* p. 35). Perec's choice of a letter-memory for his published self-depiction is clearly a choice, a choice of identity as a man of letters. But what letter was it, really? As the papers published by Philippe Lejeune show, Perec's first recall was of a Hebrew letter that was very close in shape to a tav; later on, with the help of an unidentified friend writing Hebrew in cursive script, he amended and rotated the original shape until it fitted his purpose. The result was a manifestly nonexistent, Hebrew-seeming squiggle that is in reality nothing other than a regularised mirror-image of Perec's own handwritten first initial, G. Perec's first memory is thus nothing of the sort; it is rather a (re)construction of his origin in writing.

Nothing in the writing of Perec's childhood memory is innocent. It is hardly surprising that he found his work on it such a heavy burden, for he was juggling with such brilliance as to mystify even himself. The pseudo-Hebrew letter that he had recovered, Perec claimed, was not a

---

[1] See, for example, Marcel Benabou, "Perec's Jewishness", *RCF* 77–87 and Philippe Lejeune, "La Lettre Hébraïque", in *MO* 210–231.

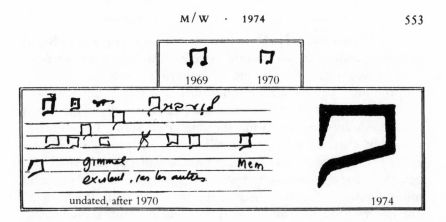

gimmel, *which I like to think could be the initial of my first name* (how far could he go? the best means of defence is attack!), but it could *just about masquerade as a "men" or "M"*. The entire passage is a masquerade. There is no Hebrew letter called men,[1] as Perec well knew (see the composite figure above), and the letter represented could not pass even for a very poorly drawn mem. But M is W turned upside down: **WM** shows it more clearly. The name of the clue is therefore also falsified, to alert readers of Hebrew to the game being played with reverse-G, whilst keeping goyim in the swirling mist. It is a diabolical game to play with the *memory* of a Jewish childhood,[2] and perhaps the most devious example of Perec's simultaneous assertion and denial of his Jewishness. It has taken a long time to understand what he intended by it.

M is mentioned as a symbol or letter nowhere else in the book, and the textual work carried out by Perec around the *I'm not telling* of the blank page on which it all hinges makes the lost thread of the **MW** inversion look like a significant clue. *M* can stand for *mother* in English, as in French (*mère*) and German (*Mutter*). But in Germany (and *Germany is the central figure of my book*, Perec said – on German radio)[3] the letter was best known as the title of a film about a child-murderer.

M was made by Fritz Lang in 1931 and banned by the Nazis as soon as they took power, in 1933. It is a free adaptation of the story

[1] The English translator first believed *men* to be a misprint, and corrected it to *mem*. He apologises for his excess of zeal.

[2] Marcel Benabou has also pointed out that the other "first memory" [*W* 14] plays on another French word for memory, *souvenir*: it is a memory of a coin, or a *sou*-venir.

[3] *Autoren im Dialog*, broadcast by SR on 9 August 1975, offers one of Perec's most substantial explanations of *W or The Memory of Childhood*, in conversation with Eugen Helmle.

of Peter Kürten, the Düsseldorf child-murderer, transposed to Berlin
and to an authentic underworld setting. Thirty-two members of
Lang's cast were arrested by the police during shooting.

In the film, a psychopathic child-killer is at large. Police surveillance increases and disturbs normal business; the underworld acts to
find the murderer so that normal thieving may resume. The murderer
(played by Peter Lorre) gives himself away by whistling a particular
melody from Grieg's *Peer Gynt* each time he knifes another child. His
signature tune is identified by a blind beggar with a musical ear, who
enlists the help of a street urchin; the boy is to chalk the letter M
(for *murderer*) on his palm, contrive to collide with the whistling
psychopath as if by accident, and, in so doing, clap his chalked hand
on the man's shoulder. The sighted will then easily be able to track
down the man labelled M. The camera watches the lad chalk the letter
onto his palm not from over his shoulder but front on, and what the
spectator sees is

W

At first seeing, a child might well marvel at the transformation of *W*
into *M*, or the reverse, especially a child who had difficulty with
left-right orientation. It is not known whether Perec saw the film as
a child, but virtually certain that he both viewed it and read the script
(translated into French by Volker Schlöndorff)[1] in 1964, when a print
of the long-lost film was found and released in Paris (and throughout
Europe) to huge acclaim. But the plot thickens.

The police are in pursuit of the murderer, using conventional police
methods. They trace a suspect – the culprit, in fact, though they do
not yet know that – back to his lodgings. His landlady can only say
that her tenant has disappeared. But before the plainclothesmen ring
the doorbell, Lang plants what turns out to be a massive clue to the
unity of Perec's "Gaspard cycle" and his childhood autobiography in
a close-up of the doorbell and the nameplate above it, which reads:

Frau Elisabeth Winckler

"M" is caught by the underworld and subjected to a trial by thieves,
which is interrupted by the police. The threepenny-opera court hands

---

[1] *L'Avant-scène Cinéma* no. 39 (July–August 1964); see also above, p. 301.

over its quarry to the law, and the fiction ends with a leather-sleeved arm on Peter Lorre's marked shoulder, with a voice-over intoning: "Im Namen des Gesetzes . . ." ("In the name of the law . . .").

Just as you are about to rise from your seat and make for the exit, Lang dissolves and cuts to

LAW COURT

Three judges seated. Sound of public standing. The magistrates put on black caps . . . then the chairman reads out the sentence. (Sound continuity from previous sequence)

Presiding Judge: . . . of the German people, we . . .

Flash to Frau Beckman sitting in the corridor of the law courts with three other women. She sighs and says: "That won't bring our children back to us! *Mothers, take better care of your children!*"

Thus M confronts you at the end with the carelessness of mothers with their children. M turned on its head is W, whose mathematical value must therefore relate to the carelessness of children with their mothers. It is as if the whole structure of *W or The Memory of Childhood* had been designed to hide and transmit a certain feeling that Perec would not have been the only bereaved child to internalise, and to bury in the empty fortress of his soul. Memories of his mother are virtually absent from Perec's childhood autobiography. What had made him forget? Not just the injunction given to him at Villard-de-Lans, which he would never manage to forgive, but also guilt at having *failed to look after his mother.* To lose one parent is a misfortune; to lose two smacks of carelessness. The upside-down M addresses Perec's guilt directly and insinuates it, unseen, into our own:

Children, take better care of your mothers!

The "M/W interface" has at least three independent sources: Pierre Lartigue, "Que balbutie Perec", *L'Humanité*, 23 December 1976; Jacques Roubaud, "Préparation d'un portrait formel de Georges Perec", *L'Arc* 76 (1979), pp. 54–60; and David Bellos, "Georges Perec and the Art of Deception"(1989 Percival Lecture for the Manchester Literary and Philosophical Society), *Manchester Memoirs*, vol. 128 (1990), pp. 107–118.

Based in part on the recollections of Ela Bienenfeld, Raymond Howard, Bianca Lamblin, Sylvia Lamblin-Richardson, Maurice Nadeau, Bernard Queysanne, Marie-Claude Lavallard-Rousseau, and Bernard Zitzerman.

CHAPTER 53

Rue Linné

1974–1975

Rue Linné was where Perec settled and where he wrote *Life A User's Manual*. The street is broad but not a main thoroughfare. It leads from the tower blocks and windswept plaza of the Jussieu University campus past a metro station, and two corner cafés, Le Nemrod and L'Epsilon, up a gentle slope to the back entrance of the Jardin des Plantes. Rue Linné is well supplied with restaurants, bars, bookshops, and newsagents and even has a specialist games-and-puzzle shop. In the 1970s it was already a centre for reprographics; over the years it has become the Savile Row of self-service photocopying boutiques, used by students from the Jussieu campus and writers from all corners of Paris.

Number 13 is an L-shaped apartment block, with the narrower arm facing the street. To reach the rear stairs which lead to Perec's mezzanine flat, you pass through a cobbled courtyard that is not as quaint as that of Rue de Quatrefages but surprisingly pleasant all the same, with a tree growing in one corner and several tubs of plants.

Perec's flat, once renovated, struck visitors as being like a railway train. You enter a tiny hall which gives on to the little kitchen, and then you pass into the main room with its marble fireplace and French windows opening onto the paved courtyard at the rear, which Perec insisted on calling his gardenlet (he would send out invitations to "gardenlet-parties"). The main room gives on to the study, which is similarly graced with French windows to the courtyard; the study leads on to the bedroom; and the bedroom is connected to the bathroom, at the back of the train. None of the rooms is especially large, and without the light that it has from the high-walled open space behind, the flat might easily be claustrophobic. It is far away from the noise of the street, however, and the silence must have been welcome to a man who had spent two years sleeping less than fifty metres from an overhead metro line.

Before Perec moved in, another flat came up for sale on the fifth floor of the block. Paulette had rejected Perec's proposal of proximate noncohabitation at Avenue de Ségur, but Rue Linné suited her better, and she bought the flat upstairs. From then on Paulette would always be near at hand. Perec showed his works in progress to her and often popped upstairs for a drink or a meal; for her part, Paulette would frequently call in on the mezzanine floor on her way out to the shops, or back from them. She remained Madame Perec in law, and in practice remained a central member of the writer's family of friends.

In 1974 Denoël, which had been taken over by Gallimard, decided to drop *Cause commune*. The journal's editors protested in a joint letter to *Le Monde*,[1] and Christian Bourgois rode to the rescue. From 1975 *Cause commune* appeared not as a review but as an unconventional and irregular paperback series in Bourgois's "10/18" collection. Perec continued to serve on the editorial board, but he published fewer pieces in the new format.

Nadeau's position at Denoël was now fragile, for Les Lettres nouvelles was losing money, as it nearly always had. Nevertheless, he accepted Perec's *W or The Memory of Childhood* for the series. Because *La Boutique obscure* had formed the first volume of the Cause Commune collection published jointly by Denoël and Gonthier, *W or The Memory of Childhood* was only the fourth, not the fifth, of the "five next books" after *Things* on which Les Lettres nouvelles had right of first refusal. But however it was counted, Nadeau wanted to launch Perec's autobiography with an illustrated jacket, not in the plain "tombstone" covers which have always been the mark of literary publishing in France. Perec asked Christine Lipinska, Suzanne's daughter, who was now pursuing a career in film, to accompany him to Rue Vilin and to take a reel of black and white photographs of what was left of the street. Number 24 was still standing, and on the wall one could just see the old inscription *Coiffure Dames*, which Perec liked to think was the sign for his mother's hairdressing business.[2] Perec decided to use a plain image of the wall with its inscription as the cover design for the first edition of his childhood autobiography, overprinted with a stencilled *W* in the same sharp shade of yellow

[1] Jean Duvignaud, Paul Virilio, and Georges Perec, letter to the editor, *Le Monde*, 31 May 1974.

[2] Enhanced enlargements of these and later photographs reveal another inscription which cannot be deciphered with certainty. The later photographs also show that the sign originally said *Coiffure de Dames*. The fascinating story of how time peeled away what had obscured the sign on number 24 Rue Vilin is told in Robert Bober's entrancing television film, *En Remontant la Rue Vilin* (INA, 1992).

that had been used for the star he had never worn. The second part of the title, "or The Memory of Childhood", does not appear on the jacket – because it is there, in effect, in the photograph of Rue Vilin.

In the second week of October 1974, Perec and Queysanne travelled to Thonon-les-Bains, on the French side of the lake of Geneva, for a screening of *A Man Asleep* at the local film festival. They put up in a rather old-fashioned grand hotel which also served as a training college for apprentice waiters and chefs. In the cavernous and half-empty dining room, a superfluity of young and hesitant servers hovered and twisted at the serving hatch. Each false move was signalled by the supervisor with a special hand-sign. When the silent sign was made, the apprentice had to go back to the serving hatch and start the ballet over again. Whilst waiting for the soup, which had been almost delivered half a dozen times, Perec and Queysanne reflected that their "Man Asleep" could not have been a woman – at any rate, not in France. No woman could have loitered around Paris like that without being followed, harassed, and picked up. That evening Perec dashed off a two-page synopsis for a work to be called *L'Oeil de l'autre* ("The Eye of the Other"), which he expanded into a fifteen-page outline on his return to Paris:

> *The story takes place nowadays, in Paris or another large city; it lasts a few weeks and describes the development, or rather the collapse, of a young woman who feels she is being followed, watched, and spied upon uninterruptedly.*
>
> *The opening of the film will establish the atmosphere and the circumstances in which this obsession with the eye of the other will arise and develop; the scenes will be handled realistically, so that the viewer never knows, at any point in the film, if what he or she is seeing is the product of the young woman's sick mind or a response to a threat in reality.*

L'Oeil de l'autre was eventually made as a film by Queysanne, with Noureddine Mechri as scriptwriter and a cast that included Regis Henrion (as a waiter) and Marcel Cuvelier, but Perec took little part in its development beyond that first short scenario. He had imagined it at the very start as a television film, not a cinema work – just like another Perec-Queysanne invention of 1974, a series (which might have turned into a soap) about *the social climbing of an entirely parasitic character* [who,] *by force of personality and casualness alone,* [. . .] *terrorises and fascinates a group of executives whom he exploits without shame.* The latter project (draft title: *Le Journal d'un arriviste* ["The Diary of a Climber"]) never materialised, and Perec went back to enthusing about Kubrick's *2001*. When *Star Wars* came out, he loved it: that was real cinema for you!

Esther Bienenfeld died of lung cancer on 21 November 1974. She had expressed the wish to be cremated, and Perec attended the ceremony at the colombarium at Père Lachaise. He recorded the event in a brief note slipped into one of the envelopes of *Lieux* and left shortly afterward for London, to present *A Man Asleep* at the British Film Institute, and then went on to stay with Sylvia and James Richardson at Griffydam, a tiny village roughly equidistant from Nottingham and Loughborough, where the young couple had their respective academic attachments. Perec arrived with presents – recordings of *Il Trovatore* and *The Marriage of Figaro* – and stayed a fortnight with his mathematical goddaughter and her husband, an ergonomist. *W* was now in production but Perec did not have the proofs sent on to him: incredible as it may now seem for a work written with such meticulous care, Perec simply left a brief set of instructions with Paulette, who checked the proofs for him in Paris. Sylvia says that Perec did not even mention his forthcoming autobiography during his stay in England. What he got down to at Griffydam was his year-end joke-booklet gift for friends. For 1974 he chose contorted puns on English proverbs, entitling the collection "Les Adventures de Dixion Harry" [*V* 53–65]. It seems he consulted James and Sylvia rather more than he did the dixionarry.

On the plane back to Le Bourget from East Midlands Airport, he scribbled down a memory-text for his time-capsule project, which he had taken up once more, perhaps because the refabrication of memories for *W* was over and done.

As the winter of 1974 turned to the spring of 1975, Perec seemed to be more at home with himself and began to pay more attention to his health. He used a bicycle (for a time) to get from Rue Linné to the lab (there was no direct metro line, and the number 86 bus could take ages to negotiate Place de La Bastille); he began to see a dentist in Boulevard Saint-Germain; and he dropped cigarettes for cigarillos, which Harry Mathews had told him were less harmful to the lungs. "Do you inhale them?" Harry asked. *No more than I have to,* Perec replied.[1] He even gave up smoking before lunch, for a while. As the analysis with Pontalis began to wind down and as the publication of *W or The Memory of Childhood* approached, things were coming together for Perec in his new home at Rue Linné.

He also made new friends. Harry Mathews took him along to meet Marie-Claude de Brunhoff, a colleague of Harry's former companion, Maxine Groffsky. Marie-Claude's husband, Laurent, was the son and successor of Jean de Brunhoff, the inventor of Babar. The Brunhoffs' daughter, Anne, hoped to become a professional photographer, and she shot two reels of Perec and Mathews, in January 1975, in the family flat in Boulevard Saint-Germain (illustrations 38 and 39 are from this set). "Perec brought the sun into our lives", Marie-Claude says. Of course he also got himself mothered in this new family environment. "But everyone wanted to mother Perec!" she adds.

Perec was now relatively free, or at any rate he was free of the childhood memories that he had taken so long to (re)write, and he had no immediate obligations hanging over him. When Bernard Queysanne obtained a commission for a short on Gustave Flaubert, Perec was delighted to write the script (for five hundred francs) and to experiment with verbal and visual structures. The text is a pastiche of a paragraph from a literature textbook; in the film it is read twice over, phrase by phrase, with the punctuation pronounced, exactly as it would be in a dictation at school. The images, meanwhile – stills of Flaubert, of Louise Colet, and of the house at Croisset which had just been reopened as a Flaubert museum – recur in strict order according to the rules of the sestina, making the six-minute *Gustave Flaubert* by Perec and Queysanne the first example of the rigorous application of a poetic constraint to the cinema.

In February 1975, Perec accompanied his lab colleague Gautier to the Alps, for a skiing holiday at Tignes. He had not done any winter sports, or any sport, for that matter, for fifteen years, and he had lost his childhood ease on the slopes. He fell a few times, found he was out of puff, and decided he was not up to it any more. He was too old for that sort of thing now, he said, with a grumpy grin that failed to mask his disappointment.

One rather splendid compensation came shortly afterwards through Queysanne's professional contacts. The Canadian film-

---

[1] Harry Mathews, *The Orchard* (Flint, MI: Bamberger Books, 1988), p. 10.

makers, Daniel Bertolino and François Floquet, had spent years in the jungles of Africa, South America, and Sumatra filming primitive peoples who resisted assimilation and had naturally proved hard to find. They were now editing their cans of anthropological film in Montreal, and needed a writer to script the voice-over commentary. They asked Queysanne, who suggested Perec, who jumped at the job and set off for Canada, by way of New York, in April 1975. He spent two weeks in Montreal on expenses, learning and writing about these "avoidance specialists" who were not creatures of Roger Price's imagination, but real and hauntingly beautiful people, such as the Anadalams of Sumatra. Chapter 25 of *Life A User's Manual* contains a long extract from the text of this film, released as *Aho! Les Hommes de la Forêt*.[1]

Perec did an equally fascinating commentary for French television as well. Michel Pamart (who had once been a marginal member of Lg) and Claude Ventura had collected home movies shot in France in the 1920s and 1930s for a series of three documentary programmes to be called *La Vie filmée des Français* ("French Lives on Film"). Perec wrote and read the commentary to Part II, dealing with the 1930s, and ended up talking as much about himself as about the life of the French on film, because, as he said later in an interview, *One of the movies was filmed in my own childhood quartier, and it was just as if I was there with my mother, my parents, in the picture!* [*Jsn* 85].

Between Griffydam, Tignes, Montreal and the scripts on Flaubert and home movies, sessions with Pontalis continued in what had become a rather irregular fashion, whilst *W or The Memory of Childhood* went through proofs, printing, and binding. On 14 April 1975 Perec called in at Denoël to sign and dispatch review and gift copies. One was inscribed, *For J.-B Pontalis, beyond the here and now, these traces which he helped me to recover, with my friendship* [*MO* 136]. Did Perec mean memory-traces? Or *traces*, signs written on a page, the lost fragments of texts drafted in 1970 before the analysis began?

W or The Memory of Childhood has a dedication printed on the page: *To E*, without the full stop one might expect after an initial letter. One day when Ela called at Rue Linné to take him out for dinner, Perec asked his sister-cousin what she thought of the dedication. She asked hesitantly whether she would be right to take it as a homage to her mother Esther – and to herself, Ela?

[1] It is sometimes referred to as *Aho! Au coeur du monde primitif.*

Georges's eye twinkled affirmatively. Then he added: *My parents, too.*

Ela raised an eyebrow, quizzically.

Pour eux, Perec explained. *Pour e-u-x.*

For "them": for his missing, missed parents.

🍁

From Perec's diary for 24 April 1975: *5:00 P.M. Pontalis: J.-B. P's "gratitude" for my dedication. The paradox of W, a book not written for other people* [MO 138]. Perec attended two more sessions, missed two, and then came to the couch for the last time on 3 June 1975: *Simple and obvious end of the analysis. Except that I make a mistake of 100 francs paying P.* [MO 138].

How did Perec himself determine that his analysis was complete? His judgment must have been connected with the composition, the publication, and the reception of *W or The Memory of Childhood,* but in ways that can perhaps never be entirely elucidated. A few years later the film director Jean-Paul Rappeneau asked Perec to tell him what it was like to be in analysis, and more especially to explain how, once in, one could ever get out of analysis again. *Well,* Perec replied,

> *one day you get fed up with complaining. As for me, I moaned yet again to my analyst that I wasn't doing enough work. He interrupted and made me recite the list of everything I had written during the analysis, and it made me think: hang on, that's not so bad after all.*

🍁

Whatever Perec was like on the couch, he was certainly the worst patient his dentist had ever had, and he nearly drove her to despair. He would turn up for appointments armed with excuses, often pathetically thin ones: he had a cold and it wasn't a good day for an injection; he was feeling sad and didn't want to hear the sound of the drill; couldn't she just put it all off for another little while? Or else he would ring up in advance to say that he was at a meeting that was dragging on. Did she mind if he was late? She did? So would it be more convenient to cancel? When he did turn up, the dentist would have to distract him with tricks normally reserved for whining infants. On three out of every four appointments she got no dental work done at all. But once she stung Perec's pride: his jaws were so rotten that he would have to have all his remaining teeth out. "But you're too cowardly, aren't you?" she said. "You'll go on suffering until they fall out on their own!" That day she got one of Perec's rotten teeth into the bin.

The first reviews of *W or The Memory of Childhood* began to appear towards the end of May 1975. They all described Perec's work in respectful tones (*you don't attack concentration-camp literature*, as Perec had said), but they hardly came to grips with the book itself: *W* left most of its first readers bewildered and almost wordless. It had a special kind of reception amongst Jewish readers of Perec's own generation, many of whom had similar histories and were having similar difficulties in coming to terms, in early middle age, with absent memories of their own childhoods, spent under false names, in Catholic families, in hiding, and so on. But it would be some time before echoes of that reception reached the author.

Perec had sent one of the first copies of *W or The Memory of Childhood* to Eugen Helmle, who promptly proposed a bilingual reading from it on radio, in the series entitled *Autoren im Dialog,* run by Arnfried Astl, the head of the *Literaturabteilung* at SR. The *Johann Wolfang von Goethe* whisked Perec to Saarbrücken once again on Thursday 5 June, two days after his last appointment with Pontalis. At dinner Eugen brought out bottles of vintage Bordeaux, which he had recently begun to collect. The next morning the two friends went over to the studios at Halberg, checked the passages to be read in French and in German, and did a dry run so as to hear how their act sounded on tape. Afterwards they chatted. More by accident than by design, the tape recorder was still running. Why, Eugen asked, did the first, false Gaspard Winckler take refuge in Germany, near the Luxembourg border? Was it because Perec recognised the new Germany as a land of asylum, a safe place to be? No, it wasn't that, Perec replied, though that was not to say that he didn't regard modern Germany as a safe place. Rather, Winckler went to Germany because *Germany is the central figure of my book*. The introduction of the word *Germany* in the first pages of *W* had allowed him to establish a network of German words (from *Luxemburger Wort* on page 16 to *Schnell, los Mensch,* on page 164), German names (Pfister, Gustafson, Westerman, and so on), and German references (on p. 103, for example) without returning the subject to Germany in any explicit way.

But how did he feel about coming to Germany, the country responsible for the death of both of his parents? Perec gave a hesitant, meandering reply, in the course of which he made the following declaration, of which the afterthought is perhaps the most significant part:

> *If I come to Germany, if I come to Germany to talk about my book*
> *W, it's because I think, as far as I'm concerned, that it's very*
> *important that this book be known in Germany, because it is a way*
> *of bearing witness and maybe of helping people to understand, of*
> *adding something that will help to make people understand how the*
> *concentration-camp system exists and what a terrible burden it placed*
> *on huge numbers of people during the war – and long after.*

Like all survivors of the *shoah* Perec could never be relieved of that burden entirely. But with *W or The Memory of Childhood* he had succeeded in sharing its weight with others. Few enjoyed the experience: *W or The Memory of Childhood* did not sell well in France; in Germany, it was a disaster.

Unpublished sources include drafts of *L'Oeil de l'autre, Journal d'un arriviste,* and *Gustave Flaubert,* in the possession of Bernard Queysanne, and letters from Georges Perec to Paulette Perec and Christian Bourgois.

The tape recording of the discussion prior to *Autoren im Dialog* was consulted by courtesy of AGP.

For the reception of *W or The Memory of Childhood,* see: *Le Monde,* 23 May 1975 (Roger-Pol Droit); *Le Nouvel Observateur,* 26 May 1975 (Jean Duvignaud); *La Quinzaine littéraire,* 1 June 1975 (Jean-Baptiste Mauroux); *L'Humanité,* 12 June 1975 (André Stil); *Le Quotidien de Paris,* 13 June 1975 (Jean-Marc Roberts); *L'Express,* 29 July 1975 (Mathieu Galey). There were remaindered copies to be had free from *La Quinzaine littéraire* long after Nadeau had left Denoël. Perec's diary note in June 1975 that thirty-five hundred copies may have been sold (reproduced by Lejeune, *MO* 138) was just whistling in the wind. Helmle has confirmed that only about four hundred copies of the first German edition were sold, and the remainder pulped.

Other information used in this chapter was supplied by Ela Bienenfeld, Catherine Binet, Robert Bober, Marie-Claude and Laurent de Brunhoff, Nicole Doukhan, Henri Gautier, Eugen Helmle, Bernard Queysanne, Christine Lipinska, Harry Mathews, Jean-Paul Rappeneau, James and Sylvia Richardson, and Luc Rosenzweig.

CHAPTER 54

Catherine

Summer 1975

Perec's trip to Neuweiler in early June 1975 to read from *W or The Memory of Childhood* was, in effect, his farewell to German radio. New avenues were being opened in the French media, and Perec was looking forward to a planned meeting with Pierre Emmanuel, head of INA, the recently established "creative" branch of the state-run television service. Eugen Helmle was thus unable to tempt his old friend back into *Hörspiel* again, and *Wie ein Hund* remained an unrealised plan. On this last working trip to the Saar, Perec used his leisure moments in Helmle's attic room to catch up on overdue pieces for *Lieux*. What he recorded in them, however, consisted less of memories than transcriptions of intense, elaborate and freshly-dreamt dreams.

Pierre Emmanuel's plan was for a series of twelve twenty-minute television "essays" by writers invited to use a camera as if it were a pen – to tell a story, make a statement, or express whatever personal themes they wished to put on the screen. At the launch meeting, held on 23 June 1975 at the Musée des Arts et Traditions Populaires, Perec asked if he, for example, might make an autobiographical film about the day he ran away from home, adapting a story he had written long before and not thought good enough to publish. The idea was accepted in principle; he was asked to send in the script.

By 1975, Perec had not had a significant emotional and sexual relationship with a woman for several years. Towards the end of 1974, he had been to a party held in the flat of Catherine Binet, and he had first tried to establish a relationship with her shortly afterwards by telephoning, late at night, in a state of great distress. Catherine grasped that her caller was appealing for help but he did not take up her offer of a spare bed for the night; instead, he called again next day to apologise for his bad manners. He called her again, on and off, over the following weeks and months, but every date that they tried to fix was overtaken by some other event: the skiing holiday with Gautier ruled out a planned rendezvous in February, the trip to Montreal made April a difficult month, and it was June in the end before they could both keep their first dinner date *à deux*. By then, Perec and Catherine knew each other quite well from their long-running, good-humoured rapport on the phone.

Catherine, who was eight years younger than Perec, came from a medical family which had settled at Bressuire, a small town in the west of France. After her baccalaureate, she entered *hypokhâgne* at a lycée in Tours, where one of her teachers was the founder-director of the annual Festival of Short Films. She went on to study English at Poitiers and then went up to Paris, ostensibly to enrol in an interpreters' school. But her heart was already in the cinema, and instead of proceeding as her family intended her to, she took the first job she could find in an editing studio. Thenceforth Catherine's whole life would be in film. She worked with Marcel Hannoun, coscripting and codirecting one of his films, and then made a short on the surrealist painter Hans Bellmer, whom she knew well. In June 1975 she had just finished writing the script of her first full-length film, *Les Jeux de la Comtesse Dolingen de Gratz*, a complex puzzle drawing on *Dunkler Frühling* by Unica Zürn (Hans Bellmer's companion), Bram Stoker's *Dracula*, and a story from real life. Her next step was to apply to the CAR, for without an "advance on receipts" she would have no prospect of finding a producer to finance her demanding and difficult film. Perec was in the opposite position: he had no problems about finding a producer for *Les Lieux d'une fugue*, since INA would play that role for him, but he was not at all sure how to turn his childhood story into a television film.

On 23 June 1975 Georges Perec and Catherine Binet met for a meal, towards eight in the evening, at the Saint-Claude, a brasserie on Boulevard Saint-Germain. Perec arrived early, as he usually did, except for dental appointments. They left the restaurant later, and became lovers the same night.

The date and the time are solemnly inscribed in chapter 99 of *Life A User's Manual*. The vast, frozen frame of Perec's great novel comes to life towards eight in the evening on 23 June 1975, when the seventy-five-year-old Percival Bartlebooth dies. *Don't you see*, Perec later explained to Catherine, *it's when the old man died.*

Perec gave Catherine copies of all his books except *Les Revenentes* and they dined together many times in the days following 23 June. Over a dish of skate in black butter sauce at Le Balzar, a drop of grease stained Catherine's blouse. To save her from embarrassment, Perec dipped his finger in the sauce-boat and smeared grease onto his own Indian shirt. Catherine had never dreamt of such charm. Perec's smiling eyes and childish grin made his otherwise ugly face almost beautiful. Was it love at first sight? Not exactly, says Catherine. With hindsight they could see that they had both been deferring their encounter for months, for fear of acknowledging true feelings too promptly. One night, however, Perec phoned to tell Catherine directly that he loved her and had rearranged his other affairs. In his diary he noted: *Told B. I loved C.*

On 18 July Perec left Paris, and Catherine, for a holiday at the Brunhoffs' holiday home at Ars-en-Ré. There was no bridge to the island of Ré in those days, so Perec caught the flat-bottomed ferry across the narrow channel from the rail-head at La Rochelle, Jean Duvignaud's hometown. A few days later he went back to the pier with Laurent de Brunhoff to meet Harry Mathews. Laurent drove them back along the narrow sand-spit island to the white-painted Brunhoff house near the sea. On Saturday, 19 July, Perec reported to Catherine:

> *The house is very beautiful, not very big, but white all over, and it has a garden, in the middle of a little village, Ars-en-Ré, which is full of rather smart people on holiday. This morning (more exactly, from noon to 3:00 P.M.) we went to the beach. A lady novelist to the left of us, a press attaché to the right of us, and publishers, writers, and so on more or less all around. It was a bit irritating, like being on the terrace chez Lipp, but it was not really too bad. It's the first time in ten years that I've been "on holiday" on a beach, and it was really quite odd. I swam a little. Protected from the sun's rays by an immense gandura (or jellaba, or jebba, or burnoose) with a hood, I began to read L'Homme-Jasmin.[1] But you can't read properly on a beach and I dipped into it just enough to be sure that I will plunge into it very soon. This morning I did hardly any work, but I feel that I am going to. On the train I think I solved some of the problems that I have been pondering about my television short story – no real images yet, even less actual shots,*

[1] The French translation of *Der Mann im Jasmin*, by Unica Zürn.

but choices which will help me to see a little better what it is that I want to make. At least I hope so.

It's been a long time since I last wrote a letter. It's not easy to tell you all that I feel: all that has happened these last weeks. I don't know how to say it because words always seem to me to be slightly off the point: what they concern is not writing, not the blank page, nostalgia, memories, but you and me and what lies before us: everything there is beneath the word love – the upheaval of desire, the unique emotion, and the calm joy that you give me, and the amazement, the plain amazement, the insatiable amazement (for instance, I would like to know every minute of your life and tell you every minute of mine) and laughter and everything.

There you are. Now I'll get down to L'Homme-Jasmin *and one of the sixteen pieces of work I planned to do here (if only in order to finish off one of them!). I'll be back sooner than I said, not on 1 August but on 30 or 31 July. My American friend, Harry Mathews, who is here, has a house in Venice and has offered to lend it to us or to have us there as guests for a few days in September. It sounds wonderful to me. But I'll go with you wherever you want to go.*

He was in a letter-writing mood, keen to keep in touch. The following Wednesday he wrote to his cousin Ela:

Dear Lili

It's the first time I've really had a holiday in ten years. We go to the beach, we go on bicycle rides. The house is all white, with a little garden, and the weather is fine. I've got a bit of sunburn but it's not too bad.

I'm doing just enough work to be able to say that I'm not doing nothing. I read a bit. I do watercolours.

Mathews and Perec had fun at Ré and kept the Brunhoffs in stitches. There is no photograph to be found of Perec bicycling on the beach, but the sheikh-of-Araby attire which he needed to protect him from the sun was a source of unending and good-humoured mirth. Perec by the telephone provoked a different kind of a smile. He hovered about it, not knowing whether to ring, hoping she would ring first. Would she have him? Would she not? He spoke to Harry about Catherine: she was beautiful, regal, imperious, and determined to make her film; she would not necessarily be an easy person to live with, but she was – without any doubt – the woman that he wanted. Harry was pleased to see Perec in decisive mood in matters that had previously given him much anguish, and put it down in large measure to the beneficial effect of psychoanalysis. Perec wrote to Catherine again on 23 July:

> *I think I really needed this respite. Over the last year a whole series of events has occurred. Meeting you was the last link in a chain whose order seems to me to be evidence of a not-yet-explicit necessity that is, I feel, fundamental. [. . .] I mean that I am pulling myself together and feel pulled-together, but how can I tell you that in a letter?*

The work that Perec "pulled together" during his island holiday consisted of further heterogrammatic "esartunilo+" poems, probably the most demanding of all the exercises he ever undertook. He and Harry went back to Paris after ten delightful days by the sea, and on the train Perec polished off another stunning heterogram in *d*, the one which forms poem 28 of *Alphabets*. Mathews writes of the end of their journey:

> I remember arriving with Georges Perec at Gare d'Austerlitz in the summer of 1975. Although on the lookout for Catherine B., he failed to see her where she stood solitary and beautiful at the end of the platform; I had to point her out to him.[1]

Three nights later Harry and Maxine Groffsky, now Perec's literary agent for the English-speaking world, dropped in at Rue Linné to collect Perec, Catherine, and Nour, who was visiting. After picking up Marcel Benabou, they all went out for dinner: it was Maxine's farewell to France. Perec hoped that she would get *W or The Memory of Childhood* published in English translation. Harry's sample chapter from *A Man Asleep* had already appeared in the *Paris Review* – but *W*, he told Catherine, was sure to appeal more to *les Amerloques* than it did to the French.

In September Perec took Harry up on his offer of a loan of his rented share of the Casa Pisis in Venice. Ostensibly he went to attend the showing of *A Man Asleep* at the Film Festival, but in practice Perec's second sojourn in the city of serenity was a storybook

---

[1] Harry Mathews, *The Orchard* (Flint, MI: Bamberger Books, 1988), p. 2.

honeymoon. After the open-air showing of the film (*Il Dormiveglia*, in the sub-titled Italian version)[1] in Campo Santa Margherita, Perec and Catherine attended a grand party at the house of Loredana Balboni, a close friend of Harry Mathews and a well-known society figure. It was the night of the historical regatta, which had, that year, a Japanese theme. The guests at Loredana's vast canalside palazzo, with its marble floors and its walls covered with modern art, threw sweetmeats from the balcony to the Japanese visitors in traditional dress standing on the punts below. Suddenly Perec grew even more excited: *Look! Look! There's Monica Vitti!* he cried. As the actress glided past in a gondola, she looked up at the Casa Balboni and shouted, "Michelangelo! Michelangelo!" Perec and Catherine had not realised before that the distinguished gentleman who had been watching motor racing on television in the lounge was none other than Michelangelo Antonioni. He could no longer be found in the house, but Franca Baratto, an old friend from Paris and from Lg now resident in Venice, assured Catherine that he would return. Later that evening, after a spectacular summer storm which turned the sky, the water and the whole city green and black, Catherine was indeed introduced to the maestro of the Italian screen.

Loredana's was not the only party held that night, for the whole of Venetian society was celebrating the Film Festival and the regatta combined. Much later, Perec and Catherine boarded a launch to take them to a veritable Xanadu where they revived their flagging spirits at dawn with lobster and champagne.

Catherine left Perec alone in the flat to write for a respectable number of hours every day. He had brought with him his plans for a huge novel based on the Knight's Tour problem and on the bi-square of order ten, which he explained to Catherine. When she returned to the flat at the end of each afternoon, Perec would make her talk about where she had been, what she had eaten, about art and literature and film, and he approached matters great and small with equally unpretentious and equally passionate interest. On some occasions he went sightseeing with her. He would stop to admire the exteriors but he would not enter any of the churches in Venice. At

---

[1] It was well received and widely reviewed, principally as a film by Queysanne; see *Corriere della sera*, *Avanti!*, *Il Gazzettino* (with an illustration of Franz Kafka, "alla cui opera si è ispirato il regista Bernard Queysanne"), *Paese Sera*, and *La Stampa*, all for 3 September 1975.

Perec's suggestion the two of them visited the Jewish quarter, the original ghetto, but he would not enter the synagogue, either: he told Catherine that he had never been in one in his life.

Catherine read all the books Perec had given her, and she was moved most of all by *W or The Memory of Childhood*. She reread her lover's twin-track autobiography more than once, discovering in it at each reading a different book. She began to question the nature of her own perplexity and then reread it once again, with care. There were some curious lapses in it, she thought. For example, the uniform of the novices on the island of W is described on page 99 as having stitched on the back a plain triangle with the apex pointing down, but when the triangle is mentioned a second time, on page 146, it is said to be pointing up. It struck Catherine that the first triangle placed over the second would make a six-pointed star – the Star of David. Perec told Catherine that he had not intended to smuggle in a sign of his Jewish identity in that way, but he was not displeased that it was there.

In Venice Perec worked not on his puzzle-novel but on *Alphabets*, a work that had been transformed from a crossword defence into a celebration of the summer of 1975 and of the poetry that he had now found in his life. He had a new heterogram-poem to read to Catherine nearly every night. She bought a handmade manuscript book from a craftsman and asked Perec to write out a fair copy of *Alphabets* in it for her. The thick and grainy paper was too absorbent for the ink of Perec's felt-tip pen, however, and Catherine's manuscript of *Alphabets* was never completed.

In Paris, some time later, Jacqueline de Guitaut caught sight of a couple with their arms around each other looking up at the equestrian statue of Henri IV by the banks of the Seine. It was a common enough sight at that infinitely romantic and much photographed spot. On this occasion, however, it touched Guitaut's heart. It was Georges Perec and Catherine Binet.

PART III
1975–1982

I detest what's called psychology, especially in fiction. I prefer books in which characters are described by their actions, their gestures, and their surroundings. [. . .] It's something that belongs to the great tradition of realism in the English and German novel of the nineteenth century, which I've exaggerated a little, almost taking it to hyperrealism.

Georges Perec, speaking in Warsaw on 5 April 1981

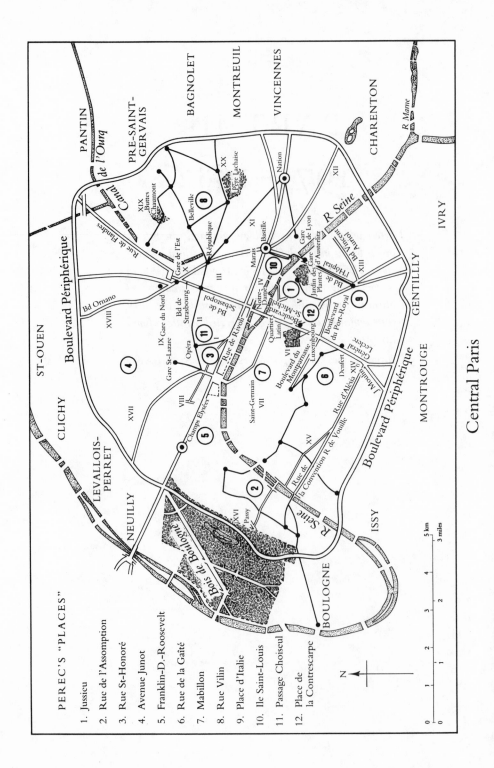

PEREC'S "PLACES"

1. Jussieu
2. Rue de l'Assomption
3. Rue St-Honoré
4. Avenue Junot
5. Franklin-D.-Roosevelt
6. Rue de la Gaîté
7. Mabillon
8. Rue Vilin
9. Place d'Italie
10. Ile Saint-Louis
11. Passage Choiseul
12. Place de
    la Contrescarpe

Central Paris

CHAPTER 55

A Writer's Living

The summer of 1975 was a turning point in the life and work of Georges Perec. He had brought his interrogation of the past to term with the publication of *W or The Memory of Childhood*, he had concluded his course of psychoanalysis, and he had found at last a relationship to which he could commit himself entirely. He would soon be forty. He had accumulated a treasury of techniques, ranging from a mastery of zero-degree description to a mastery of the alphabet, from the art of enumeration to the art of writing dreams. In his files and ledgers he had in stock well-developed plans for more than one major work and a host of shorter ones. He had his own places in Paris – Rue Linné, OuLiPo, *Cause commune*, Le Balzar, the BPR – and a set of rural retreats, at Chambroutet (the family home of Catherine Binet, near Bressuire, in the department of Deux-Sèvres), at Ars-en-Ré, and at Harry Mathews's house at Lans-en-Vercors. He was just about ready to open the door of his treasury and to bring his energy to bear on the construction of his life in words.

Not long before Perec first dined out with Catherine Binet, CHU Saint-Antoine burnt to the ground. The neurophysiology laboratory was transferred first to Pavillon Lemierre, a separate hospital building unaffected by the fire, and then, for several years, to the CNRS research campus at Gif-sur-Yvette. Perec had to travel out on the *ligne de Sceaux* (now much improved and renamed RER "B") to the last-but-one-stop on the line. He resented it. He was too old to waste time.

He had always aspired to being a book-a-year man, and now he wanted to be a professional writer, a man of letters full-time. He had almost kept the rhythm from 1965 to 1969, and had resumed it from 1973 with *La Boutique obscure*, *Espèces d'espaces* (published in autumn 1974) and *W or The Memory of Childhood*. The gap in 1970–72 was explained by the Andé crisis. In 1976–77, however, a new gap intervened for a quite different reason: Perec's editor, Maurice Nadeau, who had stuck by him for ten years, got the sack.

These two almost simultaneous mishaps at the lab and at Denoël could have been taken tragically, and might well have sunk another man for good. They gave Perec much cause for complaining, for whining, even, in front of some of his friends. At bottom, however, he was no longer prepared to bow before the blows of fate.

Nadeau's misfortune provided Perec with an opportunity to reorganise his publishing affairs. He wanted terms that would allow him to escape from the CNRS and to live as a writer full-time. But was he free to make new terms? *La Boutique obscure*, the one and only volume of Denoël's *Cause commune* collection, did not count, strictly speaking, as the last of the "five next books" after *Things* on which Les Lettres nouvelles (owned by Denoël, now an imprint of Gallimard) had first refusal. Even after Nadeau's departure, Denoël could claim with some justification that Perec still owed it one further book. He proposed *Je me souviens* ("I Remember") to complete his contractual obligation, and the firm turned it down. At the same time, he asked for the terms he had requested from Le Seuil many years before: advances on his next books to be paid month by month, in imitation of a salary. In such circumstances, Denoël agreed to count the post-*Things* books it had already published and the one it had rejected as fulfilling Perec's commitment, and let him go. He would have to look elsewhere for his living.

Perec had long been an obsessive and jubilant solver of crossword puzzles, and had played at setting his own for almost the same length of time. He must have been selling crosswords for anonymous publication as early as 1971, since a scribbled budget forecast for 1972 shows a line of income under "X-wds"; in any case, he had never made a secret of his ardent ambition to be the weekly puzzle provider in a mass-circulation magazine. In the winter of 1975–76, when Perec's lab job had become a bind and his position with Denoël was still unclear, Ela sought to help her cousin to achieve at least this one of his lesser aims. She arranged to meet Robert Franck, the nephew of Germaine Franck, "Big Jacques" Bienenfeld's last wife, and a long-standing acquaintance. Franck was a self-taught and enterprising journalist at *Le Point*, an illustrated weekly news magazine set up by a splinter from *L'Express*. She asked him whether his publication had a vacancy for a crossword-puzzle setter. Franck wasn't sure, but he promised to look into it. Ela followed up on the matter and was soon able to put Perec in touch with the back-pages editor of *Le Point*, who took him on that summer. His first puzzle appeared in August 1976, and from then on there was not a blank week for six years. The pay was less than grand (400 francs per puzzle at the start, raised in stages to 850 francs by 1981), but it came every month, on the nail. *Le Point* was the first step in Perec's plan to make a living as well as a life in words.

In 1976 Perec also joined the readers' panel at France-Culture, whose job it was to select radio plays for production from the piles of unsolicited manuscripts that were regularly sent in. His fellow readers were his old teacher Jean Duvignaud, Geneviève Serreau (Nadeau's assistant at Les Lettres nouvelles and *La Quinzaine*), Georges Conchon, Pierre Andreux, and René Farabet (a radio producer under Alain Trutat at the ACR). It was not a big money-spinner, obviously, but a second enjoyable job that could be relied on for a regular fee.

In the first months of 1976 a rising editor at Flammarion had a telephone call from a colleague, alerting him to a rumour that the author of *Things* was in search of a new publisher. He looked up Perec in the telephone book, gave him a ring, and arranged to meet him for a meal at Le Rostand. Paul Otchakovsky-Laurens – P.O.L. for short – was a young man, and he looked even younger than his years. He listened to Perec's problems and plans with rapt interest. There was a vast novel in preparation, a backlist of unpublished writing, and uncountably many works projected for the future: novels, plays, poetry, and essays of all sorts. What Perec wanted was a publisher able to pay him advances on royalties in the form of a monthly salary substitute. It made sense, even if it was an unusual arrangement, and P.O.L. was eager to take the idea up with his superiors.

Not long after this meeting, Paul Otchakovsky-Laurens's position at Flammarion became precarious. The Perec proposal gathered dust in a tray of matters pending, or in a file marked RIP.

In publishing terms Perec was a has-been, a now middle-aged winner of a premature prize, a writer who had failed to live up to the success of *Things*, but P.O.L. did not share that cruelly commercial view. He had not read everything that Perec had published to date, but he had no doubt whatsoever that he was dealing with a major writer who would do his list credit, even if he did not bring high sales. There was also a spark between Perec and P.O.L.: they liked each other, and each grasped that the other was a man alone.

Perec was certainly quite alone in French literature. He belonged to no school, and though he had some individual admirers of weight (Mauriac, Grenier, and Pingaud, for example), he had no fan club, no standard-bearers in the press, nor bespectacled scholars in French universities directing theses on his earlier work. He was not on any publisher's readers' panel, he was not a book reviewer for any newspaper or magazine. Perec had little influence on his own account, and nobody of influence behind him. (Raymond Queneau, who *was* a man of influence, never used it directly on behalf of members of OuLiPo, only on behalf of the group.) Perec had not even been abroad on a speaking tour funded by the French government, that first symbol of established status in French intellectual life. He was not in a strong position. Unfortunately, at this point – in mid-1976 – neither was P.O.L.

Perec began to write the running text of *Life A User's Manual* in the autumn of 1976. The novel had been on his mind and in his planning schedules for years, and from the start, the plan called "Life" had been envisaged as a bigger book by far than any he had previously written. In 1976 Perec also needed it to be the means by which he would spend the second half of his life as a writer. He could have chosen to make his re-entry by another vehicle – for *Life A User's Manual* was not the only big book that he had stored up and planned in some detail. In principle, he could have decided to follow the track of *W or The Memory of Childhood* by launching into *L'Arbre*; or to pursue the path of his *Cause commune* pieces by reworking the material accumulated in the envelopes of *Lieux*. He might even have decided to use the success of *A Man Asleep* to relaunch a film version of *Things*. He did none of these things. *Life A User's Manual* imposed itself not simply as a "next book" amongst others, but as the book which would swallow up and surpass them all. This underlying dynamic had in fact already led to the abandonment of *Lieux* (the last text was written in September 1975); *W or The Memory of Childhood* had taken the steam out of *L'Arbre*. Perec needed to offer prospective publishers a book that could appeal to a wide public, so as to justify paying him monthly advances and thereby allow him to resign from the lab, but financial calculations of that sort could hardly have been preponderant in the literary choices Perec made. In fact, when he

26. The Gardens of Dar Henson, Hammamet, Tunisia, 1960. See *Things*, page 117

27. The interior of Dar Henson, Hammamet, Tunisia, 1960

28. *Opposite:* The Moulin d'Andé in 1965

29. Perec in a cap, Paris, 1966. *(Copyright © 1993 Babette Mangolte, all rights of reproduction reserved)*

Non, lui dit-il d'abord, pardon, pardon, j'ai voulu vous voir.

Mais Faustin l'ignora, quoiqu'il la suppliât.

Plus tord, tout fut hallucination : il crut à un champign‑
l'intoxication d'

malgré qu'il avant tout à fait disparu ; la vision d'aut‑

l'avant vu grain, il folichonnait, il imaginait tout : un casin

voi mais, un jour, il vit la scission, ou plutôt la duplicat

sal non loin de l'aquarium l'action mot pour mot trait pa

Là, la fiction d'Ismaïl no su so‑

t mais il y avait pas (là s'inaugurait l'incon istant mai

qui l'unissait au roman

la fiction d'Ismaïl   j'aperçois qu

tait, portant un plat ; il allait sur lui, l'ignorant ; d'instinct, Ismaï

sur un bahut. Ismaïl allait au bahut, avançait la main sur l'al

tau, nul Goliath n'aurait pu à l'instant saisir l'allu .

30. From the manuscript of *La Disparition*

31. Georges Perec at Andé in 1968

32. *Above:* Jean
Duvignaud
around 1960

34. *Right:* Eugen
Helmle

33. *Above:* Philippe Drogoz

35. *Below:* Georges Perec with Paolo Boni (left)
in the artist's studio

36. & 37. Georges Perec and Jacques Roubaud playing Go at the Moulin d'Andé in 1969

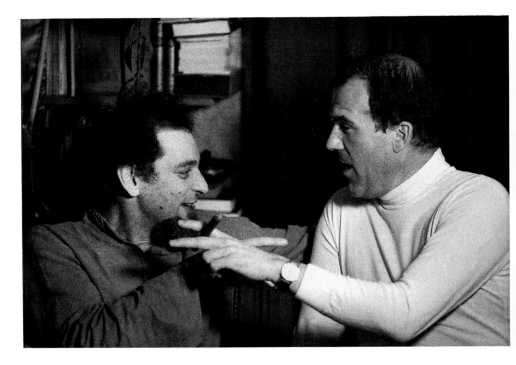

38. & 39. Georges Perec and Harry Mathews, Paris, January 1975

40. The OuLiPo in the garden of Francois le Lionnais, Boulogne-sur-Seine,
23 September 1975. See key diagram

1 Jacques Roubaud; 2 Paul Fournel; 3 Michèle Métail; 4 Italo Calvino; 5 Harry
Mathews; 6 Luc Etienne; 7 Georges Perec; 8 Marcel Benabou; 9 Jacques Bens;
10 Paul Braffort; 11 Jean Lescure; 12 Jacques Duchateau; 13 Noël Arnaud;
14 François le Lionnais; 15 Raymond Queneau; 16 Jean Queval; 17 Claude Berge;
18 André Blavier

41. Georges Perec in a hat, Ars-en-Ré, July 1975

42. Catherine Binet, Paris 1974

43. Georges Perec and Bernard Zitzerman filming *Les Lieux d'une Fugue*, Paris, June 1976

44. Catherine Binet (on the right), Bernard Zitzerman and Georges Perec filming, as above

45. *Opposite:* With Marie-Claude de Brunhoff at the party for *Life A User's Manual*, Paris, September 1978

46. *Right:* Georges
Perec and Robert
Bober in the courtyard
of Rue Linné, 1980

47. *Below:* Georges
Perec, Christian
Bourgois, Alain
Robbe-Grillet, Paris,
November 1978.

48. Georges Perec on the roof of the World Trade Center, New York, in 1979

49. Georges Perec at Rue Linné, October 1978. The painting on the wall is
Gérard Guyomard's *L'Evêché d'Exeter*, an "illustration" of *Les Revenentes*

finally began to draft *Life A User's Manual* in October 1976, he did not know whether *anyone* would publish it; and he did not know *who* would publish it until the book was very nearly complete.

As soon as the great book was under way, Perec naturally sought a means of returning to the publishing scene. He wrote out a prospectus to describe the life in words that he envisaged, typed it up neatly with his name and the date at the top, and set off for a vernissage where he thought (or perhaps knew) he would find the keen young publisher he had talked to some months before. Perec's 1976 self-presentation shows how much things had changed since 1969, when he wrote a nine-page prospectus-letter to Maurice Nadeau (*see* p. 437). Then he had been seeking sympathy, approval, and complicity from a mentor of a much older generation than his own; now, in 1976, he wrote a prospective autobibliography that was no less ambitious, but couched in an impersonal, almost administrative style, for a man who was his junior by a decade or more. At the vernissage of paintings by Colette Deblé (the wife of the poet Bernard Noël), Perec found Paul Otchakovsky-Laurens, and greeted him as if their meeting were pure chance. With timid defiance, with modest pride and a still-uncontrollable blush, Perec put the list of his unwritten works in the hand of P.O.L., as if to say, Is this enough?

The terms he requested were the same as before: advances on royalties to be paid in monthly instalments, like a salary, and a commitment in principle to take on board his entire writing life, in all the nineteen parts laid out in the prospectus. A similar proposal was made to Gallimard, the firm that had issued his first contract in 1959 and then let him down. To be published by Gallimard, the most prestigious house in Paris – to appear, like Jacques Roubaud, between the cream covers of the *nrf* collection – was a dream of youth that Perec had not yet absolutely abandoned. Gallimard turned Perec down again. Rumour has it that someone on the board declared that Gallimard would not publish crossword puzzles whilst *he* was still there.

P.O.L. made better progress on the Perec front in 1977 than he had the year before. A monthly salary substitute to allow Perec to write full-time was agreed by Flammarion, as was an annual rhythm of publication ad infinitum. So what would Perec's 1977 volume be? Not *Life A User's Manual*; it would not be ready in time. It would be easier to finish *Je me souviens* first. Unlike Denoël, P.O.L. was open to the idea of a book made up only of numbered sentences beginning "I remember", and so, as he wrote chapters 30 to 40 of *Life A User's Manual* in May and June 1977, Perec plunged into a great flurry of "I remembers", not even bothering to copy out the last 131 of them into the ledger that he had so neatly begun in 1973. He drew the line at a nice prime, "I remember" number 479, added a "blank" number 480 – *I remember (to be continued . . .)* – as a final flourish against closure, and had the typescript ready by the end of June.

In July 1977, P.O.L became unsure whether he would be able to stay with Flammarion. He discussed his situation with Jean-Etienne Cohen-Séat, the literary director of the huge Hachette publishing concern, and a deal was done. Hachette's interests ranged from dictionaries to newspapers, by way of annuals, academic books, school equipment, printing and distribution, but the long-established giant of the industry had never played a major role in literary publishing and none at all in the avant-garde. P.O.L. was to plug this gap in the firm's activities and to create his own collection, under the imprint "Hachette/ Collection P.O.L.". As the director of his own series he would have an entirely free hand in the choice of texts, with no readers' panel looking over his shoulder or breathing down his neck. It was a tremendous opportunity for a young publisher, and a demanding one, for he would have to attract a new stable of writers at great speed. Even before he announced his resignation from Flammarion, P.O.L. took Georges Perec to dine at Marty's restaurant and told him of his impending move. Perec was taken aback, perhaps because Hachette – the "octopus" of the French book trade, seen until then as a gobbling monster, not as a protector of the arts – was one of the few publishers that he would not have thought of approaching himself. P.O.L. asked Perec if he would join him in his new adventure. *I think so*, Perec replied. Later, he said to Catherine, *P.O.L is utterly mad. I've decided to go with him.*

P.O.L.'s resignation from Flammarion became public knowledge in August 1977 (Perec wrote in a huge burst that month, composing chapters 58 to 70 in virtually final form) and he took up his post as director of "Hachette/ P.O.L." in November (by which time Perec had reached Chapter 82). His first task was to set up a contract for *Life A User's Manual*. Perec's first gift to P.O.L., meanwhile, was to suggest an alphabetic design for the new logo he would need – the POL in line 2 picked out in red:

From 1 January 1978 Perec received a monthly payment of advances on royalties. It was not much of a salary, but, with the crossword money and the readers' panel fees, it provided an adequate foundation for a freelance life. Perec did not resign from the lab on the spot. He discussed his prospects at length with Marie-Claude de Brunhoff, who warned him not to rush into unnecessary risks. But by the summer of 1978 Perec had finished *Life A User's Manual* and Paris was already buzzing with advance publicity for "the novel of the year", which seemed well set to cause a sensation. Perec finally took the plunge and resigned from the CNRS with effect from 1 September. Seventeen years of work which had often been a pleasure and at times even a passion came to a natural and necessary end.

P.O.L. was able to increase Perec's monthly advances in 1979, and later that year he also began to pay him a small retainer as a literary consultant. Perec read perhaps three manuscripts in all for P.O.L., and in each instance telephoned in his advice; he never penned a full reader's report.

The success of *Life A User's Manual* and the modest way in which Perec had arranged to draw on his earnings might have meant that he would never need to write for money again. But things did not work out that way.

Based on information and documents kindly supplied by Ela Bienenfeld, Catherine Binet, Marie-Claude de Brunhoff, Paul Fournel, Dr Henry Gautier, Professor André Hugelin and the secretarial staff of CNRS LA 38, Claude Imbert and the administrative staff of *Le Point*, Paul Otchakovsky-Laurens, Maurice Nadeau, Alain Trutat, and the secretarial staff of the drama reading panel at France-Culture.

Appendix to Chapter 55

The 1976 Prospectus

This is a slightly abridged and lightly annotated translation of the four-page typescript that Perec gave to Paul Otchakovsky-Laurens in December 1976.

The titles of books that were not yet written in 1976 and of works that have not yet appeared in English translation are given in French.

Books and articles that were subsequently written and eventually published in book form are indicated by references in square brackets.

The original document is reproduced in *Cahiers Georges Perec I* (Proceedings of the Colloque Perec at the Centre Culturel International de Cérisy-La-Salle, 1984; © P.O.L. 1985.)

Georges Perec   December 1976

An attempt at a description of a schedule
of work for the years to come

This programme is laid out following four main directions, which, moreover, most often overlap:

– an autobiographical current, exemplified by *W*
– a fictional current, exemplified by *A Man Asleep* or by *La Disparition*
– a "daily-life" current, exemplified by *Things* or by *Espèces d'espaces*
– an "Oulipian" current, exemplified by *Die Maschine* or by *Alphabets*

The plans that follow are not really in chronological order; the aim is more to give an idea of work resulting in one book completed – and published – each year.

1. *LA VIE, MODE D'EMPLOI*   [L]

The book I am now writing: it's a jigsaw-novel that describes a block of flats in Paris with its façade removed; it will be a big book – between 600 and 800 pages – and I expect to finish it by the end of 1977.

2. *L'ARBRE – HISTOIRE D'ESTHER ET DE SES FRÈRES*

A plan that goes back to 1966, a kind of family saga narrating, in the form of a biographical dictionary and an exploded family tree, the story of my aunt, my father, and my uncle. It also will be a big book.

3. *LE VOYAGE A KAIROUAN* ("Journey to Kairouan")

This will perhaps be a novel in letters. It tells the story of the journey that Klee, Moilliet, and Macke made to Tunisia in April 1914. The novel is centred not on Klee but on Macke, who was killed in Champagne a few weeks after his return.

4. *LES CHOSES COMMUNES*

Under this title I would like to gather three series of texts, mostly short:

4a. *LIEUX OÙ J'AI DORMI* [*see PC* 25–29]

What's involved is describing from (distant) memory the bedrooms I have lived in (cf *Espèces d'espaces*, p. 31).

4b. *JE ME SOUVIENS* [*Jms*]

A book of banal memories, belonging to all, generally not catalogued in history, but prompting minute bouts of nostalgia [. . .]

4c. *NOTES DE CHEVET* ("Bedside Notes") [*see PC* 165–166]

An attempt to transpose to the world of today the pillow book of Sei Shonagon.

5. *TENTATIVE DE DESCRIPTION DE QUELQUES LIEUX PARISIENS* [*see inf*]

Cf *Espèces d'espaces*, p. 76. The plan, which should have extended over twelve years, has been practically abandoned and transformed: the "places" involved have been tackled from different angles: I have written a poem ("La Clôture") about Rue Vilin; I have made a film (*Les Lieux d'une fugue*) about the Franklin-Roosevelt junction; I am planning a radio broadcast on Mabillon. Nonetheless, texts exist in plenty, and it would perhaps be interesting to collect them together, to sort them, and to comment on some of them.

6. A COLLECTIVE NOVEL

For some years Italo Calvino, Harry Mathews, and I have planned to write a trilingual novel together (cf the renga by Paz-Roubaud-Sanguinetti-Tomlinson). But we are only at the preliminary stages.

7. A DETECTIVE NOVEL [*53D*]

I have always wanted to write a "classical" detective novel: perfect crime, sealed room, etc.

8. A SCIENCE-FICTION NOVEL

I have only one idea to launch it, but it amuses me a great deal: a world where letters (alphabetic) replace work and money; life would be an endless Scrabble match . . .

9. CHILDREN'S BOOKS

Not yet a plan, but an ambition, a wish. [*see* p. 682]

10. AN ADVENTURE NOVEL

Or several of them. I began to work on this idea in 1972, in response to a vague proposal from Hachette that was later abandoned, but it is a type of writing that attracts me a lot.

11. LE LIVRE DES 2000 PHRASES ("The Book of the Two Thousand Sentences")

A (Swiss) linguist did a survey of the two thousand commonest sentences in the French language and sorted them under the situations to which they relate; the idea is to write a novel – or a play – using all and only these sentences; the effect you would get seems likely to me to be even more killing than that of *The Bald Prima Donna*.

12. LE ROMAN DU XIXᵉ SIÈCLE ("The Novel of the Nineteenth Century")

This is another very old project: take an anthology of nineteenth-century literature [. . .] and harmonise the extracts quoted in it so as to end up with a story made from fragments of *Adolphe*, *Atala*, and so on, right down to Zola.

Miscellaneous texts suitable for publication in book form:

13. DRAMA, RADIO DRAMA (*HÖRSPIELE*)

13a. *Die Maschine* (in German, published in Germany by Reklam)
[*M*]
13b. *Tagstimmen* (in German)
13c. *Konzertstück* (in German)
13d. *L'Augmentation*   [*Th*]
13e. *Fonctionnement du système nerveux dans la tête*
13f. *La Poche Parmentier*   [*Th*]
13g. *Anacoluthon* (planned)
13h. *Wie ein Hund* (bilingual: a Kafka bestiary)
[*see* pp. 388–389, 470–471]
13i. *Histoire universelle* (planned, with Marcel Benabou)
13j. *L'Art effaré* (planned libretto for an opera written only with words made from notes: *La Ré Fa Ré*)   [*see.* pp 426–427, 534]

14. POEMS

14a "Ulcérations" (published in a limited edition)   [*Clô*]
14b "La Clôture" (ditto)   [*Clô*]
14c "Métaux" (on engravings by Boni, in progress)   [*Clô*]

15. OULIPIAN EXERCISES

15a. The Great Palindrome   [*Clô*]
15b. The little palindrome   [*Clô*]

15c. "Microtraductions"   [*Atlas*]
15d. *Les Horreurs de la guerre*, an alphabetic drama   [*Atlas*]
15e. "Lieux communs travaillés"   [*V*]
15f. "Les Adventures de Dixion Harry"   [*V*]
15g. "Le Petit Abécédaire illustré"   [*V*]
15h. "Version latines"   [*V*]
15i. The Knight's-Tour Problem
15j. "La Cantatrice Sauve"   [*BibOl* 16]
15k. etc.

16. ARTICLES
16a. On Robert Antelme
16b. "Ecriture et Mass-Media"
16c. "Lire"   [*PC* 109–128]
16d. "Tentative d'inventaire . . ."   [*inf* 97–106]
16e. "Douze Regards obliques"   [*PC* 43–58]
16f. Various pieces from *Cause commune* (1972–1976)
                             [*PC* 77–88, *inf* 9–14, *Jsn* 67–74]
17. CROSSWORDS (one each week in *Le Point* for the past year)
                                               [*MC* I, *MC* II]

18. TRANSLATIONS
I have translated two of Harry Mathews's three novels; I expect to translate his future works, and his poems.

19. Plans that are still vague but nonetheless firm:

19a. *Dix-sept vues du canal de l'Ourcq* (seventeen texts on seventeen engravings by Pierre Getzler: neither the texts nor the engravings exist, but we have been thinking about it for several years.)

19b. *Vie du général Eblé*. I have always wanted to write a life of General Eblé.   [*see* pp. 473–474]

19c. *Fragments d'un Ninipotch*. One of my first novels; I dropped it, but I have often thought that like Thomas Mann with *Felix Krull* I would come back to this plan.   [*see* pp. 292–293]

CHAPTER 56

Hiding and Showing

During his cord-trousered years Perec made a firm distinction between his *job* at the lab and his *work* as a writer, just as his friends differentiated between *achievement* and *success*. The value-system of the 1960s made obscurity respectable for artists and intellectuals, but in the 1970s oblivion no longer seemed a moral imperative. The Moulin d'Andé remained proud of its discretion, of course, but Andé concerned Perec no longer. Queneau, by contrast, decided, around the turn of the decade, that OuLiPo should cease to be quite so confidential. Its first public act as a group was to publish the "Ex-Cape" volume in a mass-market paperback, which came out in 1973. Once the bulk of its first ten years' work was out in that form, OuLiPo launched its own series of booklets, La Bibliothèque Oulipienne.[1] Perec and Paul Fournel were responsible for managing these semi-private editions of Oulipian "exercise" texts, printed in runs of 150 or 200 numbered copies. The first volume, which came back from the printers in August 1974, was Perec's "Ulcérations". Later that year *Le Magazine littéraire*, edited by Jean-Jacques Brochier, published a "Dossier OuLiPo", bringing the group to wider public attention,[2] and in 1975 OuLiPo at last resolved to appear in the flesh before an audience – at a Brussels exhibition in honour of Raymond Queneau, part of a Common Market culture festival called Europalia 75.[3] In preparation for the event a photographer went to the house of François Le Lionnais at Boulogne-sur-Seine on 23 September 1975, and took a colour shot of the members present at the 170th meeting

---

[1] Collectively republished by Ramsay in two volumes (in 1987) and by Seghers in three (in 1990).

[2] Perec's contribution was "Qu'est-ce que la littérature potentielle", *Le Magazine littéraire* No. 94 (November 1974), pp. 22–23. Despite its title, this is not an explanation of OuLiPo but a demonstration of (more and less murderous) transformations of the opening sentence of Marcel Proust's *Remembrance of Things Past*.

[3] Perec played a role in planning the exhibition itself. See André Blavier and Raymond Queneau, *Lettres croisées 1949–1976* (Brussels: Labor, 1988), pp. 327–328.

of OuLiPo; the faces of absent members were pasted in later to produce the famous group portrait now available as a picture postcard
(illustration 40).

Perec had no reservations about OuLiPo's gradual movement away
from the ghetto of private literature towards brighter and more public
light. As for himself, he was known in the mid-1970s (though known
is hardly the right word) less for being an Oulipian writer than as the
codirector of a prestigious, prizewinning film. An illustrated monthly
magazine, *Présences et regards*, when it did an unprecedented special
issue on Perec in October 1975, put on its cover Anne de Brunhoff's
photograph of the writer pulling his wide-eyed, Charles-Trenet-like
face beneath the headline "The Man Awake", punning on the title
of the film, *A Man Asleep*. The centrepiece of the issue was "Les
Lieux d'une fugue", the understated narrative of the day Perec ran
away from home, out of which he now planned to make a
television film.

Between OuLiPo's farcically subversive panel discussion at Europalia in October 1975 and the commencement of *Life A User's Manual*
twelve months later, Perec was without a publisher for his fiction.
He did a few jobs for French radio in that period, taking part in
programmes about Jean Duvignaud[1] and about the literature of
dreams,[2] and he also interviewed Maurice Nadeau at some length on
the occasion of his "retirement" from literary publishing.[3] But there
was no successor-programme to AudioPerec and nothing that contributed to raising Perec's standing as a radio writer to the level that
Die Maschine still gave him east of the Rhine.

As OuLiPo went public, Perec's work went through a more private
phase. He brought out two books in 1976 and neither was like anything he had produced before. They were handsome material objects,
and they were books of poems.

La Clôture appeared first, in January 1976. It consists of a box
containing seventeen heterogrammatic poems handprinted on

[1] "Rencontre avec Jean Duvignaud", broadcast by France-Culture on 25 May
1975.

[2] "Le Rêve et le langage", discussion on dream-writing with Germaine
Rouvre, recorded on 16 February 1976, broadcast by France-Culture on 20 April
1976

[3] "Entretiens avec Maurice Nadeau", produced by Georges Perec for France-
Culture. Recorded on 11 June, broadcast in five instalments on 17–21 November
1975.

unnumbered loose leaves of fine paper and seventeen black-and-white photographs of Rue Vilin by Christine Lipinska. It was produced in one hundred signed and numbered copies, and was priced (for subscribers only) at 110 francs, one hundredth of the production cost of the set.

The poems of *La Clôture* are twelve-letter heterograms of *esartunil-oc*+1, the additional letter being freely chosen for each line, like a joker in the pack. Seventeen poems each of twelve lines, and with each line containing twelve letters, make 2,448 alphabetic characters in all. Bernard Magné believes the numbers were chosen so as to produce a total whose digits secretly commemorate number 24 Rue Vilin, the explicit subject of most of the photographs and the meta-phorical subject of the poems themselves.[1] Magné may well be right: *La Clôture* was a private work in the material sense, and it represents a highly personal use of the apparently impersonal heterogram form.

The title refers to the hoardings (*clôture* in French) put up around the sites of demolished houses in Rue Vilin that can be seen on several of the photographs included in the set. But *clôture* also has the abstract meaning of "closure", or "closing-off". *La Clôture* is thus a double farewell to Perec's childhood in Belleville, to his absent memories, and to the mother he could not really recall. In that sense, *La Clôture* was a way of bringing to term some of the subject-matter of *W or The Memory of Childhood*, just as the concurrent publication of "Les Lieux d'une fugue" released material that might have gone into the autobiography but was in the end dropped. *La Clôture* also closes off the twelve-year time-capsule project, *Lieux,* which had been invented in January 1969 as a way of assuaging the pain of Perec's relationship with Suzanne. Perec finally abandoned *Lieux* in September 1975 on his return from his Venetian idyll with Catherine. She had come to fill the space that cried out for love; Perec no longer needed *Lieux.* He scribbled the last, almost derisory "places" text of his time-capsule project after taking Catherine with him late one night not to Ile Saint-Louis, but to Rue Vilin [*inf* 31].

The emotional filiation of *La Clôture* is complex. The seventeen poems relate indirectly to Suzanne by way of her daughter, who took the photographs, and also by way of *Lieux,* which they continue and displace (*see* p. 583, under "Tentative"). Through its visual and verbal

---

[1] Bernard Magné, "Les Poèmes hétérogrammatiques", *Cahiers Georges Perec 5* (Paris: Editions du Limon, 1992), p. 60.

commemoration of Rue Vilin, *La Clôture* also gives voice to Perec's nostalgia for his lost maternal hearth, and, by virtue of their form, the poems address his feelings for Catherine, the "muse" of his main output of heterogram poems. These converging relations of an almost private poetic work suggest a close connection between Perec's feelings about the loss of his mother and his loss of Suzanne. His recently completed analysis may even have led him to recognise consciously that although the two events were quite different in kind, the pain he had felt in the second case was profoundly related to the pain of the first.

The first edition of "La Clôture" did not hide the constraint by which the poems were generated, since it gave the letter-grids alongside the running text. In an edition of one hundred signed copies the broader issue of whether "private" constraints should or should not be revealed to the public hardly arose. This is the last poem of the set, with a literal translation appended:

CARPLUSENTOI	Car plus en toi s'unit l'archéologue
SUNITLARCHEO	criant son écart, plus il saigne court
LOGUECRIANTS	
ONECARTPLUSI	La porte s'incurve: ni sa clôture, ni
LSAIGNECOURT	blocus à ton désir tu.
LAPORTESINCU	
RVENISACLOTU	L'accalmie (ton sûr port au silence
RENIBLOCUSAT	conquis): l'art?
ONDESIRTULAC	
CALMIETONSUR	*For the more the archaeologist*
PORTAUSILENC	*merges in you, screaming his*
ECONQUISLART	*difference, the more he bleeds short.*
	The door bends in: not its closing,
	nor blockade against your unspoken
	desire
	The calm (your safe haven where
	silence is assured): art?

At the meeting of OuLiPo on 10 December 1975 Perec collected subscriptions for *La Clôture*, and the minutes record "general admiration. Perec stunned by own exploit." *Alphabets*, the much larger set of anagram-poetry begun in 1974 on the back of "Ulcérations", was itself more than half done, with about a hundred poems now finished out of the 176 that the published volume would necessarily contain, but unless Perec could find a publisher to take on such an unusual work, he would have to produce another samizdat book or publish *Alphabets* in the Bibliothèque Oulipienne.

Perec's relations with Michel Delormes, the owner-director of the small firm of Galilée, went back to 1973 and the contract for *Espèces d'espaces*, and they had continued in neighbourly fashion since both men lived and worked at the same end of Rue Linné. Galilée's speciality was expensive art books (it also had a small general list in which it published Jacques Derrida, amongst others), so Delormes suggested that he could take on *Alphabets* if it were not just a book of poems but an art book as well. Extracts of *Espèces d'espaces* had already been used to decorate another art book published by Galilée,[1] and Perec accepted Delormes's proposal for his heterogram-book. A Yugoslav artist working in Paris was commissioned to draw on and around Perec's typescript: it was not a collaboration of the usual kind, as Perec later pointed out,[2] since he neither wrote for Dado, the artist, nor had any contact with him until the work was done.[3]

All the poems of *Alphabets* are regular heterograms of *esartunilo*+1 (*see* pp. 535–536) but some of them have additional "superconstraints" imposed on the already diabolically difficult *esartunilo* rules. For example, the first of the "+W" set, dedicated to the American poet John Ashbery, imitates his "Into the Dusk-Charged Air" by including the name of a river in each line. Others pattern their 11 x 11 letter squares into double and triple acrostics. Far from being hidden by the book's design, these spectacular alphabetic exploits are highlighted in the layout of the pages, and one of them is printed on the back cover of the book for all to see:

---

[1] Antonio Corpora and Georges Perec, *L'Arbre et l'Isaar à Lenggries* (Paris: Galilée, 1976). The book contains twelve etchings by Corpora and two extracts from *Espèces d'espaces*.

[2] "L'Art et le livre illustré", a talk given at the Association culturelle italo-française at Bologna in November 1981 and partly published by Patrizia Molteni in *Ici-Perec* (Montreuil: Bibliothèque Robert-Desnos, 1992).

[3] The second edition of *Alphabets* (Paris: Galilée, 1985) has additional colour plates by Dado. Mireille Ribière, "Alphabets déchiffré", *Cahiers Georges Perec 5* (Paris: Editions du Limon, 1992), pp. 140–142, provides a detailed comparison of the two editions.

LANGESOURIT	L'ange sourit
ALORSGEINTU	Alors geint un glas tiré où
NGLASTIREOU	grelot a su nier salut
GRELOTASUNI	
ERSALUTONGI	On gisait.
SAITOLURNEG	
OURANTLESIG	O, l'urne, gourant le si guignart,
UIGNARTLESO	le sorti sang, élu, oint, eu, gras
RTISANGELUO	lotion à sûr gel!
INTEUGRASLO	*The angel smiles*
TIONASURGEL	*Then a tocsin moans, rung where a*
	cowbell could deny salvation
	We lay at rest.
	O urn! misleading the unlucky B,
	lost blood, the elect, the anointed, the
	had, the fat,
	lotion sure to freeze!

Alphabets is Perec's largest poetical work but it is not always appreciated by readers devoted to his other work. The fragmented syntax and the use of occasionally mis-spelt, archaic, and rare words create considerable difficulties of reading; the complex combination of constraints shows dazzling virtuosity, but dazzle can also make poetry hard to see. Like the Great Palindrome, however, *Alphabets* provides moments of startling poetic splendour. It would be wrong not to struggle with it just because it makes demands on its readers as unusual as those Perec made on himself.

Perec treated the composition of his alphabet-poems as one of his "scales" or "routines" in the winter of 1975–76. Whereas in previous years he had used train journeys and trips abroad to write his memory pieces for *Lieux*, he now used them to write the remaining *Alphabets*, in an ordinary pad of squared paper. A typewriter is of course no more use for writing a heterogram than it is for setting or solving a crossword puzzle, and it is therefore no coincidence that, once the poems were done, Perec used just the same kinds of Rhodia pads on his twice- or thrice-weekly journeys to and from Gif-sur-Yvette to polish off his regular work for *Le Point*.

When Perec started writing *Life A User's Manual* in the autumn of 1976, he had not a single following amongst readers but rather several small groups of fans attached to different parts of his work. His crosswords had already established themselves as quite special ones and there were puzzle fiends who waited anxiously for the next issue of *Le Point* (just as Perec still looked forward to *Le Nouvel Observateur*) in order to turn straight to the back page and get down to solving obliquely witty clues. *Alphabets* had received few notices, but they were important and enthusiastic ones: in *L'Humanité* Pierre Lartigue made manifest the connection among Fritz Lang's *M*, Perec's *W*, and the autobiographical dimension of poetry written under hard constraint; and Jacques Roubaud wrote at length about his fellow-Oulipian's work in *La Quinzaine littéraire*.[1] But the great work in progress was intended for a far wider public than yet knew Perec's name, and so the writer took every opportunity that arose to present himself to the public through the media. Without a publishing contract, however, and thus without a press service to make arrangements for him, Perec did not have many such opportunities. The interviews that he gave in 1977, whilst of extremely high quality, were few and far between.

On 1 February 1977 Perec recorded substantial extracts from *A Man Asleep*, from his poetry, from his translations of Harry Mathews's novels, and from his Japanese pillow-book project, and was interviewed by Bernard Noël.[2] It was in this programme that Perec first explained the main story of *Life A User's Manual* in public. Shortly after, Claude Bonnefoy interviewed Perec for *Les Nouvelles littéraires*, specifically on the book that he "had not finished writing yet".[3] He also wrote the back-panel copy for a paperback edition of

---

[1] Pierre Lartigue, "Que balbutie Perec?", *L'Humanité*, 23 December 1976; Jacques Roubaud, "Ecrit sous la contrainte", *La Quinzaine littéraire*, 16 December 1976.

[2] "Poésie ininterrompue: Georges Perec", broadcast by France-Culture on 20 February 1977.

[3] "Des Règles pour être libre", *Les Nouvelles littéraires*, 10 March 1977, p. 21.

Queneau's *Un Rude Hiver*, for which he was paid a fee so small as to make him angry, but which nonetheless got his name in front of a few thousand more pairs of eyes. Part of Perec's work may have been almost almost private in nature, but he wanted the public to know about him, and most especially about the big book that he knew he would finish soon.

Perec reported on the progress of *Life A User's Manual* at meetings of OuLiPo, which were held at Rue Linné from April until the end of 1976 and thereafter were rotated around the rest of the group for the best part of a year. In spring 1978, the members convened once again in Perec's flat, where one of the major issues they discussed was whether or not Oulipian writers should explain the constraints they used in works intended for a wider audience. Some of them, including Harry Mathews, took the view that constraints were no more a part of the finished work than the scaffolding that contractors put up in order to build a house: once the house is finished the scaffolding has no interest, except to rival contractors. Italo Calvino. who had become a full member in 1973, put the opposite point: there was a whole genre of twentieth century literature, he said, beginning with Gide's diary of the composition of *The Counterfeiters*, concerned with how writing was done. The task of Oulipians was to educate the public further and to make the understanding of constraint an integral part of reading the work.

OuLiPo itself had by then taken on an educational role in the form of writing workshops held every summer at Villeneuve-lès-Avignon. Perec enjoyed working with his fellow-Oulipians and with the students who paid to attend these special creative-writing schools – but on the broad issue of whether Oulipian rules should be kept private or made public, Perec held, simultaneously and awkwardly, the views of both Mathews and Calvino. The machinery of *Life A User's Manual*, unlike that of *Alphabets*, was quite invisible to the reader, and Perec was proud to have hidden the works so effectively, but he was also proud of how he had done it, and he liked to explain. He did so at a meeting of a literary and linguistic study group, the Cercle Polivanoff, on 17 May 1978; then he regretted having done so, and said he would never be so indiscreet again. In the end, he went public in a different way, which must have seemed to many at that time to be almost complete.

In 1979 Bernard Pingaud, who had been a strong supporter of Perec's in the columns of *La Quinzaine littéraire*, proposed to devote issue 76 of *L'Arc* to the author of *Life A User's Manual*. *L'Arc* was (and remains) an irregular literary journal every issue of which is a special number devoted to a single author, and Perec accepted a consecration that put him in the same series as Raymond Queneau, Jules Verne, James Joyce, Michel Butor, Herman Melville, Raymond Roussel, Alexandre Dumas, Robert Musil, and Vladimir Nabokov, amongst the kin that he recognised as his own. The Perec issue contained pieces by friends – Harry Mathews, Julio Cortázar (introduced to Perec by Marie-Claude de Brunhoff), Jacques Roubaud, Paul Virilio, and Paul Otchakovsky-Laurens – a stipple portrait by Pierre Getzler, and a fine cover photograph from a set that Anne de Brunhoff had done in 1978. The volume also contains childhood photographs[1] and two essays on Perec's autobiographical writing. Most important for the turn that Perec criticism would take, however, were Perec's own three contributions: the last release of texts from *Lieux*, the "real" descriptions of Rue de l'Assomption, to which little attention was paid; "Quatre figures pour *La Vie mode d'emploi*" ("Four Figures for *Life A User's Manual*"), a brief, almost cryptic explanation of four of the constraints used to generate the novel (the apartment house, the knight's tour, the bi-square, and the resulting chapter-specifications); and a scripted interview with Jean-Marie Le Sidaner, in which Perec supplied in addition a key to the the list-poem in Chapter 51 of his novel:

> The "Compendium" that constitutes the centre of Life A User's Manual *and lists 179 of its characters is a poem subject to two rules, one of which can easily be checked: each line contains sixty typographical signs, with spaces between words counting as signs.*

Thus, for example:

```
123456789012345678901234567890123456789012345678901234567890
The historian who used pseudonyms to publish rubbishy novels
The librarian collecting proof that Hitler continues to live
A blind man tuning a Russian prima donna's grand piano-forte
```

---

[1] Those described on pages 50 and 103–104 of *W or The Memory of Childhood* (the first is illustration 7) and one showing Perec on top of the "large rock" referred to on page 78 of the same book.

Perec's ambiguity about hiding and showing the machinery of his work is exemplified by this tantalising explanation, for whilst he says that there are two rules operating in this part of the novel, he does not say – anywhere! – what the *second* rule is. What he chose to include in *L'Arc* constitutes a half-intentional tease. He certainly disclosed more than Queneau usually did about the construction of his novels, but it was less than Calvino would have revealed, if Calvino had followed the argument he put to OuLiPo. Perec had once again become *like a child playing hide-and-seek, who doesn't know what he fears or wants the most: to stay hidden, or to be found* [*W* 7]. *L'Arc* set readers looking and brought some of them to Perec's door. A labyrinth, Harry Mathews had said long before, leads only to the outside of itself. Perec's writing was coming to resemble a labyrinth of fearsome complexity, and it is by no means certain that Perec wanted his readers to find the way out.

Based in part on information provided by Catherine Binet, Marie-Claude de Brunhoff, Paul Fournel, Harry Mathews, and the archives of OuLiPo.

CHAPTER 57

A View of the Works

The idea that the origin of life lay in an unprogrammed "inclination" or "bending" of atoms passing through an eternal void goes back to the earliest Greek philosophers by way of Lucretius, who coined the Latin word *clinamen* for it. Defined by the Oxford English Dictionary as "a bias or inclination", clinamen was taken up by an irreverent avant-garde group of former surrealists who, taking their cue from Alfred Jarry, the author of *Ubu Roi*, pursued his "science of imaginary solutions" and constituted themselves as the College of Pataphysics. Raymond Queneau, Boris Vian, François le Lionnais, Stanley Chapman, Noël Arnaud, Ludwig Harig and Eugen Helmle were all members of the College and held one or another of the obscure and pompous titles ("Transcendent Satrap", "Regent of General Pataphysics", "Major Conferant of the Order of the Grande Gidouille") that it awarded. OuLiPo in fact began as an official "subcommission" of the College,[1] even if most second generation Oulipians, including Georges Perec, regarded pataphysics as nothing more than a youthful aberration of their elders. Clinamen was therefore present from the start in Oulipian thinking about literature and it became a central element in Perec's later applications of Oulipian constraint. In his case, of course, the concept fell on ready ground: he knew that his lineage had begun with a kind of mistake, and that the first mythical bearer of his name had been dubbed Gapman because of it. Moreover, Paul Klee's assertion that genius is "an error in the system" had been one of Perec's mottos since the days of La Ligne générale and was the source of one of his recurrent puns, trotted out like a leitmotiv whenever he crossed swords with a woman bearing a particular name: *L'Eugénie, c'est l'erreur dans le système.*

For Perec, the attraction of the writing devices proposed by

[1] See Jean Lescure, "Brief History of the Oulipo" in Warren F. Motte, Jr., ed., *Oulipo. A Primer of Potential Literature* (Lincoln: Nebraska University Press, 1986), pp. 32–39, and also "The Collège de Pataphysique and the Oulipo" on pp. 48–50 of the same volume.

OuLiPo was, first and foremost, their rigour: lipograms, palindromes and heterograms either are or are not; they cannot be only
half done. Their hard-edged simplicity makes them subversive of
traditional or, to be more precise, romantic approaches to writing.
The target-texts of Perec's more aggressive Oulipian exercises makes
his literary-historical position plain: he never sought to murder Ron-
sard or Racine, but tackled only monsters of soulful self-expression
such as Goethe, Verlaine and Proust. But the subversive dynamic of
formal constraint naturally led self-reflective Oulipians to play at
cheating at their own games. Indeed, the best-known Oulipian rule-
device, S+7, is easy to cheat on and its practitioners admit to
obtaining some of their more startling effects by unseen adjustments
to the rule. Such adjustments or conscious errors introduced into
the application of hard-edged constraints were what OuLiPo called
clinamens. Perec was already the champion of unadjusted contraint:
there is no *e* in *La Disparition* (despite the rumour reported above on
page 402) nor is there a letter out of place in the Great Palindrome.
In *Alphabets* Perec had loosened his *esartunilo* straitjacket now and
again, but he went much further in *Life A User's Manual*, which is
quite different from all of his other writing in this respect. Perec's
masterpiece is an Oulipian work, but one that is based on the "bending" of *all* of its constraints.[1]

W or The Memory of Childhood is not a true example of Oulipian
clinamen since it has no explicit formal constraints to bend. Perec
falsified dates, details, speculations, references and quotations, as we
have seen, but the rules that were broken were the informal conventions of the autobiographical genre. There were two literary aims in
the historical and personal subterfuges of *W or The Memory of Childhood*: to make the burden of guilt inescapable at the book's end; and
to bring into autobiography the kind of truth which can only ever
emerge from gaps. The challenge he took on was to use consistent
falsification to communicate otherwise unutterable emotions.
Although there is probably something "wrong" in every apparently
factual statement of *W or The Memory of Childhood*, the work's artistic
intention is nonetheless to embody truth.

In *Les Lieux d'une fugue* Perec sought to apply an Oulipian constraint to the making of a film. INA gave its formal go-ahead to the

---

[1] See Bernard Magné, "*La Vie mode d'emploi*, texte oulipien?" in *Pérécollages
1981–1988* (Toulouse: Presses universitaires du Mirail, 1989), pp. 153–164.

project in November 1975 and shooting took place from 14 June to 2 July 1976. Bernard Zitzerman ("Zizi"), hired by Queysanne for *A Man Asleep*, was behind the camera again, and most of the locations used were the real ones of Perec's childhood escapade – Franklin-Roosevelt, the stamp market at the Carré Marigny, and the metro.[1] No child appears in the film; the absence of the protagonist communicates the emotion of absence that is so striking in the written text. Schumann's *Kreisleriana*, played at first hesitantly and then repeated with increasing confidence, forms the sound track, which is an aural commemoration of Lili's piano practice at Rue de l'Assomption. However, the real work of the film came in the editing stage, done by Perec with the assiduous technical assistance of Catherine. The minutes of OuLiPo for the meeting of 3 August 1976 carry the following report:

> GP is currently completing a film that lends itself well to Oulipian treatment. The main idea of the editing was to use a precise permutation of themes, lengths, and so on. GP did not manage to do so entirely for mainly practical reasons (for example, rigorous application of the system would have led to sequences of one second, etc.).
>
> GP: *Actually, although I abandoned the original yoke in all its strictness, the viewer will still have an impression of formal rigour, which comes basically from the fact that the film is constructed entirely of discrete and recurrent elements.*

The rhythmic repetition of elements in a sestina-like sequence may be the reason for the non-standard length of *Les Lieux d'une fugue*: it lasts neither twenty minutes, as originally planned for the series, nor fifty-two, the conventional length of one-hour television slots, but exactly forty-two.

When Perec made his first television film he had already had the "works" of *Life A User's Manual* in place for some time and he was nearly ready to turn them on. He had been collecting material for his great novel for a decade – some of it even comes from his very earliest adult years, as we have seen. The "works" that he had designed

[1] The only notable substitution was the use of the gardens near the Grand-Palais for the sequences relating to the child's escapade at the Parc de Saint-Cloud.

allowed him to store scraps and drafts in one or another of the ninety-nine files he had opened, one for each of the ninety-nine chapters of the book. Why were there not to be one hundred chapters? Because the organising constraint, the knight's tour of the 10 x 10 grid mapped onto a cross-section of the block of flats, would be "bent" or "adjusted" by the conscious omission of the sixty-sixth move (into the bottom left-hand corner of the board). The abstract move itself had to be made, otherwise the knight would get stuck and fail to complete its tour, but there would be no chapter corresponding to that sixty-sixth move. The spatial clinamen is absolutely fundamental to the "works" of Perec's great book.

Perec may have chosen the number 66 either because it mimics the novel's starting point on grid square 6,6 or because it mirrors the inevitable number of the last chapter, 99; as 66 and 99 can also be seen as representations of German opening and closing quotation marks, the choice of move sixty-six for the gap may have been intended as a secret signal of the presence of unacknowledged quotations in the book, or, even more abstrusely, of the text's status as "text".[1] However, most scholars interpret the open space at the bottom left-hand corner of 11 Rue Simon-Crubellier as a confirming echo of the letter presented in *W or The Memory of Childhood* as Perec's first memory of childhood, shown and described as a squiggle *shaped like a square with a gap in its lower left-hand corner* [*W* 13].

The chapter-plan of *Life A User's Manual*, derived from a real solution of the knight's tour problem (given above on page 515) is therefore as shown overleaf. Not only was a piece chipped out of the underlying spatial structure of Perec's blockbuster but bends were also programmed into the distribution machine. As was explained on pages 514–516 above, Perec adopted twenty-one different bi-squares of order 10 to distribute material from twenty-one different pairs of lists around his tableau. The list of lists is shown on page 602.[2] The last pair, lists 41 and 42, operated in a different way from the others, and lists 39 and 40 were vicious jokers whose role was to disrupt most of the rest of the works.

---

[1] This interpretation was first proposed by Andrew Leak.

[2] The following account of Perec's formal machinery draws on Bernard Magné's many articles, in particular "Du registre au chapitre: Le 'Cahier des charges' de *La Vie mode d'emploi* de Georges Perec" in Béatrice Didier and Jacques Neefs, eds., *Penser, Classer, Ecrire de Pascal à Perec* (Paris: Presses universitaires de Vincennes, 1990), pp. 181–200.

	1	2	3	4	5	6	7	8	9	0
1	59	83	15	10	57	48	7	52	45	54
2	97	11	58	82	16	9	46	55	6	51
3	84	60	96	14	47	56	49	8	53	44
4	12	98	81	86	95	17	28	43	50	5
5	61	85	13	18	27	79	94	4	41	30
6	99	70	26	80	87	♞	42	29	93	3
7	25	62	88	69	19	36	78	2	31	40
8	71	65	20	23	89	68	34	37	77	92
9	63	24	66	73	35	22	90	75	39	32
0		72	64	21	67	74	38	33	91	76

The Chapter-plan of *Life A User's Manual*

Lists 39 and 40 contain nothing beyond the numbers 1 to 10. Distributed by means of their own bi-square around the one hundred locations (minus one) of the block at 11 Rue Simon-Crubellier, these numbers indicated which of the *groups* of constraints (as labelled in the lower right-hand corners of the boxes on page 602) were to be applied with a gap in them (list 39, *manque*) and which of the groups were to be applied with something wrong in them (list 40, *faux*). The bi-square obviously gave the number 10 ten times in all for each of the lists. There were therefore nineteen chapters (2 x 10 minus 1, the location for which the bi-square gives 10 for both lists at once) in which either "gap" or "wrong" applied to the group of constraints that included "gap" and "wrong". Perec's impish machine thus allowed him to apply "gap" in such cases by *not* missing out any other constraint in the group ("gapping the gap") or by missing out a constraint in a group *not* determined by the bi-square number ("wronging the gap") or by *not* getting anything wrong at all ("gapping the wrong"). An odd machine, by any standards, and one that would have tickled the College of Pataphysics by taking clinamen to a mind-boggling, recursive extreme.

The "works" that generated the text of *Life A User's Manual* thus had inside them a self-wiping device reminiscent of legendary frauds perpetrated by an inserted routine instructing a bank's computer to transfer a million dollars to a numbered account and then to erase all the lines of the routine including the self-erasing instruction. In Greek philosophy the clinamen was held to be the origin of life; in *Life*, the clinamen programmed into the works allowed the author to adapt or disregard pretty well any of the constraints as he pleased. But Perec did not set things up that way solely in order to have secret fun. He really did believe that, if he allowed it to work perfectly, then his system would have no life; and that was not his aim.

One effect of "gap" and "wrong" is to make it not just hard but completely impossible to work back from the text of the novel to its spatial and arithmetical designs. Perec presented himself in *L'Arc* and elsewhere as having been only the minder of a beautiful text-generating machine. However, to some extent the potty professor demonstrating the "four figures" of *Life A User's Manual* was also laughing up his loose-cuffed Indian sleeve. No one but he could have "minded" such a quirky machine.

Lists 41 and 42, laid out on page 603, are not subject to "gap" and "wrong". Perec's ten "couples", coming from Latin mythology, German folk-tale, Russian, French, and English literature, Bolshevik symbolism, American cinema and especially from the horrors of modern history[1] are uncoupled from each other eighty-nine (out of ninety-nine) times by the bi-square distribution device. Nonetheless, their regulated recurrence[2] lays down a mosaic, so to speak, that represents important fragments of the author's personal world, including things he liked (Laurel and Hardy), disliked (Vichy

---

[1] "Labourage et Pâturage sont les deux mamelles de la France" ("Arable and livestock farming are the two teats of France") was one of the slogans of Vichy France; *NN*, standing for *Nacht und Nebel* ("Night and Fog") was sown onto the tunics of *Sonderkommandos* in the extermination camps of Nazi Germany (thence the title of Alain Resnais's documentary on Auschwitz, *Night and Fog*); *Ashes and Diamonds* is the title of Andrzej Wajda's harrowing film about the failed uprising of the Warsaw ghetto in 1944.

[2] The items sometimes appear in disguise. For example, Ulverston, given as the birthplace of Bartlebooth's uncle James Sherwood on page 82, was also where Stan Laurel was born. "Ulverston" thus implements the bi-square's requirement to mention item 1 of List 42 in the chapter corresponding to grid location 6,9.

1.	Position			21.	Fabrics (substance)	
2.	Activity			22.	Colours	
3.	Quotations 1			23.	Accessories	
4.	Quotations 2	**1**		24.	Jewels	**6**
5.	Number			25.	Reading	
6.	Role			26.	Music	
7.	Third sector			27.	Pictures	
8.	Motive?	**2**		28.	Books	**7**
9.	Walls			29.	Drink	
10.	Floors			30.	Food	
11.	Period			31.	Small furniture	
12.	Place	**3**		32.	Toys	**8**
13.	Style			33.	Feelings	
14.	Furniture			34.	Paint	
15.	Length			35.	Surfaces	
16.	Miscellaneous	**4**		36.	Volumes	**9**
17.	Age/Sex			37.	Flowers	
18.	Animals			38.	Trinkets	
19.	Clothes			39.	*Manque*	
20.	Fabrics (nature)	**5**		40.	*Faux*	**10**
	41. Couple 1				42. Couple 2	

The "List of Lists" of *Life A User's Manual*

France), and some he had probably not even read (*Pride and Prejudice*).

Perec first operated his bi-squares to determine the forty-two items to be included each chapter, constituting its unique *cahier des charges* ("specification"). However, as in *Alphabets,* where he overlaid decorative patterns on an already tightly constrained form, Perec increased the "specifications" of many chapters far beyond the requirements of the "four figures" of his explicit machine. The most spectacular example of a voluntary additional "spec" is the "Compendium" of Chapter 51. It is not only a list-poem describing Valène's envisaged portrait of the building with the facade removed, in 179 lines each of sixty characters and spaces (*see* p. 594), but also an acrostic, spelling

	List 41			List 42
1	Laurel	and		Hardy
2	Sickle	and		Hammer
3	Racine	and		Shakespeare
4	Philemon	and		Baucis
5	Crime	and		Punishment
6	Pride	and		Prejudice
7	Night	and		Fog
8	Ashes	and		Diamonds
9	Arable	and		Livestock
0	Beauty	and the		Beast

The "Couples" Lists of *Life A User's Manual*

out, from top right to bottom left, the word *âme* ("soul").[1] Perec himself revealed the superconstraint of chapter 59, the "hypographic appearance" (sounds hidden in the sounds of another word or words) of the names of OuLiPo and its twenty-three members in the descriptions of Hutting's coded portraits [*Atlas* 394–395]. Many chapters contain unacknowledged quotations beyond those called for by the specifications of Lists 3 and 4 as well as allusions to pictures and books not generated by Lists 27 and 28.[2] Perec's additions to the specifications established by the elaborate machinery of *Life A User's Manual* are not the only "bends" in the works: he also omitted a fair number of the specs that his self-invented machine had produced. Apart from the patchy implementation of the *cahiers des charges*, how-

[1] Perec explained this superconstraint to his translator, Eugen Helmle. As there is no three-letter word meaning "soul" in German, Helmle obtained Perec's approval to replace *âme* with *ich* ("I") in the German version of *Life A User's Manual*. Helmle handed on Perec's explanations to the English translator, who used *e*, *g*, and *o* to replace the key-letters of the Great Acrostic.

[2] The literary quotations smuggled into *Life A User's Manual* are laid out in detail by Ewa Pawlikowska in *Texte en main* no. 6 (1986), pp. 70–98. See also David Bellos, "Literary Quotations in Georges Perec's *La Vie mode d'emploi*", *French Studies* XLI (1987), pp. 181–194. On the paintings, see Bernard Magné, "Lavis mode d'emploi", *Cahiers Georges Perec* I (Paris: P.O.L., 1985), pp. 232–246. A huge panel showing the pictorial insertions of *Life A User's Manual*, designed by Patrizia Molteni, was exhibited at the Bibliothèque Robert-Desnos at Montreuil in April 1992.

ever, the nature of the specifications themselves calls into question the status of the bi-square as a text-generating device.

No part of the works of *Life A User's Manual* is directly responsible for the characters of the main story or for those of the vast majority of the minor ones, and Perec's narratives themselves seem to be entirely independent of the chapter-specifications produced by the bi-square machine. Let us consider what features of the novel the specifications do purport to control. List 15, if respected, sets a formal feature, the length of each chapter (in lines or pages). Lists 3 and 4 set textual insertions, but only in the vaguest way: the quotation-commands do not specify actual texts but only the names of authors from whose voluminous works Perec was free to choose whatever phrase or passage best suited the situation. List 7, entitled "Third sector", sets most of the paste-ins that constitute the visible text-decorations of *Life A User's Manual*. ("Third sector" is a term invented by François le Lionnais for the many varieties of anonymous and ephemeral printed matter that the British call bumph. The ten varieties used by Perec were newspaper cuttings, bibliographies, rules and regulations, announcements of births, marriages and deaths, recipes, pharmaceutical prospectuses, diaries or calendars, theatre programmes, dictionaries, and user's manuals.) Lists 9, 10, 14, 31, 32, 34, 35, 36, 37, and 38 specify visible aspects of the decorations and furnishings of the rooms in which the chapters are placed, and Lists 1, 17, 19, 20, 21, 22, 23, and 24 mostly determine the spatial relations and visible attire of the characters painted into the scene. Most of the other lists scatter fragments of culture around the novel – ten types of reading matter (including "third sector" again) for characters to dip into, ten types of music for them to hear (List 26), ten pictures for Perec to borrow from (List 27), ten books he must allude to (List 28), and ten types of drink and ten types of food to place on tables and bars. What about the stories themselves, and the characters, and their reminiscences and feelings? There is indeed a list labelled Feelings, but to specify one single "feeling" for each of the chapters of this vast and passionate novel is a derisory function for its generating machine. As Perec once said to Jean-Paul Rappeneau in a different context (*see* p. 424) but in the same line of thought: *Feelings? You can put those in at the end.*

★

The one constraint to which *Life A User's Manual* adheres wthout deviation save the structural clinamen of move sixty-six is the knight's tour of the block or board. Perec wrote the manuscript of his novel on the recto pages of a ledger and on the verso page facing the start of each chapter he drew a 10 x 10 box of squares with the chapters done so far marked by cross-hatching, so as to keep a visual check on his novel's lurching path around the apartment block. He also kept a tally of how many of the forty-two constraints he had managed to use in each chapter – as far as chapter 42, after which he gave up his accounting and just wrote on.[1] Only eighteen of the first forty-two chapters respect all forty-two specifications, by Perec's reckoning. Chapter 5, containing the very brief story of an unmarried mother, Geneviève Foulerot, has the lowest score of all, twenty-four. However, the grandiose generating machine that Perec sketched out in "Quatres figures pour *La Vie mode d'emploi*" and that we have inspected so far covers no more than a part of Perec's "works". Three quite separate devices impose other subtle patterns on the novel, with startling effect.[2]

The first of Perec's supplementary rules is a requirement to allude in each chapter to one of his other works (not excluding his unpublished early works, such as *Les Errants* [see p. 5] or not-yet-written ones, such as *Récits d'Ellis Island* [L 499]). This rule of regular self-reference prompts the comical story of the Réols' bedroom suite in chapter 98, which "inscribes" the theme of promotion-frustration from *L'Augmentation* whilst giving it a happier outcome, just as it accounts for the story of Grégoire Simpson in chapter 52, which encapsulates the main narrative of *A Man Asleep*, with a less ambiguous though still indeterminate ending. The most spectacular implementation of the self-reference rule is provided (once again) by the "Compendium" of chapter 51. The acrostic that it contains calls for three sets of sixty lines, so that the three key letters, *a*, *m* and *e*, can move step by step from position 60 in the first lines of their respective sets to position 1 in line 60. But there are only 179, not 180, lines in the "Compendium". The one that is missing is the last line of set three in which the letter *e* would have moved to position 1. The *absence* of the line starting with *e* "refers" to *La Disparition*, the novel

---

[1] Bernard Magné, "The Limits of Constraint", *RCF*, pp. 111–123.

[2] These were the rules that Perec explained to the Cercle Polivanoff (and then regretted having done so), mentioned above on page 593.

in which no *e* appears; but that is only the most superficial explanation of this dazzling inscription of Perec-Peretz, Man of Gaps, at the very heart – the very soul – of his oeuvre.

Earlier pages of this biography may have prompted readers of *Life A User's Manual* to recognise otherwise obscure instances of the self-reference rule, such as the passage from the commentary of *Aho! Les hommes de la forêt* (*see* p. 561) slotted into the story of Appenzzell in chapter 25 or the probable reminiscence in chapter 42 of the horoscopes that Perec translated at 203 Rue Saint-Honoré. Tracking down Perec's self-inscriptions is a game that the novel allows readers to play, and it would hardly be in the spirit of OuLiPo to suggest that playing textual games is wrong. Nonetheless the self-reference rule also has a serious literary aim: most writers repeat themselves willy-nilly, but Perec does not – because his rule *regulates* regurgitation and, in so doing, spins a spidery coherence over his oeuvre as a whole.

The second supplementary rule is a requirement to mention in each chapter some object or event that occurred or came to the writer's attention during the drafting of the chapter. The inscription of Perec's life-in-writing in *Life A User's Manual* may be responsible for details ranging from the Beirut War Memorial [if *PC* 17 is read as a gloss on *L* 156] to references to books that friends asked to borrow or offered to lend, but in principle and in practice this rule leaves traces that only the author could see, as if he wished to mark his own passage in invisible ink.

The third supplementary rule is based on the novel's master plan, the 10 x 10 board on which the knight makes its tour. As in continental chess notation, each square of Perec's grid has a pair of coordinates that identify it unambiguously: chapter 1 is located on grid square 6,6, for example, and chapter 99 takes place in the room located on grid square 1,6.[1] Perec's third rule required him to include the relevant coordinates in the text of every chapter, which he very nearly managed to do. Thus the estate agent climbing the stairs in chapter 1 (coordinates: 6,6) carries key rings bearing miniature effigies of a *bottle of Marie Brizard* apéritif, *a golf tee and a wasp, a double-six domino and a plastic octagonal token* [*L* 4–5]; the educational postcard found on the stairs in chapter 94 (coordinates: 7,5) is number 57 of the *Great*

---

[1] Column, then row, starting with 1 at the top left-hand corner. The grids on pages 184 and 186 of *French Studies* XLI (1987) were incorrectly numbered.

American Writers series; and so on.[1] The double-marking of the novel's spatial design is nearly always implemented by digits, all the easier to see in a book in which most other numbers are written out as literals.

The coordinate-insertion rule turns out to be far more than a mere decoration or even a regulated tracing of the master plan. Perec was not a mathematician by any means, but arithmetical curiosities discussed at OuLiPo did not simply flow over him like the maths lessons at Collège Geoffroy Saint-Hilaire. In *Life A User's Manual* he attributes to the fantastical polymath adventurer of chapter 78, Carel van Loorens, a *note on Goldbach's problem, proposing that any number* n *be the sum of* K *primes* [L 372].[2] As Perec must have known from mathematical Oulipians, no one has ever come up with a proof of Goldbach's hypothesis despite the fact that trivial demonstrations of it are easy to find. The main story of Perec's novel is structured so as to produce a less trivial demonstration of the "problem" tackled by Carel van Loorens, in the following way. Percival Bartlebooth spends twenty years of his life painting five hundred watercolours which are then turned into jigsaw puzzles by Gaspard Winckler and he proposes to devote the following twenty years to solving the puzzles he has had set for him. Ill health, the increasing difficulty of Winckler's puzzles, and the machinations of a giant hotel chain slow him down and he has only reached puzzle number 439 when he dies. In Bartlebooth's study, described for the first and only time in chapter 99 (coordinates: 1,6), there are therefore sixty-one unopened boxes of puzzles remaining on the shelves ($500-439=61$). The endgame position thus consists of two primes and moreover of the *only* two primes that add up to 500. One of the numbers is given in digits because 1 and 6 are *also* the coordinates of the room in which the last chapter is set.[3] Perec's achievement – not his having provided a demonstration of Goldbach's hypothesis, but his definitive demon-

---

[1] Perec allowed himself to use the digits in either order, but he does not seem to have ever used the same number twice.

[2] According to the *Encyclopaedia Britannica*, Goldbach claimed only that every *even* natural number is equal to the sum of two primes (a prime is a number that is divisible without remainder only by itself and by 1) and that every natural number greater than 2, even or odd, is equal to the sum of *three* primes.

[3] See David Bellos, "Georges Perec's Puzzling Style", *Scripsi* (Melbourne) V.1 (1988), pp. 63–77.

stration that the structure of *Life* had been shaped inexorably from the start – has the miraculous quality of great art.

Like *Les Lieux d'une fugue*, though on a far grander scale, *Life A User's Manual* is intentionally constructed from *discrete and recurrent elements*. This feature is the main cause of the impressive and pleasing *impression of formal rigour* that the novel gives to the reader. He or she does not need to be conversant with the complex workings of Perec's rule-bending machine in order to respond to the text, but an inspection of the "works" hidden beneath 11 Rue Simon-Crubellier nonetheless offers an amazing perspective on what the author constructed on the site.

CHAPTER 58

Friends and Relations

When Perec arrived at Saarbrücken in June 1975, a few days after his last session with Pontalis, he found Eugen and Margrit Hemle more comfortably off than before. The satirical radio serial that Eugen had coscripted, *Papa, Charly hat gesagt*, ("Dad, Charly told me") had been adapted for the stage and was now out as a paperback book, selling hundreds of thousands of copies. The Helmles had turned the lower ground floor of their house into a swimming pool, and had also begun collecting vintage Bordeaux. They shared their food-and-wine culture with Perec, who was no beginner in such matters (Paulette had always been a first-rate cook), though he still had things to learn about *grands crus classés* Bordeaux. Back in Paris, friends dropped in at Rue Linné on 1 August 1975 to watch episode two of *La Vie filmée des Français* on a television specially hired for the occasion,[1] and in the course of the evening Perec and Catherine opened four different Saint-Emilions – a 1961, a 1962, a 1970, and a venerable 1949, a bottle or two of which probably accounted even then for the whole of a television scriptwriter's fee.

Harry Mathews moved back from Italy to France in 1975 and divided his time between Lans-en-Vercors and a Paris flat in Rue de Varenne. Despite the lab, the metro, the absence of a publisher, and the uncertain prospects for Catherine's film, the winter of 1975–76 was a sociable and happy season for Perec and Catherine. They had dinners in plenty at Le Balzar, Marty's and Le Buisson Ardent, with Mathews, with other *oulipotes*, and with friends of Catherine, such as Julien Etcheverry, a photographer and jack-of-all-trades, who shared and developed Perec's taste for larks and japes and became one of the writer's warmest, unconditional pals.

Galilée, the publishers of *Alphabets*, introduced Perec to Paolo Boni, an Italian painter living in Paris. He and his wife, the American photographer Cuchi White, soon befriended Perec and Catherine. Perec visited Boni's studio at Alésia several times and was fascinated

---

[1] Perec never owned a television set.

by the tools and materials that the artist used to create images in semi-relief, which comprised metals as well as ink and paint. Perec agreed to write poems to accompany a limited edition of Boni's "graphisculptures". These seven particularly complex heterograms, collectively entitled "Métaux", were composed in December 1976, in the wake of *Alphabets*.[1]

A year earlier, Harry Mathews had presented to the 172nd meeting of OuLiPo a word-list, soon to be known as the Mathews Corpus, consisting of lexical items that exist in both English and French but have different meanings in each language. *Arrondissement*, for instance, a French word used in English with identical meaning, does not belong to the Mathews corpus, nor does *building*, *standing*, or *footing*, English words used in a similar sense in French or "Franglais". The words of the Mathews corpus require a sideways shift of the eye or tongue to be seen as bilingual: *rue*, *don*, *clot*, *mine*, and so on. Perec made one elegant contribution of his own, the word *surgeon* ("sucker", in horticultural French). The obvious use of the Mathews Corpus is as an aid to writing texts that are simultaneously and equally English and French – linguistic equivalents of birefractory images, W. H. Hill cartoons, or some kinds of trompe-l'oeil painting. A mad idea – but an entrancing one for a writer with increasingly global ambitions.

Perec set off for Germany again in February 1976, flying directly to Berlin with Pierre Emmanuel, to participate in a week-long Franco-German Literary Colloquium at the Wannsee villa, directed by Walter Höllerer. Eugen Helmle, Ludwig Harig, several colleagues from SR, and a whole clutch of Parisians, including Jean Lescure, Michel Tournier, Claude Simon, and the novelist and playwright Rezvani were there, as well as journalists and publishers' representatives. Perec teamed up for most of the time with the poet Bernard Noël, and also went out for a meal with Helmle and Michel Tournier, whose radio play *Le Fétichiste* ("The Fetishist") had recently been broadcast by SR. Tournier and Perec had little in common as writers, but at dinner they got on very well. No, he had not got round to writing *Wie ein Hund*, Perec told his German translator, but he would, he promised vaguely, when he had managed to finish his film.

The Wannsee villa is the building in which Hitler's cabinet decided

---

[1] See Bernard Magné, "Les Poèmes hétérogrammatiques", *Cahiers Georges Perec* 5 (Paris: Editions du Limon, 1992), pp. 17–24.

on the Final Solution in 1942. Perec did not talk about his feelings on that score, but he did walk down to the lake and stare in moody fascination at the icy water where Heinrich von Kleist had drowned himself in 1811.

Perec's main social event of the season, however, which took place not long after his visit to Berlin, was a huge party to celebrate his fortieth birthday. An affectionate crowd of perhaps a hundred friends old and new crammed into the writer's "railway-train" mezzanine flat. Mathews turned up at Rue Linné in a printed T-shirt depicting the coloured outline of a double-breasted white jacket, completed by an elegant shirt-and-tie ensemble between the lapels and a foulard in the breast-pocket. Rappeneau brought the glamour of the big screen to the soirée, and when the Slovak translator of *Things*, Michaela Jurovská, squeezed in the door, Perec yelled out the title, *Veci*! *Veci*! as if it were a new kind of greeting in French. Those who stayed through the whole riotous night got a bowl of Perec's favourite dish, buttered pasta, at dawn.[1]

Marie-Claude de Brunhoff, a literary scout for American publishers, kept in regular touch with Maxine Groffsky, now an agent in New York. Maxine persuaded New Directions to consider *W or The Memory of Childhood*; Perec reported to Mathews that Walter Abish was also going to put in a word on his behalf. Working the other way, Perec translated Mathews's poem "Milk Plasma" into French and urged Denoël to acquire the rights to *The Sinking of the Odradek Stadium*, which he proposed to translate now that *Tlooth* was out in French. New York was coming to replace Saarbrücken as Perec's main foreign antenna. His loving friendship with Harry was the most obvious reason, but it also went hand in hand with his interest in translation, which he had more ample means to develop in the English domain than in German. But translation was endemic to Perec's writing from the start: the first words of *Things* – not Perec's own, it is true, but still the first words to be printed – are in English, and numerous other examples of interlingual penetration in Perec's French and German works have been mentioned throughout this

---

[1] "A Georges Perec", *La Bibliothèque oulipienne* (Paris: Ramsay, 1987), vol. 2, pp. 87–97.

book. Mathews's *Odradek*, however, is quite untranslatable – which is precisely why Perec wanted to translate it.

The Sinking of the Odradek Stadium consists of an exchange of letters between Zachary McCaltex, a treasure hunter in postmodern Miami, and Twang Panattapam, his inamorata and archival assistant in Italy, who is a native of the Kingdom of Pan-Nam, where she half-learnt English in a half-Italian school and mastered typing not at all. Her first letter to Zachary begins:

> Pan persns knwo base bal. The giappan-like trade-for mishn play with it in our capatal any times. To morrow to work be gin. It's cleen eccepts for the talk. The in-habits live in draems.[1]

The translator had to invent a deviant French language carefully graded to represent Twang's improving grasp of syntax and typing in the course of the correspondence. It was not a question of whether Perec's English was up to it. What he had to concoct was a Gallic Twang's Pan-Italic mistyping of French.

Collaboration with Mathews was pursued in a spoof article on Raymond Roussel, put together in 1976–77. At much the same time, *Cause commune* proposed to do an issue on *La Ruse*, ("Cunning") and Perec, who was still a member of the editorial board, agreed to write an account of his psychoanalysis for it. He also decided to open the envelopes of *Lieux*, now that the project itself was dead, and to publish some of the description texts under titles all beginning *Tentative de description* . . . ("Draft of a description . . ."). Perhaps to keep faith with the peripatetic composition of these pieces, Perec chose to publish them in different places, the oddest of which was the *Nouvelle Revue de psychanalyse*, edited by his former analyst, Jean-Bertrand Pontalis.[2] The Roussel pastiche (for a serious literary journal, *L'Arc*), the account of psychoanalysis (for a mostly sociological review), and the release of time-capsule texts (in a leading French psychoanalytical journal) overlapped chronologically and were closely connected, if in rather complicated ways.

The rule of "Roussel and Venice" [*CSL* 73–115] is that everything

---

[1] Harry Mathews, *The Sinking of the Odradek Stadium* (1971; repr. Manchester: Carcanet Press, 1985), pp. 6–7.

[2] Perec was taken aback, to say the least, by the article in *Nouvelle Revue de Psychanalyse* (quoted on pages 476–477 above) in which Pontalis discussed the case of a client identified by the name of Suzanne's youngest child, Stéphane.

in it must at once look plausible and be false. The authors' intention was to be faithful to Roussel's practice and so produce a homage truer than any piece in the scholarly mode that they skewer. Roussel had never been to Venice and none of the places, books, and articles mentioned by Perec and Mathews exist outside of the works of Roussel, Thomas Mann (*Death in Venice!*) and the pasticheurs themselves. Carson College, Fitchwinder University, Rosamund Flexner (Arnold's mother?), the Grifalconis, the Venetian printer Quarli and many other fictional echoes and anticipations of *The Conversions* and *Life A User's Manual* are woven into "Roussel and Venice". However, the article also includes, at Perec's suggestion, a reasonably accurate résumé of a real psychoanalytical study, "Introject – Incorporate. Mourning *or* Melancholia",[1] that seems less a learned joke than a clue to Perec's conception of himself and of the way he was concurrently writing his masterpiece.

> *Incorporation may thus be defined as a delusion which does all it can to change the world rather than allow the slightest alteration in the subject. It achieves this goal by means of a literal and unshakeable vision of the world. While the process of introjection discovers metaphor and symbol [. . .] incorporation stresses the unique, "objective" meaning of words and things, and whenever it encounters metaphorical objects, systematically de-metaphorises them.*[2]

> [*CSL* 84]

Perec's description of his own analysis, entitled "Les Lieux d'une ruse" ("Backtracking")[3] is an account not of the theory but of the experience of the talking cure. Written not long after the Roussel article was completed in December 1976, that is to say whilst the composition of *Life A User's Manual* was in full swing, "Les Lieux d'une ruse" [*PC* 59–72] is one of Perec's gravest and most demanding texts. Few people can read it without being drawn into the process of self-examination that the essay describes. This is Perec's conclusion:

> *All I can say of the actual process that allowed me to escape from*

---

[1] N. Abraham and M. Torok, "Introjecter – Incorporer. Deuil *ou* Mélancolie", *Nouvelle Revue de Psychanalyse* no. 6 (1972).

[2] Translated by Harry Mathews and Antony Melville. Published as "Roussel and Venice. Sketch of a Melancholic Geography", *Atlas Anthology* 3 (1985), pp. 69–86.

[3] The English title was suggested by Andrew Leak as an improvement on any literal rendering such as "The Places of a Piece of Cunning".

these repetitive and burdensome acrobatics and gave me access to my
own story and to my own voice is that it was infinitely slow. It was
the process of analysis itself, but I only realised that afterwards.
What had to give way first was my armour: the hard shell that hid
my desire to write had to crack; the high wall of prefabricated mem-
ories had to crumble; my sanctuaries of rationalisation had to be
reduced to dust. I had to go back over my tracks and travel once more
along the path I had trod, whose thread I had lost.

There is nothing I can say about the buried place that I reached.
I know there was a place and that its trace is evermore marked in
me and in the texts that I write. It took the time that it took for my
story to come together: a story that offered itself to me one day,
surprised, bewildered, forceful, like a memory restored to its own
space, like a gesture or a tenderness resurrected. That day the analyst
heard what I had to say to him, what for four years he had listened
to without hearing, for the simple reason that I had not been telling
him that I was not saying it to myself.   [PC 71–72]

Since Perec's analysis began in May 1971, the reference to "what for
four years [the analyst] had listened to without hearing" situates the
discovery of the "buried place" in the summer of 1975, that is to say
more than six months after *W or the Memory of Childhood* was finished.
What Perec acknowledges in this simultaneously lucid and impenetrable passage is that his "hard shell" had cracked *after* the completion
of his autobiography, and the trace of what emerged from the crack,
the effect of what he had finally been able to hear himself saying,
something like a "gesture or tenderness resurrected", was imprinted
on all that he had written, was writing and would write thereafter.

"Tenderness" is not immediately apparent in *Alphabets* and *La Clôture*, but, as we have seen, Perec's surge of poetic activity in 1975–
76 was inspired in large part by his relationship with Catherine.
However, we have also already looked in detail at the ways in which
Perec chipped and cracked the "hard shell" of the knight's tour and
bi-square before beginning to draft *Life A User's Manual*. It seems
likely that he distorted the workings of his machinery not just in
order to implement the Oulipian notion of clinamen, but, more fundamentally, to humanise his work and to write his new self into it.
Read in this way, "Les Lieux d'une ruse" presents *W or the Memory
of Childhood* not as the "output" of Perec's psychoanalysis, but as the
literary evidence of his psychological defences (the "high wall of

prefabricated memories"). The trace of the self-knowledge that Perec gained from Pontalis is rather to be found in the construction, the stories, and the meaning of *Life*.

In "Roussel and Venice", the résumé of the article on incorporation purports to explain Roussel's "literal apprehension of the world", that is to say his use of words as objects, as the preferred mechanism of melancholia. Melancholia is said to be the emotional corollary of incorporation, and introjection its analytical opposite, defined (in the pastiche, but also in the original article) as the product of mourning. Whatever may be true of Roussel, Perec, long unable to grieve, had had no alternative but to follow the melancholic path. The rewritten analytical passage buried in a collaborative text constituted in all other respects by fake information is a characteristically Perecquian way of declaring himself. Perec's sources, only slightly rewritten, also say this about incorporation, à propos of Roussel and quite possibly of Perec too:

> *Outside of delirium and some bouts of obsessive-depressive behaviour, the incorporation fantasy is difficult to diagnose. It is effectively hidden beneath a variety of masks, such as "normality", "personality", "perversion".*   [CSL 85]

Michel Rybalka, the coauthor of a vast bibliography of Jean–Paul Sartre and a professor of French in the United States, had reviewed *A Man Asleep* when it appeared and sent an offprint to the author along with a note asking to meet him. An intermittent friendship ensued from this approach, and Perec would take Rybalka out for a drink or a meal and quizz him on the latest developments in literary theory whenever the latter was in Paris. In 1977, two years after the end of the Vietnam war, Rybalka was asked by an immigrant student to help him to get his wife and family from Hanoi to the United States. Since France was one of the few nations that had diplomatic relations with Vietnam, Rybalka took the necessary steps on his next visit to Paris. He had not quite completed his mission before he had to return to the States, and so he asked Perec and Catherine to pursue the case in his stead. They were happy to assist: Catherine went to the airport to meet the bewildered and frightened emigrants when finally they came, put them up at her flat in Rue Vineuse for the several weeks that it took to obtain their entry permits to the United

States, took the children out for walks, and was horrified when, at the sight of a police helicopter, one of them screamed and ran away to hide.[1]

It was also through Catherine that Perec met the filmmaker Robert Bober, on whom *W or the Memory of Childhood* had made a great impression. He took a copy of Perec's book with him when he went to Poland in 1975 to make a film about his own roots, *Réfugié provenant d'Allemagne, apatride d'origine polonaise* ("Refugee from Germany, Stateless Person of Polish Origin", the words entered on Bober's first French identity papers). In fact, he placed Perec's childhood autobiography alongside *Souvenirs obscurs d'un juif polonais né en France* ("Obscure Memories of a Polish Jew Born in France"), by the "revolutionary hooligan" Pierre Goldmann (one of the few other Jews to have been educated at Collège Geoffroy Saint-Hilaire at Etampes), on a shelf of French books by first and second generation Jewish immigrants that appears in a repeated sequence of the film. Bober had long wanted to meet Perec and to work with him when he discovered that one of his assistants was the oldest friend of Perec's companion, Catherine.

Once contact had been established, Bober got down to explaining his plan. Ellis Island, the port of entry for seaborne immigrants to the United States from 1894 until 1954, was to be reopened as a tourist site. Bober's great-grandfather had travelled from Poland to America, and had even shaved off his beard on the crossing in order to look less Jewish on arrival in the land of opportunity. However, his sacrilegious act served no purpose, since the medical inspectors at Ellis Island diagnosed him as having trachoma and shipped the elder Bober back to Poland again. For that reason, Ellis Island was part of Bober's family's founding myth, connected to the hazy questions of why it was neither Polish, nor German, nor American, but French. A film about Ellis Island would for him be in some way parallel to *W or The Memory of Childhood*, and he wanted to make it in collaboration with Perec. The writer did not accept Bober's proposal at first, though he got on very well with the man. His real objection, he said to Catherine, was that he did not want to tackle a nostalgic and explicitly Jewish theme. Bober persisted, however, passing reminders to Perec through Catherine, whom he had taken on to edit another one

---

[1] Michel Rybalka, "Du Marché aux timbres à la guerre du Vietnam", *Cahiers Georges Perec IV* (Paris: Editions du Limon, 1990), pp. 43–46.

of his films. It eventually emerged that Ellis Island, far from being a well-cared-for heritage site, was no more than a set of derelict buildings inhabited by mice and birds. It was the idea of making a film about *dereliction* that finally swayed Perec's mind, and he agreed to Bober's plan before the end of 1977. They arranged to visit New York together in June 1978 to inspect the site and to track down people who had entered America by way of Ellis Island – through which, but for chance, Bober's ascendants, and Perec's too, might have passed.

Perec entered a synagogue for the first time in his life to attend the bar mitzvah of Robert Bober's elder son. He put on a yarmulke and a fringed shawl and stood in the congregation with a broad grin on his face. Catherine watched the ceremony from the gallery and smiled at Perec's ignorance of what he was supposed to do. Perec met Bober's father on this family occasion. Knowing how Perec's name was spelt, the elder Bober naturally greeted him as "Peretz", which brought an even wider grin to the writer's face. All the same, even at this less anguished time of his life, Perec felt uneasy amongst traditional Jews. He did not like the way Catherine was made to feel an outsider and confided to her: *I don't like being* entre Juifs.

Perec had no reservations about Yiddish food, however, and took Catherine and Julien Etcheverry more than once to a celebrated Jewish restaurant in Rue des Rosiers. On one high-spirited occasion, he and Julien devised a means of leaving without paying the bill – and it came off. A few yards down the street they burst out laughing at their coup until tears were streaming down their cheeks. They had done it not out of malice or criminal intent but to prove that they could beat even Goldenberg's famously sharp-witted staff. And the best of it was that Catherine had not seen a thing!

Perec's friends and relations in the later 1970s formed nothing like a socially coherent "set". He was as much at ease with *l'ami américain* as he was with Paolo Boni; he could have fun with Julien Etcheverry in the thirteenth arrondissement and then dance the night away in Andy Warhol's Saint-Germain flat; he enjoyed joking with Philippe Drogoz as well as dropping in on a party at the house of Princess Marina of Greece; he was as fond of his old, rather puritan pal Pierre Getzler as he was of his erratic "brother" Noureddine Mechri. He naturally lacked anything resembling a British sense of class (save for his consistent scorn of business people), but his social life was now almost as cosmopolitan as Paris itself, and it connected him to a worldwide network of friends. In *Life A User's Manual*, Percival Bartlebooth circumnavigates the globe, like Phileas Fogg, though in more leisurely fashion; but the global dimension of Perec's vast novel is not only a reminiscence of Jules Verne. It also represents its author's way of being in the world.

Unpublished sources include letters from Georges Perec to Eugen Helmle and Harry Mathews, and the recollections of Stella Baruk, Catherine Binet, Robert Bober, Paolo Boni, Marie-Claude de Brunhoff, Julien Etcheverry, Maxine Groffsky, Eugen Helmle, Harry Mathews, Michel Rybalka and Cuchi White.

CHAPTER 59

Life A User's Manual

Raymond Queneau died on 26 October 1976. Georges Perec was at Chambroutet and decided to return immediately to Paris with Catherine. On the train he took out the pad he always had with him and began to write. From Rue Linné he telephoned Harry Mathews at Lans-en-Vercors. Mathews recalls:

> We had lost the man who authorized our lives as writers – a trustworthy, irreplaceable father. I learned later that each of us that evening reread Queneau's poems about death, the very ones we had read aloud to each other a few weeks before.

The funeral was on 28 October. Afterwards, OuLiPo met at Marcel Benabou's house.

> At the OuLiPo meeting that followed Queneau's funeral, and where it was obvious, plain obvious, that we all had a duty to persevere, Perec cried, and quoted "L'Explication des métaphores":[1]

Mais ni dieu ni démon l'homme s'est égaré
Mince comme un cheveu, ample comme l'aurore
Les naseaux écumants, les deux yeux révulsés,
Et les deux mains en avant pour tâter un décor

- D'ailleurs inexistant. C'est qu'il est égaré;
Il n'est pas assez mince, il n'est pas assez ample:
Trop de muscles tordus, trop de salive usée.
Le calme reviendra lorsqu'il verra le Temple
De sa forme assurer sa propre éternité.[2]

The next day Perec got out a fresh black leather-bound ledger, of the kind he had used for *L'Arbre* and *Je me souviens* and copied out first of all the words he had scribbled down on the train:

---

[1] A Georges Perec (Paris: La Bibliothèque oulipienne, 1984), p. 18.

[2] Raymond Queneau, *Les Ziaux* (1943), in *L'Instant Fatal* précédé de *Les Ziaux* (Paris: Gallimard, 1966), p. 75. [English translation, *see* p. 635].

In Memory of Raymond Queneau

Life A User's Manual

He wrote the first paragraphs of chapter 1 on 29 October 1976. They were in the first person.

Life A User's Manual was written in less than eighteen months and was finished in manuscript on 5 April 1978, at 7:25 P.M. precisely, *heure de Paris*. Stendhal had dictated *The Charterhouse of Parma* even faster, in fifty-three days flat, but the ex-consul had had all his time to himself. Perec, for his part, had to go to the lab at Gif-sur-Yvette; he went as little as he could, but he could not skip it entirely. He knocked off his weekly crossword for *Le Point* in a couple of hours, but that was still two hours a week taken out. He was granted a form of sabbatical by OuLiPo – not an excuse to miss meetings (his absence from meetings was always minuted as "inexcusable") but relief from the task of cutting up vegetables for the monthly luncheons at Rue Linné. But Perec dropped almost nothing else whilst he wrote his great work, which was not even his sole writing concern in the course of those eighteen jubilant months. He also wrote "Roussel and Venice", "Les Lieux d'une Ruse", the poems of *Métaux*, and the last parts of *Je me souviens*. He put together his prospectus; reworked and published four excerpts from *Lieux*; translated and published parts of *Odradek* and of Mathews's poetry; negotiated with Gallimard, Flammarion, and Hachette; he went to parties and had dinners with (amongst dozens of others) John Ashbery, the Brunhoffs, and the Bobers; looked after Vietnamese migrants; attended nearly all of the meetings of OuLiPo; played with the Mathews Corpus; had working breaks away in Corsica (with Catherine and Julien), at Chambroutet, Lans-en-Vercors, and Villeneuve-lès-Avignon; saw plays (on 6 November 1976, for instance, *La Belle Hélène*, by André Roussin; on 2 April 1977, Severo Sarduy's *La Plage*); and went to concerts (on 10 May 1977, for instance, *La Fosse d'orchestre*, by Philippe Drogoz, developed from one of his own ideas) and the cinema. Just about the only thing Perec did *not* do during the writing of *Life A User's Manual* were watch television and take any exercise.

The composition of the saga of 11 Rue Simon-Crubellier was organised like a building contract. The planning had taken years and now provided detailed instructions about the shape and the decoration of each room. As Perec proceeded to put things in their right places in the black ledger (a second one would be needed eventually for a work of this size) he entered the date of each work session (bar some that he forgot) and thus left an unambiguous trace of his passage. The book was written from beginning to end in a single, sustained, and majestic sweep. There are some corrections and crossings-out, some paragraphs moved from one place to another, and some insertions written on the facing pages; and a few particularly sticky sections had to be written out over and over again on loose sheets of paper until they were ready to place. (It is worth noting that there is no apparent relationship between the formal constraints and the difficulty Perec had with these latter passages.) But the changes made by Perec to *Life A User's Manual* are almost nothing when compared to those made in manuscript by Flaubert or by Proust, or in second, third, or nth proofs by Balzac. The "first-go" text of Perec's masterpiece is extraordinarily fluent and close to the final, printed book. The achievement is so singular, in fact, that for a time it was believed, by people close to Perec himself, that the author had copied out a pseudo-manuscript in longhand *after* composing the novel directly on a typewriter, so as to have an *objet* as well as a work of art to sell.

Progress on site was reported to Catherine (Perec read her pages in the evening, after he had typed up the day's work), to Harry (who was given pieces to read well before the work was finished), and, in almost formal terms, to OuLiPo. At the last meeting to be held for the time being at Rue Linné, on 27 January 1977, whilst others were laying the table for lunch, Perec explicated the "mode of functioning" of the book. On 12 May he announced: *I'm up to chapter 31 of my big book. 200 pp. ms. finished.* On 25 August he gave his next update: chapter 59 done, together with its punning list of the names of the members of OuLiPo (a carbon copy of the list was handed in to the definitively provisional secretary, for archiving). On 7 December 1977 Perec recited the first pages of the novel at a public reading at the Pompidou Centre. By January 1978 he was already outlining his programme for the spring and summer – a reading of *Life A User's Manual* on 15 May, followed two days later by a lecture at the Cercle

Polivanoff, to explain (up to a point) how the novel had been written – for he knew then that by April it would be finished, and he had a contract at last, which meant that it would be published.

The calendar of composition, shown opposite, tells an otherwise almost unbelievable story.

Let us imagine a man whose wealth is equalled only by his indifference to what wealth generally brings, a man of exceptional arrogance who wishes to fix, to describe, and to exhaust not the whole world – merely to state such an ambition is enough to invalidate it – but a constituted fragment of the world: in the face of the inextricable incoherence of things, he will set out to execute a (necessarily limited) programme right the way through, in all its irreducible, intact entirety.   [L 117]

The "Bartlebooth synopsis", first invented *at the end of 1969 whilst laboriously recomposing a huge puzzle of the port of La Rochelle,*[1] can easily be read as a statement of intent by the writer Perec G., as he gave up the ambitions of La Ligne générale (*merely to state such an ambition is enough to invalidate it*) for the "exceptional arrogance" of an Oulipian champion.

In other words, Bartlebooth resolved one day that his whole life would be organised around a single project, an arbitrarily constrained programme with no purpose outside its own completion. [L 117]

Perec's own life was not so simple, but his *Life* is indeed organised around a single project – the one to be described. The first mirror is put in place, and it reflects an established conceit, that of art for art's sake.

On the table opposite, copied out from the manuscript book, blanks have been left for chapters that contain no dated paragraphs; however, there is no reason to suppose that the chapters were not written in sequence. Where only one date is given for a chapter it probably represents the date of completion. With the exception of the first draft of chapters 1 to 8, where Perec toyed – as he had done with *Things* – with the idea of using first-person narration, the manuscript is close to the published version. The preamble, taken from chapter 44 with variations, and the epigraph from Jules Verne were added at typescript stage.

[1] "Quatre figures pour *La Vie mode d'emploi*", *L'Arc* 76 (1979), p. 50.

Chapter			
1	29–31	October	**1976**
2	1–4	November	
3	12		
4	14		
5	27		
6	28–29		
7	12–14	December	
8	8–18	January	**1977**
9	20		
10	21		
11	25–28		
12			
13	6	February	
14	8–9		
15	11		
16	12		
17	19		
18	22		
19	26		
20	27–28		
21	4	March	
22	23–29		
23	31	March to 1 April	
24	3	April	
25	8–9		
26	15–16		
27	19–22		
28	25–27		
29			
30	3–4	May	
31	6–10		
32	15		
33	19		
34	20–21		
35	22		
36			
37	23		
38	24–27		
39	28–29		
40	5–6	June	
41	7–9		
42	10		
43	23–29		
44	1–3	July	
45	4		
46	5–6		
47	7		
48	8		
49	9–10		
50	12		

Chapter			
51	16	July	**1977**
52	17–18		
53	20		
54	23		
55	24–25		
56	27		
57	29–30		
58	2–4	August	
59	9		
60	11–12		
61	13–14		
62	15		
63			
64	17		
65	20–22		
66	23–24		
67			
68	225		
69	27–28		
70			
71	4–5	September	
72	7		
73	27		
74	29		
75	30		
76	1	October	
77			
78	9–14		
79	15		
80	25–27		
81			
82	30		
83	16	November	
84	19–20		
85	23		
86	25		
87	2–3	December	
88	12–13	January	**1978**
89	14		
90			
91	15–17		
92			
93			
94	18		
95	28–29		
96	14–25	February	
97	28		
98	4	March	
99	2–5	April	
Epilogue		*Paris. 5 avril 1978, 19h 25*	

> *The idea occurred to him when he was twenty. At first it was only*
> *a vague idea, a question looming* – what should I do? – *with an*
> *answer taking shape:* nothing. *Money, power, art, women did not*
> *interest Bartlebooth. Nor did science, nor even gambling. There*
> *were only neckties and horses that just about did, or, to put it another*
> *way, beneath these futile illustrations (but thousands of people do*
> *order their lives effectively around their ties, and far greater numbers*
> *do so around their weekend horse-riding) there stirred, dimly, a*
> *certain idea of perfection.*   [L 117–118]

Bartlebooth is Bartleby (*what should I do? Nothing*), and he is Barnabooth, measuring out a life in neckties and racehorses. He is Perec at
the age of twenty (*what should I do? Nothing*), Perec reading *Bartleby*
("Ah, Bartleby! Ah, humanity!") and Perec reading *A. O. Barnabooth*
(or at least the first twenty pages).

> *It grew over the following months and came to rest on three guiding*
> *principles.*
>   *The first was moral: the plan should not have to do with an*
> *exploit or record, it would be neither a peak to scale nor an ocean*
> *floor to reach. What Bartlebooth would do would not be heroic, or*
> *spectacular; it would be something simple and discreet, difficult of*
> *course but not impossibly so, controlled from start to finish and*
> *conversely controlling every detail of the life of the man engaged*
> *upon it.*   [L 118]

Perec's exploits and records (*La Disparition*, the Great Palindrome)
belong elsewhere; Bartlebooth's plan does not mirror that kind of
writing. But this book is controlled from start to finish by a plan that
prompts every detail of the *Life* within life (or of the life within *Life*)
upon which the writer is engaged.

> *The second was logical: all recourse to chance would be ruled out,*
> *and the project would make time and space serve as the abstract*
> *coordinates plotting the ineluctable recursion of identical events occur-*
> *ring inevitably in their allotted places, on their allotted dates.*
>   [L 118]

Perec had tried this already, in his radio plays and in the serial version
of *W*, where time and timing serve as coordinates, and also in *Lieux*,
with its ineluctable recursion of identical events occurring on their
allotted dates.

The third was aesthetic: the plan would be useless, since gratuit-
ousness was the sole guarantor of its rigour, and would destroy itself
as it proceeded; its perfection would be circular: a series of events
which when concatenated nullify each other: starting from nothing,
passing through precise operations on finished objects, Bartlebooth
would end up with nothing.   [L 118]

Perec and Bartlebooth join and part company here, at the most intoxicating point of the plan. Yes, the idea of a series of texts that when
concatenated nullify each other is a formal intuition, a fantasy, an
ambition of all Perec's work with words, from *L'Attentat de Sarajevo*
to *Things* and *W or The Memory of Childhood*. But no, he did not end
up with nothing. He ended up with aesthetic objects, solid things,
his own books – including, most obviously, *Life A User's Manual*.

Thus a concrete programme was designed, which can be stated suc-
cinctly as follows.
For ten years, from 1925 to 1935, Bartlebooth would acquire the
art of painting watercolours.
For twenty years, from 1935 to 1955, he would travel the world,
painting, at the rate of one watercolour each fortnight, five hundred
seascapes of identical format (royal, 65cm x 50cm) depicting seaports.
When each view was done, he would dispatch it to a specialist
craftsman (Gaspard Winckler) who would glue it to a thin wooden
backing board and cut it into a jigsaw puzzle of seven hundred and
fifty pieces.
For twenty years, from 1955 to 1975, Bartlebooth, on his return
to France, would reassemble the jigsaw puzzles in order, at a rate,
once again, of one puzzle a fortnight. As each puzzle was finished,
the seascape would be "retexturised" so that it could be removed
from its backing, returned to the place where it had been painted –
twenty years before – and dipped in a detergent solution whence
would emerge a clean and unmarked sheet of Whatman paper.
Thus no trace would remain of an operation which would have
been, throughout a period of fifty years, the sole motivation and
unique activity of its author.   [L 118–119]

What Bartlebooth leaves out of his plan is death. "The novel is
death," Roland Barthes had declared long before, to echo and con-
found André Malraux. "It transforms life into destiny, memory into
a useful action, and the passing of time into a meaningly directional

flow.''[1] The Bartlebooth narrative answers Perec's former mentor with a vengeance: mortality transforms the puzzler's self-invented destiny into a novel whose name is *life*.

Life is lived forwards and understood backwards, if it can ever be understood at all. That is the simple basis of all storytelling, and Perec's challenge to narrative exploits the ancient procedure of "deferred release" to the maximum, on a grand scale. One might even take the view that every one of the other stories contained in *Life A User's Manual* (Perec lists 107 of them in the "Alphabetical Checklist" on pages 575–578, but there are a great many more) is designed to delay the completion of the Bartlebooth plot, which can only bring the novel itself to an end. At all events, the plotting of the last chapter was ineluctable from the start, once the layout of the flats at 11 Rue Simon-Crubellier had been worked out and the knight's tour had been mapped onto the block.

Many of the other stories mirror Bartlebooth's, if imperfectly: they are tales of characters with *projects*, of which most – though not all – end in failure. The novel's predominant tone of "life as clinamen", however, reflects the process of writing not one bit. Valène fails to complete his picture of the block of flats, but Perec succeeds in completing his.

In terms of technique, *Life a User's Manual* is a *Meisterstück*, designed to demonstrate the writer's mastery of all the skills of his craft. Perec shows that he can tell fairy stories, that he can construct a novel in letters, an adventure narrative, a business saga, a dream sequence, a detective story, a family drama, a sporting history; he demonstrates that he has mastered comic techniques, the creation of pathos, historical reconstruction, and many non-narrative forms of writing, from the table of contents to the kitchen recipe, the equipment catalogue, the reflective essay, the dictionary entry, the newspaper résumé, and (of course!) the bibliography and index.[2]

Life A User's Manual is therefore devoid of anything that could be called a characteristic style. Perec's talents as a writer of pastiche here find their grandest and most nearly invisible application. As in some

---

[1] *Writing Degree Zero* (1953), trans. Annette Lavers and Colin Smith (London: Cape, 1967), chapter 3.

[2] Perec's monstrously long index is really part of his novel, not simply an appendix to it. It provides solutions to the brainteasers on page 415, numerous narrative connections through names and dates, and much else.

vast symphony of words, Perec arranges, sets, and orchestrates themes that come from elsewhere and that each have their own style. As Nabokov's Sebastian Knight maintained: "It is not the parts that matter, it is their combination."

Lists 3 and 4, "Quotations 1" and "Quotations 2", also ensure that Perec's chapters reset actual passages from the works of twenty different English, American, Irish, German, Italian, Argentinian, and French authors. In the Postscript on page 579 Perec gives a character-istically impenetrable elucidation of his borrowings – an alphabetical listing of the authors of the ten books of List 28 to which allusions are made jumbled together with the twenty authors of the programmed quotations, listed below.

List 3		List 4
0	Butor	Calvino
1	Flaubert	Mann
2	Sterne	Nabokov
3	Proust	Roubaud
4	Kafka	Mathews
5	Leiris	Rabelais
6	Roussel	Freud
7	Queneau	Stendhal
8	Verne	Joyce
9	Borges	Lowry

The "Quotations" Lists of *Life A User's Manual*

One effect of the incorporation of world literature in *Life A User's Manual* by means of a couple of hundred quotations ranging in length from a few words to long paragraphs is that readers can still hear familiar echoes even when they have access to the novel only through one or another of its translations. The story of the "acrobat who did not want to get off his trapeze ever again", for example, is not just reminiscent of Kafka, it *is* Kafka's "A Fasting Artist" (or very nearly), irrespective of the language in which the reader recalls or rereads it; and the doll's house displayed in the wall cabinet of Madame Moreau's lounge is described not in Joycean fashion, but in the actual words used by James Joyce in *Ulysses,* for Bloom's fantasy of his "ultimate ambition".[1] Perec's literary borrowings in *Life A*

---

[1] See Gabriel Josipovici, "Perec's Homage to James Joyce (and Tradition)", *The Yearbook of English Studies* 15 (1985), pp. 179–200.

User's Manual are not different in principle from his use of the words of others in *A Man Asleep*, but they are handled in a much more playful way. Many longer quotations are actually set off as quotations under misleadingly plausible attributions: the lines said to be from Ibn Zaydun on page 321 come almost verbatim from Proust; Cadignan's portrait of Dr Dinteville's ancestor on pages 49–50 is in reality Rabelais's portrait of Panurge; and the "sight test cards" found amongst Troyan's junk on page 197 come from Freud's account of one of his own dreams.[1] Perec's aim in this jubilant *détournement* of literature is not to entice readers into playing hunt-the-author (although he must have known that some readers would play at it obsessively, and that others would denounce the game itself as improper, if not pernicious), but to create that unique and disturbing atmosphere common to fiction and to dreams, in which things seem at once familiar and strange.

The multiplicity of narrative and linguistic styles[2] in *Life A User's Manual* corresponds to the explicit theme of fragmentation in the main narrative. Bartlebooth takes five hundred "snapshots" of his life – five hundred seascapes painted at the rate of one each fortnight over a period of twenty years – and then has them fragmented into 750 pieces each, making a grand total of 375,000 odd-shaped slivers of experience. The chapter-plan of the novel is similarly a plotted fragmentation of a "slice" of Parisian life into a hundred pieces (minus one!), whilst the 400 elements (excluding "gap" and "wrong", which operate only on the elements themselves) distributed by the application of the bi-squares constitute a parody of the very idea of fragmentation, taking it to mind-boggling (though rational) excess. The challenge of fragmentation is imperfectly met by Bartlebooth, who solves only 439 of the 500 puzzles, and incompletely, too, by the writer, who fails to incorporate all of his constraints in chapters that are allegedly put together from pre-set pieces, like jigsaw puzzles.

---

[1] An almost complete inventory of Perec's programmed borrowings, their sources, and their locations in the French text, is given by Ewa Pawlikowska in "Dossier Georges Perec", *Texte en main* 6 (1986), pp. 70–98.

[2] The stylistic diversity is even more marked in the English translation than in the original. This is partly because there are far greater differences between the languages of Joyce, Sterne and Nabokov than between their French translations; partly because Perec used his cunning specifically to mask French-language insertions (such as Rabelais) that would otherwise be visible; and partly because things just turned out that way.

But this is all essentially "cover" (defined as a duplicitous process by Ferri the Eyetie, in chapter 73); the real challenge of fragmentation is the one facing the reader of Perec's novel, which is subtitled *romans*, "novels", in the plural, as if to underscore this very point. For there are only two characters in the book who really interest Perec, as he himself explained:

> Writing a novel is not like narrating something related directly to the real world. It's a matter of establishing a game between reader and writer. It's related to seduction.[1]

> Despite appearances, puzzling is not a solitary game: every move the puzzler makes, the puzzle-maker has made before.　[L 191]

One of the games that Perec appears to be playing with some of his readers is that of nods and winks. Alongside offcuts of world literature, *Life A User's Manual* contains numerous snippets from the lives of Perec's friends. Marcel Benabou crops up (on page 263) as the author of an article that he might just have written, in a journal that could perhaps have published it and that readers of "Roussel and Venice" may recall; David Landes and Abd-el-Kader Zghal are likewise credited with articles that they did not actually write but might have (page 48); an old friend of Perec's, the painter Gérard Guyomard, appears (on page 23) as the skilful separator of two Bellmer drawings done on two sides of the same sheet of art paper (a true story);[2] a poster that hangs in Claude Burgelin's kitchen is put up again in the flat on the third-floor right, in chapter 29; François Le Lionnais is anagrammed into the detective François-Léon Salini; and the English joke-barometer in the Brunhoffs' house at Ars-en-Ré is installed in a pub near Charing Cross (on page 445). Jacques Lederer's Hot Peppers are inscribed on page 43, Helmle's address figures on page 140, Marcenac-Burgelin-Benabou are present both in Marcel-Emile Burnachs on page 238 and Florentin Gilet-Burnachs on pages 386–388; the Lamblin house at Nivillers is invoked on page 270; and Bernard Quilliet's theatrical opinions are offered on page 364, together with a sideways account of the Hammamet Theatre Festival,

---

[1] Georges Perec, interview with Jacqueline Piatier, *Le Monde*, 29 September 1978.

[2] See David Bellos, "Perec et Saussure. A propos de *La Vie mode d'emploi*", *Parcours Perec* (Lyon: Presses universitaires de Lyon, 1990), pp. 91–95.

in which Jean Duvignaud was involved. The inscriptions go even further, in a sense: the subplot involving pornographic watches is based on information requested from and supplied by David Landes, and the paleographic erudition of the "Terra Consobrinia" story was winkled out of Marcel Benabou. Perec wrote or spoke to all the people concerned to ask their permission to include their names, their achievements, or their learning in his novel. He was not settling scores with them; his novel is there to honour them, and the OuLiPo, and the books that Perec loved and wished not only to represent but to *incorporate* in his magnum opus. "Perec's whole oeuvre", Claude Burgelin writes with privileged insight, "is a work of approval and reconciliation."[1]

Nabokov reserved particular scorn for literary researchers who tried to identify the real-life sources of objects scattered around his works like "lost property". Perec's systematic return of lost property to its place in a world that is more *constructed* than any other constitutes a gigantic red herring for readers who mistake a nod for a wink, marquetry for influence, or gossip for literary interpretation. *Life A User's Manual* is not "about" the literary texts that it incorporates any more than it is "about" David Landes, Marcel Benabou, or whoever it was who went to London to have an abortion. True to Perec's Bartleboothian design, his life is fragmented into myriad inanimate pieces – names, places, splinters of his and others' learning and life stories – and recomposed into an order that tells its *own* story. If there is life in that story, it is because Perec has put it there, not because he has borrowed it from others. Perec's modesty, like Bartlebooth's, is not without its own arrogance.

One of the "big dippers" [*PC* 68] enjoyed by sentimental readers is the story of Cinoc, the "suffering word-snuffer" whose name is discussed at length in chapter 60.

> Obviously the concierge didn't dare address him as "Nutcase" by pronouncing the name "Sinok". She questioned Valène, who suggested "Cinosh", Winckler, who was for "Chinoch", Morellet, who inclined towards "Sinots", Mademoiselle Crespi, who proposed "Chinosh", François Gratiolet, who prescribed "Tsinoc" [. . .]. A delegation went to ask the principal person concerned, who replied that he didn't know himself which was the most proper

way of pronouncing his name. His family's original surname, the one which his great-grandfather, a saddler from Szczyrk, had purchased officially from the Registry Office of the County of Krakow, was Kleinhof: but from generation to generation, from passport renewal to passport renewal, either because the Austrian or German officials weren't bribed sufficiently, or because they were dealing with staff of Hungarian or Poldevian or Moravian or Polish origin who read "v" and wrote it as "ff", or who saw "c" and heard it as "tz", or because they came up against people who never needed to try very hard to become somewhat illiterate and hard of hearing when having to give identity papers to Jews, the name had retained nothing of its original pronunciation and spelling and Cinoc remembered his father telling him that his father had told him of having cousins called Klajnhoff, Keinhof, Klinov, Szinowcz, Linhaus, etc. How had Kleinhof become Cinoc? Cinoc really did not know.

Poldevia is a land that exists most notably in Raymond Queneau's novel *Pierrot mon ami*. *Kleinhof* is a plausible German translation of *Castelot*, the presumed name of Claude Burgelin's Huguenot ancestors (regallicised from a no less plausible German transformation, *Bürglein*);[1] Cinoc-*synoque*-сынок was the Polish-Russian pet name that the father of Perec's first girlfriend gave to Voijin Čolak-Antić, called Ciga, a real person who also appears as a character in *L'Attentat de Sarajevo*; and Roger Kleman had relations by the names of Kleimann, Kleiman, Kleyman, Klajnman, Le Queffelec and Mozes.[2] The story, piercing though it may be, in fact has almost nothing to do with the history of Perec's own name; nonetheless, it is made to echo the falsified history of *Peretz* given in *W or The Memory of Childhood*, through confusion about the sound of the initial and terminal *c*. The reader of *Life A User's Manual* smiles at chapter 60; the reader of Perec's larger published oeuvre hears the echo and thinks of the poor orphan whose name must also have been mangled by anti-Semitic registrars' clerks. The author pulls the strings, whilst acknowledging three friends and one master in a single paragraph. But it is not impossible that Perec dazzled even himself with his juggling. How

---

[1] Thus the envoi on page 299 of Claude Burgelin's *Georges Perec* (Paris: Le Seuil, 1989): "Avec les très vifs remerciements de Nick Linhaus", a reference to an American cousin of Cinoc's [*L* 499].

[2] Obituary notice of Eugène (Jacques) Kleyman, *Le Monde*, 14 February 1989.

had *Peretz* become *Perec*? Did Perec himself really know any more?

The main plot of *Life A User's Manual* is a game for two or three players. Valène, the self-effacing painter-narrator, Winckler, the puzzle-cutter, and Bartlebooth, the millionaire watercolourist, conduct the three-handed match, and Perec plays their cards against the reader. Winckler dies first, in 1973, but not before Bartlebooth's plan has begun to go astray. The old man has trouble with his eyes; the attempted treatment fails, and he goes blind. His puzzle solving falls behind schedule, and the puzzles themselves get harder; still he perseveres, with obsessive anger, with help, and by touch alone. The "real" world then impinges on his scheme in the form of an art collector working on behalf of a colossal company with unlimited purchasing power. Bartlebooth's plan to leave no trace is thwarted. In the end, however, he is undone not by the onslaught of the art-buying Beyssandre but by the cunning of Winckler, given shape long before in the deceptive forms of the puzzle pieces he has cut.

Bartlebooth's death in error is revealed to be the posthumous implementation of Winckler's revenge, but what is nowhere stated in this vast novel is the puzzle-cutter's motive. Verlaine's prose version of the poem that lies near the root of the Gaspard theme in Perec's work (*see* pp. 108–109) provides one misty source of the plot (in that fantasy, "Scénario pour un ballet" ["Sketch for a ballet"], the Gaspard Hauser character murders a millionaire who is his natural father) but the plot of *Le Condottiere* obviously provides a more powerful and personal origin . Although Perec cannot have believed that *the first more or less complete novel I managed to write* [*W* 108] would be accessible to the reader of *Life A User's Manual* in any foreseeable span of time, that strange and long-lost combination of art history, forgery, resentment, self-hatred and violence is plainly what lies behind Gaspard Winckler's *long and meticulous, patiently laid plot of revenge* [*L* 6].

Harry Mathews has suggested that Winckler's revenge on Bartlebooth can be read as social-cum-political parable: the revenge of the worker-artisan on the irresponsible owner of capital.[1] The plot also has numerous echoes in other stories of revenge told in the book, notably the tales of Sven Ericsson and Elisabeth de Beaumont-Breidel, and in the mysterious conclusion of the drama of Blanche

[1] Harry Mathews, "That Ephemeral Thing", *New York Review of Books*, 6 June 1988.

Gardel and Cyrille Altamont. The indisputable presence of parallel themes elsewhere in Perec's work, however, cannot assail the unanalysed, unanalysable *givenness* of Winckler's resentment as it is presented in *Life A User's Manual*. A striking inversion of *W or The Memory of Childhood*, Winckler's revenge, simultaneously the assertion of his life and the memory of his death, is not so much a work of art as an artful trap laid down for an opponent who is himself intent on dissolving absolutely the craftsman's lifelong career. What also survives, nonetheless, if only under almost impenetrable disguise, is the energy and anger of the first Gaspard Winckler. The murder plot of *Life A User's Manual* is in effect Perec's final transformation of his first real self-assertion in writing.

Chapter 99 opens with a description of Bartlebooth's study, the novel's inner sanctum, the place where the puzzles are done. The volume of Thomas Mann on the bookshelf comes from Rue de l'Assomption, but the image on the 439th puzzle (which Bartlebooth himself cannot see) belongs less to this world than to myth: *it depicts a little port in the Dardanelles, at the mouth of the river which the Ancient Greeks called Maiandros, Meander* [L 493]. It is the one seascape out of all those mentioned that Bartlebooth cannot have painted on site. As Jacques Roubaud has explained:

> The river Meander was allegedly the son of Ocean by his sister Thetys, the goddess of the sea's riches, and the sibling of the world's three thousand waterways that flow into the sea. Meander was the only one amongst them to be reluctant and to delay his unavoidable end – to put off meeting his father Ocean and his mother the mother of the sea, to mingle with them "in the dusk-charged air".[1]

In Greek mythology, the story of Meander figures both the tortuousness of attempts to defer the moment of dying and the impossibility of doing so forever. Naturally, Bartlebooth, the inventor of a flawed plan of life that omits his own mortality, fails to solve a puzzle representing a port at the mouth of the mythical Meander. Ineluctably, the depiction of Meander's death as a river (of the place where it returns to the sea) coincides with the death of both the hero and the novel. More profoundly, Meander's dying is also the river's

[1] Jacques Roubaud, *The Great Fire of London*, trans. Dominic di Bernardi (Lisle, Ill.: Dalkey Archive Press, 1991), p. 256.

final return to its Mother: the mysterious last piece shaped like a W that Bartlebooth cannot insert into the one remaining X-shaped gap is thus a mirror-inversion of the initial letter of the puzzle's three keys: *méandre*, *mort*, and *mère* (meander, death and mother).

Only as we read chapter 99 are we allowed to grasp clearly that the narrative clock has been frozen for five hundred pages, and only now can it tick on to exactly eight o'clock of the evening on 23 June 1975 when, as Perec said to Catherine, "the old man died".[1] This minimal animation brings the novel simultaneously to life and to an end.

> It is the twenty-third of June nineteen seventy-five, and it is eight o'clock in the evening. Seated at his jigsaw puzzle, Bartlebooth has just died. On the tablecloth, somewhere in the crepuscular sky of the four hundred and thirty-ninth puzzle, the black hole of the sole piece not yet filled in has the almost perfect shape of an X. But the ironical thing, which could have been foreseen long ago, is that the piece the dead man holds between his fingers is shaped like a W.   [L 497]

According to Roubaud, the signature at the centre of the 439th puzzle is "M, the mirror image of W [. . .] the signature that constraint – any constraint – forever attempts to show and to hide by leaving a void". However, that cannot be *quite* right – because the gap or void in the puzzle is said to be shaped like an *x*. W, Winckler's mark, and Perec's too, is what is left in the old man's hand. It was to begin with the code-name for the site of Perec's adolescent fantasy (he revealed or imagined towards the end of his life that he had first named the island Wilsonia because he knew enough English as a child to think: *[I] will [be a] son*),[2] then it became the letter-symbol for the "fabricated" puzzle of his own childhood, but W stands as an almost inexhaustible *supplement* at the end of this exceptionally coherent and infinitely evocative novel. The last chapter of *Life A User's Manual* somehow transforms W into a one-letter summary of what remains when all is done.

Perec does not explain how Winckler engineered his revenge: the

---

[1] Perec used the words *vieil homme* for "old man" in his conversation with Catherine, but the ancient French pun on *vieillard/ vieil art* ("old man" and "the old art") nonetheless forms a part of the inexhaustible hinterland of meanings attached to Bartlebooth's death.

[2] "A Propos de la description", in Alain Reniès, ed. *Espace et Représentation* (Paris: Editions de la Villette, 1982), p. 346.

reader is at liberty to imagine a puzzle so artfully cut that it can be reassembled entirely whilst also allowing for a completely different resolution that fails only in respect of one piece, or else that Bartlebooth, being blind, has simply got the 439th puzzle wrong. The first alternative is very hard to imagine, but no more so than the port at the mouth of the river Meander that the puzzle represents.

What Perec shows and hides simultaneously in the central, fundamental chapter of *Life A User's Manual* naturally placed at the novel's end is not just formal constraint. Meander portrays a refusal of death. At the end of chapter VIII of *W or The Memory of Childhood*, Perec had explained that *writing* is *the memory of their death and the assertion of my life*. The ending of *Life A User's Manual* is W(inckler)'s posthumous triumph over his paymaster and the triumph also of Thetys and Ocean over Meander; it is the inextricably convoluted mirroring of M and W (and their nonreversibility into X, the "sign of the dead father" in Perec's autobiography), a simultaneous assertion of obstinacy in life and of the life that is in writing. What Perec has created is not the epitome of a fiction concerned *solely* with its own workings, but a shimmering, many-layered pearl that may perhaps be best summed up in the banal and humbling words its author had so often borrowed, long before, from his aunt Esther: "Life goes on."

Partly based on the recollections of Marcel Benabou, Catherine Binet, Claude Burgelin, Dominique Frischer, David Landes, Harry Mathews, and Paul Otchakovsky-Laurens. The schedule of *Life A User's Manual* was transcribed from the manuscripts by Patrizia Molteni.

Here is a plain translation of the poem quoted on page 619:

Neither god nor demon, man has gone astray	*- That's not there. It's because he's astray;*
As thin as a thread, as broad as the dawn	*He's not thin enough, nor sufficiently broad:*
Nostrils foaming, both eyes upturned	*Too many wracked muscles, too much exhausted saliva*
And his hands stretched out to touch a decor	*Calm will return when he sees the Temple*
	Ensure by its form his own eternity.

CHAPTER 60

Launch into Orbit

The launch of *Life A User's Manual* was very different from the take-off of *Things*. In 1965 readers made the running, and Perec's first book acquired a large audience even before it had won a prize. In 1978 the situation was almost the reverse. Perec now had a publisher who was wholly devoted to him, and whose professional career was at stake almost as much as his own. Whereas *Things* had been an easy book to sell (short, therefore cheap, and ostensibly easy to read, with a natural market amongst the young, who buy books the most), *Life A User's Manual* was not going to be a publisher's dream. It would be huge and, with its artwork insertions and monstrous index, it would be a costly nightmare to print; it could only be a success if it was cheap, but it could not be cheap unless it was a success and could justify a very long print-run indeed. The challenge that P.O.L. took on when he took on Perec was the publishing corollary of the literary challenge laid down years before by Jacques Bens at a meeting of OuLiPo:

> I am fed up with structures that produce three little snippets of verse. Is it possible to find an Oulipian structure that would allow someone to write an eight-hundred-page novel? Until we've answered that question, all we'll have done is to improve on a few parlour-games.

Je me souviens, which launched the new imprint of Hachette/Collection P.O.L. in January 1978, earned its author a sympathetic review and a short interview in *Le Monde*, and Perec was booked for two radio performances in which he was also able to talk about *Lieux* and about the connections among his various works.[1] Perec told his

---

[1] Monique Pétillon, "Ce qu'il se passe quand il ne se passe rien", interview with Georges Perec, *Le Monde*, 10 February 1978; *Nuits magnétiques*, broadcast by France-Culture on 1 March 1978; and *Panorama*, broadcast by France-Culture on 13 April 1978.

interviewers that he had already had a score of letters from readers pointing out this or that mistake in *Je me souviens*. It had not been his intention, he said, to put in mistakes. *But that's all part of the wobble. There always is something unfixed about the past and its slight tremor.*

There was one mistake that Catherine had noticed before the book was published, in "I remember" number 440:

Je me souviens de	*I remember*
"Petit Papa c'est aujourd'hui ta fête	*"Daddy, today's your name-day*
Maman m'a dit que tu n'étais pas là.	*Mummy told me that you weren't there.*
J'avais des fleurs pour couronner	*I had flowers to crown your head . . ."*
ta tête . . ."	
(j'ai oublié la suite).	*(I've forgotten the rest)*

The song that Catherine remembered from her own childhood went: "Maman m'l'a dit *quand* tu n'étais pas là" ("Mummy told it to me *when* you weren't there"). She told Perec, who responded rather grumpily, *That's how I remember it, anyway.*

Perec's minute shift from *when* to *that* did nothing to diminish Catherine's unease with *W or The Memory of Childhood*, which she had begun reading again and was to read with even greater puzzlement once she had heard the ending of *Life A User's Manual*. Perec told her that if she found it as odd as all that, then she should write it down and show him just what she meant.

In February, Catherine had to have an alarming tumour removed from her tongue. (Fortunately, it turned out to be benign.) Robert Bober, meanwhile, had put in a formal proposal to INA for the film on Ellis Island. Perec planned to visit New York in mid-May and then to go on to see Mathews, who would be teaching French literature that semester at Bennington College, in Vermont. In March, he reported on progress in a letter to Harry:

I still haven't written the last chapter and the brief epilogue. I'm correcting the rest as I go along and setting up the index, which is a colossal job. Simultaneously P.O.L. is putting the book into production. Things are moving.

In fact, at a dinner with Harry at the Terminus Nord just before the latter's departure for the States, Perec had declared that his great book was already over and done with, finished, and off his back.

"But you're not going to publish it as it stands, are you?" Catherine said. "It's full of mistakes of basic French that any pedantic school-teacher would mark wrong."

But I've had enough of the thing! Perec exclaimed, beginning to get cross, which was something he rarely did. *I want to be rid of it!*

"But it has to be corrected!" retorted Catherine, and she made Perec give in on that score. Eager as he was to see *Life A User's Manual* in the bookstores and then to move on to something else, he was not so impatient as to let it appear in a less than perfect form.

Correcting the typescript was a mammoth task, begun even whilst Perec was still writing the last few chapters of the novel (which partly accounts for slower rhythm of composition towards the end). Catherine pencilled in her queries and suggestions on the carbon copy and went over them with Perec at the round table at Rue Linné. At the start of the work she was unable to speak, since she was still recovering from the operation on her tongue, and so Perec bought a "magic slate". Catherine would write down her comments, Perec would reply, and then pull the lever that wiped the slate clean – which is why there is no written trace of what must have been an intense, amusing, and highly technical debate. Catherine had her own firm grasp of style and there were many points that she insisted on putting right. For example, the typescript described a staircase (in chapter 1) as being *bruyant* ("noisy"). It was the people that made the noise, not the stairs, she said; there was only one correct word for it, and that was *sonore* ("echoing"). P.O.L., for his part, was most impressed with Catherine's editorial work: he had never come across such a stickler before. Perec was quite relaxed about most of the suggested alterations; he accepted real improvements without demur, except when they tangled with what he claimed was the trace of a constraint. At such points he would resist all entreaties and put up a brick wall. Given the complexity of the novel's structure, it seems strange that Perec did not feel inclined to protest rather more.

The oddest piece of French in the whole book was its title. It was simply not normal to say "*x mode d'emploi*", with no comma, colon or period between. The early written references to the book-in-progress – in *Espèces d'espaces*, in handwritten and typed OuLiPo minutes, in the 1976 prospectus given to P.O.L. himself, in Claude Bonnefoy's published interview, and on the spine of the very folder that Perec used for his notes – all mark a separation between *Vie* and *mode d'emploi.*[1] In 1978, Perec had quite a job persuading P.O.L. that the book's real title was *La Vie mode d'emploi*, with no full stop, comma or colon. *Mode d'emploi*, he insisted, was not a subtitle, but an inseparable part of his novel's proper name.

It would take a while for French readers to get used to Perec's linguistic twist; most reviews of *Life A User's Manual* corrected Perec's title with an intercalated punctuation mark. But things eventually took a different turn. The unpunctuated "formula" of "*x mode d'emploi*" was borrowed for newspaper headlines ("La Cohabitation mode d'emploi") and also, to Perec's dismay, for "Suicide mode d'emploi", a pamphlet on euthanasia that was banned by the authorities. Little by little, *La Vie mode d'emploi* simply became part of the French language. The phrase has now been copied so often that it can be found in the speech and writing of many who have never read Perec's book.

Paul Otchakovsky-Laurens and Jean-Pierre Reissner, the designer, watched over the production of *Life A User's Manual* as if their lives depended on it. The typescript was not finally completed until April 1978, but printed copies of the seven-hundred-page volume were in reviewers' hands in time for their summer reading break. This most intricate of texts was pushed through manufacturing in not much more time than is reckoned to be the absolute minimum for "instant" journalists' books.

> *Dear Harry:*
> *[. . .] Catherine's much better and will write soon. We're in the middle of correcting* Life. *It's a hell of a job. I've finished. I'm up to my neck in the index, and I've already decided to add a half-chapter.*

"Operation *Life*" began with prereleases. Chapter 55 was run off first and bound into a little booklet with a prospectus describing the novel as the "literary event of the season", for distribution at the book fair held at Nice in May 1978. Extracts from chapters 25, 37,

---

[1] Most often the form is *La Vie, mode d'emploi*, but *La Vie (mode d'emploi)* and *La Vie: mode d'emploi* are also found.

and 38 were published by Bernard Pivot in his popular reading magazine, *Lire*. The most spectacular pirouette of the book, the giant acrostic of chapter 51, was published in *Po&sie* under a mock-classical title, "Compendium libri 'De vita et modo utendi' cum CLXXVIIII ex personis quae in eo libro sunt". Booksellers were the target at Nice; ordinary readers were aimed at through *Lire*; and a smaller circle of literary opinion-makers was appealed to through *Po&sie*. By Anglo-American standards it was a very modest hype indeed.

By the time Perec wrote the epilogue of *Life A User's Manual*, in early April, he knew for certain that he would be going to New York a few weeks later, and he "inscribed" his impending journey in the penultimate page of his novel, wherein Cinoc overcomes his fear of U.S. Immigration, *which he thought still happened on Ellis Island* [*L* 499].

On 19 May 1978, a mobile recording studio drew up outside L'Atrium (Perec usually called it L'Aquarium) at Place Mabillon, on Boulevard Saint-Germain. One of the strangest experiments in radio history was about to begin. A writer well known for his attention to detail and to the "infra-ordinary" was to spend an entire day describing what passed in front of his eye, into the microphone, in real time. Obviously, Perec took a few breaks for coffee and meals and so on, and the experiment was brought to a close with about five hours of tape in the can. This was later edited by Perec and René Farabet, the producer, into a hallucinatory aural experience some two hours in length, broadcast in February 1979 as *Tentative de description de choses vues au carrefour Mabillon le 19 mai 1978*. ("An Attempt at a Description of Things Seen at Mabillon Junction on 19 May 1978").

What does the experiment prove? That trivia can become poetry when pushed beyond reasonable limits; that repetition can become rhythm. That there is a thin borderline between punishment and intoxication. And perhaps that no one but Perec could have had the combination of self-restraint (he never comments on what he sees, he just says, *another 68 bus, three red cars, a lady with a dog* . . .), modesty, and sheer gall to carry on for hours on end, to the end.

The art of enumeration is not an easy one.

From the Abbey Victoria Hotel, New York, June 1978:

> *Dear Catherine:*
> *Life in NY is exhausting [. . .] A lot of our time goes into just getting around Manhattan. This morning we went to the Statue of Liberty but not up it (too high, too crowded). But we did visit the Museum of Migrating Peoples and made contact with the superintendent of Ellis Island [. . .]. He showed us a sixty-minute film made in 1975 by British television,* Destination America. *Not bad, but we can do better. [. . .] I think of you often. I would so much like happy things to happen for you, and to be able to help make them happen. At the moment, everything seems to me to hang on your film plan. [. . .] You must now find the enormous energy to turn your dream, your words, into images, even if you have the feeling that you're taking on an impossible task. [. . .]*
> > *I love you.*

The reader who wonders why Georges Perec did not stop for a while after finishing *Life A User's Manual* – why he did not just take a break, buy a cottage, do some gardening – has not understood. Perec had resigned from the CNRS; his whole life henceforth was to be a life in words. He was on the plank, a freelance writer in a country where probably no more than a hundred people live by writing alone, with no other means of support. Perec's need to write in order to be now defined him in practical terms, and his writing became an unstoppable industry.

The series of television films set up in 1975 by Pierre Emmanuel was at last ready for broadcast, and the first to go on air was Perec's *Les Lieux d'une fugue*, on 6 July 1978. The advance reviews were favourable, and it made for an excellent launch of Perec's name into the public arena. Bianca tuned in to TF1 to watch it. She was not pleased by what she saw as the implicit portrayal of her family as hostile to the unseen boy-hero of the tale, and she rang Georges to tell him so.

So you think I'm ungrateful? he asked.

"Yes, I do."

Ela saw the film more as a homage to Rue de l'Assomption. Perec also said to her, at about that time, and in relation to his feelings about his Bienenfeld background: *You know, I've changed on that score.*

The book world of Paris was already buzzing with rumours about *Life A User's Manual*; Paul Otchakovsky-Laurens was doing his job. Michel Rybalka, back in Paris for the long summer break, decided that he, too, would do something for a writer whom he had long admired and who had been so helpful to his Vietnamese student's wife and children. Rybalka persuaded his brother-in-law, Jean-Claude Trichet, at that time special economic adviser to the Elysée, to hold a dinner party. Trichet and his wife selected influential guests: Dominique Desanti and her husband; the Oulipian Noël Arnaud; Rybalka's bibliographic collaborator Michel Contat, who wrote regularly for *Le Monde*; and Catherine and Alain Robbe-Grillet. There was a special reason for Robbe-Grillet's inclusion: he was reputed to call the shots on the Médicis Prize panel.

Perec was the last guest to arrive at the Trichet flat at Rue Mizon. He came alone, and had a summer cold. He was shy. Contat recalls:

> He was introduced to Robbe-Grillet, with surprise that they had never met before. Perec smiled a lot but said nothing; Robbe-Grillet played the role of big brother with regal ease and, well aware of why the two of them had been got together, declared in his best stage voice: "Perec, of course, Perec, I've always known you! I've been following you for years. So you want the Médicis? Be my guest!"[1]

Perec hardly opened his mouth, except to take half-hearted bites of his dinner. The Robbe-Grillets left, and the Desantis as well; finally Perec relaxed and got down to conversation with friends. Contat and Rybalka's Sartrian bibliography was one of the maddest and most brilliant books he had ever come across, he said; but he was going to do an even madder and more brilliant one, a bio-bibliography of a writer who was as prolific as Sartre but had the additional merit of not existing. Every book, every article, every tiny interview his man could have done would be listed, right down to anonymous book reviews. It would be more boring and more inspirational than Flaubert's *Bouvard et Pécuchet*, and extraordinarily hard to do. After all, it's tricky enough to cook up a fifteen-line summary of a nonexistent book that could pass muster in the *Bibliographie de la France*; imagine what it would take to simmer an entire oeuvre of over seven hundred pages . . . *Oh là là, that would be something else!*

[1] "Un biographème", *Cahiers Georges Perec IV*, pp. 34–35.

That "something else" was the old *Ninipotch* design, lightly dressed in Rybalka-Contat disguise. Like *L'Arbre* and *Wie ein Hund*, *Ninipotch* had not been abandoned (see the 1976 prospectus), but was, so to speak, just resting. The only works that Perec "abandoned" were those that he published (or let out in part, such as *Lieux*). Something not easily put down in black and white is asserted in the space described by Perec's parallel and contradictory tracks: he never wrote the same book twice; never let go of books he had not yet written or finished writing; and never failed, in every book he wrote, beginning with *La Disparition*, to "reinscribe" the work he had done before (in *Life A User's Manual* he even included work that he was planning but had not yet done).

When only Rybalka, Arnaud and Perec were left in the Trichet *salon*, the latter pair embarked on recycling every last drop in the place. At around four in the morning Rybalka could take no more and closed up for the night. Rosy-fingered dawn lit the two writers from behind as Rybalka watched them set off down Rue Mizon, arm in arm, with a purposeful if wobbly stride, to find an all-night café they remembered, perhaps near Montparnasse.

The August issue of *La Quinzaine littéraire* was devoted mainly to the theme of "Music, Words and Voice", and contained a "Chronicle of a Chronic Collaboration", a brief and charming account by Philippe Drogoz of his work over the years with Georges Perec, who added a postscript, revealing that he, for his part, would have liked to compose a musical work, *in the purest tradition of Gerard Hoffnung*, to be entitled *17 Gags pour grand orchestre* ("Seventeen Gags for a Massed Band"). *But I haven't (ever) got beyond the title*, he lamented. Amazing though it may seem, Perec had entirely forgotten the seventeen gags of *Konzertstück*, just as Drogoz had, in his "Chronicle".

That same month, Paul Fournel joined Georges Perec at the Royaumont Centre where they were to serve as joint tutors at an OuLiPo summer school. One of the participants was Jacques Jouet, who Perec suspected of having a bright future in words.

At Royaumont Perec worked on the film he was scripting for Jean-Paul Rappeneau and composed a poem for Catherine in a little pad that he brought with him to meals in the refectory. He would push his plate to one side and twist himself over his writing, his great head of hair resembling a dishevelled tent spreading over an intensely busy building site. The rule governing the poem was Oulipian, but it was also very ancient. Each line is a semi-pangram (that is to say, it uses all the letters of the alphabet once only, except the non-French *k*, *w*, *x* and *y*), minus one. The absent letter in line 1 is *c*, in line 2 *a*, in line 3 *t*, in line 4 *h*, and so on, so that the nine-line poem makes a literal gap of one word only: *Catherine*. The device is called the *belle absente*. Its mirror-image, the *beau présent*, is poetry written exclusively with the letters of the addressee's name. The latter is less difficult, especially if one can select one's friends, literally (or select them literally).

Photographers came out to Royaumont at the end of the month to prepare the press launch of *Life A User's Manual*. Perec does not look well in these photographs. In September other photographers took hundreds of other shots of the master puzzler in his flat and at P.O.L.'s office in Rue Galliéra. By then Perec had got over his cold, a recurrent malady (alongside sinusitis, with which it was connected) that he only ever called *la crève*.

Perec had had a new pair of trousers made by a tailor on Boulevard Saint-Germain in honour of the great day, 10 September. Marie-Claude de Brunhoff gave the party. Perec sat with her to draw up the guest list: he wanted no journalists or "names", just friends. Even with that restriction, Marie-Claude could still have filled a concert hall. She also ordered a very special party cake. Perec was as pleased as Punch when an edible effigy of 11 Rue Simon-Crubellier was unveiled.

Life A User's Manual was "the book of the season", "the book of the year", and "the event of 1978" even before it appeared. *L'Express* led on 11 September: "Georges Perec: all in one." It was followed by *Le Nouvel Observateur* (21 September), *Le Point* (25 September), and *Le Monde* (29 September), which headlined Jacqueline Piatier's article and interview "A Book to Play With". These were all "big spreads", with either a photograph or a caricature of the author, and all presented Perec's novel as a puzzle, a challenge, an exhaustion of the field of fiction, a work to discourage anyone else from writing novels, since it contained all of the world's stories already. What struck the first professional readers of *Life A User's Manual* most forcibly was neither Perec's sadness nor his humour but rather the book's *copia*, or fullness: Perec was "Honoré de Bazar", his novel "a jumble-sale book", an Aladdin's cave, a storehouse, "a huge cemetery piled high with sand-strewn objects, already a chronicle of the 1970s".

Perec spent a large part of September and October 1978 talking to journalists. The longest and in some ways most important interview was the hour-long programme, recorded and broadcast on 22 September, in the long-established "Radioscopie" (or "X-Radio") series on France-Inter, presented by Jacques Chancel, a star personality more accustomed to having singers, society figures, and well-groomed celebrities at his microphone. Perec was back at the studios of Radio-France, at the bottom of Rue de l'Assomption, on 12 October (for a twenty-minute discussion of his new novel with Roger Vrigny),[1] on 6 November (for a discussion and reading of extracts),[2] and again on 7 November, for a group interview with his fellow-Oulipians Paul Fournel, Jacques Bens, Paul Braffort, and Jacques Duchateau.[3]

The written interviews began to appear in October: in *L'Humanité*, in *Les Nouvelles littéraires*, in *Galerie des Arts*, in *Le Magazine littéraire*, edited by Jean-Jacques Brochier, an old friend of Jean Mailland. Perec's 1978 performances (as recorded, at least) are markedly different from those he gave in the wake of *Things*. Most of the interviews about *Life A User's Manual* were conducted at Rue Linné, and in them Perec talks about the trinkets in his flat – the pearl-grading sieves from his uncle, the Ravensburger jigsaw puzzle of an art gallery on the mantelpiece – as well as his works in progress: *L'Arbre*; a book of crosswords; *Ninipotch*; and *Le Voyage à Kairouan*, "the story of a journey that Paul Klee and August Macke made in 1914". Broadly speaking, Perec's interviewers projected an image of the writer as an intense, passionate, hardworking, ambitious, and somewhat batty puzzler. The emotional core of *Life A User's Manual* is not tackled at all, though Perec does manage to get in a number of simple glosses on his work. He points out that most of his characters are defeated by institutional obstacles, and that his work is perfectly realistic on that score. He also insists that, as all of his characters have passions in their lives, what their happy and sad stories therefore evoke overall is a sense of *jubilation*.

At the Frankfurt Book Fair in October 1978, nothing happened.

---

[1] Broadcast by France-Culture the same day.

[2] Broadcast by France-Culture on 10 November in the series *Un livre, des voix*.

[3] Broadcast by France Culture on the same day in the *Panorama* programme.

No foreign buyer was attracted to the Perec book incongruously displayed on the Hachette stand. P.O.L. was neither dismayed nor overly concerned, since Hachette had its own foreign rights department and since *Life A User's Manual* now seemed clearly destined for a successful French career. Einaudi bought the Italian rights, though not at Frankfurt; soon after, a Bulgarian house got the first translation under way. Eugen Helmle began working on Perec's masterpiece without waiting for a publisher's contract. In America, Marie-Claude de Brunhoff put her best efforts into explaining the importance of the novel to a contact at Knopf, who had *Life A User's Manual* read by the poet and translator Richard Howard before saying no. There was a general feeling that Perec was untranslatable – and besides, at that time, Paul Otchakovsky-Laurens recalls, English-language publishers consistently turned up their noses at anything French that was more than two hundred pages long.

Perec had already won the Renaudot Prize for *Things*, and was therefore not a plausible candidate for it in 1978. In fact, *Life A User's Manual* was on the short-list for the Goncourt Prize, by far the most prestigious accolade available for a French novel . . . "What would the Goncourt Prize mean to you?" asked the interviewer for *France-Soir*. *It would mean lots more readers*, Perec answered honestly. *The same as the Renaudot, thirteen years on.*[1] His five competitors were Jean-Didier Wolfromm, for *Diane Lanster*; Alain Bousquet, for *Une Mère russe*; Augustin Gomez-Arcos, for *Scène de chasse furtive*; Hortense Dufour, for *La Marie-Marraine*; and Patrick Modiano, for *Rue des Boutiques obscures*.

There were two strange "spoilers" in the overwhelmingly favourable reception for Perec's new novel. In *Le Monde*, Pierre Kyria's review of Claude Delarue's *Le Fils éternel* appeared over the following attribution: "*Le Fils éternel* by Georges Perec. Hachette, 700 pp., 65FF". And in *Valeurs actuelles*, the obscure G. Rossi Lardi attacked *Life A User's Manual* as a crib of Jean d'Ormesson's *La Gloire de l'Empire*. Perec displaced his anxiety, as he had done many times before, by making fun of it: he dashed off a pastiche of the review that the critic Mathieu Galey had not written, and took himself to task for being overambitious and exceedingly boring.

[1] *France-Soir*, 15 November 1978.

Not everyone liked *Life A User's Manual*. The most effective undermining came from François Nourissier, the journalist who had started the polemic over *Things* in *Le Nouvel Observateur* all those years before:

> *Life A User's Manual* is the archetype of the "novel of the year", a leviathan amongst goldfish, a Pompidou Centre amongst bus shelters. But there's a significant omission: what does not come to mind is the one antithetical comparison you might expect, between Balzac's *Human Comedy* and Radiguet's *Diable au corps*. Why not? Because the Perec question is not one of quantity (ten years' work, 700 pages, 750 grams) but, dare I to say it, a problem of temperature and of temperament. *Life* is a novel come in from the cold. Balzac, Radiguet, Zola, Constant, alternately huge and slender, were all hot-blooded, passionate writers . . . But Perec lives on the ice shelf. His novel is a massive iceberg drifting on the otherwise empty seascape of the contemporary French novel.
>
> To be sure, *Life* does not impose an ideology nor self-indulgent affectivity, and in itself this sterility is very hygienic. But by withdrawing himself from his creation, has the creator not left it empty?[1]

The verdict of coldness and human emptiness, though fundamentally unjustified, is one that has been repeated over the years by a number of Perec's critics, including the English novelist Anthony Burgess.[2] It is obvious that Perec's restraint in presenting his characters – he consistently refrains from offering insights into their psychology and creates pathos only through description and narrative – runs counter to long-standing traditions, and can make his novel seem almost bafflingly impersonal to readers expecting a different kind of book. It is not at all surprising that Patrick Modiano's much gloomier exercise in historical evocation, *Rue des Boutiques obscures*, won the prize. The satirical weekly *Le Canard enchaîné* gave the "real" reason for the jury's preference for a slimmer and less demanding work:

> With Modiano, sales of 300,000 at least are guaranteed. Wolfromm and his *Diane Lanster* can't be relied on for more than

---

[1] François Nourissier, "Georges Perec: Métaphysique sur ordinateur", *Le Magazine littéraire*, 14 October 1978.

[2] *The Independent*, 16 September 1987.

80,000, and, as for Perec, 30,000 at most. Out with the pim-
plies, whether they're talented or not! For a Goncourt must
do 200,000 at least, or else it's a disgrace. A prizeless
business! [1]

A week later the Médicis panel met at the Cercle Interallié to pick a
winner from Jean-Didier Wolfromm, Philippe Baussant, Alain Jouf-
froy, François-Olivier Rousseau, and Georges Perec. The members
were not of one mind. They voted, and came out with an indecisive
result. They voted again. Still unclear.

Perec was waiting for the result at his publisher's office, and word
reached him that things were not going well. He telephoned Catherine and told her he had lost. Then P.O.L.'s telephone rang, asking
him to come over with his author to the Cercle Interallié for the
announcement of the winner of the Médicis Prize. Perec rang Catherine again not fifteen minutes after his first call: *We've got it!* he
shouted down the line. The tension was high, but still Perec would
not use the *tu* form of address to his publisher, nor would he ever
show affection for him in public. They were both on the plank, and
decorum was called for. The chairman of the panel, François-Régis
Bastid, came over to congratulate Perec and told him how glad he
was to see him win the prize. Overhearing the remark, Robbe-Grillet
interrupted, with his stentorian voice: "You've got a cheek! You
didn't vote for *Life A User's Manual* one single time!"

Perec owed his Médicis Prize to the staunch support of Alain
Robbe-Grillet, promised the previous July as if in fun. Robbe-Grillet
and Jacqueline Piatier had voted for him consistently, but even so,
Perec had won only in a tiebreak, on the eighth ballot, by 6 votes to 5.

The official celebration was thrown by Hachette, with *le tout-Paris* in
attendance. Perec's own private celebration consisted of taking a
whole bunch of friends to a laser light show. As a celebrity, however,
he also had to undertake the rite of passage called *Apostrophes*.

Apostrophes was a weekly television programme conceived by Bernard Pivot and hosted by him for nearly twenty years. Concerned
exclusively with books and writing, it had an influence far greater

---

[1] *Le Canard enchâiné*, 22 November 1978.

than that of any book programme outside of France. Broadcast at peak viewing time (9:30 P.M. on Fridays), *Apostrophes* gathered half a dozen writers each week around a low table, to talk to each other and to Pivot about their new books. It was said that a "good showing" on *Apostrophes* could increase an author's sales by thirty-five thousand copies in the following week. Perec appeared on 8 December 1978 alongside Conrad Detrez, Jean Dutourd, Jacques Brenner, Antoine Brunier, and Alain Robbe-Grillet. Over the years Perec had acquired greater ease in talking about his own work – but if the tongue-tied, self-critical non-orator of the Warwick lecture was a thing of the past, Perec was still a reserved and unassertive participant in any public debate. The *Apostrophes* line-up was doubly unfortunate, because alongside the expansive Robbe-Grillet sat Jean Dutourd, the critic who had panned *L'Augmentation* years before and provoked Perec into one of his rare bouts of bitterness in writing. Perhaps for these reasons, Perec was even shier than usual under the hot lights of Pivot's studio lounge. In fact he hardly managed to put a word in edgeways: Robbe-Grillet stole the whole show.

Perec was better able to use the opportunity offered by the Médicis Prize to make a considered statement about his work in a brief text that is also, in part, a reply to his critics. It appeared in *Le Figaro* on 8 December and was no doubt read by many people a few minutes or a few hours before they switched on A2 to watch *Apostrophes*. It asks to be read with respectful attention, for it is in effect a perfect résumé of Perec's whole life in words.

> *When I attempt to state what I have tried to do as a writer since I began, what occurs to me first of all is that I have never written two books of the same kind, nor ever wanted to reuse a formula, or a system, or an approach already developed in some earlier work.*
>
> *This systematic versatility has baffled more than one critic seeking to put his finger on the "characteristics" of my writing, and in all probability it has also disheartened some of my readers. It has earned me the reputation of being some sort of computer or machine for producing texts. As I see it, I should rather compare myself to a farmer with many fields: in one field he grows beet, in another wheat, in a third alfalfa, and so on. In like manner, the books I have written belong to four different fields, four different modes of questioning, which, in the last analysis, perhaps address the same problem, but approach it from different perspectives, each of which corresponds, for me, to a specific kind of literary work.*

The first of these modes could be called sociological: it has to do with looking at the ordinary and the everyday. It is this mode of questioning that underlies texts such as Things, Espèces d'espaces, Tentative de description d'un lieu parisien, and the work done by the team at Cause commune directed by Jean Duvignaud and Paul Virilio. The second mode is of an autobiographical kind: W or The Memory of Childhood, La Boutique obscure, Je me souviens, Lieux où j'ai dormi, etc. The third is the ludic mode, which relates to my liking for constraints, exploits, and "exercises", and gives rise to all the work based on the notions and devices gleaned from OuLiPo's experiments: palindromes, lipograms, pangrams, anagrams, isograms, acrostics, crosswords, and so on. The fourth and last is the novelistic mode, and it grows from my love of stories and adventures, from my wish to write books to be read at a gallop: Life A User's Manual is the obvious example.

This is a rather arbitrary distribution, which could be refined considerably. Almost none of my books is entirely devoid of autobiographical traces (for example, an allusion to one of the day's events in a chapter in progress); likewise, almost none is assembled without recourse to one or another Oulipian structure or constraint, even if only symbolically, without the relevant constraint or structure constraining me in the least.

Actually, beyond these four horizons that define the compass of my work – the world around me, my own history, language, fiction – I think my ambition as a writer would be to run through the whole gamut of the literature of my age without ever feeling I was going back on myself or treading ground I had trod before, and to write every kind of thing that it is possible for a man to write nowadays: big books and small ones, novels and poems, plays, libretti, crime fiction, adventure stories, science fiction, serials and children's books . . .

I have never felt at ease in talking about my work in theoretical or abstract terms. Even if what I produce seems to stem from a long-worked-out programme, from a long-standing plan, I believe far more that I find my direction by following my nose. From the books I have written, in the order I have written them, I get the sometimes reassuring and sometimes uneasy feeling (uneasy because it is always suspended on a "projected" work, on an incompletion pointing to the unsayable, the desperate object of writing's desire) that they map out a path, mark a space, signpost a fumbling route, *describe the specific staging posts of a search that has no why but only a how: I feel confusedly that the books I have written are inscribed and find their meaning in the overall image that I have of literature, but it seems to me that I shall never quite grasp that image entirely, that it belongs for me to a region beyond writing, to the question of "why I write", which I can never answer except by writing, and thus deferring forever the very moment when, by my ceasing to write, that image would visibly cohere, like a jigsaw puzzle inexorably brought to its completion.* [RCF 21–22]

Unpublished sources include letters from Georges Perec to Catherine Binet and Harry Mathews, documents in the possession of Catherine Binet, and information provided by Ela Bienenfeld, Catherine Binet, Marie-Claude de Brunhoff, Philippe Drogoz, Paul Fournel, Bianca Lamblin, Harry Mathews, Paul Otchakovsky-Laurens, and Michel Rybalka.

CHAPTER 61

Working for the Screen

Perec began to lay plans for his life after *Life* before the novel was even half written, and the cinema was, if not the foundation, then at least a large wing of the edifice that he sought to design. Marie-Claude de Brunhoff put him in touch with a specialised agent, Jean-Paul Faure (the grandson of Elie Faure, the art historian, and a good friend of Robert Scipion), and he told him what he had in mind. For all its long love affair with the silver screen, France had never really recognised script writing as a profession. Perec had codirected one adaptation of his own work and taken sole charge of a second; what he wanted now was to put his pen at the service of others, and to earn what his talents were worth. There was room in Paris for maybe half a dozen well-paid screenwriters, and Perec wanted to be one of them. Faure was glad to act on his behalf.

Years before, Perec and Jean-Paul Rappeneau had wanted to make a film together, and they began to see each other again in the winter of 1977–78. After a jolly and bibulous dinner they scrawled a joint affidavit declaring that the undersigned WOULD make a film together in MARCH 1978, if not sooner. The first film job that came Perec's way, however, was of a rather different kind.

The director Alain Corneau had written an adaptation of a low-life thriller by Jim Thompson, *A Hell of a Woman*, had found a producer, and engaged a cast. But he had a problem with the dialogue, and especially with the speech of the main character, called Frank. He wanted the spoken language to be made up of clichés and stereotypes, in order to communicate directly the absence of an inner core, but he was not sure how to achieve the desired effect in words. He spoke of the problem to his producer, Maurice Bernart, who mentioned it to his companion, Florence Delay, who knew Jacques Roubaud well and sought his advice. Roubaud in turn suggested that she ask Perec, for he knew that his fellow Oulipian was after just such work. The name came back by the same route in reverse to Alain Corneau, who was both surprised and delighted, for he thought Perec far too important to work as a mere hack. He rang Rue Linné, put his request to the writer, and got an affirmative reply on the spot.

When Perec turned up for the first working session in Corneau's magnificent Marais flat, the two men had a strange sensation of having met each other before. It dawned on them that they must have stood many times in the same queues at the Cinémathèque and the Salle des Agriculteurs, where both had acquired their youthful film culture. One result of their common past was that they had common strong "likes" (musical comedies) and "don't likes" (the French "New Wave"). Perec was still a very shy man; at dinner it was as if his wit were bubbling under a lid he could hardly lift. He was nervous about showing Corneau and his companion, Nadine Trintignant, the tape of *Les Lieux d'une fugue*. He told them he would love to make films himself but found the problems daunting.

As there is hardly any dialogue at all in Perec's published oeuvre, even including his German radio plays, Corneau's script required Perec to master what was for him a new technique, which he did in his customary way, that is to say by reinventing it. The dialogue of what was eventually released as *Série noire* ("B-Movie")[1] is written in a language almost entirely constructed from clichés, quotations, and set phrases, and every phrase uttered is repeated elsewhere in the film. The work was done quickly, with pleasure and satisfaction on both sides, in April and May 1978. Perec persuaded Corneau that Thompson's book was really a modern transposition of the Orpheus myth and Corneau guessed that Perec identified to a degree with the hero, played, in the film, by Patrick Dewaere. It was shot in the winter of 1978–79, on location, in Paris. When it came out in the spring, Perec was disappointed that some of the scenes that he liked had been cut, but he was nonetheless proud of having had a key role in the making of a "real" commercial movie.[2]

In between writing the dialogue of *Série noire* and correcting the typescript of the last chapters of *Life* and the proofs of the earlier parts, Perec got down to his long-deferred collaboration with Rappeneau. They planned to work in Rappeneau's study, a ground-floor room that was separate from the main upstairs flat and protected from the world by a wheel-operated door, like a Nautilus. When at last they were sitting side by side in the director's hermetic cogitorium,

---

[1] The working title of the film before release was *Moonlight Fiesta*.

[2] *L'Avant-scène Cinéma* no. 233 (1979) contains the full script of *Série noire*.

Rappeneau had an urge to brush his hair. "I'll just pop out and buy a brush," he said. "It's quicker than going back upstairs." Rappeneau was not quite as bald then as he is now, but he was always very hesitant about his film projects.

Perec and Rappeneau invented a story together. Then they doubted whether it could be a film. Then they argued about it and found themselves going round in circles. Perec tried to square it all up as simply as he could, and to keep it really simple he wrote it out in his best schoolbook hand, on lined exercise-book paper, as an answer to an essay question set at school:

Michel Dobronetsz   Royal College of Klagenfurt

Form I

Ist year

Composition

Question: On your father's death you learn that he was the last legitimate claimant to the throne of a long-forgotten kingdom, Carinthia. But neither he nor your grandfather had measured up to defending the rights of a nation sacrificed, and in the eyes of Carinthians in exile, the name Dobronetsz has become synonymous with cowardice and betrayal. What do you do to refurbish your name with its lost dignity?

The answer was eventually drafted in the autumn of 1978, in between interviews with the author of *Life A User's Manual* and the winner of the Médicis Prize. The story takes political prescience to what must have seemed at that time to be the verge of bad taste. This is how Perec and Rappeneau presented their project:

> *Europe is a mosaic of peoples and cultures artificially grouped into roughly thirty states and welded into two opposing blocs.*
>
> *Beneath the apparent stability of the two systems and alliances, tensions and conflicts are never far from the surface: practically all the European states, in the West and in the East, have minority problems that even without becoming outright wars, as in Ireland, keep the whole continent in a continual state of crisis. Examples hardly require listing: Flemings and Walloons, Basques, Breton*

separatists, Occitans, Corsicans, Slovenes, Transylvanian Magyars, Cypriots, and so on.

It is not beyond the bounds of imagination that a crisis of this kind, if it occurred in one of the hot spots constituted in international terms by the frontier between East and West, could seriously threaten "the order and the security of the world".

On this grave subject, we wish to make a light comedy.

Synopsis

A group of monarchist fanatics attempts to restore to the throne of Carinthia (a former Central European kingdom now on the Austrian edge of Hungary) the last descendant of the former reigning family. He is a thirty-year-old Frenchman whom nothing has apparently prepared for such an unusual destiny and who will learn at much the same time as the audience the nature and the scale of the terrifying mission that is being thrust upon him.

In an imaginary whirl, not to say a madcap atmosphere of carousing, passion, and intrigue, a parenthesis is opened in the rigid world of international relations, and the ungroomed prince comes, step by step, to fulfil the great nostalgic dream of a small and dispossessed people. His challenge will be more cheeky than utopian; his battles will be as much against himself as against the real world, and will cause him, within the timespan of the film, to confront most of the powers and institutions that control the balance of power in Europe.

La Couronne de Fer
("The Iron Crown")

Comedy with moments of high emotion

Script for a film by
Georges Perec and Jean-Paul Rappeneau

By the time the script for *La Couronne de Fer* was typed up, another film adventure had already taken off. Perec was sauntering along Rue du Cherche-Midi one day in October 1978, after window-shopping for curios at Saint-Sulpice, when he found himself accosted by a large and excited young man. Perec was just the man he'd been looking for! He needed a writer to help with his film! Wait a tick! And the athlete dashed upstairs – for they just happened to be at the foot of his stair – and came tumbling down again a few minutes later with a typescript in his hand. Perec, amused and flattered at being picked up in the street, was still waiting at the kerb. The typescript the other pressed into his hand was called *Alfred et Marie*. Perec promised to look at it and to ring back in a couple of weeks. He was, he said, rather tied up just then.

Perec actually read the script straightaway, and rang the young giant of Rue du Cherche-Midi two days later.

Your script has the atmosphere of Queneau, he said to Gérard Zingg. *I'm rather taken with it . . .*

Over the following weeks Perec and Catherine got to know Zingg quite well. He had been a promising tennis player in the French national team, but had given up sport as well as a career based on his training in political science in order to devote himself to his real love, the cinema. Perec and Catherine went to see Zingg's first film, *La Nuit tous les chats sont gris* ("At Night all Cats are Black") and were impressed; but they were even more impressed by the young director himself. Zingg rapidly became a close friend, a chap they could summon for dinner at a half-hour's notice, a chum they could laugh with and on occasion even cry with. Unlike some of Perec's older friends, Zingg got on well with Catherine, and he was as much at ease with Perec's proletarian "beast" Julien as he was with *rentier* Harry.

Perec rewrote *Alfred et Marie* over a long weekend in November 1978 at Harry Mathews's house near Lans-en-Vercors. He used loose sheets from the stock of the JBSA, which he still visited from time to time at 62 Rue Lafayette. Jacqueline Benoît-Lévy, who had begun there as a stringer in 1926, was now chairman and managing director; she was in the process of winding the firm down, for she was long past retiring age. Perec was welcome to have the ledgers and the foolscap sheets of heavy paper, marked up in two columns for "entries" and "exits" of natural pearls, each one with its own unique identifying number. Perec decorated his new manuscript with doodles, caricatures and self-portraits, and he decorated Zingg's story – a domestic drama set for the most part at the end of the runway at Orly, involving small-time boxing, and a dance hall at Place Clichy – with self-quotations, or rather, with narrative elaborations of plots laid in *Life A User's Manual*. For example, René Marquiseaux reappears in *Alfred et Marie* as the manager of the Boxing-Club du Val-de-Marne; Remi Plassaert comes onto the dance floor with Isabelle Gratiolet; and part of the action is set in a hotel whose name will be familiar to followers of the career of Léon Marcia: the Hôtel de l'Aveyron.

Alfred et Marie provided Perec with an opportunity to develop the simulated spoken French that he had first tried out in the dialogue of *Série noire*. However, the setting and the action of Zingg's film, reminiscent of Queneau's novels of suburban Paris, prompted Perec to go further in the construction of a dialogue-language that sounds absolutely natural but is in fact entirely composed. The result is a charming, imaginative script that is an unpretentious homage to the least Oulipian aspect of Raymond Queneau, and at the same time an expression of Perec's attention to humble and ordinary lives.

Alfred et Marie was not made as a film because Columbia, Zingg's producer, changed its policy in 1979, and cancelled all non-American projects. *La Couronne de fer*, for its part, was not made because Rappeneau got cold feet. The film industry is a lottery; Perec's luck was no worse than many others'.

No such obstacles stood in the way of the television documentary that he was committed to making with Robert Bober in New York, where they both went to prospect in June 1978. The crew flew out for the actual making of the film in mid-April 1979; Perec got his draft script to Bober only just in time. It consisted of a dozen or so brief delineations of "scenes" on unnumbered pages, which could be shuffled into an order at a later stage. Perec promised his collaborator a full shooting script by the time he himself arrived in New York. He was to leave a little later, and go by a slower route.

Although the cinema was by no means a new interest, film work had now come to occupy a larger space in Perec's life than ever before, and his relationship with Catherine was obviously an important factor in this development. Catherine herself first obtained a modest "advance on receipts" for *Les Jeux de la Comtesse Dolingen de Gratz* in 1976, but, despite intense efforts, she failed to secure adequate financial backing before the time limit on the advance ran out, in January 1979. Perec was angered almost as much as she was by the stony commercialism of film financiers ("your film just isn't referential", one of them told her)[1] and he decided that if no one else would put up the money to make Catherine's film, then he would. At first

[1] Isabelle Jordan, "Entretien avec Catherine Binet", *Positif* no. 96 (January 1982), p. 25.

Catherine refused the offer: it seemed mad. Harry Mathews thought so too; such a gesture would be more foolish than kind, and Perec was likely to lose all he had. Why risk what you have taken your whole life to acquire? Gérard Zingg asked him. *If Catherine doesn't make her film, she'll go mad! And so will I!* Perec said.

The deal was set up at a dinner at Goldenberg's restaurant in the Marais. Perec and Julien launched a joint attack on Catherine: the unending saga of her unmade film was getting them down, they said, and they were now not far short of believing that what she really wanted was to have an eternal cause for complaint, rather than to take the risk of actually making her film. She wasn't up to it, was she? And that was the fact of the matter. Catherine was outraged at the taunting and played into Perec's hands. How dared he suggest that she did not have the courage to carry through a project that had been her sole creative concern for five years? Well, if she really meant what she said, the two men pointed out to her, she would not go on refusing the only finance that had been offered to her.

The upshot of the "Goldenberg sting" was the formation in April 1979 of Les Films du Nautile, a production company (named after Captain Nemo's submarine) half of whose shares belonged to Catherine in return for the rights to *Les Jeux de la Comtesse Dolingen de Gratz* and her earnings as a director for ten years, and the other half to Perec, who put up 200,000 francs and also committed future royalty income from Hachette (mainly for sales of *Life A User's Manual*) estimated (in April 1979) at 400,000 francs. A fresh bid was prepared for the CAR, and Maurice Bernart's company, Prospectacle, agreed to cover the costs of processing the film at the GTC laboratories. That would still leave a gap in the budget: unlike *A Man Asleep,* the new film required locations, costumes, accessories, and a cast that could not be got hold of for free; in the end, the whole project would cost about two million francs. To make up the deficit, Perec circulated a letter to every last one of his relatives, friends and acquaintances, including some he had no wish ever to see again, requesting a loan, small or large, to help finance the film. It was an extraordinary thing for a man in Perec's position to do. He was convinced that it would be an extraordinary film.

It was not the most peaceful of times. Gambling and filmmaking are both high-stress activities, and gambling all you have on a film to be made by the person you love no doubt heightens pressure to a quite special degree. On the night before Perec was due to embark for New York (via Halifax) at Le Havre, he and Catherine dined late and drank too much; Perec overslept, and for the only time in his life he arrived at Gare Saint-Lazare as the train was pulling out (he normally insisted on turning up at airports and stations a good hour before he needed to be there). Catherine had to drive him down the motorway in a hung-over panic to the gangplank of the S.S. *Atlantic-Cognac*, a container ship as huge as a rectangular whale. She had always dreamt of a long sea voyage on just such a vessel. She was jealous of Perec's adventure, and he knew it.

Perec's six-week absence in America gave him and Catherine time to reflect on their relationship, which had hit its lowest point so far. The film was now a daunting challenge for them both, but it was not the greatest difficulty that they faced. Perec was not impotent, but he had always suffered from premature ejaculation and now felt acutely miserable for often leaving Catherine unsatisfied. "I've been cuck-olded often enough before," he said; she too should take a lover, since, despite his psychoanalysis, he was still unable to fill a lover's role as well as he ought. Whilst Perec was away in America, however, Catherine turned to his best friend and "brother", Noureddine Mechri, for advice on a subject about which the writer was quite naturally extremely discreet; in addition, hoping to give Perec a salu-tary shock, she got down at long last to her essay on what his auto-biography was really about.

In all, Perec spent five weeks in North America, and it was whilst he was there that he heard that Catherine had succeeded in getting a new and larger advance on receipts for the film. *Hip Hip Hip Hurrah!* he scribbled on a postcard to Harry. Making his own film on Ellis Island, meanwhile, turned out to be an exhausting experience. He accompanied the film crew all over Manhattan to conduct interviews in his fluent if accented English with former emigrants from Poland, Russia, and Italy (some of whose accents were far heavier than his) who had first entered America through Ellis Island; on many evenings he got back to his room at the Abbey Victoria Hotel feeling quite wiped out. All the same, he saw old friends in the city, including Babette Mangolte and Kate Manheim; went out to Amagansett, on Long Island, for a weekend with his cousin Simone; and up to Ver-mont again, for a weekend with Harry Mathews, before going on to

Montreal for a publicity tour. He caught a cold from Canadian air conditioning and flew back to New York with sinusitis and a buzzing in the ears. That did not stop him from dining with the Liebermans (*see* p. 21) or dropping in on Elia Kazan (who was not there: Perec's half-serious idea was to ask him to codirect a film version of *W or The Memory of Childhood*, with Stanley Kubrick!), or from meeting other Bienenfeld relatives and friends in plenty. He also dined with his agent:

> *Maxine Groffsky is very pessimistic about an American edition of* Life A User's Manual. *She thinks I won't have more than 750 readers and that not one of the major or middling U.S. publishers will risk publishing it. Nonetheless, there was an article in this Sunday's* New York Times *on literary life in Paris, which said nice things about the book and described it as "the most talked-about current success" – but Maxine says that doesn't make any difference. She reckons the only chance of seeing it in English is 1) to commission a translation and 2) to offer it ready-translated to Calder in London. In short, nothing very cheering to look forward to on the Anglo-Saxon front in the next five years.*[1]

When Perec got back to Paris in June 1979 Catherine gave him her unfinished 32-page study of *W or The Memory of Childhood* to read. It was less an essay than a montage of quotations, designed to show that Perec had inscribed his sexual anxieties into a text that appears not to speak of such matters one bit. He was taken aback by it, and moved to tears. *Nobody*, he said to Catherine, *nobody has ever taught me so much about myself*. He made her promise to complete the work one day.

---

[1] Letter from Georges Perec to Paul Otchakovsky-Laurens, 7 May 1979.

Unpublished sources include the typescript of *La Couronne de Fer*, in the possession of Jean-Paul Rappeneau, manuscript and typescript versions of *Alfred et Marie*, in the possession of Gérard Zingg, drafts for *Récits d'Ellis Island*, in the possession of Robert Bober, and letters from Georges Perec to Catherine Binet, Harry Mathews, and Paul Otchakovsky-Laurens.

This chapter also draws on the recollections of Robert Bober, Alain Corneau, Jean-Paul Faure, Simone Kaplan, Jean-Paul Rappeneau, Nadine Trintignant, and Gérard Zingg and is especially indebted to Catherine Binet for the passages concerning Les Films du Nautile and Perec's sexual problems.

CHAPTER 62

The Artist on his Trapeze

Life A User's Manual made Perec a national celebrity, but it fell short of propelling him into global orbit, as *Things* had done (if briefly) in 1965–1966. In Paris Perec was now occasionally recognised in the street, and an informal fan club arose, made up in part by young reader-collectors of Perecquiana, and in part by academics with an interest in formal writing. Now and then Perec held court, uneasily, at Rue Linné. He allowed scholars to glimpse the machinery that had set *Life A User's Manual* in motion, and handed round copies of his current exercises in poetry. Such are the obligations attendant on being a serious writer nowadays; it was not an aspect of the curriculum that Perec enjoyed very much.

Perec's life as a professional writer was a quiet and modest one. *Life A User's Manual* sold well in its first edition and was soon reprinted for a book club in hardcover; it came out as a thick massmarket paperback in 1980.[1] His income came to no more than a middle-class salary, but – Les Films du Nautile aside – Perec had no need of grand hotels and Rolls-Royces. He permitted himself a few new extravagances, adopting Catherine's taste for champagne (a drink he had previously spurned), and taking her on two winter jaunts, in February and November 1979, to Denis Island, in the Seychelles – where he had a bad bout of sun allergy that left him sore for weeks afterwards. He was now free to enjoy himself as a juggler of words, whether for exercise, to keep himself in trim, or just for the fun of it. He undertook some star turns without giving them a great deal of thought in advance. He agreed, for example, to write a preface for a book about glasses. Perec had never worn spectacles in his life! As the deadline loomed, he realised that he had nothing to say, so he dashed round to get some help from his optically shortsighted friend Julien Etcheverry.

[1] For the Livres de poche edition Perec made a small number of corrections and changes to the text. As these alterations have not yet been incorporated in the reprints of the "big" Hachette edition, the Livres de poche is the reference text.

He took some spectacles from "The Beast's" box of spare and obsolete pairs, tried them on, felt horribly dizzy, followed Julien's advice and sat down, opened up an encyclopaedia, and wrote up a lightweight, professional squib in a couple of hours [*PC* 133–150].

Perec and Paulette had not lived together for ten years, but they remained neighbours and chums and were still legally man and wife. Ela thought it wrong that Perec should carry on being responsible (for example) for Paulette's income-tax returns (*but I get an extra allowance for it*, he interjected), and she prodded him to arrange a proper divorce. The papers were finally drawn up, and the divorce was granted on 24 June 1980. Perec and Catherine both abhorred the idea of going through the formalities of marriage again, and so they remained unmarried partners for life. Perhaps Catherine might make him the father of a little goy, Perec said with a smile. In fact, as he knew, Catherine could not bear a child before having an operation; and in any case, the film had to come first.

It must have been at about this time that Perec had a long conversation about children with Bianca's daughter Sylvia, who was thinking along those lines herself. He would have liked to have had a child with Paulette, he told her. He would have liked to know that he would not be the last of his line.

Many of the shorter pieces that Perec wrote in the years after *Life A User's Manual* were turned out quickly and easily, by a wordsmith confident of being a master of his craft. He wrote prefaces, poems, permutation games, puzzles, crosswords, film dialogues, film scripts, translations (of prose and of poetry), pastiches, tautograms, essays, homages to friends, a book review for *Le Monde*, an article for *Le Nouvel Observateur*, and even a piece for *Vogue*, every one of which (except perhaps the last) is a model of its kind. Perec's pen was for hire, on terms of his own making. He had at last got where he wanted to be. It surely did not matter that he had no project of magnitude in the works to take the place of *Life A User's Manual*, for the time being at least: even Perec's imagination needed time before casting off afresh; even Perec's energy needed time to renew itself.

Perec's book-a-year rhythm was maintained with Hachette/P.O.L. without a great deal of effort. *Je me souviens* and *Life A User's Manual* had both appeared in 1978, and therefore Perec was off the hook for 1979. In 1980 Hachette/P.O.L. published *La Clôture et autres poèmes*, and in 1981, the sequence continued with *Théâtre I*,[1] which brought together the two plays that had been performed on stage in France, *L'Augmentation* and *La Poche Parmentier*.

La Clôture contains most of Perec's pre-1979 poetry excluding *Alphabets* but including, quite properly, the palindromes[2] together with a rather extraordinary exercise originally written in 1976–77 for the OuLiPo's collective homage to Raymond Queneau. "Dos Caddy d'Aisselles" is a syllabic palindrome of Gérard de Nerval's "El Desdichado", which is to say that it takes that haunting sonnet and places its syllables in reverse order, "resemanticising" them by a method that is close to that of the pun or homophone game. Nerval's first line,

> Je suis le ténébreux, le veuf, l'inconsolé
> ("I am the dark, the widowed, the unconsoled")

thus yields Perec's last:

> *Les sauts qu'ont l'Un: veuf, l'Hébreu n'était. Le suis-je?*
> ("The leaps which the One has; the Hebrew was not bereaved. Am I?")

Perec pursued a secondary booktrack as well. In 1979 Mazarine brought out the first volume of his collected crosswords, and Balland commissioned a novella for L'Instant Romanesque, a series of "short texts by great writers", "savouring the pleasure of talking about subjects that make no great demands".[3] *Un Cabinet d'amateur* ("A Cabinet Picture") is a ninety-page narrative description of a painting similar to the one depicted on the jigsaw puzzle that Perec had shown to journalists interviewing him in October 1978:[4] a "gallery portrait", a painting of a collection of paintings, a genre usually called *Kunstkabinett* in German. Perec's fictional *"cabinet d'amateur"*, by the German-

---

[1] The title suggests that Perec planned a second volume of theatre work but it is not known whether he intended it to include French versions of his other German radio plays or unspecified new works for the stage.

[2] For the Great Palindrome, *see* pp. 428–430. The "little palindrome" was written for the catalogue of an exhibition of paintings by Pierre Getzler at Galerie Camille Renault in 1970.

[3] Balland, L'Instant Romanesque, an imprint under the direction of Brigitte Massot, publisher's blurb (back panel and inside flap, respectively).

[4] Jean-Louis Ezine, "L'Impossible Monsieur Perec", *Les Nouvelles littéraires*, 6 October 1978, gives the details: 3000 pieces, 1207 x 797 mm, showing W. van Haecht, *Galeriebesuch*.

American artist Heinrich Kürz, represents itself in the collection it represents and in its self-representation represents itself once again, like a fractal, ad infinitum, just as on a packet of cornflakes one can see a little girl eating cornflakes and beside her a packet on which a little girl can be seen eating cornflakes, and so on. Heinrich Kürz's eye-teaser, painted for the Pittsburgh brewing magnate Hermann Raffke, makes slight changes to the contents of the pictures at each level of nested rerepresentation, mocking *mise en abyme* and fracturing the principle of fractalisation. When it is exhibited in 1913, for the German-American community's celebration of the silver jubilee of Kaiser Wilhelm II, it becomes a cult picture.

> *Nobody ever seemed to tire of comparing the originals with Kürz's tinier and tinier reproductions [. . .]. The day after some fellow equipped with a jeweller's glass climbed onto the shoulders of two mates and declared that you could see very precisely the seated man, the easel with the portrait of the tattooed man, and then again the painting with the seated man, and then one last time the painting reduced to a thin line no more than 0.5mm long, several dozen visitors came with every kind of magnifying and weaver's glasses, setting off a cult that caused the businesses of every optical-equipment supplier in the city to boom.* [UCDA 21–22]

Perec's irony – that it is the opticians who make a mint off the painting, not the artist himself – cannot hide the fact that *Un Cabinet d'amateur* invites the same kind of microscopic scrutiny, that it is a work that feeds tantalising crumbs to text-peckers and threatens to drive them crazy. *Un Cabinet d'amateur* contains sentences copied out *with mistakes* from *Life A User's Manual*, and introduces a new cross-quotation game. The clues are the sale-catalogue numbers of the paintings portrayed by Kürz, which "refer" to the number of the chapter in Perec's larger work from which a detail has been taken to "generate" the painting in question. The game is even more self-regarding than that, however, since most of the "snips" from *Life A User's Manual* are themselves snipped from elsewhere, and Perec uses *Un Cabinet d'amateur* to give convoluted clues to the originals from which his masterpiece was made. *Un Cabinet d'amateur* as a whole can be taken to mean that for Perec, the only formants of his writing had already been written, that his art was now nothing more than a text-generation game. The book is full of nods and winks directed at non-textual friends and relations – Harry Mathews (a reference to

"Bennington University Press" on page 60), to Cousin Simone ("The Yacht Basin at Amagansett", on page 77), to the Brunhoffs' ("Miss Ursule Boulou", mentioned on page 82, is named after their cat), Saarbrücken friends (the railway station at Sankt-Wendel, a ghastly modern construction, is beautified on page 50 into a kitsch pseudo-painting, *La Gare de Saint-Wendel*, to amuse them) – but much of Perec's unserious purpose remains hidden from readers who have only French. Some knowledge of English is required to raise a smile when one meets an art critic called Greenback, a book published at Hoaxville, or a painting bought by the Budweiser Foundation; and there is an equal sufficiency of transparent (and far more ribald) clues in German. However, there is also a simple message communicated by Perec's spoof, which places a hoax painting in hoax German in Pittsburgh. Perec is, in a sense, taking leave of his German friends in Saarbrücken, and announcing, with kindness and wit, that the external reference point for his work will henceforth be the States.

All of the paintings in the collection depicted by Kürz are forgeries, as is the story itself, which Perec cooked up, he says by way of conclusion, solely "for the pleasure – and the frisson – of *faire-semblant*" [*UCDA* 90], which in this context means the schoolboyish thrill of taking his (French-only) readers for a ride. Possibly the cruellest cut comes in the title itself: *"un cabinet d'amateur"* is indistinguishable in speech from *"un cabinet d'amateurs"* – a bunch of amateurs, poring over Perec's texts with a spy glass or loupe and finding not fractals but a textual noose.

Un Cabinet d'amateur is, additionally, an element in the construction of a personal myth whereby Perec had first wanted to be a painter. There had always been painters among his close friends – Pierre Getzler "since forever", Gérard Guyomard for almost as long; he had known art collectors (Raymond Queneau, Eugen Helmle) since the mid-sixties; and he had always had a strong eye and a passionate interest in the visual (his first published words, at the beginning of *Things*, were *Your eye, first of all*). In the 1970s Perec had met more French and American artists through Harry Mathews; he had got to know Luc Simon, and Guy de Rougemont, and found much pleasure in the work and in the company of Paolo Boni, amongst others. He was not averse to making connections between his own work and that of the "hyperrealists" in painting, and was happy to write texts for Peter Stämpfli's and Jacques Poli's exhibition catalogues. *Un Cabinet d'amateur* shows off simulated art-historical erudition, based on what was in fact a very wide knowledge of the field; it fitted perfectly into and contributed to one of the images that Perec liked now to project of himself, that of a frustrated painter who had chosen writing as second-best – the inverse of Serge Valène in *Life A User's Manual*, a frustrated storyteller who teaches Bartlebooth how to paint but barely manages to start on the canvas that was already occupied by Perec.

A similarly self-negating motif is handled to more haunting effect in *The Winter Journey*, a four-page short story written towards the end of 1979. It concerns a lost book by someone named Hugo Vernier, also called *The Winter Journey*, which impossibly prefigures the poetry of the later nineteenth century (and thus permits Perec to indulge his talent for cleverly modified quotation whilst simultaneously pursuing his growing interest in poetic form and diction). *The Winter Journey* is one of the most controlled, most densely evocative prose texts that Perec ever wrote, and despite its structural similarity to a Borgesian time-warp tale or to a pirouette by a French Eco, it must count as the finest expression of Perec's verbal art in miniature. Its plot has the form of a wry joke – a man, Vincent Degraël, devotes his life to the search for the life and works of a writer who could not have existed – and in that way it resembles the short-story outlines that constitute the chapter-narratives of *Life A User's Manual*. Like many of those tales, but unlike *Un Cabinet d'amateur*, *The Winter Journey* is the story of a madman (Degraël dies in the psychiatric clinic at Verrières, where Stendhal's *The Red and the Black* begins) bent on a passion that is not mad at all.[1]

These two "looped" texts, to which one could add the slightly later Anglo-French "Still Life/Style Leaf"[2] and "Promenades dans Londres" ("Walks around London" [*inf* 77–87] – a text cobbled together from quotations that encourages the unsuspecting Air France traveller to visit only those parts of London that figure in the works of Jules Verne, Stendhal, and Georges Perec), belong to what is now called postmodernism, or, in a probably more evanescent French jargon, the school of "*néotexte*". All use recursion as a constitutive device; all incorporate other texts ("Still Life/Style Leaf" taking the

---

[1] *The Winter Journey* was published in English translation in London in *Encounter* (July 1985), in New York in *Conjunctions* no. 12 (1988), and in Greensboro (Pa.) in a handprinted limited edition by Post-Industrial Press (1990).

[2] Trans. Harry Mathews, *Yale French Studies* no. 61 (1982), pp. 299–305.

process to a logical conclusion by reincorporating itself); and all resemble to a degree the art of the trick cyclist or the self-absorbed artiste on his high trapeze. Perec had already retold Kafka's story of the trapezist who did not want to come down:[1]

> *The acrobat, in a fit of pride, cut the rope he could have come down by and began to perform, at ever-faster pace, an uninterrupted succession of grand circles. This supreme performance lasted two hours and caused fifty-three spectators to pass out.*   [L 45]

Perec's urge to write did not diminish when *Life A User's Manual* was out of the way. On the contrary, writing now defined Perec almost entirely, and he began to live more and more inside Kafka's acrobat-fantasy. On a trip he made to Saarbrücken and Sankt-Wendel in 1980, for example, Perec missed out on excursions and entertainments because he *needed* to write. He had always admired writers who, like Thomas Mann and Tolstoy, were able to create a whole fictional universe. Perec, for his part, had now created his life in words. His later writings reflect his reluctance to come down from the trapeze, his real difficulty in coming down to earth.

On Perec and "*néotexte*", see (for example) Bernard Magné, "Quelques problèmes de l'énonciation en régime fictionnel: l'exemple de *La Vie mode d'emploi*", in *Pérécollages 1981–1988* (Toulouse: Presses universitaires du Mirail, 1989), pp. 61–98; or, more generally, Jean Ricardou, *Problèmes du nouveau roman* (Paris: Le Seuil, 1978).

Based in part on information provided by Ela Bienenfeld, Catherine Binet, Marie-Claude de Brunhoff, Eugen Helmle, Leo Kornbrust, Julien Etcheverry, and Luc Simon.

---

[1] From "A Fasting Artist," in *Stories 1904–1914*, trans. J. A. Underwood (London: Futura, 1983), p. 231.

CHAPTER 63

Perec the Poet

Georges Perec came to poetry late in life, and by a singularly circuitous path. Like the question of Jewishness, poetry was not on his syllabus between the ages of twenty and forty, or thereabouts. His idea of it, acquired no doubt from French lessons at school, was at the antipodes of all his youthful aspirations: poetry was sentiment, imagination, individuality, whereas what the young man valued was the epic, the real, and irony. Perec's literary identity as a "man of prose" was hardened by his initial position in OuLiPo. Jacques Roubaud had been co-opted first, as the poet of the next generation, and competition could not arise within the group.

Die Maschine, Perec's first Oulipian work, is an intentional derision of poetry, but its pseudo-computerised autopsy of Goethe's lyric goes far beyond that intention. The *Zitatenexplosion* with which the radio play concludes presents a multilingual anthology of poems about silence and death, and in so doing creates its own poetic effect through accumulation, repetition, translation, and rhythm. Had Perec wished, he could have identified exactly the same characteristics in his prose: accumulation (of objects, of descriptions, of adjectives), repetition (of sentence-formulas, of the words of others), translation (of Kafka, Melville, Joyce, and much else) and rhythm (Flaubert's triple rhythm, for instance) characterise Perec's first novels as well as his later prose poems. But there is no reason to suppose that Perec would have been pleased in the 1960s to be considered a poet, even if only a potential one.

The constraint of the lipogram on *e* liberated Perec's narrative imagination: *La Disparition* reassured him that with an adequate restriction he, too, could invent stories and adventures. The constraint of the palindrome, tackled the following year, led Perec towards a particular kind of poetry – the poetry of image, of fractured syntax, of "bursts" of charged words. Still, Perec did not see his Great Palindrome as being poetic until Harry Mathews either needled or bludgeoned his pal into recognising that constrictive form was the tool by which all poetry was made. As we have seen, the first Perec publication to be explicitly labelled as poetic was in English (so to speak), in a special issue of the magazine *Roy Rogers* given over to one-line poems. It was Mathews's idea, but Perec went along with it. The one-line Perec poem, from the middle of the Great Palindrome, is

. . .

From that modest beginning (how modest can one get?) grew a substantial poetic oeuvre which, seen as a whole, redefines the notion of poetry almost entirely. Texts classified as poetry took the place of *Lieux* in the mid-1970s, and from 1978 the reinvention of poetic form was at the centre of Perec's work. His redefinition of the field of poetry, however, also has a retroactive implication for works that we have up to now treated just as prose.

Accumulation is perhaps not in itself a guarantee of poetic effect. It becomes perceptible as a device only when it goes "too far", and Perec knew how to take it always a little further than that, to the point where boredom acquires an intoxicating, rhythmical quality. There are accumulation-poems in nearly every corner of Perec's work, from the whimsical *Espèces d'espaces* (*see* pp. 544–545) to *La Disparition*, from *Life A User's Manual* (in the list of the contents of Madame Altamont's cellar, for instance, on pages 153–155) to *Alphabets*, which is (also) an *accumulation* of the maddeningly exact number of 11 x 16 *onzains* that its design requires. In most cases, accumulation is used in conjunction with other forms, devices, and intentions. It engenders poetry virtually by its own force in the list of everything Perec ate and drank in 1974 [*inf* 97–106], and in the radio broadcast of the people, objects, and vehicles seen over a period of hours at Place Mabillon (*see* p. 640).

The kind of poetry learnt at school has repetition-patterns of pho-nemes (at rhyme-ends), of stress (in English metre), and of number (in French metre, as in twelve-syllable alexandrines). Perec's poetry steps sideways, employing repetition-elements that are predomi-nantly alphabetic. One might say that before OuLiPo, French poetry was first of all a matter of counting up to twelve, whilst Perec makes it as easy as knowing one's ABC.

Perec's variations on the *esartunilo* generator (principally "Ulcér-ations" [1974], *Alphabets* [1974–76], *La Clôture* [1975], and *Métaux* [1976]) gave way, in 1978, to two more ancient alphabetic forms. The first of these, the device of the *belle absente* (*see* p. 644) was used only rarely by Perec, for *Catherine* and for *OuLiPo* [*Atlas* 213].

The complementary repetition-rule, which called for the poem to be made from the letters *present* in the name of the addressee, or the subject, allowed Perec to write far more. *Beaux présents* abound in Perec's occasional writing after 1978; they became his personal form of poetic congratulation and celebration, for which he borrowed the classical term of *epithalamium* (defined by the Oxford English Dictionary as "nuptial song or poem in praise of the bride and bridegroom").

The *beau présent* is an example of what Perec began to call, in 1979–81, *contrainte douce*, or "soft constraint" – that is, a formal rule, but not a fearsomely limiting one. He continued to use and to develop more or less "soft" contraints for the composition of poetry, of which the following is a far from comprehensive list:

> THE PRISONER'S CONSTRAINT. You have only one small piece of paper and want to write the longest message possible on it. In order not to waste paper, you must use only those letters that (in French handwriting) have no "heads" above the line or "tails" below (that is to say, *a, c, e, i, m, n, o, r, s, u, v, w,* and *x*). Example: *ouvre ces serrures caverneuses . . .*
>
> VOCALIC SEQUENCE. Use the vowels as they appear in alphabetic sequence, or in reverse. Example: *Un noir éclat sur son silex mat* [*Atlas* 263–264].
>
> INCREMENTAL LEAPFROG. Write a text such that the first letter reappears in 3rd, 6th, 10th, 15th, 21st (etc.) position, with the gap incrementing by one letter at each leap. Such a text can be typed out as a right-angled triangle, with the hypotenuse made of the key-letter repeated. Example: *A la grave saison* shown on page 690 below.
>
> SNOWBALL. Write a text in which each word has one more character than the previous word (or a poem in which each line has one more word than the previous line). Example in English (by Harry Mathews): "O to see man's stern poetic thought publicly espousing recklessly imaginative mathematical inventiveness . . ."[1]
>
> SQUARE POEM. Write a text measuring 4 x 4 x 4 x 4: letters to word, words to line, lines to stanza, stanzas to poem. Example: "Rail" [*Atlas* 228–229].

[1] Printed in full in Warren Motte, Jr., *Oulipo. A Primer of Potential Literature* (Lincoln: Nebraska University Press, 1986), p. 25.

TAUTOGRAM. Write a text in which all the words begin with the same letter. Example: "Chapitre Cent Cinquante-cinq".

Translation is another and quite special kind of writing under constraint, and the books that Perec translated were themselves the products of constricted form. Translating poetry therefore had a natural place at the centre of Perec's writerly activity, though he was never very sure that he could pull it off. He produced versions of Mathews for an anthology of American poetry published in France, and he would have liked to translate much more. When he was in Australia, in 1981, he made a particular point of scouting for new poets to bring into French.

Perec's espousal of translation as a poetic concern from the mid-1970s on makes the poetic potential of some of his earlier work more apparent. What was PALF, the dictionary exercise with Benabou, if not translation? What are the translations at the centre of *La Disparition* if not poetry? Or the murderous "micro-translations" of Verlaine? Less precisely, the incorporation of modified quotation in *A Man Asleep*, in *Life A User's Manual*, and throughout the rest of Perec's oeuvre is not unrelated to the perception of poetry as being a matter of shifting things around, which is what translators also do, in a sense.

Perec's poetry is associated with his interest in visual art, and more specifically in the visual potential of writing both in and alongside art. *Alphabets* and the original edition of *La Clôture* both contain texts and images; the poems of *Métaux* were written for an artbook, and many of Perec's other poems were published in exhibition catalogues. Perhaps the most rarefied development of Perec's "artpoetry" is to be found in *Trompe-l'œil*, a boxed and unbound book brought out in a limited edition (now a collector's item) consisting of photographs by Cuchi White and short poems by Georges Perec. The colour photographs are doubly deceptive since they all represent walls (or sections of walls) of mostly Italian and English buildings painted in order to fool the eye; the poems, for their part, are "double" in a different way since they are composed in words of the Mathews Corpus and have meaning (well, a kind of meaning, at least) in English and in French simultaneously, and thus deceive the ear as well as the eye.

If Perec's explicit poetry is for the most part not structured by sound-rhythm, many of his so-called prose texts are. The alphabetic generators of his poetry regularise line length, letter repetition, and occasionally word length or number (of poems, of lines, and so on); as a corollary, they fragment syntax, vocabulary, and sound-rhythm. That is why prosaic readers are often reluctant to grant *Alphabets*, "Ulcérations", and the rest the status of "real" poetry. Conversely, the fragmentation of memory in *Je me souviens* and the regularity imposed by all sentences' beginning with the same phrase make that book, unexpectedly and magically, a poem, even by the most prosaic of definitions. Accumulation and repetition combine to achieve a result that goes far beyond the recording of shared recollections. A single "I remember" is not a poem; a dozen "I remember"s are not (yet) a poem. A couple of hundred? Maybe. It was not until number 479 that Perec was sure he had written something that was epic (in its persistence), realistic (in its attention to detail), ironic (in its self-deflations, such as "I've forgotten the rest"), *and also a poem*. The later history of the work is remarkable. The celebrated actor Sami Frey "performed" *Je me souviens* on stage, in a production in which nothing happened except that Frey recited the text as he would a poem whilst riding a bicycle on stationary rollers (in oblique homage to Perec's "*Petit Vélo*"). The show was a huge success, and a revolution. People who, like Perec at the age of twenty, would have turned up their noses at a poetry recital (or a history lecture) sat entranced by a poetry recital that was also a modestly autobiographical lesson in modern history.[1]

Perec's ear for rhythm over long stretches also allowed him to cut up entries from an equipment supplier's catalogue and to rearrange them into a magnificent poem of modern living, at the end of chapter 20 of *Life A User's Manual*. Elsewhere he exploited arithmetical devices to regularise the repetitions of similarly "everyday" material – including kitchen recipes [*PC* 89–108][2] and holiday postcard messages [*inf* 33–67]. The permutational rules of these texts are very simple, and the results would probably be tiresome were it not for two characteristically Perecquian features: exhaustiveness (without which, in the former case, the intoxication of eighty-one recipes each calling for one of only three variations on each of four cooking steps [$3^4=81$] could fall very flat) and disruption, through the introduction

---

[1] Sami Frey's recital of *Je me souviens* has been published as a cassette by Editions des Femmes.

[2] In English as "81 Easy-Cook Recipes for Beginners", trans. David Bellos, *RCF*, pp. 34–43.

(particularly in the second case) of naggingly insignificant alterations of the formulas used.

The attention to sound-rhythm is a consistent feature of Perec's prose, especially of the later period. The most rigorously rhythmical of all of Perec's texts is the Franco-German stage-and-radio play, *L'Augmentation*, but *Life A User's Manual* also works surprisingly well as a recitation-text.[1] However, the commentary that Perec wrote for the first episode of the film that he made with Robert Bober about Ellis Island (the second episode consists of the interviews with former emigrants) represents perhaps the furthest point that he reached in the development of a rhythmic but not formally regulated language for voice performance. The text was not finalised until the filming was complete and it was designed to be read as a voice-over by Perec himself. In the published book of the film, his poetic intention is signalled by a layout that looks like free verse. Accumulation, repetition, the mixture of languages, aural rhythm and a discreet, Oulipian decoration (picked out here in boldface) mark many passages of Perec's "alternative autobiography" as high points of modern poetic prose, or verse. For these reasons we must at last listen to Perec speaking in French:

> *pendant toutes ces années, les navires à vapeur de la Cunard Line, de la Red Star Line, de l'Anchor Line, de l'Italian Line, de la Hamburg-Amerika Line, de la Holland-Amerika Line, sillonèrent l'Atlantique nord*

> *Ils partaient de **R**otterdam, de **B**rême, de **G**öteborg, de **P**alerme, d'**I**stanbul, de **N**aples, d'**A**nvers, de Liverpool, de Lübeck, de Salonique, de Bristol, de Riga, de Cork, de Dunkerque, de Stettin, de Hambourg, de Marseille, de Gênes, de Danzig, de Cherbourg, du Pirée, de Trieste, de Londres, de Fiume, du Havre, d'Odessa, de Tallinn, de Southampton*

> *ils s'appelaient le* Darmstadt, *le* Fürst Bismarck, *le* Staatendam, *le* Kaiser Wilhelm, *le* Königin Luise, *le* Westernland, *le* Pennland, *le* Bohemia, *le* Polynesia, *le* Prinzess Irene, *le* Princeton, *l'*Umbria, *le* Lusitania, *l'*Adriatic, *le* Coronia, *le*

---

[1] A serialised version recorded at performances at the Avignon Festival in 1988 (adapted and produced by René Farabet) has been broadcast twice by France-Culture.

Mauretania, *le* San Giovanni, *le* Giuseppe Verdi, *le* Patricia, *le* Duca degli Abruzzi, *le* New Amsterdam, *le* Martha Washington, *le* Turingia, *le* Titanic, *le* Lidia, *le* Susquehanna, *l'*Albert-Balin, *le* Hansington, *le* Columbus, *le* Reliance, *le* Blücher

> *mais la plupart de ceux qui, au terme*
> *de leur harassant voyage, découvraient Manhattan*
> *émergeant de la brume, savaient que leur épreuve*
> *n'était pas tout à fait terminée*

> *il leur fallait encore passer par Ellis Island*
> *cette île que,*
> *dans toutes les langues d'Europe*
> *on a surnommée l'île des larmes*

> *tränen insel*
> *vispa pleatchou*
> *island of tears*
> *isola delle lacrime*
> *'to nisson ton' sakrion*
> *ostrov slosz*
> *traieren insel*

The centre of *Life A User's Manual* is a poem that has been mentioned several times already. The 179 lines describing the elements in Valène's imagined painting of 11 Rue Simon-Crubellier comprise a showpiece of many types of constraint used elsewhere in Perec's poetry, all overlaid on each other. The "Compendium" is doubly regulated by number (in that it consists of three letter-squares, each 60 x 60);[1] it is ordered by letter-repetition (since it forms an acrostic); it is an exercise in accumulation (of story outlines), in repetition (of the formula, of phrasing), and in rhythm; and, finally, it is deregulated – at the end, like everything else that is central to Perec's great novel – by an archetypal clinamen, a voided last line that would have made it too "perfect". It is a remarkable achievement on each of these scores, but its point is strikingly simple, as simple as that of *Die*

---

[1] Spaces between words, hyphens, and commas counting as characters, as on a typewriter keyboard.

Maschine: to say that poetry is precisely what *cannot* quite be said out loud, a "soft breathing" spelled out here in the word AME ("soul") and represented in the story of the Golem by an aleph pronounced as an *e*.

Perec pursued poetry with increasing intensity after 1978, and tended either to soften or to mask the alphabetical constraints involved. *La Clôture et autres poèmes* was the first book he published with Hachette/P.O.L. after *Life A User's Manual*, and to the displeasure of some, it omits the letter-box grids displayed in earlier publications of his isogrammatic poetry. It represents the next stage in the long argument amongst the members of OuLiPo, and in Perec's own mind, about "hiding" and "showing", and the form chosen reflects Perec's growing wish to be read as a poet, and indeed to be one, outside and beyond the technical exploits and props he had used to unlock his poetic soul. It had been a long and circuitous journey, in the course of which he had redefined writing, fashioned brand-new tools, and refurbished many older ones, but he did, in the end, see the distant shore. He wrote two poems without any constraint, just like that. One is called "Un poème" [*Clô* 85]; the other is called "L'Eternité".

Beaux Présents

The "soft-constraint" poetry that Perec composed out of the letters in the name of the person being addressed, or celebrated (or in one case, the letters of the poem's subject, "Farewell to Venice"), are works of circumstance, and were mostly printed or duplicated in small numbers of copies for the people involved. With two exceptions, all of the poems commemorate happy occasions (exhibitions, marriages, anniversaries, or birthdays). The list that follows contains all the *beaux présents* by Perec that I have been able to find; republication details are given where appropriate. Three of the poems have been translated by Harry Mathews (*Paris Review* no. 112 [Winter 1989]), who has also used the device in one of his own poems in English – following a precedent set by Ben Jonson and John Donne.

"Epithalame pour l'exposition de Claude Berge"
  For an exhibition of Berge's sculptures, "Personnages insolites", 21 April
  – 21 May 1978.
"11 x (11+11) + 11"
  In *Jacques Poli: Peintures entomologiques, 1978–1979*, pp. 16–18. Paris:
  Galerie Adrien Maeght, 1979.
"A Marie-France Mitrofanoff"
  For an exhibition of paintings at Galerie de la FRAC, April–May 1980.
  In *Anthologie arbitraire d'une nouvelle poésie française, 1960–1982*, ed. Michel
  Deguy, p. 210. Paris: Flammarion, 1982.
"A Marie-Jeanne Hoffenbach"
  For an exhibition of paintings at Galerie de la FRAC, April–May 1980.
"Epithalame pour Marc Cholodenko"
  11 May 1980. In Deguy, *Anthologie arbitraire*, p. 213.
"Epithalame pour Frank Venaille"
  14 May 1980. In Deguy, *Anthologie arbitraire*, p. 211.
"Epithalame de Sophie Binet et Michel Dominault"
  Written for their marriage on 24 May 1980. In Deguy, *Anthologie arbitraire*,
  p. 215. Also in Georges Perec, "Epithalames", pp. 9–10. Paris: La Bibli-
  othèque Oulipienne, number 19, 1982. Reprinted in *La Bibliothèque oulipienne*, vol. 2, pp. 5–6. Paris: Editions Ramsay, 1987

"Elégie de Pierre et de Denise Getzler"
6 June 1980. *Art-presse*, no. 39 (July-August 1980), p. 14.

"Texte lu aux noces d'Alix-Cléo Blanchette et de Jacques Roubaud"
15 June 1980. In Perec, "Epithalames", pp. 13–14. Reprinted in *La Bibliothèque Oulipienne*, vol. 2, pp. 9–10.

"A Jacques Vallet"
Le Fou parle, no. 14 (October 1980), p. 4.

"Le Pacte"
For Titi and Jean-Luc Parant. *Le Bout des bordes*, no. 5/6 (29 October – 29 November 1980), p. 19.

"Alphabet pour Stämpfli"
In *Peter Stämpfli. Œuvres récentes*, catalogue of an exhibition at the Centre Georges Pompidou, Paris, 26 November 1980–11 January 1981.

"Anagrammes de Georges Condominas"
In *Orients: Mélanges offerts à Georges Condominas pour ses soixante ans*. Paris: Sudestasie/Privat, 1981.

"Noce de Kmar Bendana & Noureddine Mechri"
15 August 1981. Nineteen typed copies numbered A–S handmade by Georges Perec at the University of Queensland on 2–3 September 1981. In Perec, "Epithalames", pp. 15–26. Reprinted in *La Bibliothèque oulipienne*, vol. 2, pp. 13–22.

"Adieu à Venise"
Written in Brisbane, September 1981. *Action poétique*, no. 88 (1982), unnumbered page.

"jfa"
For Jean-François Adam
In *Index*, Ecole Normale Supérieure de Saint-Cloud, March 1982.

CHAPTER 64

Fifty-three Days in Australia

By the end of 1979 nearly all of Perec's friends had responded to his appeal for funds for Les Films du Nautile and there was almost enough in the kitty to shoot *Les Jeux de la Comtesse Dolingen de Gratz*. Countess Dolingen, who is actually seen in the film for barely fifteen seconds, is a character taken from *Dracula* (it is she who saves Jonathan Harker, the narrator-hero, from a horrible death on Walpurgisnacht), but there is a more insistent allusion in the film to Bram Stoker's classic horror story: "The Dead Travel Fast".

Since the script called for location shots including trees in full leaf, plans were laid for filming in late summer 1980. The financing of the film remained touch-and-go to the last minute, and Perec took on some writing jobs in 1980 for straightforward pecuniary reasons – for example, contracting to write four articles for the in-flight magazine of Air France to defray the cost of first-class transatlantic travel for one of the film's leading actresses. (Only two of the set [*inf* 69–76 and 77–87] were actually written.) But although film finance was a major headache throughout 1980 it did not stop Perec from pressing forward on many other fronts. He completed his translation of Mathews's *The Sinking of the Odradek Stadium*, a model of witty and creative transposition; turned out two erudite spoofs, one in collaboration with his goddaughter Sylvia [*CSL* 34–52], the other [*CSL* 53–66] for the cartoonist Gotlib, a great admirer of *Life A User's Manual* (there was even some discussion of Gotlib's transforming "Mr Eveready" into a cartoon strip); experimented with permutated fragmentation in "Fragments de désert et de culture" ("Fragments of Desert and Culture") and with a new kind of elision of fiction and reality in "J.R.: Tentative de saturation onomastique" ("J.R.: Attempt at Onomastic Saturation"); and of course continued to turn out his crosswords every week for *Le Point*. Perec also collaborated with Jacques Bens on other kinds of games-and-puzzle columns for magazines including *Télérama*, *Jeune-Afrique* and *Ça m'intéresse*, the latter now run by one of the earliest ex-members of Lg, Jean-Pierre Sergent. If Perec's film-producer months were far from barren from a literary point of view, there was nonetheless a large overlap between the prospectus of work "for the years to come" that he had handed to Paul Otchakovsky-Laurens in December 1976 and the answers that he gave in a piece published in 1980 under the unadorned title "Questions Réponses" ("Questions Answers").

QUESTION: What is it, inside or outside of literature, that makes you write?

ANSWER: *Perhaps, above all, nowadays, it is the force of habit, a kind of inertia that makes me go on with something that began sufficiently long ago for the question to be no longer "what makes me write" but "how far have I got in my schedule?" Anyway, what else could I do but write?*

QUESTION: What is your plan of work for the next ten years?

ANSWER: *First of all, there are things to finish off straightaway – this piece for instance.*

Then there are day-by-day things, what I call my "scales" (short anagrammatic or heterogrammatic or lipogrammatic or homophonic texts, etc.), or the composition of crosswords (making up the grids, looking for definitions), or updating and sorting out of things that are already quite old, or things to put in order, to revise, to collect;

then things that are more or less in progress to get properly launched or finished off at last, but that don't all depend entirely on me: translations (Mathews, maybe one day Ashbery), film scripts (mostly vague projects that rarely attract the interest of producers), a text about Getzler's "studio landscapes", a text for Gérard Guyomard, a book with Jacques Poli, another one with Le Boulch', an "offcut" for Emmanuel Hocquard, a radio play, etc.;

then plans that are beginning to take shape, to be filled out: one of the sequels of Choses communes, *called* L'Herbier des Villes *("The Urban Herbarium"); then a kind of "family romance" that has been in progress for years; a perhaps epistolary novel narrating the journey made by Klee, Moilliet, and Macke to Tunisia in April 1914;*

then "New Year's Resolution" projects: to go back to writing for the stage, to write short stories;

then things that are still pretty vague: a "pillow book" inspired by Sei Shonagon, Lieux où j'ai dormi, *a text on Kafka (a bestiary), a play using all of and only the 2,000 most common sentences in the French language, as established by a Swiss linguist;*

then desires, some of which are nagging ones, but which nothing has yet come to nourish: to write books for children, adventure stories for adolescents, detective stories (with mysteries), science-fiction stories, and a three-hander with Calvino and Mathews;

then things that might have been done, haven't been done, but perhaps could be done: the libretto of L'Art effaré, for Philippe Drogoz, the "Dix-sept Vues du canal de l'Ourcq" on prints (yet to be done) by Pierre Getzler, a "novel of the nineteenth century" incorporating and unifying extracts from an anthology of French literature from Madame de Staël to Emile Zola, etc.;

then distant plans, for later on: to tell the the story of the life of General Eblé, to resume the "Ninipotch Fragments" begun around the age of twenty, to write a "Daily Life in the Age of the Stage-coach", to write a book on the Golem (which I have never really read);

and then also, from time to time: to read

Etc.[1]

The "year of the film" was also marked by an illustrious harvest for the grim reaper. Roland Barthes was knocked down by a car in front of the Sorbonne and died a few days later, on 6 March 1980. Not long after, Jean-Paul Sartre, who had been in declining health for some years, passed away. Before the shooting of *Les Jeux de la Comtesse Dolingen de Gratz* began, another, more bizarre shock occurred on the Left Bank. Louis Althusser, the philosophy don at Ecole Normale Supérieure who had taught a whole generation of left-wing intellectuals now in their forties and fifties, strangled his wife and was interned in a psychiatric hospital. Savage wits declared that he had at last done something that the proletariat could understand. Perec, for his part, was most upset and late one night telephoned his old left-wing friend Marie-Noëlle Thibault. He sounded hyperexcited, half drunk, possibly even in a dangerous state, so Marie-Noëlle got up, drove across Paris to Rue Linné, and took Perec out for a night ride, to calm him down. Tears were streaming down Perec's face, for he could barely stop giggling over the vicious pun he had just invented: *Althusser trop fort!* [2]

---

[1] *Action poétique*, no. 81 (May 1980), pp. 38–39.

[2] "Althusser [is] too strong" → "Al! tu serres trop fort" → "Al, you're pressing too hard!"

Perec had thought of collaborating on a series of children's books with Jacques Roubaud some years before, and had approached the firm of Nathan for an advance. "Show us some first," he was told. The project never got off the ground, but a similar idea arose over dinner with Laurent de Brunhoff, whose Babar albums sold in huge numbers in France and abroad. A new series with Brunhoff drawings and Perec texts would be a guaranteed world-beater! Laurent asked Perec for a story-line, to get his visual imagination into gear. Perec wrote his text for tots in tiny writing on both sides of a filing card only 125 x 75 millimetres in size:

There was once a little man who was so little that no one could see him. It was a great nuisance for him.

I can't even tell you what he was called because nobody had thought to give him a name – since nobody had ever seen him. And the mannikin was all alone and sad. It was no good shouting at people in his loudest voice; he was so little and his voice so small that no one saw or heard him. "Hey, Sir!" "Psst, Lady!" he would shout with all his might, but it was no use at all.

All the same, the mannikin thought to himself, it's not right, there must be somewhere more comfortable for a chap like me.

And that is how the little man got the idea of going to the four corners of the big wide world.

And when I say the big wide world, I mean it really was big and wide.

To give you an idea, for him a flea was the size of an elephant, an umbrella like a Boing 747, a match the size of a sequoia, a grain of sand like a lump of rock, a postage stamp like a huge carpet, and a saucer as big as Wembley Stadium (he held the world record for one-millimetre hurdles).

Being so small in a world so large was not without its benefits. Every morning the mannikin took a bath in a dewdrop (Please turn over)

(for he was as clean as he was tiny), and he breakfasted on a quarter of a half of a third of a tenth of a segment of milk chocolate (for he was a little guzzler, too). Then he dressed. He was very elegant and took great care with his clothes. He had a very smart suit of a thread of raw wool, a greatcoat made out of a rose petal, a bonnet of artichoke fur, and a delightful tie made from a blade of baby grass.

And so on the day our story begins, after taking his bath in a dewdrop, breakfasting on a quarter of a half of a third of a tenth of a segment of milk chocolate, and putting on his suit, his greatcoat, his bonnet, and his tie (he always put on his tie last), the mannikin set off on his way. But first he filled his pockets with his three greatest treasures: a flask of ticklemetose, a packet of adirondacks, and a magnificent three-hole flute which had been custom-made for him from the quill of the littlest wattle of the tiniest feather of the minutest

hummingbird ever seen. Then he caught the first dragonfly that passed. Fortu-
nately it wasn't too crowded, and he had no trouble in finding a seat.

The "vague projects" for film scripts mentioned in Perec's "answers" included an adaptation of Stefan Zweig's chess-novel, *The Royal Game* (under the title *Dumbo*) and two different conceptions of transposing *La Disparition* to the screen. The conundrum was to identify the "alphabet" of film so as to be able to omit one of its elements, in imitation of the lipogram: the unconvincing solution that he came up with in a proposal for a film to be called *Signe particulier néant* ("Distinguishing Features Nil") was the "constraint" of a story told on screen without the faces of any the characters ever being seen. Another, more developed version was entitled *Vous souvenez-vous de Griffin?* ("Do you remember Griffin?") – Griffin being the usually forgotten name of H. G. Wells's "invisible man".

As far as can be told, the three projects that were at the forefront of Perec's mind as he emerged from his period as a film producer were the "Urban Herbarium", for which he collected and began to sort the diverse kinds of loose bumph (*feuilles volantes*, or "flying leaves", in French) that an observant city dweller can pick up on the forest floor; the "family romance" begun long before as *L'Arbre*; and a detective novel, for which Perec signed a contract with P.O.L. in February 1981. Taken together, the three projects fit fairly well into the fourfold crop-rotation model that Perec had conceived for his literary farm in his 1976 prospectus and again in the *Figaro* article of 1978. The "social" Perec would grow in *L'Herbier des Villes*, the autobiographer would reap the long-planted field of the "family romance", and the narrator would bud again in the detective novel, in which a new game would be offered to the reader, under apparently familiar rules. Perec was ready to move forward along paths that he had prepared for himself, even if the turns that those paths would take, in works that were still to be written, would add new vistas to the landscape of his oeuvre.

Shot in the summer of 1980, edited in the autumn, shown privately in the first months of the new year, *Les Jeux de la Comtesse* went to Cannes in May 1981. Its producer and financier wrote an introduction for the press:

> *There are two distinct levels in* Les Jeux de la Comtesse Dolingen
> de Gratz. *The first level could be called "real": it is the story of a*

separated couple; the abandoned wife, Louise, makes films (and acts them out inside her head), whilst the husband takes lonely refuge in his country house and in his obsession with sculptures of angels, which he collects. The second level, explicitly presented as fictional, is a story written by a little girl who dies of love in the end. Very soon however the two levels begin to overlap and to merge, and a network or system of alternately transparent and obscure, tenuous and arbitrary correspondences entwines the two tales as if, despite their being very different at the start, they were the two sides of the same coin, mirror images reflecting in minutely changing light the same themes and motifs: loneliness, silence, attentiveness and seclusion . . .

This special nesting automatically arouses a kind of disturbance, a feeling of the uncanny in which the very preciseness of gestures, the strict, punctilious organisation of details, and the establishment of an unseen network of meanings bring all the film's elements together and seem to suggest, without ever pointing to it explicitly, an endpoint beyond which the two tales, welded together by the extremity and clarity of their desire, would form a single story.

One enters this film as one enters a labyrinth in which a few well-placed mirrors suffice to create the illusion of an infinite number of paths. Here they include prints of Jules Verne and Hans Bellmer, red roses, locks and keys, white veils lightly ruffled by wind, and a hundred other plays on image and sound, making a puzzle whose pieces must be collected by the viewer. At the end of the journey, when time and space no longer quite obey the normal rules, where Edgar Poe answers Dracula and Captain Nemo responds to Bluebeard, what remains in all its violence and emotion is the story of a love so strong that it turned to crime, to suicide and maybe madness, before being turned into a film.

Although it was favourably received as a work of film art, *Les Jeux* did not appeal to commercial distributors, and there seemed little prospect of Les Films du Nautile ever getting its investment back. Perec, for his part, had already arranged to live cheaply for most of 1981. Invitations to speak in diverse places had been arriving in the letterbox at Rue Linné in increasing quantities ever since the publication of *Life A User's Manual* and the award of the Médicis Prize, but only when Catherine's film was finished did Perec allow himself to take up any more than occasional engagements away from home.

By the end of 1980, however, he was free of material obligations towards the film, and since his principal resource (his royalties from Hachette) had been largely swallowed up by Les Films du Nautile, he also needed to live as much as possible for free. Perec therefore spent a good part of 1981 on a wandering trail mapped out for him by academic and cultural agencies offering him his travel costs and living expenses. In February, he went with Harry Mathews to give a talk at the Maison de la Culture in Grenoble, wincing when he was introduced to the audience not as a writer but as *le scripteur*.[1] In April he travelled to Poland, with the poet Claude Roy, at the expense of the French government (*see* p. 8). In Warsaw, he was interviewed in French by a perceptive young critic who asked him whether, as a Jew of Eastern European extraction, he recognised himself in what Kafka had said in one of his letters to Milena:

> *We both know, after all, enough typical examples of Western Jews, I am as far as I know the most typical Western Jew among them. This means, expressed with exaggeration, that not one calm second is granted me, nothing is granted me, everything has to be earned, not only the present and the future, but the past too – something after all which perhaps every human being has inherited, this too must be earned, it is perhaps the hardest work.*[2]

Perec was so struck by the question that he copied out the whole quotation in a letter he wrote to Ela, saying that it really was time he got down to writing *L'Arbre*, but perhaps without paying too much heed to history or to the reminiscences of those Bienenfeld relatives and connections, such as Aunt Ada and Tournier (the former accountant of the JBSA) who were still alive. As if to prompt him to take up once again his family saga, the arms of the town of Lubartów, which he had just visited, consisted of two lions on either side of a *tree*. In answering his interviewer, Perec naturally welcomed a quotation from Kafka as a definition of himself:

> *I think that corresponds exactly to what I could state on my own behalf.*

[1] The talk was published as "Ce qui stimule ma racontouze: entretien avec Claudette Oriol-Boyer le 18 février 1981", *Textes en main*, no. 1 (1984), pp. 49–59.

[2] *Letters to Milena*, trans. Tania and James Stern (London: Penguin Books, 1983), p. 174.

In the book I am going to write about the history of my family, which I have been planning for a long time, I can put that very precisely as an epigraph. When I say that nothing is given to me, that I have to acquire everything, that's what I wrote at the end of Espèces d'espaces. *I have no house, no family, I have no attic, so to speak, I have no roots, I don't know what they are.* [1]

In fact, the epigraph Perec had chosen for *L'Arbre* long before was a line from Alfred de Vigny: "Si j'écris leur histoire, ils descendront de moi" ("If I write their history they will be my descendants").

In the spring of 1981 Perec said to Catherine, *I'm going to Australia to write a book in fifty-three days.* The invitation to spend a period as writer-in-residence at the University of Queensland had in fact been made the previous year by Jean-Michel Raynaud, a lecturer in the French Department at Brisbane; with the writer's agreement, he put up Perec's name to the Australia Council for one of its coveted, nine-week Visiting Writer awards. Although that bid failed, the University of Queensland had already set aside a sum of money for Perec's visit; in addition, the French government was willing to pay the writer's fare provided he also spoke at other Australian universities; and so in the spring of 1981 a composite deal was put together, calling for Perec to spend one month in residence at St Lucia, the Brisbane campus, and a further three weeks on tour. What with the long flights out and back, Perec would be away for exactly fifty-three days, the same length of time as Stendhal had taken to dictate his last work, *The Charterhouse of Parma.* The Australian schedule only became precise after Perec's return from Poland, but it was probably in anticipation of it that he had already signed a contract with P.O.L. for a new novel, already entitled "*53 Days*". On 4 May 1981, Perec wrote to Raynaud:

I'm just beginning my long dance of hesitation around a text which will perhaps end up as a novel; that is my dearest wish, at any rate. At all events, according to my schedule I should write a good part of it in Australia.

[1] Ewa Pawlikowska, interview with Georges Perec, *Littératures* (Toulouse) 7 (1983), p. 76. (The interview was first published in Polish translation in *Literature na Swiece* (Warsaw) no. 12 (1982), pp. 337–355.)

It is not clear how much work Perec actually did on the book before he left for Australia at the end of August. What is certain is that he did a great number of other things in the intervening months, as he always did. He was overjoyed at François Mitterrand's election victory on 10 May 1981 and joined in the public celebrations at Place de la Bastille. He spent ten days working on a film script with Pascal Aubier at Veules-les-Roses,[1] finished a remarkable article on "thinking and sorting" for an issue of *Le Genre humain* (the typescript was handed to the editor, Maurice Olender, on 2 July), went to Albi to speak at a conference on "space and representation", taught at the Oulipo summer school at Villeneuve-lès-Avignon, and dashed over to Hammam-Lif for the wedding of his old friend Noureddinne Mechri (*but when's Zghal going to get here?* he kept on asking, but his other Tunisian pal from Etampes never turned up); he could hardly have had time to turn around on the spot before leaving again on Friday, 28 August, for Bahrain (*see* p. 18), Sydney (a one-night stop), and Brisbane, where he landed on Monday, 31 August, to take up his duties as writer in residence for the month of September, in the antipodean and subtropical spring. Back in Paris in late October, he made a one-day dash to Copenhagen for a lecture and then set off again on a speaking tour of Italy in November. In December, he stayed overnight in Rouen after a showing of one of his films at Petit-Quévilly, and spent Christmas at Chambroutet. It was a glamorous and exciting programme for the year, but also a punishing routine.

Perec was picked up at Brisbane airport by Raynaud, who drove him to his temporary digs at Spot Flats, a block of self-catering units so named because the owners had thought fit to advertise their property by painting polychrome spots all over the outside walls. Perec's room overlooked the Brisbane River, if you stretched your neck a bit, and gave a more direct view of the mail-sorting office. It was Perec's choice to live alone; he did not want to be a burden on his hosts.

The next day Raynaud took him to the campus at St Lucia and showed him his office in the pink sandstone quad.

---

[1] An adaptation of Michel Martens's novel, *Adieu ma mie*, renamed *Adieu la vie* and subsequently *A Tire d'aile*.

Dear Catherine:

[. . .] My office is very large. I can spread myself out. I have the use of a typewriter so heavenly that I am dreaming of buying one like it for myself. The purple jacaranda flowers are beginning to come out and I've seen orchids like never before.

Bye Bye registra mia[1]

G

Raynaud's electronic Olivetti ET 221 had page-memory and a daisy-wheel printer. Raynaud offered to lend it to Perec, but as the writer did not dare take it back to his room, he spent most of his time in Raynaud's office, learning to use the machine. He soon produced a poetry booklet and a beautifully laid out announcement of his writing workshop on gadgetry that he mastered with voluptous intensity.

Dear Harry & Mary:

It's a fine life, the life of a writerinresidence, *even if it is occasionally too lonesome. I'm working fairly well, getting about a bit, and I'll get about even more in the first half of October.*

I'm doing an Oulipo workshop that is going very well and the further developments *of which will perhaps amount to an invitation for four or five Oulipians to come out to run a polyglot workshop for a fortnight or so [. . .]*

The attached text in O seems to me to be a masterpiece whose dying fall is as fine as if not finer than the Sistine ceiling. Did it almost all on my tod, cross my heart and swear to die, without a dictionary, in two hours flat! Am astonishé. *Since then, I've found dozens of words in Webster's. I thank you, Harry, for having made me make such progress in English*

So long folks

Lov

G

Perec's only duty at Brisbane was to teach one class a week, on Friday afternoons. Most of the staff of the department attended, as did a visiting professor from England (*see* p. 369) and a clutch of final-year students. Perec took them through the basic Oulipian principles, but his main aim was to get his class writing, under constraint.

Students of French at the University of Queensland in the

---

[1] In this and subsequent quotations from Perec's letters, words in roman type are as they appear in the original.

MORTON'S OB.

Poor Morton Longford Thornton (so good sport, DSO,
honor.shortstop of Boston's Kobolds)...

To hop-scotch from Oxford to Toronto, door-to-door,
took two months, non-stop !
So cold, downtown !
Took two hot bowls of grog, 'cos O'Connor's scotch's
too strong (no Gordon's, nor Old Crow, nor Rosso
d'Orgosolo).

Fond of good food, soon holds powwow to look for
Woolworth's worth-of goods.
From noon to two o'clock, got frost frogs (no odors...),
pop-corn, good Old Port, box of "bonbons", lots of
voodoo worms, cow chops, coco roots, pot of Morgon
(sort of...), common hot-dogs, corn on cobs, softs,
doz.of sorgho rolls, cool borsch...

Follows to borrow from Mormon folks two forks, two
spoons, Color-TV, Oblomov, snow-proof boots, Soho go-go
dolls, formol, shocks, stocks & bonds, Pogo, fox-trots,
Rock'n Roll songbook, Wordsworth's, Doctor Spock's,
orthodox ponchos, Mongol cookbooks, Orlon golf socks,
Tlooth, oz.of bolts, rococo combs...

Slow now ! Stop ! Got no room & short of gold !! Toss
on odd. Won ? No, don't know how : lost. OK ?

Cops go on. Frown. Scowl. Don't nod. Told Thornton's
wrong. Don't co-op nor comfort.
Sobs.
Got shot.
Lost blood.
Knock down for good...

So long now, poor poor Morton Longford Thornton...

O, Mom's Son, born for Crown of Thorns & Cross, Who
proctors floods & storms, O, Lord, from Whom crowds of
morons look for Horn to blow on Doom's, show sorrow,
stoop and bow, tomorrow, to drop two words on Poor
Morton's tomb ! Broom off gloom of fog, throw down
ghosts of no-good & horror ! Don't lock front-doors of
World's Roof, O, Son of God, Who condocts Chords of
Swords & Words !

                                        GP

```
A
LA
GRA
VESA
ISONA
CCOMPA
GNELESA
RCHERSDA
MERIQUEDA
NSLEURINFA
MEETDETESTA
BLEPEREGRINA
TIONSOISLECHA
MPIONDELEUREXA
CTESOLITUDELECA
LMEBLOCCHUDUDESA
STREOBSCURDESORMA
ISPORTEURDUNSENSCA
MOUFLETEMONTRELEFFA
REMENTDETONREVESITRA
NQUILLEUNENUITDECHIRA
NTETECOUTELESILENCEORA
GEUXDESINDIENSIROQUOISA
QUELQUECHOSEDEGROTESQUEA
VECCESETOILESINFINITESIMA
LESCESTUNDESERTDEPIERRESCA
SSEESENMILLIONSDEPETITSECLA
TSMEURTRIERSOUNULETRENEVIVRA
```

A la grave saison accompagne les archers d'Amérique dans leur infâme & détestable pérégrination. Sois le champion de leur exacte solitude. Le calme bloc chu du désastre obscur désormais porteur d'un sens camouflé te montre l'effarement de ton rêve si tranquille. Une nuit déchirante t'écoute. Le silence orageux des Indiens Iroquois a quelque chose de grotesque avec ces étoiles infini-tésimales. C'est un désert de pierres cassées en millions de petits éclats meurtriers où nul être ne vivra.....

Georges Perec

** ATELIER OULIPIEN **

*Writing workshop
led by*

GEORGES PEREC
*French writer
at present visiting the French Department*

ALL WELCOME!

*The first meeting of those interested in participating in the workshop
will be held on Friday 4th September
from 3 pm to 5 pm in room 86.6 (French Department).*

Regular time will be arranged at this meeting.

(southern) spring of 1981 learnt how to write tautograms, univocalics and *beaux présents* from an unrivalled master of those forms. Some of their efforts were rather good, and Perec presented them to OuLiPo on his return. He also got the class to help him with his detective novel, setting as a problem the expansion of Stendhal's famous definition of the novel as "a mirror paraded along a road" after it was reduced to a Roussellian structure with only the first letters of the main words left in (indicated here in bold face):

Un **R**oman est un **m**iroir qui se **p**romène le **l**ong de la **r**oute
Un R est un M qui se P le L de la R

The procedure could be simulated in English by:

A Novel is a Mirror that you Hold to Life
A N is a M that you H to L

which would permit reexpansions such as "A name is a moniker that you hesitate to lengthen", "A neurosis is a maladjustment that you heighten to lyricism", "A novelist is a manipulator that you have to lampoon", and so on. Amongst the many expansions that Perec brought back from Australia are *Un roman est un miracle qui se prophétise le leitmotiv de la résonance* ("A novel is a miracle foretelling for itself the theme of resonance") and *Un romancier est un maniaque qui se propose le lemme de la réalité* ("A novelist is a maniac who sets himself the lemma of reality") [*53D* 210].

Perec got to know no one in Brisbane outside the university. He went in to his office most days, and joined the other members of his department for lunch. They would take postprandial strolls together around the lush campus, over lawns where plovers pecked, past strange subtropical trees, such as the kapok, which Perec dubbed the "'esticle tree" (*l'arbre à 'ouilles*) for its spherical and grossly pendulous pods. Perec did not talk a great deal about his current work, but he listened to conversations about university business and academic anxieties over the policies of the Walter-Mittyish peanut farmer who had been the premier of Queensland for a decade already. There were dark rumours about the stadium that was being constructed for the 1982 Commonwealth Games.

Perec was extremely grateful to Brisbane for giving him a month of peace in which he could live exclusively as a writer. He had planned his thank-you gift before leaving Paris, and had brought with him manuscripts of his poem for Stämpfli and of the "Epithalames", one of the preparatory sheets for chapter 50 of *Life A User's Manual*, the proofs of *La Clôture*, photocopies of typescripts of as-yet-unpublished poems, offprints of rare items (such as "Experimental Demonstration", Perec's one piece up to that time in quasi-English), and the famous 1975 photograph of OuLiPo, as well as copies of most of his published books, to donate to the university library. These artifacts served first of all for an exhibition of the works of the current writer in residence, who, with unprecedented modesty, insisted on organising and laying out the exhibits and typing up all the legend-cards himself. Shortly before the exhibition was due to open, Ann Freadman, a colleague in the French Department, came over to the library to see how Perec was getting on. It was all done; Perec had slipped away already. She granted herself a private viewing of the manuscripts and books, and had quite a shock when she came to the last item in the case, a copy of *Un Cabinet d'amateur*. The legend read:

HIS LAST NOVEL

Ann rushed to find Perec, to explain to him the difference between "latest" and "last" and to make him change the card. Perec did not like making mistakes in English. He looked glum, and then grinned evasively and said, *It's too late now, anyway*.

Perec's temporary colleagues – Jean-Michel Raynaud, Ann Freadman, Peter Cryle, Keith Atkinson, Christine Mestre, and others – were hospitable and generous with their time, and as a result, Perec saw most of the sights of the Brisbane area. He was given a tour of the "Three Faces of Paradise" comprising (1) a lake and waterfall in the forest, where Tarzan must have first seen Jane take a dip; (2) a hilltop road with views of the ocean and the forest, called Paradise Avenue; and (3) Surfer's Paradise, an Australian version of Miami Beach. He went down to Sandgate (This Beach is Not Shark-Proof! says the sign) and looked out from the jetty towards Moreton Island. He went for a walk in the rain-forest at Manorina National Park (during which he grumbled that he couldn't seem to catch his breath), and for long car rides in search of roaming marsupials, which he claimed had really been invented by a worldwide conspiracy of zoos. Perec did not seem truly interested in what he saw. The long car rides were more an excuse for chatting, nearly always about one or another of the three things that were uppermost in Perec's mind at that time: his friends, Jacques Roubaud and Harry Mathews in particular; Catherine and her film; and *Life A User's Manual*. What he most often remarked upon as he was whisked through the spectacular and varied scenery of Queensland was material he had already put in his book. But the southern roadside scene also turned out to allude directly to *Les Jeux de la Comtesse Dolingen de Gratz*, as he reported in a letter to Catherine:

> *Seen at speed, from a car, on a signpost, a poster with the words* "The Dead Travel Fast"*! Before I twigged properly,* we were far away!

Australian road safety campaigners had probably lifted the phrase, as Catherine had, from Bram Stoker, who for his part had borrowed it from one of the most popular German ballads of the eighteenth century, Gottfried August Bürger's *Lenore*. So there was really nothing new in Perec's use of modified quotation in his fiction – except for the degree of conscious control.

The department was taken aback by the way their visiting writer behaved. He was not like the previous occupant of the post, Michel Butor, a nervous, defensive man who lived the role of the Great Writer. Perec presented himself not as a representative of French culture but as a son of Polish Jews who happened to write in French. His modesty verged on the ridiculous. Everyone knew how worried he was about Catherine's film. It had been selected as the official French entry for the Venice Film Festival, and the verdict of the jury (chaired that year by Calvino, whom Perec knew well) would be crucial not only for Catherine's self-esteem but his own financial prospects also. Why didn't he telephone to find out what was happening? *You mean I can use the phone?* Ann Freadman spelt it out in words of one syllable: "You can phone France if you want, for free." Perec's profuse gratitude was out of proportion to the favour offered, in Australian eyes. He was bewildered, too, by the freedom of Queensland manners, and was not quite sure, when he was asked if he wanted a shower, exactly what sort of proposal was being made. He turned the offer down with a blush and sat staring hard at his feet as his hostess crossed the lounge, from bedroom to bathroom and back, quite properly dressed, Brisbane-fashion, in a towel.

One evening, at the Raynauds' home, Perec explained to the children that the jigsaw they were doing was not a real puzzle at all, since it had the solution printed on the box. "Okay, Mr Clever," they said as they deftly removed the lid from the writer's sight, "you show us." Perec got down on all fours and puzzled away. Dinner was deferred until it could be put off no longer; the puzzle-master at last conceded defeat, with a grin. He was starving.

Opinions vary as to what it was that Perec got up to in Australia. He worked for many hours on the Olivetti ET 221, but he may or may not have been typing *"53 Days"*. Few of the sheets amongst the surviving drafts of that novel were done on the Australian machine, but that may only mean that he threw away the Brisbane stage when he typed out the next version, at Rue Linné. Perec certainly made some notes for his novel in the university library, he certainly got his Friday class to play with its envisaged enigmas, and he certainly jotted down some of his ideas and plans on paper bought in Australia, but his correspondence suggests that he did not get very far with the text. On Monday 21 September, for example, he wrote to Paul Otchakovsky-Laurens: *I'm working on my novel. It's not going as fast as I had hoped. It's very complicated. But I'm making headway all the same. I'm also writing poems . . .* A week later, he reported to Catherine:

> *My stay here is drawing to a close. I leave for Adelaide the day after tomorrrow. Three weeks with a lot of travelling. That depresses me because my book is very much on my mind. I have almost written a half of the first chapter and I am itching to get into it completely.*

A good number of the notes for the later chapters of *"53 Days"* include material that Perec could only have collected in the last few days before he returned to Paris (for example, the names of the stations on the Sydney suburban railway system, to be given to a stick of parachutists dropped into southeastern France [*53D* 224])[1], and it is most probable that he came back from Australia not with a half-completed novel but with a work well advanced in the planning and plotting stages. For quite different reasons, some of Perec's former colleagues at Brisbane are convinced that the detective story was actually an alibi, and that their writer in residence in fact spent his time reading poetry in English, learning to use the page-memory feature on the Olivetti machine, experimenting with tautograms and

---

[1] Andrew P. Riemer, "In Search of Georges Perec", *Sydney Morning Herald*, 15 January 1990.

univocalic constraints, writing letters, and composing poems, many of which he then scrapped.

Perec's lecture tour took him to Adelaide, Melbourne, Canberra, Sydney, and Wollongong. He was entirely unknown in Australia except as the author of a set text on several universities' first-year French Studies syllabus (*Things*, of course, first taught down under not by Ross Chambers, Oulipo's Australian member, but by Colin Nettlebeck, who had encountered the text during his time in California). Some of Perec's talks were presentations of the work of OuLiPo, but he generally found his audience on these occasions looking at him as if he were a being from outer space (though they would probably have been more interested if he really *had* been a man from Mars). Twice, in Brisbane and in Canberra, he was able to screen the English-language version of the film of *A Man Asleep*,[1] but everywhere else he had to talk about *Things*. It got him down. More than once he ended up talking far more about himself, about how he had become a writer, about the mistakes he had made with *Les Errants*: he often finished well short of the time allotted to him. He preferred answering questions to holding forth and always answered cooperatively. Word got around that Perec gave "good value", quite unlike the standard-issue visiting speaker recycling last year's learned article from the proofs laid out in front of his eyes.

In Melbourne Perec was able to stay with Jacques Servières, a neurophysiologist friend of Julien Etcheverry, who was at that time on secondment to Monash University. In Sydney he lodged with Ivan Barko, a professor of French. Perec was not a burdensome houseguest; he wanted nothing more than a desk to sit at and time to write on it. However, whilst staying with the Barkos Perec did pursue two tracks other than that of the detective novel he was so eager to complete (or still trying to solve). In the Brisbane telephone book (Perec always scoured telephone books when in foreign lands) he had come across a Walter Peretz, whom he called. Walter said that his brother Kurt, who lived in Sydney, was the more knowledgeable when it came to family history, and so Perec called Kurt and arranged to meet in Sydney. The rendezvous was fixed at the Jewish Circle in

[1] "Dream-Theme Movie by French Novelist", *University News* (St Lucia), 16 September 1981.

the centre of town, and Kurt Peretz invited the French writer to dine
at his home. That evening Perec seemed to be under pressure; he
looked very tired, and admitted to having money worries. Try as
they might, Perec and Peretz could not figure out how they were
related, and finally concluded that they were not (*see* p. 10).

Perec also pursued poetry in Sydney, and got in touch with John
Forbes and Mark O'Connor. They met at The Courthouse in New-
town, with the writer Meaghan Morris and a translator, Julie Rose,
acting as linguistic go-betweens. Perec talked to Forbes about his
poetry, about *Magic Sam,* and about the work of Ken Bolton. Whenever one of the two women spoke, Perec would direct his answer to
Forbes. They formed the view that Perec was the most ungallant
Frenchman they had ever met and surmised that he was gay. It did
not occur to them then that the winner of the 1978 Médicis Prize was
just terribly shy.

On the last night of Perec's stay in Australia, a group of Ivan
Barko's colleagues at the University of Sydney held a party to draw
the visiting writer's tour to a close. There were drinks and snacks on
the patio, in the gentle evening sun. Perec seemed hesitant, homesick,
ill at ease. At one point some parakeets swooped down and ate crumbs
from his hands; the bright and noisy birds settled on Perec's shoulders
and in his hair, as if they, too, thought it was a nest, beneath which
a grey, tired face lit up with joy, like a child's.

On Perec and Australia, see also Jean-Michel Raynaud, *Pour un Perec lettré,
chiffré* (Lille: Presses universitaires, 1987).

Unpublished sources used in this chapter include the children's-story outline,
in the possession of Laurent de Brunhoff, a draft proposal for *Signe particulier
néant* in the possession of Paul Otchakovsky-Laurens, letters from Georges
Perec to Keith Atkinson, Ela Bienenfeld, Catherine Binet, Harry Mathews,
Paul Otchakovsky-Laurens, and Jean-Michel Raynaud, tape-recordings of
lectures given at the Universities of Adelaide and Melbourne, and the holdings of the University of Queensland Library (Fryer Collection mss 2291).

Other information was provided by Ivan Barko, Kmar Bendana-Mechri,
Ela Bienenfeld, Catherine Binet, Jacques Birnberg, Peter Cryle, John Forbes,
Ann Freadman, Ian Laurie, Harry Mathews, Colin Nettlebeck, Ewa Pawli-
kowska, Julie Rose, Jacques Roubaud, Claude Roy, Jacques Servières, Marie-
Noëlle Thibault, and Evelyn Wynn. I am indebted to Peter Craven and
Jean-Michel Raynaud for advice and for helping me to track down many of
the people who met Perec in Australia.

CHAPTER 65

The Murder of Robert Serval

Catherine collected Perec from the airport on his return from Australia in the grey dawn of 19 October 1981. He was tired from the long flight and the loss of a whole calendar night but he stayed up all the same and went out for dinner with Ela at the normal French time, even though his body must have been just about ready for breakfast. He downed his usual amount of wine and spirits and topped it off with the Barkos' standard remedy for jetlag, a large green sleeping pill. Ela was a little alarmed. The next day Perec rang her to apologise for not looking after himself properly. In future, he would take better care of himself, he really would. But he looked drawn for days afterwards; the Australian sunshine did not seem to have done him much good.

Catherine's film had been acclaimed at the Venice film festival in September, but it had not won the top prize, nor had its French distributor yet decided to release it commercially. The production company would be insolvent unless the film was shown soon; for the time being, the only recourse was to borrow more money to keep Les Films du Nautile afloat. Harry had had a windfall and was prepared to lend his pal enough to tide the company over. Perec wrote out an informal letter of understanding, to register both the loan and the main point – that the undersigned would never permit money matters to affect their relationship, for better or for worse.

Cramped living was something that Perec, like most Parisians, had had to put up with all his life, but now, fresh from a six-week experience of spread-out Australian homes and university offices, Rue Linné seemed far too small. In Australia he had dreamt up solutions to his lack of working space in Paris: perhaps he could rent a writing-office from Paul Otchakovsky-Laurens, so as to have a place to go to in the morning and to come back from at night, like a real office worker. At other times he fantasised about having a flat as grand as Calvino's in Rome, or even bigger, with a room for crosswords, a room for poetry, and another room just for novels; or else, like the superrich imagined in *Espèces d'espaces*, he could have a home organised along chronological lines, with a Monday room, a Tuesday room, a Wednesday room, and so on. For a more practical approach to his accommodation problem, Perec turned to Ela. She put him in touch with a woman she had first got to know during the war, at Villard-de-Lans, and who now had a spare room in her spacious apartment near Les Gobelins. Perec went round to see it, found the room suitably large and light, and accepted the kind offer. He would move in once he had sorted himself out. There would be no extra telephone, and the address would be kept confidential, for he wanted peace and quiet for his work, as well as greater convenience. He would not tell anyone where the place was – save for Catherine, of course. Perhaps not even Catherine, he muttered on one occasion. It was going to be an utterly secret retreat.

In the weeks following his return from Australia, Perec got down to typing up the first chapters of "53 Days". He pasted in Gino's Restaurant in Brisbane, where he had eaten pizza and pasta with colleagues from the French Department, and reversed the Australian red wine that he had enjoyed there, Hill of Grace, into the nom de guerre of a murdered nightclub hostess, Grace Hillof. He sprinkled the text with many other antipodean hints, some of which, based on political gossip, do not figure in the English translation of the book.

Perec told his friends that "53 Days" was to be a "literary thriller", and the structure that he adopted was by now a familiar one: it was to consist of two parts of thirteen and fifteen chapters respectively, of which the second would undo everything set up in the first. Chapter 1 is narrated by a French teacher of mathematics living in Grianta, a fictional North African city not unlike Tunis or Sfax, who is alerted by the French consul that a crime novelist called Serval, normally resident in a local grand hotel, has disappeared. Serval's name may well be a contraction of Serge Valène, the only pseudonym that Perec himself ever used (see p. 210), and in "53 Days" it is the pseudonym of a man who (it turns out) was at school with the book's narrator at Etampes, the hometown of the Serge Valène who taught Bartle-booth to paint watercolours in Life A User's Manual (page 60) and the site of Perec's own secondary education. In chapter 2 the narrator muses on his memories of Collège Geoffroy Saint-Hilaire, but he cannot remember a boy by the name of Stéphane Réal, as Serval was apparently called.

Serval-Réal has left the consul with an *unfinished* typescript, which he said would hold the clue to his whereabouts if, as he feared, he should go missing. Chapters 3 and 4 give a résumé of Serval's work in progress, which itself deals with a puzzle of a similar sort set in a Nordic "Fernland" that is partly a counterimage of the sweltering city of Grianta and partly a cocktail of Danish allusions picked up on Perec's day-trip to Copenhagen. In chapters 5 and 6, the narrator ponders on techniques for discovering secrets inscribed in texts, and in chapter 7 he interrogates the crime writer's former typist, Lise Carpenter, whose name echoes the trade of one of the first Gaspard Wincklers. Carpenter explains how Serval regularly constructed his stories from borrowed material, even going so far as to copy whole pages out of other books. He had in fact once given her a little sermon about incorporation:

> "You must never believe, young lady, that I make things up. All I do is purloin diverse details from here and there so as to connect up my own story. Everyone does likewise – and I don't just mean crime writers! Look at Antoine Berthet! or Bovary! Three quarters of Balzac comes from news items, and when it's not the real or half-real world that inspires a writer, then it's someone else's fiction, or for want of anything better, his own! Do you know how many Don Carloses have been written? Not far short of fifty! And there is one that begins with this entirely unambiguous warning: 'This story is drawn from Spanish, French, Italian, and Flemish authors who have written about the period in which it is set. The principal amongst them are M de Thou, Aubigné, Brantôme, Cabrera, Adriana, Natalis Comes, Dupleix, Mathieu, Mayerne, Mézeray, Le Laboureur sur Castelnau, Strada, Meteren, the historian of Don Juan of Austria, the eulogies of Father Hilarion da Costa, a Spanish book on the words and deeds of Philip II, an account of the death and burial of his son, etc. It is also drawn from manuscript and printed sources pertaining to the story, including a little book in verse entitled Diogenes, which deals with it exhaustively, and a manuscript by M de Peiresc directly on the same subject.'"

[53D 57]

The reader of W or The Memory of Childhood may recall, and is perhaps expected to recall, that in that text Peiresc is given as the Provençal form of Perec's family name [W 36], and we must therefore suspect that the writer of "53 Days" (though at this point the identity of that writer remains a mystery) has planted a cryptic clue of precisely the kind that the narrator is now trying to identify, with the help of a *typist* called *Carpenter*, in Serval's mystery text, tantalisingly entitled *The Crypt*. However, the passage quoted by Serval (and then by Carpenter, and then by the narrator, who gives it to us) is not a forgery but a slightly modified extract from the works of an eighteenth-century French author called Saint-Réal, to whom Stendhal twice attributes the definition of a novel as "a mirror paraded along a road", even though Saint-Réal never wrote it (at least, not in that form). There is perhaps even more to this mirror-game than meets the reader's eye. Saint-Réal is "equivalent" to Stéphane Réal if both names are contracted to St Réal, as they might be on a class-list, for instance. Perec had been in Australia, where the natural world is bewilderingly oriented the other way round (the sun is in the north, one goes south to cooler weather, and so on). St Real the other way round, and in English, gives *real st* . . . . Could that perhaps point to the *real Stéphane*, which is to say Georges Perec as he appears in Jean-Bertrand Pontalis's piece in *Nouvelle Revue de Psychanalyse* (*see* p. 476)?

The labyrinth of *"53 Days"* seems to be wound around unfathomably complex hedges of self-inscription. Some of these almost presuppose a biography to give them sense: the twin inscriptions of Etampes and of Stendhal, for example, become comprehensible when Perec's first literary embarrassment in his *classe de philosophie* is recalled; the allusions to North Africa, to the "Crubelier archipelago" [sic], to Rue de Quatrefages, to the Black Hand, and so forth, are fragments of Perec's own life and reading, many of them used in earlier published works; and the story of the statue of Diocletian in *"53 Days"* echoes an episode in *Le Condottiere*. The name Marcellus Claudius Burnachus reinscribes Perec's old friends Burgelin, Marcenac, and Benabou (Benabou's Latin learning was also plundered, for the fabricated epigraph to chapter 11), as well as nearly every one of his own published novels, from *A Man Asleep* to *Life A User's Manual*. Yet none of these nods, all of which are superficially similar to the winks of *Un Cabinet d'amateur*, has yet led readers of *"53 Days"* outside of the maze.

Perec left Paris again on 24 November for a speaking tour of Italy, and took his detective puzzle with him. He had begun to work out how part 2 might deconstruct all that had been set up in part 1, which now formed an *unfinished* diary-novel entitled *53 Days* (the quotation marks in the title of the whole book – *"53 Days"* – serve to inscribe that inner work). He had not been at his best since his return from

Australia, and now he had a nagging ache in his leg, or his hip, or his lower back. At first he called it sciatica. Harry Mathews suggested phenylbutazone, which he had found useful for back pain. Whilst waiting for his plane at Orly Airport, Perec caught a cold; when he landed, he jotted down in the pad that he was using for "*53 Days*": *Rome. Rhume.*

Throughout his eight-day Italian tour – which went without much geographical logic to Naples, Bari, Venice, Turin, Bologna and then Florence – Perec kept his manuscript with him, and made a show of anxiety about losing his heavy and bulging briefcase, because, he said, he simply had to finish the thing soon. Nearly every day in that circuitous week Perec had to get himself and his luggage from a hotel to a station, or from a station to a hotel, and it did the ache in his leg no good at all. Nor did his cold get any better. He sent postcards home, and in many of them gave his standard negative fitness-report: *je suis mal fichu* ("I'm feeling lousy"). Perec never admitted to being ill with anything in particular; every affliction he had or might have had in his life (apart from toothache) was only ever referred to in conversation or in correspondence as *la crève*, meaning a dripping nose, double pneumonia, or anything in between. Many of Perec's friends in fact believed him to be a man who was never ill. He was more open in the postcard he sent Catherine: *I may be called Georges, but I'm not up to slaying the dragon that has blocked up my ears and made my voice all husky. I've stopped smoking (because I had to).* If only he had had a little tin of James Sherwood's cough pastilles! They were decorated with the *hexagonal vignette of a knight in armour driving his lance through the ghost of influenza personified as a grumpy old man lying flat on his stomach in a fog-enshrouded landscape* [L 82], the knight in question being Saint George, and the landscape an Italian one, as painted by Vittore Carpaccio.[1]

In Venice, few people attended the lecture Perec gave on constraint and creativity. In Turin he found himself by happy chance in the same hotel as Kate Manheim and her husband, Richard Foreman. The unexpected meeting put Perec back on form. Over dinner he confessed that one of the things he would really like to do before he

---

[1] Vittore Carpaccio, *St George Slaying The Dragon* (Scuola San Giorgio degli Schiavoni, Venice) replaces *The Dream of St Ursula* as the "pictorial quotation" in chapter 22 of *Life A User's Manual*, respecting the WRONG for that chapter. From Patrizia Molteni, "Perec and Painting", PhD dissertation, University of Manchester.

died was to act in one of Foreman's plays. The next day, at Bologna, Perec was able to stay with Paolo Boni and Cuchi White. He spent as much time as he could writing *"53 Days"*, but he did not want to miss the chance of seeing the city's treasures in the company of two pairs of painterly eyes, and he pushed himself hard to enjoy every last bit of Italian art on view. It was in Bologna that the main event of the tour was to take place: a round-table discussion on art and the illustrated book with Boni, White and Michel Butor, who failed to turn up. Perec gave an ordered account of the seven different illustrated books he had been involved in, and an unpretentious statement of what pleased him about books that were art objects in themselves.[1] From Bologna, Boni drove Perec first to Vicchio di Mugello (to meet members of his family) and then on to Florence, where the Bologna round table was repeated. It did not occur to Boni that there was anything wrong with the irrepressible and good-humoured Perec that could not be put right by a good rest and a less punishing schedule.

Perec threw himself back into *"53 Days"* in December 1981. He had another commitment that would soon be overdue, an article on Agatha Christie's *The Murder of Roger Ackroyd* (a book famous for breaking one of the cardinal rules of mystery writing) but it was a different Christie novel, already incorporated and fragmented in the text of *Life A User's Manual*, that informed *"53 Days"*.

> *The first model* [for Serval's puzzle-text, *The Crypt*] *comes from* And Then There Were None.[2] *As is well known, nine unconvicted culprits are executed in this book by a judge who makes it seem as if he is the tenth (but not the last) victim. The magistrate-murderer is called Lawrence Wargrave, which is indeed the name Serval has given to the author of* The Magistrate Is the Murderer.
>
> [53D 57–58]

But Lawrence Wargrave is the name that *Perec* gave to the author of a crime novel called *The Magistrate Is the Murderer*, in *Life A User's Manual* (page 264)! The third model for Serval's *The Crypt*, meanwhile, is Bill Ballinger's *The Tooth and the Nail*, devoured by the

---

[1] Perec's contribution to the discussion, a tape recording of which was discovered and transcribed by Patrizia Molteni, has been published in part in *Ici-Perec* (Montreuil: Bibliothèque Robert-Desnos, 1992).

[2] First published as *Ten Little Niggers*, then as *Ten Little Indians*. It is still called *Ten Little Niggers* in France.

teenage writer in his little bedroom at Blévy [*PC* 26], where a copy of the book itself lay in 1981 and still lies today.

The inscription of Stendhal's *The Charterhouse of Parma* in the running text of *"53 Days"* is more blatant, since the North African city in which the book begins takes its name from Grianta, the family home of Fabrice del Dongo, the hero of Stendhal's last work. LA CHARTREUSE is inscribed acrostically as well, in a 12 x 12 letter square masquerading as a list of words changed between two versions of one of the novels copied into Serval's unfinished text. But it is in an altogether different context that the real significance of La Chartreuse finally comes clear: it is the name of the mountain massif facing the Vercors. Indeed, if one approaches Grenoble from Lyon on the old road, one comes to a fork from which a side-road leads steeply up to the Chartreuse, on the left; a little further on, on the right, another road winds up through hairpin bends to Lans-en-Vercors. At that first fork in the road there is a stone slab commemorating those who fell in the uprising of July 1944: a war grave. Perec spent part of his time in Brisbane consulting history reference works about the Resistance in southeastern France in 1943–44 – that is to say, about the events that were or were not going on around him when he was a little boy at Collège Turenne. His incorporation of Agatha Christie's "War Grave" and Stendhal's "Chartreuse" into *"53 Days"* creates ominous echoes of what he had so conspicuously omitted from his childhood autobiography.

Perec's notes for the later chapters of his detective puzzle suggest that the mystery surrounding Serval dates from the same period. Had the real Serval betrayed Resistance networks to the Gestapo? Did he owe his subsequent career to occult influence, and if so, on which side? And who *was* the real Serval? Was he really called Réal? Was his disappearance from Grianta the arbitrary action of the police chief, Blabami (a name rhyming with that of another schoolboy from Etampes, Ridha Jemmali), or the work of the Black Hand, seeking to protect corrupt dealings in antiquities? Was the French Consul involved, or was it a put-up job, or the long-plotted revenge of the survivors of the Vercors debacle? In the end it turns out to be none of these; instead, Serval has been disposed of by his American wife, Patricia, in a purely formal jealousy plot. Salini, the lawyer-detective from chapter 31 of *Life A User's Manual*, reappears to ask the all-important question: Who wrote the book?

P: A novelist we met at   . He is called GP apparently
he adores these sorts of problems. We gave him a number of key
words, themes, names. It was up to him what he did with them.

S: You weren't disappointed with the result?

P: I haven't really read the book, just checked that all the allu-
sions were there. It did not displease me that false trails were laid.

S: But why the title, 53 Days?

P: It's the time it took Stendhal to write La Chartreuse de
Parme. *You didn't know? We talked about that a great deal when*
we first met. He too wanted to write a book in 53 days. That was
actually what gave us the idea of the challenge: to take 53 days to
write a novel for which we would supply this and that piece.

In fact, he took a lot longer. We had made allowances for over-
runs, but in the end we really had to breathe down his neck.

[53D 125–126]

"53 Days" is a puzzle in every way, not least because, as Jacques
Roubaud says, its fundamental constraint is less a formal than a compositional one:

> It neither resembles the single constraint of *La Disparition* nor
> the multiple rules of *Life A User's Manual*. In "53 Days" life
> appears as a puzzle endlessly destroying its own solutions.
> The multiplicity of the explanations of a death, of a murder,
> forms an allegory of a life that does not know its own end
> (just as in *Life A User's Manual* the multiplicity of lives consti-
> tuted the puzzle of a single life, the life of all). "53 Days", in
> its evocations of the war years, treason in the Resistance, and
> the Vercors tragedy, contains new biographical "keys" to
> Georges Perec, and constitutes a further stage of his "recollec-
> tion" of a lost past or another "anamnesis" of which *W or*
> *The Memory of Childhood* and *Je me souviens* are two other
> poles.

This chapter draws on information provided by Marcel Benabou, Ela Bien-enfeld, Catherine Binet, Paolo Boni, "Mme L", Kate Manheim, Jean Ray-naud, Franca Trentin-Baratto, and Gérard Zingg, as well as on unpublished letters from Georges Perec to Ela Bienenfeld, Catherine Binet, Harry Mathews, and Paul Otchakovsky-Laurens. The passage by Jacques Roubaud quoted at the end of the chapter is translated from a text written in French for publication as an afterword in the German edition of "53 Days". I am also indebted to Heather Mawhinney for several insights into the text of Perec's last work.

CHAPTER 66

"Things to Do Before I Die"

Perec pushed himself hard, as he always had, but his aching leg and his wheezing chest slowed him down. A graduate student who had met him in Melbourne came across him one day in Rue Linné and asked him how he was. *Lousy*, he replied. *Australia fucked me up.* He said other unflattering things about Australia to those of his French friends who wanted to listen. He had been bored by the place; he hadn't done all he had wanted to do; he had spent too much time travelling around. There may be a degree of projection, not to say prejudice, in these recollections; the *writer* Perec commemorated his visit to Australia in the dozens of Australian references in *"53 Days"*. However, as 1981 drew to a close, Perec was less and less inclined to think that he had had a good year. He dined with Harry Mathews on 11 December, and told him, not for the first time, how sad he was not to be anyone's heir. (In fact, he was named as a beneficiary in Ela's will, though he may not have known it, and he was designated in Mathews's will as the literary executor for Harry's works in French.) Harry was nonetheless moved by Perec's still raw feeling of disinheritance, and so he added his friend's name to the beneficiaries of his own will, to rectify the position and to make him a little happier. With hindsight, one might suspect that this little scene was Perec's upside-down way of reminding himself that his own will had yet to be made. He had been working on something that quite naturally brought such gloomy matters to mind.

Jacques Bens, one of the founding members of OuLiPo, ran a radio programme on which celebrated guests were invited to list the fifty things they would most like to do before they died. It was a light-hearted entertainment but often a revealing one. At the microphone on 12 December 1981, the day after his dinner with Harry, Georges Perec ad-libbed and chuckled and made a few jokes, but he had prepared a proper text in advance:

Some of the Things I Really Must Do before I Die

First, there are things that are very easy to do, things I could do
right now, for example:
    Take a ride in a bateau-mouche   1
    Then there are just slightly more important things, things
that imply a decision, things that I tell myself that if I did
them, then my life would become easier, for example:
    Decide to throw away a certain number of objects that I
hang on to without knowing why I am hanging on to them   2
    or else:
    Sort my bookshelves once and for all   3
    Buy a number of domestic appliances   4
    or even:
    Stop smoking (before I have to)   5
    Then there are things connected to deeper wishes for
change, for example:
    Dress in a quite different fashion   6
    Live in a hotel (in Paris)   7
    Live in the country   8
    Go and live for a good while in a foreign city (London,
for instance)   9
    Then there are things connected to dreams of time or
space. There are quite a few of those:
    Cross the intersection of the Equator and the International
Date Line   10
    Cross the Arctic Circle   11
    Experience a "timeless" state (like Siffre)   12
    Travel by submarine   13
    Go on a long sea journey   14
    Take a ride on or make a trip by hot-air balloon or by
        dirigible   15
    Go to the Kerguelen Islands (or Tristan da Cunha)   16
    Go from Morocco to Timbuktoo by camel in fifty-two
days   17
    Then, amongst all the things I do not yet know, there are some
I would like to have time to discover:
    I would like to go to the Ardennes   18

I would like to go to Bayreuth, but also to Prague and
    Vienna   19
I would like to go to the Prado   20
I would like to drink rum from a bottle found on the
seabed (like Captain Haddock in Red Rackham's Treasure*)* 21
I would like to have time to read Henry James (amongst
    others)   22
I would like to travel by canalboat   23
    Then there are lots of things that I would like to learn
but know I won't, because they would take too much time, or
because I know I would do them very badly, for instance:
    Solve Rubik's cube   24
    Learn to play the drums   25
    Learn Italian   26
    Learn to be a printer   27
    Paint   28
    Then there are things connected to my work as a writer.
There are many of these. For the most part they are vague
plans; some are quite possible, and hang only on me, for example:
    To write for tiny children   29
    To write science fiction   30
    whilst others depend on commissions:
    To write the script of an adventure movie in which
(for instance) five thousand Kirghiz horsemen sweep across the
    steppes   31
    To write a real serial   32
    To work with a cartoonist   33
    To write lyrics (for Anna Prucnal, for instance)   34
    There's one other thing I would like to do, but I don't
know where to put it
    Plant a tree (and watch it grow)   35
    And finally there are things that cannot now be envisaged
but that would have been possible not so long ago
    To get drunk with Malcolm Lowry   36
    To make the acquaintance of Vladimir Nabokov   37
    etc. etc.
    There must be many others. I choose to stop at 37.
[*Jsn* 105–109]

Perec had likewise chosen to stop *W or The Memory of Childhood* at thirty-seven chapters, to commemorate the hasard of his birth, which meant, with mathematical necessity, that he would turn 37 on 7.3.73. Perec's thirty-seventh impossible "thing to do before I die" *is* a kind of meeting with Nabokov, who would have enjoyed the implausible palindrome of Perec's secret self-inscription.

Perec had hardly been concerned with the Bulgarian translation of *Life A User's Manual,* which had appeared in 1980, and he had not been able to meet his Italian translator, whose version was not yet finished. His relationship to the German edition was naturally quite different. He had given his old friend Eugen Helmle many clues about the various constraints used, and had annotated a copy of the novel with the sources of most of the German-language quotations that it contains (though all he said at the head of some chapters was *Doesn't matter*). By the end of 1981 Helmle's text was ready, and the book's design well advanced. The translator came to Paris with his German publisher to discuss the final details with the author, for this was to be no ordinary book. It was to have two-colour printing for chapter 80, fine paper, cloth boards embossed with *GP* on the front and the *ko* symbol on the back, and a green silk bookmark stitched into the binding. *Das Leben. Gebrauchsanweisung* would be presented to the purchaser in a black cardboard box just like the boxes made by Madame Hourcade for Bartlebooth's jigsaw puzzles, and inside the box there would be not just a book but also a real Bartleboothian jigsaw puzzle. For the puzzle-picture Perec chose a coloured-in version of the black-and-white image that had been used for the jacket of the French paperback edition – Bertall's *Une Maison bourgeoise,* a well-known nineteenth-century print of a Paris apartment house with its façade removed – and himself drew in the irregular, diabolically difficult cutting lines for the publisher's appointed puzzle-cutter to cut. The German book-object was due to be launched in March 1982, happily coinciding with the sesquicentenary of Goethe's death, an event that could be relied upon to inspire repeat broadcasts of Perec and Helmle's Goethe play, *Die Maschine.* Meanwhile, in Paris, Marcel Cuvelier was arranging to revive his stage production of Perec's other great German radio success, *L'Augmentation.* Perec's European career was beginning again.

Perec and Catherine spent Christmas at Chambroutet, but since Perec was not very well, they did not go on to Ré or to Oléron for New Year's. Dr Binet, Catherine's father, was so worried about the state of the writer's health that he insisted on doing a chest X-ray. He told Perec that he ought to see a specialist when he got back to Paris, and gave him a name and an address.

In January Perec worked as hard as he could on *"53 Days"*, which he planned to finish in March, or in April at the latest. At least he knew what the jacket design would be – a reproduction of a colour postcard that Gérard Zingg had given him, showing a garish sign at Zagora, in Morocco, bearing the legend "Timbuktoo 52 Days". He made less headway than he would have wished: if only he had had a second month of summer in Brisbane, he said, he would have finished his detective novel there. In Paris, in the darkest and coldest month of the year, there were visits to doctors and to hospitals for tests, and pills and potions to take. Perec's leg was excruciatingly painful, and he was finding it increasingly difficult to breathe. He gave up his cherished cigarillos for good, and wanted to make the flat in Rue Linné a no-smoking zone.

One evening, Perec took Ela out for dinner at Le Buisson Ardent, just round the corner from Rue Linné. He looked pale and sweaty; his face had become much thinner than before. But when he rang his sister-cousin the next morning (as he now did nearly every day), he said, with the chirpy pride of a naughty schoolboy, that he was feeling better, and had even managed to smoke a couple of (really tiny) cigarettes.

"Listen, Georges," Ela said, "Do you want me to tell you what you looked like last night? You looked like a rabbi stepping into his grave!"

What? What? replied Perec. *Does my cousin thirty-seven times removed permit herself to suggest –*

"Yes, Georges. She does."

Harry Mathews left for New York, according to plan, on 21 January, after begging Perec not to tell him how the puzzle of *"53 Days"* would be solved, since he wanted to have the pleasure of working it out from the finished book. A week later Perec went into hospital for the removal of the cyst that had now been diagnosed as the immediate cause of the pain in his leg and lower back. He carried on drafting his detective novel in his hospital bed, and kept up to date with his crossword commitments. Without work to keep him going, P.O.L. thought, Perec would have been even worse off.

Although she was not privy to the list of the twenty-eight creditors of Les Films du Nautile, Ela had known for some time that Perec needed financial help. She had explained the situation to Bianca,

Sylvia, and Marianne, and they had all agreed that the proper thing to do was to put a significant sum of money at the writer's disposal. On the eve of Perec's departure for the Hôpital Chirurgical d'Ivry, Ela paid the first part of the sum into her cousin's bank account and telephoned him to let him know that it had been done. It put his mind at rest, on that score at least.

Months before, in the summer of 1981, Ela had talked to Perec about his financial problems. Wasn't he worried that his creditors – in effect, nearly every one of his friends – might in the end turn against him?

I don't think so, he said. After a moment's thought, he added, *I'll tell you what the bottom line will be: the net result will be two years lost.* At that time – before Brisbane, before Italy, before the bad leg and the wheezing lungs had even begun – two years' writing to pay off debts hardly amounted to a tragedy. Financial constraints would not stop Perec from innovating or from doing just what he wanted to do with words.

In February 1982 Perec spent most of his ten days in hospital just waiting for the result of the operation on his hip, which was in fact not a procedure to remove a cyst or lymphoma but a biopsy. On 9 February the consultant spoke to him. Catherine called to see him later in the day.

Catherine, I have something to tell you, he said. *I have a tumour. There you are.*

In truth, she knew it already. The consultant had spoken to her on the telephone before confronting the writer with his plight. He had begun by asking Catherine how he should break the news to the patient, but ended by answering his own question before she could: "Perec's not a man you can lie to," he said.

Perec did not want sympathy from outsiders, and he abhorred the idea of being an invalid. He decided to live at home during his radiotherapy, in anticipation of major surgery to remove the afflicted lung. Few people outside of the family circle were supposed to be in the know. Perec put a brave face on it and told Catherine that he intended to be not a self-pitying cripple but *the most elegant cancer patient in Paris*. His friends gathered round him. Jacques Lederer, the oldest of his affectionate pals, became his chauffeur, driving him to and from his radiotherapy appointments at La Pitié-Salpetrière, a teaching hospital in central Paris. Laurent de Brunhoff, who was a near neighbour and had an artist's steady hand, came round to give him his regular cortisone injections. Julien Etcheverry massaged Perec's swollen abdomen; soon massage was the only thing that helped him to sleep. Sylvia did a great deal behind the scenes to track the progress and treatment of her godfather's condition (she had many contacts in the medical world), and came to see him as often as she could. Paulette lent a willing hand with the shopping and housekeeping, for which Perec thanked her. "It's just normal," she said.

Perec insisted, meanwhile, that Catherine get down to work on her new film, a short for television pairing Cuchi White's trompe-l'oeil photographs with texts by Perec and Butor read in voice-over. *Les Jeux de la Comtesse* was at last due to have a commercial release. It would be screened in Paris in March and then go on to the New York film festival in April, around the time that Perec expected to go under the surgeon's knife. Catherine wanted to cancel the trip, but Perec was adamant that she should not: what was the point of her being around when he was out cold? He did not want his illness to be an event in other people's lives. It is hard to sort out how much of this was self-denial and how much self-delusion.

There were ups and downs. The pain in Perec's leg was less agonising now, but his breathing was more difficult. His chest felt as if it were encased in a suit of armour, he told Jacques, with the breathing-slit in his helmet shrinking every day. But he went to Marcel Benabou's birthday party with Catherine, and to the revival of *L'Augmentation* at Théâtre de la Huchette, where he bubbled with glee at his own old joke. He had to try not to laugh out loud, for fear of bringing on a coughing attack. On 12 February he told Marie Chaix on the telephone: *Well, okay, I'll fight it. You have to go one day or another, but now it's staring me in the face, and it's up to me to put it off as long as I can.*

To others he said that he knew he wouldn't live as long as he would have liked, that he was cross that his work would be cut short, that he had another twenty-five years' writing in him. He hardly had time to resign himself to an early death; his mood shifted between anger and determination to hang on. He took no real break from his work. He asked Jacques Lederer to help him out with the crosswords for *Le Point* if the need arose, and to accept the dedication of the now nearly complete second collection. He wrote to his publishers to suggest that *Quel Petit Vélo*, *Les Revenentes*, and *Un Cabinet d'amateur* be brought together as a single volume. His plan was to finish "*53 Days*", have his operation, convalesce somewhere – probably at

Harry's place in the Vercors, where the air was so clear – and then settle in the country. Plenty of people managed with one lung, didn't they? He had spent seventeen years working alongside specialists in respiration, so he knew how adaptable the body's main organs could be. But it would be better not to risk the polluted Paris air, he said to Henri Chavranski, so he would probably move to the Dordogne. When Babette Mangolte, alerted by Kate Manheim in New York, rang Rue Linné from Berlin, Perec sounded almost like his old self, full of plans and good cheer; but when Harry rang from New York, he did not want to speak to him. He showed an even blacker mood to others. Once he is said to have blurted out on the telephone *I've got cancer and I'm going to snuff it. So there!*

Marie Chaix and Bernard Queysanne had dinner with Perec and Catherine on Sunday, 21 February. Perec looked awful. He hardly said a word all evening; his mind seemed to be elsewhere. Afterwards, Bernard and Marie had a nightcap in a bar.

"No, it can't happen, Georges will recover," Bernard said, his eyes appealing to Marie for comfort.

"But of course he will," Marie replied. In a diary entry written that very night, she commented on her own words by adding: "Like a fool".

A week later, on Tuesday, 2 March, Laurent de Brunhoff came round for the injection routine and found Perec in a critical state. A doctor was already there, and an ambulance on its way. When it arrived, Perec got in beside the driver and Laurent climbed into the back for the journey to the Hôpital Charles-Foix at Ivry, a southern suburb of Paris. Perec had been told a few days earlier by his doctors that his tumour was inoperable.

Many people came to see Perec in his hospital bed. He was in much pain at first; later, he was given a heavier dose of morphine. In the evening Ela drove Paulette back from the hospital to Rue Linné. Perec's ex-wife, who had never ceased to be his friend and comrade, said something about the future course of convalescence that made Ela interrupt her: "Calm down, Paulette. Georges is going to die."

Catherine telephoned the hospital for news at every opportunity. On the Wednesday she slipped out of the editing studio during her

lunch-break to call from a box in the street. She got through to the
consultant. "Come at once," he said. He met Catherine in the hospital
corridor and said that if there was anything Perec wanted, she should
give it to him now. Catherine had known for weeks, but it was only
now that her lover's dying ceased to be an idea in her mind and faced
her as a brutal fact. She spent a while with Perec, who was still
conscious, and then drove back to Rue Linné to feed the cats and tidy
up, deferring with zombielike deliberation the moment of her return
to Ivry. She knew what it was that Perec would most like to see.
From the wooden box in which he kept his *fétiches* – the odds and
ends to which he was particularly attached – she took the colour slides
of number 24 Rue Vilin, and a large lead character of the letter *W*.
When she got back to the hospital, several others were around the
bed, and Perec was drifting in a haze of painkilling drugs. Catherine
had brought a slide viewer, but Perec was hardly able to see the last
images of Cécile's derelict *salon de coiffure*. The printer's *W* was laid
beside them, on the bedside table.

It was around eight in the evening, on 3 March 1982. Pierre Getzler,
Jacques Lederer and Paulette stood against the back wall of the drab
room in Hôpital Charles-Foix, at Ivry. Seeing the small crowd, Ela,
who had been in and out for much of the day, waited outside, in the
corridor. Sylvia and James were on their way. Noureddine Mechri
would soon be there too. Catherine was at the bedside, her arms
folded on the counterpane. Perec's breathing was heavy and slow.
Then it stopped.

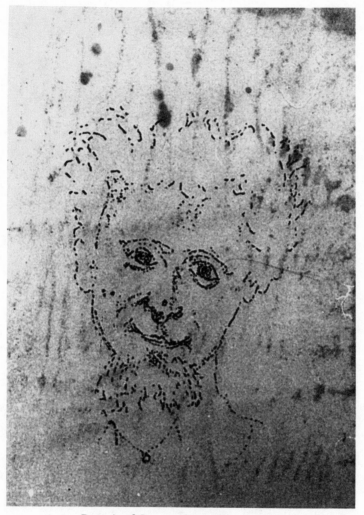

Portrait of Georges Perec, March 1982.
Gérard Zingg

From *The Minor Planets Circular*, 10 September 1984

(2187) PEREC = 1982 UJ

Discovered 17 October 1982 by E. Bowell at the Anderson Mesa Station of the Lowell Observatory.

The Works of Georges Perec

The first part of this bibliography, which is more a map than a catalogue raisonné, lists those works by Georges Perec that are (or were at one time) available (more or less) in published form. The list is divided into five subsections, each organised chronologically: books catalogued under Perec's own name (section 1); books written in collaboration (section 2); contributions to others' books (section 3); pamphlets, limited editions, self-publications and other forms of bibliographic nightmares (section 4); and periodicals (section 5). These five sections are exhaustive only in a limited sense. I believe they include everything of Perec's that has been printed to date, including prepublications of parts of works that were subsequently published in full; they do not, however, cover republications of books after their first edition (except where the current [1992] edition is significantly different), or republications of extracts in magazines, anthologies, textbooks, and so on. The five sections should, in principle, be watertight, but in practice there are items that do not fall unambiguously into one or another section (contributions to pamphlets, for example, or limited editions in collaboration). Cross-references to other sections are indicated by ⇑ (see above) or ⇓ (see below) followed by a section number and a year.

For each entry I give the title abbreviation of the published book in which the text may be read, following the scheme explained on pages xxi–xxiii; texts that either have not yet been republished or are available only in books for which no title abbreviation has been invented are signalled by a bullet (●).

I have listed, beneath each title, the languages in which translations have been published, with the year of publication; in some cases I have listed translations known to be in progress as of May 1992. These language lists are probably not exhaustive and most assuredly will rapidly become out-of-date. They are included here because the spread of Perec's work around the world is part of his biography, and a measure of his posthumous triumph.

The second part of the bibliography maps Perec's presence in non-book media: in theatre (section 6), in radio (section 7), in the cinema (section 8), in television (section 9), in music and opera (section 10), and in other media (section 11). These sections are certainly not exhaustive, nor are they watertight among themselves; they also overlap sections 1 to 5. Their purpose is, first, to show how near Perec came to writing *every kind of thing it is possible for a writer to write nowadays* [*RCF* 22], and, second, to give a glimpse of the almost infinite adaptability of Perec's works, stretching towards such unexpected horizons as a stage performance in Swedish of "243 Cartes postales en couleurs véritables".

I have not attempted to list readings of Perec's works (by Perec or by others) broadcast on French radio, not only because I have not had access to the recordings themselves, but also because I am not sure what purpose such a listing would serve (though one has been kindly drawn up by Madame Pezet). I have, however, listed (in the appendix to chapter 38 above) all the known readings of Perec's works on German radio, and in section 7 below, I have noted the few known instances of readings and adaptations on English-language radio.

The third part of this map is no more than an overview of the mountainous hinterland of Perec's work, in the absence of which I would have written a much shorter book than this. His recorded and transcribed talks and lectures, and the interviews he gave on radio (but not on television) and to newspaper journalists are catalogued in Section 12; those of his unpublished works that I have had the privilege of reading (and in some cases finding) are listed in Section 13. Section 14 is a checklist, rather than a bibliography, of Perec's unfinished works, cross-referenced to their published and unpublished fragments. Two final sections list the titles of lost works and give publication details of those of Perec's letters that have appeared in print.

Perec's work as a translator has been treated as part of his work as a writer: translated books appear in section 1 (published books), translated extracts and poems published in anthologies appear in section 3 (contributions to books) and extracts and poems published in periodicals appear at the relevant place in section 5.

First Part

SECTION 1: PUBLISHED BOOKS

Place of publication is Paris unless otherwise stated

T
Les Choses. Une histoire des années 60. Julliard, Les Lettres nouvelles, 1965. 96 pp. Current: Presses-Pocket 2224.

Translated into Bulgarian (1967), Catalan (1988), Danish (1969), Dutch (1967; retranslated 1990), English (1967; retranslated 1990), Estonian (1968), Galician (1991), German (1966 [West], 1967 ([East]), Greek (1988), Hungarian (1966), Italian (1966), Japanese (1978), Polish (1967), Portuguese (Brasiliero) (1967), Romanian (1967), Russian (1967), Slovak (1976), and Spanish (1967). Albanian and Chinese translations are also said to exist.

QPV
Quel Petit Vélo à guidon chromé au fond de la cour? Denoël, Les Lettres nouvelles, 1966. 104 pp. Current: Folio 1413.

Translated into German (1970 [West], 1985 [East])]) and Japanese (1978). Dutch, English and Greek translations are in progress.

MA
Un Homme qui dort. Denoël, Les Lettres nouvelles, 1967. 153pp.

Translated into Catalan (1990), Dutch (1968), English (1990), German (1988), Greek (1983), Hungarian (1969), Italian (1967), Japanese (1970), and Portuguese (1991; Brasiliero 1988).

D
La Disparition. Denoël, Les Lettres nouvelles, 1969. 320 pp. Current: Gallimard, Collection l'Imaginaire.

Translated into German (1986). English translation in progress. See also Times Literary Supplement (2 September 1988) and PN Review vol. 15, no. 6 (1989), p. 18.

M
Die Maschine. Übersetzung und deutsche Fassung von Eugen Helmle. Mit einem Nachwort von Werner Klippert. Stuttgart: Reklam's Universal-Bibliothek 9352, 1972. 88 pp.

●   *Les Revenentes*. Julliard, Collection Idée fixe, 1972, 1991. 128 pp.

BO   *La Boutique obscure. 124 Rêves*. Postface de Roger Bastide. Denoël, Collection Cause commune, 1973. Pages unnumbered.

EsEs   *Espèces d'espaces*. Galilée, 1974. 124 pp.

            Translated into German (1989) and Italian (1989). Extracts translated into Greek (1983).

W   *W ou le souvenir d'enfance*. Denoël, Les Lettres nouvelles, 1975. 224 pp.

            Translated into Czech (1979), Dutch (1991), English (1988), Finnish (1991), German (1978 [East], 1982 [West]), Hebrew (1991), Italian (1991), Norwegian (1984), Spanish (1987).

●   Harry Mathews, *Les Verts Champs de moutarde de l'Afghanistan* (translation of *Tlooth*). Translated by Georges Perec in collaboration with the author. Denoël, 1975. 188 pp.

●   *Alphabets*. Cent soixante-seize onzains hétérogrammatiques. Illustré par Dado. Galilée, 1976. Pages unnumbered.
         Reprinted in 1985 with additional illustrations.

Jms   *Je me souviens. Les Choses communes, I*. Hachette/ Collection P.O.L., 1978. 147 pp. Current: Hachette, Textes du XXe siècle.

            Translated into Italian (1988) and Swedish (1991). Gilbert Adair's *Myths and Memories* (London: Fontana, 1986) is an outstanding creative transposition of Perec's work to a British context.

L   *La Vie mode d'emploi. Romans*. Hachette/Collection P.O.L., 1978. 706 pp. Current: Livre de Poche 5341.

            Translated into Bulgarian (1980), English (1987), German (1982), Greek (1991), Italian (1984), Portuguese (1989), and Spanish (1988). Japanese, Dutch, Finnish, and Swedish translations are in progress.

UCDA *Un Cabinet d'amateur. Histoire d'un tableau.* Balland, Collection L'Instant romanesque, 1979. 96 pp. Current: Livre de poche 6654.

Translated into German (1989), Italian (1990), and Spanish (1989). Dutch, English and Greek translations are in progress.

MCI *Les Mots croisés I. Précédés par des considérations de l'auteur sur l'art et la manière de croiser les mots.* Mazarine, 1979. 196pp.

Clô *La Clôture et autres poèmes.* Hachette/Collection P.O.L., 1980. 96 pp.

Th *Théâtre I.* Hachette/Collection P.O.L., 1981. 136 pp.

Translated into German (1991) and Italian (1991).

● Harry Mathews, *Le Naufrage du Stade Odradek* (translation of *The Sinking of the Odradek Stadium*). Translated by Georges Perec with the collaboration of the author. Hachette/Collection P.O.L., 1981.

● *Tentative d'épuisement d'un lieu parisien.* Christian Bourgois, 1982. 64 pp. (⇓ 5: 1975)

Translated into Czech (1986).

PC *Penser/Classer.* Hachette, Textes du XXe siècle, 1985. 192 pp.

Translated into Italian (1989) and Spanish (1986). A Dutch translation is in progress.

Contains: "Notes sur ce que je cherche"(⇓ 5: 1978), "De quelques emplois du verbe habiter" (⇓ 3: 1981), "Notes concernant les objects qui sont sur ma table de travail" (⇓ 5: 1976), "Trois chambres retrouvées" (⇓ 5: 1977 and also ⇓ 14), "Notes brèves sur l'art et la manière de ranger ses livres" (⇓ 5: 1978), "Douze regards obliques" (⇓ 5: 1976), "Les Lieux d'une ruse" (⇓ 5: 1977), "Je me souviens de Malet & Isaac" (⇓ 5: 1979), "81 Fiches-cuisine à l'usage des débutants" (⇓ 3: 1980), "Considérations sur les lunettes" (⇓ 3: 1980), "Lire: esquisse socio-physiologique" (⇓ 5: 1976), "De la difficulté qu'il y a à imaginer une cité idéale" (⇓ 5: 1981), "Penser/ Classer" (⇓ 5: 1982).

MCII   *Les Mots croisés II.* P.O.L. et Mazarine, 1986. Pages unnumbered.

53D   *"53 jours". Roman.* Texte établi par Harry Mathews et Jacques Roubaud. P.O.L., 1989. 336 pp.

Translated into German (1992) and English (1992). An Italian translation is in progress.

inf   *l'infra-ordinaire.* Le Seuil, Librairie du XXᵉ siècle, 1989. 138 pp.

Translated into Greek (1991) and German (1992).

Contains: "Approches de quoi" (⇩ 5:1973), "La Rue Vilin" (⇩ 5: 1977), "243 Cartes postales en couleurs véritables" (⇩ 5: 1978), "Tout autour de Beaubourg" (⇩ 5: 1981), "Promenades dans Londres" (⇩ 5: 1981), "Le Saint des Saints" (⇩ 5: 1981), "Tentative d'inventaire des aliments liquides et solides que j'ai ingurgités au cours de l'année 1974" (⇩ 5: 1976), "Still Life/Style Leaf" (⇩ 5: 1981).

*

Jsn   *Je suis né.* Le Seuil, Librairie du XXᵉ siècle, 1990. 138 pp.

Contains: "Je suis né" (an editorial title for an extract from Perec's jottings for *W or The Memory of Childhood,* previously published by Philippe Lejeune in *CGP II,* pp. 161–162 but dropped from the republication of the relevant article in *MO*), "Les Lieux d'une fugue" (⇩ 5: 1975), "Le Saut en parachute" (⇩ 12: 1959), "Kléber Chrome" (⇩ 5: 1967, as "Une Quête en rond", but claimed in this volume to be an unpublished draft of a novel), "Lettre à Maurice Nadeau" (previously published in part by Philippe Lejeune in *CGP II,* p. 121, and republished in larger part in *MO,* pp. 95–97), "Les Gnocchis de l'automne ou réponse à quelques questions me concernant" (⇩ 5: 1972, as "Autoportrait"), "Le Rêve et le texte" (⇩ 5: 1979), "Le travail de la mémoire" (⇩ 12: 1979), "Ellis Island. Description d'un projet" (⇩ 5: 1979), "Quelques-unes des choses qu'il faudrait tout de même que je fasse avant de mourir" (⇩ 7: 1981).

V   *Voeux.* Le Seuil, Librairie du XXᵉ siècle, 1990, 192 pp.

Contains: "Petit abécédaire illustré" (⇩ 4: 1969), "Lieux communs travaillés" (⇩ 4: 1972), "Versions latines" (⇩ 4: 1973), "Les Adventures de Dixion Harry" (⇩ 4: 1974), "Petite Histoire de la musique" (⇩ 4: 1976), "Œuvres anthumes" (⇩ 4: 1978), "Gamine de blouse" (⇩ 4: 1979), "ROM POL"

($\Downarrow$ 4: 1980), "Dictionnaire des cinéastes" ($\Downarrow$ 4: 1981), "Cocktail Queneau" ($\Downarrow$ 4: 1982).

CSL   *Cantatrix Sopranica L et autres écrits scientifiques*. Le Seuil, Librairie du XXe siècle, 1991, 126 pp.

Contains: "Experimental Demonstration of the Tomatotopic Organization in the Soprano (Cantatrix sopranica L)" ($\Downarrow$ 4: 1974), "Une Amitié scientifique et littéraire. Léon Burp et Marcel Gotlib, suivi de considérations nouvelles sur la vie et l'œuvre de Romuald Saint-Sohaint" ($\Downarrow$ 4: 1980), "Distribution spatio-temporelle de Coscinoscera Victoria, Coscinoscera Tigrata Carpenteri, Coscinoscera Punctata Barton & Coscinoscera Nigrostriata d'Iputupi" ($\Downarrow$ 3: 1980), "Roussel et Venise. Esquisse d'une géographie mélancolique" ($\Downarrow$ 5: 1977).

Volumes in preparation for the Librairie du XXe siècle include "Le Voyage d'Hiver" ($\Downarrow$ 4: 1979) and a collection of literary and critical articles, both for 1992, and a collection of writings on art and artists, for 1993.

SECTION 2: BOOKS IN COLLABORATION

PTG   (With Pierre Lusson and Jacques Roubaud) *Petit Traité invitant à la découverte de l'art subtil du go*. Christian Bourgois, 1969, 152 pp.

OCR   (With Raymond Queneau, Paul Fournel, and members of OuLiPo) *Oulipo. Créations, Re-Créations, Récréations*. Gallimard, Idées, 1973.

Translated into Italian (1985).

•   (With Antonio Corpora) *L'Arbre et l'Isaar à Lenggries*. Two extracts from *Espèces d'espaces* with twelve etchings by Corpora. Galilée, 1976.

•   (With Cuchi White) *L'Œil ébloui*. Le Chêne, 1981. 80 pp. Contains "Ceci n'est pas un mur . . ." on 16 unnumbered pp. and photographs of trompe-l'oeil paintings and murals.

REI   (With Robert Bober) *Récits d'Ellis Island. Histoires d'errance et d'espoir.* Hachette/Le Sorbier, 1981 (⇓ 9).

Atlas   (With members of OuLiPo) *Atlas de littérature potentielle.* Gallimard, Idées, 1981.

CGP III   (With Marcel Benabou) *Presbytères et prolétaires. Le Dossier P.A.L.F.* . Editions du Limon, 1989. (⇓ 5: 1973).

SECTION 3: CONTRIBUTIONS TO BOOKS AND CATALOGUES

1967

●   Preface to Roger Price, *Le Cerveau à Sornettes.* Julliard, 1967.

1970

Clô   "Palindrome pour Pierre Getzler". In the catalogue of the exhibition of Getzler's paintings at Galerie Camille Renault, 1970.

1973

●   "La Vie des choses", preface to a catalogue of an exhibition held at Musée Galliéra from 12 January to 11 February 1973.

1977

●   Preface to Claudine Dannequin, *Les Enfants baillonnés.* CEDIC, 1977.

●   Back-panel copy for Raymond Queneau, *Un Rude Hiver.* Gallimard, Collection L'Imaginaire, no. 1, 1977.

●   "Petite histoire d'un texte source" (⇓ 4:1977).

1978

Clô   "Treize Vers hétérogrammatiques pour Hans Dahlem". In *Hans Dahlem. Ein Buch zum 50. Geburtstag von seinen Freunden.* Herausgegeben von Ludwig Harig und Michael Krüger, p. 56. Saarbrücken: SDV, 1978.

1979

●   Untitled preface, "Tentative d'inventaire provisoire de quelques uns des mots évoqués par la vision des tableaux de Jacques Poli", "Enumérations, 2" and "11 x (11+11) +11" in *Jacques Poli. Peintures entomologiques 1978–1979.* Exhibition catalogue. Galerie Adrien Maeght, 1979.

●   "Paolo Boni, Mecánico de lo imaginario", in *Paolo Boni pinturas y grabados.* Exhibition catalogue. Banco de Granada, April 1979. (French text, ⇓ 4: 1979.)

- *"Série noire* d'Alain Corneau". In *L'Année du cinéma 1979*, ed. Danielle Heymann and Alain Lacombe, p. 164. Calmann-Lévy, 1979.

1980

CSL "Distribution spatio-temporelle de Coscinoscera Victoria, Coscinoscera Tigrata Carpenteri, Coscinoscera Punctata Barton & Coscinoscera Nigrostriata d'Iputupi" (with Sylvia Lamblin-Richardson). In *Cartes et Figures de la Terre*, p. 394. Centre Georges-Pompidou, 1980.

PC "81 Fiches-cuisine à l'usage des débutants". In Christian Besson and Catherine Weinzaepflen, *Manger*, pp. 97–109. Liège: Editions Yellow Now and Châlons-sur-Saône: Maison de la Culture, 1980. Translated into English.

PC "Considérations sur les lunettes". In *Les Lunettes*, ed. Pierre Marly, pp. 5–9. Hachette/Massin, 1980.

- "Je me souviens des années soixante". In Maurice Achard and Anne-Marie Métaillé, *Les Années soixante en noir et blanc.* Editions AMM, 1980.

- Translations of Harry Mathews, "The Scruple Shop" (pp. 291– 295), "The Battle" (p. 297), "Deathless, Lifeless" (pp. 301– 303), "The Swimmer" (pp. 303–307), in *Vingt Poètes Américains*, ed. Jacques Roubaud and Michel Deguy. Gallimard, 1980.

1981

PC "De quelques emplois du verbe habiter" . In *Construire pour habiter*, pp. 4–5. L'Equerre-Plan Construction, 1981.

- Preface to Sylvie Weil and Louis Rameau, *Trésor des expressions françaises.* Belin, Collection Le Temps retrouvé, no. 1, 1981.

- "Alphabet pour Stämpfli". In *Peter Stämpfli: Œuvres récentes.* Catalogue of an exhibition at the Centre Georges-Pompidou, 26 November 1980–11 January 1981.

- "Anagrammes de Georges Condominas". In *Orients. Mélanges offerts à Georges Condominas pour ses soixante ans.* Sudestasie/ Privat, 1981.

- "Ceci n'est pas un mur". In Georges Perec and Cuchi White, *L'Œil ébloui.* Le Chêne, 1981. 80 pp. (⇑ 2: 1981).

1982

- Preface to Alain Barandard, *La Cathédrale de Chartres dans tous ses états.* Denoël, 1982.

- "Cinq Poèmes de Georges Perec" (pp. 207–17) and Harry Mathews, "Les Cléments et les Féroces" ("The Dexters and the Sinisters", pp. 299–301). In *Anthologie arbitraire d'une nouvelle poésie, 1960–1982*, ed. Michel Deguy. Flammarion, 1982. See the list of *beaux présents* appended to chapter 63 for details of "Cinq Poèmes".

1985

● "Jacques Roubaud". Entry in *Encyclopaedia Universalis*, 1985 supplement.

1986

● "Abécédaire". Introduction to Chica, *Les Voyageurs de l'ABC*. Magnard-Jeunesse, 1986.

● "Etérnité" (↓ 4: 1981) (p. 249), "Carte postale" (↓ 4: 1981) (p. 251), "Geôle" (p. 320). In Emmanuel Hocquard and Raquel, *Orange Export Ltd 1969–1986*. Flammarion, 1986.

SECTION 4: PAMPHLETS, SELF-PUBLICATIONS
and Other Bibliographic Nightmares

1967

● "Chemin de Pierre". In Alain Guérin, Roger Kleman, Georges Perec, and Jacques Roubaud, *Sur des dessins et des peintures de Pierre Getzler*. Exhibition catalogue, December 1967.

1969

Clô "9691. Edna d'Nilou" ("The Great Palindrome"). Perec circulated a number of copies of the original typescript, which is not laid out in the same way as any of the printed versions. These typescript copies must therefore be counted as the (almost unobtainable) first edition of the Great Palindrome.

V "Petit abécédaire illustré". Limited edition of about 100 copies, hand-made by Perec at the Moulin d'Andé. Also published in *Chroniques de l'art vivant*, 1970.

1972

V "Lieux communs travaillés". Limited edition of about 100 hand-made copies, 1972.

1973

V "Versions latines". Limited edition of about 100 hand-made copies, for 1973.

Clô "Ulcérations". Limited edition of about 100 typed copies, for 1974.

1974

CSL "Experimental Demonstration of the Tomatotopic Organisation in the Soprano (Cantatrix Sopranica L)". Typescript insertion (pages numbered 511–529) to the collection of articles presented by CNRS LA 38 to Marthe Bonvallet on her retirement in 1974. (↓ 5: 1980)

Clô   *Ulcérations.* La Bibliothèque oulipienne, no. 1 (August 1974). Numbered edition of 150 copies.

V   "Les Adventures de Dixion Harry". Stencilled typescript, 24 pp. Approximately 100 "egg-samplers" run off at Griffydam (Leicestershire) in late December 1974.

1976

Clô   *La Clôture. Dix-sept poèmes hétérogrammatiques accompagnés de dix-sept photographies de Christine Lipinska.* Imprimerie Caniel, 1976. Signed edition of 100 copies.

V   "Petite Histoire de la musique en 25 charades". 100 typescript copies numbered 197700 to 197799, distributed in early 1977.

1977

Clô   "Dos Caddy d'aisselles". In *A Raymond Queneau.* La Bibliothèque oulipienne, no. 4 (1977). 150 numbered copies.

BibOl   "Petite histoire d'un texte source". In Italo Calvino, *Piccolo sillabario illustrato.* La Bibliothèque oulipienne, no. 6 (1977). 150 numbered copies.

1978

Clô   *Trompe l'œil.* (Six Anglo-French poems.) Photographs by Cuchi White. Patrick Guérard, 1978. 125 signed and numbered copies.

●   Claude Delarue, *Le Fils éternel.* Attributed to Georges Perec in *Le Monde* (29 September 1978) and then in *Who's Who in France* (1979–80 edition) – which goes to show that it doesn't always tell you what's what.

V   "Œuvres anthumes". Privately produced and distributed in 1978, but also published in part in *Le Magazine littéraire,* no. 141 (October 1978), p. 34, under the title "Charade". (⇓ 5: 1978).

1979

●   "Paolo Boni, Mécanicien de l'imaginaire". French text unpublished (⇓ 13: 1979); published in Spanish as "Paolo Boni, Mecánico de lo imaginario" (⇑ 3: 1979).

V   "Gamine de blouse". Privately printed, 1979.

●   "Le Voyage d'hiver". In *Saisons* (Hachette, 1979), not for sale. Also in *Hachette-Informations,* no. 18 (March 1980), an internal "house" magazine (⇓ 5: 1983).

Translated into English, German, and Italian.

1980

CSL   "Une Amitié scientifique et littéraire. Léon Burp et Marcel Gotlib, suivi de considérations nouvelles sur la vie et l'oeuvre de Romuald Saint-Sohaint". Special insertion in the numbered copies ("tirage de tête") of Marcel Gotlib, *Rubrique-à-brac et Trucs en vrac.* Dargaud, 1980.

728   GEORGES PEREC · A LIFE IN WORDS

V   "ROM POL". Privately printed in an edition of perhaps 150
        copies. Also published in *Le Fou parle* no. 12 (March 1980),
        pp. 18–20.

1981

BibOl "La Cantatrice Sauve". With Claude Burgelin, Paul Fournel,
         Béatrice de Jurquet, Harry Mathews, and Jacques Bens. La
         Bibliothèque oulipienne no. 16 (1981). Limited edition of 150
         copies.
V   *Dictionnaire des cinéastes*. Privately printed.
●   "ouvre ces serrures caverneuses". Poem on a postcard
         published by Orange Export Ltd (Malakoff), 1981 (⬆ 3:
         1986).
BibOl "Noces de Kmar Bendana et Noureddine Mechri". 19 copies
         numbered A–S handmade by Georges Perec at the University of
         Queensland on 2–4 September 1981.
●   "L'Eternité". 40 numbered and signed copies published by
         Orange Export Ltd, 1981 (⬆ 3: 1986 ⬇ 5: 1983).

1982

V   "Cocktail Queneau". Limited edition printed by P.O.L. and
         distributed privately.
●   "A propos des *Jeux de la Comtesse Dolingen de Gratz*". Fly-sheet
         distributed prior to the first showing of the film (⬇ 5: 1982).
BibOl "Epithalames". La Bibliothèque oulipienne, no. 19 (March
         1982). 191 numbered copies.

1983

●   "jfa". In *Index*, Ecole Normale Supérieure de Saint-Cloud,
         March 1983). 300 copies.

1985

●   *Métaux*. Sept sonnets hétérogrammatiques accompagnés de sept
         graphisculptures de Paolo Boni. Published by Robert et Lydie
         Dutrou. 133 copies, numbered 1–15, I–XV and 1–103, on fine
         paper measuring 60 × 43 cm. Four of the sonnets, written in
         1976–77, are in *La Clôture*. The full set is reprinted in *CGP* 5.

SECTION 5: PUBLICATIONS IN
PERIODICALS

1955

●   Review of Albert Vidalie, *Les Bijoutiers du Clair de Lune*.
         Nouvelle Nrf, no. 25 (1 January 1955), p. 145.
●   Review of Jean-Pierre Richard, *Littérature et sensation*. *Nouvelle
         Nrf*, no. 28 (April 1955), p. 715.

- Review of Donald Wyndham, *Canicule. Nouvelle Nrf*, no. 28 (April 1955), p. 719.
- Review of Marcel Lallemand, *Bonheur II. Bâtir la Maison. Nouvelle Nrf*, no. 29 (May 1955), p. 931.
- Review of Félicien Marceau, *Balzac et son monde. Nouvelle Nrf*, no. 30 (June 1955), pp. 1115–1116.
- Review of René de Obaldia, *Tamerlan des Cœurs. Nouvelle Nrf*, no. 34 (October 1955), p. 789.
- Review of Henri Thomas, *La Cible. Nouvelle Nrf*, no. 35 (November 1955), pp. 967–968
- Review of Driss Chraibi, *Les Boucs. Nouvelle Nrf*, no. 36 (December 1955), p. 1163.

1957
- Review of Jacques Nantet, *Les Juifs et les Nations. Les Lettres nouvelles*, no. 45 (January 1957), pp. 134–135.
- Review of Ivo Andrić, *A Bridge on the Drina. Les Lettres nouvelles*, no. 45 (January 1957), pp. 139–40.

1959
- [Serge Valène, pseud.]."L'Enfance de Djilas au Montenegro" (review of Milovan Djilas, *Land Without Justice*). *Les Lettres nouvelles*, no. 3 (18 March 1959), p. 22.

1960
- [unsigned] "La Perpétuelle Reconquête" (with Henri Peretz). *La Nouvelle Critique* (May 1960), pp. 77–87.

1962
- "Le Nouveau Roman et le refus du réel" (with Claude Burgelin). *Partisans,* no. 3 (February 1962), pp. 108–18.
- "Pour une littérature réaliste", *Partisans*, no. 4 (April 1962), pp. 121–130.
- "Engagement ou Crise du langage?", *Partisans*, no. 7 (November 1962), pp. 171–182.

1963
- "Robert Antelme ou la vérité de la littérature". *Partisans*, no. 8 (January 1963), pp. 121–134.
- "Le VIᵉ Congrès de l'UEC". *Partisans*, no. 9 (March 1963), pp. 209–213.
- "L'Univers de la science-fiction". *Partisans*, no. 10 (May 1963), pp. 118–130.
- Review of Georges Limbour, *La Chasse au Mérou. Partisans*, no. 11 (July 1963), pp. 170–173.
- "Le Mystère Robbe-Grillet" (review of Bruce Morisette, *Les Romans de Robbe-Grillet*). *Partisans*, no. 11 (July 1963), pp. 167–170.

1964

- "*Wozzeck*, ou la méthode de l'apocalypse". *Clarté*, no. 53 (January 1964), pp. 51–53.

1966

- "Evidence du Western" (review of Raymond Bellour, editor, *Le Western*). *La Quinzaine littéraire*, no. 8 (1 July 1966), pp. 26–27.
- "L'Usure contrôlée". *Arts-Loisirs*, no. 54 (5 October 1966), p. 53.
- "L'Indestructible Rolls". *Arts-Loisirs*, no. 55 (12 October 1966), p. 12.
- "Le Papier Roi". *Arts-Loisirs*, no. 56 (19 October 1966), p. 55.
- "Les Idées du jour". *Arts-Loisirs*, no. 57 (26 October 1966), p. 10.
- "Le Vrai Petit Bistro". *Arts-Loisirs*, no. 58 (2 November 1966), p. 12.
- "Astérix au pouvoir". *Arts-Loisirs*, no. 59 (9 November 1966), p. 9.
- "Eloge du hamac". *Arts-Loisirs*, no. 61 (23 November 1966), p. 23.
- "Du lexique et des antiquaires". *Arts-Loisirs*, no. 62 (30 November 1966), p. 21.
- "La Dictature du whisky". *Arts-Loisirs*, no. 63 (7 December 1966), p. 19.
- "Esquissse d'une théorie générale des gadgets". *Arts-Loisirs*, no. 65 (21 December 1966), p. 21.

1967

- "Des Drug-stores et de leur environnement". *Arts-Loisirs*, no. 67 (4 January 1967), p. 15.
- "Le Computeur pour tous". *Arts-Loisirs*, no. 68 (11 January 1967), p. 21.
- "Le Hit-Parade". *Arts-Loisirs*, no. 69 (18 January 1967), p. 11.
- "Pour un usage rationnel du bouillon". *Arts-Loisirs*, no. 72 (8 February 1967), p. 11.
- "Principes élémentaires de la diversification". *Arts-Loisirs*, no. 73 (15 February 1967), p. 13.
- "Du Terrorisme des modes". *Arts-Loisirs*, no. 75 (1 March 1967), p. 9.

MA   "Un Homme qui dort". *Les Temps modernes*, no. 250 (March 1967), pp. 1537–1556. Prepublication of the opening section.

Jsn   "Une Quête en rond" (review of Alain Guérin, *Un Bon Départ*). *La Quinzaine littéraire*, no. 24 (15 March 1967), p. 8. The version printed in *Je suis né* is slightly different.

- "Ecriture et Mass-média". *Preuves*, no. 202 (December 1967), pp. 6–10.

1968

- "'J'ai choisi le sonnet'. Entretien avec Jacques Roubaud". *La Quinzaine littéraire*, no. 42 (1 January 1968), pp. 6–7.

D   "La Consultation". *Les Lettres nouvelles*, November-December 1968, pp. 14–25.

- "L'Art et la manière d'aborder son chef de service pour lui demander une augmentation". *Enseignement programmé*, no. 4 (December 1968). Reprinted in *Communications et langages*, no. 17 (1973), pp. 41–56, in a slightly abbreviated form. Translated into Italian.

1969

D   "Booz assoupi" and "La Mort d'un baryton". *Subsidia 'pataphysica*, no. 6 (1969), pp. 74–80.

OCR   "Histoire du lipogramme". *Les Lettres nouvelles*, June-July 1969, pp. 15–30. Translated into English and Italian.

OCR   "Les Horreurs de la guerre. Drame alphabétique". *Union des écrivains*, no. 1 (1969). Unpaginated. (⇓ 7: 1969).

W   *W*. Serial publication in *La Quinzaine littéraire*, nos. 81–94 and 96–100 (16 October 1969 to 1 August 1970). See Chapters 44 and 52 above for the relationship of this version to the book published as *W ou le souvenir d'enfance*.

1970

OCR   "Le Grand Palindrome". *Change*, no. 6 (1970), pp. 217–223. Also in *La Clôture* (⇑ 1: 1980; also ⇑ 4: 1969).

1971

BO   "Quatre Rêves particulièrement influencés par le cinéma". *Nouvelle Revue française*, no. 226 (October 1971), pp. 147–152.

1972

- "En Cent" (chapter 1 of *Les Revenentes*). *Subsidia 'pataphysica*, no. 18 (1972), pp. 70–72.

Jsn   "Autoportrait: Les Gnocchis de l'automne ou réponse à quelques questions me concernant". *Cause commune*, no. 1 (May 1972), pp. 19–20.

BO   "Six Rêves". *Cause commune*, no. 2 (June 1972), pp. 49–52.

- Harry Mathews, "Trois Tribus" (extract from *Tlooth*, translated by Georges Perec). *Les Lettres nouvelles*, no. 4 (September 1972), pp. 18–31.

- "L'Orange est proche" (review of Stanley Kubrick, *Clockwork Orange*). *Cause commune*, no. 3 (October 1972), pp. 1–2. Translated into Portuguese (1977)

- "Fonctionnement du système nerveux dans la tête". *Cause commune*, no. 3 (October 1972), pp. 42–55. (⇓ 7: 1972) Translated into German.

- (With Georges Balandier, Jean Duvignaud and Paul Virilio)

"Le Grabuge". *Cause commune*, no. 4 (November 1972), pp. 2–15.

1973

inf "Approches de quoi?" *Cause commune*, no. 5 (February 1973), pp. 3–4.
Translated into Portuguese (1977)

• "Micro-traductions. Quinze variations discrètes sur un poème connu". *Change*, no. 14 (February 1973), pp. 113–117. Fragment in *Atlas*, p. 157.

CGP III "P.A.L.F." (with Marcel Benabou). *Change*, no. 14 (February 1973), pp. 118-130.

• "Chalands et nonchalants". *Cause commune*, no. 7 (October 1973), pp. 4–5.

• "O Images, vous suffisez à mon bonheur". *La Quinzaine littéraire*, no. 172 (1 October 1973).

1974

• "*Un Homme qui dort*: lecture cinématographique". *Combat*, 4 April 1974, p. 12.

EsEs "Journal d'un usager de l'espace". *Les Nouvelles littéraires*, no. 2450 (9 September 1974), pp. 6–7.

• "Qu'est-ce que la littérature potentielle?" *Le Magazine littéraire*, no. 94 (November 1974), pp. 22–23.

• "Points de suspension" ("excerpt" from "9691 Edna d'Nilou"). *Roy Rogers* (New York), Winter 1974.

1975

Jsn "Les Lieux d'une fugue". *Présences et regards*, no. 17/18 (Autumn 1975). This publication contains printing errors. (⇓ 9: 1976)

• "Tentative d'épuisement d'un lieu parisien". *Cause commune* (Collection 10/18, no. 936), pp. 59–108. Dated 1975 for February 1976. (⇑ 1:1982)
Translated into Portuguese (1977)

1976

Jms "Je me souviens" (items 1–163). *Les Cahiers du chemin*, no. 26 (1976), pp. 83- 108.

PC "Lire: esquisse socio-physiologique". *Esprit*, no. 1 (January 1976), pp. 9–20.
Translated into Hungarian (1977).

PC "Notes concernant les objects qui sont sur ma table de travail". *Les Nouvelles littéraires*, no. 2521 (26 February 1976), p. 17.

• Harry Mathews, "Plasma Lacte" ("Milk Plasma"), translated by Georges Perec. *Action poétique*, no. 65 (May 1976), pp. 46–47.

inf "Tentative d'inventaire des aliments liquides et solides que j'ai ingurgités au cours de l'année 1974". *Action poétique*, no. 65 (May 1976), pp. 185–189.

•   "Cinq mille milliards de romans" (review of Italo Calvino, *The Castle of Crossed Destinies*). *Les Nouvelles littéraires*, no. 2531 (6 May 1976), p. 7.

•   "Alphabets" (sixteen poems from *Alphabets*). *L'Echo des Savanes*, no. 21 (June 1976), pp. 20–29.

PC   "Douze regards obliques". *Traverses*, no. 3 (1976), pp. 44–48.

1977

•   "Tentative de description de quelques lieux parisiens: guettées", *Les Lettres nouvelles*, no. 1 (February 1977), pp. 61–71 (⇓ 14, *Lieux*). The title puns on "Gaîté", the name of the street that is being described.

inf   "Tentative de description de quelques lieux parisiens: La rue Vilin". *L'Humanité*, 11 November 1977, p. 2. (⇓ 14, *Lieux*)

PC   "Trois chambres retrouvées". *Les Nouvelles littéraires*, no. 2612 (24 November 1977), p. 20. This publication contains printing errors. (⇓ 14, *Lieux où j'ai dormi*)

•   "Tentative de description de quelques lieux parisiens: Vues d'Italie". *Nouvelle Revue de Psychanalyse*, no. 16 (1977), pp. 239–246.

PC   "Les Lieux d'une ruse". *Cause commune*, new series no. 1 (1977) (Collection 10/18, no. 1143), pp. 77–88.

CSL "Roussel et Venise. Esquisse d'une géographie mélancolique" (with Harrry Mathews). *L'Arc* 68 (1977), pp. 9–25. Translated into English and German.

L   "Les Voyages de Smautf" (chapter 15 of *Life A User's Manual*). *Exit*, no. 12/13 (Autumn 1977), pp. 66–69.

1978

L   "Compendium libri 'De Vita et modo utendi' cum CLXXVIIII ex personis quae in eo libro sunt" (from chapter 51 of *Life A User's Manual*). *Poësie* 4 (1978), pp. 107–112.

L   "Histoire de l'homme qui voulait retrouver le Très-Saint Vase" (from chapter 22 of *Life A User's Manual*). *Nouvelles Impressions*, no. 1 (1978), pp. 54–64.

PC   "Notes brèves sur l'art et la manière de ranger ses livres" ("Extrait des *Notes de Chevet*, en préparation"). *L'Humidité*, no. 25 (Spring 1978), pp. 35–38.

•   "Post-scriptum" after Philippe Drogoz, "Chronique d'une collaboration chronique". *La Quinzaine littéraire*, no. 284 (1 August 1978), pp. 5–6.

•   "Des Comédiens au rabais" (review of Festival Metro Retro). *Les Nouvelles littéraires*, no. 2647 (4 August 1978), p. 11.

inf   "243 Cartes postales en couleurs véritables". *Le Fou parle*, no. 8 (October 1978), pp. 11–16.

V   "Charade". *Le Magazine littéraire*, no. 141 (October 1978), p. 34. (⇑ 4: 1978)

PC   "Notes sur ce que je cherche". *Le Figaro*, 8 December 1978, p. 28.
Translated into English.

●   "Cyd Charisse m'était conté" (review of Jean-Claude Missaien's biography of Cyd Charisse). *Les Nouvelles littéraires*, no. 2666 (21 December 1978), p. 32.

●   "Mon plus beau souvenir de Noël". *Le Nouvel Observateur*, no. 737 (23 December 1978), pp. 60–61.

1979

Jsn   "Le Rêve et le texte". *Le Nouvel Observateur*, no. 741 (22 January 1979), p. 46.

PC   "Je me souviens de Malet & Isaac". *H-Histoire*, no. 1 (March 1979), pp. 197- 209.

Jsn   "Ellis Island. Description d'un projet". *Recherches*, no. 38 (*Catalogue pour des Juifs de maintenant*) (September 1979), pp. 512–514.

Clô   "Gamme". *Les Nouvelles littéraires* (August 1979).

●   Alain Corneau, *Série noire* (full script of the film, dialogue by Georges Perec). *L'Avant-Scène Cinéma*, no. 233 (1 October 1979).

●   "Le Pacte". *Le Bout des Bordes*, no. 5/6 (29 October – 29 November 1979), p. 19.

●   "Allées et venues rue de l'Assomption". *L'Arc*, no. 76 (1979), pp. 28–34. (⇓ 14: *Lieux)*

●   "J'aime, je n'aime pas". *L'Arc*, no. 76 (1979), pp. 38–39.

Atlas   "Quatre figures pour *La Vie mode d'emploi*". *L'Arc*, no. 76 (1979), pp. 50–53.

●   "Bibliographie approximative assortie de quelques commentaires de l'auteur". *L'Arc*, no. 76 (1979), pp. 91–96. The somewhat longer original typescript is reproduced in *CGP I*.

1980

●   "Les Jeux intéressants" (with Jacques Bens). *Ça m'intéresse*, no. 1 (1980).

●   "Emprunts à Flaubert". *L'Arc*, no. 79 (1980), pp. 49–50.

V   "ROM POL". *Le Fou parle*, no. 12 (March 1980), pp. 18–20. (⇑ 4: 1980)

●   "Stations Mabillon". *Action poétique*, no. 81 (May 1980). Transcription of part of "Tentative de description de choses vues au carrefour Mabillon le 19 mai 1978" (⇓ 7: 1978).

●   "Questions-Réponses". *Action poétique*, no. 81 (May 1980), pp. 38–39.

CSL   "Experimental Demonstration of the Tomatotopic Organization in the Soprano (Cantatrix Sopranica L)". *Banana-Split*, no. 2 (June 1980), pp. 63–74.

- "Elégie de Pierre et Denise Getzler". *Art-presse*, no. 39 (July 1980), p. 14.
- "Fragments de désert et de culture". *Traverses*, no. 19 (1980), pp. 115–118.
- "Perec/rinations". In *Télérama* every week from 8 October 1980 to 1 July 1982.
- "A Jacques Vallet". *Le Fou parle*, no. 14 (October 1980), p. 41.
- "Récits d'Ellis Island: Un Film, Un Livre". *INA-Magazine*, no. 23 (December 1980), pp. 6–7. Partly in collaboration with Robert Bober.

1981

- "Emprunts à Queneau". *Les Amis de Valentin Brû*, no. 13/14 (1981), pp. 42–45.

CSL "Experimental Demonstration of the Tomatotopic Organization in the Soprano (Cantatrix Sopranica L)". *Sub-Stance* (New York), no. 29 (1981), pp. 37–45.

- "Les Jeux intéressants" (with Jacques Bens). *Ça m'intéresse*, nos. 1–17 (March 1981-July 1982).
- "J.R. Tentative de saturation onomastique". *Banana-Split*, no. 4 (1981).
- "Avez-vous lu Harry Mathews?" *Le Monde*, 3 April 1981, p. 1. Translated into English.

inf "Promenades dans Londres". *Atlas Air France*, April 1981.

- "Prise d'ecriture". *Chronique des écrits en cours*, no. 1 (May 1981), pp. 13–17.

PC "De la difficulté qu'il y a à imaginer une cité idéale". *La Quinzaine littéraire*, no. 353 (1 August 1981), p. 38.

inf "Ces bureaux qui révèlent votre personnalité" (alternative title of "Le Saint des Saints"). *Vogue/Hommes*, no. 42 (September 1981), pp. 94 and 98.

- "Un peu plus de quatre mille poèmes en prose pour Fabrizio Clerici". *Action poétique*, no. 85 (September 1981), pp. 65–72.
- "Les Jeux" (with Jacques Bens). *Jeune-Afrique*, nos. 1080–1088 (16 September–11 November 1981), nos. 1090–1095 (25 November–30 December 1981), and nos. 1097–1104 (13 January–3 March 1982).

inf "Still Life/Style Leaf". *Le Fou parle*, no. 19 (September 1981), pp. 3–6. Translated into English.

inf "Tout autour de Beaubourg". *Atlas Air France*, October 1981.

- "Chapitre Cent Cinquante-Cinq. Copie certifiée conforme". *Lectures* (Bari) no. 9 (December 1981), p. 199.

1982

PC "Penser/Classer". *Le Genre humain*, no. 2 (1982), pp 111–27.

- "Gammes. Quelle est la contrainte?" *Les Nouvelles littéraires*, no. 2828 (18 March 1982), p. 46.

● "A propos des *Jeux de la Comtesse Dolingen de Gratz*". *Les Nouvelles littéraires*, no. 2829 (25 March 1982), p. 30.

● "Adieu à Venise". *Action poétique*, no. 88 (1982). Unbound insertion.

● Harry Mathews, "Age et nuages indifférents" ("Poems after Robert Regnier I: Age and Indifferent Clouds"), translated by Georges Perec. *Chronique des écrits en cours*, no. 3 (May 1982), pp. 6–9.

1983

● "Le Voyage d'hiver". *Le Magazine littéraire*, no. 193 (March 1983), pp. 33–36. (⇑ 4: 1979)

● "L'Eternité". *Le Magazine littéraire*, no. 193 (March 1983), p. 36. Laid out more correctly in *Orange Export Ltd* (⇑ 3: 1986).

1984

CSL   "Experimental Demonstration of the Tomatotopic Organization in the Soprano (Cantatrix Sopranica L)". *Sciences et avenir*, no. 446 (April 1984), pp. 22–25.

● "Pouce-pouce: Pour Norbert Iborra". *Bulletin du Club français de la médaille*, no. 84 (1984), pp. 44–47.

1992

● "A la grave saison . . ." *Lire*, no. 197 (February 1992), p. 23.

★

Second Part

SECTION 6: THEATRE

This section includes all works written for the theatre as well as a selection of theatrical realisations of works written for other media.

Th   *La Poche Parmentier*. First performance: Théâtre de Nice, 12 February 1974.
         Translated into German by Eugen Helmle as *Der Kartoffelkessel*, performed at Stadttheater Luzern in November 1988.

Th   *L'Augmentation*. First performance: Théâtre de la Gaîté-Monparnasse, February-March 1970, directed by Marcel Cuvelier. Then, in German, as *Die Gehaltserhöhung*, directed by Annette Spola, Theater am Sozialamt, Munich, in November 1972 and subsequently at Münster, Wiesbaden, etc., between February and June 1973. Revived (in French) at Saint-Etienne in 1980 and (by Marcel Cuvelier) at Théâtre de la Huchette, Paris, in February 1982, for three months. Translated into Italian as *L'Aumento* by Enrico Groppali, directed by Alessandro Marinuzzi, performed at Udine and Trieste in 1990 and in Milan in May 1991. Translated into Swedish as *Löneförhöjningen* by Magnus Hedlund, directed by Carl Duner, performed in Stockholm in October-December 1991.
         Translated into Polish (1985).

Jms   *Je me souviens*. Directed and recited by Sami Frey. Presented at the Festival d'Avignon, July 1988; Comédie de Genève, September 1988; Festival d'automne, Paris 1988; Théâtre Mogador, Paris, January 1989; Opéra-Comique, Paris, March 1989; etc. Also recorded on video for television broadcast, and available as an audio cassette.
         Translated into Swedish as *Jag minns* by Magnus Hedlund, directed by Magnus Florin, performed in Stockholm in October-December 1991.
         Translated into Italian as *Mi Ricordo* by Guido Davico Bonino, performed and directed by Valeriano Gialli in Turin, April 1989.

L   *La Vie mode d'emploi*. Semi-dramatised reading devised by René Farabet and performed at the Festival d'Avignon in July 1988.
         (⇓ 7: 1988)

•   "243 Cartes postales en couleurs véritables". Translated as

"Tvåhundredfyrtiotre vykort" by Magnus Hedlund, directed by Magnus Florin, performed in Stockholm in October–December 1991.

W   *W ou le souvenir d'enfance*. Adapted and directed by Bernard Palmi, performed at the Théatre de la Minoterie, Marseille, December 1991.

●   "Fonctionnement du système nerveux dans la tête". Directed by Jean Guérin, presented at the Studio Berthelot, Montreuil, April 1992.

LC   *Les Choses*. Adapted by Bernard Labbé and Véronique Bernard-Maugiron, presented at the Festival d'Avignon, 1992.

SECTION 7: RADIO

This section complements the appendix to chapter 38, "RadioPerec: German Checklist", and includes (a) works written *in French* for broadcast on radio (whether in German or in French, and whether broadcast or not); (b) works broadcast on French radio (whether written for radio or not, but excluding readings of extracts from works published in books or periodicals); and the only known radio adaptation in English of a work by Georges Perec. A selection of Perec's radio interviews and talks is included in section 12 below.

1967

●   *Le Diable dans la bibliothèque*. Unpublished.
        Translated into German as *Der Teufel in der Bibliothek* by Eugen Helmle and broadcast by SR in October 1991.

1969

Th   *L'Augmentation ou, comment, quelles que soient les conditions sanitaires, psychologiques, climatiques, économiques ou autres, mettre le maximum de chances de votre côté en demandant à votre chef de service un réajustement de votre salaire*. Broadcast by SR as *Wucherungen* on 12 November 1969.
        Translated into Catalan, German, Italian, Polish, Swedish (⇑ 6).

OCR   "Les Horreurs de la Guerre. Drame alphabétique". Submitted to Radio-France as a radio play circa 1969; not accepted. (Information from Radio-France card-index.)

1970

●   *Les Extraordinaires Aventures de Monsieur Eveready*. 165 episodes. Typescript FP 103. Broadcast daily (except Sundays) by Radio-Abidjan from mid-April to 31 October 1970.

1972

- *Fonctionnement du système nerveux dans la tête* (⇑ 5: 1972).
  Broadcast as *Mechanismus des Nervensystems im Kopf* by WDR on
  15 June 1972.
  Accepted for broadcast by France-Culture, production put in
  hand by Alain Colas, but no trace of broadcast has been found.
  The relevant dossier, AL 4° Ya 9036 Rad, was missing from
  its place on the occasions I sought to consult it at the Arsenal
  Library.

- *AudioPerec*. Produced by Alain Trutat, Atelier de Création
  radiophonique no. 101, broadcast on France-Culture on 5 March
  1972. Running time 170 minutes.
  Includes: *L'Augmentation* (recorded from the stage performance
  [⇑ 6], with an additional "commentaire sonore" by Philippe
  Drogoz); "Le Petit Abécédaire illustré" (*V* and ⇑ 4: 1969) set
  to music by Philippe Drogoz; *Diminuendo* (⇓ 10); *Souvenir d'un
  voyage à Thouars* (⇓ 10), *Tagstimmen* (as broadcast by SR: see
  "RadioPerec: German Checklist" on p. 386 above); and
  "OuLiPo: Gloses et Textes" by Marcel Benabou, Luc Etienne,
  Paul Fournel, François Le Lionnais, Georges Perec, Jean Quéval,
  and Jacques Roubaud.

1974

- *186.260.374.010* (soundtrack of *Un Homme qui dort* [⇓ 8: 1973]).
  Broadcast by France-Culture (Atelier de Création
  radiophonique, no. 186) on 26 March 1974.

1975

- "Entretiens avec Maurice Nadeau". Produced by Georges
  Perec. Recorded on 11 June 1975 and broadcast by
  France-Culture in 5 instalments on 17–21 November 1975.

1977

- "Poésie ininterrompue: Georges Perec" (readings of *La
  Disparition*, *Alphabets*, *Ulcérations*, and an important interview
  with Bernard Noël [⇓ 12: 1977]). Broadcast by France-Culture
  on 20 February 1977. Running time 145 minutes.

1978

- "Tentative de description de choses vues au carrefour Mabillon
  le 19 mai 1978". Atelier de Création radiophonique, no. 381,
  directed by René Farabet, broadcast by France-Culture on 25
  February 1979. Running time approximately two hours. For the
  text, *see* "Stations Mabillon" (⇑ 5: 1980).

1981

Jsn   "Quelques-unes des choses qu'il faudrait tout de même que je
fasse avant de mourir". See above, pp. 707–708.

1988

L   *La Vie mode d'emploi.* Radio serial, edited from the recordings
of the performances at the Avignon Festival (⇑ 6), broadcast
by France-Culture in October 1988 and repeated in March 1992.

1989

L   *Life A User's Manual.* Radio play, adapted by Suzanne Kiernan
from the English translation, broadcast by Australian
Broadcasting Corporation in 1989.

SECTION 8: CINEMA

I have included in this section all the traces I have seen with my
own eyes of Perec's involvement with the cinema, excluding his
reviews of films and of books about films, and excluding also work
intended for television (⇓ 9), which, in French eyes, would be
more noble were it called film. Many of these items are (a)
collaborative, (b) unpublished, and (c) unrealised, and could
therefore also figure in section 13 and, strictly speaking, in section
14 as well. The items that exist on celluloid are marked with an
asterisk. Titles are entered under the year when the work was
(mostly) done, not under the year of completion or release.

1962

●   *La Bande magnétique* (with Michel Martens). Film-script outline.

1966

●   *Les Choses.* ("Un film en couleurs d'après le livre de Georges
Perec. Scénario, adaptation et dialogues: Raymond Bellour,
Jean Mailland, Georges Perec. Réalisation: Jean Mailland.
Production: Max Bonnafont"). Typescript booklet, 97 pp., 1966.
(A second and/or third attempt to make a film of *Les Choses*
towards the end of the 1960s may have involved Nicos Papatakis,
Noureddine Mechri, and the Bavaria studios at Munich.)

1969

●   *Le Club.* Sketch for a "mad-cap comedy", to be made with
Jean-Paul Rappeneau.

1971

●   *Des Oiseaux dans la nuit* (with Jean-François Adam). This may
be the first version of the film that was eventually made as
Retour à la bien-aimée and released in 1979.

●   *Malédiction!* ("Scénario original de Georges Perec et Jean-Pierre
Prévost. Réalisation Jean-Pierre Prévost".) Typescript
booklet, 56 pp. foolscap.

1973

★ *Un Homme qui dort*. Black and white. Length: sixty minutes. Directed by Bernard Queysanne and Georges Perec, after the novel of the same name. Produced by Dovidis (Paris) and SATPEC (Tunis). Camera: Bernard Zitzerman. Voice: Ludmila Mikael. Sole actor: Jacques Spiesser. Music: Philippe Drogoz and Eugénie Kuffler (Ensemble 010). (⇑ 7: 1974 [sound track], ⇑ 1 [text]).

Planned from 1971, shot in 1973, released in 1974. Prix Jean Vigo 1974. New copy released in 1990.

★ English-language version translated by Harry Mathews, dubbed by Shelley Duval; released in 1974 as *A Man in a Dream*.

★ Italian version (subtitled) shown at the Venice film festival in 1975 as *Il Dormiveglia*.

★ *Le F.I.A.P.* (Foyer international d'accueil de Paris). Length: six minutes. Commentary by Georges Perec. Directed by Bernard Queysanne. Produced by Pathé for the French Foreign Ministry. Released in 1974.

Le Mieux-Etre. Length: twelve minutes. Script by Georges Perec. Directed by Patrice Molinard. Produced by IRFA for the CNRS. (Information from Bernard Queysanne.) No copy has been located.

1974

★ *Gustave Flaubert. Le Travail de l'écrivain*. Length: seven and a half minutes. Dictation, 2 pp., read by Jacques Spiesser. Directed by Bernard Queysanne. Produced by Pathé for the French Foreign Ministry.

★ *L'Oeil de l'autre*. Typescript sketch, 15 pp., for a film, with Bernard Queysanne. Made as a television film in 1976 from a script by Noureddine Mechri, directed by Bernard Queysanne and produced by INA for FR3.

1975

★ *Aho! Au cœur du monde primitif*. Directed by Daniel Bertolino and François Floquet. Script by Georges Perec. Broadcast on Canadian television and shown as a film at Avignon, July 1988. The original text of Perec's script has not been located. Alternative title: *Aho! Les Hommes de la Forêt*.

1978

★ *Série noire*. Adapted from Jim Thompson, *Des Cliques et des Cloaques* (*A Hell of a Woman*, 1954), by Alain Corneau. Dialogue by Georges Perec. Directed by Alain Corneau. Released in April 1979. Original title: *Moonlight Fiesta*. Film script published in *L'Avant-Scène Cinéma*, no. 233 (1 October 1979).

• *La Couronne de fer* (with Jean-Paul Rappeneau). Typescript scenario, 34 pp. December 1978.

• *Alfred et Marie*. "Un film de Gérard Zingg. Scénario original de Philippe Dumarçay, Georges Perec et Gérard Zingg. Adaptation de Georges Perec et Gérard Zingg. Dialogues de Georges Perec". Typed booklet in sixty sequences, 1979. Also known as "Dites-le avec des fleurs".

1979

★ *Retour à la bien-aimée.* Directed by Jean-François Adam. Script and dialogues by Jean-François Adam, Jean-Claude Carrère, Georges Perec, and Benoît Jacquot. Released in 1979.

1980

● *Signe particulier néant.* Proposal, 6 ff, for an adaptation of *La Disparition* to the screen.

★ *Les Jeux de la Comtesse Dolingen de Gratz.* Directed by Catherine Binet. Produced by Georges Perec for Les Films du Nautile. Shown at Cannes, May 1981, Venice Film Festival, September 1981, New York Film Festival, March 1982. Released in Paris in March 1982.

1981

● *A Tire d'aile.* "Un film de Pascal Aubier. Scénario de Pascal Aubier. Adaptation et dialogues de Pascal Aubier et Georges Perec". Typescript booklet, 196 pp.

● *Vous souvenez-vous de Griffin?* Unfinished manuscript, related to *Signe particulier néant.*

SECTION 9: TELEVISION

● *Journal d'un arriviste.*
(Draft title: *Quelque chose à dire*). With Bernard Queysanne. Typescript, 3 ff, circa 1974. Abandoned.

★ *Les Poètes: Jacques Roubaud.*
Television portrait made in 1973, shot at Saint-Félix. Directed by Jean-Pierre Prévost. Broadcast details not known.

★ *La Vie filmée des Français* (episode 2).
Directed by Michel Pamart and Claude Ventura. Commentary written and spoken by Georges Perec. Broadcast by FR3 on 1 August 1975.

★ *Les Lieux d'une fugue.*
Colour. Length forty-two minutes. Directed by Georges Perec from his own script (⇧ 5: 1975). Text read by Marcel Cuvelier. Camera: Bernard Zitzerman. Editing: Catherine Binet. Made in 1976. Produced by INA and broadcast on TF1 on 6 July 1978 ("Caméra-Je").

*REI   *Récits d'Ellis Island. Histoires d'errance et d'espoir.*
Colour. Length: 100 minutes total. Draft script (19 ff) by
Georges Perec, commentary to part I by Georges Perec,
interviews in part II conducted (in English) by Georges Perec.
Directed by Robert Bober. Made in 1979 in New York.
Produced by INA and broadcast by TF1 on 25 and 26
November 1980.
Part I translated by Harry Mathews and read by him as a
voice-over in the English-language version, *Ellis Island
Revisited: Tales of Vagrancy and Hope,* available (in theory) from
INA and the French Foreign Ministry.

★   *Pour quelques jours encore.*
Commentary by Georges Perec. Short film by Robert Bober
on the Gare d'Orsay; other details lost.

★   *Inauguration*
Commentary by Georges Perec. Short film (following on from
Pour quelques jours encore) directed by Robert Bober and broadcast
on 23 April 1981 by TF1("Expressions"). Length: nine
minutes.

★   *Trompe l'oeil.*
Colour, 16mm. Length thirteen minutes. Scripted, edited, and
directed by Catherine Binet. Includes a reading of Georges
Perec, *L'oeil ébloui* and *Trompe-l'oeil.* Grand Prix de la
Recherche, 1982.

SECTION 10: MUSIC AND OPERA

●   *Diminuendo*
Music by Bruno Gillet. First performed at the Biennale de Paris,
1971. (⇑ 7: 1972 [AudioPerec])

CGP I   *Souvenir d'un voyage à Thouars*
Performed in 1972 by GERM, conducted by Philippe Drogoz
and Georges Perec. (⇑ 7: 1972 [AudioPerec])

●   "L'Art effaré: ouverture".
(with Philippe Drogoz). *Le Fou parle,* no. 21/22 (1982), pp. 1–
3. (⇓ 14)

●   *Konzertstück für Sprecher und Orchester*
(with Philippe Drogoz and Eugen Helmle). See "RadioPerec:
German Checklist" on page 386 for details.

●   *La Fosse d'orchestre.*
Musical experiment by Philippe Drogoz, related to *La Poche
Parmentier.* First performed at A.R.C. in 1978.

SECTION 11: MULTIMEDIA

● *Le CNRS.*
Text for a "mur audiovisuel" or permanent split-screen slideshow designed by Patrice Molinard, for IFRA, circa 1972.

Third Part

SECTION 12: TALKS, LECTURES
AND SELECTED INTERVIEWS

1959

Jsn   "Le Saut en parachute". Semi-accidental taperecording of remarks made ad lib at a meeting of *Arguments* on 10 January 1959.

1965

●   "Les Artistes devant la politique" (reply to questionnaire). *Arts*, no. 10 (1 December 1965), pp. 10–11.

RCF   "Georges Perec s'explique" (interview with Marcel Benabou and Bruno Marcenac). *Les Lettres françaises*, no. 1108 (2 December 1965), pp. 14–15. Translated into English.

1967

PAP   "Pouvoirs et limites du romancier français contemporain". Lecture, University of Warwick, May 1967.

1974

●   Luce Vigo, "Entretien avec Georges Perec et Bernard Queysanne". *La Revue du cinéma/ Image et son*, no. 284 (May 1974), pp. 68–74.

●   Jacques Grant, "Entretien avec Bernard Queysanne et Georges Perec". *Cinéma 74*, no. 189 (July 1974), pp. 46–51.

1975

●   *Autoren im Dialog* (discussion in French with Eugen Helmle about *W or The Memory of Childhood*). Broadcast by SR on 12 December 1975. Taperecording of "dry-run" discussion at AGP.

1977

●   "Des Règles pour être libre" (interview with Claude Bonnefoy). *Les Nouvelles littéraires*, 10 March 1977, p. 21.

●   Interview with Bernard Noël (⇑ 7: 1977). Broadcast by France-Culture on 20 February 1977. Transcription at AGP.

1978

●   Interview with Monique Pétillon (on *Je me souviens*). *Le Monde*, 10 February 1978, p. 17.

●   "Nuits magnétiques" (interview with G. Masse on *Lieux* and its relation to other [completed] works). Broadcast by France-Culture, 1 March 1978.

- "Radioscopie" (fifty-five minute interview with Jacques Chancel). Broadcast by France-Inter on 22 September 1978.
- "Un livre pour jouer avec" (interview with Jacqueline Piatier). *Le Monde*, 29 September 1978, p. 18.
- "Je ne veux pas finir avec la littérature" (interview with Pierre Lartigue). *L'Humanité*, 2 October 1978, p. 9.
- "L'Impossible Monsieur Perec" (interview with Jean-Louis Ezine). *Les Nouvelles littéraires*, no. 2655 (6 October 1978), p. 32.
- Interview with Alain Hervé, *Le Sauvage*, no. 60 (1 December 1978), pp. 8–25.

1979

- "Je me souviens du jazz" (interview with Philippe Carles et Francis Marmande). *Jazz-Magazine*, no. 272 (February 1979), pp. 30–34.

Jsn   "Le travail de la mémoire" (interview with Frank Venaille). *Monsieur Bloom*, no. 3 (March 1979), pp. 72–75.

- "La Semaine de Georges Perec". *Le Nouvel Observateur*, no. 785 (26 November 1979), pp. 5–6. Prompted comments on the week's entertainments and current issues.
- Interview with Jean-Marie Le Sidaner, *L'Arc*, no. 76 (1979), pp. 3–10.

1980

- "Ce qu'ils pensent de Flaubert: Georges Perec" (reply to a questionnaire). *La Quinzaine littéraire*, no. 324 (1 May 1980), p. 21.
- "Comment l'entendez-vous" (a French version of *Desert Island Discs*). Broadcast on 20 September 1980 by France-Musique. Includes fifty-one minutes of interview with Perec on Kubrick, Strauss, Mahler, Visconti, Malle, Brahms, etc., and a plan to write a film script based on Schönberg's *Verklärte Nacht*.

1981

- Interview with Claudette Oriol-Boyer. *Textes en main*, no. 1 (Spring 1981), pp. 49–59.
- Interview with Ewa Pawlikowska. *Literatura na swiece*, 1982, pp. 337–355 and *Littératures*, no. 7 (Spring 1983), pp. 69–76.
- Interview with Gabriel Simony. Published in *Jungle* no. 6 (1983), pp. 74–79, from an unverified taperecording. An unauthorised republication of this text in the form of a pamphlet was withdrawn and pulped.
- "A propos de la description", recorded talk at a conference held at Albi (Tarn) on 20–24 July 1981. Unverified transcription published in *Espace et Représentation. Actes du Colloque d'Albi du 20/24 juillet 1981*, ed. Alain Reniès. Paris, Editions de la Villette, 1982.

RCF   Interview in English with Kaye Mortley. Broadcast by Radio

Helicon (Sydney) in "The Doing of Fiction", a composite
programme about Perec that includes (inter alia) a reading of
"Still Life/ Style Leaf" in Harry Mathews's translation.
Rebroadcast three times since 1981. Parts of the English
interview were included in "Intercalaire pour Georges Perec",
broadcast by France-Culture, 4 April 1982.

- "L'art et le livre illustré". Talk on illustrated books given at
ACIF Bologna on 28 November 1981. Taperecording transcibed
by Patrizia Molteni and published in part in *Ici-Perec* (Montreuil:
Bibliothèque Robert-Desnos, 1992).
- Lecture on *Les Choses*, University of Adelaide, 1 October 1981.
Taperecording transcribed by Heather Mawhinney.
- Reading and discussion of poetry, University of Melbourne,
5 October 1981. Taperecording transcribed by Jane Byrne.
- Interview with Bernard Milluy. *Bulletin de l'Alliance française de
Melbourne*, November 1981.

SECTION 13: UNPUBLISHED WORKS

This section lists only those unpublished works that I have seen
with my own eyes, excluding the unpublished and/or unrealised
radio, cinema, television, musical, and multimedia works in sections
7 to 11 above, and the unfinished works listed in section 14.

Perec's papers in FP contain other unpublished items not
mentioned here; and there may well be other works by Perec (articles
for *La Ligne générale*, for instance) amongst the papers of his former
colleagues. In addition, some of the items listed as lost in section 15
may well be "raised" to this section, if not to section 1, in the
coming years.

Extracts from unpublished works given in translation in this book
can be located by means of the index of titles.

Some additional information about the unpublished early works
can be found in David Bellos, "Perec avant Perec", *Ecritures* 2
(April 1992), pp. 47–64.

- "Les Aventures d'Enzio, le petit roi de Sardaigne" (with
Bernard Quilliet). Strip cartoon, 14 ff. 1954–5.

- "Les Barques". Typescript story, 3 ff. Written in 1954 (but not at Rock, as claimed in *MO*). FP 48,9,3,2.
- "Le Fou". Typescript story, 14 ff. Written on 23–27 November [1956].
- "Manderre, suivi de quelques remarques". Typescript story, 34 ff. Written in December 1956, dedicated to Zoran Petrović.
- "Sommeil". A poem. Manuscript. Written circa 1956.
- *L'Attentat de Sarajevo*. *Récit*. Uncorrected carbon copy typescript, 135 ff. Written in September-October 1957.
- "La Procession. Phantasme". Typescript drama (?), 16 ff. Written in November 1957. FP 48,9,3,1. Partly reproduced in facsimile in Ribière, *Parcours Perec*, pp. 22–3.
- "Défense de Klee". Typescript essay, 3ff recto-verso. Dated 19 August 1959. Photocopy at AGP.
- *Le Condottiere*. *Roman*. Typescript, 157ff. Dated 25 August 1960. Dedicated to Jacques Lederer.
- "Henri Thomas, *John Perkins*". Typescript review. Written in 1961. FP 119, 17.
- "Situation du roman français contemporain" (on Claude Simon). Typescript dated 18 January 1961. FP 119, 13.
- "A Propos du film *Le Bonheur* d'Agnès Varda". Typescript review, 2ff. Written circa 1965.
- "Roland Barthes, *Système de la Mode*". Typescript review. Written circa 1967. FP 119,15.
- "L'Art du Hörspiel". Unfinished manuscript, 1 sheet. Written post-1970.
- "Parapèteries. L'Art du parapet". Typescript, 1f, read at OuLiPo meeting of 28 November 1974. ("Parapets" are sentences which sound as though they would be vulgar and funny if initial consonants were inverted [as in *contrepets*], but aren't.)
- "Paolo Boni, Mécanicien de l'imaginaire". (⇑ 4: 1979, 3: 1979)
- "Il y avait une fois . . .". Unfinished children's story, manuscript, 1f recto-verso.
- "L'art léger . . ." Vocalic sequence. Typescript, 1f. Typed in Australia, September 1981.
- "Morton's Ob". Univocalic in English. Typescript, 1f., typed in Australia, September 1981.

SECTION 14: UNFINISHED WORKS

This section includes only those unfinished works on which Perec made a real start, which itself has been located and seen. Planned works mentioned, even at length, in, for example, letters to friends, have not been included here unless some first-order fragment has been found.

- *Fragments d'un Ninipotch*. Jottings circa 1963–64.
- "L'Age". Scrappy drafts, circa 1968.
- *L'Arbre*. Substantial sections written in 1967, additions made up to 1971, work pursued in 1979–81. FP 58.
- *Lieux.*
  Commenced January 1969, abandoned September 1975. FP 57. Fragments published as "Tentative de description de quelques lieux parisiens: Vues d'Italie" (⇑ 5: 1977), "Tentative de description de quelques lieux parisiens: La rue Vilin" (⇑ 5: 1977, republished as "La Rue Vilin" in *inf*), "Tentative de description de quelques lieux parisiens: guettées" (⇑ 5: 1977), and "Allées et venues rue de l'Assomption" (⇑ 5: 1979).
  Further excerpts can be found in Lejeune, *La Mémoire et l'oblique*, together with a technical description of the contents of FP 57.
- *Lieux où j'ai dormi*. Conceived before July 1969. Fragment published as "Trois Chambres retrouvées" (⇑ 5: 1977) and subsequently in *Penser/Classer*.
- *L'Art effaré*. (With Philippe Drogoz, from 1968–69). Abandoned around 1973, though not definitively. Fragment published posthumously (⇑ 10).
- *Notes de Chevet*. Conceived before 1976. Fragment published as "Notes brèves sur l'art et la manière de ranger ses livres" (*L'Humidité*, no. 25 [Spring 1978], pp. 35–38), and subsequently in *Penser/Classer*. See also the 1976 prospectus (*see* p. 583).

SECTION 15: LOST WORKS

- *Les Errants*. Written in 1955–6.
- Article on the Algerian problem for *Pregled*, 1957.
- *La Nuit*. Drafted in 1958.
- *Gaspard*. Parts typed in October 1958.
- *Gaspard pas mort*. Completed in February 1959.
- "Toplicin Venac". Planned in October 1959.
- *Gradus ad Parnassum*. Written in 1960–61
- *J'avance masqué*. Written in 1961.

SECTION 16: PUBLISHED LETTERS

- To Maurice Nadeau, 12 June 1957. In Nadeau, *Grâces leur soient rendues*, pp. 430–432. Albin Michel, 1990.
- To Denise Getzler, undated (circa 1964). *Littératures*, no. 7 (Spring 1983), pp. 61–66
- To Albert Ghuislaine. Quoted in *Le Soir* (Brussels), 14–15 December 1965.
- To Indra Chakravarti, 10 June 1969. Reprinted in part in Lejeune, *La Mémoire et l'oblique*, pp. 205–207.

Jsn   To Maurice Nadeau, 7 July 1969. Reprinted in part in *Cahiers Georges Perec II*, p. 121, and in larger part in Lejeune, *La Mémoire et l'oblique*, pp. 95–97.

- To Maurice Nadeau, 8 March 1973, facsimile in Nadeau, *Grâces leur soient rendues* (Albin Michel, 1990), unnumbered page.
- To Christian Bourgois, 15 May 1975. Facsimile in *Christian Bourgois 1966–1986*, unnumbered page. Bourgois, 1986.
- To Paul Braffort, François Le Lionnais, Harry Mathews, and Raymond Queneau, prior to 12 August 1975. In Raymond Queneau, André Blavier, *Lettres Croisées, 1949–1976*, pp. 327–329. Brussels, Editions Labor, 1988.
- To Norbert Iborra, 12 December 1979. *Bulletin du Club français de la médaille*, no. 84 (2ᵉ trimestre 1984), p. 46 (facsimile).

★

A number of Perec's letters to Catherine Binet are shown and read in Catherine Binet's two-part *Film sur Georges Perec*, first broadcast on television in February 1991.

Index of Perec's Titles

This index lists all of Perec's titles mentioned in chapters 1 to 66, without distinction amongst published, unpublished, draft, planned, unwritten, collaborative and lost works. Titles in French are cross-referenced to entries in English for works available in English; in all other cases translated titles are cross-referenced to entries in French. Titles that appear only in "The Works of Georges Perec" on pages 717–750 are not indexed. Numbers followed by s refer to mentions in the sources sections at the ends of chapters. Numbers followed by n refer to footnotes.

Numbers in bold type indicate the principal references to a given subject.

Index of Names

Names of real persons are in small capitals; titles of books, films, periodicals, and paintings are in italic.

Numbers followed by s refer to mentions in the sources sections at the ends of chapters. Numbers followed by n refer to footnotes. Names that occur only in footnotes are not consistently indexed.

Numbers in bold type indicate the principal references to a given subject.

Index of Topics

Principal topics are in small capitals.

Numbers in bold type indicate the principal references to a given subject.

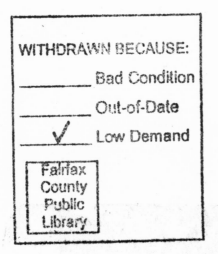